Solent-Thames Research Framework for the Historic Environment:

Resource Assessments and Research Agendas

Solent-Thames Research Framework for the Historic Environment:

Resource Assessments and Research Agendas

by Gill Hey and Jill Hind (eds)

with major contributions by
Michael Allen, Richard Bradley, Sally Crawford, Anne Dodd, Michael Fulford,
George Lambrick, Julian Munby and Francis Wenban-Smith

and county contributions by
David Allen, Tim Allen, Grenville Astill, Catherine Barnett, Vicky Basford,
Kim Biddulph, Paul Booth, David Bridgland, Owen Cambridge, Steve Clark,
Kate Cramp, Anne Dodd, Chris Dyer, Bob Edwards, Mike Farley, Steve Ford,
Julie Gardiner, Brian Giggins, David Green, Jill Greenaway, Terry Hardaker,
David Hinton, David Hopkins, Robert Hosfield, Sandy Kidd, Rebecca Loader,
Malcolm Lyne, Richard Massey, David Radford, John Rhodes, Alison Roberts,
Barbara Silva, Kim Taylor-Moore, Ruth Waller, Chris Welch,
Keith Wilkinson and Bob Zeepvat

Illustration by
Gary Jones and Julia Collins

Oxford Wessex Monograph No. 6
2014

The publication of this volume has generously been funded by English Heritage

Published by Oxford Archaeology as part of the Oxford Wessex Monograph series

Designed by Oxford Archaeology Graphics Office

Copy-edited by Tim Allen

All figures contain data reproduced from the Ordnance Survey on behalf of the controller
of Her Majesty's Stationery Office, © Crown Copyright, AL 100005569

Figure 1.3 includes data reproduced by kind permission from British Geological Survey.

Front cover: Solent foreshore, copyright Wessex Archaeology, with amendments by Laura Hart

Back cover: Hominins butcher a brown bear carcass on the banks of the Thames,
c. 300,000 years ago (MIS 9), reconstruction by Peter Lorimer

ISBN 978-0-9574672-1-7

Typeset by Production Line, Oxford
Printed in Great Britain by Berforts Information Press, Eynsham, Oxfordshire

Contents

Chapter 1 Introduction to an Archaeological Research Framework for the Solent-Thames sub-region: Resource Assessment and Resarch Agenda Background *by Jill Hind and Gill Hey*

Chapter 2 An introduction to the geoarchaeology, palaeo-environmental and archaeological science of the Solent-Thames sub-region *by Michael Allen*

Chapter 3 The Lower/Middle Palaeolithic: Resource Assessment *by Francis Wenban-Smith, with Terry Hardaker, Robert Hosfield, Rebecca Loader, Barbara Silva, Keith Wilkinson, David Bridgland, Kate Cramp and Michael Allen*

Chapter 4 The Lower/Middle Palaeolithic: Research Agenda *by Francis Wenban-Smith,*
with Terry Hardaker, Robert Hosfield, Rebecca Loader, Barbara Silva, Keith Wilkinson, David Bridgland,
Kate Cramp and Michael Allen

Chapter 5 Late Upper Palaeolithic and Mesolithic Resource Assessment *by Gill Hey*

Chapter 6   Late Upper Palaeolithic and Mesolithic Research Agenda *by Gill Hey*

Chapter 7   The Neolithic and Early Bronze Age Resource Assessment *by Richard Bradley,*
with contributions by Michael Allen and Gill Hey

Chapter 8   The Neolithic and Early Bronze Age Research Agenda *by Richard Bradley*

Chapter 9   The Later Bronze Age and Iron Age Resource Assessment *by George Lambrick*

Chapter 10 The Later Bronze Age and Iron Age Research Agenda *by George Lambrick*

Chapter 11 The Roman Period: Resource Assessment *by Michael Fulford*

Chapter 12 The Roman Period: Research Agenda *by Michael Fulford*

Chapter 13 The Early Medieval Period: Resource Assessment *by Anne Dodd with contributions from Sally Crawford and Michael Allen*

Chapter 14 The Early Medieval Period: Research Agenda *by Anne Dodd and Sally Crawford* *with contributions from Michael Allen*

Chapter 15 The Later Medieval Period: Resource Assessment *by Julian Munby*

Chapter 19 Conclusions *by Gill Hey and Jill Hind*

List of Figures

List of Tables

List of Plates

Summary

The Solent-Thames region, as recently defined by central government, comprises five counties from north to south: Buckinghamshire, Oxfordshire, Berkshire, Hampshire and the Isle of Wight, providing a N-S transect across Central Southern England. This area includes a varied geography, from the Cotswolds in the north across the chalklands of the Berkshire Downs and the heathlands of Hampshire to the south coast. It does not follow previous regional divisions of England, instead aiming to provide fresh insights into the past through the grouping of existing administrative units in a new combination.

This volume presents the first two phases of the Research Framework project for this region. The first is an assessment of the current state of archaeological knowledge within this region from Palaeolithic times to the present day, the second a series of research aims and priorities both for specific periods and for wider cross-period themes. It starts with an introduction explaining the current organisation of information about the past in the region, and a brief introduction to the environmental archaeology of the Solent-Thames area. Following this, two chapters are devoted to each major chronological period, the first presenting an overview of the resource as currently understood, the second a Research Agenda for future work. There is then a brief conclusion.

In several of the chronological periods, this region contains some of the most important and best-researched sites, or groups of sites, in England. These include the remarkable series of early Mesolithic settlements along the Kennet valley, the hillfort at Danebury

and its environs, the Roman town of Silchester and the cemetery of Lankhills, and the Saxon and medieval towns and cities of Southampton, Winchester and Oxford. The region has strong royal links in the medieval period, resulting in the preservation of Windsor Forest and the New Forest, and Oxford was the capital for King Charles I during the English Civil War. Arguably the most important ships in the naval history of Britain are housed at Portsmouth, including the Mary Rose, the best-preserved Tudor warship in Britain. Among the many country estates, Blenheim Palace, the seat of the Dukes of Marlborough, is of international renown. More recently, this region has been the focus of political dissent during the Cold War, around the nuclear facilities at Greenham Common and Upper Heyford.

The Resource Assessments are written by eminent period specialists, drawing upon county assessments prepared by local experts, which can be found online at http://oxfordarchaeology.com/research-projects-by-name/217-solent-thames-research-framework. The Research Agendas are organised under the same headings as the Resource Assessments, and the research questions are numbered for ease of reference.

The volume is one of a series covering the whole of England, and is published with the support of English Heritage. It aims to draw together the results of developer-funded, purely academic and local research within this region, and to place the results in the context of current research. It is hoped that it will be useful to all those contemplating, planning or undertaking future archaeological work within the region.

Résumé

La région du Solent-Tamise, comme définie récemment par le pouvoir central comprend 5 comtés repartis du Nord au Sud : le Buckinghamshire, l'Oxfordshire, le Berkshire, le Hampshire et enfin l'île de Wight, créant une section transversale N-S qui traverse l'Angleterre méridionale en son centre. Cette zone dessine une géographie diversifiée, à partir des Cotswolds au nord puis sillonne les hauteurs crayeuses des collines du Berkshire ainsi que les landes de l'Hampshire jusqu'à la côte sud. Elle ne suit pas les anciennes divisions régionales de l'Angleterre, mais cherche au contraire à offrir de nouvelles perspectives du passé grâce au regroupement des unités administratives existantes en un nouvel agencement.

Ce volume rassemble les deux premières phases du Projet-cadre de recherche de cette région. La première phase constitue une évaluation de l'état actuel des connaissances archéologiques au sein de la région des temps paléolithiques à nos jours ; la deuxième offre une série d'objectifs et de priorités de recherche concernant à la fois des périodes spécifiques et des sujets plus vastes portant sur plusieurs périodes. Une introduction initiale explique l'organisation actuelle de l'information sur le passé de la région, suivie par une brève introduction sur l'archéologie paléoenvironnementale de la région Solent-Tamise. Le volume enchaîne avec deux chapitres consacrés à chaque grande période chronologique, le premier proposant un panorama des ressources telles qu'elles sont appréhendées aujourd'hui, le second un programme de recherche en vue de travaux futurs. Le tout s'achève par une courte conclusion.

Pour plusieurs des périodes chronologiques, cette région conte certains des sites, ou groupes de sites, les plus importants et les mieux documentés d'Angleterre. Parmi ces derniers, on répertorie la remarquable série d'habitats du mésolithique ancien le long de la vallée de la rivière Kennet, la colline fortifiée de Danebury et ses environs, la ville romaine de Silchester et le cimetière de Lankhills, sans oublier les villes anglo-saxonnes et médiévales, plus ou moins grandes, de Southampton, Winchester et Oxford. A l'époque médiévale, la région jouit de solides liens royaux dont résultent la bonne conservation de la Forêt de Windsor et de la New Forest, puis Oxford comme capitale du roi Charles Ier durant la guerre civile britannique. Les navires les plus importants de l'histoire navale de la Grande-Bretagne sont sans doute à Portsmouth, dont la Mary Rose, le mieux préservé des navires de guerre Tudor en Grande-Bretagne. Parmi de nombreux domaines, le palais de Blenheim, siège des ducs de Marlborough, est de renommée mondiale. Plus récemment, pendant la guerre froide, la région est au cœur d'un désaccord politique, autour des installations nucléaires de la RAF Greeham Common et de la RAF Upper Heyford.

Les Evaluations des ressources, rédigées par d'éminents spécialistes par période, font usage des évaluations régionales préparées par des experts locaux. Ces documents peuvent être consultés en ligne à l'adresse suivante thehumanjourney.net/pdf-store/sthames. Les Programmes de recherche sont organisés sous les mêmes rubriques que les Evaluations de ressources ; enfin les questions relatives à la recherche sont numérotées pour faciliter la consultation.

Ce volume fait partie d'une série de publications sur l'ensemble de l'Angleterre et est publié avec le soutien de l'English Heritage, l'organisation chargée du patrimoine. Il vise à rassembler les résultats de différents types de recherche dans la région, recherche financée par les promoteurs, purement universitaire ou locale, et situe ces résultats dans le contexte de la recherche actuelle. Cet ouvrage devrait être utile à tous ceux qui envisagent, planifient ou souhaitent entreprendre des travaux archéologiques dans cette région.

Zusammenfassung

Die Solent-Thames-Region, wie sie kürzlich durch die Zentralregierung festgelegt wurde, besteht von Norden nach Süden aus fünf Grafschaften: Buckinghamshire, Oxfordshire, Berkshire, Hampshire und die Isle of Wight und bietet somit einen N-S Durchschnitt durch den zentralen Teil Südenglands. Dieses Gebiet besitzt eine abwechslungsreiche Landschaft, von den Cotswolds im Norden, über die Kreidelandschaften der Berkshire Downs sowie die Heideflächen von Hampshire bis hin zur Südküste. Dieses Gebiet stimmt jedoch nicht mit früheren regionalen Gebieten Englands überein, und bietet somit die Möglichkeit durch die Präsentation des Kulturerbes noch bestehender Verwaltungseinheiten in einer neuen Kombination die Gelegenheit für neue Einblicke in die Vergangenheit.

Dieser Band stellt die ersten beiden Phasen des Forschungsrahmen-Projektes für diese Region vor. Die erste umfasst eine Auswertung des archäologischen Wissensstandes des Gebietes vom Paläolithikum bis zum heutigen Tag, während die zweite Phase eine Reihe von Forschungszielen und -prioritäten beinhaltet, die sowohl für spezifische Epochen als auch für epochenübergreifende Thematiken definiert worden sind. Der Band beginnt mit einer Einleitung, welche die derzeitige Organisation der Information über die Vergangenheit der Region erklärt, sowie einer kurzen Einführung zur Umweltarchäologie der Solent-Thames-Region. Hierauf folgen zwei Kapitel, die den chronologischen Hauptepochen gewidmet sind. Während das erste dieser Kapitel einen Überblick über die Quellen, wie sie momentan verstanden werden, bietet, beinhaltet das zweite ein Forschungsprogramm für zukünftige Arbeiten. Anschließend folgt ein kurzes Schlusskapitel.

Dieses Gebiet umfasst einige der wichtigsten und am intensivsten untersuchten archäologischen Stätten bzw. Gruppen solcher im ganzen England. Diese schließen die bemerkenswerten früh-mesolithischen Stätten entlang des Kennet Tals, die neolithischen und bronzezeitlichen Monumentkomplexe bei Stanton Harcourt und Dorchester-on-Thames, die Bergfestung und deren Umgebung bei Danebury, die römische Stadt Silchester und den Friedhof von Lankhills, sowie die sächsischen und mittelalterlichen Städte Southampton, Winchester und Oxford ein. Das Gebiet hatte im Mittelalter enge königliche Beziehungen, woraus sich die Konservierung des Windsor Forest und des New Forest ergab, und zudem galt für König Charles' I. Oxford als Hauptstadt während des englischen Bürgerkriegs. Die vermutlich wichtigsten Schiffe der britischen Schifffahrtsgeschichte sind in Portsmouth untergebracht, und zu diesen zählt die Mary Rose, das besterhaltene Kriegsschiff der Tudorzeit in Großbritannien. Zu den zahlreichen Landgütern gehört der Blenheim Palace, der Sitz des Herzogs von Marlborough, welcher von internationalem Ruhm ist. In jüngerer Zeit, während des Kalten Krieges, stand das Gebiet im Mittelpunkt einer politischen Auseinandersetzung, vor allem wegen der kerntechnischen Anlagen bei Greenham Common und Upper Heyford.

Die Auswertungen der Quellen wurden von angesehenen Wissenschaftlern mit Spezialisierung auf die einzelnen Epochen verfasst, die sich dabei auf Bewertungen der Grafschaften durch Lokalexperten stützen. Diese stehen im Internet auf http://oxfordarchaeology.com/research-projects-by-name/217-solent-thames-research-framework zur Verfugung. Zur besseren Orientierung sind die Forschungsprogramme unter denselben Überschriften wie die Quellenbewertungen angeordnet; die Forschungsfragen sind nummeriert.

Dieser Band gehört zu einer ganz England umfassenden Reihe, welche mit der Unterstützung von English Heritage sowie der Förderung durch ALGAO South East herausgegeben wird. Ziel ist es, die Ergebnisse der archäologischen Untersuchungen in der Region zusammenzufassen, gleichgültig ob sie durch Unternehmer finanziert, rein akademisch, oder einfach örtliche Untersuchungen sind, und diese Ergebnisse in Zusammenhang mit den aktuellen Forschungen zu stellen. Es ist zu hoffen, dass dieser Band für alle nützlich sein wird, die zukünftige archäologische Arbeiten innerhalb dieser Region erwägen, planen, oder gerade durchführen.

Acknowledgements

The Solent-Thames Research Framework project was initiated by the South East Regional Group of the Association of Local Government Archaeological Officers (ALGAO) who, with English Heritage encouragement, held a regional discussion seminar, organised a tender competition for its management and funded the first project design. A number of its members went on to form part of the Steering Group. In particular we would like to acknowledge the unceasing interest and encouragement of Sandy Kidd (Buckinghamshire County Council), who chaired the group from its formation and its other ALGAO representatives: Duncan Coe, Brian Giggins, David Hopkins, Fiona Macdonald, Paul Smith and Ruth Waller. We are also grateful for the active support of all ALGAO member authorities and their staff in the project area:

Berkshire Archaeology, representing Windsor and
  Maidenhead, Reading, Bracknell Forest, Slough and
  Wokingham
Hampshire County Council
Isle of Wight Council
Milton Keynes Council
Oxford City Council
Oxfordshire County Council
Southampton Council
Test Valley Borough Council
Winchester Council
West Berkshire Council

English Heritage provided core funding to the Oxford Wessex Archaeology Joint Venture to facilitate the project and to publish the results. Kathy Perrin, English Heritage's co-ordinator for most of the project's life, was extremely supportive and provided invaluable advice from her experience of working with other research frameworks. Latterly, Helen Keeley filled this role. Dominique de Moulins, Chris Welch and Richard Massey represented English Heritage's South East Region on the Steering Group.

Other active members on the Steering Group were Mary Oliver (representing the voluntary sector), Nigel Pratt and Sarah Orr (representing HER officers), David Hinton (representing higher education) and Steve Ford (representing contracting archaeologists). With the other members of the group, they provided very helpful suggestions during the different phases of the project and commented on draft documentation.

Thirty-eight contributors wrote the 40 period county contributions, seven writing more than one. They are acknowledged at the heads of the Resource Assessment chapters and we are extremely grateful to them for attending seminars and using their knowledge to summarise the resource of their county and helping to draw up the Research Agenda items.

Without the contributions of our Lead Authors, this volume would not have been completed. We owe a huge debt of gratitude for their interest and participation in the project and that they have been able to bring their extensive knowledge to bear on the heritage environment of the Solent Thames.

Most of the work that went into this project was undertaken by very busy people in their own time and is a testament to their dedication to the historic environment of the Solent Thames region. Other work was funded by English Heritage, county archaeological services in the region, university institutions, Oxford Archaeology and Wessex Archaeology. A number of institutions also provided venues for seminars at little or no cost and we would like to acknowledge Reading University, Reading Museum, the Ashmolean Museum, English Heritage and Oxford Archaeology.

The Research Framework was set up to engage a very wide range of people with an involvement and/or interest in the historic environment of the area, whether professionals or members of the public. Many attended seminars, read online documentation and sent in their comments and, to all these people, we would like to extend our thanks.

The volume was copyedited by Tim Allen, who would like to thank all those who supplied plates. The figures were produced by Gary Jones, and the plates and cover were compiled by Julia Collins. Translations of the summary were made by Nathalie Haudecouer-Wilkes (French) and Anna Hodgkinson (German).

We hope that the results published in this volume justify the work and enthusiasm that has been devoted to its production.

Chapter 1

Introduction to an Archaeological Research Framework for the Solent-Thames sub-region: Resource Assessment and Research Agenda

by Jill Hind and Gill Hey

Introduction

This volume presents the results of the first two stages in a three-stage process for the production of a Research Framework for the historic environment covering the Solent-Thames sub-region, the western portion of the South East Region of England. The sub-region comprises the historic counties of Berkshire, Buckinghamshire, Hampshire, the Isle of Wight and Oxfordshire, including the six Berkshire Unitary Authorities, Milton Keynes, Southampton and Portsmouth (Fig. 1.1).

Following an introduction to the sub-region and its environment, and to the work undertaken as part of this study, the book is divided into sixteen chapters based on a chronological timeframe. Each period includes a chapter dealing with the *Resource Assessment* for that period in the sub-region, followed by one providing a *Research Agenda*. The *Resource Assessments*, which are the first stage of the Research Framework, describe the current level of knowledge and understanding relating to the historic environment, and explore the nature of the available resource within the area. The *Research Agendas* form the second stage, and identify those areas where there are major gaps in our current understanding and key research questions that need to be addressed. They also suggest possible methods by which this evidence could be obtained. The volume concludes with some themes which are common to many of the periods under discussion, and also some proposals for moving the Solent-Thames Research Framework project towards its next stage.

The *Research Strategy* for the sub-region will be developed in the third and final stage, and will provide a mechanism to allow Research Agenda issues to be addressed and the results reported and disseminated.

The Research Framework project

English Heritage (EH) highlighted the need for regional frameworks for the historic environment in 1996 with the publication of *Frameworks For Our Past*. The importance of Research Frameworks as a tool for ensuring that it is possible to meet long-term objectives for sustaining the historic environment, such as those identified within both previous and existing government planning guidances) was emphasised in *Power of Place* (2000). The need for Research Frameworks was also addressed by DCMS in *Historic Environment: a Force for Our Future* (2001, paras 1.10 and 1.12), and Action Point 8 in that document stated that English Heritage had been '*commissioned to frame a co-ordinated approach to research across the historic environment sector*'. The need has again been highlighted by *The Government's Statement on the Historic Environment for England 2010* (DCMS 2010) which accompanied the publication of Planning Policy Statement 5: Planning for the Historic Environment (PPS5). PPS5 set out the government's objectives for the historic environment, which are being carried forward in the National Planning Policy Framework (NPPF).

The historic environment is a non-renewable resource so particular care is needed to ensure that decisions that affect important sites, buildings and landscapes are carefully considered. Research Frameworks are important for providing sound contextual information and a basis for assessing the significance of the historic environment resource to planners, conservationists and developers. A record of the past is not as valuable as the historic asset itself so an offer to fund investigation cannot in itself be seen as justification for destruction. This is almost always the case, even if there is significant research interest, because such interest can normally be satisfied either elsewhere or by less destructive means.

Research Frameworks can also inform strategies for the preservation, utilisation and display of the historic environment. A wide variation in the state of knowledge and approaches to the conservation of the historic environment has been recognised across the country, which has hindered a structured approach to research into the past and access to the results for the public at large. Research Frameworks are an important element in the creation of a fundamental shift in the role that historic landscapes and seascapes, maritime heritage and buildings play in national life (English Heritage 2001).

The Research Frameworks initiative advocates the review of regional resources and the formulation of a policy for further research within a national, regional and local framework. It aims to facilitate decision

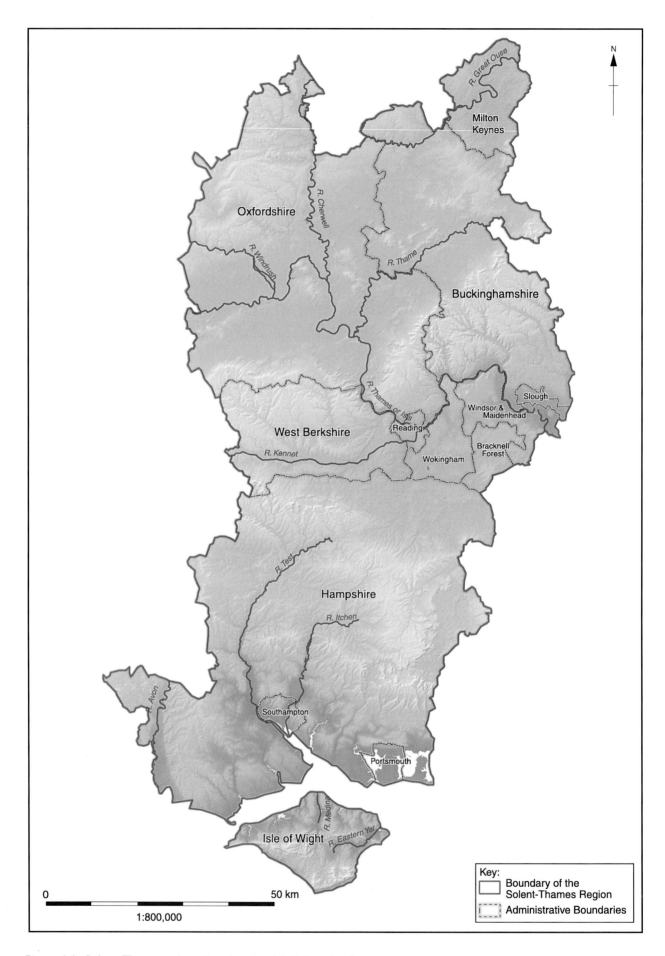

Figure 1.1 Solent-Thames sub-region showing Administrative Areas

making, to prioritise resources and to link curation, developer-funded work and research, enabling curatorial decisions to be firmly based and fairly judged. The Framework has tried to encourage the participation of all those who are active in historic environment work.

Methodology

Oxford Wessex Archaeology (OWA) is a Joint Venture combining the expertise of Oxford Archaeology and Wessex Archaeology. In 2005, OWA was invited by the Association of Local Government Archaeological Officers (ALGAO) for the South East and English Heritage to prepare a Project Design for the compilation of a Resource Assessment and Research Agenda for the sub-region and to co-ordinate this process (Oxford Wessex Archaeology 2005). This followed an extensive consultation exercise involving a wide range of interested organisations, local groups and individuals across the Solent-Thames sub-region, people in neighbouring regions who had experience of Research Frameworks, and selected national bodies who were considered to have a natural interest in the project. The project has been monitored by a Steering Group comprising representatives from those organisations, the relevant local authorities, higher education bodies and local heritage societies.

Two principal options were considered for the structure of the Research Framework: a period-based approach supplemented by a consideration of over-arching themes, and a thematic-based approach with chapters addressing specific issues covering all periods. The former was adopted as it was felt to offer the most useful product for its likely users and be more effective and practical to organise. The first stage in the process was the preparation of period Resource Assessments for each county, which were undertaken by 39 individual contributors, some covering more than one period. These were followed by consultation, both in the form of public seminars held in each county and by posting the documents on the project website as they were completed. Lead authors for each of the main periods then combined the county contributions into overall period Resource Assessments and prepared draft Research Agendas. Consultation on the draft agendas was undertaken through seminars organised on a period basis, and through web-based discussion.

Resource Assessments and Research Agendas were amended to take into account comments received and uploaded onto the Project website: http://oxford arch.co.uk/index.php?option=com_content&task=view &id=553&Itemid=277 where they remain available. Details of the County Contributors, Lead Authors and Steering Group are given in Appendix A.

The project has incorporated the philosophy that Research Frameworks should be undertaken in partner-ship with all those with historic and cultural interests at a local and regional level, and with other regional bodies. In practice, however, there were different levels of partic-ipation across the heritage sector, and strategies for engaging more fully with some curators, for example those in the built heritage sector, need more considera-tion in the final phase. The project has also tried to recognise the unique qualities of the area, and the great diversity of its population, its natural and cultural environments and potential impacts upon them.

The Solent-Thames Region

Political and administrative background

The Solent-Thames sub-region has no political or administrative existence, but is a convenient sub-division of the South East Region, reflecting the variation in character of the area and the intensity of occupation of this part of England, both now and in the past. It is also an area that, in the latter part of the 20th century and early years of the 21st, has seen immense pressure from development and rapid change, with resulting impacts on its countryside, seascapes and townscapes. The lack of a historical identity for the Solent-Thames sub-region has added to the challenges of the project, but as a transect across the heart of southern England from the South Coast to the Chilterns and Cotswolds, it has provided a new perspective upon the information from this area.

The historic counties that make up the Solent-Thames sub-region underwent significant boundary changes in the later 20th century. In 1974, a large part of North Berkshire was transferred to Oxfordshire, part becoming the Vale of the White Horse District and part joining the South Oxfordshire District. Slough and its surrounding area were transferred from Buckingham-shire to Berkshire.

In 1995, the Isle of Wight, already an independent authority, and Milton Keynes, then part of Bucking-hamshire, became Unitary Authorities. Two years later the same status was granted to the City of Southampton and the City of Portsmouth. In 1998, Berkshire ceased to exist as a local authority with the creation of the Unitary Authorities of Bracknell Forest, Reading, Slough, West Berkshire, Windsor & Maidenhead and Wokingham.

This remains the pattern for the region and these boundaries are shown on Figure 1.1.

Geology and topography

The Solent-Thames topography is shown on Figure 1.2. River valleys, mainly associated with the Thames, the former River Solent and their tributaries dominate the area. The Solent strait formed as the result of a gradual widening of the valley of the Solent River. These valleys are interspersed with the broadly west–east trending uplands of the Cotswolds, the Corallian Ridge, the Berkshire Downs and Chilterns, and the Hampshire and South Downs (Plate 1.1). There is nowhere within the region where the land rises above 300m and the majority lies below 100m.

The overall pattern of the solid geology across the region is a series of bands running from south-west to north-east and then in a more west – east orientation, as

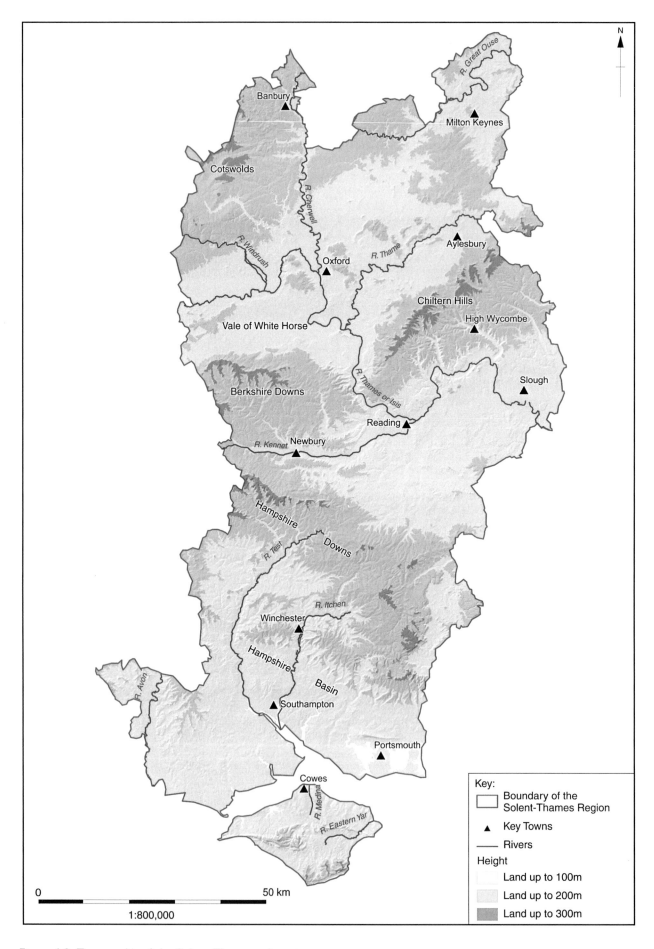

Figure 1.2 Topography of the Solent-Thames sub-region

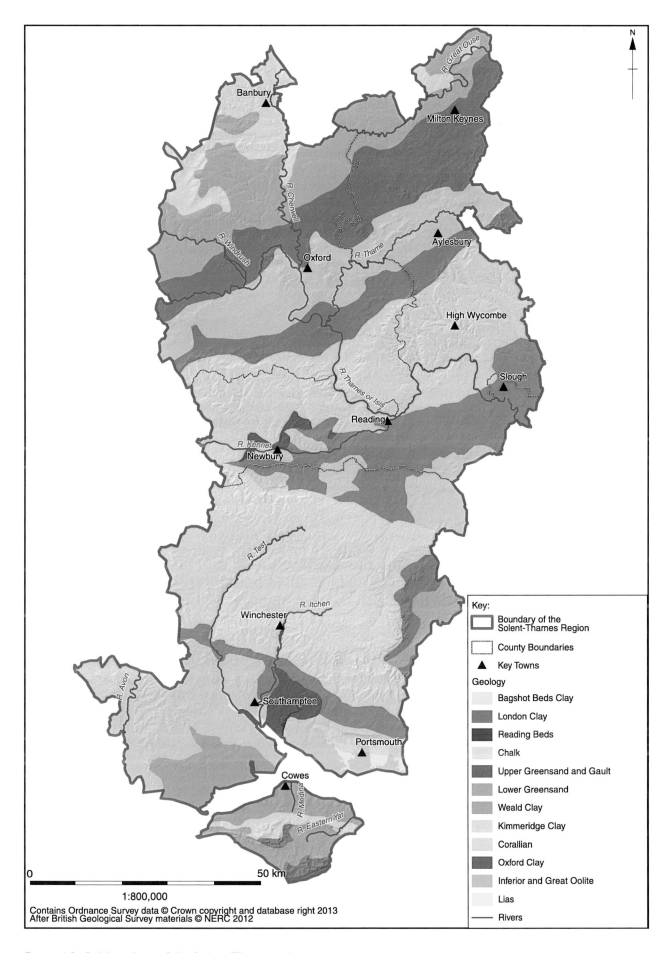

Figure 1.3 Solid geology of the Solent-Thames sub-region

Plate 1.1 Chiltern landscape, *copyright Jill Hind*

shown on Figure 1.3. Chalk, limestone and clays predominate.

The Isle of Wight has a central chalk ridge with the Needles on its western edge, and with Weald Clay to the north and Greensand to the south. In contrast to the steep southern cliffs, the northern part of the island has some distinctly marshy areas, formerly the south bank of the Solent River.

Central Hampshire is predominantly Chalk, with Bagshot Beds Clay and London Clay along the northern edge. The coastal area to the south and the New Forest to the south-west are mainly clay. The southern parts of Berkshire and Buckinghamshire are clays leading onto the dipslopes of the chalk ridge of the Chilterns to the east and the Berkshire Downs to the west.

This chalk ridge overlooks the Greensand and Gault and Kimmeridge Clay of the Vale of Aylesbury and the Vale of the White Horse, north of which is a band of Corallian limestone and sand then Oxford Clay. Oolitic limestone formations are found in the north of Oxfordshire and Buckinghamshire.

Landscape Character

The combination of its geology, topography and river systems has created a wide range of environments in the Solent-Thames sub-region and these are described in the next chapter and shown on Figure 1.6. It has also led to the recognition of distinct Landscape Character Areas, which are shown on Figure 1.4. The varied character of the landscape has also influenced how people have interacted with their environment in the past and present, for example in the vast urban expansion in the east of the region close to London. These Character Areas were mapped by what is now Natural England in 1996; parts of 23 of the 159 Countryside Character Areas defined across England are represented in the Solent-Thames sub-region.

The best of the region's countryside has been recognised and granted statutory protection, as shown on Figure 1.5. Within the Solent-Thames sub-region there are two National Parks: the New Forest in the south-west, created in 2005, and the South Downs in the south-east, which was established in 2011. Five Areas of Outstanding Natural Beauty (AONB) are also present within the area. Two of these lie on the central Chalk uplands: the North Wessex Downs and the Chilterns, which meet at the River Thames, and large parts of the Isle of Wight form another. In the north-west, the Cotswolds AONB extends into Oxfordshire, and the western tip of Hampshire lies within the Cranborne Chase and West Wiltshire Downs AONB.

Communication routes

The Solent-Thames sub-region is crossed by a number of key routes connecting to London, and linking the North and the Midlands with the South Coast. The development of these transport networks within the region is discussed in more detail in the Post-medieval and Modern Resource Assessment chapter.

There are three main motorway links. The M40 from London to the Birmingham area passes across Buckinghamshire and Oxfordshire, while the M4 from London to South Wales bisects Berkshire. The South Coast is connected to London by the M3 through Hampshire, intersecting at Southampton with the M27, which runs along the south of the county from the New Forest to Portsmouth. The key trunk roads are the A5, which crosses Milton Keynes on its way from London to North Wales, the A34, which is still the main north-south route

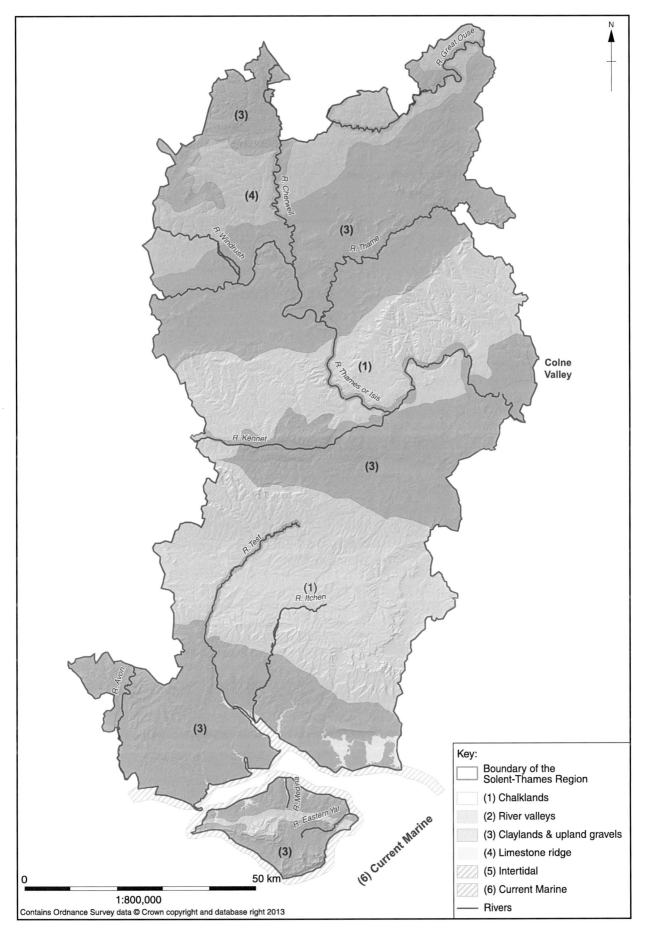

Figure 1.4 Topographic zones of the Solent-Thames sub-region

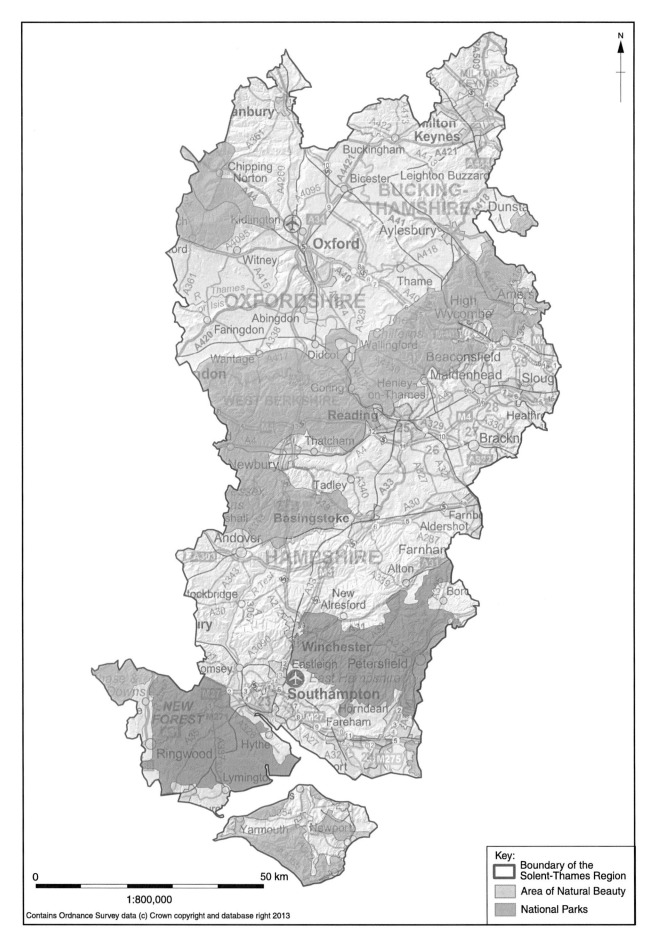

Figure 1.5 Statutory protection in the Solent-Thames sub-region

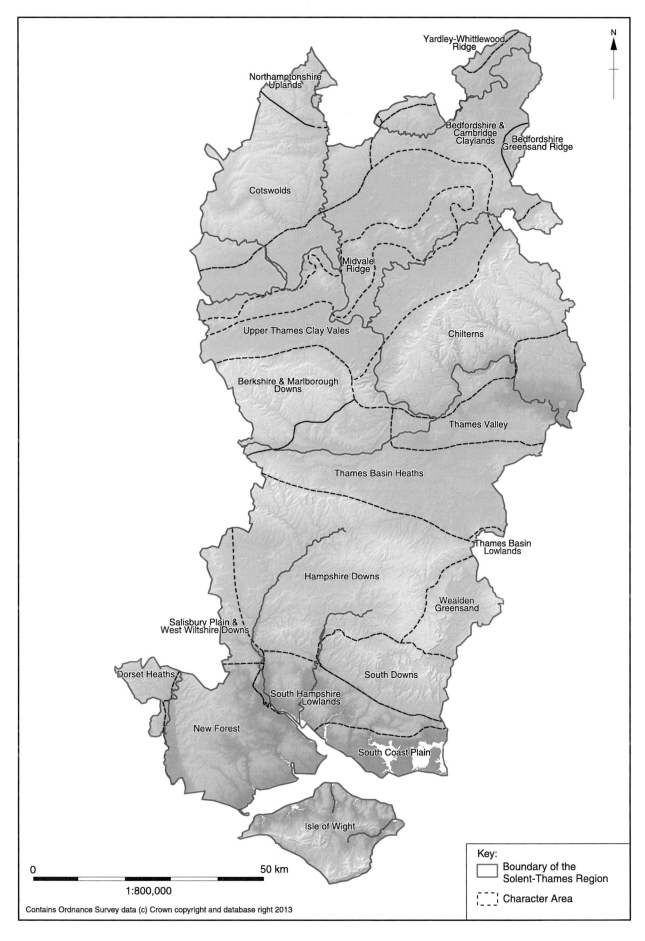

N

Yardley-Whittlewood Ridge

Northamptonshire Uplands

Bedfordshire & Cambridge Claylands

Bedfordshire Greensand Ridge

Cotswolds

Midvale Ridge

Upper Thames Clay Vales

Chilterns

Berkshire & Marlborough Downs

Thames Valley

Thames Basin Heaths

Thames Basin Lowlands

Hampshire Downs

Wealden Greensand

Salisbury Plain & West Wiltshire Downs

Dorset Heaths

South Downs

South Hampshire Lowlands

New Forest

South Coast Plain

Isle of Wight

0   50 km

1:800,000

Contains Ordnance Survey data (c) Crown copyright and database right 2013

Key:

☐ Boundary of the Solent-Thames Region

⌐ ⌐ Character Area

Figure 1.6 Environmental character areas of the Solent-Thames sub-region

Plate 1.2 Kennet and Avon canal, Berkshire, *copyright Jill Hind*

through the centre of Southern England, and the A303 linking the region to the South West.

Most of the major cities and towns in the region are served by railways. Rail use has increased since the end of the 20th century and there are ongoing projects to update stations, and to improve lines between Oxford and Bicester to provide an alternative route to London. The proposed new High Speed 2 rail service is due to run through Buckinghamshire.

Air links are more restricted. There are only two airports within the region with scheduled services: Southampton and London Oxford at Kidlington, although London Heathrow lies only just outside the region to the east.

Although rivers and canals no longer support significant commercial traffic, they have become important

Plate 1.3 HMS Warrior in Portsmouth Dockyard, Hampshire, *copyright Dave Allen*

parts of the region's leisure business (Plate 1.2). The sea is still a very important transport route. For the Isle of Wight, this is the only public link with the outside world, with vehicle ferries, catamarans and hovercraft services from Cowes, Freshwater, Ryde and Yarmouth to Lymington, Southampton, Portsmouth and Southsea. Ferry services from Portsmouth also serve Guernsey and Jersey in the Channel Islands, Caen, Cherbourg, Le Havre and St Malo in France, and Bilbao and Santander in Spain. Southampton remains one of the United Kingdom's most important ports, dealing with a substantial volume of containers, vehicles, oil and people (the last through the largest cruise liner terminal in the UK), while Portsmouth has continued to be a significant dockyard (Plate 1.3).

The nature of the archaeological evidence

The varying effects of acid and alkaline soils, the differing degree to which archaeological remains are buried below the modern ground surface, and the uneven distribution of post-depositional disturbance, has led to a complicated pattern of survival and visibility of archaeological remains in the sub-region. Environmental conditions across the sub-region and the preservation of environmental data are discussed in detail in Chapter 2.

Of particular importance in the Solent-Thames region is the presence of extensive alluvial floodplains in the river valleys, sealing and protecting pre-Roman remains, and sometimes those of a later date. The understanding of the process of alluviation and the periods during which it occurred are of great importance for appreciating what may survive in these locations. Although preservation may be good, sites can be very difficult to find. Air photography, fieldwalking and geophysical survey are seldom of use (unless overlying deposits are shallow) and the problems of examining small percentages of areas in trenched evaluations have been noted (Hey and Lacey 2001). These difficulties are exacerbated when archaeological remains are ephemeral in character, as so many earlier prehistoric settlement sites in these locations are.

Similar problems of survival and visibility apply to the intertidal areas along the Hampshire coast and the north coast of the Isle of Wight (Allen and Gardiner 2000). Here, however, the conditions can be much more dynamic, with some deposits exposed on a regular basis, in addition to those which are more deeply buried. They have received much less attention than inland environments and are more poorly understood (see Chapter 2).

Where soils are thinner and/or geologies are more susceptible to the effects of drought, air photography has been particularly successful in locating archaeological sites. This applies particularly to the gravel terraces of the main river valleys (see Plate 7.8). In the Thames Valley, for example, air photography has been important for recovering archaeological information in advance of gravel quarrying since the early decades of the 20th century. The Chalk Downs and limestone uplands also provide good cropmark evidence. The level of preservation in downland

Plate 1.4 Fieldwalking in progress at Yarnton, *copyright OA*

areas and in wooded areas can be particularly good. Other remote techniques, such as geophysical survey, have been successful in identifying sites in these environments.

Fieldwalking has a long history of use in the sub-region (Plate 1.4). For example, important Mesolithic assemblages have been recovered on the Hampshire Greensand since the 19th century, and have formed the basis for much of our chronology of the British Mesolithic (Reynier 2000). This method has provided a useful means of detecting the presence of archaeological

sites, though fieldwalking assemblages are also an indicator of their destruction. The impact of ploughing on the historic environment in the sub-region is of some concern and the subject of a number of current studies (http://www.englishheritage.org.uk/publications/ripping-up-history-archaeology-under-the-plough).

Arable cultivation can also lead to the formation of colluvial deposits, as can other processes of erosion. These events have been noted particularly in Chalklands, but can occur in small pockets elsewhere in the landscape. As with alluviation, this process serves to both protect and to hide remains sealed beneath it.

The Solent-Thames sub-region is well-populated, and contains a number of large urban centres as well as new towns and large and growing villages. House construction and related infrastructure and services have affected earlier remains, digging through and levelling off archaeological deposits and demolishing earlier buildings. These activities can however also build over and seal earlier remains and, even in our towns and cities, preservation sometimes surprises us, as the recent discovery of a Neolithic henge in the centre of Oxford, or the examples of early houses encased within later buildings have shown. Important and sometimes extensive, archaeological excavation in advance of development has been undertaken over the last few decades, for example in Milton Keynes, Southampton, Winchester and Oxford

Plate 1.5 View of excavations in progress in the French quarter, Southampton, *copyright OA*

Plate 1.6 St George's Tower, Oxford Castle, *copyright OA*

(Plates 1.5; 1.6). Such development both provides the opportunity to investigate the urban heritage and poses a threat to its survival, an issue that needs to be addressed.

Although the Solent-Thames sub-region is not thought of as an industrial area, industry has also had an important impact upon parts of its historic environment. This includes engineering such as car and ship building and a variety of manufacturing processes, especially those associated with food processing and the nuclear industry. Gravel extraction has had a significant effect on the countryside of many of the river valleys, particularly the Thames, with important archaeological remains coming to light. This activity is now beginning to have an impact on the marine environment.

Table 1.1 HER/UAD Records

HER/UAD	Number of records
Berkshire Archaeology	10611
Buckinghamshire	36983
Hampshire	45570
Isle of Wight	13445
Milton Keynes	9000
Oxfordshire	36200
Oxford City UAD	3936
Portsmouth*	
Southampton	8836
West Berkshire	9027
Winchester – UAD	5073
Winchester – excluding UAD area	6640

*At the time of writing no access to this HER was available.

Sources of information for the Historic Environment

A number of key sources of information were consulted during the compilation of the Resource Assessments and Research Agendas presented in this volume, and many of these are available to the public at large.

Historic Environment Records

The primary sources of archaeological information are the Historic Environment Records (HERs) maintained at local authority level. Oxfordshire was, in 1964, the first county to set up a Sites and Monuments Record (SMR), as they were previously called, followed by the other historic counties. Today, West Berkshire maintains its own HER, but the other Unitary Authorities in the old county have set up a joint resource, Berkshire Archaeology, based in Reading. Milton Keynes, the City of Southampton and the City of Portsmouth have their own HERs. As part of an English Heritage-funded initiative, Urban Archaeological Databases have been created for Oxford City and for Winchester. These operate in parallel with their county-based HERs, although the relevant authorities are continuing to develop their records and Winchester now has a district-wide HER.

The data on the numbers of monuments and events recorded in the HERs in 2011 is given in Table 1.1.

In addition to databases of events and monuments, HERs are repositories of unpublished archaeological reports ('grey literature'). The National Monuments Record (NMR) in Swindon, maintained by English Heritage, has a similar database and its grey literature includes many thematic surveys of industrial buildings of particular relevance for this area. The NMR also holds large collections of architectural plans and photographs, particularly air photographs. Photographs can also be seen in local record offices and local history centres.

It is now possible to access online a version of all of the Historic Environment Records of the Solent-Thames region (apart from Portsmouth). *Heritage Gateway*, maintained by English Heritage, is increasingly used as a portal for searching both local and national records, but in several instances HER information can also be searched through the respective local authority websites, which often supply additional material such as parish surveys or Historic Landscape Characterisation studies (HLC).

Local archaeological services

The provision of local authority curatorial services very largely replicates the distribution of HERs/UADs. In addition, the New Forest National Park maintains a separate Archaeological Officer. For Listed Buildings, the responsibility usually lies at a more local level, the various districts having their own Conservation Officers.

The Portable Antiquities Scheme (PAS) was established to encourage the general public to report any archaeological finds they made, enabling this information to be entered onto a database. Information from the PAS

Plate 1.7 Finds Liaison Officer at work, Isle of Wight, *copyright Isle of Wight Council*

is fed back into HERs at intervals. To facilitate recording, a network of Finds Liaison Officers (FLOs) was established. There are five FLOs covering the Solent-Thames sub-region: the Isle of Wight; Hampshire; West Berkshire and Oxfordshire; Buckinghamshire; and East Berkshire (along with Surrey) (Plate 1.7).

Designated sites

The Solent-Thames region has a rich resource and many of the sites have been recognised as of national or international significance and awarded a designated status. There is one World Heritage Site within the region: Blenheim Palace, which was inscribed in 1986 (see Plate 17.3). Scheduled Monuments range from the Neolithic Rollright Stones (see Plate 7.12) in the north of Oxfordshire to the GAMA complex at Greenham Common, Berkshire (see Plate 17.7), via iconic sites such as Carisbrooke Castle in the Isle of Wight (Plate 1.8). There is also a wide variety of Listed Buildings of very varied character. Tables 1.2-1.5 show how designation categories are distributed across the region using data from the English Heritage National Heritage List for England in 2011.

This distribution obviously partly reflects the relative size of the areas covered by the different local authority areas, as shown on Figure 1.1: Hampshire occupies by far the largest area and, although Milton Keynes was a designated New Town, it incorporated several important villages and their hinterlands. It is also affected by the urban character of many of the Unitary Authorities. Bracknell Forest and Slough in particular are fairly recent developments.

Museums, Record Offices and Local History Centres

The Solent-Thames region is well served by museums run by local authorities, by private organisations and by trusts and, in the cases of Oxford and Reading, by their Universities. In Berkshire, there are two principal museums: Reading Museum and the West Berkshire Museum in Newbury, in addition to the Museum of English Rural Life at Reading University. The Buckinghamshire Museum is located in Aylesbury and there is also a museum in Milton Keynes and the Chiltern Open Air Museum at Chalfont St Giles. Hampshire Museum Service maintains a number of museums, and there are also independent museums in Winchester and the Cities of Portsmouth and Southampton. The Isle of Wight

Plate 1.8 Donkey wheel, Carisbrooke Castle, Isle of Wight, *copyright English Heritage*

Table 1.2 Scheduled Ancient Monuments by Authority area

Local Authority	Number of Scheduled Monuments
Bracknell Forest	12
Buckinghamshire	142
City of Portsmouth	18
City of Southampton	42
Hampshire	617
Isle of Wight	120
Milton Keynes	50
Oxfordshire	298
Reading	2
Slough	2
West Berkshire	91
Windsor & Maidenhead	17
Wokingham	18

Table 1.3 Listed Buildings by Authority area

Local Authority	No Grade I listings	No Grade II* listings	No Grade II listings
Bracknell Forest	1	9	253
Buckinghamshire	135	296	5374
City of Portsmouth	12	32	406
City of Southampton	12	19	286
Hampshire	183	494	10095
Isle of Wight	29	67	1837
Milton Keynes	30	59	1001
Oxfordshire	381	689	11073
Reading	6	21	480
Slough	5	7	90
West Berkshire	42	107	1736
Windsor & Maidenhead	22	69	866
Wokingham	9	40	592

Table 1.4 Registered Parks and Gardens by Authority area

Local Authority	No of Grade I	No of Grade II*	No of Grade II
Bracknell Forest	1	2	3
Buckinghamshire	5	11	20
City of Portsmouth	0	0	3
City of Southampton	0	1	2
Hampshire	2	22	32
Isle of Wight	0	1	7
Milton Keynes	0	2	1
Oxfordshire	9	16	33
Reading	0	0	5
Slough	0	0	4
West Berkshire	0	4	10
Windsor & Maidenhead	7	1	4
Wokingham	0	4	3

Table 1.5 Registered Battlefields by Authority area

Local Authority	No Battlefields
Bracknell Forest	0
Buckinghamshire	0
City of Portsmouth	0
City of Southampton	0
Hampshire	1
Isle of Wight	0
Milton Keynes	0
Oxfordshire	2
Reading	0
Slough	0
West Berkshire	1
Windsor & Maidenhead	0
Wokingham	0

Museum Service also supports a wide range of museums, including the Museum of Island History at Newport. Oxfordshire Museum Service has its principal museum in Woodstock, but provides services to other local museums. Oxford University houses the Ashmolean Museum, the University Museum and the Pitt Rivers Museum.

Each of the counties has its own Record Office: Berkshire Record Office in Reading; the Centre for Buckinghamshire Studies in Aylesbury; Hampshire Archives and Local Studies in Winchester; the Isle of Wight Record Office in Newport; and the Oxfordshire History Centre. There are also the Southampton City Archives and Portsmouth Record Office. To supplement these, a number of the larger libraries, particularly within the Unitary Authorities, also contain a local studies collection.

Access to catalogues is available online for the Record Offices. Their websites increasingly provide direct access to many of the holdings, including for example all the enclosure maps and awards for Berkshire. 'Oxfordshire Heritage Search' includes catalogues for not just the record office, but also many

of the county's museums, with much material, including the HER, available to view.

Societies and education

Each of the historic counties of the Solent-Thames region has at least one county society covering archaeology and/or local history. Each county society produces a journal: the *Berkshire Archaeological Journal*, the *Records of Buckinghamshire*, *Hampshire Studies*, *Wight Studies* and *Oxoniensia*. In addition, archaeological work across the region is reported in two of the Council for British Archaeology journals: *CBA Wessex News*, covering Berkshire, Hampshire and the Isle of Wight, and *South Midlands Archaeology*, which includes Buckinghamshire and Oxfordshire.

The number of societies relating to the historic environment is very large, catering for a wide range of local and specialist interests. In Berkshire, Hampshire and Oxfordshire there are umbrella organisations drawing together the various local history societies for the county. The Oxfordshire *History* website provides information about the county's past and provides many useful links. The Buckinghamshire Archaeological

Society supports the Buckinghamshire Local History Network (BLHN).

There are nine universities within the region: Buckingham, Buckinghamshire New University, the Open University, Oxford, Oxford Brookes, Portsmouth, Reading, Southampton and Winchester. Of these, Buckingham is the only one not to offer any historic environment related courses. The Open University, Oxford, Reading, Southampton and Winchester all offer archaeology at undergraduate and masters level. Oxford University also offers a wide range of continuing education courses, one of the few universities anywhere in the country to continue work of this type.

Many of the universities are involved in research projects within the region. Reading University's Silchester Project is in its 15th year, for example, the *Hillforts of the Ridgeway* project carried out by the University of Oxford is nearing completion, while the University of Southampton has been commissioned by English Heritage to prepare a *Maritime and Marine Historic Environment Research Framework*. Important contributions are also made by establishments outside the region, most notably the University of Leicester, which has been one of the partners in the *Wallingford Burgh to Borough* project since 2008, and also in the Whittlewood Project, which includes the north-east of Buckinghamshire.

Key projects

The level of research activity within the Solent-Thames region is very healthy, with the impetus for work coming from all levels, from national initiatives to projects run wholly by local societies. It is impossible to discuss all of this work, but a number of key projects are described briefly below.

Urban surveys were carried out for Oxfordshire, Berkshire and Hampshire in the 1970s. With English Heritage funding, an updated version for Hampshire and the Isle of Wight has been prepared, and work is underway in Buckinghamshire. Oxford and Winchester have also been covered by another English Heritage initiative for larger towns and cities. Each has an Urban Archaeological Database prepared following careful inspection and analysis of the records of past work. These databases form the foundation for a deeper understanding of a town's development and help formulate a specific Research Agenda. In Oxford this stage of the work is well underway.

Another relevant research programme is Historic Landscape Characterisation (HLC). This has been carried out for Hampshire; West Berkshire (including the part of Oxfordshire within the North Wessex Downs AONB); Buckinghamshire and the Chilterns (extending to areas beyond the Solent-Thames Region). A Landscape Characterisation study has also been prepared for the Cotswolds AONB, which extends into Oxfordshire, and an HLC for Oxfordshire has begun in 2012.

English Heritage's National Mapping Programme has covered four areas in the Solent-Thames sub-region: the Cotswold Hills, Hampshire South Downs, Lambourn Downs and the Thames Valley, one of its pilot projects.

There have been many local research projects over the past few years involving excavation and survey, some of which have already been mentioned. These have been undertaken variously by academic, professional and non-professional groups.

The Tidgrove Project, centred on the medieval site at Tidgrove Warren, was a joint enterprise between Kingsclere Heritage Association and the University of Southampton. As a result of the work earlier occupation from the late Iron Age and Roman periods was also identified.

The Hampshire and Wight Trust for Maritime Archaeology has been involved in many projects within the region, including the *Wootton Quarr* and *Bouldnor Cliff* projects, and work in Langstone Harbour has been examining the intertidal zone further east. The Danebury Trust spent many years studying the Iron Age hillfort and its surrounding landscape and, in *Danebury Environs Project II*, work has been extended to cover the Romano-British period.

Excavations at Silchester by Reading University, examining the Roman town, its origins and hinterland started *c.* 1974 and continue to yield exciting discoveries and excellent outreach facilities, as does the work at Marcham/Frilford undertaken by the Oxford University. The hillforts of the Berkshire Downs have also received attention, as mentioned above.

A collaborative research project at Dorchester-on-Thames, involving Oxford University, Oxford Archaeology and the local residents of Dorchester co-ordinated through the local museum, is investigating its development from Neolithic ceremonial complex to medieval monastery. This highlights the important role that local, non-professionals play in archaeological research in the area. A good example of this was the recent Whiteleaf Project, near Princes Risborough in Buckinghamshire (Plate 1.9).

Plate 1.9 Work in progress at Whiteleaf, Buckinghamshire, *copyright OA*

Work continues on the Victoria County History volumes for Oxfordshire and the VCH team have combined this with the *England's Past for Everyone* initiative funded by the Heritage Lottery Fund. Two volumes, one on Burford and another on Henley-on-Thames, have been produced with the assistance of local individuals and groups. A further community initiative is in place linked to preparation of the volume covering Ewelme hundred.

A number of large developer-funded projects have also played an important role in advancing our understanding of the historic environment, for example the Eton Rowing Course, the Maidenhead to Windsor Flood Alleviation Scheme, Yarnton and other projects focused on gravel extraction, for example around Stanton Harcourt and Abingdon in Oxfordshire and Reading in Berkshire.

Oxford Archaeology is publishing four volumes in a series entitled *Thames Through Time*. This has been an Aggregate Sustainability Levy Fund project to provide an overview of the area surrounding the non-tidal section of the River Thames, where there has been so much development work in recent years. Much of this area lies within the Solent-Thames sub-region. Three volumes have been published and the Later Historical Period volume is in preparation. A *Historical Atlas of Berkshire* (ed. Joan Dils) was published in 1998 and the *Historical Atlas of Oxfordshire* (eds Tiller and Darkes) in 2010.

Chapter 2

An introduction to the geo-archaeology, palaeo-environmental and archaeological science of the Solent-Thames sub-region

by Michael J. Allen

Introductory comments

Understanding and defining the human lived-in landscape, its natural and humanly exploited resources and economy, farming and food production (i.e. the discipline we sometimes call 'environmental archaeology' – see Luff and Rowley Conwy 1994) must not be divorced from aspects of cultural, artefactual and social archaeology (Bradley 1978, 2; Allen 1996). Nevertheless, because of the number of specialists involved, and the fact that environmental archaeology has been considered an 'interest group' of its own, both environmental archaeology and archaeological science have sometimes been given research agendas in their own right. For environmental archaeology these have included Hampshire (Allen 1996) and the South West (Wilkinson & Straker 2008); for archaeological science see Bayley 1998. In this research framework, these topics will be fully covered within the successive chronologically-organised chapters.

Some topographical zones of the Solent-Thames corridor are distinctly more conducive to preservation of palaeo-environmental information or macrofossils than others (see Allen 1996). These topographic zones will be dealt in summary below, but in terms of 'environmental archaeology' nevertheless there are some comments of an introductory nature that are over-arching and embrace all periods. Certainly Luff & Rowley Conwy (1994) dislike the term 'environmental archaeology', but its longevity of use and the wide umbrella nature of the term are useful. In this review the broad 'environmental' discipline is divided into two distinct, but not wholly separate themes: land-use and landscape on the one hand, and economy and diet on the other, as has been done previously (eg Hampshire Environmental Archaeology review; Allen 1996). In general the focus is more directed on the former (i.e. land-use and landscape) than the latter in this paper, as archaeologists engage with information about diet and economy more readily, and the information is often more readily digestible or accessible.

Chronologically environmental archaeology is clearly more heavily (and integrally) involved with the earlier periods; of necessity, prehistorians have long had to deal with issues of landscapes and land-uses that differ markedly from those we engage with today. In the historic periods environmental and scientific archaeology are more concentrated upon issues of diet and economy. In the latter periods these disciplines should be engaged much more fully than is regularly the case, although this engagement should always be within a directed research framework, whether the project is undertaken for commercial or purely archaeological reasons, rather than being just a data-gathering exercise. Studies of landscape and land-use development have often been far more efficacious and productive in terms of results that are immediately understandable and usable to the archaeologist leading a project, though interpretations provided by the component specific scientific analyses have not always been so readily accessible or immediately evidently relevant. Nevertheless there are a number of environmental and scientific themes that are generally applicable, regardless of the period, and these are set out below in summary:-

- During all periods we need to define, at a much higher spatial resolution than before, the nature of the local landscape and land-use than hitherto, and then use these site-specific data to re-evaluate and redefine regional and chronological trends.

- Our understanding of food procurement economies is generally woefully poor except at the general level. If we are to advance in our understanding of communities and society in the past then this is an area that requires concerted attention.

- Advances in archaeological science are now having earth-shattering effects on our comprehension of diet, mobility and origin. Isotope analysis is isolating main dietary components (meat, plant and fish/marine composting) while other isotope suites are defining the high state of mobility within what may be large portions of prehistoric communities, as seen in the case of Cranborne lady and children found on the chalk at Monkton-up-Wimborne in Dorset (Green 2000), but who were brought up on, and revisited, Mendip (Montgomery *et al.* 2000).

- Chronology. No longer are radiocarbon dates needed to confirm the longevity of an established chronological epoch, and rarely to confirm that any item or event merely belonged to that period. Recent advances using Bayesian analysis now allows us to examine events at the generational scale in the Neolithic (Bayliss & Whittle 2007), and the results are destroying long-held assumptions of longevity of monuments or social activities.

- Spatial awareness. Developer-funded applied research archaeology is confined by the spatial parameters of the development threat. Most research-led archaeological fieldwork is however also spatially constrained by the assumptions of the researcher or pre-conceived framework of spatial distribution of activity. Commercial archaeology does however produce the opportunity for serendipitous discovery. Development is often in areas where no archaeology is known, and where the lack of recorded finds in a topographical zone may have led to a view that such areas were empty, ensuring that such areas were considered of low priority. Chance finds in dry valleys (eg Allen 2005) and concerted research on the slopes of the Thames valley (Yates 1999) have now allowed these to be added to prehistoric settlement and land-use patterns, and have forced us to re-evaluate these regions and topographic zones.

Although research themes can be addressed and specifically targeted, commercial archaeology is innately prone to unforeseen and unexpected finds despite the highly computerised and numerous SMR or HER records held by development control authorities. For instance, the location of a commercial archaeological project is precisely defined by the developer and development needs. Where these coincide with areas of few archaeological records we assume little or no archaeological return, and we must be acutely aware that this lack of records may result from a deficiency of former archaeological investigation and enquiry. Thus areas of the interfluves of the Kennet valley now seem to be the location of a number of later prehistoric sites, and are often charcoal-rich and associated with industrial activities. Only recently have these areas been recognised as of archaeological value, and our comprehension of the commensurate evidence of palaeo-environmental, landscape, land-use and the wider farming economy of these areas is even more tardy. Lacunae such as these need identifying, targeting and reviewing to ensure that such areas or topographical locations are rapidly highlighted in the HER records, and are fully accounted for in development control decisions.

Physiographic and topographic zones

Although the period by period review adequately covers the main points of future research and attention, from the environmental and geo-archaeological perspective in particular, the main building blocks or topographic zones have distinct and separate characteristics in terms of sedimentation and their potential to preserve environmental information. These factors are directly relevant to the nature of the available environmental data, and to its acquisition. Further, in some areas burial beneath colluvial, alluvial and marine sediments removes sites, cultural evidence and palaeo-environmental evidence from our immediate reconnaissance, and should not be overlooked. Both long- and short-term projects have clearly demonstrated the highly biased nature of the immediately available archaeological resource (eg Allen & Gardiner 2000; Allen 1988), and are starting to indicate patterns where whole classes of human activity are specifically located in areas that have been subjected to such burial. Recognition of this can radically change our view of activity in entire epochs, eg the Beaker/Chalcolithic period (see Allen 2005).

The Solent-Thames corridor has been divided into six basic crude topographical zones (Fig. 1.4), in which some of the principal topographic forms, characteristics with regard to palaeo-environmental preservation and geo-archaeological potential are summarily outlined.

Chalklands (Hampshire, Berkshire Downs, Chilterns)

Topography, Form and Palaeo-environmental preservation and geo-archaeological potential

The chalklands generally form one of the most significant 'uplands' of these parts of lowland Britain. They typically comprise a scarp edge or scarp slope and more gently dipping or plateau upland, bisected by a dendritic pattern of dry valleys of varying size, form and amplification. In places the chalk is mantled by drift deposits of clay-with-flints or Tertiary Clays and gravels, which give rise to locally more acidic soils (eg brown earths or argillic brown earths), rather than the characteristic calcareous rendzina- form soils that mantle much of this landform. The calcareous nature of the chalk, and thus the soils and deposits derived from it, provide potentially ideal preservation for bone and shell including land snails. In contrast, its free-draining nature leads to generally dry and heavily bioturbated soils and deposits in which pollen preservation is sparse and waterlogging rare, and thus the preservation of insect remains is extremely rare, if not unknown. Geo-archaeologically, understanding the soil history of these areas has been demonstrated to be of crucial importance (French *et al.* 2007), and the presence of localised calcareous colluvium provides significant palaeo-environmental opportunities as well as sealing and masking key locations in the landscape, often burying archaeological sites and evidence.

The Hampshire chalklands surprisingly have had relatively little palaeo-environmental attention in comparison with the central Wessex chalklands (eg Dorchester, Cranborne Chase, Stonehenge and Avebury), yet these may form the boundary between two major ecological and cultural zones. To the west are areas rich in henges and henge-type monuments and with Grooved Ware, while, in contrast Sussex contains few or no incontrovertible henges on the chalk, and Grooved Ware is conspicuous by its absence. At the same time the early woodlands are seen to differ; those in the Wessex region contain a mosaic of woodland and woodland openings, whilst Sussex seems to contain a more uniform woodland cover (Allen & Gardiner 2009). Clearly the boundary between these zones, if such exists, lie within the Solent-Thames region; indeed the Solent-Thames region *is* that boundary.

In contrast the Berkshire Downs and Chilterns (eg Whiteleaf Hill) have seen some major single-site palaeo-environmental studies, and a number of small-scale projects, but the density is generally low and synthetic overviews are almost totally absent. The chalklands are considered to be well-studied, but this is not always true (see major new interpretations of the Wessex chalk and South Downs, Allen & Scaife 2007; Allen & Gardiner 2009), particularly as regards the Berkshire Downs, Marlborough Downs and Chilterns.

River Valleys/Corridors (Class I rivers: Avon, Thames, Kennet, Thame, Colne, Test, Itchen, Great Ouse)

River valleys by their very nature often cut though, or provide a division between, physiographic and topographic zones; they are both boundaries and corridors. Individually they are largely defined by the geology through which they cut and over which they run; this circumscribes the shape and form of the valley, as well as bed form and load and the nature of any resultant alluvium.

Often rich soils may be found on the floodplain. There is water to drink from the river and pools on its margins, food (fish and fowl) and other resources (reeds, clay, gravels, flint) are plentiful, and the topography forms a natural corridor. These features attracted past human populations to visit, exploit, and utilise them. Such human activity varied from periodic short-term visits, through seasonal use, to long-term non-settlement activities, and in places, to longer-term settlement.

In economic terms, therefore, the significance of these areas is clear. In palaeo-environmental and geo-archaeological terms these are potentially very rich and highly significant. River valleys provide two main landscape elements: the former channels and the channel itself, and the floodplain and floodplain islands. River courses and channels wander across floodplains stripping out sediment and archaeological activity, sorting and transporting elements of them downstream. Unless channel avulsion (rapid channel abandonment and creation of new channels) occurs, channel forms may be tens or hundreds of metres across, cutting on one side and infilling on the other. Abandoned and infilled channels provide long sedimentary and palaeo-environmental records of the watercourse itself, and of the local and wider environment, via a combination of the sediments, land and fresh-water mollusc, plant and insect remains, and pollen (eg Anslow's Cottages

(Butterworth & Lobb 1992), and Testwood, Hampshire (Fitzpatrick *et al.* 1996).

The floodplains may provide long sequences through overbank floodplain and alluvium, and in areas of high water table these may be waterlogged (containing waterlogged plant remains and insects, as well as pollen and land and fresh-water Mollusca, or even peat). The latter can vary from small local buried 'pools' to wide and complex expanses, such as at the Denham, Colne and Rushbrook valleys in Buckinghamshire. Peat provides not only the opportunity for waterlogged remains and very good, long and detailed pollen sequences, but also the potential to date the onset, changes within and the demise of these landscape events. With their potential to reflect local, extra-local and sub-regional land-use and environment, the palaeo-environmental evidence in these locations can be of major regional or national significance. This is further heightened by the potential for human activity to be present, exceptionally well-preserved and interstratified in these sequences (eg at Runneymede).

Stream courses and valleys

Stream courses and other valleys provide similar opportunities to those in the major (class 1) river valleys, but just on a smaller scale. That does not mean that the potential for palaeo-environmental preservation or presence is any less, nor that deep and long palaeo-environmental sequences do not exist; more that the scale of human activity may be smaller. On this basis alone, this is considered to be a separate, sub-group of the major river courses.

Claylands and 'upland' gravels (New Forest, North Oxfordshire and North Buckinghamshire Vales, Thames basin)

These form large expanses of undulating ground along the coastal fringes of the Solent and New Forest to the London Basin and the Vales of Central and North Oxfordshire and North Buckinghamshire (Northamptonshire Vale, Upper Thames Vale, White Horse Vale etc). These are on varied geologies ranging from clays to sands and gravels, but generally provide low relief landforms, although varying considerably in drainage and water retention properties. Nevertheless, these zones are characterised by their heterogeneous low relief and relatively acid soils, often related to the presence of former major drainage systems. In general bone and shell survival is variable and (with local exceptions) land and fresh-water molluscan survival is poor. Nevertheless charred remains are often present, and the potential for highly localised waterlogging preserving waterlogged plant remains, insects and pollen sequences is high. These areas provide one of the widest expanses of long and intermittent use through prehistory and early history. As zones, however, we have little synthetic work on each of these regions as a whole, even if specific long-term and large research projects, for example in the Vale of the White Horse, Oxfordshire, have studied one part of a specific area (see Tingle 1991; Miles *et al.* 2003).

Limestone ridge (Cotswolds)

The Cotswolds running east-west through Oxfordshire and Buckinghamshire provide a unique and distinctive stony hard landscape. They form upland with higher relief than the surrounding areas, and sharper forms than many other zones in the Solent-Thames corridor. Today the slow-weathering Inferior and Great Oolitic limestone give rise to relatively thin, non-calcareous soils, but have been proven to generate moderate thickness of non-calcareous colluvium in dry valleys and at the foot of hill slopes, especially in Gloucestershire and West Oxfordshire. The preservation of bone and shell is moderate; land snails are poorly preserved as a result of the slow weathering and release of calcium carbonate of the limestone. On the whole, like the chalklands, these are freely to moderately freely draining with little potential for waterlogging (except in local and exceptional circumstances). Consequently insects and waterlogged plant remains are scarce except in streams and watercourses traversing or draining from the Cotswolds. Our economic information in terms of animal bones and charred seeds is moderate compared with other zones, but that of the specific landscape character and land-use is generally sparser.

Intertidal (coastal margins of Hampshire and Isle of Wight)

Topography, Form, Palaeo-environmental preservation and geo-archaeological potential

The present intertidal zones are low-lying areas poorly surveyed in archaeological terms, in which the potential for exceptional palaeo-environmental and archaeological preservation exists. Recent work in the Severn Estuary and on the Welsh coastline for example, has recovered lines of prehistoric human footprints and animal tracks (eg Bell 2007). The potential for these certainly exists along the Solent margins, but the resources needed to find these, and other important finds, have not yet materialised. High water tables provide the possibility of preservation by waterlogging, as well as the presence of most other proxy palaeo-environmental indicators. Some of these currently low-lying marine environments were completely different landscapes with fundamentally different environmental characteristics in early historic and prehistoric periods. Although coastal today and in recent historic times, in many cases these may once have been dry land. The natural inlet of Langstone harbour, for instance, was once open dry lowland, with small freshwater streams flowing across a wider and deeper coastal plain (Allen & Gardiner 2000).

Surveys of the largely muddy foreshores around Langstone Harbour (Allen & Gardiner 2000) and between Wootton and Quarr, Isle of Wight (Tomalin *et al.* 2012) are the only significant coastal margin surveys to date. The potential of other inter-tidal foreshore areas has yet to be explored from both an environmental and palaeo-environmental perspective. This zone is a narrow and temporary physiographic zone that does not necessarily represent that of the past, nor future, landscape. The potential for finding evidence of submerged forests and nationally significant palaeo-environmental and palaeo-economic evidence is high. These areas also contain the potential to obtain dated sea-level index points to refine the Solent sea-level curves (eg Long & Tooley 1995; Long *et al.* 2000) and general sea-level curves specific to defined study areas.

Current Marine (Solent)

The current sea bed is an under-explored archaeological and palaeo-environmental resource, largely due to the difficulty and expense of obtaining access to these benthic landforms and landscapes. In the Palaeolithic and through to the end of the Mesolithic periods, however, a large part of the Solent was dry land or lowland with high groundwater tables. Recent sub-bottom profiling and coring off the West Sussex coast has revealed peats and land surfaces of Mesolithic date under 30 m or more of water. There is no reason why such preservation should not occur in the Solent or off the Isle of Wight coast. In geo-archaeological terms, defining the nature and altitude of the benthic landscape in relation to known sea-levels demonstrates that there is a large landmass that was once habitable. We have yet to get to grips with this landscape conceptually, let alone define the clearly rich palaeo-environmental and palaeo-economic evidence that will be preserved there.

The sea bed also provides the last resting place of a number of land-based artefacts washed out to sea, as well as larger artefacts and marine vessels such as the *Mary Rose* dating to AD 1545 (eg Gardiner with Allen 2005) and the *Invincible*, which sank in AD 1758 (Bingeman 2010). Whilst a detailed strategy and huge effort in sampling and analysing the waterlogged palaeo-environmental remains and other scientific data was expended, with huge rewards from the *Mary Rose*, (Gardiner with Allen 2005, 302-650) the same potential was not exploited for the excavations of the *Invincible*. The potential for recovering good palaeo-economic evidence relating to food-production in southern English is high, but so too is the potential, in time, to recover early historic or prehistoric vessels – see for instance the Dover boat. The endeavours on the Mary Rose, essentially a project of the 1970s and 1980s, showed the huge resource scarcely tapped in terms of palaeo-environmental and palaeo-economic data.

Chapter 3

The Lower/Middle Palaeolithic Resource Assessment and Research Agenda

by Francis Wenban-Smith, Terry Hardaker, Robert Hosfield, Rebecca Loader,
Barbara Silva, Keith Wilkinson, David Bridgland and Kate Cramp

Introduction

This review of the Lower and Middle Palaeolithic resource in the Solent-Thames region considers the region as a whole, embracing the five county authorities of Buckinghamshire, Oxfordshire, Berkshire, Hampshire and the Isle of Wight. Previous reviews (Table 3.1) have given a detailed picture of the resource in each county. This synthesis combines this information to provide a more general overview of the nature, distribution, diversity and potential importance of the resource in the region.

Before addressing these central themes, some general background is provided on the British Palaeolithic, and the Pleistocene geological period during which it occurred. Following this, the current landscape of the Solent-Thames region is reviewed, focusing on topography, drainage and bedrock geology, but also considering the potential for paleoenvironmental and human remains ; these contemporary landscape aspects are intimately related to the present survival and distribution of Pleistocene deposits, and the story they tell of climatic change and landscape development through the long period covered by the Lower/Middle Palaeolithic.

As will become clear, the approach taken to the core object of reviewing the Lower/Middle Palaeolithic resource in the region is deposit-centred rather than find-centred. Clearly artefact finds are the most direct evidence of the Palaeolithic; but, research into, and understanding of, the period depends almost more upon the context of discovery than upon the finds themselves. Most importantly, the potential for the existence of a Palaeolithic site is initially contingent upon the presence of Pleistocene sediments; and then the questions are: what do they contain in the way of Palaeolithic remains, and how important are these remains for current research? Central to answering these questions is the nature of the sediment containing any remains, how it formed, and the taphonomy of the evidence contained. This section is based, therefore, upon reviews of the range of Pleistocene sediments within the region, their differing formation processes, and consequently the varied potential importance of any contained Palaeolithic remains. Attention is then given to the distribution, prevalence and potential of the Palaeolithic remains in the different deposits in the region, and to identification of key areas/sites.

The resource review is then followed by an interpretive overview of our current understanding of the Lower/Middle Palaeolithic in the region. This looks at the regional history of occupation within the wider national context, and presents interpretations of lifestyle and behaviour. The final section briefly reviews the end of the Lower/Middle Palaeolithic in Britain, and the transition to Upper Palaeolithic.

Background

The inheritance: the British Palaeolithic in global context

The Palaeolithic, or Old Stone Age, is the earliest period of prehistory, representing the very substantial period of time for which our main surviving evidence is lithic

Table 3.1 County reviews of the Lower and Middle Palaeolithic Resource

County	Author	Title	Link/Availability
Berkshire	Hosfield, R.	Solent–Thames Research Framework: Lower/Middle Palaeolithic Resource (Berkshire)	
Buckinghamshire	Silva, B.	An Archaeological Resource Assessment of the Lower/Middle Palaeolithic in Buckinghamshire	
Hampshire	Wilkinson, K.	The Palaeolithic of Hampshire	
Isle of Wight	Wenban-Smith, FF. & Loader, R.	The Isle of Wight: a Review of the Lower and Middle Palaeolithic Resource	
Oxfordshire	Hardaker, T.	The Lower and Middle Palaeolithic of Oxfordshire	

artefacts. Globally, the Palaeolithic begins in the east African Rift Valley over two million BP (years Before Present), with the manufacture of simple stone chopping tools by Australopithecines, a group of bipedal apes with a brain capacity not very different from the modern chimpanzee. The initial hominin expansion out of Africa took place between 1.5 and 1 million years ago, and involved eastward migration across southern Europe into Asia (Dennell 2003). The hominins at this stage, named as *Homo erectus* or *Homo ergaster*, and much more recognisably human than their Australopithecine ancestors, were capable of inhabiting a range of tropical and sub-tropical regions, but could not yet cope with the seasonality of the higher European latitudes.

The start of the British Palaeolithic is defined by the earliest hominin presence in Britain as reflected in lithic artefacts. Clearly this is therefore not an easily fixed date, but one liable to vary in conjunction with new discoveries and with improved dating of existing remains. Initial expansion into Britain and northern Europe seems to have consisted of very occasional forays during periods of warm climate between 800,000 and 500,000 BP. A few very early sites of this age are known in France and Spain, as well as one recently discovered in Britain at Pakefield on the Norfolk coast (Parfitt *et al.* 2005). These pioneer populations failed to establish themselves, however, and soon died out. Following these isolated occurrences of very early hominin presence, there then was a major range expansion northward into Britain and northern Europe *c.* 500,000 years ago. There are a number of sites from this period with evidence of stone tool manufacture (Roebroeks & van Kolfschoten 1994; 1995), associated with the early western European *Homo heidelbergensis*, named after a jawbone found in a quarry at Mauer, near Heidelberg, in Germany. The main British site is Boxgrove in West Sussex, where an extensive area of undisturbed lithic evidence is associated with abundant faunal remains and palaeo-environmental indicators, as well as fossil remains of two hominid individuals (Pitts & Roberts 1997; Roberts & Parfitt 1999). These comprise two lower front incisors from one individual, and a shinbone from another. Hominid remains from this period are so rare that the Heidelberg and Boxgrove finds comprise the full northern European skeletal record of this early ancestor.

One of the key factors to bear in mind when considering the British Palaeolithic is that it coincides with the second half of the Pleistocene geological period (aka 'The Ice Age'). During the Pleistocene, there were repeated climatic oscillations between warm, interglacial conditions and severe cold. This would have inevitably resulted in major variations in the character of day-to-day existence over time, as well as upon long-term patterns of colonisation and occupation. Between 500,000 and 425,000 BP, there was a marked deterioration in climate (the Anglian glaciation), leading to most of Britain being covered by ice, and abandonment by (or local extinction of) the hominin population. Following the end of the Anglian glaciation, Palaeolithic occupa-

tion became much more frequent in Britain, although certainly not continuous. Further periodic deteriorations in climate would have made Britain uninhabitable, and existing populations must either have again died out, or moved southward to the continent. Britain would then have become inhabitable again as the climate ameliorated. Sea levels would, however, have risen with the warming climate, and, once the straits of Dover had been created through breaching the Dover–Calais Chalk ridge, probably shortly after the end of the Anglian (Gibbard 1995), access to Britain would have been effectively obstructed during warm periods. The potential of hominids and other fauna to recolonise would have been governed by a sensitively balanced combination of the distribution of the refuge population, its rate of expansion as climate changed and the rate of sea level rise. Once a population had returned to Britain it would then be isolated from the continent by high sea-level until the following climatic deterioration. This history of contact with the northern European mainland through the Palaeolithic, and of abandonment and recolonisation of Britain, or of extinction of its population, is still poorly understood.

The Palaeolithic population of Britain seems to have flourished for at least 150,000 years following the end of the Anglian glaciation. Numerous sites of this period, often with very abundant evidence, are found across southern Britain. Then, after *c.* 250,000 BP, there seems to have been a marked decline in Palaeolithic occupation. Between this time and the end of the Palaeolithic at *c.* 10,000 BP, there again seems to have been only very sporadic incursions into Britain by the Palaeolithic populations that were relatively abundant and almost continuously present on the European continent. As is explained in more detail further below, this period of absence coincides with the spread across Europe and western Asia of the Neanderthal people, their subsequent extinction and the first appearance in Britain of anatomically modern humans in *c.* 30,000 BP.

The other key points to take on board when considering the Palaeolithic are that it is an immensely long period of time, at least 600,000 years in Britain, and that almost the only evidence of the period are stone artefacts that we recognise as humanly worked. These are found in a range of natural Pleistocene deposits, and our understanding of the Palaeolithic is mostly based upon our interpretation of the context in which lithic artefacts are found, and study of associated faunal and floral remains. These lead to dating of sites and construction of frameworks of material cultural change, climatic and palaeo-environmental reconstruction, and, on rare occasions when artefacts are undisturbed, direct reconstruction of hominin activity.

The Palaeolithic and the Pleistocene

Study of the Palaeolithic is inseparably entwined with study of the Pleistocene. During the Pleistocene the climate underwent numerous and repeated dramatic changes, oscillating between glacials – episodes of severe cold, and interglacials – episodes of warmth. Thus, rather than a single Ice Age, there were repeated ice ages throughout the Pleistocene, separated by interglacials. At the cold peak of glacial periods, ice-sheets hundreds of metres thick would have covered most of Britain, reaching on occasion as far south as London, and rendering the country uninhabitable. At the warm peak of interglacials the climate would have been warmer than the present day; mollusc species that now inhabit the Nile were abundant in British rivers, and tropical fauna, such as hippopotamus and forest elephant, were common in the landscape. For the majority of the time, however, the climate would have been somewhere between these extremes.

The start of the Pleistocene, approximately 1.8 million years BP, is marked by an initial deterioration in the climate. Following this, over sixty numbered cold and warm stages have been recognised up to the present day, based on fluctuating proportions of the oxygen isotopes O^{18} and O^{16} in deep sea foraminifera. By convention odd numbers represent warm stages and even numbers cold ones, and different stages are counted back from the present. We are therefore currently in marine isotope stage (MIS) 1, also known as the Holocene, which represents the 10,000-year warm period since the end of the last cold stage (the Devensian glaciation) (Table 3.2). The Middle and Late Pleistocene are of most relevance to British Palaeolithic archaeology, with the first occupation of Britain occurring early in the Middle Pleistocene, and continuing thereafter, albeit with a number of gaps.

Middle and Late Pleistocene climatic oscillations were sufficiently marked to have a major impact on sea level and terrestrial sedimentation regimes. In the colder periods ice sheets grew across much of the country, and arboreal forests disappeared, to be replaced by steppe or tundra. Sea levels dropped across the globe due to the amount of water locked up as ice, exposing wide areas offshore as dry land, and enhancing river channel downcutting. In the warmer periods sea levels rose as ice melted, river channels tended to be stable and prone to silting up and the development of alluvial floodplains, and forests regenerated. The range of faunal species inhabiting Britain changed in association with these climatic and environmental changes, with *in situ* evolutionary adaptations of some species to cope with these changes, or local extinction when conditions became intolerable.

Britain has been particularly sensitive to these changes, being: (a) situated at a latitude that has allowed the growth of ice sheets in cold periods, and the development of temperate forests in warm periods; and (b) periodically isolated as an island by rising sea levels and then rejoined to the continent when sea level falls. This has led to different climatic stages having reasonably distinctive sets of associated fauna and flora, which both reflect the climate and environment, and may also identify the specific MI Stage represented (eg. Plate 3.1 for the Aveley Interglacial). The study of such evidence – such as large mammals, small vertebrates, molluscs, ostracods, insects and pollen – is an integral part of Pleistocene, and Palaeolithic, research for its role in

Table 3.2 Quaternary epochs and the Marine Isotope Stage framework

Epoch	Age (BP)	MI Stage	Traditional stage (Britain)	Climate
Holocene	Present 10,000	1	Flandrian	Warm — full interglacial
Late Pleistocene	25,000 50,000 70,000 110,000 125,000	2 3 4 5a–d 5e	Devensian Ipswichian	Mainly cold; coldest in MI Stage 2 when Britain depopulated and maximum advance of Devensian ice sheets; occasional short-lived periods of relative warmth ("interstadials"), and more prolonged warmth in MI Stage 3. Warm — full interglacial
Middle Pleistocene	190,000 240,000 300,000 340,000 380,000 425,000 480,000	6 7 8 9 10 11 12	Wolstonian complex Hoxnian Anglian	Alternating periods of cold and warmth; recently recognised that this period includes more than one glacial–interglacial cycle; changes in faunal evolution and assemblage associations through the period help distinguish its different stages. Warm — full interglacial Cold — maximum extent southward of glacial ice in Britain; may incorporate interstadials that have been confused with Cromerian complex interglacials
	620,000 780,000	13–16 17–19	Cromerian complex and Beestonian glaciation	Cycles of cold and warmth; still poorly understood due to obliteration of sediments by subsequent events
Early Pleistocene	1,800,000	20–64		Cycles of cool and warm, but generally not sufficiently cold for glaciation in Britain

Plate 3.1 Reconstruction of Marsworth, Buckinghamshire, *copyright Buckinghamshire County Council*

dating Palaeolithic sites and recreating the associated palaeo-environment (Plate 3.2).

The evidence from different MI Stages, including any hominin lithic evidence, is contained in terrestrial deposits formed during the stage. In contrast to the deep-sea bed, where there has been continuous sedimentation, terrestrial deposition only occurs in specific, limited parts of the landscape. The deposits formed are also highly variable, depending upon climate and landscape situation. Furthermore, sedimentation takes place as a series of short-lived depositional events

such as land-slips or river-floods interrupted by long periods of stability and erosion. Thus the terrestrial record is relatively piecemeal, and the challenge for both Pleistocene and Palaeolithic investigation is to integrate the terrestrial evidence into the global MIS framework, based on relatively few direct stratigraphic relationships, and making maximum use of biological evidence and inferences about the sequence of deposition in major systems such as river valleys.

The current interglacial began *c.* 10,000 BP and it is generally agreed that MI Stages 2–5d, dating from

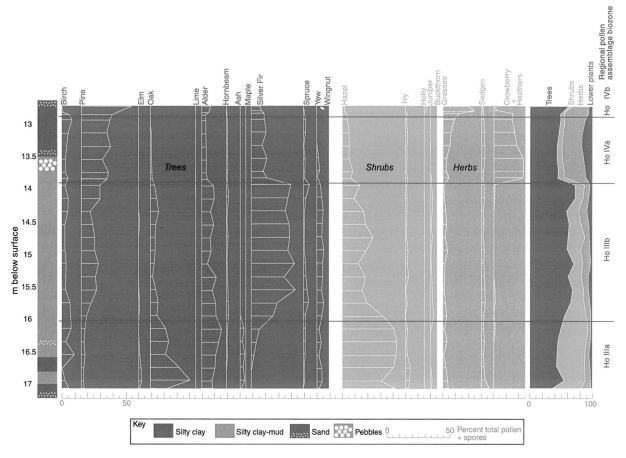

Plate 3.2 Pollen diagram from Denham, Buckinghamshire, *adapted from Gibbard 1975, Cambridge University Press with permission*

c. 10,000–115,000 BP cover the last glaciation (the Devensian), and that Stage 5e dating from *c.* 115,000––125,000 BP correlates with the short-lived peak warmth of the last interglacial (the Ipswichian) (Table 3.2). Beyond that disagreement increases, although many British workers feel confident in accepting that MI Stage 12, which ended abruptly *c.* 425,000 BP, correlates with the major British Anglian glaciation when ice-sheets reached as far south as the northern outskirts of London (Bridgland 1994).

The nature of the evidence

Our understanding of the Palaeolithic is hampered by the fact that the earliest written texts post-date the end of the Palaeolithic by thousands of years. Furthermore, unlike in later periods, there is no structural evidence such as huts, houses or monuments. It is only through the natural sediments that survive from the Pleistocene, and the archaeological and environmental evidence they contain, that we have any knowledge of the Palaeolithic. Sediments are only laid down, however, in certain locations in the landscape, and then are vulnerable to subsequent reworking or destruction. It is only under rare circumstances that lithic remains have accumulated at a point in the landscape where they are likely to be preserved, for instance on the edge of a river floodplain just before a major flooding episode, or at the foot of a slope just before a minor landslip. One should, therefore,

always remember that for any phase of the Palaeolithic, our knowledge is initially restricted by the limited circumstances where sediment formation has incorporated archaeological material; and after this, by the tiny parts of the ancient landscape that survive to the present day, most of which will only rarely happen to contain archaeological evidence.

Interpretation of the evidence we do have is then dependent upon understanding how it has become buried. Different burial processes have different implications for any archaeological evidence. Some processes lead to substantial mixing and transport of material, and this destroys fragile evidence, confusing the spatial distribution of evidence from various areas of activity and combining material from different phases of occupation and possibly periods. Other processes bury material gently, preserving faunal remains and individual areas of activity. The swiftness of burial will therefore affect whether single episodes of activity are represented, or an accumulated behavioural palimpsest. Although many types of Pleistocene sediment are known in Britain, most of which have produced at least some Palaeolithic evidence (Wymer 1995), in the Solent-Thames region there are only eight broad sediment types occurring, six of which have produced Palaeolithic remains (cf. Table 3.5). The distribution of these deposits across the Solent-Thames region, the ways in which they formed and their consequent implications for Palaeolithic studies, are discussed further below.

Plate 3.3 Photograph of excavation of a mammoth at Dix Pit, Stanton Harcourt, Oxfordshire, *Information and images courtesy of Kate Scott and Christine Buckingham, the Upper Thames Quaternary Research project*

Stone tools and waste flakes from their manufacture constitute the main type of evidence. Handaxes are the most commonly found and easily recognised type of lithic artefact, but the earliest lithic technology embraces simple core and flake strategies, and attention should also be paid to their recognition. Although stone artefacts can be damaged by some burial processes, as for example when they are caught up in a river channel or crushed under an ice sheet, they are essentially indestructible and resistant to biological decay, which is why they constitute the bulk of Palaeolithic evidence. This can of course pose problems, since one always has to consider, when interpreting stone artefacts, whether they have been moved from where they were originally discarded, and whether they represent mixed material from different periods of the Palaeolithic.

Besides lithic artefacts, which also incidentally include stones with batter marks used as percussors, artefacts can be made from organic material such as wood, bone and antler. These are much more perishable, and so are very rarely found. They are only preserved under certain combinations of swift burial, waterlogging and (usually) alkalinity of the sedimentary context. However, because of this rarity, one should be particularly aware of the possibility of their recovery from suitable contexts. These include, even from early in the Palaeolithic, wooden spears, hafted flint tools, and antler percussors for knapping. These rare discoveries serve as a constant reminder that at most sites we are missing major elements of the evidence, and that we should not overlook this when interpreting human society and behaviour from the ubiquitous stone tools and waste flakes that predominate through the Palaeolithic.

Otherwise unmodified bone and antler fossils can also show cut-marks and evidence of breakage, indicating exploitation for food.

Although no decorated/carved objects are yet known from the early, Lower/Middle phase of the Palaeolithic, there is some evidence of a capacity for ritual behaviour at this period (for instance the deposition of Neanderthal and *Homo ergaster/erectus* skeletons in association with probable grave goods in France and Spain), so it is not out of the question that evidence of this type could be found.

An important category of evidence for researching the Palaeolithic that must not be overlooked is biological/palaeo-environmental remains. These are often large mammalian, small vertebrate or molluscan, but a wide range of other evidence may be brought to bear, including pollen and ostracods (Table 3.3). They may be present at the same sites as artefactual remains, either in the same horizon or in stratigraphically related horizons; or they may be present at sites where direct artefactual evidence is absent. In both cases, they have the same value and potential for Palaeolithic research, and should be recognised as significant, even in the absence of artefacts. Faunal and floral remains can help in dating the deposit, and providing information of the local climate and environment at any particular time. They can also point up differences in species within the region (Plates 3.3; 3.4). Such information is essential if we are to carry out core research objectives such as dating sites, constructing regional and national frameworks of cultural change and development, and understanding human activity and behaviour in its environmental and landscape context.

Plate 3.4 *Elephas primogenius*, short-tusked forest elephant, Isle of Wight, *Isle of Wight Dinosaur Museum*

Besides artefactual and environmental evidence, a range of other information associated with Pleistocene deposits is relevant to Palaeolithic research objectives (cf. Table 3.3). Information on their height above OD, their three-dimensional geometry, their position in the landscape and their sedimentary characteristics are all integral to interpreting their origin and date. Other factors such as the range of lithologies represented in the solid clasts, heavy mineral signatures and the occurrence of sand bodies suitable for dating by optically stimulated luminescence (OSL) also have a role to play.

The Lower and Middle Palaeolithic in Britain

The British Palaeolithic has been divided into three broad, chronologically successive archaeological periods (Lower, Middle and Upper), based primarily on changing types of stone tool (Table 3.4). This framework was developed in the nineteenth century, before any knowledge of the types of human ancestor associated with the evidence of each period, and without much understanding of the timescale. This tripartite division has broadly stood the test of time, proving both to reflect a broad chronological succession across wide areas of

Table 3.3 Palaeolithic remains and relevant information

Category	Range	Eg., Comments
Human activities/artefacts	Lithic artefacts	Flaked stone tools and debitage, percussors
	Wooden artefacts	Spears, tool-hafts
	Bone/antler artefacts	Percussors, handaxes (known from Italy from elephant bone)
	Cut-marked faunal remains	
	Decorated/carved objects	Generally Upper Palaeolithic, but not out of the question for Lower/ Middle Palaeolithic
	Cave art	Upper Palaeolithic only
	Manuports	Unused raw material
	Features, structures	Hearths, stone pavements, pits
	Fire	Charcoal concentrations in association with hearths
Biological/ palaeo-environmental	Large vertebrates	Mammals (rhino, elephant, lion, deer horse, carnivores, etc.) birds
	Small vertebrates	Mammals (bats, mice, voles, lemmings etc.), fish, reptiles, birds, amphibians
	Plant macro-fossils	
	Pollen and diatoms	
	Molluscs	
	Insects	
	Ostracods and foraminifera	

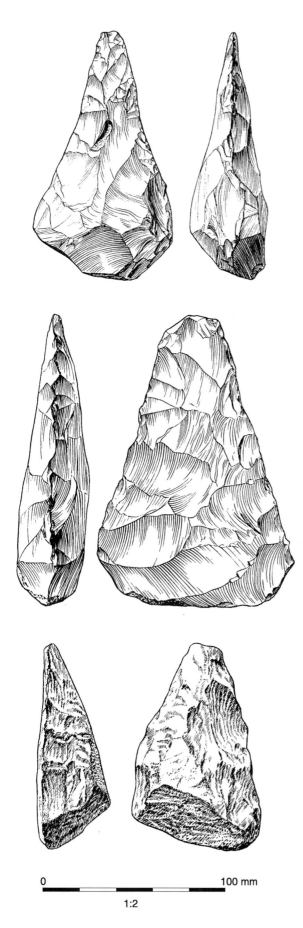

0   100 mm

1:2

Plate 3.5   Post-Anglian tools from Toots Farm, Caversham, *copyright Wymer 1968 with permission Wessex Archaeology*

Table 3.4 The Palaeolithic period in Britain

Traditional archaeological period	Updated cultural stage	Human species
Upper Palaeolithic	Upper Palaeolithic	Anatomically modern humans (*Homo sapiens sapiens*)
Middle Palaeolithic	British Mousterian -	Neanderthals (*Homo neanderthalensis*) -
Lower Palaeolithic	Lower / Middle Palaeolithic	Early pre-Neanderthals, evolving into *Homo neanderthalensis*
Lower Palaeolithic	- *Homo* cf *heidelbergensis*	-
	Homo ergaster	

Europe, and to correspond with the evolution of different hominin species. However, improved understanding, and particularly dating, of a number of sites over the last fifty years has resulted in: (a) recognition of a wide range of technological and typological variation within the Lower Palaeolithic; and (b) some confusion over the distinction between Lower and Middle Palaeolithic.

The earliest Lower Palaeolithic evidence, associated with the sporadic pre-MIS 13 incursions, constitutes simple core and flake industries, as at Pakefield (Parfitt *et al.* 2005). Subsequent Lower Palaeolithic industries (from MIS 13 through to MIS 8) are for the most part dominated by handaxes (in a wide range of shapes from ovate to sharply pointed; Plate 3.5) although there are various instances throughout this period of non-handaxe industries such as the High Lodge flake-tool industry of MIS 13 and the Clactonian of MIS 11. The transition from Lower to Middle Palaeolithic is conventionally marked by the appearance of prepared core technology (Levalloisian) and/or the manufacture of *bout coupé* handaxes. However several sites in southern England dating to MIS 9–11 contain Levalloisian material in conjunction with handaxe-dominated technology. Furthermore, it also seems that the growth of Levalloisian technology in Britain in MIS 7–8 is contemporary with a number of late handaxe industries. It is therefore difficult to make a distinction between Lower and Middle Palaeolithic based on the presence of (often only one piece) of Levallois material. In contrast, it seems that *bout coupé* handaxes are genuinely associated with a distinct phase of occupation much later than the main Levalloisian phase, at *c.* 60,000 BP in the middle of the subsequent (Devensian) glaciation (White & Jacobi 2002; Plate 3.6).

This has resulted in updating the framework of British Palaeolithic cultural stages used for this resource assessment (Table 3.4). Separation between Lower and Middle Palaeolithic has largely been abandoned. Only material

Lithic artefacts and other material culture	MI Stage	Date (BP)	Geological period
Dominance of blade technology and standardised tools made on blade blanks, personal adornment, cave art, bone/antler points and needles	2–3	10,000–35,000	Late Devensian
The appearance of *bout coupé* handaxes	3–5d	35,000–115,000	Early/Middle Devensian
Britain uninhabited	5e	115,000–125,000	Ipswichian
Still some handaxe-dominated sites, but growth of more standardised (Levalloisian) flake and blade production techniques	6–9	125,000–425,000	Hoxnian/Saalian complex
Handaxe-dominated, but appearance of more standardised flake and blade production techniques (Levalloisian); occasional industries without handaxes (Clactonian)	8–11		
Britain uninhabited	12	425,000–475,000	Anglian
Handaxe-dominated, with unstandardised flake core production techniques and simple unstandardised flake-tools; occasional industries without handaxes (High Lodge)	13	475,000–500,000	Late Cromerian
Simple flake/core industries with no standardised flake-tools	18–13	500,000–700,000 complex	Early/Middle Cromerian complex

reliably dated to before the Anglian glaciation is regarded as Lower Palaeolithic. Sites of uncertain date in the period MIS 13 to MIS 6 with any or all of handaxes, flakes/cores and Levallois material are included under the umbrella of "Lower/Middle Palaeolithic". Sites with *bout coupé* material have been attributed to a later period, which could be regarded as "true" Middle Palaeolithic, but has been renamed "British Mousterian" to avoid confusion.

So far as hominin species goes, the Lower/Middle Palaeolithic saw the gradual evolution in northwest Europe of an Archaic hominid lineage from the first colonisers (*Homo erectus/ergaster*) through *Homo heidelbergensis* into Neanderthals (*Homo neanderthalensis*). In the middle of the last, Devensian glaciation Neanderthals were suddenly replaced *c.* 35,000 BP in north-west Europe by anatomically modern humans (*Homo sapiens*

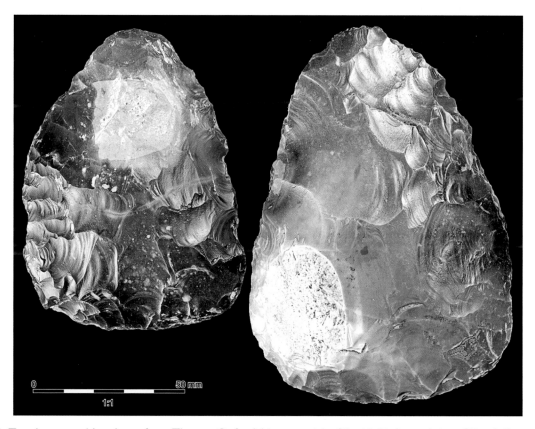

Plate 3.6 Two *bout-coupé* handaxes from Thrupp, Oxfordshire, *copyright OA with kind permission of Derek Steptoe and Geoff Cross*

sapiens), who are associated with the following Upper Palaeolithic. The suddenness of this change, the physiological differences between Neanderthals and modern humans and DNA studies (Cann 1988) all suggest that modern humans did not evolve from Neanderthals, but developed elsewhere, probably in Africa *c*. 150,000 BP, before colonising other parts of the world and replacing any pre-existing Archaic populations. Although there is evidence of a late Neanderthal British Mousterian population in the middle of the last glaciation *c*. 60,000 BP (Boismier 2003), Britain was probably unoccupied at the time of the Neanderthal–Modern transition.

Landscape and topograpy

Regional variation

As shown in Figure 1.4: Topographic Zones, the Solent-Thames region comprises a north-south transect across the middle of southern England, passing across the western end of the London Basin, the Wealden Basin and the Hampshire basin with intervening areas of higher ground. Chalk bedrock outcrops and thickens southward from within southern Oxfordshire and Buckinghamshire (here comprising the Chilterns). North of this, older Lower Cretaceous and Jurassic limestone deposits form the landscape of the northern parts of these counties (the Cotswolds), containing the upper part of the Thames, and its tributaries the Cherwell and the Thame. The Thames then heads south through Oxford and diverts across the Chilterns into the London Basin through the Goring Gap. South of this, a major synclinal fold in the Chalk forms the London Basin, which is filled with softer Tertiary sands and clays. The western end of this occurs roughly along the boundary between Berkshire and Hampshire. Here, the Kennet drains eastward towards London, joining the Thames at Reading. Further east, the Thames is joined by a number of tributaries, including, (from the north) the Wye and the Misbourne, and (from the south) the Blackwater and the Loddon.

The chalk landscape rises again southward, forming widespread chalk downland of the Wessex Downs and the Hampshire Downs. In the eastern part of Hampshire, an eroded anticlinal rift in the chalk exposes older, Lower Cretaceous sediments at the western end of the Wealden Basin. This area contains the headwaters of a number of western Wealden rivers: the Wey, the Godalming Wey, and the (western) Rother. Further south, the surface of the chalk dips again and becomes overlain by younger Tertiary sands and clays, filling the Hampshire Basin. Several rivers drain southwards across the Hampshire/Wessex Downs into the Hampshire basin, particularly the Avon, the Test and the Itchen. Just off the southern coast of Hampshire, the central east-west Chalk ridge of the Isle of Wight represents the southern edge of the Hampshire basin, with Chalk bedrock rising again, and, to the south, a further minor anticlinal exposure of older sediments forms the southern part of the Island. Thus, geologically, the Hampshire basin is very similar to the London basin, although its southern edge has been broken through by the sea between Durlston Head and the Needles, destroying the lower reaches of what would once have been a major river (the Solent River) passing east from Poole Harbour, north of the Isle of Wight, entering the English Channel southeast of Bembridge.

Palaeo-environmental and human remains

Because of the strong geo-archaeological engagement necessitated by those studying this period (eg Wymer 1999 *Southern Rivers Project*), and the geo-achaeological teams they regularly deploy (eg Boxgrove, Roberts & Parfitt 1999), most of this assessment dwells on the sedimentary and geo-archaeological architecture associated with and related to the Lower-Middle Palaeolithic resource. Nevertheless the rare, but demonstrable, survival of palaeo-environmental and human remains is not widely considered, nor are the application of some of the newer scientific techniques to biological remains. Although the data are limited, in previous studies there is an almost total lack of engagement with the lived-landscape inhabited during the Lower and Middle Palaeolithic. More significantly, there has been no direct acknowledgement of Lower Middle Palaeolithic people, despite the fact that their remains have been encountered, albeit rarely and in sparse quantity (eg Boxgrove, Happisbugh etc.).

Studies of the environment have generally been undertaken within a broad geo-archaeological framework. Balaam and Scaife's national concern 20 years ago is still apposite today. They stated that 'No concerted attempt has been made to examine possible effects, if any, of Palaeolithic man upon his local environment' (Balaam & Scaife 1987, 8). Indeed there has been little attempt to define the local lived-environment i.e., the physical and vegetational nature of the land they inhabited (see Allen 1996, 60). Until such sites come to light, or are directly searched for via modelling and mapping, it will be necessary to continue to refine knowledge of Quaternary chronology and landscape in the broadest terms, in order to understand from whence the artefact assemblages came, and in what general landscape environment the populations that created them lived. What is required for the Solent-Thames region, and the likelihood of its existence seems moderate, is *in situ* evidence accompanied by palaeo-environmental and palaeo-economic evidence.

Ex situ: the depositionary environment

The *ex situ* environment, such as riverine and glacial outwash gravels, is largely well documented for most sites. There is little engagement, however, with the environment of the origin of those artefacts. Geo-archaeological and stratigraphic investigations have studied the environment of their emplacement and deposition, but not of their origin – challenging though this may be. Defining the likely location of origin, and of human activity prior to sediments displacement, is thus key to any interpretation of human activity within the wider Palaeolithic landscape.

In situ

Most sites are comprised of allochthonous, or derived, artefacts and ecofacts, and *archaeological* sites *per se* are scarce, their rarity attracting a battery of environmental analyses to recover as much information as possible. Nevertheless, there is increasing evidence that finds may occur in 'slack-water' locations or protected quiet depositional environments in river valleys, former cliff lines (Boxgrove) and locations currently submarine (Bouldnor, Isle of Wight). The potential of these sites to contain internationally important palaeo-environmental evidence (soils, pollen, charcoal, charred plant elements, snails, as well as food detritus; animal bones, marine and riverine shells) is clearly high, and such information is desperately needed. It will provide important and rare clues into some of the basic information about the lived-in environment, local natural resources, and modification of that environment, diet and consumption.

People

Human remains are increasingly being recovered and the potential for sites similar to Boxgrove exists along the same cliff line in Hampshire. Serendipitous finds elsewhere in the country associated with fine-grained deposits (Boxgrove, Happisburgh) and coarse-grained clastic material (Swanscombe) undoubtedly exist. Clearly such finds are accorded the importance they deserve but there is little, or no, predefined research agenda for these remains. Obviously the population is small and there are too few remains to enable any real comparative studies.

Pleistocene deposits, palaeography and county landscape zones

The region contains a variety of superficial, Pleistocene deposits, reflecting its history of landscape development over the last 2 million years or so (Table 3.5). For this period more detailed consideration of deposits is required than can be obtained from the broad zones already discussed. Glacial till is present in the northern half of Buckinghamshire, and in two small patches in Oxfordshire, one in the north-east corner, and the other near Chipping Norton, reflecting the most southerly extent of a substantial ice sheet during one of the Pleistocene glaciations. It is uncertain which glaciation is responsible, but it was probably in the time range 500,000 to 250,000 BP. The remainder of the region has not been directly affected by glaciation, so any surviving Pleistocene sediments potentially reflect a greater span of Pleistocene time.

The two major groups of Pleistocene sediments in the remainder of the region are: (a) residual Clay-with-flint, capping the higher parts of the chalk downland that covers much of the region; and (b) fluvial sand/gravel terrace deposits associated with the changing drainage history of the region. These latter can be subdivided further, into: (1) a more recent group, mostly post-dating the Anglian glaciation, which are evidently associated with present-day drainage systems, lining the valley flanks of existing rivers; and (2) an older group, found at higher levels and mapped as "plateau" or "high-level" gravels, distributed with little relation to existing river valleys, and probably dating to early in the Pleistocene, or perhaps back into the Pliocene or before in some instances.

In addition to these major sediment groups, a few other types of deposits occur as minor isolated outcrops at various locations. A few small patches of diverse fluvio-glacial sediments occur in north Buckinghamshire, associated with the more widespread glacial till. Fine-grained sand/silt deposits mapped as "brickearth" occur as small patches in a number of locations across the region, present in all counties apart from Oxfordshire. These are associated with Middle Thames fluvial terrace deposits in Berkshire and Buckinghamshire, are known in southeast Hampshire in the vicinity of Portsdown Hill and the Gosport peninsula, and occur as isolated patches in the centre and on the eastern side of the Isle of Wight. As is discussed further below (see The Lower/Middle Palaeolithic resource 'Brickearth'), sedimentologically similar brickearth deposits can have formed in a variety of ways, ranging from mass-movement slopewash deposition (colluvium), floodplain water deposition (alluvium) to gentle aeolian deposition

Table 3.5 Pleistocene sediments in the Solent-Thames region, by county

Deposit	Bucks	Oxon	Berks	Hants	IoW
Glacial till	+++	+	-	-	-
Fluvio-glacial	+	-	-	-	-
Fluvial	+++	+++	+++	+++	++
High-level/plateau gravels	-	+	++	+	++
Residual (Clay-with-flints)	++	++	++	+++	++
Brickearth: (a) Head/valley	+	-	+	+	+
Brickearth: (b) Plateau	-	-	-	-	+
Head/solifluction gravels	-	++	+	+	++
Marine littoral (raised beach, intertidal/estuarine)	-	-	-	+	++

[+++ Abundant; ++ moderately common; + scarce; - none known; ? Uncertain]

Table 3.6 Solent-Thames landscape character palaeo-zones and Pleistocene sediments

County	Zone	Zone character description	Pleistocene sediments	Notes
Bucks	BU1 – Great Ouse (Upper)	Great Ouse valley, upper part and tributaries, esp. Ouzel	+++ Glacial till + Fluvio-glacial ++ Fluvial	No Palaeolithic remains known One varied patch, at Bletchley Great Ouse and Ouzel valleys
	BU2 – North Bucks Clay Lands	Undulating clay topography, low hills incised by rivers, namely the Thame and the Great Ouse	+++ Glacial till + Fluvial	No Palaeolithic remains known Thame Valley; Thame, Ouzel and Lea headwaters
	BU3 – Chilterns	Chalk hills of the Chilterns dominates a landscape incised by small valleys that in high areas is capped by clay-with-flint deposit	+ Fluvio-glacial +++ Residual (C-w-f)	Patches at Chalfont St. Giles and Beaconsfield Widespread pockets/patches
	BU4 – Middle Thames	The Middle Thames Valley, and the tributaries of the Colne and Wye rivers; this southern part of Buckinghamshire is formed by fluvial terraces as well as the floodplain itself	+ Fluvio-glacial +++ Fluvial ++ Brickearth: Head/ valley	Burnham area Extensive Thames terraces Alluvial/colluvial spreads, equiv. to Langley Silt complex
Oxon	OX1 – Cotswolds	Jurassic upland plateau of mainly soft yellow limestones	+ Glacial till + Fluvial ++ High-level/plateau gravels	Small patches Evenlode terrace patches Northern Drift
	OX2 – Upper Thames	The Upper Thames valley follows the course of the Thames and its tributary the Cherwell, whose floodplains are filled with Devensian gravels and whose slopes are intermittently occupied by older terrace gravels	++ Fluvial ++ Head/solifluction gravels	Extensive Thames and tributary terraces Wallingford Fan gravels
	OX3 – Chalk Downs	The Oxford Clay vale is occupied by Upper Jurassic rocks merging into the Cretaceous, in the far south and southeast of the county; with Thames terrace deposits between Henley and Reading	++ Fluvial ++ High-level/ plateau gravels ++ Residual (C-w-f)	Thames terraces, including Caversham Ancient Channel Pre-Anglian Thames terraces, including Winter Hill Patches on Chalk high ground
Berks	BE1 – Northwest Berks	The Thames valley upstream of Reading and the Berkshire Downs region between the northern county boundary and the northern edge of the Kennet valley	++ Residual (C-w-f)	Patches on Chalk high ground
	BE2 – East Berks	The Thames valley between Reading and Windsor	+++ Fluvial + Residual (C-w-f) + Brickearth: Head/ valley	Extensive Thames and tributary terraces Occ. patches Slough, Langley Silt complex
	BE3 – Southwest Berks	The Kennet valley from Newbury to Reading	++ Fluvial ++ High-level/ plateau gravels ++ Residual (C-w-f) + Head/solifluction gravels	Kennet terraces Pre-Anglian terraces, including Silchester Gravel Patches on Chalk high ground Savernake; possible confusion with terrace deposits
	BE4 – Southeast Berks	The Loddon and Blackwater valleys	++ Fluvial + High-level/ plateau gravels	Whitewater, Blackwater, Loddon terrace deposits Small patches
Hants	HA1a - London Basin	Thames and tributary valleys, developed in soft Tertiary deposits overlapping Chalk at the northeastern corner of the county	++ Fluvial	Whitewater, Blackwater, Loddon terrace deposits
	HA1b - Western Wealden Basin	Upper headwater area of Wealden rivers, overlying Cretaceous Gault and Greensand within western end of Wealden Basin, at eastern side of county	++ Fluvial ++ Fluvial	Upper headwaters of Wealden rivers: Wey, Godalming Wey, western Rother Upper headwaters of Wealden rivers: Wey, Godalming Wey, western Rother

Table 3.6 Solent-Thames landscape character palaeo-zones and Pleistocene sediments (continued)

County	Zone	Zone character description	Pleistocene sediments	Notes
	HA2 – Wessex Downs	Middle and Upper Chalk highlands, through which the upper valleys of the southward flowing Avon, Test, Itchen and Meon rivers are cut	+ Fluvial	Occasional patches along Bourne, Dever and Test; one more sub stantial spread at Longparish
			+++ Residual (C-w-f)	Extensive spreads capping high ground
	HA3 – Hants Basin	Lower valleys of the Avon, Test, Itchen and Meon rivers together with the extinct Solent River, developed over soft Tertiary sands/clays filling the Hampshire Basin syncline	+++ Fluvial	Extensive terrace systems associated Solent River and tributaries
			++ High-level/plateau gravels	Higher terrace patches, pre-Anglia
			++ Brickearth: Head/valley	Extensive spreads on Gosport peninsula; plus slopes of Ports Down Hill
			√ Marine littoral sediments	Limited raised beach outcrops on S-facing slope of Ports Down Hill
Isle of Wight	IoW1a - Chalk Downs (central)	The east–west central Chalk ridge, between the Needles and Culver Cliff	+ High-level/plateau gravels	Occasional patches
			+++ Residual (C-w-f)	Extensive spreads, esp. Cheverton Down
	IoW1b - Chalk Downs (south)	The Chalk high ground at the southern tip of the Island	+++ Residual (C-w-f)	St. Catherine's Hill
	IoW2 - Northern Plain (Hants Basin)	The whole part of the Island lying to the north of the central Chalk ridge; various valleys, tending to drain north into the Solent, dissecting soft Tertiary sands/clays filling the Hampshire Basin syncline	++ Fluvial	Terrace systems associated with Yar (western) and Medina
			++ High-level/plateau gravels	Substantial spreads northern and northeastern coast – uncertain age, and may include marine littoral and/or soli fluction deposits
			+ Brickearth: Head/valley	Small patches: over Medina 1st terrace deposits at Newport; cliff-section at Bembridge
			+ Brickearth: Plateau	Small patch at Downend
			++ Head/solifluction gravels	A swathe of deposits is mapped as marine along NE coast between Bembridge and Ryde – much may be of fluvial or solifluction origin; many gravels mapped as "plateau" may also be of solifluction origin
			++ Marine littoral	Much of the mapped "marine gravels" are probably of solifluc tion origin – cf. above –although raised beach (and other marine) sediments occur at Bembridge
	IoW3 - Southern Plain	The southern half of the Island lying between the two Chalk Downland areas; an undulating landscape, mostly developed over Cretaceous Lower Greensand and Gault sediments	++ Fluvial	Terrace systems associated with upper reaches of Yar (western) and the Yar (eastern)
			++ High-level/plateau gravels	Substantial spreads, esp. Bleak Down
			+ Brickearth: Head/valley	Various patches associated with upper western Yar terrace system
	IoW4 - Solent Waters	Submerged ground under the Eastern and Western Solent straits	++? Fluvial	Poorly known; sea bed bathy-metry suggests offshore sub-merged continuations of terrestrial terrace systems …
			++? Marine littoral	… these may include marine littoral sediments

[+++ Abundant; ++ moderately common; + scarce; - none known; ? Uncertain]

(loess), or as a combination of any or all of these processes, with corresponding implications for any contained archaeological material.

Coarser-grained head gravel and solifluction deposits are mapped in all counties apart from Buckinghamshire, but are not extensive. They are, however, probably more widespread than is shown by current geological mapping as: (a) substantial gravel spreads mapped as "high-level" or "plateau" gravel, or as "marine" gravel (especially on the Isle of Wight) are probably of head/solifluction origin; and (b) there are probably numerous minor unmapped head/solifluction gravel deposits filling dry valleys in, and draining out of, the chalk downland that extends across the majority of the region.

Finally, marine littoral sediments occur only in the southern coastal counties of the region, namely Hampshire and the Isle of Wight, and then are only present in two very restricted areas: (a) on the south-facing slope of Ports Down Hill, southeast Hampshire; and (b) on the eastern corner of the Isle of Wight, in the vicinity of Bembridge. At this latter location, extensive spreads of gravel extending north-west up the coastline towards Ryde are mapped as "marine". However, it is questionable whether this is a correct interpretation. Exposures in these deposits at Priory Bay show features equally suggestive of a fluvial origin in the deeper-lying gravel deposits, as well as demonstrating a substantial overburden of head/solifluction deposits (see Plate 3.10); no other sub-surface exposures have been examined.

Each county has been subdivided into a number of landscape character zones, reflecting a combination of bedrock type, geomorphology and associated Pleisto-cene sediments, and the presence/abundance of different Pleistocene sediment types in each of these landscape zones is given (Table 3.6).

The Lower/Middle Palaeolithic resource

Introduction and approach

The approach taken here to assessing the Lower/Middle Palaeolithic resource in the Solent-Thames region is deposit-centred rather than find-centred. Clearly artefact finds are the most direct evidence of the Palaeolithic, but as outlined above, research into, and understanding of, the period depend almost more upon the context of discovery, and other evidence, faunal and floral, than upon the finds themselves. Most importantly, the potential for the existence of any Palaeolithic remains at a location is initially contingent upon the presence of Pleistocene sediments; and then the questions are:

- What do they contain in the way of artefactual or other evidence?

- How important are these remains for current research?

Therefore this assessment focuses first upon the distri-bution and prevalence of Pleistocene deposits of various types, secondarily addressing the presence/ prevalence/nature of Palaeolithic remains within them, and their research potential, taking account of how they formed and the range of evidence they contain. This then provides the basis for the subsequent review of our current understanding, both of the region in its own right and also within the wider national context, addressing the history of occupation and cultural change represented, and interpretations of lifestyle and behaviour.

The resource

Glacial till

Glacial till is characteristically a clay-rich sediment containing frequent and very poorly sorted lithic (and Chalk, in areas of chalk bedrock) clasts ranging in size from fine gravel to large boulders. It is formed underneath glacial ice sheets, and as such, does not represent a situation where Palaeolithic occupation would have been possible or animal bone remains are likely to accumulate. Any artefactual or mammalian finds from a glacial till context would definitely originate from pre-existing sediments overridden by the ice sheet, and would have undergone substantial transport and reworking. The massive compression and shear stresses underneath an ice sheet are not conducive to the preser-vation of mammalian remains, should any be caught up from pre-existing sediments. Lithic artefact remains are, however, sufficiently robust not to be destroyed. Despite loss of their original provenance, they could still be of interest, as representing a remnant of occupation from some time prior to the formation of the till, which would be of importance if the till represented one of the earlier periods of glaciation. That having been said, no artefac-tual remains are attributed to glacial till in the Solent-Thames region, which only occurs in the northern half of Buckinghamshire, and in two small patches in Oxfordshire.

An important point to bear in mind is that glaciers may have over-ridden pre-existing fluvial channels or lakes, sealing the pre-existing sediments under thick layers of glacial till without destroying them. In such circumstances, the buried sediments may be of high Palaeolithic potential; therefore, although glacial till itself is of low potential, landscape areas covered by glacial till are not necessarily entirely also of low potential.

Fluvio-glacial deposits (outwash sands/gravels, pro-glacial lake sediments)

Deposits of this category are typically formed at, or near, the boundaries of ice sheets. As such, they are most liable to be present in the northern part of the Solent-Thames region, the only part subject to glaciation. Even here, they only occur in very restricted areas (Table 3.7), particularly in the vicinity of Bletchley, comprising a complex accumulation of sands, gravels and fine-grained lacustrine sediments. Artefacts from the coarser-grained of these sediments are liable to have been substantially

Table 3.7 The Lower/Middle Palaeolithic resource, Solent-Thames region: fluvio-glacial sediments

County zone	Abundance (deposits)	Key areas	Abundance (Palaeolithic remains)	Key sites	Notes
BU1	+	Bletchley; Newport Pagnell	++	Yew's End Pit; Fenny Stratford	Need to clarify provenance of arte-facts; high potential for undisturbed material and faunal remains in fine-grained sediments
BU2	-	-	-	-	-
BU3	+	Chalfont St. Giles; Gerrards Cross; Beaconsfield	+	-	-
BU4	+	Burnham	-	-	-
OX1	-	-	-	-	-
OX2	-	-	-	-	-
OX3	-	-	-	-	-
BE1	-	-	-	-	-
BE2	-	-	-	-	-
BE3	-	-	-	-	-
BE4	-	-	-	-	-
HA1a	-	-	-	-	-
HA1b	-	-	-	-	-
HA2	-	-	-	-	-
HA3	-	-	-	-	-
IoW1a	-	-	-	-	-
IoW1b	-	-	-	-	-
IoW2	-	-	-	-	-
IoW3	-	-	-	-	-
IoW4	-	-	-	-	-

[+++ Abundant; ++ moderately common; + scarce; - none known; ? Uncertain]

reworked, and hence of minimal interpretive potential. In contrast, however, any artefacts from fine-grained sediments may represent *in situ* occupation, and would thus be of high importance. These latter sediments would also have high potential for preservation of faunal and other palaeo-environmental remains. A moderately high number of Palaeolithic find spots occur in the vicinity of Bletchley (where, incidentally, there are also substantial outcrops of Terrace deposits associated with the Ouzel). It would certainly be worth giving this area some attention to clarify the distribution and strati-graphic relationships of the various Pleistocene fluvial and fluvio-glacial sediments in the vicinity, to clarify which of them contain Palaeolithic artefactual remains and to investigate for the preservation/association of biological remains.

Fluvial deposits (sand/gravel terraces, alluvium and buried channels)

The most widespread sedimentary contexts for the Lower/Middle Palaeolithic record are undoubtedly the fluvial ones, with the ubiquitous sand/gravel terrace deposits accounting for a large majority of artefacts in the various extant collections. These contexts represent (in the main) the gravel beds of rivers flowing during the colder parts of the Pleistocene, when they would have formed multiple-channelled 'braided' systems with gravel accumulating on bars between the channels, and periodic

Plate 3.7 Taplow quarry, Buckinghamshire, *copyright Buckinghamshire County Council*

phases of lower energy deposition and overbank flooding represented by sand and silt beds within the predominantly gravel sequence (as at Taplow, Buckinghamshire; Plate 3.7). These braided river gravels rarely yield artefacts in primary or near-primary context. Contained artefacts have typically been regarded as rolled from downstream transport and possibly reworked from unknown earlier sediments or land-surfaces (see Hosfield, 1999; Hosfield and Chambers, 2002).

This does not, however, mean that artefact remains from fluvial gravels are of no use for archaeological interpretation. Fluvial deposits that contain archaeological material from a reasonably wide catchment area provide a more representative sample of the range of artefacts produced over the period of occupation than evidence from a single undisturbed site, which might represent just one event. Downcutting phases would lead to some reworking of older artefacts into the new channel-bed, but the majority would be left in the correct part of the terrace sequence, preserved for the future. Older derived specimens are likely to be a rare component of assemblages from a terrace body, and also be distinctive through their greater degree of abrasion. Thus the stone tool evidence in sequences of river terraces in different basins can give a useful insight into the overall trajectory of regional cultural change and hominid presence through the long Palaeolithic period.

Artefacts from fluvial contexts may, however, be less disturbed than generally presumed. An alternative model would see artefacts as relatively immobile within the sediment load, being substantially more angular (and in the case of most handaxes, significantly larger) than most of the accompanying sand/gravel. Under this alternative model, artefacts would be subject to "churning" as channel-braids shifted, becoming abraded in the process, but would not be transported significantly downstream. Depending upon the energy of the river stream, and the vagaries of channel shifting, many artefacts may be rapidly incorporated into the forming gravel body, and not subsequently disturbed. In this case, we would need to reappraise our perspective on the interpretative potential of artefact collections from gravel bodies, as they would represent more constrained concentrations of Palaeolithic activity than is currently widely believed. Furthermore, braid bars might well have represented valuable sources of

raw material, as well as being associated with river channels that provided water and attracted game animals, so where there was rapid burial and minimal disturbance it is possible that valuable and minimally disturbed, concentrations of knapping debris might survive, particularly near former floodplain edges.

Finer-grained fluvial sediments are preserved much more rarely but, when present, can provide a plethora of valuable evidence, including fossils and datable materials, as well as better-preserved artefacts. These sediments will often represent the warmer parts of the Pleistocene, when the rivers would have had considerably less energy and would have flowed in narrower single-thread channels. The best preservation will always be in fine-grained fluvial sediments, such as the infills of abandoned channels and floodplain overbank sediments, within which artefacts can be preserved in a condition good enough to preserve signs of use-wear, and bones can be sufficiently well-preserved to reveal cut-marks.

Fluvial Terrace deposits are abundant in the region (Table 3.8), mainly associated with the Thames and its tributaries (particularly: the Thame, Cherwell, Blackwater, Loddon and Wey) and the north bank of tributaries of the Solent River (particularly: the Avon, Test and Itchen). In addition, there are fluvial deposits associated with restricted headwater stretches of the Great Ouse (in Buckinghamshire) and the western Rother (in east Hampshire).

As summarised in Table 3.8, and reviewed in more detail in the individual county resource assessment reports (cf. Table 3.1), Palaeolithic remains are abundant in many fluvial Terrace deposits, particularly: (a) along the middle Thames in Berkshire and southern Buckinghamshire; and (b) in the southern Test Valley in Romsey and Southampton. There are also a number of relatively isolated sites where great quantities of artefacts have been recovered, for instance Woodgreen on the Avon, Wolvercote on the upper Thames, on the northern outskirts of Oxford, and Priory Bay. There are also a few sites with rich mammalian and other palaeo-environmental remains, for instance Stanton Harcourt (in Oxfordshire) and Marsworth and Stoke Goldington (in Buckinghamshire) (Plate 3.8). Unfortunately we have yet to find a site that combines rich archaeological and biological remains, although no doubt such a site exists

Table 3.8. The Lower/Middle Palaeolithic resource, Solent-Thames region: fluvial sediments

County zone	Abundance (deposits)	Key areas	Abundance (Palaeolithic remains)	Key sites	Notes
BU1	++	Great Ouse (upper)	+	Stoke Goldington	Key site has rich palaeo-environmenal remains, but no artefacts known
BU2	+	Thame Valley; Thame/Ouzel/ Lea headwaters	-	Marsworth, Pitstone Quarry	Key site has rich palaeo-environmental remains, but no artefacts known
BU3	-	-	-	-	-
BU4	+++	Middle Thames Valley (Iver, Marlow, Burnham, Slough)	+++	Deverill's Pit; Cooper's Pit; Danefield Pit; Baker's Farm Pit; Lavender's Pit; Station Pit, Taplow	Overlap of this zone with Oxon and Berks; v abundant material from Boyn Hill and Lynch Hill terraces

Table 3.8. The Lower/Middle Palaeolithic resource, Solent-Thames region: fluvial sediments (continued)

County zone	Abundance (deposits)	Key areas	Abundance (Palaeolithic remains)	Key sites	Notes
OX1	+	Evenlode terrace patches	-	-	-
OX2	++	Upper Thames Valley; Oxford;	++	Stanton Harcourt, Dix Pit and Gravelly Guy Pit; Wolvercote brick pit; Cornish's Pit, Iffley	Raw material type and source is a key concern in this zone; also provenance, integrity and taphonomy of artefacts; potential for very good preservation and variety of biological material
OX3	++	Caversham Ancient Channel (most of it)	+++	Highlands Farm Pit; Kennylands Pit	
BE1	-	-	-	-	-
BE2	+++	Caversham Ancient Channel (part of it); Middle Thames Valley terrace deposits (Reading-Maidenhead-Slough)	+++	Roebuck Pit (MTV-1/67); Farthingworth Green Gravel Pit (MTV-1A/9); Smiths Pit (MTV-1A/20); Toots Farm (MTV-1A/28); Grovelands Pit (MTV-1A/52); Danefield Pit (MTV-2/8); Cannoncourt Farm Pit & Cooper's Pits (MTV-2/17); Bakers Farm Pit (MTV-2/45)	A classic area for Lower/Middle Pal archaeology: clear terrace sequence, rich archaeological material, well-researched and documented
BE3	++	Kennet and Enborne terraces; gravels between Pang and Kennet	+	Crowshott	-
BE4	++	Extensive terrace spreads associated with Blackwater and Loddon	+	Cluster of handaxe findspots at Wokingham	Needs more intensive, controlled investigations
HA1a	++	Terrace outcrops associated with upper reaches of Blackwater and Loddon	-	-	No Pal finds known, but lack of investigation
HA1b	+	Terrace outcrops Wealden headwaters of Wey (and Godalming Wey) and western Rother	-	-	No Pal finds known, but lack of investigation
HA2	+	Terrace outcrops associated with stretches of Bourne, Dever, Test, Itchen and Meon	+	Some finds at Longparish	Few Pal finds known, but lack of investigation – possibly an important, unappreciated resource (cf. Harnham)
HA3	+++	Solent river and tributaries; Avon, Test, Itchen, Hamble; plus extensive gravel spreads across New Forest	+++	Romsey Pits: Test Road, Belbins, Dunbridge; Soton sites: St James Church Pit, Highfield Pits; Portswood (mammoth reported); Warsash; Avon sites: Woodgreen, Ringwood	Are clusters (eg. at Woodgreen, Romsey, Southampton and Gosport) real patterns, or do they just reflect intensity of investigation?
IoW1a	-	-	-	-	-
IoW1b	-	-	-	-	-
IoW2	++	Yar (western); Newport	++	Afton Farm; Great Pan Farm	Levallois at Afton Farm and Great Pan Farm; not sure from which terrace level at Afton Farm
IoW3	++	Yar (western), upper stretch above Brook Bay and Chilton Chine; Yar (eastern)	+	Black Pan Farm; Ninham; mammoth teeth at Chilton Chine	-
IoW4	++?	Between Lymington and Yarmouth	++	-	Various findspots in Solent (Wessex Archaeology 2004)

[+++ Abundant; ++ moderately common; + scarce; - none known; ? Uncertain]

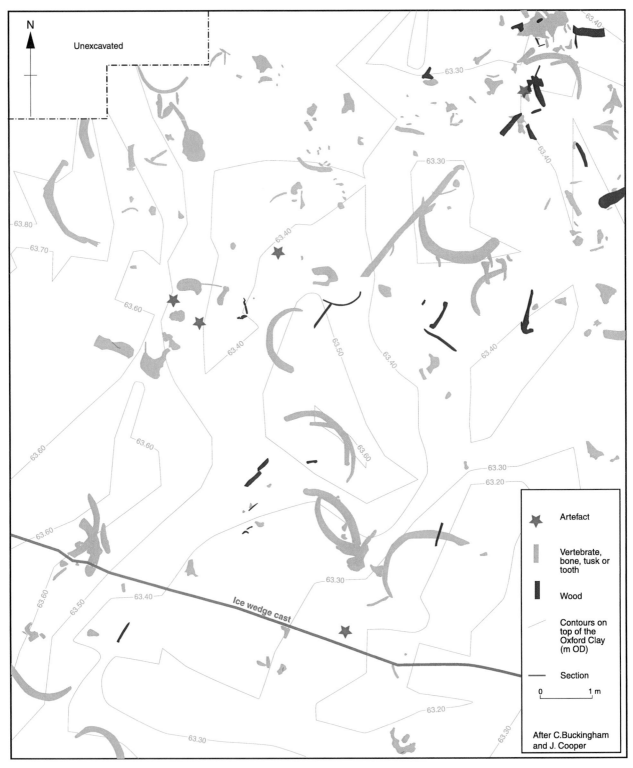

N

Unexcavated

Artefact

Vertebrate, bone, tusk or tooth

Wood

Contours on top of the Oxford Clay (m OD)

Section

Ice wedge cast

0   1 m

After C.Buckingham and J. Cooper

Plate 3.8 Plan of deposit in the Stanton Harcourt Channel, Oxfordshire, *adapted from Scott and Buckingham 1997*

somewhere in the region. Biological remains appear to be less common and less well-preserved in the southern part of the region. Rather than dismissing their potential to be present, however, this should heighten the importance attached to their discovery.

Despite the recorded richness of Palaeolithic remains in some areas, and in some terrace bodies, particularly Boyn Hill and Lynch Hill deposits in the Thames Valley, and T6 to T3 sediments in the Test Valley, there remain substantial stretches of Terrace deposits, even in areas

with a generally rich record, where few finds are recorded. This highlights two key problems in the study and interpretation of Palaeolithic material from fluvial terrace deposits, which are that: (a) despite the relatively well documented records we have of previous discoveries, we actually have very little idea of the texture and scale of artefact clustering within terrace bodies; and (b) we don't know whether the patterns we observe represent genuine archaeological distribution, or merely reflect differential intensities of recovery and investigation.

Plate 3.9 Phil Harding recording a palaeolithic deposit at Dunbridge, Hampshire, *copyright Wessex Archaeology*

For instance, at a large-scale, there are rich concentrations of findspots in Solent River (and tributary) deposits at Bournemouth (just west of the Solent-Thames region) and in Southampton. However, there are very few finds in the intervening stretches of Solent River Terrace deposits covering the New Forest. At a smaller scale, reinvestigations of specific deposits with a rich record of previously discovered finds, for instance as at Dunbridge in the Test Valley, Hampshire (Plate 3.9) have often been relatively unproductive (Harding 1998). This emphasises that we currently know too little about the distribution of artefactual material within gravel deposits. The lack of material in some otherwise rich deposits suggests that concentrations may be tightly clustered, and represent real sites, rather than be an ubiquitous background noise. If so, this would increase the interpretive potential of any clusters that were discovered.

A second point to make about the Palaeolithic potential fluvial Terrace deposits is that it may be misleading to focus upon the better-mapped and more extensive deposits of larger river channels, such as the Solent River gravels that occur across Southampton. Although generally proven to be rich in artefacts, these represent substantial depositional events by a major river, and thus any contained archaeological remains are perhaps more likely to be churned, fluvially transported or reworked. In contrast, small remnant outcrops associated with tributaries may be a more fruitful hunting ground for Palaeolithic sites, even if they appear insignificant on geological mapping, or perhaps are too small to appear at all. Although (in the former case, only just) outside the Solent-Thames region, the sites of Harnham (in Wiltshire) and Cuxton (in Kent) both exemplify this point. Harnham (Whittaker *et al.* 2004) is near to a small patch of mapped terrace gravel outcropping above the Avon, but there is no indication from the geological mapping of any reason to suspect an important site – although it is within a corridor where one could predict the likely presence of unmapped terrace outcrops. Cuxton, in contrast, is situated on a mapped outcrop, but still one so small that it is hardly noticeable compared to many other outcrops up and down the Medway Valley (Cruse 1987; Wenban-Smith 2004a). The important corollary of this is that significant Palaeolithic sites may be present, or even abundant, in tributary valleys where Pleistocene terrace deposits are scarce, minimal or even apparently absent.

High-level/plateau gravels

There are various spreads of high-level gravel patches across southern England, often capping areas of higher ground, that do not appear to be residual deposits, and yet are not sufficiently closely related to the modern drainage pattern to be identified as associated terrace deposits. These are often mapped as plateau gravels, for instance in southern Hampshire and the Isle of Wight. They can be accepted as significantly older than most deposits mapped as Terrace gravels, dating to the early Middle Pleistocene or before. The Northern Drift of Oxfordshire can also be included under this category of deposit. Palaeolithic artefacts have often been recovered from these areas (Table 3.9); several have been found on patches of plateau gravel on the Isle of Wight, for instance, and there have been a recent spate of discoveries on the Northern Drift. Other high-level gravels of pre-Anglian date associated with artefact finds include the Silchester Gravel (Berkshire) and various Solent and Test gravels in Hampshire. The key question concerning these remains is whether they are essentially later, deposited on the surface of these deposits, or whether any actually come from within these early deposits, and hence represent evidence of very early occupation of Britain?

Clay-with-flints and other residual sediments

Residual deposits can be found capping high ground where there has been little Pleistocene deposition, but the surface has been subject to exposure throughout the Pleistocene, leading to the development of sediments. The best-known residual deposits are the Clay-with-flints material that mantles the Chalk uplands in various parts of the Solent-Thames region, particularly Hampshire and Berkshire. This is now known to include a mixture of Chalk solution residue homogenized with fine-grained Tertiary sediments, representing remnants of soils built up throughout the Tertiary and Pleistocene and periodically subject to sub-aerial weathering and degradation accompanying climatic oscillations. The Clay-with-flints

Table 3.9 The Lower/Middle Palaeolithic resource, Solent-Thames region: high-level/plateau gravels

County zone	Abundance (deposits)	Key areas	Abundance (Palaeolithic remains)	Key sites	Notes
BU1	-	-	-	-	-
BU2	-	-	-	-	-
BU3	-	-	-	-	-
BU4	-	-	-	-	-
OX1	++	Northern Drift	++	Combe; Freeland	Need to establish whether Palaeolithic artefacts are residual surface finds, or are contained within Northern Drift
OX2	-	-	-	-	-
OX3	++	Winter Hill terrace	++	Kidmore End; Sonning Common	Need to establish whether Palaeolithic artefacts are residual surface finds, or are contained within terrace outcrops
BE1	-	-	-	-	-
BE2	-	-	-	-	-
BE3	++	High level Enborne terraces; Silchester gravel	++	Wash Common; Hamstead Marshall; Crowshott	Need to establish whether Palaeolithic artefacts are residual surface finds, or are within these deposits
BE4	+	High level Blackwater and Loddon terraces	+	Pine Hill	Need to establish whether Palaeolithic artefacts are residual surface finds, or are within deposits
HA1a	++	Southern edge of Silchester Gravel; Yateley Common	-	-	-
HA1b	-	-	-	-	-
HA2	-	-	-	-	-
HA3	++	Higher gravel spreads in New Forest; T8+ patches in Southampton	+	Midanbury Hill	-
IoW1a	+	Patches near Newport and Calbourne	-	-	-
IoW1b	-	-	-	-	-
IoW2	++	Extensive spreads around Cowes; various other patches, eg. in Parkhurst Forest	++	Rew Street; Norris Castle; Wootton	Need to re-assess blanket group of 'plateau gravel', and to establish whether Palaeolithic artefacts are residual surface finds, or are within these deposits
IoW3	++	Various spreads, esp. between Ventnor and Newport, and west of Sandown airport	+	Bleak Down	Need to see if any original Bleak Down gravel can be found and re-examined to establish date and formation process
IoW4	-	-	-	-	-

[+++ Abundant; ++ moderately common; + scarce; - none known; ? Uncertain]

has long been known to contain Early Palaeolithic artefacts (Dewey 1924; Willis 1947), abundantly in some locations (Halliwell & Parfitt 1993; Scott-Jackson 2000). Residual Lower/Middle Palaeolithic finds have been made across the region (Table 3.10), with rich concentrations of material known from Cliddesden and Ellisfield (near Basingstoke) and Holybourne Down (east Hampshire).

The understanding and interpretation of material from residual contexts is, however, fraught with difficulty (cf. Wenban-Smith 2001a). Any artefacts within residual deposits may have been reworked within the sediment by repeated freezing and thawing, but not been subject to down-slope movement or fluvial transport. Accordingly any archaeological evidence found in residual deposits such as Clay-with-flints, which often caps chalk on high ground in Hampshire

and Berkshire, has probably been deposited close to where it was found. There is rarely, however, any precisely stratified material, and Neolithic, Mesolithic and Palaeolithic finds can all be contained within the same horizon. Thus the archaeological material from residual deposits comes from a palimpsest representing 500,000+ years of intermittent occupation. This is not to disregard or belittle the value of such a palimpsest, whose spatial integrity over such a long period could open interesting avenues of research, but its nature needs to be recognised and understood as a prerequisite for such research. Important points for future research are to investigate whether it is possible to date artefactual material from residual deposits, and whether (and if so, how often) residual deposits contain Lower/Middle Palaeolithic material in sealed stratigraphic contexts.

Table 3.10 The Lower/Middle Palaeolithic resource, Solent-Thames region: residual sediments (Clay-with-flint)

County zone	Abundance (deposits)	Key areas	Abundance (Palaeolithic remains)	Key sites	Notes
BU1	-	-	-	-	-
BU2	-	-	-	-	-
BU3	+++	Stokenchurch; plateau N and S of River Misbourne	+	Brick Kiln Farm, Chartridge	-
BU4	-	-	-	-	-
OX1	-	-	-	-	-
OX2	-	-	-	-	-
OX3	++	Chilterns, E of Wallingford Fan Gravels	-	-	Need to investigate for Palaeolithic material
BE1	++	North Berks Downs	+	-	-
BE2	+	-	+	-	-
BE3	++	South Berks Downs	+	Hungerford-Newbury	-
BE4	-	-	-	-	-
HA1a	-	-	-	-	-
HA1b	-	-	-	-	-
HA2	+++	South of Basingstoke; East Hants	++	Cliddesden, Ellisfield and Holybourne Down	Need to see if clusters occur; need to disentangle palimpsest of Palaeolithic and later material
HA3	-	-	-	-	-
IoW1a	+++	Brighstone Down; Cheverton Down; Westridge Down	++	Cheverton Down	More than one handaxe from Cheverton Down
IoW1b	+++	Week Down; Boniface Down	-	-	-
IoW2	-	-			
IoW3	-	-	-	-	-
IoW4	-	-	-	-	-

[+++ Abundant; ++ moderately common; + scarce; - none known; ? Uncertain]

'Brickearth'

The region includes several spreads of deposits mapped as 'brick earth'. This is often presumed to be of aeolian, or loessic, origin, although such sediments are highly mobile once deposited and are often reworked by colluvial processes, perhaps often intermingling with alluvial deposits in the process. Thus most spreads of brick earth are the result of an uncertain combination of colluvial, aeolian and/or alluvial processes. Aeolian sediments are poorly represented within the British Pleistocene record, with the exception of last glacial (Devensian) coversands and loess accumulations. These are sand and silt-sized material blown out from glacial outwash plains during periods of severe climate, and then deposited at particular parts of the landscape where wind-speed dies (Catt 1977). Loess from earlier in the Pleistocene is of great importance as an archive of palaeo-climatic data (from alternations of cold-climate loess and interglacial soils) elsewhere in the world, especially central Europe and China (eg Kukla, 1975) but also including the nearby River Somme valley (Antoine et al., 2007). Much loessic material, even the majority, rapidly becomes colluvially or even fluvially reworked, rather than remaining as primary aeolian loess. From the Palaeolithic archaeological point of view, loessic deposits are potentially significant because they form progressively, burying any archaeological evidence very gently and preserving it undisturbed.

Brickearth sediments are generally scarce in the Solent-Thames region, being slightly more common and occurring as larger patches in the southern part of the region (Table 3.11). Artefactual finds, including Levalloisian material, are associated with colluvial/alluvial brickearth spreads overlying Terrace deposits of the Middle Thames at Burnham, Marlow and Slough. These deposits can be broadly equated with the Langley Silt complex of the Middle Thames, associated with rich Palaeolithic sites at Yiewsley, a little further east in the London region (Wymer 1968: 255). Thus, although not a lot of material is known from these deposits in the Solent-Thames region, they should be regarded as of high potential.

In Hampshire, there is a substantial spread of brick earth covering Solent River terrace deposits on the Gosport peninsula, in the vicinity of Fareham. No Palaeolithic artefacts are known in association with these deposits. However, a short distance to the north, on the south-facing slope of Portsdown Hill, a thick sequence of colluvial deposits is known to occur (in an area mapped as chalk bedrock); and this sequence of deposits buries the undisturbed Palaeolithic occupation floor at the Red Barns Palaeolithic site, which has produced thousands of mint condition artefacts from a very restricted area (Wenban-Smith et al. 2000). The key points arising from discovery of this site are: (a) that geological mapping of Pleistocene deposits is often erroneous; and (b) that highly significant sites can occur in unexpected situations, including (in this instance) on a slope mapped as chalk bedrock.

Finally, although entirely unmapped, recent excavations at Priory Bay have demonstrated the presence of mint condition artefacts, probably associated with an undisturbed palaeo-landsurface, within, and at the base of, fine-grained brickearth deposits exposed in the cliff section (Plate 3.10). As above, this discovery demonstrates the inadequacy of relying entirely upon geological mapping to model accurately the Palaeolithic potential of landscapes, although it can definitely provide a useful fuzzy starting point to second-guess the range of sediments likely to be present.

Head/solifluction gravels

Mass slope-movement and solifluction gravels incorporate rocks and pebbles of all sizes alongside finer grained sands and silts. The Palaeolithic remains they contain have varied depositional histories and interpretative potential. Deposits occur at the base of slopes, on the surface of valley-sides, in dry valleys and in hollows in the landscape, anywhere, in fact, where sediment destabilised by severe climatic conditions and/or de-vegetation has slipped downslope and accumulated. Despite their sometimes coarse nature, many colluvial/solifluction deposits have

Plate 3.10 Section at Priory Bay, Isle of Wight, *copyright Francis Wenban-Smith*

slipped only a short distance, leading to the relatively gentle burial of archaeological material. Others have moved a longer distance, and may also include derived material from significantly older deposits, for instance

Table 3.11 The Lower/Middle Palaeolithic resource, Solent-Thames region: head/valley brickearth

County zone	Abundance (deposits)	Key areas	Abundance (Palaeolithic remains)	Key sites	Notes
BU1	-	-	-	-	-
BU1	-	-	-	-	-
BU2	-	-	-	-	-
BU3	-	-	-	-	-
BU4	√√	Burnham; Marlow	√√	Dorney Wood; Great Western Pit	Associated faunal remains at Dorney Wood; Levallois from brickearth at Marlow (possibly equivalent to Langley Silt)
OX1	-	-	-	-	-
OX2	-	-	-	-	-
OX3	-	-	-	-	-
BE1	-	-	-	-	-
BE2	√	Slough	√	Langley Marish, Langley	Contains Levallois material, and equivalent to Langley Silt
BE3	-	-	-	-	-
BE4	-	-	-	-	-
HA1a	-	-	-	-	-
HA1b	√	Small patch at Bentley	-	-	-
HA2	-	-	-	-	-
HA3	√√	Extensive spread near Fareham, Gosport peninsula; and on slopes of Ports Down Hill, esp. S-facing	√	Red Barns	One very prolific (and in situ) site at Red Barns, buried under >2m slopewash sediments – a worrying case-study exemplifying difficulty of predictive modelling of high potential locations
IoW1a	-	-	-	-	-
IoW1b	-	-	-	-	-
IoW2	+	Small patches at: Newport, Downend, and behind cliffs between Nettlestone Point and Bembridge Foreland	+	Priory Bay; Bembridge	*In situ* horizons at Priory Bay; finds from brickearth outcropping east of Bembridge school
IoW3	++	Large spread associated with upper Yar (western), above Chilton Chine	-	-	-
IoW4	-	-	-	-	-

[+++ Abundant; ++ moderately common; + scarce; - none known; ? Uncertain]

Table 3.12 The Lower/Middle Palaeolithic resource, Solent-Thames region: head/solifluction gravels

County zone	Abundance (deposits)	Key areas	Abundance (Palaeolithic remains)	Key sites	Notes
BU1	-	-	-	-	-
BU2	-	-	-	-	-
BU3	-	-	-	-	-
BU4	-	-	-	-	-
OX1	-	-	-	-	-
OX2	++	Wallingford Fan Gravels	++	Benson, (Turners Court); Ewelme, Rumbolds Pit	Thought to be of Anglian age (MIS Stage 12)
OX3	-	-	-	-	-
BE1	-	-	-	-	-
BE2	+	Remenham	-	Remenham Church Pit	One very prolific site in solifluction deposits over terrace
BE3	++	Savernake	++	Knowle Farm	Very prolific site at Knowle Farm
BE4	-	-	-	-	-
HA1a	-	-	-	-	-
HA1b	-	-	-	-	-
HA2	-	-	-	-	-
HA3	-	-	-	-	-
IoW1a	-	-	-	-	-
IoW1b	-	-	-	-	-
IoW2	++	Priory Bay; Bembridge raised beach section	++	Warner Hotel; Bembridge School; Whitecliff Bay	Abundant material at Priory Bay and at Bembridge School
IoW3	-	-	-	-	-
IoW4	-	-	-	-	-

[+++ Abundant; ++ moderately common; + scarce; - none known; ? Uncertain]

when a landslip cascades down a dry valley tributary across a series of terrace deposits of different ages.

Solifluction gravels are recorded in Oxfordshire, Berkshire, and are known to occur, although not mapped as such, on the Isle of Wight. However deposits of this nature are likely to be significantly more abundant than shown on the geological mapping, as numerous dry valleys on the chalk downland that is common in the region are likely to be filled, at least in part, with solifluction deposits. The most notable of the solifluction deposits recorded are the Wallingford Fan Gravels in Oxfordshire, thought to date from the Anglian glaciation, which are associated with moderately abundant lithic artefacts (Table 3.12). Isolated, but prolific, sites are also known from solifluction deposits in Berkshire at Remenham Church Pit. and at Knowle Farm, Savernake, Wiltshire, close to the Berkshire border.

On the Isle of Wight, a substantial spread of solifluction gravel deposits can be observed in the Bembridge raised beach cliff section (cf. below), and these have produced artefactual remains. A substantial number of handaxes have also been produced from deposits at Bembridge School that are probably of solifluction origin. This would be of interest in its own right, if a stratigraphical relationship could be established between the artefact-bearing deposits and a datable horizons such as the Steyne Wood Clay. It is also of potential interest as indicating that there might be in the vicinity a source deposit with undisturbed remains. Coarse-grained solifluction deposits are also present in the artefact-bearing sequence in the cliff section at Priory Bay, and these too contain abundant Palaeolithic remains.

Marine littoral sediments (raised beach, estuarine, intertidal zone)

Marine littoral sediments include deposits that have undergone a range of depositional processes. Material incorporated in pebble storm beaches is likely to have undergone severe churning by wave action, and can be so severely abraded that individual artefacts are scarcely recognizable as such. In contrast material incorporated in rapidly forming fine-grained sediments in the intertidal zone, as for instance in various horizons at Boxgrove (cf. Roberts & Parfitt 1999), can be preserved entirely undisturbed. In the Solent-Thames region, marine littoral sediments occur at two locations (Table 3.13). Firstly, at Portsdown Hill, two distinct pebble storm beach deposits are preserved at two different levels, an upper level broadly equivalent to the Boxgrove raised beach, and a lower level of uncertain date. No artefactual remains are associated with either of these deposits. Secondly, at Bembridge on the Isle of Wight, the main marine sediments comprise a substantial raised beach exposed in section on the south-facing stretch of coastline west of Bembridge Foreland. This includes a major pebble storm beach, and associated offshore fine-grained sediments that contain pollen remains. The altitude of the storm beach, and the range of pollen grains, combine to suggest an Ipswichian (MIS 5e) date for the storm beach, confirmed by a recent OSL dating investigation (Wenban-Smith et al. 2005). A short distance to the northwest, in deposits developed a little inland, and well above the Ipswichian raised beach, the estuarine Steyne Wood Clay occurs, which has been dated as broadly equivalent to the

Table 3.13 The Lower/Middle Palaeolithic resource, Solent-Thames region: marine littoral sediments

County zone	Abundance (deposits)	Key areas	Abundance (Palaeolithic remains)	Key sites	Notes
BU1	-	-	-	-	-
BU2	-	-	-	-	-
BU3	-	-	-	-	-
BU4	-	-	-	-	-
OX1	-	-	-	-	-
OX2	-	-	-	-	-
OX3	-	-	-	-	-
BE1	-	-	-	-	-
BE2	-	-	-	-	-
BE3	-	-	-	-	-
BE4	-	-	-	-	-
HA1a	-	-	-	-	-
HA1b	-	-	-	-	-
HA2	-	-	-	-	-
HA3	+	Ports Down Hill	-	Cams Bridge; M27 junction 11	No Palaeolithic finds known associated with marine littoral sediments
IoW1a	-	-	-	-	-
IoW1b	-	-	-	-	-
IoW2	++	Bembridge School; Bembridge-Foreland cliff section	-	Bembridge School; Warner Hotel	Two v different sites and sets of deposits, both with good biological remains: (a) pre-Anglian Steyne Wood Clay (estuarine) at Bembridge School; (b) Ipswichian raised beach and intertidal zone, exposed in cliff section
IoW3	-	-	-	-	-
IoW4	+?	Between Bembridge and Selsey Bill?	-	-	Needs investigation

[+++ Abundant; ++ moderately common; + scarce; - none known; ? Uncertain]

Boxgrove deposits. No artefactual remains are associated with either of these deposits, although they are relatively abundant in the vicinity of the Steyne Wood Clay, suggesting that undisturbed horizons may perhaps be present not too far away.

Site distribution and concentration

A number of patterns are apparent in the distribution of Palaeolithic sites in the region. Firstly, at the largest scale, there is a broad correspondence between the occurrence of chalk bedrock and the occurrence of Palaeolithic artefact find spots. As most Palaeolithic artefacts were made out of flint, and as chalk bedrock is the source of most flint raw material, then this confirms that the majority of lithic artefacts were made and abandoned in the same general area. However, it is difficult to monitor mobility within the Chalk/flint zone. This means that extra importance should be attached to discoveries of concentrations of flint artefacts out of the chalk bedrock zone, for instance as at Wolvercote, or Priory Bay, as these sites may have important information to contribute about the mobility of Palaeolithic hominins, and the extent to which they anticipated their need for lithic artefacts, and transported them around the landscape.

Secondly, as discussed above, there are distinct areas of Pleistocene fluvial sediments where Palaeolithic artefacts seem particularly abundant, in particular, Middle Thames terrace deposits and Test Valley deposits at Romsey and Southampton, as well as a number of more isolated, but very prolific sites, such as Woodgreen

in the Avon Valley. However, we are completely in the dark as to whether these apparent distributions represent a genuine archaeological reality, or whether they are wholly a reflection of differential investigation – this uncertainty needs to be urgently investigated through controlled and systematic sieving programmes.

There are also prolific but isolated sites in residual Clay-with-flint deposits (eg. Holybourne Down, Hants), head/solifluction deposits (eg. Knowle Farm, Savernake, Wilts) and on some high-level/plateau gravels (eg. Bleak Down, Isle of Wight; Silchester Gravels, Berks). Again, we need to carry out more controlled investigations and establish whether these are genuinely isolated occurrences.

Current understanding

Regional settlement history and cultural trends

As emphasised above, we are uncertain whether the apparent distribution of sites (Fig. 3.1) is a genuine representation of archaeological reality, or merely a reflection of the differential survival of artefact-bearing deposits and their subsequent varied histories of investigation. This disclaimer having been made, certain coarse patterns can be identified.

There is little evidence of hominin presence in the northern part of the region, in the clay lands of northern Buckinghamshire. Hominin presence seems strongly correlated with the river valleys of the Middle Thames and the Test, with occasional sites in other valleys, and

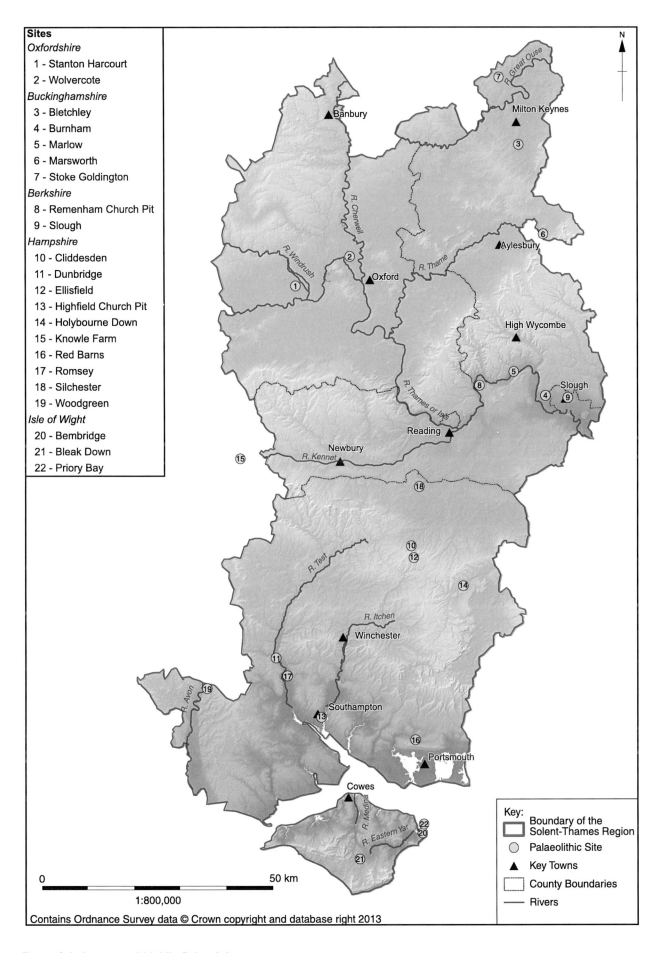

Sites

Oxfordshire
1 - Stanton Harcourt
2 - Wolvercote

Buckinghamshire
3 - Bletchley
4 - Burnham
5 - Marlow
6 - Marsworth
7 - Stoke Goldington

Berkshire
8 - Remenham Church Pit
9 - Slough

Hampshire
10 - Cliddesden
11 - Dunbridge
12 - Ellisfield
13 - Highfield Church Pit
14 - Holybourne Down
15 - Knowle Farm
16 - Red Barns
17 - Romsey
18 - Silchester
19 - Woodgreen

Isle of Wight
20 - Bembridge
21 - Bleak Down
22 - Priory Bay

Key:
▢ Boundary of the Solent-Thames Region
● Palaeolithic Site
▲ Key Towns
▢ County Boundaries
— Rivers

0   50 km

1:800,000

Contains Ordnance Survey data © Crown copyright and database right 2013

Figure 3.1 Lower and Middle Palaeolithic sites

occasional forays into the chalk uplands represented by handaxe finds from residual Clay-with-flint deposits. A key common factor in almost all areas of artefact concentration is the local availability of a good supply of flint raw material, and this may, therefore, have been a key constraint upon hominin mobility. A notable exception to this pattern is the site at Wolvercote, where an assemblage of flint handaxes apparently occurs well to the north of the nearest outcrop of chalk bedrock. This anomaly merits further investigation.

There is a consistent pattern of the earliest reliable evidence of occupation occurring in late Anglian deposits across the region (Plate 3.11). Artefacts come from the Harefield terrace of the Great Ouse (Buckinghamshire), the Wallingford Fan Gravel and Caversham Ancient Channel (Oxfordshire), the Gerrards Cross Gravel and Silchester Gravel (Berkshire) and terrace 8 of the Test Valley (Hampshire). The typological characteristics (large, well-made ovates, often with tranchet sharpening) of many handaxes from the Caversham Ancient Channel are similar to those from Boxgrove, known to date from a pre-Hoxnian interglacial episode. There are, however, also hints of earlier occupation. In Oxfordshire, a number of artefacts have been found from the surface of the Northern Drift, a deposit that formed substantially before the Anglian period, although it is uncertain whether any

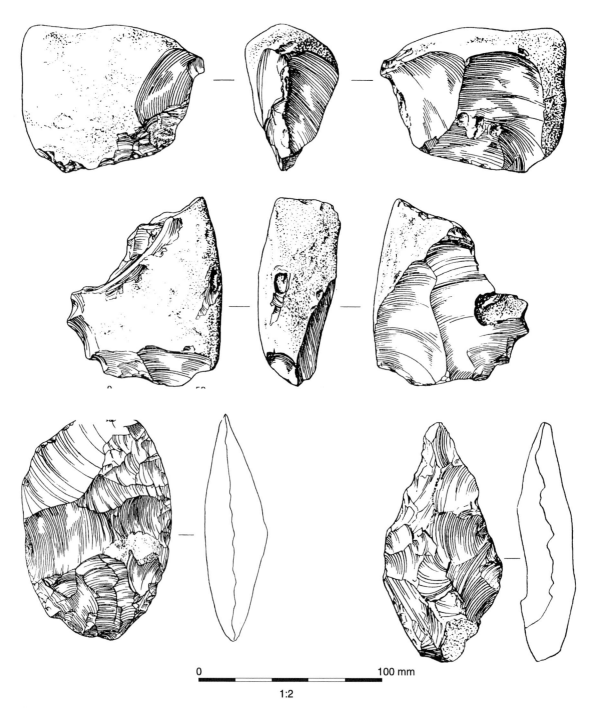

0   100 mm

1:2

Plate 3.11 Tools from the Anglian glaciation: Highlands Farm pit, *copyright Wymer 1999, 51, fig. 13 with permission Wessex Archaeology*

artefacts originate from within the deposit, rather than being intrusive surface finds of later date.

Secondly, a large collection of handaxes was recovered from within the gravel deposits that cap Bleak Down, on the Isle of Wight. These were described as stratified

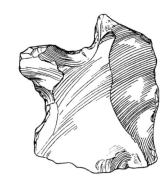

Plate 3.12 Grovelands Pit, Reading, *copyright Wymer 1968 with permission Wessex Archaeology*

fluvial deposits when first exposed early in the 20th century, but no accurate drawings were made, and no exposures have been seen in modern times. If genuinely fluvial, the high altitude of these deposits would make them substantially pre-Anglian in date. Considering the recent discovery of a simple flake/core industry at Pakefield (Parfitt *et al.* 2005) in other substantially pre-Anglian deposits, it is perhaps now time to start paying greater attention to the archaeological potential of early, high-level gravel deposits previously dismissed as of no possible archaeological importance. Handaxes appear to be a characteristic aspect of cultural adaptations in later pre-Hoxnian populations, although not of the earliest Pakefield occupation. This is perhaps another reason for the difficulty of recognising earlier activity, as handaxes are relatively easily discovered compared to small simple flakes and cores.

The climate and environment in Britain would without doubt have been too inhospitable for hominin occupation in the peak cold stages of the Anglian. After the final retreat of Anglian ice, Britain seems to have entered a relative golden age, with prolific evidence of sustained occupation in the Hoxnian (MIS 11). By far the most abundant evidence of early hominin presence in the Solent-Thames region occurs in the post-Anglian and pre-Ipswichian terrace deposits of the Middle Thames valley (Boyn Hill, Lynch Hill and Taplow terraces; Plate 3.12) and the Test valley (T7 through to T2). A case-study of artefact abundance in the Middle Thames, controlled as far as possible for intensity of investigation, has suggested that population suffered a steady decline through the period MIS 11 through to MIS 8 (Ashton & Lewis 2002). Handaxe-dominated assemblages occur throughout this period (see Plate 3.14 below), with Levallois technology first appearing in the Lynch Hill terrace. It is currently uncertain when this phase of occupation came to an end, although we are generally confident that Britain was unoccupied by the Ipswichian (MIS5e). It is widely held that Britain was unoccupied through MIS 6, and indeed there are no unequivocally dated occupation sites within MIS 7, and certainly none within the Solent-Thames region, despite a couple of rich palaeo-environmental sites (Stanton Harcourt and Marsworth).

Following the Ipswichian, Neanderthal occupation in the last glaciation is indicated by the presence of *bout coupé* handaxe finds across the region (Tyldesley 1987; White & Jacobi 2002). Most finds come from brickearth or gravel deposits broadly associated with the last glaciation, but none come from an accurately and independently dated context (see Plate 3.6 above).

Solent-Thames in national context

The overall picture of hominin colonisation and settlement in the Solent-Thames region is broadly similar to that known from other parts of Britain. In addition, many aspects of the lithic cultural record through the Lower and Middle Palaeolithic apparently mirror our understanding from other parts of Britain. However, on closer scrutiny, it becomes evident that the national understanding is primarily based upon the rich record of the Middle Thames as it passes through the Solent-Thames region, making this apparent conformity entirely illusory. The seminal surveys of both Wymer (1968) and Roe (1981), for instance, both explicitly take the record from this region as representative of Britain as a whole. Some aspects of the East Anglian record, such as the pre-Anglian occurrence of the unifacial High Lodge industry and the preponderance of twisted ovate dominant sites in MIS 11, are not represented in the Solent-Thames region. Other regions of Britain, particularly various valleys in the Solent basin – the Test Valley, the Wiltshire Avon and the Stour – have a relatively rich record of Lower/Middle Palaeolithic artefact finds, but have not yet been systematically studied for comparative purposes. A small number of studies on material from the Test Valley suggest both similarities and differences with typological patterns in the Middle Thames region. Roe (2001) identifies a co-occurrence of cleavers with sharply pointed ficron handaxes in broadly contemporary sites in both regions. In contrast, Wenban-Smith (2001b) identifies a distinctive occurrence of unifacially worked handaxes on large side-struck flakes in T4 of the Test, at Highfield Church Pit. This is clearly a topic where further work is required.

Lifestyle and behaviour

One of the fundamental questions concerns whether we can think of early hominins as 'people' at all, or whether we need to try and imagine some kind of bipedal chimpanzee, technically skilful, but lacking a level of consciousness that we would regard as typically human. Despite lack of achievements often regarded as defining 'humanity', such as animal carvings and dramatic pictures on cave walls, we should not jump to the conclusion that they lacked a human degree of consciousness. Firstly, consider the irrelevance of the lack of material evidence for technological and artistic development. Anatomically modern humans have been around for over 100,000 years, yet it is only in the last 30,000 years that cave-painting has proliferated, and only in certain parts of the world, establishing that its absence does not necessarily imply a lack of human capability. Developments during the last 10,000 years such as writing, pottery, use of metals, television, computers and space travel are not so much signs of an evolving species, but of development of technical and information storage systems, which in turn facilitate increasingly swift and complex technological change. No-one would argue that the diverse peoples of the world today are not all part of the human species, yet there are considerable contrasts, in an archaeological sense, in visible material culture between nomads of the Saharan desert, inhabitants of the Amazon rainforest and the denizens of the Solent-Thames region in the twenty-first-century.

It is also necessary to consider the positive implications of the evidence that we do have. Chimpanzees and other animals have developed a range of tool-using behaviours that exploit the innate potential of naturally found objects,

sometimes with a small amount of trimming or modification, for instance trimming twigs from a branch to leave a denuded stick. The ability to make even the simplest stone tools requires, however, the much greater ability to foresee the transformation of an innately useless lump of blunt and asymmetrical material into an entirely different sharp-edged object. Even with a clear intention in mind, the ability to achieve the desired end-product depends upon an understanding of how one specific type of stone will fracture when hit, and the ability to transmit this knowledge from one generation to the next. These abilities were developed two million years ago in Africa.

Manufacture of the sophisticated handaxes by some of the earliest inhabitants of Britain depended on visualising how the removal of single flakes would contribute to the shaping of the final artefact. Although knapping depends upon being able broadly to predict how a flint nodule will fracture, there is always some uncertainty. Tiny variations in the force or location of percussion, together with the almost incalculable complexity of how a single flaking blow will impact on the nodule as a whole, affected by factors such as supporting hand pressure and overall three-dimensional shape and balance of the nodule, lead to a certain amount of unpredictable variation. As knapping progresses, short-term objectives are being continually developed and modified to reflect the specific, and sometimes unwelcome, outcomes of attempted individual flake removal. In fact, making a handaxe is very similar to playing chess, with the same mixture of deliberate planning, often several moves ahead, and almost unconscious strategic action, based on years of experience. It seems inescapable that the Archaic hominids of the Lower and Middle Palaeolithic were capable of thought processes broadly similar to modern humans, and that their lack of technological development was fundamentally ignorance and lack of necessity rather than stupidity.

This has implications for how we understand their behaviour. While some still see the Archaic world as one of a fifteen-minute attention-span, with tools made, used and abandoned as required, it is questionable whether such strategies could have worked in the seasonal climates of north-west European latitudes with their patchily distributed raw material resources. Moreover, there are sites which show clear patterning as locations of handaxe manufacture/export or handaxe discard incompatible with a strategy of tool use and discard to meet immediate expediencies (Wenban-Smith 2004a and b). We can, therefore, reasonably imagine an Archaic world involving foraging parties going on excursions, targeting specific resources, tooling up at certain well-known raw material sources *en route* or in advance, and habitually returning, laden with food, to specific base locations or temporary camps for overnight stays (Plate 3.13). Some scarce or labour intensive equipment, such as knapping pebbles or wooden spears, was probably either cached at specific locations around the landscape or carried and cared for as personal equipment.

Socially, these Archaic humans would have functioned within a group, and life would have been dominated by

Plate 3.13 Reconstruction of a Homo Heidelbergis site, *copyright OA, drawn by Peter Lorimer*

maintaining and negotiating social status and sexual relationships within the group, embedded within day-to-today subsistence activities. Items of personal equipment such as handaxes and spears could well have been significant weapons in this social battleground, and the incredible attention paid to the size and symmetry of certain handaxes or Levallois cores probably reflects their function in the social arena rather than any practical concerns in relation to butchering efficiency. Cut-marks on animal bones from certain sites, and in particular Boxgrove, confirm the long-standing assumption that meat-eating was central to diet, an argument supported by our omnivorous dentition and the necessity for a high protein diet to support our brain development (Aiello and Wheeler 1995; Stanford and Bunn 2001). There is no sign of the controlled deliberate use of fire until late in Neanderthal development, so, through most of the Lower and Middle Palaeolithic, meat would have been eaten raw, emphasising the continual need to acquire it fresh.

A number of studies over the last decades have suggested for the Lower Palaeolithic group sizes reaching 20–40 individuals with a home territory of *c*. 30 x 30 km, with group sizes increasing to 60–80 and territorial range to *c*. 50 x 50 km in the Middle Palaeolithic (Gamble and Steele 1999).

Finally, what was the size of these early humans and what did they look like? The fragments of skeletal material that we have are sufficient to confirm a fully bipedal hominid with a brain size approaching our own, or even

exceeding it in the Neanderthal era. The tibia from Boxgrove indicates the extreme robustness of at least one very early Briton, perhaps similar to an international rugby player, and the fairly large number of continental Neanderthal remains gives a clear image of the general robustness, heavy brow ridges, long head and forward-jutting face of the final Archaics. Skeletal material from the intervening period, however, is restricted to very few specimens, none of which allows facial or post-cranial reconstruction. Look around the diversity in any gathering of more than a few people in the present day, and it is clear that the small quantity of material we have is insufficient for any generalisations concerning whole Archaic populations. It is possible that post-cranial proportions would have varied with climatic change, with cooler conditions encouraging squatter body shapes, as is the case with Neanderthals. The large size of many handaxes, hammerstones and waste knapping debitage provides an indicator, based on experience from modern experimental knapping, that Archaic hominids would have been more robust and stronger than the majority of the present-day population (Plate 3.14).

There are no archaeological indications of any form of clothing, and bearing in mind the cold climate (usually colder than the present day), one has to consider how survival was possible without fire or protective clothing in the latitudes of north-west Europe. A number of animals that colonised more northerly latitudes from a tropical origin developed increased fat and body hair to aid

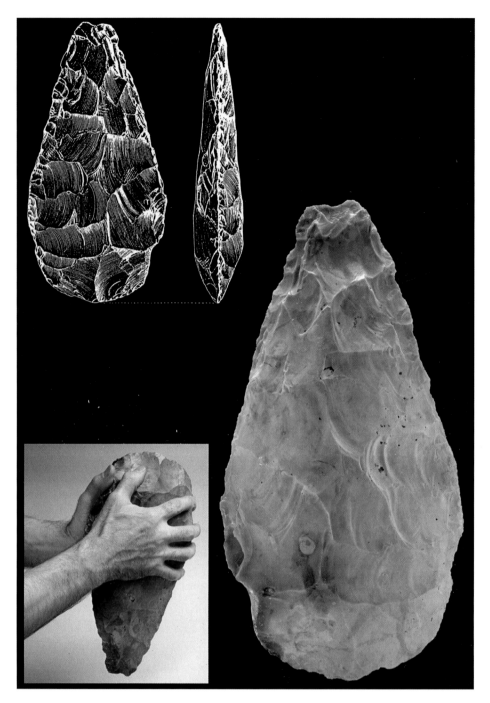

Plate 3.14 Giant handaxe from Furze Platt, Berkshire *copyright Trustees of the London Natural History Museum*

survival. These included the woolly rhinoceros and woolly mammoth, the remains of which have been found in the arctic permafrost. It seems highly likely, therefore, that Archaic humans would have been adapted in a similar way, and possessed increased subcutaneous fat and a thick furry pelt over the whole body.

Transition to the Upper Palaeolithic

The last British Mousterian occupation of Britain is represented by occasional Neanderthal incursions during the last glaciation in the time range 100,000 to 50,000 BP, mostly identified through their convenient habit of manufacturing the typologically distinctive *bout*

coupé handaxe (see Plate 3.6). The Upper Palaeolithic commences with the arrival of modern humans and their associated range of lithic and bone/antler artefacts, characterised as Aurignacian after the site of Aurignac in France (Mellars 2004). The first influx into Europe seems to have occurred from the south-west in MIS 3, *c.* 40,000 BP. There are a number of British sites with Upper Palaeolithic evidence dating between *c.* 30,000 and 26,000 bc (uncalibrated radiocarbon years), particularly Kent's Cavern in Devon and Paviland Cave on the Gower peninsular in Wales (Jacobi 1999). Early Upper Palaeolithic sites in Britain are concentrated in the south-west, and it seems possible that the route of Upper Palaeolithic colonisation of Britain was by the Atlantic sea-board. Britain appears only to have occasionally been visited by both Neanderthals and early modern humans, and never, as far as we know, contemporarily with each other. Southern Spain seem to have been the last refuge of the Neanderthals (Finlayson *et al.* 2006), and their range seems to have contracted in conjunction with the expansion of the early modern human range. It is unlikely that these two events are unrelated, although the precise nature of any competition or interaction between these two hominin groups is uncertain. It is most likely that ecological factors lie behind their apparent inability to occupy the same terrain, rather than more romantic notions of overt competition. However, there is no *a priori* reason why Britain might not have been another refuge where Neanderthals remained as early modern humans colonised increasing swathes of mainland continental Europe, and this should perhaps constitute one final question upon which to focus further research in the region.

Chapter 4

The Lower/Middle Palaeolithic: Research Agenda

by Francis Wenban-Smith,
with Terry Hardaker, Robert Hosfield, Rebecca Loader, Barbara Silva,
Francis Wenban-Smith and Keith Wilkinson

4.1 Themes and priorities

It was recognised in the 1980s that the present structure of archaeological curation and investigation in advance of development requires a framework of academic and research priorities against which to consider the significance of sites and to guide their investigation. The seminal English Heritage publication *Exploring our Past* (1991) identified three main themes – physical evolution, cultural development and global colonisation. English Heritage has subsequently taken the lead, in conjunction with the Prehistoric Society, in keeping core strategic research themes under review, with updated themes and research priorities issued in 1999 and 2008 (English Heritage/ Prehistoric Society 1999, 2008). A condensed list of national research themes is given (Table 4.1), collated from these sources, and taking account of actual ongoing research across Britain. This has led to the inclusion of an element of material cultural study, which is unaccountably omitted from the proposed national framework, despite still comprising a signifi-

cant element of the actual practice of Palaeolithic archaeology. It is suggested that all Lower/Middle Palaeolithic research within the Solent-Thames region should be related to this framework, and that much of it will be regionally specific instances of these national generalities.

Within this context, a number of specific research priorities have been discussed above, and others are given for each county in the region in the individual county reports, summarised in sections 4.5-9 below. Generally recurring themes are:

4.1.1   an improved chrono-stratigraphic framework, both for sets of deposits within clearly defined zones such as specific river valleys, and between sets of deposits in, for instance different valley systems

4.1.2   an improved understanding of the taphonomic history of artefact accumulations in all types of deposits, but especially fluvial and Clay-with-flints contexts

Table 4.1 National Lower/Middle Palaeolithic research themes

Aim	Details
N 1	Documentation of regional sequences of material cultural change
N 2	Dating of artefact-bearing deposits within regional, national and international Quaternary frameworks
N 3	Developing understanding and dating of regional Pleistocene environmental, climatic and litho-stratigraphic frameworks
N 4	Explanation of diachronic and synchronic patterns of material cultural variability
N 5	Behaviour of Archaic (pre-anatomically modern) hominids (a) at specific sites, (b) across the wider landscape
N 6	Behaviour of anatomically modern hominids (a) at specific sites, (b) across the wider landscape
N 7	Extent of contrasts in Archaic and anatomically modern human behaviour and adaptations, and in fundamental cognitive capacities
N 8	Patterns of colonisation, settlement and abandonment through the Pleistocene
N 9	The climatic and environmental context of Archaic settlement, and the relationship between climate/environment and colonisation
N 10	The history of isolation/connection between Britain and the continental mainland, and the relationship/implications for Palaeolithic settlement and cultural development/expression
N 11	Improved documentation and understanding of hominid physiological evolution
N 12	Investigation of the relationship between evolutionary, behavioural and material cultural change
N 13	Social organisation, behaviour and belief systems
N 14	Models for cultural transmission and learning
N 15	Improving models of Palaeolithic site formation and post-depositional modification

4.1.3   an improved understanding of the distribution of artefact concentrations within gravel bodies

4.1.4   clarification for a number of solifluction and high-level deposits (eg. northern Drift) of whether associated artefact finds are intrusive finds from the surface of the deposits, or whether any of these deposits contain artefacts incorporated within them contemporary with, or earleir than. their deposition

4.1.5   the improved identification, dating and technological/typological characterisation of lithic artefact assemblages, and integration into regional/national frameworks

4.1.6   to put hominin presence and activity in its climatic, environmental and landscape context, as well as within a chrono-stratigraphic framework

4.1.7   Predictive modelling for, and discovery and investigation of: (a) sites rich in faunal and other palaeo-environmental remains; (b) undisturbed sites; and (c) ideally, both together

In addition to these, at the regional and sub-regional level, it seems important to:

4.1.8   develop, compare and contrast regional and sub-regional sequences and distributions of settlement and cultural development. In particular, for instance, how does the sequence and distribution of settlement and cultural development in the Upper Thames Valley compare with those of the middle and lower parts of the Thames Valley? Likewise, how do these sequences compare with those in the Hampshire basin, and in different valleys within the Hampshire basin, such as the Avon and the Test? Fundamental to investigation of these issues is development within each region of an improved chrono-stratigraphic framework

4.1.9   look at these regional and sub-regional histories in relation to the wider national and north-west European history of settlement and colonisation, for instance as expressed in the Lower Thames Valley, East Anglia, the Sussex Raised Beaches and northern France, both from the point of view of mere chronology, and also to bring in material cultural expression

4.1.10   try to identify the original depositional environment of *ex situ* finds, and the location of regional human activity with the catchment, including searching for slack-water contexts

4.1.11   identify buried and sealed deposits/sites,

as contemporaneous palaeo-environmental evidence from *in situ* locations is exceptionally rare and would be virtually unparalleled

4.1.12   carry out detailed scientific studies in relation to any human remains, including those in fissure deposits such as Beedings, West Sussex, on the Greensand, and to attempt to isolate isotope suites for the examination of diet (meat vs plant food vs marine foods).

4.2 Specific immediately desirable projects

In the course of the resource assessment process, a number of specific and immediately desirable projects have been suggested. These are listed county by county in sections 4.5 to 4.9 below. Many of these are relevant to specific local and regional research questions. Others, however, are of more strategic importance, addressing themes that are applicable both across the region as a whole, and the nation generally. These latter include:

4.2.1   Compiling and maintaining a database of sites with mammalian and other palaeo-environmental evidence

4.2.2   Developing a GIS model of the available Palaeolithic and Pleistocene evidence to provide an overall view of the palaeo-landscape as well as a predictive tool for potentially artefact- and fossil-rich deposits

4.2.3   Modelling artefact dispersal and the formation of secondary context assemblages, with particular (but not exclusive) reference to the fluvial deposits ...

4.2.4   ... complemented by an intensive investigation of artefact distribution, vertically and horizontally, within a representative selection of specific terrace beds

4.2.5   Field-walking surveys of specific river valleys for gravel outcrops and Palaeolithic artefacts, supplemented by systematic investigation by controlled sieving

4.2.6   A typological/technological review of existing collections in specific key regions, complemented by targeted fieldwork to provide an improved chrono-stratigraphic framework for the analysed collections

4.2.7   Controlled investigation of high-level and "plateau" gravels, to identify whether artefact clusters are intrusive surface finds, or whether any of these deposits contain artefacts within them of very early date

4.3 Research methods and approaches

4.3.1 The first challenge is to identify at the earliest possible stage whether a site has any Palaeolithic potential. This can be addressed at the desk-based assessment (DBA) stage by consideration of the geological situation of the site, of whether any Pleistocene deposits are mapped in the vicinity, and whether there is a background record of Palaeolithic finds. The primary source of information is the county/unitary authority HER, supplemented by the appropriate volumes of the Southern Rivers Palaeolithic Project (Wessex Archaeology 1993a, b; 1994) or the English Rivers Palaeolithic Survey (Wessex Archaeology 1996a, b; 1997), which collated all information on known Palaeolithic findspots up to *c.* 1990.

4.3.2 There is one particularly fruitful source of information that should, whenever possible, also be taken account of at this stage. Most development projects, and particularly larger ones, carry out a range of geo-technical investigations early in the project cycle. These often involve excavation of test pits, window-samples and deeper U4 cable/percussion bore-holes. Besides the point that these in themselves have archaeological impact, and perhaps should be monitored, they also provide an excellent opportunity for archaeological knowledge to be gathered on a site, piggy-backing on the geo-technical investigations. These investigations reveal the presence and nature of any Pleistocene sediments present. All that is required is monitoring by a person with appropriate expertise, who can record the stratigraphic sequence, and observe and recover Palaeolithic remains if present.

4.3.3 It is necessary, in areas where potential is established for Pleistocene deposits and Palaeolithic remains, that special methods are applied to investigating their presence and potential. Deeper test pits need to be dug than in conventional archaeological trial-trenching, so as to allow investigation and characterisation of the Pleistocene sequence across a site. A key aspect of this is the application of: (a) standardised sedimentological recording; and (b) volume-controlled sieving of bulk samples on-site for artefacts and faunal remains. It is also necessary, when potentially suitable sediments are encountered, to sample and assess off-site for the presence and quality of biological remains such molluscs, pollen and ostracods.

4.3.4 In areas where there is not thought to be even the possibility of Pleistocene deposits, there is no need to carry out a full Palaeolithic/ Pleistocene evaluation. However, it would be good practice to at least ask the question as part of conventional evaluation: "Have Pleistocene deposits been encountered, and if so what is their nature and Palaeolithic potential?". Significant deposits may be found in unsuspected areas, and these may then require further evaluation specifically in relation to their Palaeolithic potential. Two useful case-studies in the South-East region of unexpected and highly important Palaeolithic discoveries are the sites of Red Barns, Hampshire (Wenban-Smith et al. 2000), a prolific and undisturbed Lower Palaeolithic site on a hill slope mapped as Chalk bedrock, and Swan Valley Community School, Swanscombe, Kent (Wenban-Smith & Bridgland 2001), another prolific Lower Palaeolithic site on a deposit mapped as Tertiary Thanet Sand.

4.3.5 If Palaeolithic remains are found to be present, it is advisable to take specialist advice on their potential, and on suitable methods for further study or mitigation of any impact. A wide range of options are potentially applicable depending upon the specific circumstance. In many cases a separate phase of mitigation work may not be required, and mitigation can be addressed by increasing the volume or intensity of sampling during the evaluation phase of work.

4.4 Assessment of Palaeolithic importance

4.4.1 An assessment of importance depends upon the extent to which the evidence in a particular deposit can contribute to addressing national and regional research priorities. English Heritage (1998) has published eleven criteria, any of which are deemed sufficient to identify a Palaeolithic site as of national importance (Table 4.2).

4.4.2 The English Heritage criteria successfully pinpoint a number of situations where there is particularly high potential to address a number of research priorities. It should be noted that remains in a primary undisturbed context represent just one of these criteria. Many sites without undisturbed remains may meet these criteria for national importance. Thus, by these guidelines, the absence of undisturbed primary context remains is not a basis for disregarding the potential of a Palaeolithic site and failing to carry out mitigating archaeological works. Furthermore, many sites that are not of national importance in themselves may contain good evidence that contributes to addressing national and regional research priorities, and impacts upon these should be mitigated.

Table 4.2. English Heritage (1998) criteria for Palaeolithic importance

Criterion	Notes
Any human bone is present	The only Lower/Middle Palaeolithic remains from Britain are: – one partial skull (occipital region) from Swanscombe – two incisors and a shin bone (two individuals) from Boxgrove – molar tooth from Pontnewydd (Wales)
Palaeolithic remains in primary undisturbed context	There are about a dozen British sites with undisturbed Palaeolithic remains. Less than half have both faunal and lithic remains, and have had areas of more than a few square metres excavated (cf. Wenban-Smith 2004b)
Remains from a period or geographic area where evidence is rare or previously unknown	
Organic artefacts	The only organic artefacts known from Britain from the L/M Palaeolithic are a wooden spear-point from Clacton and bone and antler percussors from Boxgrove
Well-preserved associated biological/ palaeo-environmental evidence	These are important on two counts: – May provide direct behavioural/dietary information – Provide environmental/climatic/biostratigraphic data
Evidence of lifestyle	Can include cut-marked faunal remains, particular topographic situation, artefacts when interpreted in light of their context/ distribution
Remains from different stratigraphic horizons	
Artistic evidence	Can include decorated/carved objects and rock-art. Not presently known before the Upper Palaeolithic, although should not be ruled out as a possibility for earlier periods
Evidence of hearths or structures	No evidence in Britain before the Upper Palaeolithic, but might be expected for the Middle Palaeolithic
Site can be related to exploitation of a particular resource	For instance raw material source, cave/rock-shelter, lake
Artefacts are abundant	No absolute guidelines on how abundance should be assessed. Needs to be considered together with level of investigation. If limited investigation, even low numbers of artefacts may indicate abundance

4.4.3   Finally, and this is a key strategic point, significant knowledge – ie. information that contributes to both national and regional research priorities – can be acquired, not only from single sites with obvious indisputable high quality evidence, but also from repeated observations at sites with evidence that is in itself of little apparent potential. The incremental accumulation of information from repeated observations in, for instance, a single mapped fluvial terrace can lead, over time, to a reliable picture of the density, distribution and nature of Palaeolithic remains. This can not be achieved other than through a coherent strategy of investigation that recognises this from the outset, and sets in place a standardised methodology of systematic small-scale data gathering exercises. A single event may involve excavation of a couple of test pits, sieving of eight x 100 litre gravel samples and recovery of no evidence. This in itself fails to provide sufficient information to make a more general summary of the Palaeolithic remains in a body of gravel that may cover several hundred hectares. However, once this exercise has been repeated a hundred times over a period of maybe 20 years, with hopefully at least occasional artefact recovery, then we will actually begin to both: (a) determine the distribution and prevalence of Palaeolithic remains in the gravel body under investigation; and (b) learn something that can make a major contribution to core national and regional research objectives.

4.5 Particular aims for Buckinghamshire

General aims are to:

4.5.1   Establish the evidence for the earliest human presence in Buckinghamshire.

4.5.2   Date the onset of the Middle Palaeolithic in Buckinghamshire and particularly the appearance of Levallois artefacts.

4.5.3   Compile the mammalian evidence and explore the possibility of using bio-stratigraphy to date key sites.

4.5.4   Establish the potential of the tills of the Buckinghamshire clay lands.

4.5.5   Explore the role of the Buckinghamshire landscape as a migration corridor along the major Rivers Great Ouse and Thames, as well as in the Chilterns themselves.

4.5.6   Develop a GIS model of the available Palaeolithic and Pleistocene evidence to provide an overall view of the palaeo-landscape as well as a predictive tool for potentially artefact- and fossil-rich deposits.

4.5.7   Investigate the locations and migrations of Palaeolithic peoples, within a tightly constrained geo-chronological framework, between fluvial and non-fluvial landscapes (to be identified)

Specific questions and projects:

A – Great Ouse Valley

4.5.8   To establish a firm geo-chronological framework for the major river terraces

4.5.9   Can a chronology be established for the Great Ouse terraces and can these be tied in with the Thames Valley sequence?

4.5.10   To investigate the potential of these sediments to contain palaeo-environmental evidence for Pleistocene landscapes and/or human presence

B – North Buckinghamshire clay lands projects

4.5.11   To investigate the potential of the lake sediments under Milton Keynes.

4.5.12   To investigate the possible fossil content of the River Thame Shabbington terrace

C – Chiltern Hills projects

4.5.13   To explore potentials for *in situ* finds associated with the clay-with-flints, both Palaeolithic and Pleistocene.

4.5.14   To investigate the likelihood of any Caddington-style brickearth-filled depressions with Palaeolithic potential

D – Middle Thames Valley projects

4.5.15   To date the sediments of the infilled hollow at Slade Oak Lane independently, and investigate the possibility of other proxies as well as artefacts being present.

4.5.16   To resample and establish the sedimentary composition of the brickearth deposits as being Aeolian in nature, and to establish a chronology for the loess deposits and the artefacts contained within them.

4.5.17   To explore and establish the potential for palaeo-environmental evidence, in particular mammalian remains, that could potentially be used for bio-stratigraphic dating.

4.6 Particular aims for Berkshire

Research questions

4.6.1   Does the artefactual material from Berkshire provide evidence relevant to the debate concerning the status of British handaxe and core and flake assemblages?

4.6.2   Can the Levallois material from non-terrace gravel deposits (eg brickearths) be reliably dated (eg using new techniques such as AAR (amino-acid ratio) and OSL (optically stimulated luminescence))?

4.6.3   What are the absolute geo-chronological ages of the fluvial terraces of the Thames and its tributaries?

4.6.4   Can key deposits (including brickearths and/or other sediments associated with primary context archaeology) be re-located and re-investigated using modern, multi-disciplinary techniques?

Specific projects

4.6.5   Independent geo-chronological testing of terrace chronology models (principally for zone 2, but also for zones 3 and 4), including use of AAR and OSL techniques, either through specific re-investigations of remnant deposits or PPG16-funded work in advance of development activity.

4.6.6   Re-examination of key artefact assemblages from zone 2 (eg artefacts from the Black Park, Lynch Hill and Boyn Hill terraces) with specific reference to techno-typological variability and those factors which may explain it, including: raw material quality, knapping strategies and/or 'cultural' knapping traditions, and spatial/chronological contrasts.

4.6.7   Re-examination of key artefact assemblages from zone 2 with specific reference to techno-typological variability and the degree of integrity (in terms of artefact derivation) of specific assemblages. For example, it has been suggested that there was a difference in condition between the handaxes ('waterworn') and the flake and core ('sharp') components of the Grovelands Pit material.

4.6.8   Modelling of artefact dispersal and the

formation of secondary context assemblages, with particular (but not exclusive) reference to the fluvial deposits and assemblages of zone 2 (see also bullet point above).

4.6.9   Direct, multi-disciplinary, investigation of primary context deposits (if and when such deposits are newly identified and/or re-located).

4.7   Particular aims for Oxfordshire

Research opportunities

As mentioned above, Oxfordshire offers the chance:

4.7.1   to study the Palaeolithic against a spatially variable lithic resource background – from total absence to abundance. The empty spaces may say as much as the dense clusters in helping us to understand what drove early hominids to occupy, or not occupy, terrain.

The physical features of the landscape, different though they were in the remote past, still retained the underlying geology and perhaps some of the topographic surfaces. Thus we can attempt

4.7.2   to study the part played by limestone hills, clay vales and chalk downlands in early hominin use of this region.

Specific research projects

Apart from archaeological work that precedes commercial development, these might include:

4.7.3   A further attempt to locate and date the Wolvercote Channel, excavating on land that still remains undeveloped in north Oxford.

4.7.4   A fieldwalking programme on all the remaining areas of Northern Drift to establish presence of artefacts. There is a need to clarify whether artefacts come from within the Northern Drift, or from its surface. This could be supplemented by a search of other Cotswold plateau areas away from the Drift, to test the hypothesis that lack of lithic resources meant a lack of Palaeolithic occupation.

4.7.5   Detailed study of selected Devensian gravel pits (in the course of gravel extraction) to monitor the distribution of quartzite clasts on the bedrock surface, their relationship with the micro-topography, and their association or otherwise with artefacts, with the objective of testing the theory that these surfaces are 'lag' deposits possibly of pre-MIS 6 age.

4.7.6   A further attempt to locate the Sugworth

Channel near Abingdon to amplify the data and especially to try to locate artefacts in it.

4.7.7   Placement in the public domain of the detailed and as yet unpublished supplementary data for the county collected by Roe in the course of the compilation of the Gazetteer (Roe 1968), currently held manually on a card index. This task is underway for Oxfordshire as a pilot study.

4.8   Particular aims for Hampshire

Research questions

The critical lessons to be learned from our increasing understanding of the Lower/Middle Palaeolithic, in both Hampshire and the wider UK, are the importance of an absolute chronology and the importance of the application of chronometric dating techniques to Pleistocene deposits associated with archaeological artefacts.

4.8.1   It is vital that chronometric techniques should be employed in the future on any archaeological investigation of Pleistocene strata to provide an assessment of site age that is independent of artefact typology.

There are, however, other more specific questions that could usefully be explored:

4.8.2   Do sites with properties comparable to Red Barns exist elsewhere on the Portsdown ridge? What survey-based approaches would enable their discovery?

4.8.3   Can the spatial/vertical distribution of raised marine deposits in south-eastern Hampshire be better defined? How might the archaeological significance of these deposits be determined given their present deep burial?

4.8.4.   Is it possible to develop an approach to the independent dating of artefact assemblages recovered from Clay-with-Flint strata?

4.8.5   How might river terraces designated for aggregate extraction be better investigated to determine their Palaeolithic archaeological potential?

Priority research projects

4.8.6   Given the success in the PASHCC project (Phases 1 and 2) in providing chronometric ages for key Pleistocene strata in Hampshire (Bates et al. 2004, Bates *et al.* in prep), a priority must be the publication of these key data.

4.8.7   A possible future research project building on PASHCC might be the extension of the

Boxgrove Raised Beach Mapping Project, carried out from 2003-5 (Pope and Roberts 2003), into Hampshire.

The other research questions outlined above can be addressed (presumably) by:

4.8.8   the continuation of the work by the Oxford University's unit for the study of Palaeolithic Artefacts and associated Deposits Mapped as Clay-with-Flint (PADMAC) (Anon. 2006).

4.8.9   a project to survey the Portsdown ridge and hopefully, in the case of the final question, through discussions as part of the Thames-Solent Research Agenda.

4.9 Particular aims for the Isle of Wight

Priority research aims and questions include:

4.9.1   To date the first isolation of the Island from the mainland.

4.9.2   Establish the patterns of occupation and settlement through the Lower/Middle Palaeolithic.

4.9.3   The integration, correlation and chrono-stratigraphic attribution of Plateau and Terrace gravels.

4.9.4   What is the correct interpretation of the dissected strip of Plateau gravel/marine beach deposits mapped between Cowes and Bembridge, and is there an important buried landscape comprising a raised beach or fluvial staircase preserved beneath the ground surface in this area?

4.9.5   The patterns of technological/typological change through the Palaeolithic, and their contrast/similarities with adjacent mainland areas such as the Test Valley, Bournemouth and West Sussex.

4.9.6   To discover faunal/palaeo-environmental remains in fluvial deposits

Priority research projects

As long ago as 1980 *The Vectis Report* identified six priorities for future work (Basford 1980):

4.9.7   Rescue excavation at Priory Bay

4.9.8   Observation at Great Pan Farm during proposed construction of Newport South-Eastern Relief Road

4.9.9   Monitoring of any future gravel extraction at Bleak Down.

4.9.10   Safeguarding the site at High Down for future investigation

4.9.11   Fieldwork along the south-west coast and re-examination of material from this area

4.9.12   Investigation of Pleistocene deposits at Bembridge and Steephill if these sites are threatened with disturbance.

The subsequent Southern Rivers Palaeolithic Project endorsed these recommendations, and incorporated them into a *Revised set of suggestions* (Wessex Archaeology 1993a, 172):

4.9.13   High Level Gravels: recording at prolific sites such as Bleak Down and Priory Bay

4.9.14   Bembridge Raised Beach: the location and recording of palaeoliths *in situ* if possible

4.9.15   Bembridge Steyne Wood Clay: recording to determine context of palaeoliths

4.9.16   Mousterian sites: part of the deposits remaining at Great Pan Farm should be preserved, but if this is not possible full excavation should precede any further destruction of the site

To a large extent, these priorities have still not been addressed. Fieldwork at Priory Bay has confirmed the importance of the site and identified important horizons, but the site remains vulnerable to erosion, and requires further investigation to mitigate its impact. Fieldwork at Great Pan Farm has been driven by development rather than research, so while our understanding has increased, this has raised more questions than it has answered, and further work is required if we are to resolve these.

A more robust chrono-stratigraphic framework

As well as carrying out further work at the specific sites mentioned above, understanding of the Island's Lower/Middle Palaeolithic could greatly benefit from a more robust chrono-stratigraphic framework. This could be achieved by developing a long-term programme of:

4.9.17   Field-walking survey and systematic investigation by controlled sieving of gravel deposits for Palaeolithic artefacts

4.9.18   Survey and attempted broad dating of Plateau gravel outcrops

4.9.19   Systematic OSL dating of Terrace gravels

4.9.20   Typological/technological review of existing collections

Chapter 5

Late Upper Palaeolithic and Mesolithic: Resource Assessment

by Gill Hey

(County contributions by Catherine Barnett, Mike Farley, Julie Gardiner, Gill Hey,
Rebecca Loader and Alison Roberts; palaeo-environmental contribution by Michael Allen)

Introduction

History of research

The history of research into the Late Upper Palaeolithic (LUP) and Mesolithic of the Solent-Thames region has been very variable and the extent of our understanding of settlement is thus extremely patchy. The Kennet Valley in Berkshire and the Greensand of Hampshire are amongst the best-known Mesolithic landscapes in Britain, and assemblages from the Greensand have provided the basis for national flint chronologies for the period. In contrast, relatively little is known about the Mesolithic of Oxfordshire and large parts of Buckinghamshire, with few excavations targeted at sites of this period (Fig. 5.1).

Even in Berkshire, most work on LUP and Mesolithic sites has been concentrated in the middle stretches of the River Kennet, focusing on a few large sites such as Thatcham and Wawcott (Wymer 1962; Lobb and Rose 1996), as this is where the pressure for gravel and other development was originally most intense. Research projects have followed because of the known quality of the resource. Excavation in advance of development in the lower Kennet around Reading, survey work on the Downs and survey and research excavation in the Upper Kennet Valley, mostly undertaken more recently, have all revealed finds and sites of 10th to 5th millennium date (Richards 1978; Ford 1987a; Whittle 1990; S Allen 2005). These tend to confirm the clustering of activity in the middle Kennet, at least for the early Mesolithic period.

Similarly, the highly visible scatters of Mesolithic flintwork on the light ploughsoils of the Hampshire Greensand attracted collectors from the 19th century onwards (Rankine 1953; Gardiner 1984). These substantial assemblages, sometimes associated with hearths, were compiled into a database and studied by Roger Jacobi, forming the basis for his chronology of the British Mesolithic (Jacobi 1978; 1981; Wymer 1977), which has been little altered since (Reynier 2000). It is only in recent decades that work in other parts of the county, especially around the Solent and largely related to development control work, has started to redress this imbalance (Allen and Gardiner 2000; Gardiner 2002; Field 2008).

A particular concern with coastal erosion, and a growing recognition of the extent and good preservation of the submerged Mesolithic landscape, has also led to work around the coasts of both Hampshire and the Isle of Wight and, more recently, underwater (Allen and Gardiner 2000; Momber 2000; Plate 5.1). The recent publication of the project at Wootton-Quarr on the north coast of Wight funded by English Heritage is of particular significance (Tomalin *et al.* 2012). Other work on LUP and Mesolithic sites on the Isle of Wight has tended to focus on the eroding cliff lines to the southwest of the island, the Medina Estuary or the Greensand to the south of the island (Poole 1936; Rankine 1956; Palmer 1977). Early work suggested that there were two groups present: one using heavy tranchet axes, gravers and a few microliths on the coast, and another on the Greensand utilising lighter axes, and more microliths and petit tranchet arrowheads (Poole 1936). More recently, Palmer suggested that these assemblages were, in fact, utilised by a single population, but with variation in finds reflecting different activities (Palmer 1977).

Traditionally, most work in Buckinghamshire has been conducted in the south of the county, on the outskirts of London, especially related to gravel extraction in the lower Colne Valley. The site at Iver is particularly well-known (Lacaille 1963), but the quality of preservation of both Late Upper Palaeolithic and Mesolithic sites in the Denham and Uxbridge area (straddling the Buckinghamshire/Middlesex county boundary) has only recently become apparent. Exceptions are the collections made by Peake at Kimble Farm, Turville close to the Oxfordshire border (Peake 1917) and work undertaken at the important site of Stratford's Yard, Chesham (Stainton 1989). A few Chilterns upland sites have also been investigated, for example Bolter End (Millard 1965). More recently, Mesolithic material has emerged as the result of gravel extraction and flood alleviation schemes near the Thames in the Eton/Maidenhead area (Allen 1998; Hey and Barclay 2007; Allen *et al.* 2013).

In Oxfordshire, only two major sites have been excavated in recent years specifically because of their Mesolithic component: New Plantation, Fyfield and Tubney and Windmill Hill, Nettlebed (Bradley and Hey 1993; Boismier and Mepham 1995). LUP and Mesolithic material has also come from other major excavations within the Thames Valley, for example Gravelly Guy, Stanton Harcourt and Gatehampton Farm, Goring (Holgate 2004; Brown 1995) and sustained smaller-scale

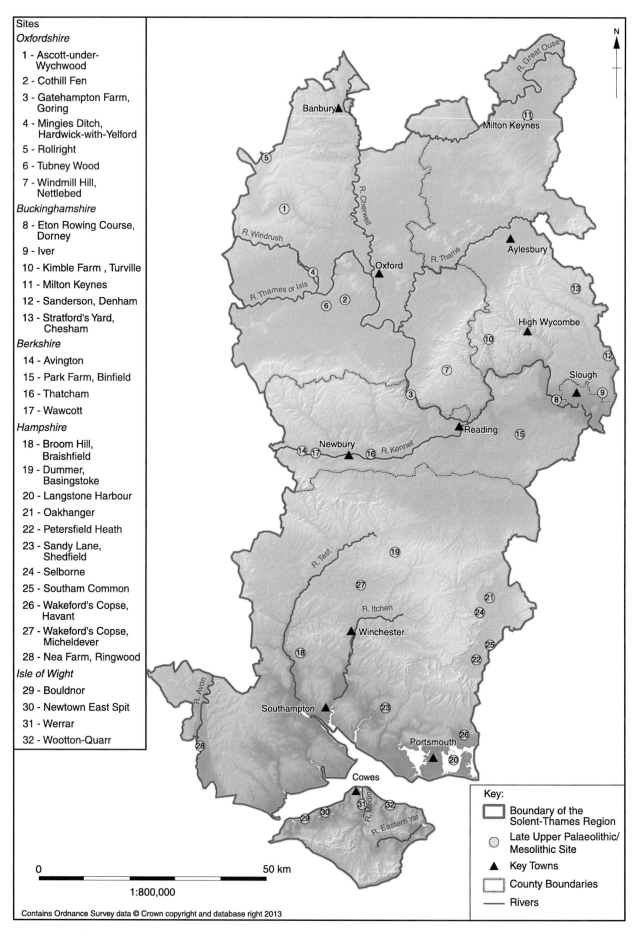

Sites

Oxfordshire

1 - Ascott-under-Wychwood
2 - Cothill Fen
3 - Gatehampton Farm, Goring
4 - Mingies Ditch, Hardwick-with-Yelford
5 - Rollright
6 - Tubney Wood
7 - Windmill Hill, Nettlebed

Buckinghamshire

8 - Eton Rowing Course, Dorney
9 - Iver
10 - Kimble Farm , Turville
11 - Milton Keynes
12 - Sanderson, Denham
13 - Stratford's Yard, Chesham

Berkshire

14 - Avington
15 - Park Farm, Binfield
16 - Thatcham
17 - Wawcott

Hampshire

18 - Broom Hill, Braishfield
19 - Dummer, Basingstoke
20 - Langstone Harbour
21 - Oakhanger
22 - Petersfield Heath
23 - Sandy Lane, Shedfield
24 - Selborne
25 - Southam Common
26 - Wakeford's Copse, Havant
27 - Wakeford's Copse, Micheldever
28 - Nea Farm, Ringwood

Isle of Wight

29 - Bouldnor
30 - Newtown East Spit
31 - Werrar
32 - Wootton-Quarr

0   50 km

1:800,000

Contains Ordnance Survey data © Crown copyright and database right 2013

Key:

☐ Boundary of the Solent-Thames Region

○ Late Upper Palaeolithic/ Mesolithic Site

▲ Key Towns

☐ County Boundaries

— Rivers

Figure 5.1 Late Upper Palaeolithic and Mesolithic sites mentioned in the text

Plate 5.1 Underwater archaeology in progress at Bouldnor Cliff off the Isle of Wight, *copyright Richard Brooks, Maritime Archaeology Trust*

investigations and collections around Abingdon (Abingdon Area Archaeological and Historical Society various), all of these largely the result of gravel extraction. Otherwise, activity is generally deduced from fieldwalking material, with a concentration of sites on the Corallian Ridge and more sparse spreads on the Cotswolds and the Downs, or finds that have been dredged from the Thames (Case 1952-3; Holgate 1988b; Ford 1987b).

Chronology

Conventional sequence and artefact chronologies

The start of the Late Upper Palaeolithic is traditionally dated to the end of the Last Glacial Maximum (LGM; around 13,000 BP), a time when only modern humans were present in Britain (Barton 1997). Three main industrial traditions are currently recognised for this period: Creswellian (*c* 13,000–12,000 BP), Final Palaeolithic (*c* 12,000–10,700 BP) and Long Blade or Epipalaeolithic (*c* 10,700–9,800 BP), and all of these have direct affinities with industries on the European mainland, to which south-east England was attached at that time. The Creswellian represents the earliest reoccupation of Britain following the LGM (Barton *et al.* 2003). The diagnostic artefact for this industry is the bi-truncated angle-backed 'Cheddar point', although it can also be defined on the basis of technological features such as the presence of blades with butts *en éperon*. Although sites were originally believed to be situated at upland margins, more finds are now

coming to light from open-air locations in southern England; for example, the lower half of a Cheddar point has been found at Mingies Ditch, Oxfordshire (Barton 1993). (Plate 5.2)

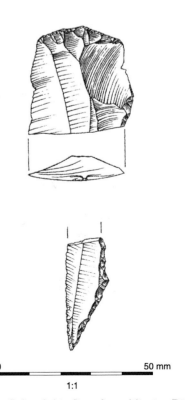

0   50 mm

1:1

Plate 5.2 Upper Palaeolithic flints from Mingies Ditch, Hardwick, Oxon., *copyright OA*

Final Upper Palaeolithic industries appear to be much more regionally diverse (Barton and Roberts 1996), with a greater variety of tools than in the Creswellian phase, including curve-backed, straight-backed, tanged and Penknife points and blade-end scrapers. Long Blade assemblages seem to occur at the very end of the Pleistocene and beginning of the Holocene, and may overlap with the earliest Mesolithic. They were defined for Britain by Barton and are mainly found in floodplain or river valleys close to the sources of high-quality, *in-situ* flint (Barton 1998). Unsurprisingly, the technology is characterised by the production of very long blades, commonly heavily edge-damaged blades known as 'bruised blades', but assemblages also include end

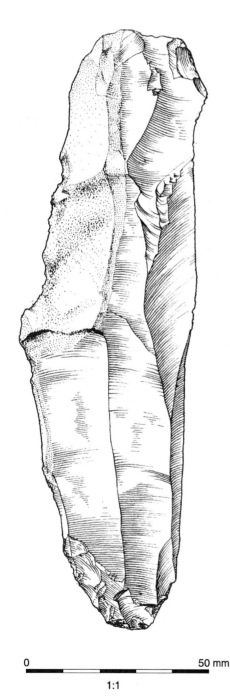

0   50 mm

1:1

Plate 5.3 Long blade from Gatehampton Farm, Oxfordshire, *copyright OA, drawn by Jeff Wallis*

scrapers and burins as well as microliths (Barton and Roberts 2004). (Plate 5.3)

Diagnostically early Mesolithic assemblages are represented by simple microlith forms (oblique points and broad triangles) with a range of other equipment, including end scrapers, microdenticulates, burins, awls and bifacially-flaked axeheads or adzes (ibid., 342). Where assemblages are of reasonable size, it may be possible to distinguish chronological traits within early Mesolithic groups (Reynier 1998). Earliest, 'Star Carr' assemblages, represented by microliths with broad oblique points, isosceles triangles and trapezoids, have been found as far south as Thatcham (III), Berkshire. Slightly later, 'Deepcar' assemblages, perhaps dating from around 9,400 years ago, have more slender oblique points, with few isosceles triangles and trapezoids. Later early Mesolithic 'Horsham' assemblages (after around 9,000 years ago), with distinctive basally-retouched microlith forms, are more common and widely dispersed (Barton and Roberts 2004).

Small geometric and more varied microlith forms are the defining characteristics of late Mesolithic assemblages; smaller microliths, and especially rod forms, are seen as indicative of very late dates (*ibid.*). In addition, adzes and axes seem more common on later Mesolithic sites (Gardiner 1988).

There are, however, many sites that are of uncertain date within the Mesolithic period because they lack diagnostic elements, including many of the lithic scatters listed in county HERs. Additionally, there can be serious difficulties in distinguishing between late Mesolithic and early Neolithic assemblages that lack the diagnostic Mesolithic microliths or Neolithic leaf-shaped arrowheads.

Scientific dating

Late Upper Palaeolithic

An OSL date of 10,250 BC ± 1,100 years came from the Long Blade site at Crown Acres in the Kennet Valley, from sediments enclosing the assemblage (Barton *et al.* 1998).

The Long Blade site at Three Ways Wharf, nearby in Middlesex, yielded horse bone dating to 10650-9650 and 10050-9250 cal BC (OxA-1788: 10270±100 BP; OxA-1902: 10010±120 BP), and peat overlying a newly-discovered site at Sanderson in the lower Colne Valley was dated to 8710–8340 cal BC (Lab no: 9300±50 BP), providing a *terminus ante quem* for that site (Lewis with Rackham 2011; Farley 2009, 16).

Early Mesolithic

A number of conventional and AMS dates exist, in particular for Thatcham. These show that activity associated with a Mesolithic material culture started in the area within 300 years of the start of the Holocene (10,900-9,700 cal BC; Q-659: 10,365±170 BP; Wymer 1962), comparable with Star Carr in the Vale of Pickering (Mellars and Dark 1998; Dark 2000a), the two forming the earliest Mesolithic sites recorded in Britain. It is suggested activity may have existed even earlier in the Holocene at Thatcham and at the nearby Chamberhouse Farm, with Final Upper Palaeolithic culture continuing beyond the end of the Lateglacial (Barton and Roberts 2004; Wessex Archaeology 2005a). Overlap of the two cultures or continuity in settlement is feasible in places if not proven. Chisham provides a complete list for Berkshire (http://oxfordarchaeology. com/research-projects-by-name/217-Solent-Thames-research-framework).

In Buckinghamshire, a date of 9150-8730 cal BC (OxA-14088: 9540±45 BP) was obtained for an aurochs bone associated with a lakeside flint scatter at the Eton

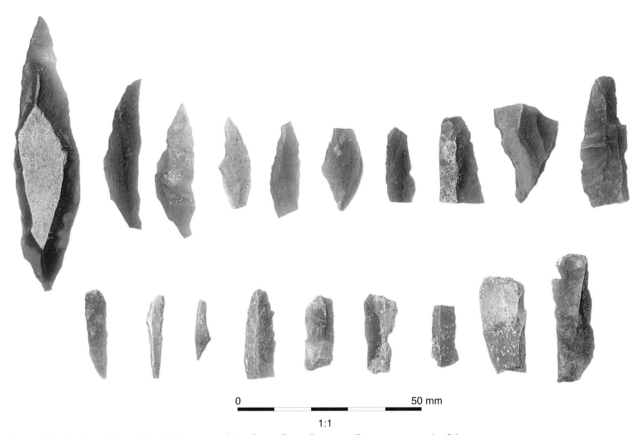

Plate 5.4 Early and late Mesolithic microliths from Eton Rowing Course, *copyright OA*

Table 5.1 Radiocarbon dates for Mesolithic sites in Hampshire (Gardiner)

Site	Context	Material	Lab ref	BP determination	Date cal. BC at 2 sigma
Oakhanger VII	Level II	hazelnuts	Q1489	9225±200	9200-7900
	Level II	pinus charcoal	Q1491	9100±160	8750-7750
	Level II	pinus charcoal	Q1493	9040±160	8700-7600
	Level II	pinus charcoal	Q1490	8995±160	8600-7600
	Level II	pinus charcoal	Q1492	8975±1600	8550-7600
	Level II 8450-7550	pinus charcoal	Q1494	8885±160	
		scots pine charcoal and hazelnut	F 68	6380±115	5650-5050
		scots pine charcoal and hazelnut	F 69	6380±110	5650-5050
Longmoor	L1, podsol	hazelnut	OxA-376	8930±100	8300-7700
	L3 podsol	hazelnut	OxA 377	8760±110	8250-7550
	L3	oak/birch charcoal	HAR 4475	6060±110	5300-4700
Broom Hill, Braishfield	base of Pit III	wood charcoal	Q1192	8540±150	8200-7100
		wood charcoal	Q1528	8515±150	8000-7000
		wood charcoal	Q1383	8315±150	7650-6800
	top infill of Pit III	wood charcoal	Q1460	7750±120	7050-6350
	above Pit III	wood charcoal	Q1191	7220±120	6400-5800
	Pit II hearth	wood charcoal	Q1128	6535±125	5720-5260
Oakhanger V		pinus sylvestris charcoal	BM 221	7869±104	7100-6500
Micheldever R4	pre barrow	oak charcoal	HAR 1043	6904±170	6200-5450
Wakefords Copse	hearth in pit 8	charcoal	HAR 233	5680±120	4800-4250

Rowing Course, and a date of 9220-8740 cal BC (OxA-9411: 9560±55 BP) from adjacent peat deposits that included charred bullrush seeds and stems (Allen *et al.* 2013).

Eleven dates also come from Hampshire:

- Six dates come from Oakhanger VII, one 9200-7900 cal BC (Q1489: 9225±200 BP) and others all falling between 8750 and 7550 cal BC (Q1490-4; Table 5.1).

- Two dates from Longmoor Inclosure I, Hampshire for Horsham assemblages: 8300-7700 and 8250-7750 cal BC (see Table 5.1)

- Three dates around the middle of the 8th millennium come from Broom Hill, from the bottom of a pit (Pit III, see Table 5.1)

(note that a number of these come from wood charcoal whose species is not specified).

Late Mesolithic

Although few radiocarbon dates are available, these suggest an overlap between diagnostically early and late assemblages.

At Broom Hill, an assemblage of microliths and other late Mesolithic types overlay the layer at the bottom of the pit yielding the three dates around the middle of the 8th millennium cal BC listed above. Charcoal from the layer above provided a date of 7050-6450 cal BC (Q-1460: 7830±120 BP). Two more dates from above Pit III and from Pit II hearth are mid 7th to early 6th millennium and mid to late 6th millennium respectively (Table 5.1).

One result from Oakhanger V is very late 8th or 7th millennium in date and two from Oakhanger VII lie in the mid and late 6th millennium (Table 5.1).

A late 7th to mid 6th millennium date came from below the Micheldever R4 barrow, and a hearth in a pit at Wakeford's Copse yielded a 5th millennium date (*ibid.*).

A tree bole at the base of a cliff at Bouldnor on the Isle of Wight produced a date of 6430-6120 cal BC (GU-5420: 7440±60 BP), and a *terminus ante quem* is provided at Wootton-Quarr by a sample of charcoal from sediment overlying the flint scatter of 3630-3110 cal BC (OxA-7183: 4645±65 BP).

There are late 6th and 5th millennium dates from Ascott-under-Wychwood on roe deer from an early Neolithic midden and beech charcoal from a posthole (Bayliss *et al.* 2007). A very late Mesolithic date of 4360-3780 cal BC (BM-449: 5260±130 BP; Froom 1972) came from a hearth at Wawcott (Lobb and Rose 1996).

In Buckinghamshire, late Mesolithic radiocarbon dates have come from Stratford's Yard, Chesham, where a *bos primigenius* bone was dated to 5010-4500 cal BC (BM-2404: 5890±100 BP; Stainton 1989), from the Eton Rowing Course, where a tree-throw hole containing struck flint was dated to 5220-4940 cal BC (OxA-9412:

6130±45 BP), and from the Misbourne Railway Viaduct site, on the floor of the Misbourne, where seven radiocarbon dates were obtained. Three of these were late Mesolithic (OxA-601: 6190±90 BP; OxA-618: 5970±100 BP; OxA-619: 6100±120 BP), but others produced both very early, late glacial and post-Mesolithic results.

Environment and geoarchaeology

River valleys

Major river valley corridors have been the location of important Late Upper Palaeolithic and Mesolithic sites, as described below. In many cases these were buried under a mantle of alluvium, albeit sometimes thin, retarding discovery and indicating that other significant sites may be present beneath blankets of alluvium in other less-well explored areas (eg M Allen 1991b, 51). Importantly, those alluvial and riverine contexts that are associated with peats or tufas, as in the Kennet valley, provide key stratigraphic sequences from which to obtain geo-archaeological information about sites and their regional context, and to extract a detailed stratified palaeo-environmental record (pollen, snails, ostracods, etc). The concentration of sites in river valleys demonstrates the attraction of such localities, but the precise nature of activity in its ecotonal setting, and how it relates to the local environmental resources and the wider landscape, is rarely fully addressed.

Where they survive, faunal remains can provide further key information about animal resources and carcass preparation, and of Palaeolithic and Mesolithic life-styles. Soil micromorphological evidence at Nea Farm, Avon valley, provides indication of soil development in the warmer Alleröd to early Younger Dryas periods, and includes evidence of on-site activity. This lies on weakly calcareous soils and drift geology leading to poor to no bone preservation and no shells (land snails), but other areas may well exist in which such palaeo-environmental and economic data will survive, perhaps in the Middle Kennet and Lower Colne Valleys. The recently published site at Three Ways Wharf, Uxbridge, just outside our region, certainly had good bone preservation and provided considerable faunal information (Lewis with Rackham 2011).

Current coastal and sub-marine

Geo-archaeologically, sites in present day near-coastal, coastal, intertidal and submarine locations provide whole physical lowland, terrestrial landscapes that have rarely been satisfactorily brought into the reconstruction of Mesolithic lifeways. Just outside the Solent-Thames area, work off the Sussex coast has recovered habitable, dated Mesolithic land surfaces, containing charcoal at *c.* -36 m below current sea level. Large portions of the sea-bed in the later Upper Palaeolithic and earlier Mesolithic were large lowland landscapes capable of supporting whole ecosystems and hunting-foraging communities. Often trapped within the sediments is stratified detailed palaeo-environmental information which allows detailed and imaginative reconstruction of large topographic zones virtually never considered in studies of Mesolithic activity.

Clay and other lowlands

In-situ palaeo-environmental evidence beyond the river corridors, both *sensu stricto* and *sensu lato*, is desperately lacking. Recent finds of Late Upper Palaeolithic sites at Nea Farm, Somerly, near Ringwood, Hampshire (Barton *et al.* 2009) and just outside the Solent-Thames area, at Deer Park Farm, Cranborne Chase, Dorset (Green *et al.* 1998), demonstrate their presence. Geo-archaeological and sediment micromorphological studies (eg French 2007, 389-9) clearly provide key taphonomic and formation data. Less readily accessible is the contemporaneous palaeo-environmental material.

Open-air sites on rising ground do exist (see Deer Park Farm, Green *et al.* 1998) and have significant, if restricted, palaeo-environmental potential (see French 2007), but the low density of artefacts makes them difficult to identify.

Chalkland: a superficial lack of evidence

The broad expanses of the Chalklands seem, superficially, only to contain scatters of flints, and there is no palaeo-environmental evidence to accompany the evidence of considerable activity. Outside the region, long and stratified palaeo-environmental sequences from local colluvial sequences and well-dated palaeo-environmental evidence in subsoil hollows indicate the potential for fragmented survival of data that can be used for re-evaluating early Holocene Chalkland history (Allen and Gardiner 2009). Little comparable palaeo-environmental data has been recovered from the Solent-Thames Chalklands to date. Glimpses of Mesolithic woodland from the land snails on Twyford Down, Winchester, Hampshire, indicated closed deciduous woodland (M Allen 2000a, 138-142), but also that the adjacent river valley may have been more open (M Allen 2000b; Waton 1982; 1986).

Key Mesolithic vantage points and local colluvial burial

Many physiographic zones seem superficially to be ones of open landscape in which typically only surface Mesolithic sites may occur. These tend to provide relatively rich artefact assemblages with some spatial patterning, but few contemporaneous deposits or soils from which to obtain proxy palaeo-environmental data or even contemporary geo-archaeological information. Recent research in South East England is, however, just starting to indicate that, within these landscapes, there are key bluff locations with excellent vantage and

viewpoints (Allen and Scaife 2007). More significantly, however, many of these locations are ones where shallow and highly-localised colluvial deposits may have buried, sealed, preserved and protected evidence of Mesolithic activity. They provide new topographic locations in which to look for evidence of Mesolithic activity, and it is likely that such sites occur within the Solent-Thames region.

Late Upper Palaeolithic

Creswellian and Final Upper Palaeolithic

Around 12,600 years ago, the climate and vegetation was only just recovering from the Last Glacial Maximum (LGM). At Mingies Ditch in the Lower Windrush Valley (Robinson 1993), a sample from a channel in the floodplain gravel contained arctic fauna and flora, including an arctic-alpine species of beetle (*Helophorus glacialis*) and fruit scales and leaves of dwarf birch (*Betula nana*; Late Devensian Zone III; 11,150 – 10,650 cal BC; HAR-8356: 10860± 130 BP; *ibid.*, 7-9). No trees were present, although pollen analysis suggested that clumps of birch and pine grew beyond the edge of the floodplain terrace. Slightly later, an open landscape was recorded from a channel at Lot's Hole in the Middle Thames, where a basal date of 10670-10150 cal BC (AA-44401 (GU-9488): 10,490±75 BP) was measured (Allen *et al.* 2013). Birch scrub, juniper-*empetrum* heath and dwarf arctic-alpine vegetation covered the higher ground, and tall herb meadows, ruderal and aquatic communities the low lying areas. In the channels *Isoetes*, which requires deep, clear water was present. In addition, there was standing, open water locally with floating leafed aquatics, surrounded by a *Carex/Equisetum* reedswamp. An open environment with light tree cover (predominantly birch and pine with some willow) was present in the base of a pollen sequence from the Upper Thames at Cothill Fen on the Corallian Ridge (Day 1991, 465). This however can only be dated as being before 8650–7900 cal BC (OxA-2114: 9070±1100 BP). It is thought that, gradually, the landscape became more wooded. Work in the Kennet Valley, both by the Kennet Valley Project and subsequently, shows an open and relatively unstable Lateglacial environment in terms of sedimentation and hydrology, including high-energy, braided river channels (Chartres 1975; Cheetham 1975; Holyoak 1980; Collins 1994; Collins *et al.* 1996). As warming began at the start of the Holocene, a highly dynamic period of environmental fluctuation followed, resulting in the deposition of thick bodies of calcareous marl in West Berkshire. Subsequently the landscape stabilised, with soil formation and the establishment of open aspen-birch-pine woodland.

The only known Creswellian stage find from the region is the Cheddar point found at Mingies Ditch, Oxfordshire (Barton 1993) referred to above, but there is more evidence for activity dating to the Final Upper Palaeolithic. People seem to have used a greater variety and more local sources of flint, and the evidence suggests a pattern of short-lived and seasonal settlement, with open-air sites which seem to represent places where people congregated close to the spring or autumn migration routes of herding animals (Barton 1997, 128). It is possible that, at first, there was long-distance mobility, with groups moving in and out of Britain (Jacobi 1981) but, with more closed habitats, people may have ranged less widely.

Hengistbury Head, Dorset (Barton 1992), just west of the Solent-Thames region, used to be the only excavated open-air site in Britain, but two new sites have recently come to light nearby in Hampshire which will add considerably to knowledge about this period. One of these, Nea Farm, Somerley, New Forest, Hampshire, on the first gravel terrace of the River Avon, has recently been excavated (Barton *et al.* 2009; Plates 5.5 and 5.6). At present there are only a few diagnostic artefacts from Oxfordshire, most of which have come from gravel extraction sites (for example Mingies Ditch, Hardwick and Drayton Cursus), though some others have recently been identified by Alison Roberts in the Ashmolean collections. To date, all seem to have been recovered from the Thames river valley but, given the context of their discovery, this is perhaps unsurprising. A possible tanged point was recovered at '100 Acres' pit in the lower Colne Valley, also in a riverine environment (Lacaille 1963; Wymer 1977).

Long Blade sites

Human activity probably ceased in Britain during the Loch Lomond Stadial or Younger Dryas, a short but very cold period (*c* 10,800 – 10,000 BP) when there was a reversion to arctic temperatures and a tundra environment. Reindeer arrived and other, small mammals only found in northern Scandinavia today. There seems to have been a very sudden recovery from these glacial conditions, with temperatures rising to those similar to today within a period of less than 50 years. Human beings followed soon afterwards, as shown by the presence of sites with Long Blades, as well as the scrapers, microliths and burins already mentioned above. The absence of hearths and quantities of burnt flint associated with these sites has led Barton to suggest that they represent short-term occupation events (Barton 1997).

It has been suggested that the edge damage found on 'Bruised Blades' is the result of working hard materials such as wood or antler (Barton 1986), although they may also have been used to trim and repair the ends of sandstone hammers for flint knapping. Other tools suggest a bow-hunting technology. As already noted, Long Blade sites are mainly found on the floodplain or in river valleys close to the sources of high-quality, *in-situ* flint (Barton 1986). The site at Gatehampton Farm, Goring, Oxfordshire, in the narrow Goring Gap where the Thames has forced its way through the Chalk ridge, was thus in a classic location. Despite the fact that bone did not survive, the flint assemblage was interpreted by Barton (1995) as representing a kill/butchery site. Near Milton Keynes, in the north-east of our region, a large concentration of 'narrow blade industry' flints was found in ploughsoil at Little Woolstone by the Ouzel (Mike Farley pers. comm.).

There are a number of important Long Blade sites not far from Goring in the Kennet Valley, Berkshire, including Avington IV – with an OSL date of 10,250 BC ± 1,100 years (Froom 1970, 2005; Barton and Froom

Plate 5.5 Long blades *in situ* at Nea Farm, Ringwood, Hampshire, *copyright TVAS*

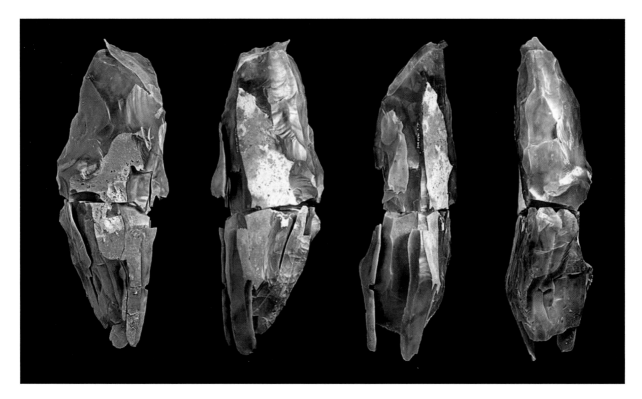

Plate 5.6 Refitting long blades from Nea Farm, Ringwood, Hampshire, *copyright TVAS and Nick Barton*

1986; Barton 1989; Barton *et al.* 1998), Wawcott XII (Froom 1970, 2005) and Crown Acres (Campbell 1977; Barton 1986; Froom 2005). As with Goring, they were all open sites with a high proportion of blade waste to retouched pieces. At Crown Acres, the Long Blade horizon appears to lie in sandy marl below a site of early Mesolithic date, both being sealed by peat (Barton 1986, 84). Avington VI is the best stratified, with 6000 artefacts seemingly *in situ* on and within possible colluvial or solifluced clay with a fine (overbank) alluvial input. Typologically, the artefacts are similar to sites on the Continent where they have been associated with the killing and processing of large game (Bokelmann 1991; Fischer 1991; Larsson 1991). No animal bones have been found on the Kennet Valley sites and environmental preservation was poor, but there was some indication of an open flora at Avington VI (Holyoak 1980).

Further down the Thames Valley, recent work by MoLAS at the Sanderson site between the Colne and the Colnbrook in Buckinghamshire has yielded relatively large flakes which may be of Upper Palaeolithic date within an otherwise early Mesolithic assemblage (Lakin 2006). At Denham nearby, *in-situ* long blade material has been found during evaluations by Wessex Archaeology (2005b). This site was sealed by peat over 2 m deep dated to 8710–8340 cal BC (9300±50) and indicating a late cold stage herb/juniper assemblage. Close by, across the county boundary in Middlesex, is the well-known long-blade site at Three Ways Wharf with associated animal bone, including horse dating to 10650-9650 and 10050–9250 cal BC (Lab no: 10270±100 BP; Lab no: 10010±120 BP; Lewis 1991). The flint assemblage from this site is broadly comparable with that from Avington IV.

The Isle of Wight was part of mainland Britain, though divided from present-day Hampshire by the great Solent River. The offshore zone of the northern coast of the island is thought to offer potential for the survival of material of this period that would have lain within the river valley (Momber 2000; 2001; Hampshire and Wight Trust for Maritime Archaeology (HWTMA) 2005; Wessex Archaeology 2004a). A thin scatter of finds from the south-west coast of the island was thought by early antiquaries to be of Upper Palaeolithic date, but the identifications are open to question and would merit reassessment.

Landscape and land use in the Mesolithic

Early Mesolithic landscapes

By around 9,000 BC temperate conditions were beginning to lead to an expansion in woodland (juniper, birch, pine and hazel) and woodland animals such as elk, roe deer, pig and beaver were present. This did not occur uniformly, however, for some regions experienced retarded vegetation development, and it is in some of these areas that early human activity is found (Simmons *et al.* 1981; Allen and Gardiner 2009). The appearance of diagnostic Mesolithic tools suggests specialist wood-working equipment (transversely sharpened axes and adzes) and more flexible tool kits with items suited to a mobile lifestyle and hunting small game within a more enclosed setting. The Mingies Ditch environmental sequences show that by 9150–8300 cal BC (HAR-8366: 7430± 110 BP) all the species present can be found growing in England today, with birch and willow and some pine and juniper (Robinson 1993, 9). Half the terrestrial pollen was from grasses, however, indicating a relatively open environment; evidence from Yarnton nearby suggests that the numerous, anastomised channels of the River Thames were free-flowing at this time (OSL date of 9450–6850 BC; Robinson in prep.). The Cothill sequence shows a rise of pine, hazel and elm on the Corallian Ridge, with birch and willow declining, and then oak and later hazel increasing at the expense of pine (Day 1991). The pollen from peat adjacent to a Thames-side stream at Little Marlow is consistent with this environmental reconstruction (Richmond *et al*. 2006).

From the 9th millennium BC, dense thickets of hazel existed in the Kennet Valley, with colonisation of common deciduous types such as oak, elm then lime and alder following soon after (Holyoak 1980, Chisham 2004). Peat formation occurred on the floodplains and low terraces of the Rivers Kennet and Loddon, and tufa was deposited at a number of sites both here and south of the Chilterns, for example in the Misbourne valley at Gerrards Cross (Barfield 1977). This was the result of increasing spring activity fed by calcium-rich water coming off the Chalk uplands. Less peat formed or has been preserved around the Thames, where erosion followed by alluviation to a considerable depth seems to have occurred. Although significant woodland cover was certainly present from the early Mesolithic, indications are that, in the Kennet, a mosaic of small gaps remained, notably at the river margins where there was low-growing herb and grass flora. These persisted through

natural gap formation, and appear to have been maintained by grazing herbivores, possibly also by beavers (Evans 1975, 88), and also by human activity. Molluscan (and occasionally pollen) studies on the Chalk have shown that open grassland and scrub vegetation in the Lateglacial was followed there by the spread of deciduous woodland in the early Holocene, contrary to the assumption that such areas have always been grassland (Waton 1982; 1983a; 1983b; 1986; Evans *et al*. 1993; Allen 1992; Birbeck 2000).

At the Eton Rowing Course in the Middle Thames valley, peat preservation was variable, but there were well-preserved areas of backswamp adjacent to, and within, elements of the braided channel system (Allen *et al*. 2013). The earliest peat was dated to 9220–8740 cal BC (OxA-9411: 9560±55 BP), and indicated extensive reedswamp dominated by *Schoenoplectus lacustris* (true bulrush), and vegetation on dry ground dominated by *Pinus*. A dense scatter of struck flints was found along the swamp edge only 50m away, and an aurochs bone from this gave a very similar radiocarbon date, 9150–8730 cal BC (OxA-14088: 9540±45 BP). The bulrush included some charred stem fragments and seeds, perhaps suggesting the burning of dead reed swamp vegetation in winter, to facilitate fishing or encourage grazing animals. Charred culm and leaf fragments of *Phragmites australis* (common reed) from the lakeside peat at the Star Carr Mesolithic settlement were interpreted as being derived from the deliberate burning of reed beds (Hather 1998). Episodes of burning there

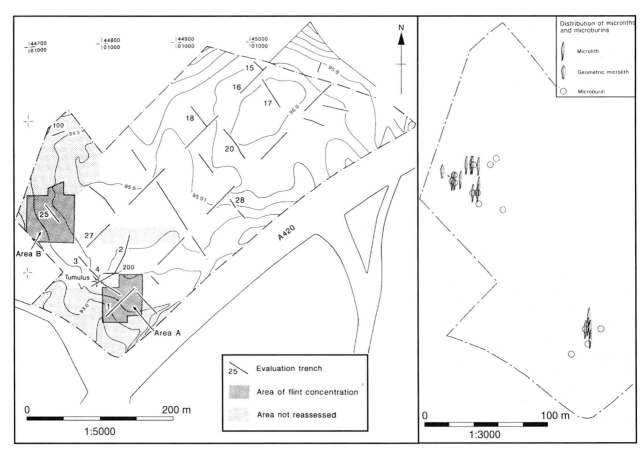

Plate 5.7 Plan of flint scatters at Tubney, Oxfordshire (adapted from Oxoniensia 1993), *copyright OA*

were dated as occurring between 8750 BC and 8250 BC (Mellars and Dark 1998).

In the Upper Thames, the distribution of Mesolithic sites along the river valley is striking, but many are undated and it is uncertain what proportion of these are of early date. There are however certainly early elements at North Stoke and Goring (Ford 1987b; Brown 1995), and probably also at Abingdon (information from the Abingdon Area Archaeological and Historical Society; Allen and Kamash 2008, 67). There is a noted concentration of early Mesolithic sites on the Corallian Ridge, of which Tubney Wood is a good example (Bradley and Hey 1993; Plate 5.7). Many of these are situated near the scarp overlooking the Thames Valley, and they may have provided single locations with a number of different environmental niches within easy reach. The site at Tubney seems to have been visited on a number of occasions, but there was evidence of more permanent occupation with a range of domestic activities taking place in addition to hunting (Bradley and Hey 1993).

The Cotswold sites (eg Ascott-under-Wychwood, Benson and Whittle 2007) and those on the Chilterns (eg Nettlebed, Peake 1913; Kimble Farm, Turville, Peake 1917; and Marline's Sandpit, Bolter End, Millard 1965) are further away from the main river valley, although the Cotswold sites are often near to tributary rivers and streams. It seems probable that woodland cover was not as dense in these higher areas as on the intermediate valley slopes, and clearings would have provided important areas of resource aggregation.

North of the Chilterns, the area which has received the most intensive archaeological investigation is Milton Keynes, where Williams (in Croft and Mynard 1993, 5-10 and fig. 3) notes the discovery of 'significant quantities of Mesolithic flints, including microliths and large numbers of narrow blades ... in both the Ouse valley and its tributaries, the River Ouzel and Loughton Brook'. No specific Mesolithic sites appear to have been excavated or published from the Milton Keynes area, however. It is possible that the geomorphological history of these valleys has led to only limited alluviation, and thus the evidence has not been well-preserved. Evidence further down the Thames in Oxfordshire, Buckinghamshire and Berkshire reinforces the significance of rivers in the distribution of Mesolithic sites, perhaps as routeways, but also as important sources of plant and animal food, both in the river and on its banks. A concentration of adzes has been found in the river around Goring, although whether these were the result of casual loss or deliberate deposition is debatable.

Even though rising water levels in the Kennet Valley resulted in deeply-buried early Mesolithic sites (Hawkes and Heaton 1993), it is apparent that there is a significant concentration of early Mesolithic sites on low terraces and bluffs in the valley of the Middle Kennet and its tributaries, and in the Kennet/Thames confluence area. By contrast, there is a near-absence of known sites along the Loddon (Ford 1997a), Whistley Court Farm, Wokingham being the exception (Harding and Richards

Plate 5.8 Struck flints, bones and skull from Thatcham, Berkshire (from Wymer's notebook), *with kind permission from the family of John Wymer*

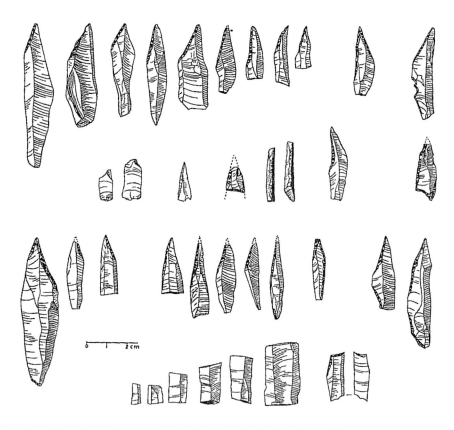

Plate 5.9 Flint tools from Thatcham, *with kind permission from the family of John Wymer*

1982). At Thatcham Reedbeds five major early Mesolithic lithic concentrations (Sites I-V) were associated with hearths and substantial animal bone assemblages (Plates 5.8 and 5.9). Approximately 16,000 flakes and spalls, 1,200 blade-like flakes, 280 cores, 285 microliths, 17 axe-adzes, 130 scrapers, 15 awls, six hammerstones and a variety of other flint implements were found, demonstrating intense *in-situ* activity (Wymer 1958; 1959; 1960; 1962; 1963; Churchill 1962). Nearby concentrations occurred at Newbury Sewage Works (Healy *et al.* 1992) and Lower Way and Chamberhouse Farm Newbury (Wymer 1977; Wessex Archaeology 2005a) and other substantial early assemblages are found in the wider area which are thought to contain stratified assemblages (Lobb and Rose 1996).

At the Eton Rowing Course, limited evaluation along the edge of a backswamp of the Thames revealed several thousand struck flints including early microliths dated to 9150-8730 cal BC (Allen *et al.* 2013). This extensive Early Mesolithic site is part of a wider spread of activity, evidence for which came from the Maidenhead Flood Alleviation Scheme, especially around Taplow, and from Holyport, Bray (Allen 1998; Allen *et al.* 2013; Ames 1993). A number of important sites with large early assemblages are also known in the braided river system of the lower Colne Valley, for example '100 Acres' and Boyer's Pit, Denham and Sandstone, Iver (Lacaille 1963; Wymer 1977), another important area of resource aggregation (Plate 5.10). The river is fed by the Chess, Misbourne and Alderbourne rivers, which cut through the chalk of the Chilterns and themselves contain infilled late and post-

glacial sediments. At Sandstone, the flint lay upon basal floodplain gravels and sands and was overlain by peat, containing predominantly hazel and pine pollen, 'pieces of tree' and a red deer tine, the whole defined as Late Boreal (Mitchell in Lacaille 1963). This deposit was overlain by mud and tufa thought to be the sediments of a local pond or lake and containing some oak pollen and molluscs. Early Mesolithic flint was also found at the Wessex Archaeology evaluation at Denham in association with animal bone (Wessex Archaeology 2005b). A sample of wild boar was dated to 8470–8250 cal BC (9131±45 BP).

Other areas in the north of the Solent-Thames region appear, on present evidence, to be little used in the early Mesolithic, for example the Vales of Aylesbury and the White Horse and the boulder clay of East of Berkshire (Wymer 1977; Ford 1987a). Only light scatters of Mesolithic flint have been recovered from the Berkshire Downs (Richards 1978) and other slopes away from the Thames. Ford (1992, 263) noted that only 13% of known sites in the area come from ridges, hilltops and dry valleys on the Chalklands and, although this may be partially explained by the activities of particular individuals like Froom in the Wawcott area, low-lying areas do seem to have been preferred. The distribution of tool types represented may indicate transitory use of the lower Kennet and more specialised activity in the uplands where many tranchet adzes have been recovered (S. Allen pers. comm.; 2005), with an occupation focus in the Middle Kennet. However, Ford (1992) felt that the few sites outside the valley were also settlements, though smaller.

Plate 5.10 Excavation of flint scatter at Denham, Buckinghamshire, *copyright MoLAs*

Virtually all known early Mesolithic sites in Hampshire are concentrated on the Greensand in the north-east of the county around Oakhanger, Petersfield Heath, Sleaford Heath, Selborne, Trottsford and Kingsley (Clark 1932; Rankine 1949; 1953; Jacobi 1981). These include some substantial assemblages, for example Oakhanger sites V and VII produced approximately 85,000 and over 100,000 pieces respectively (dates between 9200 and 7550 cal BC; see above, Table 5.1). Sites away from the Greensand are relatively few, and most of these, such as Sandy Lane, Shedfield and Abbey Wells, Woolton Hill (Draper 1953; 1968; Wymer 1977, 112; Gardiner 1988), are again generally associated with sands and gravels rather than with the Chalk that dominates the county's geology. Smaller early scatters may be apparent amongst material collected in a few locations around Basingstoke, for example at Dummer and Bradley (Gardiner 1988), but given the amount of fieldwork on the Chalk, this distribution seems likely to be genuine.

Major flint assemblages containing Horsham points are concentrated just to the east of the region, in East Sussex and Surrey, with 'outliers' on the Hampshire Greensand in amongst the distribution of early sites. However, some assemblages from Chalkland areas, such as Salt Hill East Meon, Windmill Hill and Butser Hill (Draper 1968), have also produced small numbers of Horsham points. These industries can now be seen to have a sporadic but widespread distribution across the southern Chalk, even reaching Cranborne Chase, though their main distribution continues to be periph-eral to it. The only other substantial assemblage in Hampshire to incorporate Horsham points is Broom

Hill, Braishfield, which is again located on sandy substrate (O'Malley and Jacobi 1978). One area that seems so far to be largely devoid of Mesolithic flintwork is the eastern part of the New Forest, though this may reflect land use and the absence of collectors.

The present coastal plain, with its generally gentle topography and sand and gravel deposits was, in the Mesolithic, incised by a series of relatively deep river valleys running south from the Chalk. These were far inland in the Mesolithic period (Allen and Gardiner 2000). Pollen evidence from Langstone Harbour indicates that they contained open grass and sedge environments bordered by flat plateau areas supporting light deciduous woodland and open grassland (Scaife 2000). A pollen sequence from Testwood, Southampton, also indicated a gradual change from pine and juniper in the 9th millennium cal BC to a more open, semi-deciduous woodland including oak, elm and hazel by the middle of the 8th millennium (Scaife pers. comm.). As such, this region would have seen high biodiversity, and the extensive flint scatters reported from the shores of all the major harbours suggest widespread exploitation of the lowland plain. The intertidal and underwater resource of the Solent harbours has particular potential for the preservation of organic materials and pollen sequences.

Jacobi (1981) drew particular attention to the presence of many Mesolithic flint scatters at or below present tide level all along the Hampshire coastline. Such sites, from Christchurch Harbour in the west to Chichester Harbour and Selsey in the east, were well known to local collectors such as Rankine and Draper, and many thousands of implements have been recovered from foreshore sites (Rankine 1951; 1956; Draper 1951; 1968; Bradley and Hooper 1975; Jacobi 1981; Gardiner 1984; 1987; 1988; Cartwright 1982). Most scatters can be seen to be eroding out of the soft clay margins of the harbours onto the foreshore, and it is clear that the material represents extensive exploitation of former dry land rather than of a coastal environment.

Lying on the southern banks of the Solent River, the Isle of Wight would have been very close to the southern coastline of Britain in the early Mesolithic, and in many ways the environment would have resembled that to the north (Allen and Gardiner 2000). On the Isle of Wight, sites have also been discovered eroding out of banks and cliffs or on the modern shoreline, for example at Werrar on the west bank of the Medina, Newtown East Spit, on the south-west coast, between Wootton and Quarr and at Bouldnor (Poole 1936; Clifford 1936; Scaife 1987; Loader 2006; Tomalin *et al.* 2012; Momber 2000; 2004; McInnes *et al.* 2001; HWTMA 2005). A number of these sites are probably late Mesolithic in date. Undoubtedly, archaeological investigation has been more intense in coastal areas in recent years, and this may have biased the distribution maps. Nevertheless, fieldwalking in the Wootton-Quarr hinterland has found little evidence of Mesolithic activity (Tomalin *et al.* 2012). The Greensand, in the south of the island, has also revealed a number of Mesolithic sites, largely as a result of fieldwalking. Excavations have been few, but an amateur archaeologist digging in the garden of The Wakes, Shorwell, produced nearly 1200 waste flakes and over 400 hundred implements, including scrapers, microliths, gravers, burins, awls and a small pick (Bennett 1966). Some Neolithic material was also present, but the assemblage has not been systematically studied.

Later Mesolithic landscapes

It is in the south of the region that the most dramatic environmental change occurred during the Mesolithic period, when rising water levels breached the land bridge with Continental Europe, and Britain became an island. The Isle of Wight became separated from England at this time and a coastal environment was established in these areas for the first time for around 25,000 years. The dating of this event remains uncertain, but the most commonly accepted view is 6900 – 5800 BC, or possibly a little later (Tomalin *et al.* 2012). In the lower Thames Estuary, it is estimated that, between *c.* 7950–5900 cal BC, sea levels were rising at around 13 mm per year (Devoy 1979), although the tidal reach of the Thames was way below that of today (Sidell and Wilkinson 2004).

On the Isle of Wight and the Hampshire coast, rapidly changing sea levels had a significant impact, not only on the whole terrestrial environmental and coastal landscape but also on the nature, presence and distribution of exploitable resources. Picks and tranchet adzes have been recovered from the north coast and the Medina Estuary (Tomalin *et al.* 2012), and worked and burnt flints have been found below sea level at Bouldnor, with humanly-

modified timbers at *c.* -11 m OD. The distribution of sites shows a marked concentration on the coast and in the river valleys, in particular the Medina.

The present coastal plain of Hampshire would have been far inland in the late Mesolithic; evidence from Langstone Harbour shows that it remained a river valley with an open, grassy hinterland and not a marine environment (Allen and Gardiner 2000). It only really started to become a coastal environment in the Bronze Age; tidal inlets only occurred from the later Bronze Age and Iron Age. Numerous small, late Mesolithic scatters have been found on the foreshore and around the islands of the harbour, some associated with hearths, animal bone and burnt flint, suggesting short-stay visits, probably lasting only a few days at a time (*ibid.*). Both Jacobi (1981) and Wymer (1977; 1996) commented on the comparative lack of late Mesolithic flint sites in Hampshire, excepting those early sites in the western Weald which also had late Mesolithic components, for example Kingsley and Oakhanger III and IX (Rankine 1952; 1953).

Recent work has indicated the widespread occurrence of flint scatters both off and on the Chalk. Many thousands of pieces were recovered from a sandpit at Broom Hill, Braishfield, in the lower Test Valley, where 80% of the microlithic component comprises rods and scalene triangles and over 100 adzes. Radiocarbon dates are again few but span the period 6400–5260 cal BC (Appendix 1; O'Malley and Jacobi 1978). The East Hampshire Field Survey (Shennan 1985) showed that, outside of the main concentrations, there is a generalised scatter of broadly later Mesolithic material spreading across to the western edge of the Chalk, especially in areas capped by clay-with-flints. Excavations at Southam Common, just 5 km south of Oakhanger, identified several small, dense flint scatters associated with hearths (Thames Valley Archaeological Services (TVAS) 1989; Gardiner 2002). Southam reflects a pattern that is most noticeable away from the Greensand, where sites tend to be discrete, of limited extent, and to contain small assemblages, often associated with hearths or possibly pits. Such sites also tend to cluster over relatively small areas. This pattern has been confirmed by larger-scale, more systematic surveys (Schofield 1995; Gardiner 2002). Sites are usually located on sandy substrates or on superficial deposits overlying the Chalk, for example at Windmill Hill, Chalton and Butser Hill, in southern Hampshire (Draper 1968; Gardiner 1988).

Direct evidence for the vegetation of the Hampshire Wealden Greensand is lacking, but pollen evidence from the adjacent area of Sussex demonstrated dramatic change from hazel-dominated open woodland to heathland species, especially heathers, during the course of the early Mesolithic (Simmons *et al.* 1981; Garton 1980); whether anthropogenic factors were involved is not known. This may have encouraged more widespread use of the landscape. The distribution of Hampshire's late Mesolithic sites indicates the importance of river valleys as communication routes as well as favoured areas for settlement. Penetration of the Chalk uplands seems to have been accomplished via major rivers and their tributaries, and the presence of axes and adzes may indicate clearance of the upland forests at this time.

The Upper and Middle Thames Valley was quite heavily wooded by the 7th millennium cal BC, and closed alder woodland prevailed on the floodplain by the mid-6th millennium. Mixed deciduous woodland appeared to be present over much of the valley by the 5th millennium, with alder growing in the valley bottoms and lime, oak, hazel, ash and elm on the better drained gravel terraces and higher slopes (Day 1991; Needham 1992; Robinson 1993, 9-12; Scaife 2000; Keith-Lucas 2000; Branch and Green 2004). Under climax vegetation, channels in the Upper Thames ceased to flow, many subsidiary river channels silted and the floodplain became quite dry; alder trees were growing in the base of channels at Yarnton by 4460–4250 cal BC (OxA-10713; 5535±50). The hydrology of the Middle Thames was affected by sea-level rises, the changing gradient of the river creating wetter valley-bottom conditions and encouraging peat formation.

The late Mesolithic is comparatively poorly represented in the Kennet Valley, in both artefactual remains and dated layers or sites. However, several late Mesolithic sites are known, including those which show long-term use, notably Wawcott Sites XV and XXX (Froom 1976; Froom et al. 1993), and others where small discrete clusters appear to represent short-term events, for example Wawcott III (Froom 1976). In addition, finds for the later period are more prevalent in East Berkshire, and to the west at Avebury and the headwaters of the Kennet where, conversely, there is little evidence for early Mesolithic activity (Ford 1987a; Lobb and Rose 1996). It may be that increasing waterlogging within the valley bottoms (Holgate 1988; Healy et al. 1992; Evans et al. 1993), while it might not have created conditions unfavourable to settlement and exploitation (Whittle 1990), may have changed patterns of settlement and land use. Once again, the picture seems to be of smaller groups moving over more extensive and varied territories.

Elsewhere in the Thames Valley and its catchment, most later Mesolithic activity seems to be related to rivers and water courses, a pattern already observed for Hampshire. Sites such as Gravelly Guy, Kidlington Lock Crescent, Abingdon (various), North Stoke and Goring demonstrate activity on the gravel terraces and floodplain of the Upper Thames. In the Middle Thames, major sites have been found at Jennings Yard, Windsor (Hawkes and Heaton 1993), Park Farm, Binfield (Roberts 1995), which lies on raised ground overlooking the river valley, and Moor Farm, Holyport, in Bray (Ames 1993). A number of sites have also come to light in south Buckinghamshire, for example Fulmer in the Alderbourne Valley (Farley 1978). Work in the Eton area has produced scatters and in-situ deposits of late Mesolithic flint (Allen et al. 2013). These were often found on riverside locations, with tools often on levées on the banks of palaeochannels and in situ knapping sites on the adjacent floodplain. At the Misbourne Railway Viaduct site, on the floor of the Misbourne, small flint

assemblages were found associated with animal bone: aurochs, red deer, wild pig, roe deer and small numbers of beaver, wild cat, otter, badger and possibly pine martin bones (Farley 1983; Wilson in Farley 1983). Seven radiocarbon dates were obtained, three of which are late Mesolithic (grouped between 5350 and 4610 cal BC; see above), but the others are both very early and post-Mesolithic.

Robin Holgate's model of late Mesolithic activity in the Thames Valley postulated short-stay or base camps on the terrace edges adjacent to rivers with task-specific sites on the upper slopes (Holgate 1988). He thought that increasing utilisation of upland areas may have been related to the increased importance of hunting ungulates as part of food-gathering strategies. Recent work suggests more activity on the floodplain than he anticipated, but also few large sites in any location. It is the case, however, as he argued, that microliths are more numerous in upland assemblages, with fewer tranchet adzes or axe-sharpening flakes (ibid., 74-6). The evidence is, perhaps, more consistent with small and mobile groups exploiting many different environments according to resource availability, need and inclination.

To summarise, it still seems to be the case that in the early Mesolithic sites on sandy geologies were favoured, whether this was the Corallian Ridge in Oxfordshire or the Hampshire Greensand. These naturally acidic soils would have produced distinctive combinations of vegetation and resources, encouraging repeated occupation of traditional hunting and foraging grounds. Sites seem to have been preferentially positioned on scarps, bluffs and slopes overlooking watercourses or arranged along springlines, and these are locations also favoured in river valleys such as the Kennet and the Lower Colne Valley. They would have provided optimal environments for the exploitation of a range of resources and for the congregation of communities, probably at specific times of the year, in areas with a good and constant water supply. Large assemblages probably represent the repeated use of a favoured site for many generations.

In the late Mesolithic, resource exploitation and land use seems to have changed. Smaller sites are found over a much wider range of geologies and topographies, but the presence of nearby water remains an important factor in site choice. River valleys became increasingly utilised. Referring to Hampshire, Julie Gardiner notes that 'in general, the largest and most complex assemblages are still those that are located on the sands and we can envisage the regular movement of smaller groups of people along the river valleys penetrating the Chalklands in search of seasonal resources and/or on hunting trips'. This seems to be a situation that applies over much of our region.

Social organisation and settlement

As elsewhere across Britain, the evidence for Mesolithic social organisation in the Solent-Thames region is slim. As Julie Gardiner points out in her county contribution for Hampshire, the idea of seasonal movements, with the coming together of small groups in so-called base camps at particular times of the year, is a now well-rehearsed explanation of Mesolithic lifeways, and there is little to contradict this view in the current evidence. What we may be seeing, however, is greater mobility through time, with new areas gradually being drawn into the seasonal cycle (Hey *et al.* 2011b). Whether this reflects a perceived need for new 'territory'; an increase in the variety of available natural resources; changes in the character of resource utilisation by animals resulting from climatic and vegetation changes; or changes in social organisation, is impossible to tell. An apparent uniformity of tool traditions across the region, despite the changing technology and environment of the times is interesting in this context, and might point to widespread communication between groups and the maintenance of longer-distance ties.

It is unfortunately the case that, even where the range of environments within the locality of a particular site is described, the dynamics of the exploitation of the wider resource base by the people who used those sites is rarely considered, even when the proxy palaeo-environmental data has been retrieved and reported upon. Integration of palaeo-environmental records to discriminate between local resources and those obtained from further afield can not only provide an understanding of social and economic activity on site but also that of wider Mesolithic economies. Additionally, more effort could be expended on defining the seasons or seasonality of site occupation, whether long or short term, for example from various plant and animal foods. A study of red deer teeth from the Thatcham site indicated that killing took place there at least in late summer/early autumn and in winter (Carter 2001); periodic visits at other times of the year, and not necessarily in a set seasonal pattern, was also considered possible (ibid.). Understanding seasonality is one way of addressing issues of community mobility, social economy and resource territories, as well as providing evidence of diet throughout the year, and not just at one particular location.

Aggregation sites

The vast majority of Mesolithic finds recovered in the region have been from disturbed contexts. Where sites do lie on the surface, without vertical stratigraphy or nearby contemporary deposits from which to obtain proxy palaeo-environmental data, geoarchaeology, soil and sediment micromorphology can help to elucidate more precisely the taphonomy of lithic scatters, although it can be difficult to ascertain whether finds and the deposits in which they are found are contemporary (*cf* pollen and flints from La Sagesse; Conneller and Ellis 2007). At La Sagesse, Romsey, Hampshire, like many other sites, the clear patterning in the flintwork shows that it retains some spatial integrity, even if it is no longer in its precise original position. Pedogenesis and minor sediment movement have resulted in the artefacts being moved vertically with some lateral displacement. This

largely occurred as a result of soil formation processes during increased vegetation growth many millennia later; the pollen reflects the later vegetation event and not that relating to the Mesolithic flint deposition.

Nevertheless, some sites do survive, usually buried beneath alluvium or peat on valley floors, with evidence of hearths, intact surfaces and *in-situ* flint spreads. Recent work in South East England has also revealed highly-localised colluvial benches in key topographical locations that might provide glimpses of the data lost in open sites (Allen 2008a; 2008b).

Surfaces and *in-situ* deposits

The five early Mesolithic sites at Thatcham Reedbeds (Sites I-V) included hearths associated with substantial animal bone and flint assemblages, with a great variety of tool types than is normally present. Intense *in-situ* activity seems to be represented (Wymer 1958; 1959; 1960; 1962; 1963; Churchill 1962), as it does at a number of nearby sites, for example Newbury Sewage Works (Healy *et al.* 1992) and Lower Way and Chamberhouse Farm Newbury (Wymer 1977; Wessex Archaeology 2005a). Some of these sites appear to contain stratified assemblages (Lobb and Rose 1996). Wymer suggested that charcoal spreads exposed at Thatcham, which were around 20 m in diameter, represented hut sites, perhaps of a band of a few dozen individuals who returned to this place periodically (Wymer 1962, 336-7).

A possible working floor has been claimed for a site at Gerrards Cross in the Misbourne Valley (Barfield 1977), with an assemblage, which includes two core axes, four axe-sharpening flakes and three microliths, associated with flint-rich gravels, but Neolithic material is also present and it is hard to disentangle the evidence. Small-scale clusters of flintwork on the floodplain at Eton appear to represent *in-situ* activity, perhaps temporary encampments and short-lived activity areas (Allen *et al.* 2013).

The association between substantial early Mesolithic flint assemblages and hearths on the Hampshire Greensand has already been noted above, as has the numerous small late Mesolithic scatters with hearths associated with animal bone and burnt flint at Langstone Harbour and elsewhere on the Hampshire coast; at Langstone Harbour inter-site patterning was revealed (Allen and Gardiner 2000).

In a more unusual environment, material found beneath the Neolithic long cairn at Ascott-under-Wychwood in the Cotswolds suggests midden accumulation in both the early and late Mesolithic (Benson and Whittle 2007).

Structures

Mesolithic structures are very rare nationally, although a few stake-built houses have come to light in recent years (Pederson and Waddington 2007). Some kind of tented structure was suggested for a series of pits and possible stakeholes at Wakeford's Copse, Havant (Bradley and Lewis 1974), and for a sub-circular arrangement of postholes associated with a pit at Broom Hill, Braishfield, in the latter case associated with a vast assemblage of flintwork and other pits (O'Malley and Jacobi 1978; Jacobi 1981). In neither case did these suggestions meet with universal agreement. However, the similarity of the Broom Hill 'structure' to those recently-excavated further north at Howick, Northumberland, East Barns, Lothian and Ronaldsway on the Isle of Man (Pederson and Waddington 2007) shows that its original interpretation may be correct and it merits reappraisal. Stakehole structures are also now more widely accepted (eg Bayliss and Woodman 2009). Claims have been made for temporary shelters or windbreaks at Wawcott (Froom 1972; 1976; Hey with Robinson 2011, fig. 10.17) and Stout (1994, 9) proposed a stakehole hut or shelter in the Earley Water Meadows near the Thames at Broken Brow, but these have not been verified.

Wymer (1958, 31-32) suggested that a pile structure with associated flints in the peat at Bartholomew Street, Newbury might be Mesolithic, and a dug out butt-ended ditch at Thatcham was identified as a possible fishtrap (Wymer 1963, 46), although it is now thought to be a beaver-cut channel (Wymer 1991, 27). A substantial flintwork assemblage, radiocarbon dated to around 4800 cal BC, was excavated at Bowman's Farm near Romsey where it was thought to have been associated with structures represented by ring-slots (Green 1991; 1996), but these 'structures' have since been re-appraised as belonging with Iron Age activity on the site; some might be tree-throw holes.(Plate 5.11)

Activities

A range of activities is represented by assemblages from what would conventionally be described as base camps (Mellars' 'balanced assemblages'; Mellars 1976). At these sites, tools include those for cutting and for plant and animal food preparation and processing (for example at Tubney, Oxfordshire, where the high proportion of microdenticulates was suggested to be linked to plant-food processing), working bone, antler or wood (such as at Windmill Hill, Nettlebed), processing skins and hides (at both Tubney and Windmill Hill) and making and rejuvenating the tools needed to undertake these tasks (Bradley and Hey 1993; Boismier 1995). Tranchet axes from Goring may suggest deliberate tree clearance (Brown 1995).

The evidence from the Kennet Valley indicates home-base sites visited time after time, as discussed above (Plate 5.12). Use-wear analysis of the flintwork assemblages from the two Thatcham Sewage Works sites (Grace 1992; Healy et al. 1992) gives some indication that wood-cutting was carried out in both areas. The working of harder materials, such as antler and bone, including boring and whittling of these, seems to have dominated activity on the earlier, southern site; in contrast, tasks such as scraping softer material (like hides) and cutting soft plants (such as roots and tubers) was more common in the northern area. A difference in function is implied, showing different activities taking place at different times. With only one probable projectile point and little animal bone, there was little evidence of hunting or butchery.

Plate 5.11 Excavation at Bowman's Farm, Hampshire, *copyright Frank Green, New Forest Trust*

Bone tools from Thatcham, such as points, pins, the point of a bodkin and a punch (Wymer 1962, 351-3), indicate the preparation of clothes and fabric for bedding and shelters, such as tents (Plate 5.13). Another rare find in the area was of mastic still adhering to a flint flake where it had probably been hafted into a wooden handle. Analysis showed that it had been prepared with resin, probably of birch, mixed with clay and a lipid or beeswax (Roberts et al. 1998).

A number of sites have yielded palimpsest assemblages, created by small task groups engaged in a variety of subsistence activities and repeatedly occupying the same location, for example at Windmill Hill, Nettlebed (Boismier and Mepham 1995, 18). At this site these activities included core preparation and reduction, tool manufacture, use and rejuvenation of a variety of tools used in working bone, antler or wood, and processing skins (ibid.). At Tubney, successive episodes of activity also seemed to be represented, and included hide preparation, food preparation and microlith manufacture. This might be a more accurate way of describing sites that had previously been considered to be base or short-stay camps, for example Gravelly Guy, Oxfordshire, where cutting, scraping and engraving tools were being used, microliths produced and axes sharpened (Holgate 2004). The early settlement activity at Ascott-under-Wychwood was suggested to be of some duration

Plate 5.12 Reconstruction of Mesolithic settlement at Thatcham, *with kind permission of the family of John Wymer*

and included microlith manufacture and tool use; the late assemblage probably represents short visits rather than prolonged stays (Cramp 2007).

Hunting and gathering strategies

Hunting and gathering seems to have been focused on river resources, on the mosaic of clearings around the river and on less densely-wooded upland areas. The Corallian Ridge, for example, may have been seen as an advantageous site from which to observe animals, but also to exploit a wide range of environmental niches, from the sandy ridge to the valley bottom of the Thames.

Faunal remains from early Mesolithic sites are relatively common, showing the presence and exploitation of a wide range of species for food, fur and other resources. At Thatcham these included pike, mallard, crane, goldeneye duck, hedgehog, watervole, hare, badger, beaver, fox, pine marten, wildcat, red deer, roe deer, wild boar, wild horse and aurochs (King 1962). Carter (2001) assessed the age at death from tooth development of six immature red deer (*Cervus elaphus*)

specimens and suggested that killing took place in at least late summer/autumn and winter. Domestication of dogs is also evidenced. Red deer and roe deer were generally favoured, but wild boar was also a common food source, and at Chamberhouse Farm, Faraday Road and Greenham Dairy Farm, all in the Newbury/Thatcham area, butchered wild boar remains dominated the on-site early Mesolithic assemblages (Sheridan *et al.* 1967; Carter 1976; Ellis *et al.* 2003; Chisham 2004). Interestingly, isotopic analysis of a human humerus recovered at Thatcham suggests a diet lacking in freshwater fish as well as marine sources, with similar results for a dog bone also found at the site (Schulting and Richards 2000).

At the late Mesolithic sites at Wawcott, the only large herbivore types to be recorded were red deer and wild cattle (Carter 1976; Froom 1976). Wild cattle, red deer, wild pig and roe deer were all found at the late Mesolithic site of Stratford's Yard, Chesham, Buckinghamshire (Grigson 1989), along with charred hazelnut shells; a radiocarbon date of 5010–4500 cal BC (BM-2404: 5890±100 BP) was obtained on a *Bos primigenius* bone (Stainton 1989).

Contrary to the traditional view, there is no evidence for seasonal population movements to follow deer migrations in the Kennet Valley. Few sites have been identified on the Chalk, while temporary sites with evidence of deer hunting have been found in the lowlands, for example at Ufton Green and Faraday Road (Allen and Allen 1997; Chisham 2004; Ellis *et al.* 2003), where herbivores might have congregated around water sources. The distribution of tool types suggests upland-lowland site differentiation by specialist task rather than by hunting or season.

Hunting sites have been identified in other parts of the region. At Rollright, high up on the Cotswolds, a knapping scatter is interpreted as one or more individuals carrying a flint-working toolkit and manufacturing or repairing hunting equipment on the spot (Holgate 1988b, 90). Sites around South Stoke and Goring in the Goring Gap may represent more frequent hunting visits, while individual microliths found in the landscape across the region may represent tools lost during hunting expeditions.

Apart from the evidence from microwear analysis on tools (see above), evidence of plant food remains is slight, the exception being the common discovery of charred hazelnut shells. An assemblage of 120 charred hazelnut fragments reported by Scaife (1992) at

Plate 5.13 Detail of bone pin and antlers from Thatcham, *copyright the family of John Wymer*

Newbury Sewage Works indicates at least autumnal use of the site, although storage was also considered to be possible.

Interference in the landscape

Childe (1931) suggested over 80 years ago that the introduction of picks and adzes to the Mesolithic toolkit was part of Mesolithic human adaptation to the increasingly wooded environment in general, and tree clearance in particular. Nevertheless, the extent to which Mesolithic populations modified their physical environment remains controversial, although evidence continues to mount for at least some interference in the woodland vegetation (eg Dennell 1983; Mellars 1975; Tipping 2004).

Repeated phases of small patch burning of both the dry terrace edge and wetland landscapes occurred during the early Mesolithic occupation of Thatcham, dated to between 9150–8600 and 7950–7520 cal BC (AA-55303: 9480±68 BP; AA-55308: 8629±82 BP; Chisham 2004), a pattern mirrored in the nearby, contemporary sequence at Woolhampton (ibid.). Charred *Carex* sp. nutlets, associated with a peak in landscape burning in the floodplain peat dated to 8480–8230 cal BC (AA-55306: 9,134±65 BP; ibid.), might indicate late summer activity, assuming the nutlets burnt on the stem. On the other hand, no evidence of burning other than local hearths was found at the more temporary hunting site at Ufton Green *c.* 15 km downriver. This might indicate a pattern of interference in the vegetation around major foci of activity, related to pathways and the encouragement of specific resources (ibid.). Hints of Mesolithic impact on the vegetation were also observed at the Eton Rowing Course (Allen *et al.* 2013) and at Charnham Lane, Hungerford (Keith-Lucas 2002).

The Kennet valley is blanketed by varying depths of calcareous silty loessic alluvium which has largely eroded from the interfluves (Evans *et al.* 1993). It extends for many kilometres along the Kennet valley and presumably indicates the removal of a considerable soil mantle from the interfluves and it changed the landscape character significantly. It is presumed that the mechanism behind the exposure of soil was deforestation, but palaeo-environmental evidence has yet to confirm, elaborate upon, or refute this.

Although woodland was the dominant feature of the Mesolithic landscape in the Upper Thames, there is little direct evidence for woodland clearance, with the exception of the quantities of charcoal found in the Cothill Fen cores by Petra Day and suggested by her to be the result of human clearance of the pine woodland on the Corallian Ridge at around 8800 – 7700 BP (Day 1991, 465). This coincides with what appears to be the period of most intense use of this landscape, providing support for her hypothesis (Bradley and Hey 1993). Additionally, there are many indications that some clearings in the woodland were used, perhaps opportunistically at first, but then repeatedly, suggesting that they were maintained by humans and assisted by fauna (for example at Ascott-under-Wychwood; Benson and Whittle 2007). The discovery of tranchet adzes at Goring may indicate deliberate tree clearance there (Brown 1995).

Exploitation of other natural resources

Although there is some utilisation of larger flint nodules from the river gravels, the use of good-quality flint occurs probably on most Mesolithic sites. There is no evidence for flint mines during this period, and nodules seem all to have been retrieved from surface deposits and exposed faces. In the Kennet Valley, for example, assemblages are dominated by high-quality flint from the Chalk, requiring short-distance importation from exposures and outcrops, with material being brought to sites as pre-prepared cores (eg Hawkes and Heaton 1993, 12). But there is some local use of lower-quality material taken from the London Clay and from river gravels, for example at Holyport (Ames 1993) and Thatcham. The site at Stratford's Yard, Chesham could be associated with the exploitation of flint on the valley slopes of the Chilterns. Five horizons, lying above river gravels and sealed beneath colluvium, yielded over 34 cores and in excess of 300 struck flakes, along with some 49 microliths, including scalene triangles and rods of the narrow blade tradition, scrapers, a tranchet adze and two sharpening flakes (Stainton 1989).

In the north of the region, the majority of flint recovered has been brought over a great distance, for example sites in the north of Oxfordshire, such as Rollright, where high-quality flint is found. Thus people moved over long distances to acquire important resources, or they exchanged materials with neighbouring groups.

It has been suggested that the people making short-stay visits to the Langstone Harbour area were largely concerned with the procurement of large flint nodules from the Bracklesham Beds (Allen and Gardiner 2000). These would have been exposed in river cliffs and gravels, and were used to make adzes and other core tools as well as flake and blade tools. Significantly, nearly all the tranchet adzes and sharpening flakes recovered during the recent Langstone Harbour survey are made of chalk flint, indicating that, whatever the local flint was to be used for, the visitors brought their own adzes with them and took some of them away again. The restricted range of forms and lack of processing tools suggests that items were being manufactured here and removed for use elsewhere.

A variety of stone sources was used on the Isle of Wight, including the good-quality grey-black flint found during the Wootton-Quarr survey, but local gravel flint seems to have been used too, for example at Werrar and Newtown (Loader 2006; Poole 1936; Tomalin *et al.* 2012). Chert is also available on the Island, and was exploited for use as picks amongst other purposes.

In Hampshire, there was a change through the Mesolithic from the use of generally poor-quality, small-size nodules available in the river gravels and

Greensands to the much larger and generally better-quality material derived from the tertiary beds in the south of the county and, especially, from the Chalk. The majority of Mesolithic flint tools are small and easily portable but, increasingly, high-quality raw material was needed in order to produce the small, precise, fine blades from carefully prepared cores that characterise the later assemblages. There was also an increase in the production of tranchet adzes and large core tools that required the availability of large, quality nodules. Like Neolithic polished axeheads, these tools were in use for many hundreds of years and it is very difficult to trace their development closely. Gardiner (1988) however found that the vast majority occur on the upland Chalk, particularly in the areas covered by clay-with-flints where they were probably made, but, significantly, the remainder are very widely spread, with comparatively few in the Mesolithic 'heartlands' of the Greensand belt. In other words, they mirror the pattern of late Mesolithic flint distributions much more closely than they do that of the earlier sites. It is reasonable to assume that communities moving into the flint-rich areas and encountering this resource would have collected sufficient for their own needs, if not for the wider community, presumably carrying away roughouts or finished items rather than predominantly unworked nodules.

Funerary and ritual practices

There are no known human burials from these periods. The only certain find of Mesolithic human bone is of a humerus recovered from a flood deposit below the occupation site at Thatcham, probably of a woman (Brothwell in Wymer 1962, 355). Three human skulls were also reported by Silus Palmer as coming from the peat at Halfway, Thatcham near red deer antlers (Palmer 1872-5; Wymer 1958), but they have not been dated and their whereabouts are unknown. No human remains from rivers in the region have yet been dated to the Mesolithic period. It can be surmised that treatment and disposal of the dead was conducted away from living sites and was thorough, for example by cremation and the scattering of remains or by excarnation. It has been suggested (Barton et al. 1995) that there was long-distance transport of remains to coastal regions, where the few inhumations of the period are to be found, but no inhumations have been found so far on the Hampshire coast or the Isle of Wight, and this explanation seems unlikely.

There may be some evidence in the Solent-Thames region of deposits that seem to be the result of special, rather than day-to-day, activity. An inverted red deer skullcap and antlers were found above the ground surface at Thatcham, with a battered antler beam propped up against them and knapping waste to one side (Warren 2006, 24-5; Wymer 1962). This might indicate the inclusion of ritual practice into the more mundane task of flint tool preparation. It has also been suggested that

the large groups of animal bone found at the contemporary lake edge of many of the Thatcham sites is the result of deliberate acts of deposition (Chatterton 2006, 103-4). A skeleton of an aurochs with microliths embedded into its sinus region alongside the horn (sic) of a red deer was found in the same area (ibid. 104).

It is possible that at least some of the picks and adzes dredged from the river near to Goring could be the result of deliberate deposition, and the placing of finds within tree-throw holes has been observed at Gatehampton Farm, Goring and also on the Eton Rowing Course and the Maidenhead Flood Alleviation Scheme (Brown 1995, 80-1; Lamdin-Whymark 2008). Although there was no evidence of formal structuring of this material, it was clearly deliberately deposited and demonstrates an intimate link between people and their natural woodland environment. Such actions may have been seen as a way of replacing things retrieved from the holes, for example flint nodules exposed when the trees fell over (Carew et al. 2006).

Material culture

Aside from flint tools, there is a paucity of material culture associated with Mesolithic sites. These were mobile communities whose possessions would have been easily carried and who had no tradition of manufacturing artefacts from durable materials; we may not recognise collected natural items even if they survived.

Tools made from animal bone and antler include needles at Thatcham, and these objects show that clothes and objects were made from organic materials which have not survived, as already discussed. A single bone spearhead, apparently unique in the British Mesolithic and resembling a Palaeolithic type, was found with the early Mesolithic assemblages at Thatcham (Wymer 1963). Antler was also used for picks, an example of which was recovered from the Eton Rowing Course in Buckinghamshire (Plate 5.15). Traces of ochre were found at Thatcham (Wymer 1963), and small, natural,

0   100 mm

Plate 5.14 Pebble macehead from Eton Rowing Course, *copyright OA*

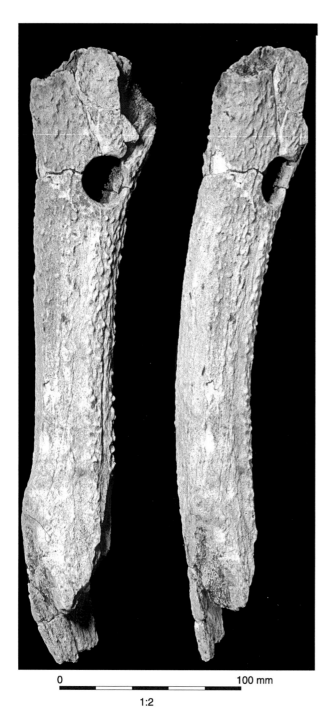

0 |_____| 100 mm

1:2

perforated pebbles may have been for clothing or strung as jewellery.

Otherwise, material culture is confined to flint artefacts and occasional objects made from Greensand/ Portland chert and other stone where this was easily accessed, for example the use of sandstone for pebble maceheads (Roe 1979). A river pebble was used to make a macehead found at the Eton Rowing Course (Plate 5.14).

Several chert maceheads recorded in the Isle of Wight HER may be Mesolithic in date. In addition, although few have been analysed, this collection is believed to contain examples made in non-local stone. Occasionally chert objects are found away from their source, for example the Dorset chert axe found at Wawcott (Froom 1963; 1972).

Becoming Neolithic

None of the late Mesolithic sites so far investigated in the Solent-Thames area have ever yielded pottery or the remains of domesticated plants or animals, and there are no other signs of emerging Neolithic culture, such as monument construction or burial of the dead (Schulting 2000). Where Mesolithic and Neolithic sites are discovered in the same locality, as they often are, they are either disturbed or the Neolithic material is stratified above Mesolithic remains. Radiocarbon dating of some sites, for example Ascott-under-Wychwood (Benson and Whittle 2007) has tended to show a gap in time between these episodes of activity.

Plate 5.15 Antler pick or mattock from the Eton Rowing Course, *copyright OA*

Chapter 6

Late Upper Palaeolithic and Mesolithic: Research Agenda

by Gill Hey

6.1 Nature of the evidence

A number of nationally important sites of Late Upper Palaeolithic (LUP) and Mesolithic date lie within the region, in particular sites with *in-situ* deposits in the Middle Kennet Valley, such as Thatcham. In addition, there are *in-situ* scatters with hearths on the floodplain of the Middle Thames and probably in the Lower Colne Valley, and less-securely stratified but dense flint spreads also associated with hearths in the Hampshire Greensand. Other areas may have similar remains, albeit surviving in smaller pockets, but they have not been so intensively examined, either because they are less visible or because development pressure is less intense.

Recent work has shown that the level of activity during these periods was undoubtedly greater than had been appreciated previously, but an understanding of its distribution and character is subject to distortion because investigation has been so uneven across these counties. In addition, the nature of much of the surviving evidence consists of disturbed material in the ploughzone, making identification and characterisation of LUP and Mesolithic sites difficult. Improving our understanding of the potential of these assemblages, and the most effective ways in which they can be investigated, is of key importance. This can be addressed in a number of ways:

6.1.1 The extent to which developer-funded work can change our understanding of the extent of LUP and Mesolithic activity in this region needs to be recognised, and sites of these dates should be more actively sought when devising mitigation strategies.

6.1.2 Our effectiveness in recovering what can be small scatters of material should be reviewed, and we need to improve the use we make of this material to provide a model of landscape exploitation and social structures across the region.

6.1.3 Fieldwalking for LUP and Mesolithic material should become a more routine part of field evaluation.

6.1.4 The extent to which LUP and Mesolithic sites lie buried beneath alluvium and colluvium should be more fully investigated. This would shed light on whether the density of sites known in the Middle Kennet and Lower Colne Valleys is a factor of preservation biases or of genuine Mesolithic preferences for these areas in the past.

6.1.5 Palaeo-environmental and geo-archaeological sampling should play a much more important role in the identification of sites, in elucidating the range of human activity and in developing a better understanding of variation across the region.

6.1.6 There are a number of sites investigated some time ago that should be published, for example the work undertaken in the Misbourne Valley, Buckinghamshire, and at the 'Wakes' on the Isle of Wight.

6.1.7 The re-examination of some old assemblages would also make an important contribution to our understanding of these periods, for example those from the Hambleden Valley in Buckinghamshire, those in Milton Keynes and the early Mesolithic assemblages from Oxfordshire and the Vale of Aylesbury. Re-assessment is also needed of material from the Thames and some of the other rivers in our catchment, for example material found in the Kennet.

6.1.8 Some new excavations are needed of old sites in order to test established interpretations, as suggested for 'hazel-nut plant bed' on the Isle of Wight and the land surface at Werrar (Poole 1936). Further field collection would also expand the evidence base, for example on ploughed Lower Greensand on the Isle of Wight.

6.1.9 Integration is needed of the results of underwater/foreshore archaeology, especially in the Solent, where previously dry-ground sites could be well preserved beneath the modern sea level.

6.2 Chronology

Chronologies for this period have traditionally been based on typographic sequences, but scientific techniques are increasingly able to provide much more precise dates from which to revise the current model.

6.2.1   There should be a concerted effort to improve our chronological understanding of LUP and Mesolithic flint scatters using scientific dating, particularly OSL.

6.2.2   The collection of samples suitable for scientific dating techniques needs to be a routine part of investigations.

6.2.3   More material should be radiocarbon-dated in order to establishing a more reliable chronology.

6.3 Landscape and land use

For a period from which there is little structural evidence and only limited survival of material culture, landscape studies and environmental sampling are of particular importance. A more detailed understanding of the character of the varied landscape areas present in the region would be extremely valuable, and the relationship between these and human activity needs more investigation.

6.3.1   Excavations in river valleys should be much more clearly focused on the wider use of these locations for settlement and the impact of settlement upon the surrounding landscape.

6.3.2   More work needs to be done to identify sites away from river valleys and coastal/intertidal areas, particularly open sites.

6.3.3   Investigation is needed into human manipulation of the woodland, if indeed this was taking place. This should not only rely on generalised interpretations from pollen diagrams, but on more carefully directed research in order to identify and model these activities on site. For example, some sites have the potential to yield stratified sequences with pollen and also identifiable inwashed charcoal.

6.3.4   More detailed exploration is needed of changes in landscape use over time and how these relate to climate change and vegetation succession.

6.3.5   The impact of changing sea levels on the populations who lived in the Solent area should be investigated, from a physical perspective and that of changing food resources. Did erosion increase in lower river valleys as a consequence of rising sea levels, with subsequent impacts on the landscape over a more extensive area?

6.3.6   Analysis of insect assemblages, where found, is especially important because of their rapid response to climatic and environmental change. Isotope studies on insect assemblages should be considered.

6.3.7   Evidence is needed of regional variation in the types of biological assemblages found at different geographical locations, for example the Hampshire Basin versus the Chalk.

6.3.8   Sites that are well stratified producing a wide range of well-preserved biological remains are rare, and can be regarded as of national importance. They should be carefully sampled wherever possible and analysed with particular attention to site formation processes to provide a detailed picture of local habitat and environmental history. The seasonal use of particular sites can be elucidated in this way, for example, using faunal remains and other proxy indicators.

6.3.9   It seems likely that the growth of underwater archaeology will greatly increase the number of sites producing well-preserved biological remains in the Solent. The development and refining of methodologies to recover this material provides an interesting challenge for the next decade, and should greatly increase our understanding of the exploitation of these landscapes.

6.3.10   Research is needed into evidence for animals browsing under woodland conditions in the late Mesolithic/ early Neolithic and the dating and reasons for the Elm Decline. *Scolytus scolytus*, an insect which can be a vector for Dutch Elm Disease, was recovered in late Mesolithic deposits at Runnymede, although it does not always carry the disease (Robinson 2000b, 149).

6.4 Society

The limited range of archaeological evidence for this period provides significant challenges for understanding the composition of social groups and the inter-relationship between the communities who inhabited the region.

6.4.1   Ways to shed light on mobility, group range and group size need to be investigated. More work on understanding the seasonal use of particular sites would be one way of addressing this issue (see above).

6.4.2 There is the potential in this area to undertake valuable research into the differences (or similarities) between LUP society and settlement and that of the early Mesolithic.

6.4.3 There should be more awareness of the potential to investigate, and attempts to gather evidence for, LUP and Mesolithic beliefs and ideologies, for example the identification of instances of ritual activity.

6.4.4 Some human remains from rivers may be Mesolithic in date and, if so, information from them may contribute to understanding burial practices and ritual, in addition to potentially providing evidence for appearance, pathology etc of Mesolithic people.

6.4.5 More microwear analysis on flint tools would provide a much better understanding of activities on site, including food resources used, food preparation methods, textile and other craft activities, and construction practices.

6.4.6 Any charred material found in association with human activity should be given the highest priority. Distinguishing between charcoal assemblages derived from wild fires and those from domestic areas should be possible through the use of reflectance analysis.

6.4.7 The collection of food remains from bulk soil samples is a priority for understanding diet during this period. In addition, a more holistic approach should be taken to investigating evidence of diet, based on integrating evidence from many sites. Should human remains come to light, isotope work to investigate diet, as well as the distances over which people moved, would be extremely important.

6.4.8 Mesolithic shell middens require further attention. Data should be compared to that from the many examples in Brittany.

6.5 Material culture

Stone tools are the main surviving evidence for material culture from this period and they need to be studied in a variety of ways.

6.5.1 Innovative methods of analysis or lines of thought should be sought in order to gain a better understanding of this material. Samples should be collected and preserved in anticipation of new methods being applied.

6.5.2 Some re-assessment of the raw materials used for tools, their sources and the distance over which they have been brought is needed

6.6 Predictive modelling

Predictive modelling can be a useful tool for any archaeological period, but the full potential of the technique remains to be realised for the Mesolithic. Geo-archaeological sampling should assist in this.

6.6.1 Models should be developed and tested as predictive tools to locate archaeological sites and explain land use.

6.6.2 Particular landscapes that are under threat, and where good research projects could be developed, need to be identified and targeted. Examples include the Denham preferred mineral area and the area around Abingdon, Oxfordshire.

6.6.3 More work in the Solent area, both in areas presently 'offshore' but also horizons in submerged river estuaries, should prove a fruitful source of evidence and help to understand the impact of coastal change.

Chapter 7

The Neolithic and Early Bronze Age: Resource Assessment

by Richard Bradley

(County contributions by Kim Biddulph, Steve Ford, Julie Gardiner, Gill Hey and Ruth Waller; palaeoenvironmental contribution by Mike Allen)

Introduction

The nature of the evidence

It is often claimed that linear projects such as pipelines or major roads provide a novel perspective on the past. They cannot represent a 'random sample' of archaeological observations because each element does not have the same chance of being selected. Instead, their course is essentially arbitrary and bears no obvious relationship to the geography of any particular period. For that reason the results of monitoring these developments are often surprising, and it is those surprises that provide a stimulus for rethinking archaeological orthodoxies. Regions prove to have been settled where few sites had been known before; rich burials are found outside the small concentrations on which the literature had been based; new kinds of monument are revealed and familiar forms occur in unfamiliar settings. It is not the most obvious way of conducting research, but sometimes the results of this work offer a perspective out of which new approaches to the past can develop.

The same should be true of the Regional Research Assessments, of which this publication is an example. They are concerned with regions of the country which have been selected on the basis of modern administrative arrangements. They lack any real geographical unity, and the relationships between their component parts may well have changed over time. On the other hand, like the road schemes that have done so much to widen the scope of prehistoric archaeology, the process of bringing together what is known about these areas of land can be remarkably productive. A distribution of key sites and other selected sites is shown in Figure 7.1.

As it happens, the area selected for the Solent-Thames Research Assessment has many of these advantages. Like the building of pipelines, it makes archaeologists think harder about some areas that have not played a major part in writings about prehistory – the Isle of Wight, for example, or the Buckinghamshire Chilterns. Quite by chance, it also avoids a region whose monuments have been over-emphasised in accounts of prehistoric Britain. It is an important challenge to write about the Neolithic period without discussing Hambledon Hill, Stonehenge, Avebury and Durrington Walls, just as it is important to think about an early Bronze Age that does not depend on the rich burials found on the Dorset and Wiltshire chalk. Not only does the Solent-Thames corridor avoid these famous groups of monuments, it covers an area in which certain kinds of structure seem to be rare or absent. Causewayed enclosures are unusual outside the Thames Valley and southern Cotswolds; long barrows of classic form are not represented across the entire study area; henges are uncommon or take unusual forms, and rich early Bronze Age cemeteries are the exception rather than the norm. That may not be an impediment to research, for it can be argued that, within the wider context of British prehistory, developments in the heart of earlier prehistoric Wessex were altogether exceptional. A framework of more general application may depend on fieldwork in other regions, in particular the major river valleys and the North Sea coast.

A few basic points need to be made at the outset. Some of these observations apply to the entire prehistoric sequence; others are specific to the period between 4000 and 1500 BC that provides the subject of this chapter.

Inherited landscapes and Neolithic and early Bronze Age land use

It is no longer satisfactory to suppose that the earlier prehistoric landscape was covered by a continuous canopy of trees (Allen and Gardiner 2009). By the beginning of the Neolithic period some areas had been modified by burning – both deliberate and accidental – and others by natural events, especially storms (Brown 1997). The vegetation cover will also have been affected by the activities of wild animals, by the ecological preferences of different kinds of woodland, and during the Neolithic period by such practices as coppicing and pollarding. There was greater variation than is generally supposed, and recent research in Cranborne Chase and on the Yorkshire Wolds suggests that certain areas of chalk downland may never have been covered by primary forest in the way that is commonly supposed (French *et al.* 2007; Allen and Scaife 2007). That is especially important because both these regions contain an unusual concentration of

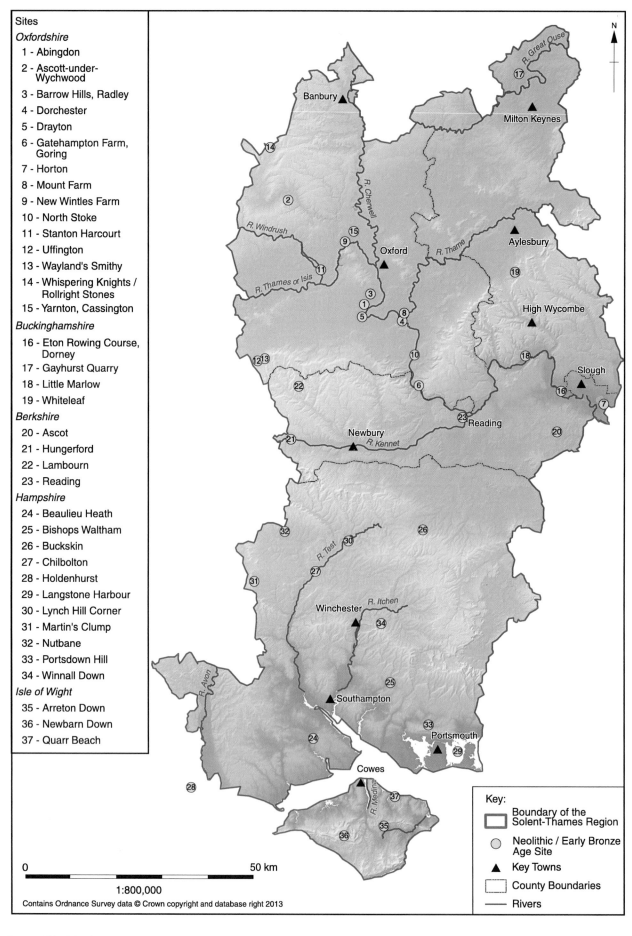

Sites

Oxfordshire

1 - Abingdon
2 - Ascott-under-Wychwood
3 - Barrow Hills, Radley
4 - Dorchester
5 - Drayton
6 - Gatehampton Farm, Goring
7 - Horton
8 - Mount Farm
9 - New Wintles Farm
10 - North Stoke
11 - Stanton Harcourt
12 - Uffington
13 - Wayland's Smithy
14 - Whispering Knights / Rollright Stones
15 - Yarnton, Cassington

Buckinghamshire

16 - Eton Rowing Course, Dorney
17 - Gayhurst Quarry
18 - Little Marlow
19 - Whiteleaf

Berkshire

20 - Ascot
21 - Hungerford
22 - Lambourn
23 - Reading

Hampshire

24 - Beaulieu Heath
25 - Bishops Waltham
26 - Buckskin
27 - Chilbolton
28 - Holdenhurst
29 - Langstone Harbour
30 - Lynch Hill Corner
31 - Martin's Clump
32 - Nutbane
33 - Portsdown Hill
34 - Winnall Down

Isle of Wight

35 - Arreton Down
36 - Newbarn Down
37 - Quarr Beach

Key:

Boundary of the Solent-Thames Region

Neolithic / Early Bronze Age Site

Key Towns

County Boundaries

Rivers

0   50 km

1:800,000

Contains Ordnance Survey data © Crown copyright and database right 2013

Figure 7.1 Neolithic and Early Bronze Age sites mentioned in the text

Neolithic monuments. By contrast, there is little to suggest the existence of comparable environments in the study area (Robinson 1992a and b; Hey et al. 2011 b; Field 2004; 2008).

The pattern of prehistoric activity cannot be reconstructed on the basis of modern land use. There are areas that provide evidence of continuous occupation, for example the Thames gravels (Barclay et al. 1996), while there are others that show signs of intensive activity in certain phases and little evidence of occupation in others. The character of the local soils has changed significantly. The clay-with-flints which caps the chalk was intensively used in the Mesolithic and Neolithic periods but was less densely settled during later phases. Similarly, the heathland soils of the New Forest and perhaps the Hampshire Greensand saw a peak of activity during the Bronze Age, but since then they seem to have been regarded as marginal land (Field 2008).

The increase in the number of palaeo-environmental datasets has improved the resolution at which we can look at landscapes and land-use, whether for individual sites or across whole regions (Allen 1997a and b; Allen and Gardiner 2009). We can now start to re-address some key questions surrounding the presence and use of 'farmed' produce, and whether this indicates a wholly farming economy. The Neolithic may partly be defined by the presence of farming activities, but Neolithic communities may have had a risk-averse strategy which involved hunting and gathering as well as farming (Jones 2000; Moffett et al. 1989; Robinson 2000). In addition, the use of domesticated resources does not require a sedentary lifestyle. The issue as to whether the economy of these communities becomes largely, or wholly, based around a domesticated food supply requires further study.

While there may be some relationship between the extent of open ground and the choice of certain regions for monument building, it is not correct to use the frequency of earthwork structures to estimate the intensity of occupation in any part of the study area. The construction of such monuments certainly required a significant labour force, but its members could have been drawn from a wider region. Elsewhere in England, some monument complexes are associated with evidence of nearby settlement, but there are others where it is absent (Bradley 2006). In the same way, it is incorrect to suppose that areas that lack large concentrations of field monuments were less intensively occupied. Within the Solent-Thames corridor, some of the greatest concentrations of worked flints come from the chalk downland around Basingstoke and from the Chilterns, where the density of monuments is unusually low (Gardiner 1984; 1988; Holgate 1988a; Field 2004). Moreover, current work on the dating of Neolithic long barrows and enclosures suggests that they could have been constructed during quite specific phases, and that they were often short-lived (Whittle, Barclay et al. 2007). Thus their occurrence may prove to be the exception rather than the rule.

Some of the changes to the natural environment that took place during or after this period have severely biased the archaeological record. In the valleys of major rivers like that of the Thames, occupation sites and some of the smaller monuments have been buried beneath later deposits of alluvium (Robinson 1992b; Evans 1992a; Parker and Robinson 2003). Others were preserved because they occupied the hollows left by former channels and escaped destruction by the plough. On the chalk there is another source of bias, for not only has much of the original topsoil been lost by erosion, this process had led to the accumulation of deep deposits of hill wash on the valley floors. Recent work in Sussex and Kent has shown that these had buried some of the elusive living sites of the Neolithic and Early Bronze Age (Allen and Scaife 2007). Similar evidence has been identified on the Chilterns and it is probable that the same process happened in other parts of the study area (Evans 1972; Evans and Valentine 1974).

Archaeologists still assign a special status to the archaeology of the chalk. That needs careful consideration. It is true that it is an area with an unusual density of field monuments, but this is only partly due to developments during the prehistoric period. To a large extent the prominence of chalkland monuments is the result of later land use. These structures escaped some of the destructive activities that affected their lowland counterparts. For example, it is often supposed that early Bronze Age burial mounds were sited in prominent positions, yet their overall distribution is most obviously related to important valleys, as it is on the Isle of Wight (Allen and Scaife 2007). The earthworks on the hills have escaped the damage experienced by barrows on the lower ground, and yet it is often the case that a distribution of standing mounds gives way to one of ring ditches. They are discovered by different methods and sometimes they are treated as different kinds of monuments.

The survival of so many earthworks on the high downland introduces yet another bias, for it is often supposed that they were located along 'ridgeways': long distance paths extending between major groups of monuments. The antiquity of these routes is very doubtful. Their course is not reflected by later prehistoric field systems and land boundaries, suggesting that such features as the Berkshire Ridgeway or the Icknield Way did not exist until long after the period discussed here (Harrison 2003). Instead it seems as if the main communications were along the valleys and around the coast. It is likely that rivers were often more significant than land routes. That would certainly help to explain the distribution of major monument complexes beside the Thames, for they are often at confluences (Barclay et al. 1996). One interpretation of this evidence is these structures were built where they were particularly accessible. (Plate 7.1)

The traditional emphasis on the Wessex chalk has overlooked the possibility that it was simply the upland component of an enormous territory (or territories), extending along the river valleys to the Channel coast. The importance of the river gravels is widely accepted – and

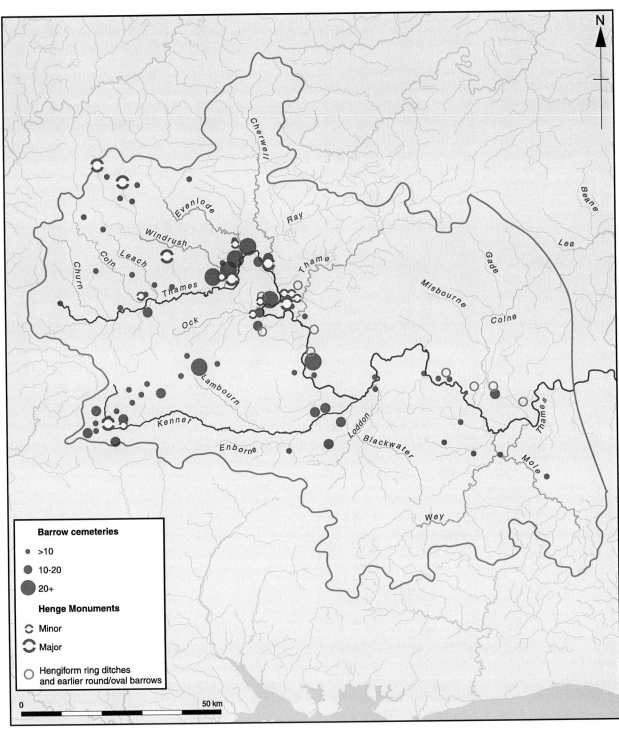

Plate 7.1 Henge monuments and major barrow groups on the Thames, *copyright OA*

has been since the development of archaeological air photography. In addition to their obvious attraction as places of animal aggregation, valleys would have provided resources such as reeds, coppice carr woodland, muds, clays, sands and gavels used for potting clays and temper, flooring, walling, roofing and lining features, matting and basketry, and a number of these items would probably have been removed and utilised elsewhere. On the other hand, the significance of the Hampshire Basin has been largely overlooked. Not only does it contain concentrations of earlier prehistoric finds, recent research has shown that many of the most distinctive artefacts of the

Neolithic period have been discovered near to the coast of Hampshire, Dorset and West Sussex (Field 2004; 2008). The same applies to some exceptional early Bronze Age burials. Their distribution is not limited to the rivers discharging into the English Channel, but there are problems in investigating parts of the surrounding area, for it is difficult to identify subsoil features in the local brickearths, nor do they respond well to aerial reconnaissance. It is worth remembering that this is the part of the study area with the easiest access to the monuments on the chalk. The same was surely true of the Isle of Wight where too much fieldwork remains unpublished.

Recent work in Langstone Harbour, and at Bouldner Cliff and Wootton-Quarr on the Isle of Wight (Allen and Gardiner 2000; Momber 2000; Tomalin *et al.* 2012), has provided further examples of deeply buried peat sequences like those known in Southampton and Portsmouth harbours (Godwin and Godwin 1940; Everard 1954). The Mesolithic rapid sea-level rise of *c.* 100 m had a profound effect on the landscape and the availability of resources, and subsequent coastal attrition has removed or submerged parts of the Neolithic landscape, some of which survive in the current subtidal and submarine landscape. Just as work on the Severn Estuary and the South Wales coastline has demonstrated the presence of important and unique archaeological evidence (structures, economic and landscape development evidence and very human histories including the presence of the footprints of children), there is good reason to believe that comparable data exist on the Solent fringes.

Questions of prehistoric geography suggest another observation. For a long time the prehistory of southern England was been written using models devised for the archaeology of Wessex. But where did Wessex end? Was its northern limit along the Berkshire Downs, where the Bronze Age barrow cemetery at Lambourn is very similar to those on Salisbury Plain, or did it reach as far as the River Thames, where the monuments at Radley Barrow Hills also share similar characteristics? It is worth considering whether such monuments were typical or exceptional. In the same way, it is certainly tempting to compare the major groups of sites at Dorchester-on-Thames and Stanton Harcourt with similar concentrations of henges and round barrows on the Wessex chalk, but this is to overlook a vital difference. Enclosures like Durrington Walls, Marden or Mount Pleasant are associated with enormous numbers of artefacts and animal bones. In the superficially similar monuments of the Thames Valley they do not occur. Nor are they found at Avebury. Although the latter site is located on the chalk, it is at the headwaters of the River Kennet and directly linked to the Thames by this major tributary. Perhaps it might be wiser to think in terms of two related but largely autonomous areas, and to study each in its own terms.

The archaeology of the Chilterns raises a similar problem. To the south this area is obviously related to the archaeology of the Middle Thames, but to the north it overlooks an extensive tract of lower ground which extends beyond the county of Buckinghamshire, and thus outside the study area. In some phases its archaeology has close connections with that of the East Midlands (Bradley 2006). As in many other cases, it is impossible to discuss the earlier prehistory of the Solent-Thames region without transgressing its boundaries.

Chronology

Finally, it is essential to make proper use of current chronologies. Unfortunately, the most detailed sequence applies to only one area: the Upper Thames and the Cotswolds (Whittle, Barclay *et al.* 2007). No doubt it will play a part in future research, but at present this model should not be used across a larger region; indeed, a different phasing is already proposed for the Avebury area. Otherwise the period labels applied to earlier prehistory are rather unsatisfactory and say more about the development of the discipline than they do about the material being studied (Whittle and Bayliss 2007).

It is not quite clear when the Neolithic period began or when the Mesolithic ended. Nor has it been demonstrated that the artefact assemblages to which these terms refer were ever actually used together. At present the Mesolithic/Neolithic transition may have happened by 4000 BC or as late as 3800 BC (Whittle 2007). That has important implications for the rate of change. Early Neolithic ceramics were undecorated, and certain styles of pottery and monuments can be assigned to a Middle Neolithic phase, but that scheme does not extend to surface flintwork which provides one of the main clues to the distribution of settlement.

There have been changes in the dating of Neolithic pottery and it is now known that Peterborough Ware was used during the Middle Neolithic period; before it had been assigned to the Late Neolithic. That has important implications for the classification and chronology of field monuments. The Late Neolithic period saw the end of that ceramic tradition and its gradual replacement by Grooved Ware. It is possible to identify the flint artefacts of the Late Neolithic but the same technology continued with little modification into the early metal age, so that once again different categories of material cannot be dated with the same amount of precision.

The problem does not end with the first use of metalwork. It would be logical (and consistent with Continental usage) to talk of a Copper Age associated with the first use of Beaker pottery, but British archaeologists have taken a different course, writing either of a 'metal-using Neolithic' or assigning this phase, quite inappropriately, to an 'Early Bronze Age'. Finer subdivisions have been suggested on the basis of Beaker pottery and the classification of the oldest metal artefacts, but these schemes need finer resolution through radiocarbon dating. The first use of bronze followed at about 2200 BC, and the period between then and the beginning of the middle Bronze Age is subdivided on the basis of the artefacts found in burials and hoards. Such work requires further refinement, as there is practically no absolute dating evidence for the graves of the Wessex Early Bronze Age. In any case it is hard to apply such schemes to surface finds or to discoveries of domestic sites.

As a result of these difficulties, the account that follows must be expressed in very general terms. Except where more exact information is available it will distinguish between just three periods: an earlier Neolithic which combines the early and middle phases and ran from about 4000 to 3000 BC or a little later; a late (here later) Neolithic period extending to about 2200 BC; and an early Bronze Age which lasted until the middle of the 2nd millennium BC.

The Earlier Neolithic

Landscape, settlement and land use

The earliest Neolithic settlement: transitions

Although the study area extends down to the English Channel coast, there is little evidence for how the Neolithic period began or for the respective roles of indigenous hunter gatherers and immigrants from the Continent. Even so, enough is known to establish that cereals, domesticated livestock and fine pottery had all been introduced from the European mainland (Whittle and Cummings 2007). The remains of cereals are mostly found towards the beginning of the Neolithic period, and wild plant foods, particularly hazelnuts, are more common during subsequent phases (Hey *et al.* 2011b; Plate 7.2). Wild animals, however, contributed little to the diet, and some species may have been hunted for their pelts (Serjeantson 2006, 119-21).

There are certain areas in which it is possible to compare the distributions of artefacts belonging to both Mesolithic and Neolithic traditions. The clearest evidence probably comes from the Kennet Valley where there is evidence for a long Mesolithic sequence (Hey *et al.* 2011b). The local environment had been modified by burning, and it seems possible that salmon fishing was important as well as the hunting of large game. Although the river rises in the heart of the Avebury complex, the distributions of diagnostic Mesolithic and Neolithic material only partially overlap (Richards 1978; Whittle 1990). In particular, there is less Neolithic evidence than one might expect from the valley between Hungerford and the confluence of the Kennet and the Thames (Ford 1987a). This may form part of a wider pattern as fieldwork across the Dorset border in Cranborne Chase suggests that the distribution of earlier Neolithic artefacts and monuments complemented that of late Mesolithic rod microliths. A similar pattern has been postulated in the Windrush Valley and part of the middle Thames Valley (Barclay 2000; 2007).

0   100 mm

Plate 7.2 Lump of Early Neolithic bread from Yarnton, Oxfordshire, *copyright OA*

In other cases artefacts belonging to both traditions are found together, but it is impossible to tell whether they were used simultaneously. That is true on the clay-with-flints which mantles areas of the Hampshire chalk, and the same applies to the evidence from sites in some of the major river valleys, such as the Eton Rowing Course on the Thames or Chesham on the Colne (Gardiner 1988; Holgate 1988; Hey and Barclay 2007; Allen *et al.* 2013). Unless deeply stratified deposits like those in the Fenland can be found it will be difficult to make much use of this evidence. A suitable site was recorded in the 1930s in the Newtown Estuary on the Isle of Wight (IWCAHES 2000). In any case a radiocarbon chronology is essential. One site where this has been achieved is the chambered cairn at Ascott-under-Wychwood, which had been built over a land surface with successive episodes of Mesolithic and Neolithic occupation (Benson and Whittle 2007).

Resource exploitation

It is clear that land was being cleared from the beginning of this period, although there is insufficient environmental evidence from the study area to shed much light on this process. On the other hand, small-scale excavations on the Hampshire/Wiltshire border have located extensive groups of flint mines at Easton Down and Martin's Clump (Fowler 1986). They were producing axes suitable for felling trees. Much less is known about these complexes than their well-known equivalents on the South Downs where the main period of production was during the earlier Neolithic. Martin's Clump has one radiocarbon date from the very beginning of this period, but the only date from Easton Down spans the middle and late Neolithic periods and its reliability has been questioned (Barber *et al.* 1999). There is not enough evidence to establish the chronology of the complex as a whole. It has been claimed that there were other flint mines at Peppard Common in south Oxfordshire (Peake 1913), but here it seems more likely that a medieval chalk quarry had been dug through a surface scatter of Neolithic artefacts.

Occupation sites and structures

It is commonly supposed that evidence of earlier Neolithic settlement is difficult to identify. To some extent this is true, as some of the excavated assemblages are very small. Moreover, much of the relevant material may have been deposited in pits when a living site was abandoned, making it particularly difficult to locate from surface finds; that was particularly true during the middle Neolithic phase (J Thomas 1999; Pollard 1999; Lamdin-Whymark 2008). Such pits can be found in isolation or as clearly-defined clusters. They may also be scattered over an extensive area of land. It is hard to interpret these patterns, which presumably reflect differences in the duration and intensity of occupation, although it is clear from radiocarbon dating that certain preferred locations were returned to several times. On the other hand, large scale field survey has been quite successful in establishing the extent of Neolithic settlement in a number of different areas. That is particularly true around the Goring Gap in the Thames Valley where the mapping of artefacts in the modern ploughsoil has documented a progressive expansion in the settled area, extending from the land beside the river onto the lower slopes of the Chilterns (Ford 1987b). More evidence has been recovered by surface collection around the confluence of the Thames and the Ock, in East Berkshire, the Avon and Meon valleys and again on the west Berkshire Downs (information from Abingdon Area Archaeological Society; Ford 1987a; Richards 1978; Field 2008). They are consistent with the broader patterns identified in studies of provenanced museum and private collections by Julie Gardiner and Robin Holgate (Gardiner 1988; Holgate 1988).

Recent fieldwork in two areas has added a new dimension to these studies. The first is the Middle Thames near to Eton (Plate 7.3). At the Eton Rowing Course it seems that earlier Neolithic settlement took place close to the river, but in this case the evidence was not a small flint scatter or a group of pits, but extensive middens that included large quantities of artefacts and faunal remains (Allen et al. 2004; 2013). Smaller foci were certainly identified nearby, one of them where arrowheads were being made (Lamdin-Whymark 2008). Again such discoveries raise the question of whether certain places were occupied more intensively, or for longer periods, than others. It may be significant that until these deposits were found by excavation, the densest surface scatters of earlier Neolithic artefacts came from the sites of causewayed enclosures. There is at least one such monument near to the middens at the

Eton Rowing Course, so the similarity between such deposits may be more than a coincidence (Plate 7.4). Indeed, given the dating evidence from such monuments, the activities associated with the earliest middens may be the precursors of those associated with enclosures (Bradley 2006; Lamdin-Whymark 2008). Another important field project took place on Quarr Beach on the Isle of Wight where ephemeral timber structures are still preserved in the intertidal zone. They probably result from specialised activities rather than sedentary occupation, and include the remains of three timber trackways and those of a possible fish trap located in a palaeochannel (Tomalin et al. 2012).

Such evidence is exceptional. In discussing earlier Neolithic settlement it is usual to distinguish between three widespread phenomena: occupation sites characterised by pits; those where occupation debris had accumulated on a land surface; and the few examples where traces of buildings survive. That may be inappropriate, for it is clear that even where pits or tree holes were filled with a carefully selected group of material it had probably been collected from a midden (Evans et al. 1999; Lamdin-Whymark 2008). In an initial phase these deposits were usually placed in the hollows left by fallen trees, but in later phases pits were used in a similar way. They may have been dug for the purpose. It is important to establish why some middens were left intact whilst others were dispersed. Guttmann (2005) has suggested that this happened because they were reused as cultivation plots. In the same way, the striking absence of houses from settlement sites in the study area can be interpreted in more than one way. It may provide

Plate 7.3 Uncovering the early Neolithic midden at the Eton Rowing Course, Dorney, Buckinghamshire, *copyright OA*

Plate 7.4 Aerial view of the Thames showing gravel terraces, floodplain and palaeochannels at Dorney, Buckinghamshire

evidence of a mobile pattern of settlement in which few places were occupied continuously or for long, but it is also possible that the domestic buildings did not make use of uprights bedded in the subsoil. The discovery of a plank-built trackway in Somerset which dates from the beginning of this phase may be relevant here (Coles and Coles 1986).

The structural evidence from the study area is meagre, but it gives the same impression of diversity. There was at least one timber structure beneath the cairn at Ascott-under-Wychwood on the Cotswolds (Benson and Whittle 2007), as there was at the comparable site of Hazleton North in Gloucestershire (Saville 1990). These were accompanied by middens. The excavated features at Ascott allow more than one interpretation. They may either represent two small buildings with a hearth in between them, or the excavated postholes might mark the positions of the end walls of a rectangular structure 9 m long and 4 m wide; that is suggested by the distribution of artefacts on the site. On the other hand, traces of a larger building of a kind more familiar in Ireland and Western Britain have been found on the Thames floodplain at Yarnton (Hey *et al.* in prep.; Plate 7.5). It was so substantial – it measured about 20 m by 14 m – that similar features would have been recognised on other sites if they had occurred. The Yarnton 'house' may have been a domestic dwelling, but, like the large timber halls of this phase in Scotland, it was associated with a limited number of artefacts. It also included a small amount of cremated bone. A slightly later structure, perhaps

belonging to the end of the 4th millennium cal BC, has recently been identified at Horton, Berkshire. It was *c.* 8 m by 5 m, and defined by a wall trench in which uprights and the traces of plank walling could be discerned (Alistair Barclay pers. comm.; Hey *et al.* 2011b, Figs 11.8 and 11.11)

Ceremony, ritual and religion

The domestic site at Ascott-under-Wychwood was buried beneath a chambered cairn (Benson and Whittle 2007). That connection is important, for the monuments of earlier Neolithic date are complex structures. There are three kinds to consider. They probably appeared in the study area in the following order: first, long barrows and related monuments, then causewayed enclosures, and, finally, cursuses. Their distributions are not the same. The mounds are found across most parts of the Solent-Thames region, but causewayed enclosures and cursuses are mainly a feature of the Thames, its tributaries and the southern edge of the Cotswolds. The contrast should not be exaggerated, as causewayed enclosures are common in Sussex, Wiltshire and Dorset, and cursuses and related monuments occur on the Wessex chalk.

Funerary monuments

The long mounds show considerable diversity. Properly speaking, they can be divided between barrows on the chalk and the river gravels, and cairns on the Oxfordshire

Plate 7.5   Neolithic house from Yarnton, Oxfordshire, *copyright OA*

Cotswolds. Other structures, like that at Holdenhurst on the Channel coast, were partly built out of turf. Although the forms of the mounds range from sub-oval monuments to long rectangular structures, their building was often the last event in a lengthy sequence (Field 2006). The wooden structures concealed beneath them are very varied, and the same is true to a lesser extent of the megalithic chambers identified on the Cotswolds and the Berkshire Downs (Darvill 2004).

Some of the best-excavated structures are actually the most problematical. The Holdenhurst long barrow near Christchurch did not include a mortuary structure apart from a slight oval mound (Piggott 1937), whereas the example at Nutbane was preceded by a sequence of large timber buildings (Mallet Morgan 1959). In this case the finished monument was set on fire: a practice more common in Northern Britain. The megalithic tombs are almost as diverse. The cairn at Ascott-under-Wychwood was constructed in a series of bays and underwent some modification before it was completed (Benson and Whittle 2007). The deposits of human remains were enclosed within side chambers of quite modest proportions and accumulated over a period of between three and five generations. Wayland's Smithy was a more massive trapezoidal monument with a considerable forecourt bounded by tall standing stones (Whittle 1991; Plate 7.6). They provided access to a set of transepted chambers conceived on an equally extravagant scale. An unusual feature is that it overlay the remains of a smaller oval barrow with a mortuary structure defined by two split tree trunks. In this case the

deposits of human remains had accumulated over a single generation. On the Cotswolds the equivalents of these early timber structures could be the portal tombs of the Whispering Knights and the Hoar Stone, neither of which may have covered by a cairn (Lambrick 1988).

Little is known about the contents of these stone chambers, but Ascott-under-Wychwood was associated with the bones of about twenty people whose remains had been treated in a variety of different ways. Some were introduced to the monument as intact bodies, but other corpses were incomplete. The timber monument at Wayland's Smithy was significantly later in date (Whittle, Bayliss and Wysocki 2007). It housed the remains of about fourteen people who had been placed there as intact bodies; few of the bones from the megalithic tomb on the same site now survive. In neither case do the burials seem to have acknowledged any differences of status, although it is clear that only a small section of the population can be represented by the finds from such monuments. At both Wayland's Smithy and Ascott-under-Wychwood at least one, and possibly more, of the people buried had been killed by an arrow.

Wayland's Smithy illustrates another important point, for the earliest mound was built between forty and a hundred years after the burials were deposited (*ibid.*). Although an entire monograph has been devoted to the long barrows of Hampshire (RCHME 1979), they had little in common until their use came to an end. It was only then that a mound or cairn was built to 'close' these sites. Moreover, the distinctive structures that were often concealed beneath them can also be found in isolation,

Plate 7.6 Long barrow at Wayland's Smithy, Oxfordshire, *copyright OA*

although this is rarely acknowledged. It is probably true of rectangular ditched enclosures, like the example at Dorchester-on-Thames which was associated with a human jaw, and of the distinctive structures in which other human remains were deposited (Whittle *et al.* 1992). An isolated example was identified at Radley Barrow Hills (Bradley 1992), and another was inside an insubstantial enclosure at New Wintles Farm in the Upper Thames (Kenward 1982). There were Neolithic graves that may never have been accompanied by a mound, like the small cemetery outside the Abingdon causewayed enclosure (Barclay and Halpin 1999) or two other flat graves found during excavation at the Eton Rowing Course (Allen *et al.* 2000; 2013).

Not all the mortuary monuments were long barrows or long cairns. Oval barrows were at least as important and may have had a wider distribution than is apparent without excavation. Such structures had a lengthy history and were often defined on three sides by a ditch which was later extended to close off access to the monument. Again they occur in a variety of different sizes, from the ephemeral oval mounds found at sites like Radley Barrow Hills to more considerable earthworks. An U-ditched barrow at Horton in the Middle Thames was later enclosed by a ring ditch associated with Peterborough Ware (Ford and Pine 2003), whilst the recently re-excavated site at Whiteleaf on the Chilterns was probably associated with a timber structure comparable to that at Wayland's Smithy (Hey *et al.* 2007). Again it was not buried immediately, and the barrow was not built over it for another hundred years. That earthwork was rebuilt several centuries later towards the end of the middle Neolithic period. Other monuments of this type covered shallow graves, sometimes those of intact bodies accompanied by distinctive artefacts. A variant of the oval barrow is an earthwork enclosure at Freshwater on the Isle of Wight (Tomalin 1980). It shares its characteristic ground plan but in this case no mound was constructed.

The study area also contains the sites of a number of Neolithic round barrows. The best known example is at Linch Hill Corner near Stanton Harcourt in the Upper Thames, where a single body was accompanied by grave goods similar to those from the oval mound at Barrow Hills (Grimes 1960). Other examples are recorded at Mount Farm, Berinsfield and at Newnham Murren, Wallingford in Oxfordshire, at Park Farm, Lambourn in Berkshire and Five Knolls nearby in Bedfordshire (Lambrick 2010; Moorey 1982; Richards 1986-90; J Dyer 1991). There may have been another example at Winnall Down in Hampshire (Fasham 1985). It is likely that similar monuments once existed across most of the study area, although they have seldom been recognised. That has happened for two reasons. Some examples have been wrongly identified as 'hengiform enclosures': the sites of circular earthworks allied to the henge monuments of the later Neolithic period. In some cases it seems more likely that the ditch enclosed a mound. Sites have also been dated to that phase because they are associated with Peterborough Ware, a style of pottery which is now known to have developed during the later

4th millennium BC. Neolithic round barrows had a shorter history than was once supposed, and in England there is no convincing evidence that they were employed for burials between about 3000 BC and the Beaker period (Bradley 2006). It is likely that round and oval barrows originated at much the same time as the classic long mounds and long cairns, but it remains a possibility that in southern England they were used after the building of the larger mortuary monuments had lapsed.

How were all these structures related to other features of the landscape? Their relationship to the settlement evidence is very varied. There are certainly cases in which substantial monuments were created within the domestic landscape. If the chambered cairn at Ascott-under-Wychwood was built over an earlier occupation site, the old land surface beneath Wayland's Smithy had been tilled (Benson and Whittle 2007; Whittle 1991, 92). There are also cases in which prominent mounds, like the recently identified example at Uffington in Oxfordshire (Miles *et al.* 2003), may have overlooked more distant areas of settlement (see also Plate 7.7). On the chalk individual monuments were often situated along the heads or flanks of valleys overlooking lower ground. Their distribution sometimes follows the springline. But all these examples relate to the 'classic' forms of monuments that are still preserved on the downland and the Cotswolds. They are massive structures associated with substantial ditches or quarries. The remains of such monuments would be easy to identify from the air or by geophysical survey, and yet their distribution rarely extends down into the river valleys. There are a few examples in the Upper Thames (Hey *et al.* 2011b), but they are quite exceptional. Otherwise the lower ground contains a much wider variety of monuments, including smaller mounds and enclosures, oval or U-ditched barrows, round barrows and ring ditches (Bradley 2006). Most of them have been identified as a result of excavation on the gravels, and it is likely that they were more common than presently appears. It seems quite possible that they were also more closely integrated into the settled landscape – perhaps it was only the larger structures that had to be viewed from a distance

It is often suggested that the distribution of long barrows was closely allied to that of causewayed enclosures, but this is another case in which the evidence from the Wessex chalk has been treated as the norm. It is certainly true that there are such enclosures around the edges of the main concentrations of long barrows in Sussex, Dorset and Wiltshire, but this does not seem to have happened in Hampshire or on the Chilterns. Nor is a similar pattern clearly recognisable on the Cotswolds. Instead, the distribution of causewayed enclosures extends along the Thames and its tributaries (Plate 7.8), with significant gaps between the main concentrations of monuments (Oswald *et al.* 2001). If these enclosures are connected with mortuary monuments, then they are probably the small oval and circular structures associated with inhumation burials. The closest connection between the two types is probably at Abingdon where the Radley oval barrow was one of a pair built alongside an older

Plate 7.7 Long barrow at Inkpen Beacon, Combe Gibbet, *copyright West Berkshire Council*

Plate 7.8 Cropmark of the causewayed enclosure at Buckland, Oxfordshire, *copyright English Heritage National Monuments Record*

causewayed enclosure. Like that enclosure, the excavated monument was associated with carefully placed deposits of antler and human bone (Bradley 1992). The primary burials were of two adults associated with an arrowhead, a polished knife and a belt ornament.

Ceremonial monuments

In fact the Abingdon causewayed enclosure is the only example in the Solent-Thames corridor to have been excavated on any scale. Even this work poses problems, for none of the excavations took place recently. Leeds (1927a; 1928) examined the site before it was generally accepted that the distribution of such monuments extended beyond the chalk, and Avery's work was conducted and published on the premise that this was an occupation site (Avery 1982). It is possible to recognise some features that Abingdon shares with more recently investigated sites – the presence of inhumation burials and disarticulated human bones, the lavish consumption of meat, the deposition of considerable deposits of cultural material in its inner ditch – but the work was not on a sufficient scale to permit a fuller discussion. At one time it seemed possible that its earthworks were constructed in sequence – first a causewayed ditch associated with deposits of cultural material, and then a continuous defensive barrier enclosing a larger area (Case 1956a) – but this hypothesis was based on analogy with monuments in other regions and is not supported by radiocarbon dating (Bradley 1986). Still less can be said about similar enclosures at Gatehampton (T Allen et al.1995) and Eton Wick (Ford 1991-3) where the excavation merely confirmed the Neolithic character of the monuments. The latter site is chiefly of interest because of its proximity to the middens at Eton Rowing Lake. The small scale of the fieldwork carried out at these sites needs to be redressed in the future.

Both long barrows and causewayed enclosures form parts of broader traditions with their origins in Continental Europe. That is not true of cursus monuments or bank barrows, which were first built in Scotland. The earliest examples were contemporary with causewayed enclosures in the south, but those found in the study area are significantly later in date (Barclay and Bayliss 1999). In some parts of the country cursuses or bank barrows cut across the sites of older causewayed enclosures, but in the Solent-Thames corridor these different kinds of earthwork were generally located in different areas (Barclay et al. 2003; Loveday 2006). Although both groups could be close to the Thames and its tributaries, cursuses seem to have been built in the gaps in the distribution of existing enclosures. The classification of these earthworks has created difficulties. All are elongated monuments which generally take the form of long rectangular or oval enclosures with an internal bank, but the unusually narrow example at North Stoke (Case 1982a) was probably a bank barrow with a central spine of excavated gravel – there would not have been enough room for an open space within it. In fact the remains of an axial bank can be recognised on aerial photographs of the site.

The cursus monuments of the study area tend to be found in groups, although it is not clear whether they were all used at the same time. At Drayton it seems possible that two of these monuments were built end to end on either side of a stream (Barclay et al. 2003), but in other cases they ran roughly parallel to a major watercourse or approached it at right angles. Thus the Dorchester-on-Thames cursus approaches the River Thame but it may also be aligned on the midwinter sunrise (Bradley and Chambers 1988). None of the monuments attains the exceptional length of the Dorset or Rudston cursuses, nor is the modest bank barrow at North Stoke of similar length to the recently excavated example at Stanwell in the Middle Thames.

Rather than causewayed enclosures, cursuses are associated with oval barrows, with U-ditched barrows or enclosures and with smaller rectangular earthworks, all of which seem to be related to the tradition of long mounds. The Drayton cursus is found with one of the few conventional long barrows on the river gravels and points towards an excavated site associated with earlier Neolithic pottery at Corporation Farm, Abingdon (Barclay et al. 2003). This has been interpreted as an early henge but may have been another oval barrow. In fact the precise relationship between these features varies from site to site. An individual monument may be aligned on an older enclosure, as happened at Dorchester-on-Thames and North Stoke (Whittle et al. 1992; Case 1982a); it may incorporate existing monuments in its path, for example at Dorchester-on-Thames and perhaps the nearby site at Stadhampton; or other mounds may be built beside it, reflecting its long axis. The clearest examples of this pattern are found at Drayton and Benson (Barclay et al. 2003).

It is difficult to say much about the roles played by these extraordinary structures even though a substantial length of the Dorchester-on-Thames cursus has been stripped and smaller excavations have taken place at Drayton and at Lechlade just outside the region in Gloucestershire. Few artefacts have been found on these sites and until comparatively recently it was assumed, quite wrongly, that they were built during the later Neolithic period. That was partly because it had been difficult to find suitable samples for radiocarbon dating. Bank barrows may be interpreted as massively extended long mounds, and cursuses perhaps stood in a similar relationship to the elongated enclosures associated with mortuary monuments. It is certainly true that their main association is with human remains. Few of these have been found, and even fewer have been directly dated, but disarticulated fragments of human bone are associated with the monuments at Dorchester-on-Thames and Drayton (Whittle et al. 1992; Barclay et al. 2003). Still more important is the way in which these structures seem to be integrated with Neolithic funerary monuments of kinds described earlier in this chapter. Although cursuses are often described as processional avenues, not all of them are provided with entrances and this interpretation may be incorrect. Alternatively, they may originally have been open, and the terminals were

Plate 7.9 Peterborough Ware pit from Dorney, Buckinghamshire, *copyright OA*

added later to 'close' these monuments (Barclay and Harding 1999 and papers therein). The problem needs investigating by targeted excavation.

The areas around the causewayed enclosures and cursuses include a number of pits, some containing whole vessels, as at Lake End Road West, Dorney, Buckinghamshire (Plates 7.9; 7.10), others whose contents had apparently been selected from middens. The Middle Thames Valley, however, also has evidence for the purposeful deposition of artefacts in the river itself, some of which may have accompanied human remains (Bradley 1990). The main artefacts selected for this purpose were axeheads, often of non-local origin,

and vessels of Peterborough Ware. This practice continued during the later Neolithic period.

The Later Neolithic

Landscape, settlement and land use

It is not always easy to synchronise the chronology of Neolithic monuments with that of flintwork. Still more rarely is it possible to harmonise the dating of this material with the currency of particular pottery styles. Nevertheless the results of fieldwalking still provide some indications of the changing pattern of settlement.

Field surveys and studies of older collections show that a greater area of the landscape was occupied during this phase (Holgate 1988; Gardiner 1988). Recent work in Langstone Harbour suggests that more use was also being made of specialised environments (Allen and Gardiner 2000), and the same may be true on the Isle of Wight where ephemeral wooden structures were still being built in the intertidal zone at Quarr and at Pelhamfields Beach (Tomalin *et al.* 2012). At the same time, there are indications that certain areas were being more intensively occupied during this phase. One was almost certainly the clay-with-flints, which was both an important focus of settlement and a significant source of lithic raw material. The density of surface finds increased and so did their diversity. No longer are settlements marked by small scatters of worked flints. Instead domestic debris spreads over a more extensive area. To some extent this is due to different cultural practices as

Plate 7.10 Peterborough Ware bowl from Dorney, Buckinhamshire, *copyright OA*

there is less reason to believe that the remains of middens were buried when occupation ceased (Lamdin-Whymark 2008). Even so it seems likely that occupation sites were larger and that settlement was more sustained.

Occupation sites and structures

Unfortunately, there is little structural evidence to relate to these general trends. The main information is still provided by the contents of pits, some of which were carefully organised on their deposition in the ground (J Thomas 1999). This is a particular feature of those associated with Grooved Ware and is most apparent in the vicinity of monuments (Barclay 1999; Bradley 2006), although the distribution of later Neolithic pits extends into areas like the Vale of Aylesbury where such earthworks have yet to be found. Few intact surfaces have been preserved, although it did happen at a number of sites on the Isle of Wight where a large number of artefacts were preserved beneath later mounds (Grinsell and Sherwin 1940; Tomalin 1980). There is similar evidence from the Bronze Age round barrow at Bishop's Waltham in Hampshire and from similar sites on the Berkshire Down (Ashbee 1957; Richards 1986-90). Only one domestic building can be attributed to this phase. This is a sub-rectangular structure at Yarnton in the Upper Thames that was associated with Grooved Ware (Hey et al. 2011b, Fig. 11.28). There is comparable evidence from recent excavations at Durrington Walls, but in Cranborne Chase the buildings of this same date are small and circular (Barrett et al. 1991). It is not clear whether the use of round houses was a new development, as a group of post holes at Yarnton dating from about 3600 BC is interpreted as a small circular building (Hey et al. 2011b, Fig. 11.12). Later Neolithic buildings were often insubstantial, and the same applies to those of the Beaker ceramic phase which seem to have been equally ephemeral. Their remains are usually marked by small concentrations of stake holes, like those at Snail Down in Wiltshire. None is recorded from the Solent-Thames corridor, but pits associated with Beaker pottery are widely distributed.

Ceremony, ritual and religion

The archaeology of this period is characterised by discontinuity. The forms of the major monuments do not seem to be directly related to those of the previous phase, nor are they always found in the same areas. Moreover, the Grooved Ware tradition which is usually associated with the construction and use of henges seems to have originated in Northern Britain and possibly in Ireland (Harding 2003; Bradley 2006).

The significance of these points is not always appreciated, perhaps because the field archaeology of the Wessex chalk has distorted prehistorians' perceptions of its wider context. For example, it is often asserted that causewayed enclosures were the direct precursors of henge monuments. That seems most unlikely as there is an interval of perhaps five hundred years between the

uses of these traditions in the south. Moreover, the two kinds of enclosures actually have little in common apart from an approximately circular outline. The last diminutive earthworks in the older tradition seem to be exactly circular, but they still possessed internal banks and were employed in the same ways as their predecessors. One example was the earthwork at Stonehenge, which has lent its name to a style of prehistoric architecture to which it does not belong. In the Solent-Thames corridor its closest counterpart may be a small enclosure at Radley (Oswald et al. 2001). This is known only from crop marks and remains unexcavated.

There seems no reason to postulate the continuous development of enclosures in southern England when the earliest henges have been identified in Northern Britain, where they developed together with Grooved Ware. Both were adopted in lowland England at a later date, although it is unlikely that enormous monuments such as Mount Pleasant and Durrington Walls were among the first to be built there (Bradley 2006). Even in Wessex it is clear that smaller henges predate these massive structures. So do the earliest deposits of Grooved Ware.

The evidence from the Wessex chalk is deceptive in yet another way, for it has been used to emphasise the spatial continuity between causewayed enclosures and major henges. There are problems with this scheme, for the distances between supposedly successive monuments actually vary greatly, and this interpretation was put forward before it was recognised that cursuses were used in between the latest causewayed enclosures and the construction of henges. Nevertheless it had been tempting to postulate a process of social evolution extending throughout the Neolithic period and even into the Early Bronze Age. That attractive notion must be abandoned.

There is no such evidence from the study area. Here there are four major henges, all of them in the Upper Thames (Barclay et al. 1996), the last only recently identified by Ford beneath the city of Oxford (Plate 7.11; Hey et al. 2011b). None corresponds to the site of a causewayed enclosure, but one is located beside an older cursus. Moreover even these henges are smaller than the well known examples on the Wessex chalk, the only exception being the group of earthwork enclosures at Knowlton. Moreover, the henges identified in the Thames Valley lack some of the principal associations of the well known examples on the downland. They are not accompanied by large circular mounds like those at Knowlton, Marden or Silbury Hill, nor is there any evidence of nearby palisaded enclosures such as those at West Kennet or Greyhound Yard, Dorchester, Dorset. Two of the sites in the study area have been excavated on a large scale and did not enclose enormous timber structures of the type found in Dorset, Wiltshire or south-west England (Whittle et al. 1992; Barclay et al. 1995). Not only are these monuments of a rather different kind, none has been discovered in the remaining parts of the Solent-Thames corridor, where later Neolithic monuments appear to be rare or absent.

Plate 7.11   Henge monument ditch at Keble College, Oxford, *copyright TVAS*

The same applies to the region east of the study area. Possible henges have been suggested on the South Downs in Sussex, but none is convincing, and only a single example is clearly documented in Kent.

One of the Oxfordshire monuments, Big Rings at Dorchester-on-Thames, is even more distinctive (Whittle *et al.* 1992; Loveday 1999). Like Condicote on the Gloucestershire Cotswolds, it was defined not by one ditch but by two, and in this case the earthworks were widely spaced. This unusual procedure can only be paralleled among the henge monuments of north-east England, again emphasising the point that this tradition was not of local origin (Harding 2003). The sequence of monuments at Dorchester-on-Thames has further implications, for the enclosure of Big Rings was built alongside a major cursus. There is no evidence of a causewayed enclosure in the vicinity.

The Dorchester-on-Thames cursus had led between a series of pre-existing earthworks, including an oval ditched enclosure and the likely remains of a round barrow. This alignment faced the midwinter sunrise and seems to have retained its importance for several hundred years (Bradley and Chambers 1988). During the later Neolithic period a series of small circular monuments was built in its path and others were constructed just outside it. Despite the lapse of time, they shared its orientation. Most of these structures had a single entrance, but their perimeters were defined in a variety of different ways. Some were surrounded by ditches; some were probably circles of pits, although this has been questioned (Gibson 1992); and in at least one case there was a ring of massive upright posts. Individual examples were rebuilt, but it is not clear how many of them were used simultaneously. Even so, it is probably

correct to compare them with the features of a henge. There was a similar pit circle on the nearby site at Mount Farm (Lambrick 2010).

When the monuments at Dorchester-on-Thames went out of out use they provided the focus for deposits of cremated human bone (Atkinson *et al.* 1951). That evidence has been misunderstood in an attempt to relate these sites to the archaeological sequence at Stonehenge. The cremations were located in the upper fillings of the ditches and post sockets, and do not appear to have occurred in primary contexts. For that reason it is illogical to describe the monuments as 'enclosed cremation cemeteries'.

The major henge at Dorchester-on-Thames is the site of Big Rings, excavated in the 1950s and published after an almost unprecedented delay in 1992 (Whittle *et al.* 1992). This site poses problems, for the excavation report claims that it was of Beaker date. Of course that might be correct, but the section drawings of ditch raise the possibility that only the secondary filling of this earthwork was excavated; the primary levels may not have been identified – a common occurrence on the river gravels. This monument incorporated a smaller circular enclosure in one of its entrances and instituted a new alignment for the complex. There was no sign of any post or stone setting inside it.

The Big Rings has some features in common with the other extensively excavated henge, the Devil's Quoits at Stanton Harcourt (Barclay *et al.* 1995). Again the first excavator did not recognise the lower filling of the ditch, although he did identify the sockets for a single ring of monoliths inside the enclosure (Grimes 1960). Subsequent work by Margaret Gray not only established the true scale of the earthwork perimeter, it also found a small circular post setting in the centre of the monument. In this case, it was possible to suggest that the earthwork predated the adoption of Beaker ceramics. There is nothing to show whether the banks and ditch were the first structures on this site. Whilst that sequence is widely assumed, it has been questioned by recent research and in some cases it is demonstrably incorrect (Bradley 2006). In the same way, it is usually supposed that timber structures were earlier than those of stone, but it is perfectly possible that both these elements were combined in a single architectural scheme. Close to Devil's Quoits there were other monuments, whose dating remains uncertain, but one of them was a post circle not unlike the Later Neolithic structures associated with the cursus at Dorchester-on-Thames (Barclay 1995). There was also a circular ditched enclosure comparable to a small henge, and a series of pits containing Peterborough Ware and Grooved Ware.

Similar features are found at another site, Radley Barrow Hills, which was first used during the earlier Neolithic period. Here two oval barrows and a series of Neolithic burials had been located close to a causewayed enclosure (Barclay and Halpin 1999). Their histories may have overlapped, but in this case the earliest pit deposits are those associated with Grooved Ware, suggesting a hiatus of several hundred years between the first generations of monuments at Radley and those of the later Neolithic. When activity resumed, at least one new structure was built there. This was another small circular enclosure. It was associated with deposits of antler and with pottery in the Grooved Ware tradition, and in many respects it compares with the miniature henges at Stanton Harcourt and Dorchester-on-Thames. Perhaps their distribution will extend into other regions of the study area, but apart from an undated timber setting at Rockbourne on the edge of Cranborne Chase, a segmented ring ditch at Green Park, Reading, and a few examples on the Wessex chalk, this has yet to happen (Barrett et al. 1991; Brossler et al. 2004). Such monuments are difficult to identify – still less, to date – without total excavation, but it is possible that they really were more common in the north of the study area. Small monuments of similar character are often found in the Midlands and East Anglia and it is conceivable that they belong to a regional tradition that rarely extended far into the Solent-Thames corridor. That remains to be established in future work.

One of the pits at Barrow Hills included a bone point made from the ulna of a white-tailed eagle, and part of a Grooved Ware vessel decorated with two opposed spirals (Barclay and Halpin 1999). That provides another indication of the cultural connections between the study area and Northern Britain, for the same design has been identified in a variety of other media in the west of Scotland, Orkney, Anglesey and even in the Boyne Valley north of Dublin (Barclay 1999). A further set of long distance connections is illustrated by the movement of non-local artefacts to different parts of the study area. They consist of axeheads, most of them originating from quarries in highland Britain (Bradley and Edmonds 1993). They are quite common in the study area, although there are larger concentrations of such material around the major ceremonial centres of Wessex. In the study area they come from three different contexts. A small number have been discovered in pits together with later Neolithic artefacts, but others are chance finds. A significant proportion of the imported objects come from the River Thames in Berkshire and Buckinghamshire (Holgate 1988; Bradley 1990). The latter group lacks much dating evidence, but it does seem as if such artefacts were distributed over greater distances during the later Neolithic period. The areas where they had been made include Cornwall, Cumbria, North Wales and the East Midlands.

Yet another long distance connection may also be relevant here. This concerns the Rollright Stones on the Oxfordshire Cotswolds (Lambrick 1988). The form of this monument is unusual as the monoliths are closely spaced and define a circular enclosure with a single clearly defined entrance. In both respects this site is very different from the Devil's Quoits (Plate 7.12). The distinctive configuration of the Rollright Stones has features in common with a number of monuments in northern England which are assumed to be of later Neolithic date. This has not be been demonstrated by excavation, but one reason for stressing the exotic character of the Cotswold monument is that is its layout is very similar to that of the Swinside stone circle in Cumbria. Just as the henges at Dorchester-on-Thames and Condicote may refer to structures found in northeast England, the Rollright Stones represent another monument of exotic type.

Plate 7.12 Rollright Stones, Oxfordshire – view from the air, *copyright Rollright Trust*

Beaker settlement and the end of the Neolithic

Such long distance connections anticipate a still more drastic development. This was the appearance of Beaker pottery and the earliest metalwork: an assemblage with its origins in Continental Europe (Clarke 1970).

This is not the place to rehearse the complex arguments concerning the interpretation of Beakers and their associations, for that is a problem that extends far beyond the confines of the study area. It is quite possible that this material was first introduced by immigrants, but the only way of showing this unambiguously is through the isotopic analysis of human teeth. This method has certainly suggested the 'Amesbury Archer' was one such migrant, but it is necessary to take this approach to a large sample of human remains before any conclusion can be reached. Fortunately, this work is now in progress (The Beaker Isotope Project, University of Sheffield). Similar analysis of isotopes can also address the issue of the distance over which animals were grazed, traded and brought to ceremonial sites. In any case, the movement of people often forms only part of a more complex pattern of alliance and exchange and it seems improbable that the introduction of Beakers was any exception; if portable artefacts were moving over longer distances, that may have been true of marriage partners as well. Some combination of these different ideas might explain why the new kinds of material culture are so often associated with regions and even monuments that were important during the Grooved Ware phase. It does not follow that these developments were entirely peaceful. One of the people buried at Barrow Hills had probably been killed by an arrow, and archery equipment and daggers often feature among the grave goods of this period.

In the Solent-Thames corridor the earliest Beakers can be associated with copper artefacts and gold ornaments. Their appearance marks the inception of a new tradition of inhumation burial associated with small round barrows and with flat graves, but some of these were close to existing monuments (Bradley 2006; Garwood 2007). It may be no accident that the richly furnished burial at Amesbury was near to a Grooved Ware pit circle and not far from Woodhenge and Durrington Walls. In the same way, the earliest metalwork in the Upper Thames was associated with burials at Radley Barrow Hills, whilst there were others near to the Devils' Quoits (Barclay and Halpin 1999; Barclay *et al.* 1995). Yet another rich grave was associated with a round barrow immediately outside the north entrance of Big Rings, Dorchester-on-Thames (Whittle *et al.* 1992). Of course that simple equation does not apply to every case. A burial at Chilbolton in the Test valley contained gold ornaments like those at Barrow Hills but it was not associated with an older monument (Russel 1990). In fact there may have been considerable regional variation. Whilst the early Beaker graves in the Upper Thames could be located close to structures with an established significance, their counterparts in the Stonehenge area seem to have been set apart from the monument itself (Bradley 2006).

That is very striking, as Beaker pottery was perhaps associated with the first stone building on that famous site (Cleal *et al.* 1995). Its occurrence there forms part of a more general pattern, for ceramics of this kind were not only deposited in a number of Wessex henges, their distribution could even echo that of the existing deposits of Grooved Ware and other artefacts within these monuments. The same idea may be relevant to the interpretation of Big Rings, where a significant deposit of Beaker material was found in the enclosure ditch (Whittle *et al.* 1992). As suggested earlier, it may not date the original construction of the monument and could have been placed there during a later phase. The same was perhaps the case at Condicote on the Gloucestershire Cotswolds (Saville 1983).

The Early Bronze Age

As mentioned earlier, the definition of this period presents certain difficulties, if only because metal artefacts are found in such a limited number of contexts. Copper was alloyed with tin from approximately 2200 BC and from that period onwards other parts of the archaeological record began to change significantly. Although Beaker pottery remained in use, it was supplemented, and eventually replaced, by new ceramic styles. Round barrows became much more conspicuous features of the landscape and sometimes developed into entire cemeteries. At the same time, henge monuments gradually went out of use.

Landscape, settlement and land use

Few of these changes are clearly reflected in the settlement evidence from this phase, which is remarkably meagre. Beaker pits are quite widely distributed but provide less evidence of structured deposition than those associated with Grooved Ware. There are comparatively few pits associated with other early Bronze Age ceramic styles, and only occasionally can the lithic scatters of this period be distinguished from those of the later Neolithic, the main difference being the presence of small thumbnail scrapers and the use of barbed and tanged arrowheads (Gardiner 1988; Barclay *et al.* 1996). The greatest concentration of the latter type is in the area around Bournemouth and Christchurch that was formerly in Hampshire but now forms part of Dorset (Field 2008).

There is little structural evidence from this period. Excavation at Yarnton has identified the position of a small round house associated with sherds of Biconical Urn, and there was a series of post holes of similar date at Easton Lane, Winchester on the Hampshire chalk (Hey *et al.* 2011b, Fig. 13.9; Fasham *et al.* 1989). Another settlement associated with round houses was at Gore Down, Chale on the Isle of Wight (Currie 2002). One reason why such settlements have been so difficult to find is because the remains of domestic buildings were relatively slight. This is certainly suggested by a small stake-built structure preserved beneath an early Bronze

Age round barrow at Shrewton in Wiltshire (Green and Rollo-Smith 1984). Another possibility is that settlements were increasingly located in valleys where their remains might be buried beneath substantial deposits of hill wash. This has been demonstrated at a series of sites on the South Downs (Allen 2005a), and there is no reason why a similar situation could not have occurred more widely. Early Bronze Age deposits were preserved at Charnham Lane, Hungerford, in the Kennet Valley, and an early Bronze Age house was found at Yarnton beneath a layer of alluvium (Ford 2002; Hey *et al.* in prep.).

In three cases there are suggestions of more specialised activities. Recent fieldwork has recorded the remains of ephemeral timber structures on the foreshore of the Isle of Wight (Tomalin *et al.* 2012). Those at Fishbourne Beach and Quarr Beach have radiocarbon dates during this period. So do the burnt mounds at Little Marlow in Buckinghamshire which belong to an enigmatic class of field monument that is usually dated to the Later Bronze Age (Richmond *et al.* 2006). Other examples with similar dates are now known at the Eton Rowing Course and at Yarnton. Their function is still in doubt, and they may have been employed for cooking, as open air saunas or for a variety of industrial activities. The last of these specialised activities was the deposition of elaborate artefacts in the Thames and its tributaries. This continued during the early Bronze Age, but now the offerings included metalwork that might otherwise have been placed in graves (Bradley 1990). That is a special feature of the closing years of this period.

Ceremony, ritual and religion

The rarity of domestic sites is especially frustrating since so many burial mounds survive from this period, either as standing mounds or as ring ditches in cultivated land. Even so, it is clear that the settled area expanded. There are large numbers of round barrows in the New Forest, a region where there is little indication of sustained Neolithic activity (Field 2008). The same is true of the Hampshire Greensand. Both regions had been occupied during the Mesolithic period, but may have been used less intensively since that time. There are indications that the sites of some of these barrows had recently been cleared of woodland and that the local soils were unable to sustain a long period of settlement. One example was Ascot in Berkshire where a bell barrow sealed a series of spade furrows associated with cereal pollen (Bradley and Keith-Lucas 1975). Again the site had not been used for long before the monument was built. With the exception of a mound on Beaulieu Heath in Hampshire which contained an amber necklace, few artefacts are associated with these earthworks.

As the evidence from these two areas shows, the distribution of burial mounds is by no mean confined to the uplands, although few mounds remain intact on the lower ground. For example, all the standing mounds on the Isle of Wight are on the higher downland, but even here their distribution emphasises the importance of lowland areas – they are most often found around the heads of coombes close to the spring line (Tomalin

Plate 7.13 Aerial view of the Lambourn Seven Barrows, Berkshire, *English Heritage Photo Library*

1996). Air photography suggests that in the Solent-Thames corridor other barrows were built in the valleys but have since been destroyed. The large groups of burial mounds at Lambourn on the Berkshire Downs or at Burghclere on the Hampshire chalk occupy just this position. They are probably chance survivals of what was once a more general pattern. (Plate 7.13)

At one time it was supposed that the main groups of early Bronze Age barrows were located in 'ritual landscapes' from which everyday activities were excluded. There is no evidence for this proposition which is influenced by an outmoded conception of ritual. Field survey on the West Berkshire Downs provides no support for this assumption (Richards 1978; 1986-90). The great barrow cemetery at Lambourn is not only located close to a spring, it is found in an area with a considerable quantity of worked flint. The same is true of other major cemeteries. Large scale gravel extraction in the Upper Thames suggests a similar pattern in which pits containing domestic artefacts are found near to major groups of burials, but do not extend right up to them (Barclay *et al.* 1996).

The distribution of these monuments has other implications that are not always recognised. This is because the contents of early Bronze Age graves are analysed for evidence of social status. While not necessarily wrong, this procedure often takes place at the expense of spatial analysis. It is easy enough to suppose that graves containing metalwork are indications of high status, but the spacing of the individual barrow groups does not support the suggestion of an overarching social hierarchy of the kind associated with a 'chiefdom'. Some mounds do seem to have been genuinely isolated and others have been found in pairs, but just as often they occur in groups which may be regarded as cemeteries (Bradley 2006). These clusters of funerary monuments are usually located not far from one another. This point was originally made in a study of the ring ditches along the River Ouse, but its implications have still to be taken seriously. The spacing of these groups of monuments suggests that most of them belonged to local communities of no great size (Case 1986). Any distinctions between them may have been minor and quite short-lived.

There are two important exceptions to this argument, and both concern burial mounds that were either particularly elaborate or covered exceptional groups of artefacts. They are particularly common in the vicinity of older monuments. That has long been accepted for the great concentrations of round barrows near to Stonehenge, Avebury, Knowlton and Mount Pleasant, but it is just as true of examples in the Thames valley and on the Berkshire Downs. The small area around Stonehenge contained a particular concentration of linear cemeteries which seem to have developed towards the end of this period (Woodward and Woodward 1996). There are at least two further examples in the study area, the first at Radley Barrow Hills, where it was aligned on the position of the Abingdon causewayed enclosure, and the other at

Lambourn, where the cemetery was orientated on an older long barrow (Barclay and Halpin 1999; Richards 1986-90; Woodward 2000). The Lambourn cemetery was excavated many years ago and the results are difficult to interpret (Case 1956b), but it is clear that the cemetery at Radley had an exceptional range of contents. Not only did it begin with the early Beaker flat graves mentioned earlier, the burials were associated with more metalwork than any other group recorded on the Thames gravels (Garwood 1999). A large barrow cemetery may also have formed around the Oxford henge.

Another complex burial was found at Stanton Harcourt, where it was associated with the largest of the round barrows that developed around the Devil's Quoits (Harden and Treweeks 1945). Again this site was used over a lengthy period and its role as a cemetery may have started with a series of Beaker graves, one of them of exceptional complexity. Such finds emphasise another important point. There do seem to have been significant variations in the sizes of different mounds. This has wider implications. The richer burial mounds around Stonehenge tend to be larger than the others, and were usually constructed on higher ground (Woodward and Woodward 1996). There are hints of a similar distinction among the excavated ring ditches on the Upper Thames gravels. The same idea may also help to explain the distinctive ridgetop siting of some of the round barrows on the Chilterns and of others on isolated hilltops overlooking the Vale of Aylesbury (Dyer 1961). The prominent positions of such monuments may have added to their visual impact.

If these arguments are correct, the study area may contain not one series of early Bronze Age burials but two (Bradley 2006). The simpler and smaller mounds appear in clusters that may have formed the cemeteries of local communities. These were fairly regularly spaced across the chalk and the river gravels, and their construction does not seem to have made extravagant demands on human labour. Nor were the offerings provided for the dead exceptionally elaborate ones. That was not always the case with the second group of burials. They involved a variety of different types of mounds and were often located, not in relation to nearby settlement areas, but to the ceremonial centres of the recent past. They can include a wider variety of grave goods, and it seems likely that they were the burial places of people who did not live in the immediate area. If there was a social elite during the early Bronze Age, this is where evidence for its existence should be sought.

Unfortunately, this outline over-simplifies a number of issues. Few of the barrows were the burial places of a single individual. Where the remains of a mound survive it often contains a number of separate graves, some of which may even have been reused; an outstanding example is a recently excavated barrow at Gayhurst Quarry in Buckinghamshire (Chapman 2007). There could be further burials outside the monuments altogether. In the linear cemetery at Radley Barrow Hills the axis of the cemetery was reflected by a row of urned cremation burials that would never have been discovered in a less ambitious excavation (Barclay and Halpin 1999). The investigation of ring ditches often obscures these points simply because so many deposits have been lost. That can also happen because the barrow ditches are only sampled. Still more evidence is overlooked when barrows are excavated piecemeal and the areas in between them are neglected. The potential of these areas is amply demonstrated by work on the gravels of the study area which is locating an increasing number of flat graves. The first to be identified were associated with Beaker pottery, but now it is becoming clear that they extend throughout this period. They can also be found on the chalk. For example, at Easton Lane, Winchester in Hampshire there were several pits containing inhumations and cremations associated with Collared Urns (Fasham *et al.* 1989).

Where mounds have been well preserved and well excavated – a rare occurrence in the Solent-Thames corridor – it is clear that some of them developed incrementally, so that their outward appearance is no guide to their internal structure. The largest barrows can encapsulate the remains of smaller monuments, and often the earthworks cover the site of what was once a flat cemetery. In one sense the building of barrows was really a process that was undertaken intermittently; the 'finished' form of the monument was simply the state that it had reached when that process was discontinued (Woodward 2000). In another sense, like the long barrows considered earlier, the building of a round barrow was sometimes a way of 'closing' activity on a particular site. It is as important to work out the details of those processes as it is to classify the end results. Again that can only happen in those instances where

monuments survive above ground, as at Arreton Down on the Isle of Wight (Plate 7.14).

Even where there is evidence that the people who built these barrows had a particular design in view, it is important to acknowledge the evidence for regional variation. In practice most studies of these earthworks have been influenced by the typology developed by Grinsell for well preserved monuments on the Wessex chalk, but he himself acknowledged that this scheme does not work well among the neighbouring barrows of the New Forest (Grinsell 1938-40). Case (1963) has also attempted to classify the monuments of the Upper Thames on the basis of their ground plans and the patterns of silting in their ditches. His scheme differs from that of Grinsell, but that is no reason to reject either of these classifications. What is perhaps more significant is the way in which specialised types of barrow that are a special feature of the Wessex chalk are occasionally found in more distant areas. That certainly applies to the cemetery at Lambourn on the West Berkshire Downs, and it probably applies to the levelled monuments at Radley Barrow Hills. In such cases the forms of the mounds might have signified long distance connections as effectively as the objects buried in the grave. It is surely significant that such monuments should be a particular feature of these sites, for there are not many others in the study area. In Hampshire, however, Tomalin has suggested that there were smaller concentrations between the Beaulieu and Lymington Rivers and in the headwaters of the Test and the Meon (Tomalin 1996).

There are a few indications of other sources of variation among what might seem to be a homogeneous distribution of earthwork mounds. Sometimes the grave

Plate 7.14 Barrow on Arreton Down, Isle of Wight, *copyright P Page*

itself was incorporated in an elaborate timber structure, as happened at two sites on Beaulieu Heath and on the earlier site at Chilbolton (Russel 1990). The body might have been placed in an elaborate tree-trunk coffin like that at Bishop's Waltham (Ashbee 1957). Other coffins have been identified at Barrow Hills, and possible traces of biers have been recognised there and at Dorchester-on-Thames (Barclay and Halpin 1999; Whittle *et al.* 1992). Corpses could also have been cremated on a pyre that made extravagant demands on fuel. This was a particular feature of the later early Bronze Age, and the remains of pyres were probably found in the excavation of Cassington Barrow 6 near to Yarnton in the Upper Thames valley (Leeds 1936) – an unusual monument that can perhaps be compared with the disc barrows found on the chalk.

Round barrows were not only places where the dead were buried; they were also where they were commemorated. This is often difficult to document, but there are some important exceptions. Many sites were originally enclosed by a ring of wooden posts or stakes, and there were sometimes several concentric circles of uprights. They have been identified during excavations on the West Berkshire Downs (Richards 1986-90), but such features have a much wider distribution. Two of the most convincing were at Arreton Down and Newbarn Down on the Isle of Wight (Alexander *et al.* 1960). At Charnham Lane, Hungerford, a related monument was defined by a circle of pits with a burnt area at its centre (Ford 2002). In this case no barrow had been built, but this structure was associated with an Aldbourne Cup, a kind of pottery which is otherwise peculiar to burials. Even where barrows were built they were not just for the dead. At Buckskin in Hampshire one of those monuments was constructed over a low platform of turf (M J Allen *et al.* 1995). It was enclosed by a setting of stakes and seems to have provided a kind of stage on which food could be prepared and consumed. Here there was evidence of bonfires and placed deposits of animal bones. At Gayhurst Quarry in Buckinghamshire it is clear that massive feasts took place, as a barrow ditch was filled with cattle bones (Chapman 2007). Again such evidence might be missing in levelled monuments, or might not be recognised in only partial excavation.

There are two broader issues that must also be considered here: the chronology of these monuments and their connections with other areas (Bradley 2006).

There were three main trends on the development of these mounds over time. The first has been mentioned already and is undoubtedly the simplest: certain barrows increased in size. Beaker graves were covered only by a small circular mound, if they were covered at all, whereas some of the barrows built towards the end of the early Bronze Age were enormous. The second trend is a change in the burial rite, from an initial emphasis on inhumation to a greater use of cremation. That has important implications for the interpretation of the objects found with the dead. Inhumation burials usually contain a series of intact offerings; some of the items deposited with a

cremation burial may have passed through the pyre, and others could have been totally destroyed. The final point is apparent from the analysis of Barrow Hills and comparable studies in Wessex and Sussex. The linear cemeteries at Lambourn and Radley are exceptional in a region with much less structured groups of burial mounds (although a third example may be partly buried beneath modern houses in North Oxford), but they are also unusual in relation to a wider region, for this rather rigid design is mainly found close to Stonehenge. It may have facilitated processions through the burial ground (Garwood 1999), but it is clear that it was one of the last developments to take place before the construction of round barrows slowed down in the later second millennium BC.

That introduces a further question. How far is it appropriate to compare the round barrows of the study area with the famous examples on the Wessex chalk? It is all too easy to focus on the richly furnished graves at the expense of their wider context. Perhaps it is the very fact that there are so few precise equivalents for practice in Wessex that lends those few examples their special character. Otherwise the smaller, less formal cluster of monuments, with their rather stereotyped grave assemblage, have more in common with sites in the Midlands and East Anglia than with the areas further to the south. Indeed, the great deposit of cattle bones around the barrow at Gayhurst Quarry recalls a similar find from a mound at Irthlingborough in Northamptonshire rather than any example in Wiltshire or Dorset. In that respect the evidence of early Bronze Age round barrows recalls the evidence of later Neolithic monuments in the study area.

Two important points remain to be considered: the absolute chronology of early Bronze Age artefacts in the study area; and the evidence they provide for long distance contacts. The first topic requires much more research, for despite the prominent part played by burials in central southern England in general accounts of this period, their dating is not particularly secure. It depends very largely on comparison with the archaeology of other regions, some of them in Britain and Ireland, and others in Continental Europe (Garwood 2007). To some extend the problem would be resolved through the direct dating of cremated bone: a method which has revolutionised the study of prehistoric Scotland but which has hardly been attempted in southern England. A reluctance to employ this method has held back studies of the local Bronze Age.

We do not have to look as far as Continental Europe, which lies outside the scope of this volume, for long distance contacts, for there is evidence of the growing importance of contact along the south coast of Britain during this period. This seems to have been far more than the lowland periphery of Wessex, and isolated finds from barrows and metalwork hoards along the English Channel suggest that yet another important axis may have been forming at this time. It extended well beyond the Solent-Thames corridor to run from Cornwall to

Kent and certainly incorporated the Isle of Wight, where two important hoards have been found (Sherwin 1936; Piggott 1947). The burials themselves extend from Rillaton in south-west England to Ringlemere in Kent, but only the burials from Portsdown Hill overlooking Portsmouth in Hampshire fall within the artificial limits of the present study area. In a recent monograph Stuart Needham (2006) has referred to this network as the beginnings of a 'Channel Bronze Age'. It was an axis that would increase in importance during later phases, but even in its early beginnings its significance must not be underestimated.

Chapter 8

The Neolithic and Early Bronze Age: Research Agenda

by Richard Bradley, with contributions by Michael Allen and Gill Hey

8.1 Nature of the evidence

A strength of the Solent-Thames region is that it enables us to look at very diverse areas and study the differences and similarities between them. Its physical diversity provides many opportunities for landscape reconstruction, from riverine environments with their alluvial silts, uplands with associated colluvial deposits to coastal and marine environments. There is also considerable variety in the evidence for human activity, in the realms of settlement, economy and beliefs. This evidence has considerable potential to shed light on the character of regional diversity at the time. Questions and issues to explore include:

8.1.1   why do some areas have major monuments and others do not, and why do some monuments have different distributions to others?

8.1.2   why is deposition in rivers favoured in some areas (for example the Middle Thames), whereas deposition in graves is more common elsewhere (such as the Upper Thames and Hampshire). Was there deliberate deposition in the sea?

8.1.3   comparing the character of ceremonial activity in areas where 'typical' monuments (eg henges) are rare with those from conventionally-accepted monument complexes

8.1.4   comparing the character of settlement in those areas that were comparatively populous from an early period with those where settlement was sparse.

8.2 Chronology

Much more precise chronologies are now available for some parts of the region (particularly the Upper Thames and the Cotswolds) and for some periods (mainly the earlier Neolithic) and these have demonstrated, not only that some of our widely-accepted sequences were erroneous, but also how much can be gained in terms of understanding the social dynamics of early communities. Priorities for research can be stated as follows:

8.2.1   Better dating of key sites and deposits, especially beyond the Cotswolds and the Upper Thames, in order to improve an understanding of chronological sequences across the region. This should include, in particular:

8.2.2   identifying and investigating sites with both late Mesolithic and early Neolithic material present, especially where these can be linked to environmental and datable sequences

8.2.3   better dating of the wide range of earlier Neolithic funerary monuments

8.2.4   better refinement of early Bronze Age chronologies, for example the dating of early Bronze Age 'Wessex' burials – linking burials and settlement evidence, where this exists

8.2.5   investigating sites with good environmental sequences with potential for environmental reconstruction

8.2.6   full analysis of well-dated lithic assemblages to aid with the dating of surface finds from field survey

8.2.7   dating residues on ceramics, particularly Peterborough Ware and 'urn' traditions of early Bronze Age date.

8.3 Landscape and land use

Over the course of the Neolithic and early Bronze Age, a dramatic change occurred in the landscape of the region which, for the first time, was achieved by human rather than natural means. Tree clearance occurred on an unprecedented scale, creating pasture for domesticated animals and small cultivation plots, both the animals reared and cereals grown being new introductions from the Continent at the beginning of the Neolithic. The speed of change, the relative and changing importance of animals and cereals and the impact of their introduction on human populations remains hotly contested. Key areas for study comprise:

8.3.1   Investigating the process of tree clearance, especially in relation to expanding settlement and new monument complexes

8.3.2   Examining direct evidence for cultivation, for example ard marks below barrows, in addition to appropriate environmental samples

8.3.3   Investigating the reasons (social and environmental) behind the episodic use of some apparently more fragile landscapes in the region. For example, the reduction in the use of clay-with-flint after the Neolithic, and the more intensive, but relatively short-lived use of the Hampshire Greensand and New Forest in the Bronze Age, following an apparent period of disuse since Mesolithic

8.3.4   Obtaining more and larger animal bone assemblages in order to gain a better understanding of herd composition and the primary uses of domesticated animals.

8.4 Settlement

Identifying and characterising Neolithic and early Bronze Age settlement sites continues to be highly problematic. Issues and questions to address include:

8.4.1   Establishing the extent and character of settlement away from monument complexes, especially in areas where early settlement has traditionally been thought to be thin (eg Hampshire Basin, the Vale of Aylesbury, Vale of the White Horse. Extending areas of fieldwalking.

8.4.2   Is the impression that there is more extensive and denser settlement in the later Neolithic in many parts of the region real and, if so, does increasing population have an impact on other aspects of human activity, such as ceremony and ritual activity and burial practices?

8.4.3   Why is there comparatively little evidence of early Bronze Age settlement, and to what extent can the distribution of round barrows and ring ditches be used to elucidate the picture?

8.4.4   The better characterisation of settlement sites – what they are and what they should look like? For example, buried ground surfaces and their assemblages should be compared with material acquired in fieldwalking?

8.4.5   Identifying and examining buried sites, especially beneath colluvium off the chalk and preserved ground surfaces below both alluvium

and prehistoric monuments such as ring ditches. This should include the use of the widest possible range of relevant environmental techniques.

8.4.6   Further examination of the extent and character of midden sites, some of our most important and least investigated early Neolithic sites. To what extent are middens actually a feature of 'settlement' and to what extent a result of special events and gatherings? Were middens cultivated in the Neolithic, and how did the material in them come to be deposited or redeposited?. Advancing the recognition of middens in flint scatters (see also 8.4.4 above).

8.4.7   Does the character of settlement change between the early and later Neolithic, with greater mobility and emphasis on pastoralism?

8.5 Burial

The investigation of Neolithic and early Bronze Age burial monuments goes back to the beginnings of our discipline. Nevertheless, the sheer range of burial types emerging, initially from aerial photography, but more recently from large-scale developer-funded archaeology, has been unexpected. Recently-dated examples confound our preconceptions. Key areas for study, questions to address and recommendations for future approaches are as follows:

8.5.1   A much better understanding is needed of date range of the very varied burial monuments of the 4th millennium – portal dolmens, mortuary enclosures, oval barrows, small long barrows in river valleys, U-shaped enclosures, round and segmented ring ditches. These should be compared with the better-known sequences of cairns and long barrows on the chalk and limestone. Do these, apparently more simple structures also have extended sequences, as the Radley oval barrow suggests?

8.5.2   What is the relationship of these small burial monuments to the settlement evidence? Are smaller monuments found in areas of settlement?

8.5.3   What is the significance of small burial monuments in relation to monuments and the development of monument complexes?

8.5.4   Even though the number and range of burial monuments are more numerous than we had imagined, it is clear that most people would not have been buried at these sites. How were most dead bodies treated? What happened in the 3rd millennium when burial monuments were few? Was cremation burial more common throughout than we have imagined?

8.5.5   Recent work has also highlighted the extent and importance of unmarked inhumation and cremation burials, throughout the period. The extent and relative significance of these merits further attention.

8.5.6   The human bones found in the excavation of cursuses should be dated as a matter of course.

8.5.7   Were some bodies deposited in rivers, along with distinctive Neolithic and early Bronze Age artefacts?

8.5.8   It has become apparent that early Bronze Age barrows are very complex, in terms of their contents and forms and the burial practices and other ritual activities associated with them, such as processions. Some of this evidence is found in the upper deposits of the barrows or beyond their physical extents and can be easily damaged if not recognised. Further analysis of their chronology and function is needed and recognition of the ritual use of these sites.

8.5.9   Piecemeal sampling of prehistoric burial mounds is likely to provide misleading results and should be avoided.

8.5.10   The areas around, and in between, barrows should be excavated as well as the mounds and ditches.

8.5.11   Flat graves and flat cemeteries are not likely to be discovered by piecemeal sampling. A better approach is strip, map and sample.

8.6 Ceremony and monuments

It may be thought that our major monuments and monument complexes are well understood, but this is far from the case. Most of our best-known monuments were examined rapidly in advance of development (mainly gravel extraction) many years ago, without the benefit of modern analytical techniques. Priorities for the future include:

8.6.1   The Thames Valley has one of the densest concentrations of causewayed enclosures in the country and yet only Abingdon has seen excavation on any scale in this region, and this was a long time ago (in the 1920s, 1954 and 1963) and in advance of development. A better understanding of causewayed enclosures is needed – their date, longevity of use and character of deposits. Are they all alike or are closely-spaced monuments complementary?

Are the more nearly-circular monuments of later date?

8.6.2   What is the relationship between causewayed enclosures and cursuses and why were cursuses constructed away from the earlier monuments? How were cursuses used and what is their link with small funerary monuments? Why do circular monuments that were the scene of feasting and other communal ritual activities go out of fashion?

8.6.3   What was the role of the large henges and why are they only found in the north of the region? What is their relation to small henge monuments?

8.6.4   Why and how did some monuments attract further monument building – pit and post circles and small ditched enclosures – and become more important complexes? Could these be described as pilgrimage sites?

8.7 Specialised activities (crafts, industries and exchange)

8.7.1   Easton Down and Martin's Clump are the only certainly known flint mines in our region. Over what period of time were they in use? Where did the majority of the flint used in the region come from, and how did people acquire it?

8.7.2   Burnt mounds are usually thought of as a later Bronze Age phenomenon, but a few are now dated to the early Bronze Age (or even late Neolithic). Are these more common than we had imagined? What is their link to settlement?

8.7.3   What is the extent, function and date of timber structures that are increasingly coming to light in coastal areas (for example in Langstone Harbour and at Wootton Quarr)?

8.7.4   Environments such as coastal zones and waterholes have revealed a range of wooden artefacts. What can we deduce about Neolithic and early Bronze Age woodworking? What do we know of other crafts?

8.7.5   What is the evidence of early metalworking in the region?

8.8 Links with the outside world

The character of the region means that links with the outside world were potentially diverse. Techniques for studying these, and key questions to address, include:

8.8.1 Investigate the potential long distance links with the region via the movement of artefacts and similarities in the morphology of monuments. For example, links between the Upper Thames Valley and the north of Britain can be approached through stone axes, Grooved Ware pottery, small late Neolithic circular enclosures and henges, and through the similarities between the Rollright Stones and Cumbrian stone circles. Links between the Hampshire Basin and the Continent might include the evidence of jadeite axes. Another area of high potential is links with the South West of England along the coast.

8.8.2 Isotope analysis on both human and animal bones (eg C, N, Pb, Sr) and creation of a wider database of isotope results in order to address the issue of the origin and mobility of individuals, communities and their animals

8.8.3 What can we say about the beginnings of the 'Channel Bronze Age'?

8.8.4 What impact did the introduction of metal have on society in the Solent-Thames region? Can this be seen in the high-status burials of the area and in aspects of everyday life?

Chapter 9

The Later Bronze Age and Iron Age: Resource Assessment

by George Lambrick

Background

Studies carried out for the Solent-Thames Research Framework

This overview is based (with some additions and modifications) on accounts of late prehistoric period compiled on a county-by-county basis, all of which follow the project's common thematic structure. An advantage of the thematic approach is that there is scope to consider how trajectories of change differed across space and time within the area.

The study for Buckinghamshire was written by Sandy Kidd, for Oxfordshire by Tim Allen and the author, for Berkshire by Steve Ford, for Hampshire by Dave Allen and for the Isle of Wight by Ruth Waller. Environmental background was supplied by George Lambrick with input from Michael Allen.

Regional and national research context

There have been various previous reviews of different aspects of late prehistory in the area, and various conferences have outlined key research issues. Few span the full period covered here, and they all vary in geographical scope, but although some are now becoming quite elderly, they are all still useful (cf Barrett and Bradley 1980a and b; Brück 2001; Cunliffe and Miles 1984; Fitzpatrick and Morris 1994; Champion and Collis 1996; Haselgrove and Pope 2007; Haselgrove and Moore 2007; Lambrick with Robinson 2009). *Understanding the British Iron Age: an Agenda for Action* (Haselgrove 2000) is the most recent attempt at a national research framework for the latter part of the period.

It is also worth noting that under the national initiative, *Exploring Our Past*, regional research frameworks have been or are being developed for adjacent regions which adopt the same period and thematic structure.

The Solent-Thames Area

The Solent-Thames area is an artificial modern administrative construct that spans several different geological and topographical areas, as shown on Figures 1.1-1.4 and 1.6.

Although in detail the present day landscape has been determined by relatively recent historical and modern land use, mapping of its historic character has strongly demonstrated the long-term significance of geology and topography on land division and usage through to the present day (eg Lambrick and Bramhill 1999). Modern grading of land has most of the Area as Grade 3 with significant areas of Grade 2 and more rarely Grade 1 on the main calcareous river gravels and upper Greensand bench. Much the largest area of poor soils (Grade 5) is in the New Forest, with another significant area represented by Otmoor (Oxon), while fairly impoverished (Grade 4) land occurs mostly on the tertiary sands and clays and some of the wetter clay vales.

The geographical diversity of the region can now be mapped digitally in terms of a very wide range of geological, topographical, hydrological, vegetational and historical characteristics that can be used as the basis for analysing existing archaeological data. So far, however, very few if any attempts have been made to do this.

In some respects the natural diversity of the area and its lack of a clear historical or geographical rationale has advantages, because it means that no assumptions can be made that change was uniform across the area: instead it demands consideration of sub-regional differences and contrasts. For many parts of the Solent-Thames area, patterns are likely to be more similar to those in adjacent counties beyond its limits than to other areas within it. It is much more realistic to think of the area as a transect across different geographical and cultural entities that it impinges upon than as a coherent area in itself.

A key issue for late prehistoric Britain is its varying regional character. The Solent-Thames area offers the opportunity for taking a fresh look at some of the best-studied regions for the period in terms of their diversity and differences in the trajectory of change, rather than pursuing the more usual quest for similarity of development.

Nature of the evidence base

General scale and character of investigations

The way in which later prehistoric sites and finds are recorded in county Historic Environment Records (HER) is rather variable and it is not always easy to

Table 9.1 Numbers of later prehistoric HER records

County	Later Bronze Age	Iron Age
Buckinghamshire & Milton Keynes	144	1622
Oxfordshire	42 (but 897 gen BA)	485
Berkshire	Not provided	Not provided
Hampshire	Not provided	Not provided
Isle of Wight	31	118

Table 9.2 Solent-Thames records in the Later Prehistoric Pottery Gazetteer

County	No Sites/ collections	% Published
Buckinghamshire & Milton Keynes	261	21.8
Oxfordshire*	195	33.8
Berkshire*	272	31.8
Hampshire	387	20.4
Isle of Wight	57	14

NB the low figure for Oxfordshire compared with Berkshire is because many sites in the Vale of White Horse and some in South Oxfordshire are listed according to pre-1974 county boundaries under Berkshire.

extract data, so the following figures (Tables 9.1 and 9.2) give only a broad-brush indication of the scale of the known resource. To put this into perspective, the Buckinghamshire figures for the period represent up to about 10 % of entries in the HER.

Another way of looking at this is through the records of *The Later Prehistoric Pottery Gazetteer* (www.arch. soton.ac.uk/Projects). Compiled in 1999, this provides a breakdown of collections in the Solent-Thames area (Table 9.2).

In terms of large excavations, of 27 substantive open area excavations in Buckinghamshire, 15 have been fully published, whilst a further 9 are progressing towards publication. In Oxfordshire at least 30 major area excavations, including some complete excavations of settlements, have either been published or are very close to publication. In Berkshire there have been about 20

substantial excavations, the majority of which have been published. Hampshire has 14 sites with 'sizeable' collections (3,000 sherds or more) all of which are from the chalk, with all but one published, and there are some other substantial excavations with lower yields of pottery. On the Isle of Wight most excavations have mostly been small-scale though the enclosure at Knighton produced a reasonably substantial collection of pottery. Of specific sites, Danebury with 158,000 sherds is exceptional in the whole Solent-Thames area. Since this information was compiled (2008) there have been many more excavations large and small, and many publications, as the references cited indicate.

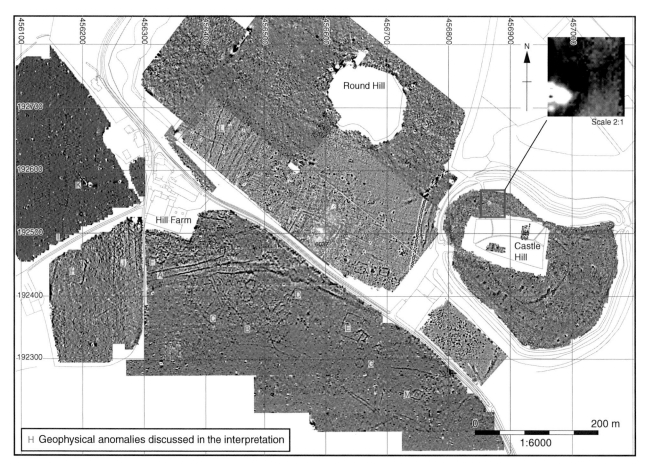

H Geophysical anomalies discussed in the interpretation

Plate 9.1 Geophysical survey in and around Castle Hill, Little Wittenham, Oxfordshire, *copyright OA, with kind thanks to Time Team*

Plate 9.2 Reconstruction of the settlement at Pennylands, Milton Keynes, *copyright R Williams*

History of investigation

In Buckinghamshire later prehistoric sites have been recognised since the 19th century, but there was little pioneering excavation.

In Oxfordshire later prehistoric sites have been recorded since the 16th century, when Leland wrote about the earthworks on Castle Hill, Little Wittenham (Leland 1964, 120; Gelling 1974, 128). Interest and knowledge grew from the mid-19th century onwards, with the excavations of Stephen Stone at Standlake (1847) and Boyd Dawkins (1862; 1864) and Rolleston (1884) at Yarnton. There was increasing concern at the destruction of prehistoric monuments in the later 19th century, and the levelling of part of the earthworks at Dyke Hills, near Dorchester-upon-Thames became a particular cause célèbre in the campaign that led to the passing of the first Ancient Monuments Act in 1882 (Lane-Fox 1870; Cook and Rowley 1985, 18-20).

Some of Hampshire's prominent Iron Age earthworks received honourable mention in the 17th and 18th centuries from Camden, Aubrey and Stukeley, but it was not until the second half of the 19th century that excavation on an Iron Age site took place. In 1858 Augustus Franks worked at Danebury, and later Dr J C Stevens reported upon a number of 'pit-dwellings' (probably storage pits) at Hurstbourne railway station (Cunliffe 2000, 10; Stevens 1888, 25).

On the Isle of Wight much evidence gathered by antiquaries remains unreliable eg Late Bronze Age urnfields. Very little new data from this period was recovered in the intervening years.

The development of aerial photography in the 1920s and 1930s, notably by Major W G Allen in the Thames Valley and O G S Crawford in Wessex, led to an explosion of information about buried sites on the river gravels and chalk (and to a lesser extent on limestone and other free-draining soils). These pioneers were followed by Derek Riley, J K St Joseph, Arnold Baker and others. New discoveries continue to be made, even

in well-surveyed areas (Featherstone and Bewley 2000). Many undated cropmark sites are probably of later Bronze Age or Iron Age origin, though dating on purely morphological grounds is of very variable reliability.

Other non-intrusive site prospection and recording techniques (fieldwalking, earthwork survey and geophysics) have also played their part in enhancing the record.

In the late 1950s and 1960s, when magnetometry was first being developed, the use of geophysics coupled with targeted excavation was pioneered by the Oxford University Archaeological Society in a series of hillfort investigations in Oxfordshire and south Northamptonshire. In recent years a similar approach with more sophisticated modern equipment has been revived with the Wessex hillfort project (Payne *et al.* 2006) and work along the Berkshire Downs and at Little Wittenham (Miles *et al.* 2003; Lock *et al.* 2005; Allen *et al.* 2010), not to mention many other surveys of settlements and religious sites (Plate 9.1).

Approaches to excavations have also changed over the years, many early ones being small-scale trenches or salvage areas, the scale gradually increasing especially through the 1970s to 1990s. A few excavations such as Danebury and Gravelly Guy, Stanton Harcourt, reflect very complete recovery of material from large area excavations, but most reflect less complete levels of sampling, and in recent years the trend has been towards recording much larger areas with lower levels of sampling. However, there has been relatively little academic research into the pros and cons of sampling strategies since the 1980s.

Biases in geographical coverage of investigation

In Buckinghamshire there has been a heavy bias in excavation towards the Milton Keynes area and along the Thames valley, but also more recently around Aylesbury, which remains an area of growth. Plate 9.2

For a long while the pressure of development in Oxfordshire was most evident in the gravel and sandpits

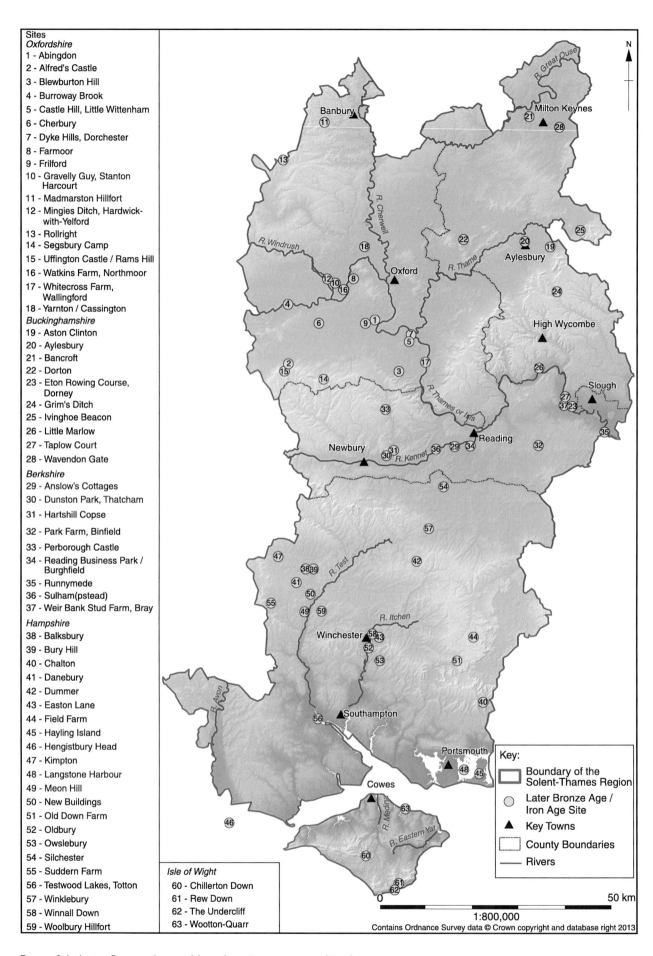

Sites

Oxfordshire
1 - Abingdon
2 - Alfred's Castle
3 - Blewburton Hill
4 - Burroway Brook
5 - Castle Hill, Little Wittenham
6 - Cherbury
7 - Dyke Hills, Dorchester
8 - Farmoor
9 - Frilford
10 - Gravelly Guy, Stanton Harcourt
11 - Madmarston Hillfort
12 - Mingies Ditch, Hardwick-with-Yelford
13 - Rollright
14 - Segsbury Camp
15 - Uffington Castle / Rams Hill
16 - Watkins Farm, Northmoor
17 - Whitecross Farm, Wallingford
18 - Yarnton / Cassington

Buckinghamshire
19 - Aston Clinton
20 - Aylesbury
21 - Bancroft
22 - Dorton
23 - Eton Rowing Course, Dorney
24 - Grim's Ditch
25 - Ivinghoe Beacon
26 - Little Marlow
27 - Taplow Court
28 - Wavendon Gate

Berkshire
29 - Anslow's Cottages
30 - Dunston Park, Thatcham
31 - Hartshill Copse
32 - Park Farm, Binfield
33 - Perborough Castle
34 - Reading Business Park / Burghfield
35 - Runnymede
36 - Sulham(pstead)
37 - Weir Bank Stud Farm, Bray

Hampshire
38 - Balksbury
39 - Bury Hill
40 - Chalton
41 - Danebury
42 - Dummer
43 - Easton Lane
44 - Field Farm
45 - Hayling Island
46 - Hengistbury Head
47 - Kimpton
48 - Langstone Harbour
49 - Meon Hill
50 - New Buildings
51 - Old Down Farm
52 - Oldbury
53 - Owslebury
54 - Silchester
55 - Suddern Farm
56 - Testwood Lakes, Totton
57 - Winklebury
58 - Winnall Down
59 - Woolbury Hillfort

Isle of Wight
60 - Chillerton Down
61 - Rew Down
62 - The Undercliff
63 - Wootton-Quarr

Figure 9.1 Later Bronze Age and Iron Age sites mentioned in the text

of the valleys, but development around towns like Bicester, Banbury and Didcot has provided new foci for archaeological investigation. Understanding of the Cotswolds in later prehistory still lags behind that of the valley, but has begun to be addressed (Lang 2009). While recent work along the Ridgeway and outlying chalk hills has started to redress the balance for the Berkshire Downs, this has still been of a somewhat restricted character. Recent work on the Corallian Ridge and in the Vale of White Horse has also begun to fill out the picture.

In Berkshire there has again been a major concentration of investigation on the Middle Thames and lower Kennet gravels, especially in the areas west of Reading and between Maidenhead and Slough. There has been growing investigation in some parts of the tertiary beds eg in the vicinity of Burghfield, but still only limited work on the dip slope of the Berkshire Downs compared with the recent focus of research along the Ridgeway in Oxfordshire.

In Hampshire the study of chalkland sites (around Danebury, Andover, Basingstoke, and down the M3 corridor past Winchester) has held a pre-eminent position in the study of late prehistory not only in the county but nationally. In the non-calcareous parts of the county field surveys, gravel quarrying, road building and urban development have added to the picture, although in comparatively sporadic fashion, except for the major late Iron Age regional tribal centre at Calleva Atrebatum (Silchester).

On the Isle of Wight most work has again concentrated on the central chalk ridge where most sites are

known, but there has been an increasing amount of work in recent years on the coastal areas.

An important aspect of the geographical coverage has been the interplay between development-led archaeology and university and other research projects. The latter have made a major contribution to rectifying some of the biases, and in some instances have provided the backbone of research, notably for the Cotswolds, the Chilterns, the Berkshire Downs and outlying hills, Silchester, parts of the Hampshire chalk and the coastal plain.

Taking these patterns overall, it is clear that there are substantial geographical biases in the record, but useful progress has been made in recent years to begin to redress these. The distribution of key sites is shown in Figure 9.1.

A further important feature of the Solent-Thames area as a resource for studying later prehistory is that it includes several of the most intensively studied local areas for late prehistoric archaeology in Britain. Particularly notable in this respect are the areas around Milton Keynes (Buckinghamshire); Stanton Harcourt, Cassington/Yarnton and Abingdon (Oxfordshire); the Lower Kennet valley (Berkshire); Silchester; Danebury (Plate 9.3) and its environs (Hampshire). Some other areas with a more recent history of major investigations, such as the Maidenhead to Slough section of the middle Thames valley and Frilford/Marcham and the Oxfordshire Ridgeway are emerging as further important foci of investigations. These various 'hotspots' of later prehistoric archaeology thus provide an excellent resource for comparative studies across the Solent-

Plate 9.3 Aerial view of Danebury hillfort, Hampshire, *copyright Oxford Institute of Archaeology*

Thames area, which is especially valuable in the wider context of our better understanding of its variability in settlement patterns, land use and cultural associations.

Chronology

The dating of most sites still rests on ceramic typology as few produce other dateable finds. The chronology of the later Bronze and Iron Ages in the Solent-Thames area can be divided by broad pottery styles into the following main phases, though these are not equally clear-cut, nor necessarily contemporaneous across the area:

i.   Deverel Rimbury (globular and bucket urns) 1700–1500 to 1200–1000 BC

ii.   Post- Deverel Rimbury (plain ware) 1200–1000 to 850–750 BC

iii. Late Bronze Age to earliest Iron Age (decorated ware akin to All Cannings Cross) 850–750 to *c.* 600

iv.   Early Iron Age (angular vessels) *c.* 600 to 400–350

v.   Middle Iron Age (slack-profiled assemblages, globular bowls and jars or saucepan pots) 400–350 to 100 to 50BC

vi.   Late Iron Age (handmade and wheel-turned vessels, especially necked jars and bowls) 100–50BC to 50AD

On current understanding these broad phases break down across the area as shown in Table 9.3.

For the later Bronze Age the ceramic phasing is based on pioneering work carried out in the late 1970's (Barrett 1980a & b). This drew on several of the sites excavated at that time at Runnymede (Longley 1976) and in the Kennet Valley (Bradley *et al.* 1980), for which radiocarbon dates were available. However, while the basic identification of a later Bronze Age ceramic tradition remains unchallenged, Elaine Morris (Morris 2013) has suggested that the 'sequence' in which late Bronze Age 'plain ware' follows Deverel Rimbury pottery, and gives way to decorated late Bronze Age pottery looks increasingly dubious. In the light of many more recent radiocarbon dates, there appears to be more of an overlap of plain ware with the more distinctive earlier and later styles, between which there may have been less separation than has been supposed.

There is also significant regional variation in ceramic chronologies and the issues that arise for interpretation. In northern Buckinghamshire the model used is generally that of David Knight (1984, 2002) which sees the Deverel Rimbury phase as somewhat later than in other parts of the area. Here there are also difficulties in distinguishing a clear latest Bronze Age/ earliest Iron Age phase, and some overlap between early to middle and middle to late Iron Age characteristics, as more up-to-date styles do not always seem to be present.

Similar issues arise for Berkshire, and for the middle to late Iron Age to Oxfordshire, where it is suspected that at some sites middle Iron Age styles may have lasted almost until the Roman conquest, even though on others late Iron Age pottery was being introduced 100 years earlier.

In Hampshire the detailed sequence at Danebury has allowed the middle and later Iron Age to be subdivided, giving six rather than three or four ceramic phases for the Iron Age (Cunliffe and Poole 1991b). It must be stressed however that the available chronological framework indicated in the table above provides only approximate dating. Danebury is exceptional and while it has greatly clarified the middle to late Iron Age ceramic sequence at least for central Hampshire, the vast majority of the Solent-Thames area has seen no systematic attempts to refine or provide secure absolute dating for the basic sequences first defined 20 years ago or more (Barrett 1980; De Roche 1977; 1978; Lambrick 1984; Saunders 1971; Knight 1984; 2002).

Scientific dating

Over the last thirty years radiocarbon dating has been applied, mostly very sporadically, to many later prehistoric sites in the Solent-Thames area. This has resulted in a growing body of determinations from an increasingly wide range of sites and contexts, though most of them have tended to be burials and other specific deposits rather than defining sequences. For example in Buckinghamshire radiocarbon dating has been used on about 40% of open area excavations with between 2 and 4 dates per site. Amongst a growing plethora of determinations, very few significant programmes of radiocarbon dating have been undertaken, Yarnton, Eton Rowing Course, Runnymede (just outside the area in Surrey) and Danebury being the main exceptions.

The radiocarbon curve has a particularly pronounced deviation between 800 and 400 cal BC and this has severely limited the use of radiocarbon dating. However, improvements in pre-treatment of samples, the develop-

Table 9.3 Chronology of later prehistoric pottery phases

	Deverel Rimbury	*Post DR Plainware*	*LBA/EIA*	*EIA*	*MIA*	*LIA*
N Bucks	1500-1000	1000-800	800-300	400-50AD	50-50AD	
Oxon	1600-1100	1100-800	800-600	600-350	350-0/50AD	50-50AD
S Bucks/ Berks	1700-1200	1200-850	850-400	400-100	100-50AD	
Hants/ IoW	1600-1100	1100-800	800-600	600-350	350-100	100-50AD
					(D)250-100	(D)50-50AD

(D) = additional ceramic phases in the Danebury sequence

ment of AMS dating and high-precision approaches, and the dating of multiple samples have established a variety of means of reducing the error margins. The application of Bayesian statistical analysis can also significantly refine the precision of the dating where samples can be put into series. An example of effective application of such methods is the dating of the middle Iron Age cemetery at Yarnton (Hey *et al.* 1999) and the very early iron working site at Hartshill Copse, Berkshire (Collard *et al.* 2006).

Other forms of scientific dating, such as Optical Stimulated Luminescence dating, Thermo-luminescence dating and Thermo-remanent Magnetic dating, have all been used on occasion, but the accuracy of these types of dating (at best offering 5-10% accuracy, i.e. ± 200 years, and often with ranges of 500 years or so) is of rather limited value. Nevertheless, the use of OSL dating for the Uffington White Horse is a particularly interesting application (Miles *et al.* 2003).

Dendrochronology was used to date some of the repairs to the waterfront structures at Testwood Lakes, Hampshire, to the 1450s BC (Bowijk and Groves 1997; Fitzpatrick and Ellis 2000; Plate 9.4). In most cases, however, preserved timber, for example at Runnymede, the Eton Rowing Course and Whitecross Farm Wallingford, have had too few rings to allow successful dating.

Plate 9.4 Testwood Lakes wooden timbers *in situ*, Hampshire, *copyright Wessex Archaeology*

Metalwork

A national programme for close scientific dating of some individual items or deposits has taken place, including some from the Solent-Thames area. This has led to a very much clearer chronology for Bronze Age metalwork, which is especially important for interpreting individual items, hoards and river finds and their wider social and economic implications (Needham *et al.* 1997; Needham 2007). There has not been a comparable effort to date Iron Age weaponry and other metalwork, not least because of problems with the calibration curve.

The scarcity of Bronze Age and Iron Age metalwork on most ordinary settlement sites, however, together with the potential for redeposition and curation as heirlooms or scrap metal, means that such metalwork is usually of only limited use for dating settlement sites. The role of brooches, potentially datable to within 50 years, has been of value in relation to Iron Age ceramics at Danebury (Cunliffe 2000, 79), but again they are not numerous on most settlements.

The development of coinage towards the end of the period presents similar issues, as very few occur in well-stratified contexts. Their chronological value is probably more in the context of the political and economic power of the new ruling elites of the late Iron Age than as routine numismatic dating evidence for this period (Gwilt and Haselgrove 1997; Creighton 2000).

Other chronologically distinctive artefacts

There are a number of types of object that, although not especially sensitive to change over long periods, are sufficiently common to be useful chronological markers. These include the distinctively late Bronze Age perforated clay slabs which occur in the middle Thames valley, and the switch from cylindrical or pyramidal 'loomweights' in the middle to late Bronze Age to triangular ones in the Iron Age. Other distinctively Iron Age objects such as weaving combs and grooved and polished metapodials can also be helpful indicators.

Inheritance

The period reviewed here represents the transition from 'monument-dominated landscapes and mobile settlement patterns to that of more permanent settlement and a greater emphasis on agricultural production' (English Heritage 1991, 36). It has been considered that the onset of the Middle Bronze Age defined this in cultural terms and, more importantly, in physical evidence (Ellison 1981) and this view has tended to persist (eg D Yates 2007). But there is no reason to expect such a transition to have been synchronous right across the Solent-Thames area, and there is growing evidence that it was not (Lambrick with Robinson 2009, 377-93).

Landscape

It is clear that in many areas a relatively open landscape was inherited from the earlier Bronze Age. This is suggested by the pollen sequences from Little Marlow (Richmond *et al.* 2006), and Sydlings Copse, Oxon (Day 1993), and by pollen from peat on tertiary sands and clays in the Newbury area and New Forest. Molluscan evidence from barrows in the Ouse and Ouzel valleys at Milton Keynes indicates the same picture (Green, 1974). On the Isle of Wight pollen evidence shows large scale woodland clearance during the Bronze Age creating downland and heathland around the central and southern chalk where the barrow cemeteries were situated (Scaife 1987).

Broad patterns of clearance and landuse appear to have influenced the character of later settlement, as at Stanton Harcourt, Oxfordshire (Lambrick 1992b; Lambrick and Allen 2004). A similar respect for pre-existing sacred sites has been argued for the barrow cemetery at Radley (Allen 2000, 11-12) and at Oxford (Lambrick 2013).

Barrows were also utilised in the setting out of middle to late Bronze Age/Iron Age boundary ditches and field systems, or were given apparent 'special status' within them, Examples include Mount Farm Dorchester (Lambrick 2010) Reading Business Park (Moore and Jennings 1992), Eton Rowing Course (Allen *et al.* 2000) and a number of sites in Hampshire (Cook and Dacre 1985, 7; Cunliffe 2000, 159).

Settlement pattern

The idea of a pattern of 'settlement' before the middle Bronze Age raises one of the most fundamental issues for the period, since there is very little evidence of permanent settlement. Life-styles were dominated by patterns of 'residential mobility' (Barrett 1994, 136-46; Brück 2000, 281-5) and the influence of such mobility on how communities interacted and shared resources is a fundamental part of the inheritance from earlier periods that is likely to have influenced how land came to be divided, enclosed and settled over the next 1,500 years in which more permanently settled farming developed.

Many later prehistoric sites produce rather ephemeral traces of earlier activity, as in the case of several later Bronze Age enclosures and settlements like Ivinghoe Beacon, Rams Hill and Taplow Court (Cotton and Frere, 1968; Brown, 2001; Bradley and Ellison 1975; Needham and Ambers 1994; Allen *et al.* 2009). Several enclosed settlements and forts in Hampshire have evidence of at least some earlier prehistoric activity.

It seems clear that major late prehistoric enclosed forts, settlements and other sites were often sited in places that had seen some significant earlier use, but major monuments tended to be avoided – and in some cases clearly respected and reused.

Funerary and ceremonial monuments and customs

Examples of round barrows attracting Middle Bronze Age (Deverel-Rimbury) secondary burials have long been known and are now widely recognised across the Solent-Thames area (Green, 1974; Allen *et al.* 2000; Barclay and Halpin 1999, 162-3 and 167; Hamlin 1963, 7-9; Barclay *et al.* 1995, 94-5; Lambrick 2010; Butterworth and Lobb 1992; Piggott 1938; McGregor, 1962; Walker and Farwell 2000; Entwhistle 2001). At Kimpton, Hampshire a standing sarsen stone (subsequently broken) was the focal point of the remarkably long-lived (2100 to 600 BC) urn cemetery (Dacre and Ellison 1981).

There is little evidence for stone and timber circles attracting particular respect or reuse in later prehistory (eg Lambrick 1988), but there may be a continuing tradition of constructing of post-circles in the Upper Thames Valley (Allen and Kamash 2008, 72-5; Lambrick with Robinson 2009, 329-31; Lambrick 2010, 24-7; see also Williams 1946-7).

Although the tradition of building major ceremonial and funerary monuments mostly died out, some earlier prehistoric ceremonial like henges and barrows continued to be respected. However, it is noticeable that cursuses were not. At Dorchester-on-Thames a field system (probably of Middle Bronze Age date) was aligned on the Big Rings henge but cut across the more ancient cursus ditches (Whittle *et al.* 1992), a pattern also evident just outside the area at Lechlade (Glos) and Staines (Surrey). It thus seems likely that whatever sacred traditions were once associated with these enigmatic enclosures, they had not survived.

Some ancient monuments that were visible as earthworks were reused at much later periods. For example some long barrows in Hampshire apparently served as *loci consecrati* for Late Iron Age and Romano-British communities (Massey 2006), and a similar phenomenon is evident at Uffington (Miles *et al.* 2003). At some Hampshire barrows large quantities of abraded Roman pottery were placed on barrows or in their ditches as votive deposits, but it is uncertain to what extent this implies continuous veneration throughout the later prehistoric period (Knocker 1963; Cook and Dacre 1985).

The natural environment and landscape change

Climate and climatic change

It has long been recognised that the climate changed in this period from a warmer drier climate in the Bronze Age to a wetter cooler climate in the Iron Age (eg Lamb 1981). A variety of lines of evidence has been cited to support this, including extrapolations from oxygen isotope ratios trapped in ice cores, preserved remains of fauna and flora sensitive to climate fluctuations and hydrological and geomorphological changes, including sea level change (Anderson *et al.* 2007; Needham and

Macklin 1992; Tomalin *et al.* 2012). In the case of hydrological change in river catchments, a key issue is the need to distinguish between change attributable to climate from the effects of human intervention through forest clearance and land management, which, in the Thames valley has been argued to be a more significant driver of change (Robinson and Lambrick 1984; Lambrick with Robinson 2009, 29-39).

One possible indication of late prehistoric cooling of the climate from the region comes from deposits at Yarnton and the Wilsford Shaft near Stonehenge with a high proportion of dung beetles of the genus *Onthofagus*, which are now rare or extinct in Britain but typical of mid-France. In the absence of any obvious ecological reasons for their abundance around 1600–1350 cal BC it is thought that they reflect the warmer climate adduced from other, more generalised evidence such as oxygen istope ratios.

General environment

Molluscs and pollen together with field systems, droveways and the large-scale land-division like the Chiltern Grims Ditch suggest extensive clearance by the middle/late Iron Age and before. The appearance of beech at Little Marlow, both as pollen and fuel, and also at Taplow (Coleman and Collard, 2005) suggests that Chiltern beech woods could have originated during the 1st millennium BC.

Pollen sequences and other biological data from the Upper Thames valley suggest that permanent clearance of forest cover was earlier on the gravel terraces than the surrounding hillsides or floodplain, and continued through the middle to late Bronze Age, but with some cleared areas on surrounding hills remaining rough grazing or heathland through the Iron Age (Lambrick with Robinson 2009, 34-51).

Based upon environmental evidence from the floodplain of the Upper Thames Valley, there is a well-established model for the chronology of increasing clearance and run-off in later prehistory leading to flooding and later alluviation by the end of the period (Robinson and Lambrick 1984; Robinson 1992a; Robinson 1992b; Lambrick 1992b), but the pattern is rather different in the Middle Thames (Lambrick with Robinson 2009, 29-34).

On the Berkshire Downs and their outliers, evidence from both Rams Hill and Castle Hill suggests cleared grassland and periodic regeneration on the chalk in the late Bronze Age (Bradley and Ellison 1975; Allen *et al.* 2010, 89-93 and 203-14). On the Hampshire chalk there is good evidence from sites like Easton Lane and Twyford Down both of clearance and some regeneration and of long-established grassland with some arable, but probably with localised stands of ancient woodland (Fasham *et al.* 1989; Walker and Farwell 2000). During the Iron Age the landscape became much more open, and was dominated by mixed farming. An issue that only some of these studies have addressed (eg Allen *et al.* 2010) is how far wider conditions of regeneration can be extrapolated from samples derived from ditches that may have become wooded but could still have functioned as boundaries and/or barriers.

Pollen evidence from sites in the New Forest, where Bronze Age burnt mounds and barrows are numerous, indicates a rapid decline in soil fertility and onset of acidic heathland conditions (Tubbs 2001).

On the Isle of Wight pollen evidence shows large-scale woodland clearance during the Bronze Age creating downland and heathland around the central and southern chalk where the barrow cemeteries were situated (Scaife 1987). Such clearance seems to have persisted into the later prehistoric period. The midden sites and hearths on the south coast indicate use of a mix of land-based and marine resources.

Soils, erosion and alluviation

As farming became more established and larger areas were managed landscapes (see below) there was an impact on the natural environment. This is evident in many pollen spectra, and colluvial studies have been highly profitable in determining palaeo-environmental chronologies (eg Bell 1983; Allen 1992) occasionally defining sites and whole periods of evidence not otherwise recorded in the archaeological record (Allen 2005). The most comprehensive studies of colluvium have been carried out in adjacent regions on the Sussex and Wiltshire chalklands, and relatively little comparably systematic research has been undertaken on the Hampshire, Berkshire and Marlborough Downs or the Chilterns and Cotswolds, despite the presence of important sites related to and buried by hillwash or alluvium. There are however some notable exceptions: Uffington (Miles *et al.* 2003) and Aston Clinton (Masefield 2008). Some attempts have been made to analyse the nature and quantity of erosion products in the form of colluvium, alluvium and aeolian deposits (eg Favis-Mortlock *et al.* 1997). Burrin and Scaife (Burrin and Scaife 1984; 1988; Scaife and Burrin 1992) clearly show that colluvial deposition is just one part of a larger sediment history for which both alluvial and (where relevant) marine sediment records need to be considered.

The less pronounced topography of river gravels limits the value of such colluvial deposits, but can nonetheless be valuable at terrace edges or in major features such as waterholes (Lambrick with Robinson 2009; Lambrick 2010) The environmental evidence from alluvial sites can provide the environmental context of the floodplain and its settlement and occupation parameters (eg Lambrick and Robinson 1979; Allen and Robinson 1993; Allen 2008b). The accumulation of alluvial silt provides a genuine generalisation about conditions of erosion within the upstream catchment, which may indicate a significant degree of human intervention, possibly eclipsing any climatic contribution (Robinson and Lambrick 1984; Robinson 1992b; Lambrick 1992b), but attempts to map the origin of such deposits have been disappointing (Limbrey and Robinson 1988).

Farming

The emergence of permanent sedentary farming settlements has been assumed to occur across the Solent-Thames region from the Isle of Wight to Buckinghamshire by the Middle Bronze, but the dynamics of change in relation to possible variations in population growth have only begun to be explored. West of the region, research in the upper Allen valley suggests that whatever the process of field system development, there is no evidence for agrarian intensification. (M J Allen pers. comm.).

On the Thames gravels Lambrick (with Robinson 2009, 377-87) has explored the varied chronology and spatial distribution of the transition to sedentary farming; of the possible changing social basis of land management; of the emergence of specialist pastoral farming alongside mixed farms; and the possibility that some degree of mobile pastoralism still survived. The assumption that the establishment of field systems and permananet farming settlments go hand-in-hand is also challenged.

This approach to understanding the dynamics of change suggests a much more complex chronological and spatial picture than more traditional models of simple periods of major change (eg D Yates 1999; 2007) would suggest. It emphasises the need to define the farming economies of specific farm units, the land units, and ultimately to examine the possibility, if not the probability, of regional variation and specialisation, and of complex trade economies of secondary products and materials less readily seen in the material archaeological evidence.

Fields

The chalklands of Hampshire, along with much of Wessex, saw a major transition from an open to an enclosed landscape between 1600 and 800 BC. In the middle Bronze Age, coaxial field systems were set out, with ridge-top linear ditches sometimes providing a base line. Trackways and rectilinear enclosures were also created but contemporary settlements were apparently rare and unenclosed. Molluscan evidence from the Windy Dido field system adjacent to the Quarley linear ditches indicates that they were constructed in long-established open grassland (Evans in Cunliffe and Poole 2000). Pre-existing round barrows were either left alone, presumably in areas of pasture, or employed as laying-out markers (Crawford and Keiller 1928, 154; Cunliffe 2000, 159; Cook and Dacre 1985, 7). Away from the chalk in Hampshire the background picture is less clear, but a wide range of sites and finds shows that the exploitation of heathland, river valleys and coastal fringe were significant in their own way. On the heathland soils of the New Forest enclosures and fields are rare but not unknown (Pasmore 2000).

On the Isle of Wight there are four field systems dated on stylistic grounds to the Iron Age to Roman periods and an earthwork enclosure (possibly for livestock)

dated to the Iron Age on typological grounds, but again not securely dated.

The pattern of late prehistoric land division in the river valley and vales of the Solent-Thames area tends to be somewhat different. Middle to late Bronze Age ditched field systems have been investigated in the Middle Thames and Lower Kennet and Colne valleys in southern Buckinghamshire and northern Berkshire. These include Kingsmead, Horton (Wessex Archaeology 2006), Eton Rowing Course (Allen and Mitchell, 2001) The Lea, Denham (Coleman *et al.* 2004), Weir Bank Stud Farm, Bray (Barnes and Cleal 1995), Reading Business Park and Green Park (Moore and Jennings 1992; Brossler 2004) and Moores Farm (Brossler *et al.* 2013). Parts of middle and late Bronze Age field systems are also increasingly being found in the southern part of Oxfordshire on the gravels round Dorchester, Didcot, Appleford and Radley, and also further west along the foot of the Upper Greensand bench in the Vale of White Horse (Lambrick 1992a; Ruben and Ford 1992; Mudd 1995; Hearne 2000; Booth and Simmonds 2009).

Overall, some of these rectilinear fields were established on co-axial layouts in which some sub-division appears to have taken place, but others were more agglomerative with evidence of phases of accretion. These do not seem to have undergone much development in later prehistory, though some fields (eg at Appleford and Denham) were redefined in the Roman period. There are different views as to whether such fields were entirely abandoned (D Yates 1999; 2001; 2007) or may have continued in use as hedged enclosures without their ditches being recut, which would help explain such Roman reuse (Lambrick with Robinson 2009, 80-84).

So far such fields seem to be lacking on the Corallian Ridge and on the gravels to the north, though possible early Iron Age fields have been found at Lady Lamb Farm, Fairford just outside the area (Roberts 1993). Early fields are also absent so far from clay vales, and have not yet been found on the Tertiary sands and clays of Berkshire and Hampshire. A single ditch and droveway high on the Cotswolds at Rollright hints at late Bronze Age or early Iron Age fields (Lambrick 1988), but virtually nothing is known of the potential extent or character of such field systems.

Ditched fields, paddocks and trackways are increasingly evident for the Iron Age in the river valleys and other non-chalkland parts of the Solent-Thames area, and mainly appear to be associated with pastoral farming (Lambrick with Robinson 2009, 83-90. Apart from an unusual early Iron Age droveway with attached fields at Wickham, most are middle to late Iron Age and were probably used for stock management (Williams and Zeepvat 1994; C Stevens 2004; Lambrick 2010; Birbeck 2001; Bourn 2002). Extensive paddocks also appear to be part of some low-lying middle Iron Age pastoral farmsteads at Port Meadow, Oxford (Lambrick and MacDonald 1985a; Lambrick with Robinson 2009, 87-8), and there are small paddocks or cultivation plots adjacent to some settlement enclosures (Allen and Robinson 1993; Allen 1990; Hey 1995; Cromarty *et al.*

Plate 9.5 Reconstruction of the double-ditched farmstead at Mingies Ditch, Oxfordshire, *copyright OA, drawn by Danyon Rey*

1999). By the late Iron Age large areas of rectilinear ditched enclosures, paddocks or "closes" become evident (Lambrick with Robinson 2009, 88-90; Williams and Zeepvat 1994; Parkhouse and Bonner 1997). A late Iron Age co-axial field system is known from Arborfield, south-east of Reading (Lobb and Morris, 1991-3).

In all these areas evidence of the physical form of field and paddock boundaries other than ditches or lynchets is patchy, but physical traces and waterlogged remains cumulatively suggest a variety of forms from permeable boundaries, to hedges, hedge banks, fences, hurdles and natural watercourses (Lambrick with Robinson 2009, 56-62). More tentatively, charred plant remains and snails have been cited as possibly indicating hedges (Clapham 2000; Allen in Davies *et al.* 2002). Apart from seeking to understand the appearance of the landscape, an appreciation of the possible above ground form of boundaries is often crucial to understanding the layout, use and longterm survival of enclosed areas for which the subsoil evidence provides only a very partial picture (Lambrick with Robinson 2009, 56-8).

Archaeologists have been good at defining, recording and mapping field systems especially across the chalk of southern England (Bowen 1961; Palmer 1984), but less attention has been paid to defining their use and how they operated, as for example Pryor (1996) has done in the fens, though the potential has been recognised (Lambrick with Robinson 2009, 246-9 and Figs. 7.8 and 7.9). Such information is important for understanding how farming communities managed the land. In the past it has largely been assumed, but seldom questioned, that fields were for crops, and as discussed by Lambrick (with Robinson 2009, 380-7) there are good reasons to suggest that the origin of many ditched fields on the gravels may have been to manage pasture. On the limestone and chalk hills of the region, tillage and soil disturbance clearly created lynches, but that does not necessarily reflect their origin or indicate exclusive use as arable (Allen 2008a).

Some form of rotation of arable, fallow and pasture is likely, but few if any attempts have been made to investigate this. Charred and waterlogged remains often reflect a mixture of habitats that could reflect rotation, but the complexities of different distribution and depositional (and post-depositional) processes prevent firm attribution to rotational farming. Using land snail analysis to detect and differentiate between grazed or trampled grassland and prehistoric arable habitats is not always easy, nor even always possible (Evans 1972), but improvements in species diversity indices and other statistical means, coupled with the increasing body of soil/sediment and snail data, offers some potential to explore this.

Large-scale land division

While the establishment of field systems can be traced back to the middle Bronze Age, larger scale ditched land divisions are mostly later. In the Chilterns, several small linear earthworks are known on the Chiltern scarp, notably at Whiteleaf Hill (Hey *et al.* 2007; Wise 1991). By analogy with `cross ridge dykes' found in the eastern Chilterns, these have been presumed to be later Bronze Age/early Iron Age local territorial boundaries(Bryant and Burleigh 1995). A possibly similar pattern of cross ridge dykes is evident on the ridge between the Kennet and Enborne to the south of Newbury, though they are as yet undated.

Large linear boundary ditches dating to the late Bronze Age are known on the Berkshire Downs, forming `ranch' boundaries. Late Bronze Age linear ditches have been found at Alfred's Castle, apparently associated with an extensive field system (Gosden and Lock 2001). A lynchet sealed by the early Iron Age rampart at Rams Hill (Bradley and Ellison 1975) is good evidence of the existence of late Bronze Age or early Iron Age arable fields on the Berkshire Downs, but most of the very extensive rectilinear and coaxial field systems are thought to be late Iron Age or Roman in origin (Bowden *et al.* 1993).

On the Hampshire chalk in the Late Bronze Age new linear ditch systems were created. These sometimes related to what already existed, either man-made features or focal points like hilltops, but sometimes cut across established fields to create new tracts of territory (Bowen and Fowler 1978; Bradley *et al.* 1994). Many of these survived into and throughout the Iron Age as new types of enclosure were established, either large as at Balksbury, Winklebury and Danebury or small as at New Buildings and (possibly) Meon Hill and Old Down Farm (Cunliffe 2000, 154). At Easton Down, a middle to late Bronze Age boundary that had been part of a field system seems to have persisted as a boundary through to the middle Iron Age (Fasham *et al.* 1989). In many other cases late prehistoric linear boundaries lasted even longer, and some still survive as parish boundaries and along trackways.

There is also increasing evidence of ditched boundaries dividing up the river valleys, including so-called meander cut-off boundaries defining large areas of dry ground surrounded by watercourses, as at Lechlade, Culham and the Eton Rowing Course (Boyle *et al.* 1998; Allen *et al.* forthcoming). Other examples of early to middle Iron Age ditched land divisions anything from 250 to over 800m long have been found near Aylesbury, and in Oxfordshire at Bicester, Yarnton and Little Wittenham (Parkhouse and Bonner 1997; Ellis *et al.* 2000; Hey *et al.* 2011a; Allen *et al.* 2010, 266-7). These can variously be seen as demarcating areas of settlement or paddocks from more open areas, dividing areas of different intensity of landuse, or acting as boundaries between farming settlements (Lambrick with Robinson 2009, 62-8).

Animal husbandry

For the middle Bronze Age faunal remains are generally scarce, though with isolated exceptions, and animal bones are much more common in many late Bronze Age and Iron Age assemblages than earlier ones.

Ellen Hambleton (1999) carried out a comparison of the evidence for Iron Age animal husbandry in the Upper Thames valley and on the Hampshire chalk, and a decade later reviewed the evidence for Southern Britain in later prehistory (Hambleton 2008). Her principal conclusion was that although the husbandry of sheep and pigs were similar, there was a different strategy for cattle husbandry in the Upper Thames valley (more cattle probably kept in larger herds with fewer surviving till old age for traction and secondary products). Lambrick (with Robinson 2009, 240-9) has reviewed the proportion of species representation in relation to different topographical parts of the Upper Thames valley, showing both differences over time, but also much more variation in species proportion within topographical zones than has previously been supposed, and that horse rearing may have been significant in some parts of the Thames valley.

Both Hambleton and Lambrick have noted the complexity of chronological, regional and topographical trends in herd composition and management. For example, Hambleton (2008) has commented on the correlation of herd composition with environmental factors and found an overall trend to increasing numbers of sheep over the period as a whole across southern England, but with variations within this, also finding differences in the management of animals for meat, dairy or secondary products. Lambrick has noted an increase in cattle numbers in the Iron Age Thames valley, but the topographical differences suggest that this could reflect a higher proportion of later sites being on lower-lying ground.

Throughout the period wild species such as red and roe deer are rare, except for a small assemblage at Anslow's Cottages, Burghfield, near Reading (Butterworth and Lobb 1992). They occur regularly enough in small numbers to show that their low presence declines from *c.* 5% to less than 1-2% over the period. Various birds and mammals are known, bones, feathers and fur

Plate 9.6   Bronze Age wooden structure being recorded at low tide, Isle of Wight, *copyright Isle of Wight Council*

as well as meat may have been utilised, if they were not casual bones from dead individuals.

Fish bones are very rare on later prehistoric settlements, and Hambleton (2008, 102-3) suggests that along with wild birds, small mammals and herpetofauna they may be 'natural chance incorporations' noting that there was probably a taboo against eating fish throughout the period (Dobney and Ervynck 2007). Nonetheless, fish bones do occasionally occur, sometimes in hillforts and/or special deposits perhaps reflecting feasting or ceremonial or religious activities (Allen *et al.* 2010, 82-4 and 255-6). That fish were sometimes deliberately caught (at least in the late Bronze Age and early Iron Age) is suggested by one of two Late Bronze Age foreshore structures at Wootton-Quarr on the Isle of Wight interpreted as a fish trap (Plate 9.6), and by another in London, where the Thames Archaeological Survey discovered part of an early Iron Age fish trap dated to 790–390 cal BC at Vauxhall (Tomalin *et al.* 2012; Cohen 2010). In general, however, there was probably a taboo against eating fish throughout the period (Dobney and Ervynck 2007).

A key issue highlighted by such studies is the need to recover sufficiently large animal bone assemblages to enable detailed analysis. This is especially relevant for later Bronze Age and many early Iron Age sites where the general occurrence of domestic debris can be relatively sparse.

Crop husbandry

Crop husbandry has been especially well studied for the Iron Age on the Hampshire chalkland and in the Thames valley (Jones 1984; Campbell 2000; Lambrick with Robinson 2009, 249-60). Evidence for cereals (spelt wheat, occasionally emmer and six-row hulled barley) has been recovered from a large number of settlements across the Solent-Thames area. Oats, and occasionally rye are also recorded, but seldom in sufficient quantity to suggest they were being deliberately planted and grown. The introduction of bread wheat as a main crop occurred on some sites in the late Iron Age, as shown at Barton Court Farm (Miles 1986).

In terms of other crops, flax was also found at middle to late Bronze Age settlements in the Middle and Upper Thames valley, but it does not occur in Iron Age ones, possibly suggesting a switch to wool and animal fats as the preferred sources of yarn and oils. Good evidence for other crops is scarce, but probably include opium poppy (eg at Whitecross Farm in the late Bronze Age), peas and field beans. More doubtful is the growing of brassicas (eg wild turnip), which occur in sufficient numbers on some Hampshire sites to suggest they were deliberately grown, but occur only at a low level elsewhere (Gill Campbell and Mark Robinson pers. comm.).

A striking feature of the later Bronze Age is a switch in emphasis from growing emmer to spelt wheat, which became predominant across the whole Solent-Thames area and beyond by the early Iron Age. Spelt wheat has now been found in Oxfordshire in middle Bronze Age contexts both at Appleford Sidings and at Yarnton, a grain from the latter giving a radiocarbon date of 1740–1410 cal BC.

Emmer has increasingly been found in Iron Age contexts in some regions (Carruthers 2008; Stevens 2008; 2009; Pelling 2012), but on the Hampshire chalk and in the Thames valley it is still rare in Iron Age crop residues before the late Iron Age and there has been much debate about the reasons for this, usually in the context of climate change and autumn sowing (Jones 1984; van der Veen 1992; van der Veen and Palmer 1997). Experiments by Mark Robinson suggest that the complete dominance of spelt over emmer could have arisen from recurrent autumn sowing of 'maslin' crops mixing the two wheats, which would have resulted in spelt producing bigger yields, quite quickly displacing emmer in the resultant resown crops (Lambrick with Robinson 2009, 258).

Other areas of ongoing debate concern the possibility of extrapolating changing trends of soil fertility and drainage from the weeds species associated with crop remains, and the extent to which it is possible to discern communities that were the main arable 'producers' from others who may have mainly been 'consumers,' (Jones 1985; Van der Veen 1987; 1999; Stevens 2003; van der Veen and Jones 2007). Much of this remains open to question (not least because of the complex taphonomic factors that influence the character of charred crop and weeds remains as found in the ground. Lambrick (with Robinson 2009, 388-9) has questioned whether the character of charred crop remains alone is sufficient to provide answers.

While there is much to debate about the detailed interpretation of relatively rich charred plant assemblages, an even more fundamental issue is the great variability in the concentration of cereal remains found on settlement sites, which varies both in time and geographically across the region. In general, concentrations are higher on Upper Thames Valley sites, excluding the floodplain, than on sites in the Middle Thames Valley but not as high as on settlements on the Hampshire Chalk. In contrast, although cereals were used in the Bedfordshire Ouse Valley, concentrations are very low and occur in company with wild food plant remains, producing assemblages that resemble Neolithic charred assemblages from the Thames Valley (Robinson, unpublished). On some later Bronze Age and Iron Age sites charred crop remains are very rare, and occasionally are more like earlier prehistoric samples than typical Iron Age ones. Many features are devoid of such material with only occasional concentrations, as at Hartshill Copse where 90% of the 2289 charred plant remains recovered came from a single context (Collard *et al.* 2006, 378). A near-absence of charred crop remains seems to persist well into the Iron Age in some areas (eg Powell *et al.* 2010, 93) and this seems commonest in the Middle Thames valley where querns are also relatively infrequent. One possibility is that earlier practices of crop husbandry on a small horticultural scale for family consumption may have persisted for some farming communities long after larger-scale farming had taken off in parts of the Upper Thames gravels and Hampshire chalk. These latter areas may have acted as the breadbasket of a wider region.

Subsistence and surplus

There have been some attempts (eg Lambrick and Allen 2004; Cunliffe and Poole 2000a, b) to use experimental and other data coupled with indicators of land availability to try to model whether farming settlements are likely to have been self-sufficient in agricultural terms or would have been generating a surplus. This approach is seldom feasible where settlements are incompletely excavated and there is little or no way of estimating the extent and character of the land they farmed; however, the overall indications from current evidence are that while the exchange of prestige goods (and perhaps livestock wealth) was an important economic driver in the late Bronze Age, the production and exchange of an agricultural surplus derived from mixed farming became a much more important driving force in the Iron Age.

Settlement patterns and social organisation

Regionalism

The idea of regional cultural identity in later prehistory has been a topic of much debate, stemming partly from ideas prevalent in the middle of the 20th century about different waves of continental immigrants. Cunliffe (1974 onwards) has long propounded the concept of more home-grown ceramic 'style zones,' and while this approach has been questioned and challenged (eg Collis 1994; 1996; Hill 1995), no alternative models for regional variation in the development of ceramic traditions have been developed. There are also hints at more localised differences in stylistic design that may be relevant (Lambrick 1984), and fabric analysis has shown a number of chronological trends or preferences that are consistent from one site to another in particular areas. These reflect broad preferences (eg in the use of calcined flint or quartzite or broad character of filler) as well as differences in local geology, but the possible complexity of how recurrent variation may reflect 'regional' variation at very different geographical and cultural scales has not been fully explored.

Some other indications of regional variation, such as the distribution of 'banjo' enclosures, have been altered by subsequent survey, but still show regional clustering (Lang 2009). The clearest indication of regional cultural entities comes from the distribution of late Iron Age tribal coinage, but here again there are significant complexities in the interpretation of the economic and political role of coinage at this period and the extent to which they reflect cultural, tribal, economic or political regions – or how far back any regional divisions can be traced (Haselgrove 1989; Creighton 2000).

The emergence of permanent settlement

During the late prehistoric period scattered farmsteads and sometimes villages increasingly came to replace much more ephemeral traces of domestic and farming activity, but rather little attention has been paid to quite how, when and why the emergence of settled farming communities came about – or over how long a period and whether or not it was synchronous across different areas. Lambrick (with Robinson 2009, 384-7) has suggested that in the Thames valley the transition from earlier Bronze Age residential mobility to later prehistoric farms, settlement groups and villages may have occurred quite gradually and by no means synchronously, and was not obviously associated with the enclosure of land into fields. Initially the coalescing of domestic occupation may have taken the form of recurrent but highly scattered occupation across extensive areas (both within and separate from enclosed field systems), which in due course gave way to more compact, organised settlement forms (eg at Reading Business Park, Berkshire, or Cassington West, Oxfordshire. By the early to middle Iron Age compact tightly constrained settlements, often indicative of more permanent year-round settlement, were typically located on topographical and/or landuse divisions.

In the middle Iron Age the integration of settlement and landuse was even more strongly emphasised in the appearance of pastoral farmsteads on low-lying land (see Plate 9.5 above), occasionally including short-lived seasonal occupation of regularly inundated floodplain, as at Farmoor (Lambrick and Robinson 1979). Some slight traces of late prehistoric domestic activity not dissimilar to earlier periods may indicate that residential mobility never really died out. On the other hand, the emergence of compact farm units closely integrated into landuse management may reflect a transition (occurring at different times up and down the valley) from an essentially family-based form of agriculture to one that was rather more communal in character.

While ideas about the development of late prehistoric settlement in the Thames valley have been coloured by the emergence of open settlements along the valley floor, those concerning the chalk south of the Thames valley have been equally coloured by the focus on how major communal enclosures (late Bronze Age hilltop enclosures and hillforts) developed together with enclosed settlements. Many of the latter began in the middle Bronze Age. Nonetheless, the character of widely scattered sparse middle Bronze Age occupation over large areas, such as that at Chalton, as compared with more compact forms of settlement that emerged later in the Iron Age, may reflect a similar pattern. Similarly, the presence of low levels of later Bronze Age occupation on the sites of Iron Age enclosed settlements, which in some cases also exhibit quite sparse levels of occupation, suggests a sequence of change in the basic character and permanence of settlement that has yet to be fully unravelled.

Settlement forms and hierarchies?

Traditionally, defensive enclosures, enclosed farmsteads and open settlements have been seen as reflecting a hierarchy of settlement forms reflecting different social status and/or relationships. However, the role of defensive enclosures as settlements is clearly very variable and a more pertinent way of looking at this may be the extent to which the need for communal labour and its organisation reflected social groups and hierarchies controlling supply of labour. For example interesting issues have been raised in the case of Alfred's Castle, Oxfordshire, which has ditches like those of a hillfort, but in size and location is much more like an settlement enclosure (Gosden and Lock 2001).

Across the Solent-Thames area as a whole there is considerable variety in the distribution and character of late prehistoric enclosures. For example, they are much commoner on the Hampshire chalk and the Cotswolds than in the Thames valley. Some have very little trace of settlement activity, others were clearly permanent farms of some importance. They differ greatly in date, size and form, some being very simple, others much more substantial. For example two large rectilinear enclosures in the Test valley, at Flint Farm (Cunliffe and Poole 2008) and Fir Hill, Bossington (Brown 2009), were earlier than the 'Danebury Environs' model of settlement change would have predicted. In addition, the Bossington site, sited on clay-with-flints, included an unusual early Iron Age triple-ditched enclosure c. 25m in diameter that was not known from the air photographs.

Although morphologically some particularly distinctive 'types' of enclosure occur, detailed analysis has repeatedly shown that even the most obvious of these (such as 'banjo' enclosures) are seldom as clear-cut as first appears from the crude snapshot impressions of form provided by air photography.

There has been much discussion about the socio-economic and cosmological symbolism of enclosure ditches round settlements (eg Hingley 1984a; 1984b; 1999; Hill 1995; Collis 1996), and also whether the apparent increase in such enclosures from around 400 cal BC is indicative of a change in social relationships (T Moore 2006; Hill 2007). However, the idea that physical boundedness in the form of ditches was especially indicative of social relations is problematic. Sharply-defined boundaries not marked by ditches are evident in some open settlements (Lambrick and Allen 2004), and the character (and even presence or absence) of settlement within enclosures is very variable. In some cases enclosed settlements had unenclosed phases. Some sites like banjo enclosures with highly developed ditch systems attached (eg Featherstone and Bewley 2000) are much more elaborate than very simple forms.

While ditches are archaeologically rewarding features that can reveal abstract concerns about boundaries as well as practical needs, it can be argued that archaeologists' fixation on their symbolic meaning has distracted attention from the great variability in size, permanence, longevity and form (or absence) of settlement that they enclose. These variations may have been much more significant socially than the increasingly tired and over-simplistic distinction between 'enclosed' and 'unenclosed' forms.

Social hierarchies within settlements

Material evidence of status is ambiguous and does not seem to correlate much with settlement form. For example the quality of pottery and other finds from Watkins Farm (Allen 1990) contrasts with that from the otherwise similar enclosed farmstead nearby at Mingies Ditch (Allen and Robinson 1993), and is more like the large open settlement at Gravelly Guy (Lambrick and Allen 2004). Especially large or elaborate round houses can occur within defensive forts and both enclosed and open settlements at various periods (eg Bancroft, Milton Keynes; Dunston Park, Thatcham), and may reflect a variety of social significances, in some cases probably as much communal as individual.

The role of communal earthworks

One way in which some distinction can be made in site hierarchies – though this does not equate to settlements – is that some entailed large scale earthworks, best seen as communal undertakings. To some extent this is a relative consideration: what may have been a large undertaking for a small late Bronze Age community would have been trivial for a more populous Iron Age one, but nonetheless their construction would have demanded significant resources and had political

meaning symbolising the authority of leaders over their communities.

Territorial land division

Major ditched boundaries were a new feature of late prehistory, reflecting growing concern with control of land as a resource. Such boundaries have variously been interpreted as political/communal boundaries and/or connected with large scale stock management. The major linear earthworks on the Chilterns collectively known as Grims Ditch form a major land boundary running for c. 27.5km on high ground between Bradenham and Pitstone in three discontinuous sections. Limited trenching has produced small fragments of Iron Age pottery, and some evidence of grassland. The Berkshire Grims Ditch along the crest of the Downs overlooking the Vale of the White Horse probably acted as a similar territorial boundary (Ford 1982a), whereas other linear ditches following the generally north-south ridges on the downs to the south may have been smaller community subdivisions (Ford 1982b). The so-called 'Wessex Linear' ditches in Hampshire and Wiltshire are similarly thought to be concerned with defining rather than defending territory (Cunliffe 2000).

A new stage of constructing large-scale dyke systems marking territorial areas is evident in the late Iron Age. The South Oxfordshire Grims Ditch crossing the end of the Chilterns east of Wallingford, and the Aves Ditch east of the Cherwell are thought to be late Iron Age territorial boundaries (Cromarty et al. 2006; Sauer 1999; Sauer 2005a), and their locations bear some correspondence to the distributions of Late Iron Age coins (Sellwood 1984; Allen 2000; Lambrick with Robinson 2009, 361-75). The Grims Ditch at Aldermaston may be another territorial boundary of this date, possibly related to the nearby *oppidum* at Calleva Atrebatum (Silchester), or could be post-Roman, but recent investigation failed to provide good dating evidence.

Communal and defensive enclosures

Cunliffe (2005) has suggested that a communal enclosure or hillfort is best thought of as *"an enclosed place constructed in a highly-visible location to serve as a focus (if sporadic) for communal activity."* As such, they share common characteristics of enclosure, visibility and communal functions, but may fulfil very different roles, which can include:

*   The act of building as a demonstration of group cohesion
*   Enclosure used for communal pastoral activities
*   Defined space for social/religious interactions
*   Storage for communal surplus
*   Settlement for a community on a cyclic basis
*   Settlement for a community on a permanent basis
*   Settlement for elite and entourage
*   Focus for redistribution and production

* Defence in time of unrest
* Territorial marker

For Wessex, Cunliffe (2005) has summarised the evidence as follows:

* Most of the hillforts built in the 6th to 5th centuries BC continued to be developed to the 2nd century BC, although this need not imply continuous use
* Many of the hillforts built in the 5th–4th century BC were short-lived
* There appears to have been a period in the early 3rd century BC when forts with two gates had one blocked
* The few distinctive late hillforts, of the early 1st century BC, did not develop from earlier forts (although in the case of Bury Hill 2 it occupied part of the site of a long-abandoned early fort)

The results from excavation and the Wessex Hillfort geophysical surveys suggest that five broadly defined arrangements of internal can be identified:

* No recognisable activity
* Limited pit scatters usually clustered in discrete areas
* Dense, even pit scatters
* Zones of pits interspersed with circular structures
* Complexes of enclosures associated with circular structures and pits

But in the northern part of the Solent-Thames area – including the Berkshire Downs – the pattern is not so clear, and in particular there is very little evidence for similar patterns of 'developed hillforts' and dense organised patterns of internal activity. This may well be because the trajectory of social economic and political development was rather different, with the broad characteristics of the earlier forms lasting longer.

Late Bronze Age hilltop and valley enclosures

The late Bronze Age hilltop enclosures at Rams Hill and Castle Hill Little Wittenham, both in Oxfordshire) and at Taplow Court in Buckinghamshire (Plate 9.7), all lie within later, early Iron Age, hillforts. A Late Bronze Age date has also been suggested for the early palisade at Blewburton Hill (Harding 1976b) but is not proven, while much of the pottery from Chastleton appears to belong to the latest Bronze Age or earliest Iron Age. In Buckinghamshire it is possible, but by no means certain that the late Bronze Age settlement at Ivinghoe Beacon was within a defensive enclosure.

Reconsideration of the radiocarbon evidence suggests that Rams Hill originated in the last quarter of the 2nd millennium cal. BC, with Phase 2 between 1070 and 890 cal BC, whereas the dating from Castle Hill lies between 1050 and 900 cal BC (Needham and Ambers 1994; Allen *et al.* 2010). Both Rams Hill and Taplow

Plate 9.7 Excavation at Taplow Hillfort, Buckingham-shire, *copyright OA*

consisted of a series of palisades and dump defences (Allen *et al.* 2009). The enclosure at Castle Hill has contemporary settlement 200m away on the plateau below the hill, and a similar situation may exist at Taplow (Coleman and Collard 2005). In both cases concentrations of contemporary metalwork have been recovered from the reaches of the Thames that they overlook. It would not be at all surprising if there were not other comparable sites (Windsor being an obvious potential example) but the evidence for the much quoted possible example of Marshall's Hill, Reading (Bradley 1984, 121) is dubious (see Seaby 1932).

The possibly palisaded island midden sites at Runnymede and Whitecross Farm might fall into a similar category of enclosures on the valley floor, while Ford (1991-3, 316) has suggested one at Eton Wick, though this is far less clear.

The late Bronze Age hilltop enclosures at Rams Hill, Castle Hill and at Taplow Court are all quite small enclosures of *c.* 1ha (as are the riverine sites). In contrast, the possible example at Bozedown (Berks) and those in Hampshire such as Balksbury, Danebury (outer enclosure) and Walbury, were much larger enclosures of over 10ha. The Balksbury enclosure was constructed in the 9th or 8th century and continued in use for about 200 years, with at least two refurbishments, but with only very sparse evidence of fourposters and possible roundhouses inside. There is so far no evidence for Late Bronze Age hilltop enclosures in The Isle of Wight.

Plate 9.8 View of excavations at Aylesbury, showing the hillfort ditch, *copyright Mike Farley*

Late Bronze Age hilltop enclosures were probably not permanently occupied though they often have evidence of at least some domestic occupation with a thin scatter of pits, roundhouses and four posters. At Balksbury and Ivinghoe (if it was enclosed) there were rich midden deposits but this need not indicate permanent occupation (see below). Both Rams Hill and Winklebury have evidence of periodic remodelling or refurbishment, possibly with intervening periods of abandonment, and at Rams Hill, Castle Hill and Balksbury the late Bronze Age enclosures seem to have been abandoned before they were replaced by the much larger Iron Age fortifications.

Hillforts

In Buckinghamshire seventeen 'hillforts' can be identified with confidence whilst a further five possible examples are known (8.5 to 1 hectare). There are three possible undated valley forts. Two forts are definitely early (Ivinghoe and Taplow Court) with evidence of occupation; some others are suspected. The hillforts at Aylesbury (Farley and Jones 2012), Cholesbury (Kimble 1933) and Danesfield, Medmenham (Keevil and Campbell 1991) were occupied during the middle Iron Age but only Cholesbury has late Iron Age occupation (Plate 9.8). The nature and scale of internal occupation is nowhere clear due to the limited internal areas investigated and somewhat disappointing results from geophysical survey.

In Oxfordshire there are about 27 Iron Age forts. A scatter of them occurs on the Cotswold dipslope and on the Corallian ridge and chalk outliers within the valley south of the Thames. The greatest concentration is to be found along the scarp of the Berkshire Downs and outlying hills, with one fort at Bozedown east of the Thames. There are also valley forts at Burroway Brook and Cherbury Camp, as well as the late Iron Age enclosed *oppida* at Cassington Big Ring, Abingdon and Dyke Hills, Dorchester-on-Thames.

Including those which superseded late Bronze Age defensive enclosures, most investigated hillforts in Oxfordshire appear to be of Early Iron Age origin. Blewburton, Castle Hill and Segsbury clearly continued in use into the Middle Iron Age, and Cherbury and Madmarston (near Banbury) may only have been created in the Middle Iron Age. Most are around 6 ha in size, but Bozedown Camp, Segsbury Camp and Cherbury Camp are much larger, *c.* 10 ha. Segsbury may have post-dated the earliest Iron Age hillforts on the Ridgeway, possibly reflecting the emergence of a larger community than the more numerous but smaller early sites (Lock *et al.* 2005, 140-141).

In Berkshire seven hillforts are now included within the county boundary but none of these has been investigated to any great extent. Their distribution, mainly across the better soils of West Berkshire is largely what might be expected, and the hillfort at Caesars Camp on the poor heathland soils of south east Berkshire may be connected with the exploitation of iron deposits found in Tertiary geological outcrops nearby (Ford 1987a, 80).

There are about 40 hillforts in Hampshire (Hogg 1979), of which 10 have seen some form of excavation. Although the combined work at all the others would comfortably fit within the 2.5ha investigated at Danebury, significant areas have been examined at Winklebury, Balksbury, Woolbury and Bury Hill. Most appear to have been built by the 5th century BC and they display a significant range of diversity in terms of chronological development and internal settlement and other features, with Danebury acting as a type site in displaying all the stages of development and yet being unusual in doing so. The Danebury Environs and Wessex Hillfort projects have done much to demonstrate the great variety of sequence and levels and kinds of internal occupation (Cunliffe and Poole 2000 a-d; Cunliffe 2005).

On the Isle of Wight remains of a possibly unfinished Iron Age hill fort, including an earthwork rampart and ditch, survive at Chillerton Down; a possible defensive-double ditch has been identified at Yaverland; and at Castle Hill, Mottistone the earthworks of a possible small defensive site (*c* 55m x 58m across) have been identified (Basford 1980; Currie 2003).

Valley forts

Forts in valley floor locations include Burroway on the Thames floodplain, with evidence of a timber- framed rampart and of early Iron Age origin, and Cherbury, probably of early/middle Iron Age origin, on a spur of land defined by two streams on the Corallian dip slope at Pusey.

Valley locations become a key element of major defensible sites in the middle to Late Iron Age in the Upper Thames area, with Abingdon Vineyard (*c* 25ha) and Dyke Hills, Dorchester (33ha) on the Thames and Salmonsbury (22.5ha) on the Windrush just outside the area (Allen 1991; 1993; Allen in Henig and Booth 2000; Dunning 1976). Cassington Big Rings is a fourth, smaller enclosure (*c* 10ha) of rather different character and probably unfinished (Case 1982b). The dating of the defences at Salmondsbury is probably middle to late Iron Age, Abingdon later middle Iron Age to early Roman and Cassington late Iron Age to very early Roman. The dating for Dyke Hills is still uncertain. In Hampshire the site of Oram's Arbour predating the Roman town at Winchester (Whinney 1994), overlooked by the earlier fort on St Catherines Hill, bears some resemblance to the sequence of Castle Hill, Little Wittenham followed by Dyke Hills preceding the Roman town at Dorchester on Thames. No exactly comparable sites are identifiable in Buckinghamshire, Berkshire or the Isle of Wight.

Internal activity in forts

Geophysical surveys have now been carried out upon a wide range of hillforts in the Solent-Thames area, pioneered in the early days of magnetometry at Madmarston and Rainsborough (Fowler 1960; Avery *et al.* 1967, Appendix 1) with more recent systematic surveys at other forts on the Cotswolds, at Cherbury on the Corallian Ridge, at Castle Hill, Little Wittenham, various Chiltern forts, several along the Ridgeway and a significant number on the Wessex chalk (Lang 2009; Wintle *et al.* 2009; Allen *et al.* 2010; Gover 2000; Payne, Corney and Cunliffe 2006).

These surveys together with aerial photography suggest that most of the Oxfordshire hillforts did not contain very dense internal activity, although Segsbury has a fair concentration of pits towards the centre of the interior, together with a spread of penannular ditched enclosures, as does the valley fort at Cherbury. At Ivinghoe there remains an issue of whether the fairly dense late Bronze Age and early Iron Age occupation is actually an earlier open settlement (Brown 2001).

In Hampshire the very dense pit clusters and lines of four-post structures of so-called 'developed hillforts' like Danebury contrast with other (often earlier) sites with much sparser indications of settlement (Plate 9.9). Most forts within the Danebury study area were short-lived, whereas Danebury itself was refortified at various stages up until its abandonment in the late middle Iron Age, by when its interior had become a dense mass of pits, houses and other features respecting clearly established roads. It is thought that it may have developed a 'special relationship' with the New Buildings complex, where the limited evidence of internal use despite substantial defences suggests a different role for some forts, perhaps with the developed Danebury acting as a stronghold, massive communal store and political centre surrounded by more symbolic territorial markers (Cunliffe 2000). One of the results of the Wessex Hillfort project has been to show that rather few forts had such densely occupied interiors as Danebury (Payne *et al.* 2006).

Plate 9.9 Excavation within Danebury hillfort, Hampshire, *copyright Institute of Archaeology, Oxford*

It has long been recognised that Iron Age forts (and perhaps some of their late Bronze Age predecessors) were also sacred places where a good deal of ritualistic communal activity took place. At Castle Hill a very large early Iron Age pit was found containing evidence of feasting, and there was a high occurrence of human remains, including complete bodies, partly mutilated remains and single placed bones (Allen *et al.* 2010). While the fort was largely abandoned in terms of occupation, the ramparts, interior and the immediate surroundings remained a place of burial into the Roman period. At Uffington aspects of the probable communal use of the fort in association with the maintenance of the White Horse may well have been the foundation of traditions that lasted into the modern era. At Blewburton, the burial of a man with a horse, associated with a pot split above and below the burial with an adze-hammer beneath, were found in the hillfort ditch (Collins 1952-3). At Aylesbury a remarkable complex of human burials associated with the remains of kids and lambs has been recorded (Farley and Jones 2012). Danebury has produced a very considerable number of human burials, both complete, partial, mutilated and fragmentary, as well as possible shrine structures.

The richness of this evidence and related results from large scale excavation of Danebury together with a few other forts like Winklebury and various enclosed settlements has formed the basis of several important individual research projects, and a very extensive long-running debate has developed about the interpretation of the evidence, much of which goes to the heart of the nature of Iron Age society (eg Hill 1995, 1996; Collis 1996; Cunliffe 2005)

The substantial achievements of mainly non-development led archaeological research projects like Danebury, Danebury Environs, Wessex Hillforts, Uffington and the Ridgeway and the Wittenhams, together with smaller scale projects, make the Solent-Thames area a particularly rich resources for hillfort studies. The results have begun to show both similarities and great variety in how hillforts developed and were used, both chronologically and regionally; the sheer richness and variety of the evidence now available, however, leaves a great deal still to be learnt about what this tells us of late prehistoric society.

External settlements close to hillforts

A missing ingredient in most investigations of hillforts, which has only recently started to be rectified, is the role of external settlements. A number of forts in the northern half of the Solent-Thames area are now known to have significant external settlements, as at Madmarston, Castle Hill and Cherbury in Oxfordshire and perhaps Taplow in Buckinghamshire. Only those at Castle Hill and Taplow have been investigated by excavation. The Castle Hill external settlement at 700 m long and 200-300 m wide, is one of the largest late prehistoric settlements known in the Thames Valley, with evidence of extensive pits, paddocks, four posters and roundhouses (Allen *et al.* 2010; see Plate 9.1).

However, the extent to which Iron Age forts had external settlements may well be under-estimated since surveys such as the recent Wessex Hillfort project (Payne *et al.* 2006) seldom cover external areas as thoroughly as interiors. Where they did, there are some indications of external activity, though not necessarily on the scale of the examples such as Castle Hill.

Middens

The most notable aspect of these late Bronze Age and Iron Age sites, which mostly occur either on hilltops or floodplains, are the thick deposits of artefact-rich dark soil that sometimes cover significant areas and often (though not always) share distinctive characteristics of high status objects, human skull fragments, animal bone suggestive of meat consumption and many late Bronze Age bronze objects. There is much debate about their possible roles as trading emporia engaged in the distribution of valuable bronze metalwork or, probably more likely, ceremonial gathering places engaged in communal recycling of material culture (Needham 1991).

Runnymede Bridge (Longley 1980; Needham 1991) located on a former island in the Thames on the easternmost edge of the Solent-Thames area, was surrounded by wooden revetments and perhaps a palisaded enclosure, possibly with landing stages for boats. Whitecross Farm, near Wallingford seems to have been similar, but on a much smaller scale.

Outside the hillfort at Castle Hill, Little Wittenham (Oxon) is an extensivel midden of late Bronze Age to early Iron Age date, up to 0.4m deep and at least 50m (possibly 100m) across, with a chalk and pebble platform, clay spreads and postholes forming an horizon within it (Rhodes 1948; Wessex Archaeology 2004b; Allen *et al.* 2010). Lambrick (with Robinson 2009, 340-1) suggests that the rich late Bronze Age to middle Iron Age site at Woodeaton 0.15 to 0.4m thick and perhaps up to 120m or more across is likely to be a similar sort of site (cf Harding 1987), and is unusual in extending well into the middle Iron Age (possibly after a break in use) and subsequently becoming the site of a Romano-celtic temple.

In Buckinghamshire, the late Bronze Age occupation horizon with an important collection of late Bronze Age metalwork at Ivinghoe may be a similar kind of deposit. In Hampshire the accumulation of rich colluvial deposits at Balksbury and possibly Winklebury may arguably be equated with these types of late Bronze Age/Early Iron Age 'midden' deposits. On the Isle of Wight the Undercliff, on the south east coast, has a number of midden deposits ranging in date from Bronze Age to the medieval period (Sherwin unpubl.; Preece 1986). A possible late Bronze Age midden site has been investigated at Binnel, and Iron Age material from Gills Cliff (Trott and Tomalin 2003).

Apart from Runnymede, no middens are yet known that compare in size with the major midden sites like All Cannings Cross, Potterne or Chisenbury in the Vale of

Plate 9.10 Reconstruction of the late Bronze Age eyot at Whitecross Farm, Wallingford, Oxfordshire, *copyright OA*

Pewsey, Wiltshire, which are up to 3m thick (Lawson 2000; McOmish 1996) or even the substantial midden at Whitchurch, Warwickshire 300m x 175m and 0.75m thick (Waddington and Sharples 2010). Nevertheless they share a number of similar characteristics, and the more recent though small scale excavations at Whitecross Farm and Castle Hill have produced signifi- cant palaeoenvironmnetal evidence (Plate 9.10). However, the scale of these sites and richness of deposits is very variable, and it is not yet clear how far there is a sharp distinction between them and the more regular occurrence of smaller scale midden-like deposits within and around settlements. These are often 'trapped' within the backfill of large features such as waterholes, as at Green Park (Brossler *et al.* 2004), and sometimes as general settlement edge deposits as at Cassington West (Lambrick with Robinson 2009, Fig. 4.8).

Burnt mounds

These heaps of fire cracked flint are most often found close to water and are often thought to be cooking places utilised by mobile transhumant groups, though many other possible uses (including saunas and cloth-making) have been put forward. Their function may vary over time, and more application of lipid residues and other chemical analyses might help define, or negate various potential practices.

A large burnt mound was dated by association with Late Bronze Age pottery at Green Park, Reading and sealed a pit with a C14 date of 880–860 cal BC (Brossler *et al.* 2004, 39) and at Barkham Square, Wokingham the mound was dated by two C14 determinations of 1400- 800 and 810–410 cal BC (Torrance and Ford 2003, 93). A very much smaller 'mound' at Turnpike School, Newbury produced a C14 date of 1000–800 cal BC (Pine 2010).

At least 300 Burnt Mound sites are recorded in the New Forest,(Pasmore and Pallister 1967; O'Drisceoil, 1988; Pasmore 2000), and they also occur elsewhere, as at Harbridge in the Avon Valley (Shennan 1999) and Hatch near Old Basing (Oram 2006). Few seem to conform to the 'model' type of burnt mound with a trough surrounded by a crescent-shaped heap of discarded burnt stone (Raymond 1987; Oram 2006). Mainly late Bronze Age, a middle Bronze Age date of 1454–1370 cal BC (KIA26695) was obtained from a burnt mound deposit at Greywell Road, Basingstoke (Oram 2006) and there is increasing evidence for burnt mounds from the earlier Bronze Age and even the late Neolithic (Beamish and Ripper 2000; Allen *et al.* 2013). The availability of improved radiometric dating and Bayesian modelling should enable the chronology and longevity, and even the sequence of activity of burnt mounds to be established.

Burnt flint is also significant at some burial sites, including Mount Farm near Dorchester and Field Farm,

Burghfield, and has been found with Deverel-Rimbury vessels at Langstone Harbour (Allen and Gardiner 2000) and on Twyford Down (Walker and Farwell 2000).

The built environment

The ground plans of hundreds of buildings of the later Bronze Age and Iron Age have been excavated across the area, and a number of studies have reviewed their form and possible practical and cosmological reasons that underpinned their design (Allen *et al.* 1984; Fitzpatrick and Morris 1994; Brück 1999; Parker Pearson 1993; Oswald 1997; Pope 2007; Lambrick with Robinson 2009, 143-49).

A number of broad chronological trends appear to apply to most of the Solent-Thames area, with relatively straightforward, simple post-built roundhouses (occasionally with porch/vestibule structures marking their entrances) evident from the middle Bronze Age onwards, eg at Yarnton, Weir Bank Stud Farm Bray and Chalton (see Fig.9.1). Post-built houses become much commoner in the later Bronze Age and into the early Iron Age across the region, and include some larger examples, as at Bancroft, Stanton Harcourt and Cassington, Dunston Park, Balksbury, Old Down Farm and Winnall Down (see Fig. 9.1). The Bancroft example, 18.6m across with three post-rings surrounded by a drainage gully and structured deposits of late Bronze Age ceramics, a saddle quern and pig bones, is exceptional (Williams and Zeepvat 1994).

In the middle Iron Age there appears to be a wide range of variation both in construction type (post-built,

stake- and plank-walled and probably turf-constructed) and the more common provision of drainage gullies or small enclosures surrounding them. The sequence of especially well-preserved buildings stratified within the Iron Age quarry hollows at Danebury remains exceptional for the detail revealed of different construction methods including the possibility of impermanent, basket-built construction (Cunliffe 1984b). For the most part this is within a more restricted size range, but with much less regular evidence of earth-fast posts (Plate 9.11). Since there is no good evidence of this arising from any particular technical invention, it seems to be part of a change in fashion in which posts ceased to be as decoratively or symbolically important.

The large number of ground plans now available offers the potential for more insights into stylistic or symbolic fashions and details of design. For example some houses have axial or paired posts, and Lambrick (with Robinson 2009, 139) has noted how some later Bronze Age houses have entrances that taper outwards, whereas most Iron Age ones are splayed outwards suggesting rather different social indications of privacy or welcome. Apart from structural evidence, there is increasing evidence from the distribution of artefacts and small pits etc how the use of buildings reflect both cosmological and practical aspects of design. This is especially striking for example at Hartshill Copse (Collard *et al.* 2006; see also Plate 9.16 below). There is also growing evidence of external as well as internal living, as at Mingies Ditch and Weir Bank Stud Farm.

In the Thames valley a number of large rectangular buildings, some with over a dozen postholes have been identified, as exemplified from recent work at Cassington

Plate 9.11 House without posts at Danebury, Hampshire, copyright Oxford Institute of Archaeology

(LBA), Yarnton (E/MIA) and Radley (IA) (Hey *et al.* 2011a, Fig. 3.4; Cotswold Archaeology 2004). Possible D-shaped structures of late Bronze Age and Early Iron Age date have been identified at Yarnton (Hey *et al.* 2011a, Fig. 3.5); also semicircular ones there and at Farmoor (Lambrick with Robinson 1979) and Little Wittenham (Allen *et al.* 2010, 125-6). Nevertheless, rectangular buildings are still very unusual in later prehistory and it is by no means certain what they were used for.

In the late Iron Age the normal form of buildings is still far from certain. Although there is quite good evidence for the continuation of roundhouses, eg at Park Farm Binfield, Berks (Roberts 1995), any evidence of houses is far less common than earlier in the Iron Age. The possibility that there was more use of rectangular sleeper beam construction is one possibility, as revealed by the admittedly exceptional case of Calleva (Silchester).

The number and diversity of four-post structures continues to grow; various examples with differing numbers of posts have been identified at Hill Farm outside Castle Hill, Little Wittenham (Allen *et al.* 2010). Lambrick (with Robinson 2009, 272-4) has observed that a number of probably pastoral settlements in the Upper Thames valley such as Mingies Ditch and Groundwell Farm have a particular form of four-post structures with very large postholes (denoted as 'mega-posters'). The postholes are sometimes linked by trenches, and at Groundwell Farm, Wiltshire, these are very similar to rectangular sets of parallel trenches, though it is not clear what they were for. The use of four-posters remains somewhat uncertain, and while some are associated with charred crop remains, their very common association with settlements that have an emphasis on pastoral farming suggests that they were certainly not always granaries. Bradley (2005) has indicated the variety of roles, both functional and symbolic, that such structures have long performed.

Funerary customs

Over the period the means of disposing of the dead varied, with rites involving cremation becoming uncommon by the early Iron Age, and recurring in the late Iron Age mainly as a result of new cultural influences alongside older ones. However, although this is archaeologically distinctive, it is not clear that it was a primary consideration in how the human remains were treated compared with other factors such as where remains were disposed of, whether or not deaths were natural, and the likelihood that most dead people were not accorded formal burial. For much of the Iron Age it is suspected that most bodies were exposed and may have been scattered into the environment and if this was partly concerned with the removal of corruptible flesh the apparent contrast with cremation may have been less significant than first appears. The complexities of interpreting human remains that are found are thus compounded by relative ignorance about how the majority of dead people may have been treated and what superstitions and beliefs were paramount.

Funerary monuments

A small number of round barrows are recorded with secondary cremation burials ('urnfields') such as Mound 1 in the Lambourn Seven Barrows where 112 cremation burials (and one child inhumation) were recorded (Case 1956b), and Standlake, with mostly unurned cremations. However these are unusually large, and smaller groups of half a dozen cremations and/or inhumations, as at Field Farm Burghfield, Stanton Harcourt, Mount Farm, Dorchester, and Eton Rowing Course are more typical (Lambrick with Robinson 2009, 294-8). Amongst the latest instances of continued use of earlier funerary monuments are some late Bronze Age burials at Barrow Hills (Barclay and Halpin 1999).

Satellite burials, i.e. single burials on the margins of ring ditches of middle or earlier Bronze Age date are also recorded, as at Mount Farm (Lambrick 2010), Heron's House and Field Farm Burghfield (Bradley and Richards 1979; Butterworth and Lobb 1992), and Eton Rowing Course (Allen *et al.* 2000).

Over the northern part of the Solent-Thames area very few barrows were newly-built in the Middle Bronze Age, but a number are known for Berkshire and south Buckinghamshire, notably a small 1.8m high barrow at Sunningdale with 25 urned cremations, and ring ditches of possible middle Bronze Age origin at Cippenham near Slough, Field Farm Burghfield and Eton Rowing Course (Lambrick with Robinson 2009, 298-300). In general barrows with primary Deverel Rimbury burials are very much commoner closer to the Deverel Rimbury heartland in Dorset and South Wiltshire, and to some extent Hampshire.

Flat cemeteries

Several middle Bronze Age flat cremation cemeteries are known from the Solent-Thames area, mostly southwards from the Middle Thames (Ellison 1980). A middle Bronze Age cemetery of about 15 Deverel Rimbury urned cremations at Stokenchurch is one of the most northerly. Some are old finds of large cemeteries such as Dummer, Hants, with over 70 inverted urns (Ellison 1980), medium sized groups like Sulham Berks with 17 surviving of a potentially larger group (Barrett 1973), but others were only very small, as with the five urns at Shortheath Lane, Sulhampstead (Butterworth and Lobb 1992). Some of the cremations are not burials as such but are token deposits of pyre debris. A noticeable feature of later Bronze Age urnfields is that almost all large ones were late nineteenth or early twentieth century discoveries, suggesting some bias in discovery processes (Lambrick and Robinson, 2009, 303).

In Hampshire both Easton Down (R7) and Twyford Down have revealed mixed rite cemeteries. At Easton Down the sequence is unclear but at Twyford Down two phases of burial could be distinguished, both involving cremation and inhumation burials associated with Deverel Rimbury pottery (Walker and Farwell 2000). On the Isle of Wight known later Bronze Age urnfield sites (groups of 40, ?70 and 11) show a different distribution from earlier barrows with only Rew Down on the Middle to Upper Chalk.

Iron Age cemeteries are very much rarer than Bronze Age urnfields, but a small number have been found in recent years, including a middle Iron Age example of 35 individuals at Yarnton in Oxfordshire (Hey *et al.* 1999). In Hampshire 18 early Iron Age burials (mostly adolescents an children) occurred in clusters at Winnall Down; 28 middle Iron Age burials were found in an Iron Age quarry at Suddern Farm; and at Owslebury 16 mainly late Iron Age burials were found in a cemetery that continued in use into the early Roman period (Fasham 1985; Cunliffe and Poole 2000, vol 2, pt 3, 153-74; Collis 1994, 108). The reasons for these unusual cemeteries are obscure, though for Yarnton it is suggested that they might be victims of disease. The Winnall Down burials were in small clusters around the settlement and small groups of burials are know on other sites, such as three close to a boundary between two areas of settlement at Berwick Salome (Oxfordshire) (Wilson 2008).

The occasional use of Iron Age buildings as formal burial places is suggested by three associated with a post-built roundhouse at Spring Road, Abingdon (Allen and Kamash 2008) and two in the stake-walled building at Frilford (Harding 1987).

Isolated burials and human remains within fields and near boundaries

A significant number of single urned cremation burials have been recorded across the Solent-Thames area (Ellison 1980), one recent example being at Old Way Lane, Cippenham, Slough (Ford *et al.* 2003, 105). Apparently isolated late Bronze Age and Iron Age burials also occur, such as the recent find of a bagged or bound body at Sutton Courtenay south of Abingdon (Gill Hey pers comm).

These cases may reflect a practice of disposing of human remains in small clusters in open areas or in and around fields, as was apparently the case with small urnfields at the Eton Rowing Course and at Appleford Sidings. Individual isolated examples are known at Weir Bank Stud Farm, Reading Business Park and Green Park, Reading in Berkshire, and at The Lea, Denham in Buckinghamshire (Lambrick with Robinson 2009, 306-11). A cluster of late Bronze examples were associated with ditches adjacent to a palaeochannel at Marsh Lane East on the Maidenhead-Windsor flood channel (Allen *et al.* forthcoming). At Twyford Down some of the cremation vessels were arranged in two alignments at regular intervals (Walker and Farwell 2000), which might be suggestive of an association with an above ground hedge or fence line.

Iron Age inhumations in or close to ditches outside settlements have been recorded just outside the area at Roughground Farm, Lechlade and Horcott in Gloucestershire. At Watchfied (West Oxfordshire) a double inhumation of a woman and child was placed within a funnel entrance area of a field system, with another burial of a young woman and perinatal infant close to one of the boundaries (Birkbeck 2001).

Burials in and around settlements

Apart from the relatively clustered groups of burials occurring as cemeteries, or more isolated burials associated with boundaries, human remains were often disposed of in and around settlements, often in a manner that suggests a degree of ritualistic behaviour.

Burials in or close to the boundaries of enclosed settlements and hillforts are well-attested (cf Hill 1995), and some such as a possibly severed head at Aylesbury and a double burial of a woman and child at Cassington Big Ring could be foundation sacrifices. The collection of human and animal skeletons associated with the hillfort at Aylesbury (Farley and Jones 2012) is without parallel in the region (Plate 9.12), although the remarkable burial of a man and a horse with a ritually broken pot and an adze hammer at Blewburton, which might be a closing deposit (Lambrick with Robinson 2009, 324-5), has similarities on a smaller scale.

Both the occurrence and character of these remains suggest that activities connected with disposal of the dead were especially associated with communal enclosures, some hillforts like Danebury, Aylesbury and Castle Hill being particularly prolific (Cunliffe 1995). These include cases of mutilation and very possibly ritual killing. However, none of this was confined to such places.

Double inhumations, often of women and children (conceivably mothers and their offspring), which could reflect ritual killings have been found in a variety of contexts, including pits within hillforts at Castle Hill Little Wittenham (Allen *et al.* 2010, 257) and Danebury (Cunliffe and Poole 1994, 421), in the ditch of Cassington Big Ring (Case 1982b) and in two graves associated with a field system at Watchfield (described above). Other double or multiple burials include infants or adults and infants at Old Down Farm and Winnalll Down (Wait 1985, 372-3, 376-83).

The practice of disposing of human remains in and around ordinary farming settlements can be traced back at least to the late Bronze Age, with cremations and inhumations occurring for example at Cassington West and Reading Business Park. There are a few instances of early Iron Age cremations associated with houses at Yarnton, but for the most part Iron Age remains found in settlements are a mixture of single bones, partial bodies and complete inhumations. The extent to which some individual bones represent accidental deposition (eg of curated fragments from excarnated bodies) is debatable; the placing of some (especially skull fragments) was clearly deliberate.

The rate of occurrence of human remains within farming settlements is highly variable in the Upper Thames valley, sites like Gravelly Guy, Mount Farm and Bourton on the Water (just into Gloucestershire) having much greater densities of human remains than comparable sites such as Ashville, Yarnton or Coxwell

Plate 9.12 Human and animal bone deposit at Aylesbury, *copyright Mike Farley*

Road Faringdon (Lambrick with Robinson 2009, 313-5). In Buckinghamshire such pit burials have not so far been found, despite the extent of work at Milton Keynes, suggesting some regional variation in the practice. Elsewhere the practice seems to have become commoner through the early to middle Iron Age, but is much less common in the late Iron Age.

Detailed burial practices were examined by Wait (1985) demonstrating a substantial degree of variation in detailed practice (including for example whether graves were dug and how bodies were disposed of on the bottom or within the fill of storage pits or ditches and how they were oriented).

Late Iron Age high status burials

Grave goods are only rarely found in the burials of the later Bronze Age and Iron Age, but in the late Iron Age social differentiation began to be manifested through the grave goods accompanying burials. High status late Iron Age burials are rare within the Solent-Thames region, but include the warrior inhumation burial at Owslebury, Hampshire (Collis 1994). Other inhumation burials at Owslebury were accompanied by pots, and in one case a wooden box. A cremation burial with a bucket was found at Blagden Copse, Hurstbourne Tarrant (Dewar 1929) and there were early finds described as bucket fittings from Silkstead near Winchester, although their provenance and identification is now regarded as uncertain (H Rees pers. Comm.). In Buckinghamshire a rich cremation burial at Dorton was found that had contained three amphorae, two flagons, a carinated cup, an iron hoop and timbers (possibly from a chest) and a

decorated bronze mirror (Farley 1983; Plate 9.13). This is the only Welwyn-type burial in the region, so-called after a group of rich burials found in Hertfordshire. Another mirror burial, whose cremation was otherwise accompanied by only a single pedestal pottery jar, was found at Latchmere Green, near to Silchester in

Plate 9.13 The late Iron Age mirror from Dorton, Buckinghamshire, *copyright Prehistoric Society*

Hampshire (Fulford and Creighton 1998). Late Iron Age cremations accompanied by pots are more widespread, and at Brooklands, Milton Keynes, these may have included another burial accompanied by one or more substantial metal objects, as one of the graves was robbed by nighthawks before excavation could take place (D Stansbie pers. Comm.).

Human remains in watery places

Langstone Harbour was demonstrably used as a flat cremation cemetery, most cases utilising urns that were large and heavy and probably made more or less on the spot. Several urns containing only burnt flint were found in soft mud on the foreshore, and other scatters of burnt flint could represent remains of funerary pyres and which was used as temper for the urns (Allen and Gardiner 2000, esp. Fig. 64).

Bradley and Gordon (1988) reviewed the evidence of human skulls recovered from the Thames, of which nearly 300 survive and several more were reported with original finds of metalwork. It is noticeable that while animal bones had been retained there were very few other human bones, including mandibles or cervical vertebrae, suggesting that the skulls had been selected already in a defleshed, disarticulated condition, for deposition in the river. There was a bias towards prime adult males aged between 25 and 35. Four out of six skulls that were radiocarbon dated were late Bronze Age.

Excavation of a former Thames channel at Eton Rowing Course has shown that complete pots, human and animal skulls and other bones were being placed on sandbanks within the river not far from a location traversed by a sequence of wooden structures. In this case the human bones included long bones that had perhaps been cracked to extract marrow, possibly suggesting cannibalism (Allen *et al.* 2000).

Other associations of human remains with watery places include several instances of usually fragmentary bones being found in the backfilling of waterholes. One of the most unusual examples is the whole skeleton of a young woman in a later Bronze Age waterhole at Watkins Farm, Northmoor, Oxon (Allen 1990).

Wider interpretations and social attitudes

Since Whimster (1981), Wilson (1981) and Wait (1985) undertook their various reviews of Iron Age burial practice the amount of data available has grown enormously. Although on the whole their conclusions have stood the test of time quite well, a good deal more can now be gleaned than was then the case. There has been much discussion of how Iron Age burial practices reflect social and religious attitudes meaning, but the ways in which concerns for the environment and social groups rather than the prestige of individuals was expressed has generally been reinforced in recent years, including more instances of grave goods that may relate to the manner in which people were buried, but also more examples of double inhumations, mutilations and

smashed or butchered bones with which to explore issues of human sacrifice and possible evidence of cannibalism.

There is now more indication that the preferred normative right was for the body and spirit to be released into the environment, perhaps with some watery places being specially appropriate for commemorating a warrior elite. The social opposite of that prestige may be reflected in some of the evidence of how people buried in and around settlements were treated, their bodies not released into the wider environment, but at least sometimes the victim of sacrifice. The amount of data on health and stature now available has yet to be explored fully, but Lambrick (with Robinson 2009, 321-3) has tentatively suggested that those chosen for burial in settlements were socially and perhaps economically disadvantaged, with more evidence of poor nutrition and an undue proportion of women and young adults.

There is also more scope for re-examining the detailed positioning of burials, how this varied regionally, and whether for example the association with storage pits is related to fertility and renewal (related to crop storage), or waste and discard (related to possible secondary use as latrines). In addition, there is now better evidence upon which to explore cultural trends in terms of the continuance of traditional practices alongside new influences, both through the later Bronze Age cremation rite persisting into the early Iron Age, and pit burials persisting into the Roman period.

Ceremony, ritual and religion

The construction of ceremonial monuments had largely ceased by the middle Bronze Age, though many were at least respected. In the later Bronze Age and Iron Age major communal enclosures and forts would have acted as major communal ceremonial and religious centres. From what is known of late prehistoric religion a good deal of importance was attached to natural features and groves that are difficult to identify archaeologically.

Amongst later Bronze Age ceremonial structures are a possible group of post rings in the upper Thames valley (at Spring Road, Abingdon, Standlake and perhaps at Gravelly Guy and at Langford Down, Lechlade (Lambrick with Robinson 2009, 330 Fig. 9.1). More impressive is a pair of diagonally crossing palisade screens associated with the early ironworking site at Hartshill Copse (see Plate 9.16 below). At Yarnton ditches and rows of slots may have been aligned on a sacred tree. All of these are notable as odd structures rather than having clearly associated votive deposits

At Danebury there was a succession of four rectangular structures interpreted as successive shrines in the middle of the hillfort, though they were not directly associated with votive offerings.

Iron Age shrines have been suggested as predating Romano-British temples at Frilford and Woodeaton near Oxford; the evidence at Woodeaton is circumstantial, relying principally on a possible pre-Roman palisade temenos and suitable finds. Recent unpublished geophysical evidence and the recognition of the site as an important midden has increased the likelihood of an Iron Age religious centre here, but it is far from proven. The case for Frilford was questioned (having previously been accepted) by Dennis Harding (1987) but the presence of a votive ploughshare in a curious set of post holes, and two burials in the stake-walled house, both beneath Romano British structures, is still highly unusual. The absence of late Iron Age material is not an objection to Roman reuse of a site known to be sacred (Lambrick with Robinson 2009).

By far the most convincing case of an Iron Age shrine predating a Romano-Celtic one is Hayling Island, where an Iron Age circular structure 8m in diameter was centrally placed within a courtyard 22m square defined by a ditch and lengths of palisade or hedge (King and Soffe 1994; 1998). This predated a well-built Roman temple building of similar form. Post holes and a central pit that could have held some sort of object of veneration were found, and within the courtyard there were patches of burning. Unlike other possible examples there were numerous objects such as horse gear, weaponry, brooches and currency bars, many showing signs of deliberate breakage. The almost complete absence of cattle bones in the faunal remains suggests that they were deliberately excluded.

There are a number of other possible shrine-like structures, such as a late Bronze Age to early Iron Age (1300 BC–500 BC) site on Aston Clinton bypass (Buckinghamshire) which revealed a substantial 4-post structure surrounded by a gully with a single entrance. Pits around this structure contained human bone and unusually shaped 'concertina pots' thought to mimic bronze beakers. A skull was radiocarbon dated to the middle Bronze Age, several hundred years older than the other finds. The site is interpreted as a roofed shrine or mausoleum on which remains of the dead were exposed. The skull could have been a treasured relic (Masefield 2008). A rather similar arrangement, but of late Iron Age date, was found at Smiths Field, Hardwick-with-Yelford, Oxfordshire (Allen 2000, 20, fig. 1.11). Here a shallow penannular enclosure 20m in diameter enclosed a deep, vertical-sided slot forming a square c.10m across with a cow burial at one corner. This in turn surrounded a setting of posts 4m square with a small pit or scoop set off-centre within it (Allen, 2000, 20, fig 1.11).

Warfare, defences and military installations

Weaponry and trappings of war

That "heroic" behaviour and conflict was part of the image of the elite in late prehistory can hardly be doubted, but there is little physical evidence for large-scale warfare. The trappings of warfare are widespread, with artefactual remains such as swords and daggers from both the Bronze Age and Iron Ages, and late Iron Age coins show the local Atrebatic rulers striking a fine pose as mounted warriors. The River Thames has been

an especially rich source of late prehistoric weaponry as a result of ritualistic deposition.

Jill York's analysis of bronze objects from the Thames (York 2002) showed that many were damaged, and some of that damage was probably the result of fighting, as in the case of the bronze shield from Clifton Hampden punctured by a Bronze Age spear. But much of the damage (bending and breaking swords and spears etc) was probably ritualistic and symbolic – in effect 'killing' the weapon. Similar evidence has emerged from analysis of bronze sword blades in Hampshire, which has suggested that some were used in hand to hand combat, though the examples in the Andover (Varndell 1979) and Blackmoor (Colquhoun 1979) hoards appear to have had a ritual beating before their deposition.

To a large extent such river deposition was symbolic, and it is doubtful if any was the direct result of battle or combat, though at Dorchester-on-Thames (close to Clifton Hampden) a male human pelvis was found with a late Bronze Age spearhead embedded in it (Ehrenburg, 1977). At Danebury there were numerous skeletons with sometimes lethal wounds from weaponry, but the context of their death (warfare, personal combat or sacrifice) is not entirely clear.

Most Iron Age weaponry (swords, daggers, sheaths, spearheads and shields in the Solent-Thames area come from watery deposits (Fitzpatrick 1984) but there are also some from burials in pits or graves (eg Lambrick and Allen 2004, 232, 362, Fig. 8.7; Collis 1994). Their occurrence on settlement sites with no obvious ritualistic connotations, as at Pennylands (eg Williams 1993, 23, Fig. 16 and 99-100, Pl. 13, Fig. 54) is much rarer.

There is a distinct absence of archery equipment, but slingstones would certainly have been used as projectiles in human combat. Apart from the well-known slinger's position in the main entrance to Danebury and a cache of 11,000 slingstones (Cunliffe 1984), there are some other hillforts with numerous slingstones including caches ready for use (Hirst and Rahtz 1996, 48; Lock et al. 2005, 122-3; Miles et al. 2003, 112, 185-6; Allen et al. 2010, 30, 266; Ralston 2006). Although slingstones occur quite commonly in very small numbers on settlements, where they could have been used for hunting or for personal protection, there is a distinction between this and the hundreds or thousands found on some defensive sites.

A small number of sites from the late Bronze Age onwards have produced horse equipment and there is sparse evidence for chariots, though their actual use in warfare is not directly evident. There is evidence from Bury Hill for use of the later fort as a possible 'chariot school' (Cunliffe and Poole 2000b), and late Iron Age coins depict local Atrebatic rulers as mounted warriors.

Iron Age defences and evidence of possible use in warfare

Whatever the other copious evidence for the complex roles of hillforts, they were designed at least in principle and almost certainly in practice to be defensible. But it is important to appreciate that this may have been both

Plate 9.14 The White Horse and hillfort at Uffington, Oxfordshire, *copyright OA*

symbolic and practical. For example, so-called 'guard chambers' at the entrances to some hillforts may have had multiple roles, and their use for military purposes, rather then symbolic or general use in relation to the comings and goings through hillfort entrances, has been questioned by Avery (1993).

Most Buckinghamshire hillforts have only a single rampart and, so far as is known, simple gateways. Ivinghoe and Taplow show evidence of timber-framed phases that in the latter case was augmented by a dump rampart.

In Oxfordshire timber-framed or revetted box-ramparts are known from Uffington Castle, Segsbury and Blewburton on the Berkshire Downs, and at Burroway Brook in the valley (Plate 9.14). On the limestone stone-faced ramparts occur at Rainsborough (Northants), Bladon Castle, and Cherbury, while on the chalk sarsen revetments are known at Uffington and Segsbury. Simple dump ramparts typically followed the timber-framed phases at several sites and a simple dump rampart is

known from Madmarston. Entrances have been investigated at Rainsborough, at Cherbury, Blewburton Hill and to some extent Uffington, and on a number of Hampshire hillforts, most notably Danebury (Cunliffe 1984b; 2000; 2005). Multivallate defences like those at Cherbury (probably middle Iron Age) and Rainsborough (unusually early Iron Age) are rarer than in the 'developed' hillforts of Wessex. Broadly speaking these patterns of development follow much the same pattern as that of the more numerous and varied forts of Wessex, where the major excavations at Danebury and its environs have allowed the development of a general model for how defences developed (Cunliffe 2005) (Table 9.4):

While arguments about the role of a developed hillfort like Danebury will continue, there is evidence, in the form of weapons, skeletons with wounds and gates destroyed by burning, to suggest that the elaborate fortifications were not just for show. Particularly striking is the pit with 11,300 sling stones (River Test pebbles) found near the east gate (Cunliffe 1984b).

Table 9.4 Scheme of development of hillfort defences in Wessex

Enclosure type	Characteristics	Ceramic phase	Date	Example
Early 1	vertical faced rampart	cp 2 3	6th–5th BC	Bury Hill 1
Early 2	glacis rampart	cp 3	5th–4th BC	Quarley Hill
Developed 1	entrances modified	cp 4/5 6	4th–3rd BC	Beacon Hill
Developed 2	one gate; ramparts and gate enhanced	cp 7	3rd–2nd BC	Danebury 5
Late	circular and multivallate	cp 7	late 2nd BC- early 1st AD	Bury Hill 2

There is a growing number of hillforts in southern England where wholesale burning appears to have taken place. These include Rainsborough (just outside the region), Taplow, Bladon Castle (Oxfordshire) and (from the extreme magnetic signature of a section of its southern rampart) possibly Perborough Castle (Berkshire) (Lambrick with Robinson 2009, 360-1; Payne *et al.* 2006). The valley fort at Burroway Brook (Oxfordshire) has a charred corduroy of timbers underlying an entire circuit of collapsed reddened gravel and soil ramparts that had once been timber-laced. While it is unclear if the cause of such burning in each case was the result of attack, slighting or accident, these must have been major events and the vulnerability of timber-laced ramparts to fire might have been a factor in their eventual abandonment in favour of dump ramparts of *glacis* form.

Material culture

Within settlements, the evidence of day-to-day material culture in the form of pottery and craft objects show a significant degree of variation in quality of materials, finish and decoration that suggest important differences in the social roles that material objects played that are familiar today. Deliberate deposits of groups of objects such as querns, occasionally pots, 'loomweights' and spindlewhorls are not especially common, but nevertheless occur on many ordinary settlement sites. The extent to which these should be regarded as special votive deposits or caches of valued material hidden for later recovery is often difficult to tell.

There is good evidence of structured deposition and special deposits that variously include animal skeletons, skulls and limbs, querns, spindlewhorls, metalwork, pottery and other objects, burnt stone and chalk lumps and (at least in waterlogged deposits), wooden objects (Plate 9.15). The variation and contexts of such deposits, and their occasional association with human remains, presents a highly complex picture reflecting a mixture of the rituals and beliefs that may have directly resulted in such deposits. Depositional processes range from deliberate votive placement to relatively random discard of waste from special activities, or to hoarding for later recovery (Wait 1985, Hill 1995; Lambrick and Allen 2004, 488-91).

Middle to late Bronze Age metalwork has been found across the whole area in the form of isolated finds, a few hoards and site finds. A number of summaries of classes of objects and reports on hoards have been published for Buckinghamshire (eg Farley 1972; 1973; 1991a), and for Hampshire (Lawson 1999), but Oxfordshire Berkshire and the Isle of Wight lack up-to-date reviews.

Excavations of hoards include a late Bronze Age hoard of 2 gold torcs and 3 gold bracelets found in a Post-Deverel Rimbury plainware pot dated 1150-800BC at Monkston, Milton Keynes (Needham, 2002) and a middle Bronze Age hoard of gold torcs and bracelets at Crowdown, Berks (Varndell et al. 2007). Neither of these was in association with any obvious contemporary activity. In contrast, a late Bronze Age hoard of socketed axes was found at the entrance of a roundhouse at Tower Hill, 5km south-west of Rams Hill (Miles *et al.* 2003). The late Bronze Age Petters Sportsfield hoard lies just outside the Solent-Thames area near Runnymede.

Iron Age hoards are generally less common and have not received so much attention. However, Hingley (2006) has reviewed the occurrence of iron currency bars in hoards, including several across the Solent-Thames area, and has suggested that they often occur in association with boundaries. Individual hoards include the remarkable 'Salisbury hoard' of votive miniatures from Hampshire (Stead and Renfrew 2000). Others include a number containing horse gear, such as pairs of bits from Wytham and Hagbourne Hill, Oxfordshire (Lambrick with Robinson 2009, 228-9).

A great deal of evidence of highly valued objects comes from those deposited in watery places, most notably the Thames, but also some coastal contexts. There have been several studies of or including this material, which have discussed at length the complex issues concerning the character of the material found (often weaponry) and the possible circumstances and meaning of its deposition (Ehrenberg 1977; Wait 1985; York 2002; Bradley and Gordon 1988; Bradley 1990; R Thomas 1999). With the exception of Bradley's (1990) wide ranging study of such deposition across NW Europe, however, these studies have almost all been confined to particular periods (Bronze Age, Iron Age or subdivisions between them). There has thus been relatively little detailed consideration of the phenomenon from a more general prehistoric perspective.

Crafts, trade and industry

Workshops

To a large extent craft would have been carried to in ordinary houses – but in some cases house-like buildings were perhaps built as workshops. For example at Hartshill Copse there is very good evidence of different stages of metal working being carried out in two adjacent roundhouses which also had complementary characteristics in terms of the quantity and character of

Plate 9.15 Wooden ladle from Reading Business Park, Berkshire, *copyright OA*

other finds (Collard *et al.* 2006). In general, however, it is very difficult to distinguish purpose-built workshops. There are a number of cases of D-shaped post built structures in the Upper Thames valley that have been interpreted in this light, and this might also apply to some rectangular structures and west-facing round-houses, but as Lambrick has noted, these are seldom associated with craft objects or residues, Hartshill Copse being a notable exception (Lambrick with Robinson 2009, 153-5; Collard *et al.* 2006). Recently a most unusual sunken-floored sub-rectangular building supported on four posts and measuring 3m long and 2m wide, has been found at Ewe Farm, Newington (Lambrick with Robinson 2009, 181-2). It had an entrance ramp at one end and pitched stone hearth cells or ovens overlying an original hearth at the other. It was associated with large pieces of perhaps 10-12 early Iron Age angular vessels, but there is no firm evidence of what craft activities it may have been used for (T Allen and P Booth pers. comm.)

Metalworking

An increasing number of ordinary Late Bronze Age settlement sites, as well as high status ones, contain evidence of bronze metalworking. The items range from casting drips, an unused rivet, crucibles and mould fragments (usually for spearheads and axes), to a possible tuyere and occasional casting failures (Bowden *et al.* 1993; Bradley *et al.* 1980, 244; Moore and Jennings 1992, 87; Needham 1991). At Runnymede Bridge a mis-cast razor was found still in its clay mould. Apart from the character of hoards like that at Tower Hill (Miles *et al.* 2003), there are possible hints of the existence of itinerant craftsmen from parts of syenite moulds for a typically south-western 'Sugoursey' style axe. One fragment was recently found at Castle Hill Little Wittenham, and was similar to an earlier find from Petters Sports Field, Surrey.

There is good evidence of bronze working continuing on settlement sites into the Iron Age (Northover 1984; 1995), though by then bronze metalwork had ceased to have the economic importance it had enjoyed in the late Bronze Age (Needham and Burgess 1980; Needham 2007). Nevertheless, the high technical craftsmanship in La Tene weaponry, horsegear, mirrors and other objects, emphasises the continued value of metalwork as prestige goods. An unusual later indication of metalworking linked to high status exchange is the late Iron Age evidence of manufacture of silver bars (or ingots) and other silver and gold smelts on the Isle of Wight.

The late Bronze Age ironworking site on tertiary geological outcrops at Hartshill Copse Upper Buckle-bury is of international importance, enhanced by evidence of an early Iron Age site nearby at Coopers Farm, Dunston Park (Collard *et al.* 2006; Fitzpatrick *et al.* 1995, 89-92). At Hartshill, 17 radiocarbon dates securely date the earliest iron working activity to the 10th century BC, pre-dating previous evidence for ironworking in the British Isles by three centuries. A pair

Plate 9.16 Reconstruction of the precocious iron-working site at Hartshill Copse, Berkshire, *copyright Cotswold Archaeology and West Berkshire Council*

of post-built roundhouses/workshops, respected by ceremonial fence lines, were associated with slag and hammerscale, revealing clear differences of work areas (Plate 9.16). A later enclosed settlement dated to the 5th century cal BC also produced iron slag and hammer-scale. Further areas of ironworking nearby at Coopers Farm, Dunston Park were dated to the 7th century BC.

In the mid to late Iron Age various sites south and south-east of Reading in Berkshire have produced evidence of iron production (Lobb and Morris 1991-3; Hammond 2011; Pine 2003a), prompting the suggestion of an association between these ironworking sites and the fort at Caesar's Camp, Crowthorne, on the outskirts of Bracknell.

In Buckinghamshire the most substantial (but still limited) excavated evidence for iron smelting and smithing comes from Aston Clinton Bypass from late Iron Age contexts (Masefield 2008). There is an old, somewhat doubtful reference to evidence of smelting at Cholesbury hillfort.

While evidence of Iron Age iron smelting is now less rare than it was at the time of Salter and Ehrenreich's (1984) review for central southern England, their observation that almost all domestic settlements had some evidence of smithing has if anything been reinforced. However, there needs to be some qualification to this because it has become increasingly clear that slag-like material that might in the past have been taken to indicate smithing can arise from other high temperature activities or events such as structures being destroyed by intense fires (eg Salter 2004). Sampling for hammer scale and higher density slags, which are more reliable indicators of smithing activity, has become more routine in recent years.

Pottery

Direct evidence for pottery production in terms of firing sites and wasters remains largely elusive until the very end of the Late Iron Age, when the first small temporary kilns appear eg in the Upper Thames Valley at Yarnton, Cassington and Hanborough. Distorted, over-fired, spalled and cracked pottery occurs fairly frequently (and flawed pots were often used as funerary urns) but it is very seldom possible to pinpoint on site pottery manufacture (though at Runnymede it has been suggested that there is evidence of querns being used to prepare calcined flint as pottery temper).

The ability to control firing temperatures is shown by fineware vessels of both the early and middle Iron Age, some using inlay and slip decoration for the first time in many centuries, suggesting a reasonably high level of craftsmanship. In the Iron Age there is considerable variability in fabrics in many parts of the Solent-Thames area, suggesting that a wide variety of clays were exploited on a fairly opportunistic basis, but these distributions and trends through time are mostly not well understood, though the potential is clear (Morris 1994b; 1997).

Stone working

Quarrying, in particular to obtain stone used as 'pot boilers' and also to win stones suitable to make into querns and rubbers would have been a significant craft. Making objects from stone was also noteworthy (eg Cunliffe and Poole 1991, 382-404). While querns may have been finished at the quarry, roughout spindle whorls (eg of Malmstone at Little Wittenham, shale or coal at Bourton-on-the-Water in the Cotswolds and of chalk at Gravelly Guy, Stanton Harcourt) show how stone was both procured locally and transported over long distances in a relatively robust state to avoid breakage before being worked into more delicate objects (Lambrick with Robinson 2009, 205-11).

Bone and antler working

Bone and antler working was ubiquitous and was a principal source of tools for other crafts. Techniques developed to some extent, eg through use of drills and saws in the Iron Age. Lambrick (with Robinson 2009, 225) has suggested that the degree to which antler combs and spindlewhorls were shaped, polished and decorated to make tools (as compared with unshaped bobbins etc) may say something about the role of the implement as a symbol of social status in families, personal relationships and, perhaps, in the symbolic role of the crafts for which they were used.

Leather, cordage and textiles

Although many later prehistoric implements are thought to be associated with these crafts, in only very few cases (eg spindle whorls, needles and perhaps bobbins) is their function clear. The use of combs for teasing wool, weaving, skin cleaning, personal toiletry or other activities in later prehistory is still a matter of debate. While there seems to be little question about the function of later Bronze Age cylindrical 'loomweights' the theory that Iron Age triangular 'loomweights' were really 'oven bricks' (Cunliffe and Poole 1991b) is beginning to be quoted as unquestioningly as their former attribution, though this is not yet fully accepted. The use of the highly distinctive and quite common polished and grooved sheep medapodials remains as obscure as ever.

Finds of cordage (as opposed to objects that clearly required it) are very rare indeed. Likewise, there are only very few finds of later prehistoric leather from the area, and they are not well preserved (eg Allen 1990). Actual textiles are also still very rare, as is evidence for aspects of their fabrication such as fulling and dyeing.

Plate 9.17 Ard share from the Eton Rowing Course, Buckinghamshire, *copyright OA*

Woodworking

The range of woodworking tools became wider in the late Bronze Age and Iron Age with the introduction of chisels, saws, drills and files. There is also a growing plethora of preserved worked wood and woodworking debris, both from riverbed and foreshore structures and preserved objects such as wooden bowls. Significant preserved structures have been found at Whitecross Farm, the Eton Rowing Course, Runnymede, Anslows Cottages (Berkshire) and Testwood Lakes.

An increasingly wide range of bowls and other wooden objects have been found in recent years, including one of the earliest wooden ard shares in Britain from the Eton Rowing Course (Plate 9.17). However, this still does not compare with the richness of finds from sites like Glastonbury and Meare in the Somerset levels, or Fengate in the Fens of East Anglia.

Markets, centres of exchange and trade

The existence of 'markets' or centres of exchange in prehistory has been a matter of debate, especially in relation to hillforts and midden sites as 'redistribution centres' or 'entrepôts.' While the quantity, range and quality of objects found is often suggestive of high status, it is much less clear exactly what this means in terms of why objects were brought to these sites, and to what extent forts like Danebury acted as massive stores for redistribution of agricultural produce (Cunliffe 1984a). Hill (1995, 1996) has questioned whether this interpretation of Danebury is overstated, and it is clear that many hilltop enclosures and hillforts do not have such evidence; many contain settlements no more elaborate or dense than some contemporary non-defensive enclosed and open settlements – and some less so (Cunliffe 2005). It is increasingly clear that some artefacts that might be taken to be indicative of a more central market role (such as being centres for specialist crafts like metalworking) are not always present and do not occur much more than on some ordinary settlements.

Needham has similarly argued that, contrary to tempting theories, there is rather little to suggest that riverside midden sites were primarily entrepots for river trade. He sees them more as high status communal meeting places, involved with the recycling and processing of material brought in, but not specifically related to river traffic (Needham and Spence 1996, 242-8).

The function of defensive and communal sites as centres of exchange thus seems to have been variable, and is probably better seen as a by-product of their wider communal role than as their primary raison d'être. In the later Iron Age, with more indication of centralising economic political and social power, the role of enclosures and *oppida* in controlling trade and exchange may have become more overt, as reflected in the wide range of traded goods that tend to occur on these sites. This is perhaps clearest of all in the case of Hengistbury Head where the defended headland clearly acted as an important port (Cunliffe 1987).

The principal indication of trade and exchange is the distribution of objects that came from distant sources. In Buckinghamshire, for example, there are later Bonze Age ornaments of continental origin, as there are across the Solent-Thames area (Rohl and Needham 1988). Dorset shale, Wealden greensand querns and some late Iron Age ceramics all indicate regional exchange networks. In Oxfordshire work by Fiona Roe has found that querns were both produced locally and were coming from the Derbyshire, the Welsh Marches, the Forest of Dean, the Downs and Sussex (Lambrick with Robinson 2009, 207-11). Although some of these materials may have been transported by river, there is some evidence that the Thames acted more as a boundary than a conduit of exchange. Briquetage from Droitwich (along with Malvernian pottery) is found almost exclusively north of the Thames and west of the Cherwell, whereas briquetage from Hampshire and Dorset reached areas south of the river, such as Abingdon and Castle Hill (Morris 1981; 1985; 1994a; Allen *et al.* 2010, 166-7).

In Berkshire and Hampshire broadly similar trends apply, with querns travelling significant distances (eg from Lodsworth, East Sussex) even though sarsen, a perfectly good local material, was often available. Shale roughouts and finished objects, briquetage, metal objects and ceramics again all point to well-developed extensive trading networks, in which agricultural produce is likely to have been a key basis for exchange.

On the Isle of Wight tantalising glimpses of social, economic, maritime trade and other linkages are revealed by Iron Age coinage and currency bars. There is evidence of trade in ceramics, including typical Glastonbury wares, pottery in the St Catherine's Hill/Worthy Down tradition, imported Gallo-Belgic finewares and amphorae and other material comparable to pottery from Hengistbury Head.

As the commonest material that reflects origins beyond the immediate vicinity of its discovery, pottery can be a very useful indicator of trade and exchange and of possible social affiliations. Cunliffe's ceramic 'style zones' have been very influential in considering these issues (Cunliffe 1974 to 2005) and the interpretation has gradually evolved, especially in Hampshire where the Danebury team reviewed pottery from sites within a study area of 450 km2 and further afield. The ceramic differences observed coupled with intensive radiocarbon dating changes (Orton in Cunliffe 1995) suggested territorial transitions – particularly a shift from east to west (Cunliffe 2000, 162). The pottery has also been studied from a petrological and production point of view (eg Morris 1994b; 1997) and there are alternative interpretations of its significance and the validity of the 'style zone' approach propounded by Cunliffe (eg Collis 1994, Hill 1995).

Elsewhere in the Solent-Thames area, especially the Upper Thames valley, the ceramic evidence has also revealed a complex picture, albeit with much less tight chronological control and petrological evidence. Lambrick (1984; with Robinson 2009, 203-5) has suggested that while the 'style zone' approach may have some validity in the Thames valley, the picture is complex: the sources of pottery can vary considerably at a local level from one site to another (notably Mingies Ditch and Watkins Farm); there are possible local variations of stylistic motifs within supposed 'style zones'; and pottery fabrics also vary significantly in local and distant origins, but not correlating closely with such 'zones'.

Distinguishing the influences of simple fashion, socially defined stylistic identity, and the organisation of pottery production and distribution is thus a complex challenge of multivariate analysis, not restricted to pottery alone, that still leaves many unanswered questions.

Transport and communication

As evidenced by trauma on cattle bones first noted at Ashville, Abingdon (Wilson *et al.* 1978) oxen or steers were probably the main draft animals on the farm and for transporting goods. However, the evidence of prestige attached to horses and horse gear, and possibilities of horse breeding areas in Oxfordshire and Milton Keynes, suggest that horse riding and horse-drawn vehicles were a relatively high status forms of transport. Recent work by Bendrey (2007) has revealed new diagnostic evidence for horse bitting which may give these animals a wider role. Cart and chariot fittings (nave rings and linch pins) and harness gear are familiar finds from a range of sites and increasingly objects such as terret rings are reported to the Portable Antiquities Scheme. Finds of pairs of Iron Age horse bits, such as those at Wytham and Hagbourne Hill, Oxfordshire, are also indicative of horse-drawn vehicles (Lambrick with Robinson 2009, 228-9). In Hampshire, possible vehicle and harness fittings come from a number of sites, including the putative 'chariot school' at Bury Hill (Cunliffe and Poole 2000b). The high quality craftsmanship involved, including bimetal working and elaborate decoration on some of these objects, is good evidence of the prestige attached to equine transport.

Physical remains of transport routes tend not to survive well except in localised places where hollow ways, causeways or waterlogged remains of bridges, jetties or landing stages have been buried in conditions conducive to survival. Structures have been discovered in the Rivers Test (Testwood, Hampshire), and Kennet (Anslows Cottages, Berkshire), and in the Thames at Runneymede, Eton Rowing Course and Whitecross Farm (Fitzpatrick *et al.* 1996; Lambrick with Robinson 2009, 229-35). Others have been found in current intertidal locations such as Langstone Harbour, Hampshire (Allen and Gardiner 2000). Such riverine and marine environments have high palaeo-environmental potential to elucidate detailed site chronologies and reconstructions.

Amongst the main prehistoric trackways in Southern England, the traditional explanation of Icknield Way as a route alongside the chalk escarpment from Wessex to East Anglia has been questioned (Harrison, 2003). At Aston Clinton no trace of it was found, and there was nothing to say that it might not be a post-medieval

creation (Masefield 2008). Although such routeways might be better understood as loosely defined 'zones of movement,' the emerging pattern of territories seems to be better defined by regularly spaced hillforts, trackways and cross-ridge dykes running perpendicular to the Chiltern scarp. Bull (1993) suggested that a 'bi-axial' pattern of roads and trackways across the Chilterns and north Buckinghamshire may have pre-dated the Roman road network, and similar networks have been noted in the Hertfordshire Chilterns extending into Buckinghamshire (Williamson 2002).

Very similar issues arise for the Ridgeway, the best known of all 'prehistoric' trackways in Britain, running along the scarp of the Berkshire and Marlborough Downs. Very comparable cross-ridge hollow-ways and boundaries link the Vale of White Horse to the Berkshire Downs, but as yet have not been shown to have prehistoric origins. There is growing evidence of ditches crossing its course, not only at Uffington (Miles *et al.* 2003), but also at several other points along its route. These are often revealed by deep rutting and occasionally by exposure in recent ditches or as crop- or soilmarks– as has also been observed at the southern end of the Ridgeway at Avebury. However, Gary Lock and colleagues have found that several Iron Age hillforts lie on a line defining the most theoretically efficient route along the Ridgeway, which in several cases (including Uffington) is not the present day course of the Ridgeway (Miles *et al.* 2003, 131-3).

Another celebrated ancient trackway crossing the Solent-Thames area is the Harroway crossing Hampshire, linking Salisbury Plain with the Downs of Surrey and Kent (Williams-Freeman 1915, Hawkes 1925, Crawford 1960, 78).

At a more local level, throughout the Solent-Thames area there was almost certainly a more extensive network of tracks and droveways linking fields, farmsteads and communal gathering places than is evident from the ditches (and presumably hedges), hollow ways and lynchets that survive as archaeological features. These are often best preserved either under floodplain alluvium or colluvial hillwash, including a 'lost' trackway of Iron Age origin traced along an historic parish boundary perpendicular to the Chilterns between Aylesbury and Chesham (Green and Kidd, 2006). A late Bronze Age road metalled with flint gravel which incorporated a gate or barrier has been investigated at New Buildings, Hampshire (Cunliffe 2000, 19), a pre-Roman ford crossing the Padbury Brook at Thornborough in the Ouse valley (Johnson, 1975), and various causeways crossing the Upper Thames floodplain have been investigated at Yarnton, Farmoor and Thrupp near Abingdon (Lambrick with Robinson 2009, 229-235). The former Thames channel at the Eton Rowing Course was crossed by six wooden pile-built bridges and two possible jetties, which dated between the middle Bronze Age and the middle Iron Age (Allen and Welsh 1997; Allen *et al.* forthcoming). Piles embedded in a silted channel at Whitecross Farm, Wallingford may either have been for two successive bridges or jetties (Cromarty *et al.* 2006). A late Bronze Age possible landing stage dated to

840–410 cal BC was found at Anslows Cottages, Burghfield (Butterworth and Lobb 1992). Other cases of revetted river banks, as at Lower Bolney, Oxfordshire (Campbell 1992) may be similar.

The use of the Thames and its tributaries for river transport may be suggested by traded goods, and there are possible 19th century discoveries of log boats attributed to the Bronze Age at Marlow and Wooburn (Clinch, 1905), but there are no modern confirmed cases of prehistoric river craft.

Other potential causeways have been noted in Langstone Harbour (Allen and Gardiner 2000), and waterlogged remains of timber bridges and causeways dating from 1600 to 1450BC have been found at Testwood Lakes, Totton, where one find of special significance was a cleat from a plank boat capable of cross-Channel journeys (Van de Noort 2006).

Sea crossings in the early part of the period can be inferred from finds such as the numerous bronze hoards of northern French type (Lawson 1999). By the Iron Age, trade with the Continent was well established with Christchurch Harbour and Hengistbury Head having an important role (Cunliffe 1987; Cunliffe and de Jersey 1997). The Isle of Wight was also well placed to play a role in both the Atlantic and Central European trade routes, but the available evidence has not been reviewed in recent years.

Legacy

Much of the Solent-Thames area was intensively settled and farmed by the end of the Iron Age, though some areas like the middle Thames gravels may only have been gradually re-colonised after a relatively stagnant period of development at the end of the late Bronze Age (Lambrick with Robinson 2009, 379). To the north-east and south-east there were emergent kingly rulers who had sought a peaceful and prosperous relationship with Rome; there is little evidence for Roman military activity in these areas. Silchester was probably deliberately created as a major centre that had already adopted the trappings of a Roman town and its manners, but more generally many late Iron Age sites continued to be occupied into the Roman period. Even in the less overtly pro-Roman tribal territories, such as that of the Dobunni to the west, the same pattern of uninterrupted development seems apparent. So far as there was any major disruption of settlement it had been in the late Iron Age, and was to occur again in the mid Roman period, not at the time of the conquest.

In Buckinghamshire evidence from the Roman nucleated sites is variable: Fleet Marston has some mid 1st-century occupation which probably pre-dates the conquest (Cox 1997) whilst at Magiovinium a pre-conquest field system was found on a different alignment to Watling Street and the later fields (Neal 1987).

Within the area of Atrebatic influence in Hampshire both Winchester and Silchester developed from major late Iron Age settlements. In Oxfordshire, on the putative border between three major tribal areas, the same is true of the probable Roman small town at Abingdon, while at Dorchester the Roman fort and town was established a short way from the Dyke Hills enclosure. The massive territorial area defined by the North Oxfordshire Grims Ditch was probably never completed, but was nevertheless notable for a cluster of early villas which may indicate some special legacy of land rights (Copeland 1988; Lambrick with Robinson 2009, 363-8).

Many of the practices of pit burials and disposal of bodies in and alongside boundaries and within settlements continued well into the Roman period alongside more Romanised rituals. Early Roman cremation rites (eg at Bancroft, Thornborough and Wendover) developed from the Aylesford-Swarling culture, indicating a continuity of belief also found with the worship of 'Taranis' at Wavendon Gate (Williams *et al*. 1996). Similar continuity of burial rites is evident also in Hampshire.

Except at Danesborough (Buckinghamshire), Alfred's Castle and Tidbury (Hampshire) there is little evidence for Roman use of hillforts, though both at Uffington and Castle Hill some tradition of religious use seems to have survived, as reflected in the presence of Roman cemeteries immediately adjacent (Allen *et al*. 2010), which is also suspected for Tidbury and Ashley's Copse in Hampshire. Saxon reuse is likewise less common than in western Britain, but the high status burial within the Taplow fort, which at that stage was still a prominent earthwork, is a notable exception (Allen *et al*. 2009). Saxon activity is also well-attested at Uffington where the traditions of scouring the White Horse lasted well into the post-medieval period (Miles *et al*. 2003), while in Buckinghamshire the reuse of hillforts as the location of a number of medieval churches has been noted (Kidd 2004).

Longer-term legacies can also be suggested by the survival of the co-axial patterns of trackways of the Chilterns into modern times, and perhaps even by the evidence for supposed Roman or earlier origins for early medieval multiple estates (Reed 1979, 71-77). Many prehistoric boundaries seem to have survived as later parish boundaries on the chalk.

The biggest legacies of all from this period were perhaps less directly tangible, yet far more substantial. It was in the late prehistoric period that the first fields and fully settled farms emerged within an almost fully managed landscape, and it was also the first time that a kind of politics that would be relatively familiar in modern terms emerged out of a kind of social interaction that would have seemed very odd to us now. Although subsequent periods also saw major transformations, it is becoming increasingly clear how much can be traced back to this early emergence of a society in which control and management of land and territory had become so important. In a few places it is even possible to see what may be real living legacies like the common grazing of Port Meadow just outside Oxford and the enduring symbol of identity that the White Horse has become.

Chapter 10

The Later Bronze Age and Iron Age: Research Agenda

by George Lambrick

10.1 Character of the regions, geological and topographical diversity

The Solent-Thames sub-region provides a different segment of the country from the more usual way of dividing it, using areas such as Wessex and the hillfort zone. This provides a fresh opportunity to consider the late prehistoric period.

The Solent-Thames is a meaningful cross section of the varied pattern of later prehistoric development in Southern England and ways to exploit this should be developed. These should include:

10.1.1 Investigation of the distribution of natural deposits that could provide natural pollen and insect sequences to map environmental change through the period.

10.1.2 The use of GIS and other geographical techniques to explore the interaction of major natural geological and topographical differences with social, economic or cultural factors.

10.1.3 The potential to compare the Solent-Thames with other sub-regions to investigate regionalism in late prehistory.

10.2 Nature of the evidence

There has been a considerable amount of archaeological investigation carried out across the sub-region, which has made possible the current level of understanding of the later prehistoric period. In many instances this work has been linked to development, including extensive areas of gravel extraction, particularly since the introduction of PPG16. However, there have also been a number of large-scale research projects, such as the *Danebury Environs Project* and *Hillforts of the Ridgeway*, mainly focussed on hillforts and enclosed settlements. As a result the archaeological evidence from this period may not be providing a full and accurate picture of activity. Consideration should be given to the ways and extent to which the overall picture has been distorted by biases in fieldwork and or development, including how to redress imbalances and focus on poorly surveyed areas which warrant particular attention. These might include:

10.2.1 The use of modern GIS methods to explore and counter such biases.

10.2.2 Areas which have been prone to especially little coverage or have conditions that are inherently difficult to overcome deserve most attention, for example priorities for carrying out Lidar surveys of woodland areas and the most appropriate method for addressing claylands.

10.2.3 In addition, a diverse range of 'hotspots' of later prehistoric investigation across the Solent-Thames area exists, for which comparison of results is required.

10.3 Chronology

In the past chronology was established on the basis of type series. Increasingly the use of stratigraphic sequences and scientific dating techniques has enabled more exact and refined chronologies to be prepared. Typology has produced some confusing patterns which have yet to be resolved through other methods. Much remains to be done.

10.3.1 An audit of the existing scientific and typological chronological frameworks established on a sub-regional or thematic basis is required.

10.3.2 Resolution of chronological issues identified in the audit will need:

A – Standards or criteria to enhance chronological resolution in terms of sampling strategies for artefacts and scientific dating.

B – Enhancement of the chronological framework, using techniques such as Optically Stimulated Luminescence (OSL), dendrochronology and residue analysis.

C – A programme of retrospective C14 dating with agreed priorities.

10.3.3 Excavations should be undertaken with the specific objective of refining chronologies using well-stratified artefact-rich sites.

10.4 Landscape and land use

From the later prehistoric period there is evidence for land clearance, changes in farming and organisation of the landscape, both in the form of extensive field systems and large scale land-division, often marked by substantial boundaries. Some of these changes may be related to climatic change. One of the key sources of evidence to explain these developments will come from the biological record, including pollen sequences. The full range of palaeo-environmental and geo-archaeological data should be collected, particularly from sites away from the chalk. Retrieval of sufficient environmental samples to generate such sequences and facilitate collection of other biological indicators should be routine. Any sites with large assemblages of fish, bird and shellfish remains would be of national importance. The survival of large mammals such as bear, wolf and aurochs in the Bronze Age and Iron Age countryside, and the implications this has in terms of habitat loss, is also worth consideration.

The pattern of landuse and its development across the region can be investigated through a number of research themes.

10.4.1 The extent of clearance in different parts of the Solent-Thames area, and at what periods this took place, should be explored. A cycle of clearance and regeneration may have persisted in some areas.

10.4.2 The use of newly-cleared areas, and any influence of climate on land use, need to be investigated, possibly through proxy data for temperature and rainfall. The relationship with economy across the region and with time should be considered.

10.4.3 The location and exploitation of woodland should be explored through palaeo-environmental data.

10.4.4 Farming and clearance should be explored through studies of alluvial and colluvial deposits.

Changes in agriculture, such as the introduction of new domestic animal species, perhaps including fowl, or the change to spelt and free-threshing varieties of wheat, can be explored through biological remains. Weed floras can shed light on time of sowing, soil fertility and soil drainage and the by-products of crop-processing. Evidence can also be retrieved for synanthropic species, pests and disease.

10.4.5 For field systems in the Solent-Thames area, their origin and purpose, including the reason for co-axial fields and the form taken by field boundaries, would merit further study.

10.4.6 Changes in the relationship of fields to settlements across the region should also be investigated.

10.4.7 Research may show whether fields were mainly created to control grazing. The importance of grassland management in the Iron Age economy, and the degree of specialisation of grazing farmsteads, for example whether horse raising was a major economic activity in the Thames valley, should be explored.

10.4.8 The relative effects of climate change and socio/economic factors on changes in farming need to be clarified.

10.5 Settlement

The later prehistoric period saw the development of permanent settlements, although transhumannce did not entirely disappear. Types of settlement range from scattered farmsteads, open and enclosed settlements to defensive enclosures and finally to the *oppida*. The relationship between the different kinds of settlement and social organisation, particularly social hierarchy, and changes in economy presents a number of issues. These are not specific to the region, but the number of hillforts and surrounding settlements, and later of *oppida*, the extensive relict field systems and the evidence for seasonal occupation, suggest that the Solent-Thames area would provide suitable opportunities to explore them.

10.5.1 The decline of earlier prehistoric patterns of mobile domestic activity, including whether highly dispersed later Bronze Age settlements were only seasonal places of occupation, might be tested.

10.5.2 Reasons for increases in the intensity of settlement should be explored, for example whether this reflects a switch from family to more communal management of animals and crops, and the role of land-use divisions in this process.

10.5.3 The factors that led to the common shift of settlement location in the late Iron Age need to be identified.

10.5.4 Pre-existing landuse rights may have affected the development of settled farming communities, possibly explaining differences in settlement form and patterns of change. Evidence for the emergence of such rights should be sought.

10.5.5 Classifying settlements as enclosed and unenclosed may still be useful, but differences in scale, social and economic basis of settlement may be considered in other ways.

10.5.6 The extent to which forts have Bronze Age origins and their role at that period form part of the larger issue of the purpose of hillforts, which might have been for reunions, ritual and for refuge.

10.5.7 Levels of occupation of forts still need further investigation, and the presence of external settlements immediately outside forts, and the relationships between them, requires further research.

10.5.8 If forts were not the prestige settlements then these need to be identified. Material culture may prove a better indicator of social hierarchy than size.

10.5.9 The extent to which the socio-economic basis of settlement differs across the region needs to be explored.

10.5.10 More work is required on whether the form of settlements bear a relation to their socio-economic role or to other non-morphological factors, and upon the existence of geographical and chronological variations within the region.

10.5.11 Palaeo-environmental evidence should be used to develop spatial chronologies for settlement change and to identify functions of specific sites.

10.5.12 Changes in settlement function should be compared to changes in other areas eg pottery typologies, to look for relationships between them.

10.5.13 Palaeo-environmental evidence, including lipid residues, should be used to try to elucidate the use of middens and burnt mounds.

10.6 Social organisation

In the past it had been thought that the different forms of settlement reflected some form of hierarchy in society. However, this idea has been undermined by a lack of certainty over the role of defensive enclosures and the fact that the status of material culture found does not correlate with settlement type. The likely development of cultural, tribal, economic and political regions is indicated by large-scale linear earthworks and distribution of coinage. While by no means exclusive to the Solent-Thames area, there are several important issues to be explored to which the levels of late prehistoric activity and archaeological research across the region can make a significant contribution.

10.6.1 The extent to which single family pastoral farmsteads existed needs to be determined.

10.6.2 More remains to be learnt about storage pits, such as the establishment of a minimum size, their reuse as latrines and the implications of this for burials in pits.

10.6.3 Late prehistoric health care may be better understood through bones and seeds of medicinal plants.

10.6.4 Survivors of trepanning operations may have worn their skull discs as talismans of good fortune, or these could be trophies. This might possibly be investigated through DNA or isotope studies

10.6.5 Large-scale land divisions are not well understood and there is a need to clarify their frequency, to discover whether these might have defined land rights and ownership or land use areas, and to discover who organised them.

10.6.6 The form taken by the boundaries above ground and how long they lasted merits further study.

10.6.7 The size of communities in the Iron Age, their social and economic relationships and the degree of economic specialisation need more investigation.

10.7 The built environment

The remains of many buildings dating to the late prehistoric period have now been identified across the subregion, demonstrating a wide variety of construction techniques over time, and showing increasing complexity from the Bronze Age into the Early Iron Age. Both round houses and rectangular buildings have been found. There are also large numbers of four-post structures, traditionally thought to be granaries, but as they occur at pastoral sites also, their function is not as clear cut. Given the enormous number now available for study certain questions about structures in the region may be addressed.

10.7.1 The development of the architecture of late prehistoric houses over a long time scale from the middle Bronze Age to late Iron Age may be clarified.

10.7.2 The mix of cosmological and practical influences on architecture could be investigated.

10.7.3 The role of four-posters needs better understanding. An association with pastoral farms might suggest that some were for fodder, and the 'megaposters' found at Mingies Ditch and other sites might support this theory. Further detailed study of the implications of the differing size of postholes for these structures would be valuable.

10.7.4   Sampling strategies need to be refined, giving priority to contexts associated with Bronze Age hut platforms/ roundhouses, including any postholes associated with these features, as these appear more productive than ditches. More balanced sampling of Iron Age sites, concentrating less on pits, and targeting four-post structures and ditches etc. would be beneficial.

10.8   Material culture

Everyday objects from settlements display a wide variety of quality of manufacture and design which may relate to a greater social role than is associated with such objects in the present day. Although deliberate deposits of such objects are uncommon, large numbers of deposits of higher status pottery, metalwork, querns, animal remains and other objects have been found, including those in watery contexts. The significance of both the objects and their deposition remains unclear, posing questions such as:

10.8.1   The functions of common objects like loom weights/ oven bricks; antler combs and grooved and polished metapodials.

10.8.2   Whether there was a personal and social significance in common highly finished and decorated craft tools and domestic objects.

One direction for study in the Solent-Thames area would be its pottery.

10.8.3   Detailed study of assemblages from large numbers of excavated sites would allow exploration of the distributions of pottery fabrics, changing fashions in fabrics, forms and decoration, the definition of sub-regional styles of pottery and their links to social groups.

10.9   Crafts, trade and industry

Archaeological evidence suggests that during the late prehistoric period manufacture, particularly of metalwork, involved the use of specialist craftsmen in addition to more domestic production. The extent to which the specialist remained in a particular location or travelled between sites is less easy to determine. The organisation of crafts, use of itinerant craftsmen and the extent to which all families carried out basic domestic crafts needs to be explored. Any large scale iron-working will have placed demands on the local woodland as a source of charcoal. The impact of industrial processes on the environment merits exploration. Within the Solent-Thames region questions about craft production remain. In particular,

10.9.1   Where did smithing fit into the organisation of metal working?

10.9.2   Where were the sites where pottery was manufactured, and what evidence can be used to identify and distinguish such sites?

10.10   Transport and communication

Evidence from bones suggests that oxen were the principal draft animals although possible horse breeding areas suggest that high status horse-drawn vehicles may have been used. Evidence for a road network is limited. Communication by water was probably common and a number of waterfront sites have been identified. Environmental evidence may help to extend understanding of how the water was used. However, material culture provides the best indication of long distance communication including cross-channel trade.

10.10.1   There is a need to explore patterns and axes of exchange, including the nature of the main exports from the region, possibly corn or horses.

10.10.2   The role of the Thames as a key boundary in distribution of salt from Droitwich, Hampshire and Dorset should be investigated.

10.10.3   European connections from the south coast and down the Thames and their influence on patterns of exchange at different periods should be studied.

10.10.4   More evidence for structures and waterside activities needs to be identified.

10.11   Ceremony and ritual

In comparison with other periods, the evidence for the treatment of the dead in the later prehistoric period is limited, although deposition in pits was taking place. Creation of large scale funerary monuments also decreased during this period and the number of ritual sites identified is small, although there are some sites where an earlier feature has been identified in association with one dating from the Roman period. There remain many issues to explore, to which the comparative wealth of evidence from the region can make a significant contribution. Questions include:

10.11.1   When and why people stopped building and using funerary monuments during the period?

10.11.2   The extent to which biases in fieldwork might

prevent the discovery of more urnfields and other cemeteries?

10.11.3 How frequent were cremations and inhumation burials in boundaries, fields and settlements before monuments stopped being used?

10.11.4 What were the selection criteria for pit burials? Were these the socially disadvantaged, and why does this occur with varying frequency on different sites? If (as currently appears) it was seldom more than once in a couple of generations on most sites, what is the significance of pit burial?

10.11.5 How do we define an Iron Age cemetery, and do small groups outside settlements count?

10.11.6 What other forms of formal burial like those in buildings at Frilford and Spring Road, Abingdon are there, are there chronological patterns in their occurrence, and how should we interpret them?

10.11.7 How should we interpret practices indicated by mutilated bodies and double burials, and how prevalent was human sacrifice?

10.11.8 What is the significance of differences in sex, age, health and stature of burials within cemeteries and around settlements.

In particular the region has the capacity explore the relationship between water and ritual, with some significant evidence already recovered from the Thames and from Langstone Harbour.

10.11.9 It remains to be established whether excarnation and scattering of remains on land or river was the norm?

10.11.10 What was the nature, purpose and frequency of 'special deposits' of human remains and metalwork?

10.12 Warfare, defence and military installations

Hillforts are the most imposing late prehistoric monuments, but their function is uncertain. Few show definite signs of conflict and they might have played a role in political and social organisation rather than serving a defensive role. Similarly deposits of weapons in rivers may not have been related to conflict. The extent of warfare and the politics of the period need addressing through several avenues:

10.12.1 The relationship between the major late Bronze Age and Iron Age linear ditches and the concept of territorial entities needs to be explored. The many major late Iron Age earthworks in the central part of the Upper Thames may represent major political boundaries and possible ownership differences, rather than defence.

10.12.2 The relationship between the earthworks associated with different major centres in late Iron Age and tribal political attitudes to Rome should be explored.

10.12.3 The question needs to be answered as to whether the North Oxfordshire Grims Ditch and Cassington Big Ring are unfinished.

10.12.4 More investigation is needed into the extent to which construction, maintenance and remodelling of communal enclosures and forts, with the massive deployment of labour involved, was a major means of exerting and symbolising social and political authority.

10.12.5 Evidence from settlements suggests that society was peaceful, although this conflicts somewhat with the picture from hillforts. The idea needs to be tested.

10.12.6 The level of attack on and burning of hillforts should be established, and the context of burning requires more careful consideration. Was burning always evidence of attack, or might it have been due to ritual cleansing or even to deliberate modification of the defences by the occupants?

10.12.7 There is need for review of metalwork found in rivers, considering the preponderance of weapons, their possible use in conflict, association with deposition of bodies and their relationship to politics and the role of rivers as tribal boundaries

10.13 What were the drivers and inhibitors of change?

A possible approach to the study of the later prehistoric period is to consider the evidence in relation to how changes were influenced by a variety of factors.

A - Environment
B - Population dynamics
C - Family relations
D - Communications
E - Economics
F - Technology
G - Rights and Traditions
H - Religion
J - Politics

Chapter 11

The Roman Period: Resource Assessment

by Michael Fulford

(County contributions by Paul Booth, Jill Greenaway, Malcolm Lyne, Richard Massey, David Radford and Bob Zeepvat; palaeo-environmental contribution by Michael Allen)

Introduction

The five English counties that make up the Solent-Thames sub-region form a distinctive territory, sub-rectangular in plan, which runs from towards the heart of England (and *Britannia*) south to the maritime landscape of the Solent, its estuaries and harbours and the Isle of Wight. It embraces a significant stretch of one of England's major rivers, the Thames and its watershed, involving the counties of Oxfordshire, Berkshire and Buckinghamshire, but also touches on the Ouse to the north and the rivers that drain the Hampshire basin to the south. It includes a range of distinctive geologies, of which, in spatial terms, the dominant is the chalk. As the largest island of south-east Britain, the Isle of Wight stands out as a highly distinct entity of the sub-region. Between the Island and the mainland, the sheltered waters of the Solent offer a number of natural harbours. Apart from the Hampshire coast-line (and the Isle of Wight), therefore, there are no natural boundaries to the sub-region.

Any assessment of archaeological research into the Roman period within the sub-region has to begin by taking account of its position within the larger entity of Roman Britain, since this will have an influence on the development of research agendas which might have impact beyond the sub-region. Once the context of the sub-region can be considered in relation to the larger entity of Roman Britain, assessments concerning the pre-Roman-to-Roman and Roman-to-post-Roman transitions can be developed. Culturally, Solent-Thames lies within 'Romanised' Britain, though within that generalising categorisation, there is considerable variation, whose further investigation and characterisation against the pre-Roman context is a major theme for Romano-British studies in general.

In regard to the political geography of Roman Britain (in so far as we can define boundaries), the sub-region embraces the probable entirety of one *civitas*, the Atrebates (Berkshire, Hampshire and Oxfordshire) with its *caput* at *Calleva Atrebatum* (Silchester, Hampshire). It also includes a significant proportion of a second, that of the Belgae (Hampshire) with its *caput* at *Venta Belgarum* (Winchester), a *civitas* which otherwise stretches north-west towards Bath, and smaller areas of the territories of the Catuvellauni (Buckinghamshire, Oxfordshire), the Dobunni (Oxfordshire) and the Regni (Hampshire).

Whether the Isle of Wight formed part of a mainland *civitas*, or was independently administered, we do not know.

A distinctive aspect of the *civitas* of the Atrebates is that its urban centre, along with its suburbs and cemeteries, remains a greenfield site, to be compared with other *civitas* capitals such as Aldborough (Yorkshire), Caistor St Edmunds (Norfolk) and Wroxeter (Shropshire). This degree of preservation and protection as a Scheduled Ancient Monument (SAM) adds a considerable premium to *Calleva*'s research value. Going back into the regnal period of the late Iron Age and earliest Roman period (1st century BC/1st century AD), the challenges of defining territorial boundaries, in themselves probably always fluid, are even greater. Nevertheless the sub-region contains a significant proportion of the Atrebatic kingdom with its primary centre (*oppidum*) at *Calleva*, as well as parts of the Catuvellaunian and Dobunnic territories. Although the densely populated and defended heart of the *oppidum* remains buried beneath the later, Roman town, the overall research value of this – in modern terms – undeveloped site and its environs is very considerable.

Going forward into the post-Roman period, the sub-region embraces a significant proportion of the Anglo-Saxon kingdom of Wessex, which had taken shape, with its associated ecclesiastical and political centres at Winchester and Dorchester-on-Thames (both flourishing settlements today) by the second quarter of the 7th century. Unlike for the immediate pre-Roman and Roman periods, the archaeological resource in respect of these two centres is constrained by virtue of the modern settlements that mask the underlying archaeology. To conclude, the Solent-Thames sub-region has excellent and appropriate archaeological capacity to support research agendas concerned with three, broadly-framed themes: the origins and development of complex societies in southern Britain at the end of the 1st millennium BC, the nature of Roman provincial society in 'lowland' Britain through the prism of town and its associated, rural hinterland or *civitas*, and, thirdly, the transition to post-Roman, complex society in southern England in the second half of the 1st millennium AD.

The archaeological resource of Solent-Thames has grown out of all recognition in the last 40-50 years through a huge volume of research, much of which has been published and is in the public domain (key sites are

Sites

Oxfordshire
1 - Abingdon
2 - Alchester
3 - Appleford
4 - Asthall
5 - Bablock Hythe
6 - Bampton
7 - Barton Court Farm
8 - Didcot
9 - Dorchester
10 - Frilford
11 - Gill Mill
12 - Lowbury Hill
13 - Oxford
14 - Queenford Farm
15 - Samson's Platt
16 - Shakenoak
17 - Stanford-in-the-Vale
18 - Stonesfield
19 - Wigginton
20 - Wilcote
21 - Woodeaton

Buckinghamshire
22 - Bancroft
23 - Denham
24 - Fleet Marston
25 - Latimer
26 - Magiovinium
27 - Stantonbury
28 - Cox Green, Maidenhead
29 - Thornborough
30 - Wymbush
31 - Yewden

Berkshire
32 - Caversham
33 - Maddle Farm
34 - Roden Down
35 - Thatcham
36 - Weycock Hill

Hampshire
37 - Alice Holt, Farnham
38 - Alton
39 - Appleshaw
40 - Avington
41 - Clausentum
42 - Danebury
43 - Hayling Island
44 - Hengistbury Head
45 - Lankhills
46 - Neatham
47 - New Forest
48 - Portchester
49 - Silchester
50 - Thruxton
51 - Winchester

Isle of Wight
52 - Brading
53 - Carisbrooke
54 - Fishbourne Creek

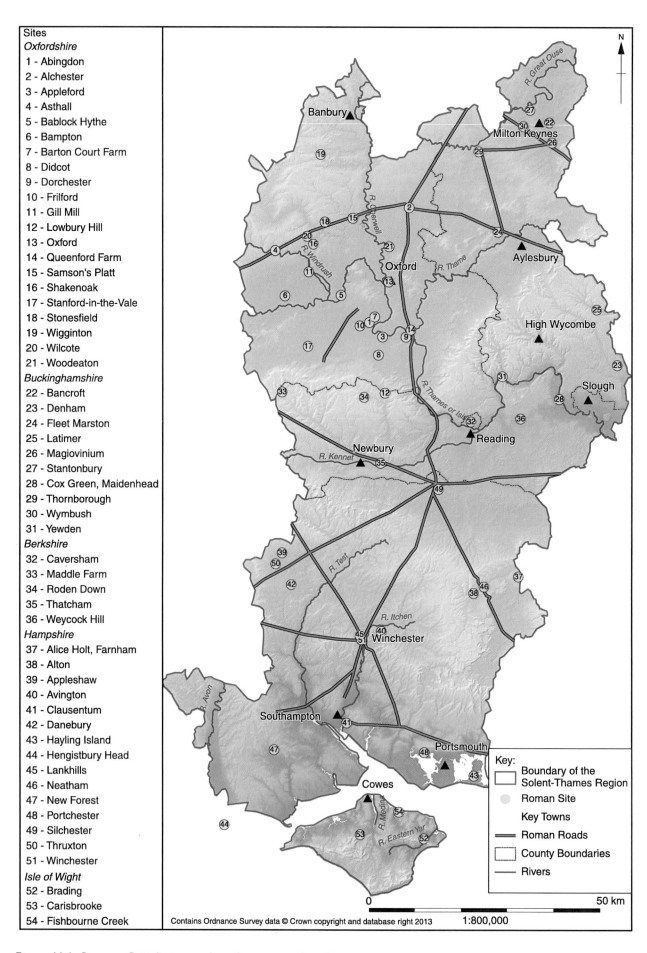

Contains Ordnance Survey data © Crown copyright and database right 2013   1:800,000

Figure 11.1 Romano-British sites and roads mentioned in the text

shown on Figure 11.1). There still remain largely untapped reservoirs of knowledge from excavations either only reported in summary form or not published at all. This unpublished work is of crucial importance for two areas of the sub-region in particular, the archaeology of Winchester and of the Isle of Wight. The problem needs addressing urgently.

Environmental evidence

By the Roman period most of the main concerns about the openness of the landscape and extent of woodland are no longer the key issues that drove much of the earlier, prehistoric research agenda. Most of the palaeo-environmental enquiry of the Romano-British period has traditionally been, and largely remains, focussed around economic issues (see Allen 1996), and on the expansion of agriculture (Van der Veen and O'Connor 1998). However, the review of recent data and current archaeological philosophies may allow the inclusion or re-introduction of some more landscape-based levels of enquiry. The resolution of interpretation required is higher than in previous periods and thus more-accurate data and better and more tightly chronologically controlled assemblages are required over space and time.

Farming

Defining the precise nature of the agricultural economy and the role of all elements in production, trade and exchange are key themes that palaeo-environmental science should address, using palynological sequences, geoarchaeology and land snails to provide a broad landscape background and charred, mineralised and waterlogged plant remains and animal bones to provide the evidence of specific produce. Farming in some parts of the region appears as a major and increasingly managed 'industry', while in others farmsteads appear to remain small and self-sufficient.

Geoarchaeological issues

Challenging, but potentially rewarding, might be the possibility of distinguishing between fields prepared using a plough (ploughed) and using an ard (arded). Two quite different soil surface microhabitats are created by the ard and the plough. More complex is the potential variation of arded field surfaces between those where minor furrows are 'scratched' in the weedy field surface for a seed bed (more like the effect of a digging stick), and that created by a heavily-driven beam ard. The two microhabitats thus produced are physically and ecologically different, and thus the plant and mollusc communities should reflect this. In the former only a small proportion of the soil surface is broken, and weeds and vegetation provide more shady mesic microhabitats for catholic snails (*Trichia hispida*, *Coclicopa* sp. etc) and some more shade-loving species (*Nesovitrea hammonis*, *Aegopinella* spp., *Punctum pygmaeum*). Deeper arding produces a more uniform broken soil surface, but does not eradicate weeds or surface vegetation, so it too provides locally less xerophile habitats than can be seen in modern fields.

The late Iron Age

The county assessments all recognise that there are no clear boundaries between Iron Age and Roman in south-eastern Britain. Distinctive, Roman material culture, mostly imported from Gaul or the Mediterranean world, is particularly evident from the last quarter of the 1st century BC, when a variety of manufactured goods and other commodities, particularly ceramics and decorative metalwork, flows into the south-east from across the Channel. On the other hand distinctive, local fabrics and wares that are dated from the later 1st century BC continue to be manufactured well after the Roman conquest into the later 1st century AD. In material culture terms, therefore, there is little to distinguish a later 1st-century BC 'pre-Roman' settlement from a later-1st century AD, early 'Roman' settlement.

Equally, it is clear from most counties that the late Iron Age/early Roman period (approximately the 1st century BC and extending into the late-1st/early 2nd century AD) was a period of major change in the countryside. This saw the emergence of numerous new settlements and types of settlements, and the abandonment or transformation of others, such as the distinctive hillforts and banjo enclosures, notable features of southern chalk landscapes. It is against this background that the rise in contacts with Gaul and the wider Roman world, and the emergence of major, nucleated settlement takes place. In our region the *oppidum* at *Calleva* is preeminent (Fulford and Timby 2000; Plate 11.1), but there are also lesser centres with – in Romanising terms – precocious material culture assemblages, such as Abingdon, Oxfordshire (T Allen 1991).

The evidence for this period is particularly well represented on the chalk, firstly by the work at the hillfort of Danebury in northern Hampshire (see Fig. 9.1 for location) and on the later prehistoric settlements associated with the Danebury Environs (Iron Age and Roman) Programmes (eg Cunliffe and Poole 2000a-e; Cunliffe 2008; Cunliffe and Poole (2008a-g)). Important excavations have also been undertaken in advance of development around Andover (eg Davies 1981; Bellamy 1991; TVAS 1997; Stevens 2004), Basingstoke (eg Northamptonshire Archaeology 2001; 2002; Oliver 1992; Oliver and Applin 1979; Wessex Archaeology 1990; 1996) and of the M3 between Winchester and Basingstoke (Fasham 1983; 1985; Fasham and Whinny 1991). Substantial work on the gravels of the Upper and, to a lesser extent, the Middle Thames has also made a significant contribution towards understanding this period of major change (Booth *et al*. 2007).

In all the above areas of research concentration, our knowledge base has been built on a significant number

Plate 11.1 Excavations at Insula IX, Silchester, Hampshire, showing the Late Iron Age phase, *copyright M Fulford*

of complete, or very extensive, modern settlement excavations associated with high quality research on both the material culture, particularly ceramics, and the biological evidence, notably faunal and charred, plant remains. It remains to be seen, however, how change affected other environments where research has been less intensive, particularly settlement on the heavier, clay soils, such as in Buckinghamshire and Oxfordshire, and in the Hampshire Basin and the northern half of the Isle of Wight.

Where imported material culture is found, it offers the possibility of establishing relatively tight site chronologies. Much of the archaeological record for this period is however dominated by settlements where reliance has to be placed on the broader framework provided by radiocarbon chronologies or less narrowly

datable material culture. Eventually, out of the rural settlement pattern of the earliest Roman period emerge the villa estates of our sub-region from the late 1st /early 2nd century onwards.

While there has been a very substantial growth in our knowledge of rural settlements and their associated agricultural economies over the last 40 years or so, particularly on the chalk and in the river valleys, there is clearly much more work to be done to set this knowledge in its full, landscape context. The sampling strategies of the Danebury Environs Programmes indicate how much can be learnt within a relatively small area from sites imperfectly preserved, either through the degradation caused by generations of cultivation, or by previous archaeological intervention. Despite this, even now, it is hard to generalise from the evidence that has been recovered. Nevertheless the model of intensive research within a limited, geographical area is one that invites further development in two respects. Firstly, for purposes of comparison, it is necessary to take research to the understudied landscapes of the sub-region, to clarify to what extent our present, limited sample is representative. Secondly, it is vital to take research in well-studied areas a stage further, in order to gain a better understanding of the 1st century BC/1st century AD, a period that sees both expansion in the number of settlements, but also, paradoxically, quite marked dislocation evident from the abandonment of settlements (cf Fulford 1992). The importance of this formative period in the history of the English landscape cannot be overstated; it provided the basis for supporting a complex pattern of urban settlement across the sub-region for over 400 years.

The Roman conquest of Southern Britain

The Roman military conquest of Britain remains of enduring interest and evidence recovered from any sub-region has, potentially, significant implications for the province at large. Until recently the sub-region has had little to contribute to a history which had little changed in half a century. However, recent, but not yet fully published excavations at Alchester (on the road leading due west from Colchester) have revealed evidence of a fort, arguably for legio ii, with dendrochronology providing a *terminus post quem* for its construction from AD 44 (Sauer 2000; 2005b). This represents a significant northwards shift in our understanding of the early work of this legion in Britain. Hitherto, on the basis of written sources, which associate this legion with the conquest of the Isle of Wight and with the capture of several *oppida*, it is assumed to have operated across the southern counties into Dorset, leading the sieges attested at hillforts (*oppida*) such as Hod Hill and Maiden Castle (eg Frere 1987, 58).

The major question of the nature of the military treatment of the Atrebates still remains. While it might seem inconceivable for there not to have been a military presence at *Calleva*, particularly as numismatic evidence suggests it was in the hands of Caratacus around the time of the invasion (Bean 2000, 205-10), the evidence so far rests on finds of military equipment and limited structural remains (cf Fulford 1993; Fulford and Timby 2000, 565-9). The Roman town otherwise seems to evolve from its pre-Roman counterpart through the pre-Flavian period with little significant change. Although the resource for understanding the Roman military presence in the sub-region during the conquest period is limited, it is difficult to see how a purposive research agenda could be developed to address this possible lacuna in our knowledge. The same is also true in relation to developing our limited understanding of the suppression of the Boudiccan revolt and the subsequent disposition of forces in the affected area. One major 'lesson' to be learned from the discoveries at Alchester is that it is not possible to predict with certainty the pattern and progress of the military conquest of the south.

The urban landscape

Large towns

The sub-region has two *civitas* capitals, both in Hampshire at Silchester (*Calleva Atrebatum*) and Winchester (*Venta Belgarum*). As it is a greenfield site, Silchester was extensively excavated in the later 19th and early 20th century, much of the work undertaken in the context of a clear research framework to determine the plan of the Roman town (eg Fox and St John Hope, 1891-1906). While plans of all the masonry-founded buildings within the walled area were indeed produced, field techniques at the time were not adequate to recover the remains of timber buildings systematically, or to address the chronology of settlement. The resultant plan appears as a single period (eg Boon 1974, foldout). Nevertheless, with its constituent public, religious and private buildings, Silchester has provided a benchmark for the interpretation of the larger towns of Roman Britain, not least of the fragmentary evidence derived from developer-led interventions in Roman towns, such as *Venta Belgarum*, now buried under medieval and modern counterparts.

Until the more recent excavations that began in the 1980s, the Victorian and Edwardian work at Silchester was assumed to have been very destructive of the archaeology within the walls. The more recent excavations have however shown that the early excavations were comparatively superficial, with extensive preservation of stratigraphy and the possibility of recovering complex histories of individual buildings and *insulae*. Research on the defences (Fulford 1984; 1997), amphitheatre (Fulford 1989; Plate 11.2) and the forum basilica (Fulford and Timby 2000) has been followed by research on the development of part of one insula from Iron Age origins through to abandonment between the 5th and the 7th century AD (Fulford *et al.* 2006; Fulford and Clarke 2011; Fulford 2012a & b). Unlike the antiquarian work modern research includes reporting of both material and biological culture. It has been estimated that at least 80 per cent of the archaeology within the walled area that was available to 19th century excavators at the start of their work still survives undamaged today. The comparable figure for the extent of preservation of the archaeology of the suburbs and cemeteries beyond the walls is surely well in excess of 90 per cent. While modern work, executed to the highest field standards, has provided the stratigraphic context lacking from the antiquarian work at Silchester, fundamental questions remain to be addressed about the origin, development and functions of the town, as well as the transition into the early medieval period. The town thus retains the capacity to address a rich variety of urban research themes of national and international interest.

Plate 11.2 Silchester amphitheatre, Hampshire, *copyright M Fulford*

In contrast, the scale and scope of excavation at Winchester has been very largely determined by opportunities offered through development work. While a considerable amount of work has been done, particularly since 1960, both within the walls and in the suburbs, very little has been fully published, of which the most significant is of the late Roman inhumation cemetery at Lankhills (Clarke 1979; Booth *et al.* 2010). Even though the biological evidence from the earlier excavation has not been published, the character and diversity of the accompanying grave goods and their disposition in relation to the body provide important insights into the social organisation of late Roman Winchester, including the possible presence of migrant groups from elsewhere in Europe, particularly from Pannonia. However, recent research on stable isotopes from a sample of the human remains at Lankhills suggests that there are no clear correlations between the character of grave goods and funerary ritual and the isotopic evidence for the origin of individuals. Nevertheless, although only one individual might be of central Danubian or Pannonian origin, about a quarter of the sampled population (40) appear to have originated from outside of Britain (Eckardt *et al.* 2009).

In addition to more recent excavation of suburbs and cemetery there has also been some important work within the walls. Our understanding of the later Iron Age, Oram's Arbour enclosure has been significantly augmented by the discovery of several round houses at the base of a complex, but fragmented sequence of occupation of a largely artisanal character in the northwest of the Roman town (Ford *et al.* 2011, 37-72).

Closer to the centre excavation of more complex occupation, including town house developments, in Middle Brook Street has added important knowledge to our understanding of residential development within the town (Zant 1993).

While finds reporting is integral to the Northgate House report (Ford *et al.* 2011), there has been separate treatment of the 'small finds' and faunal remains from excavations on the defences and in the suburbs carried out in the 1970s and 80s (Rees *et al.* 2008; Maltby 2010).

Notwithstanding our limited knowledge, perhaps one of the most important aspects to stress for the archaeology of the sub-region is the major differences between its two *civitas* capitals with all the potential that has for generating contrasting and individual urban histories and geographies. As illustration we can point to the very different topographies, origins and later histories. Silchester was located on relatively high ground, some distance from a river and very largely dependent on wells for water, Winchester on the valley side with the River Itchen on its eastern side. Silchester apparently emerged very rapidly, perhaps as a planned town, in the last quarter of the 1st century BC. Winchester, on the other hand, is certainly established in the pre-Flavian period, but, given the lack of late Iron Age activity, notably at the Oram's Arbour (Iron Age) enclosure, without clear evidence of immediate pre-conquest origins (Qualmann *et al.* 2004; Ford *et al.* 2011, 37-72).

Whether or not with continuous intramural occupation from the early 5th century AD, Winchester emerged as the principal ecclesiastical centre of the Anglo-Saxon kingdom of Wessex by about the mid-7th century

(Biddle and Kjolbye-Biddle 2007), whereas, by about that time, Silchester was abandoned (Fulford *et al.* 2006, 280-1; Fulford 2012b). For the future, Silchester and its environs have, for all practical purposes, unlimited potential for addressing carefully formulated research questions concerned with late Iron Age and Roman urbanism, unconstrained by a thriving, overlying city (cf Preston 2011). In contrast, Winchester's research agenda will be more adventitious, conditioned and constrained by the pattern of future development.

'Small towns'

The customary categorisation of towns in Roman Britain is to distinguish the larger *civitas* capitals and *coloniae* with their characteristic range of public buildings and, generally, large, defended areas from the rest which are grouped together as 'small towns', a category which includes both defended and undefended settlements. While the majority of these show some degree of planning, commonly streets or lanes offset at right angles from a single, major through route, the most conspicuous difference is in the typical absence of a forum basilica and monumental civic or religious architecture (except for the presence of *mansiones)*, and the size of the settlement. Bath is an obvious exception. In recent years there has been a tendency to contemplate the inclusion in the urban category of nucleated settlements, simply on the grounds of spatial extent, rather than on any analysis of function or social differentiation.

The sub-region boasts four typical, walled 'small towns': *Magiovinium* on Watling Street at Fenny Stratford in Buckinghamshire (Woodfield 1977; Neal 1987; Hunn *et al.*1997), Alchester in Oxfordshire (Hawkes 1927; Iliffe 1929; 1932; Booth *et al.* 2001), linked by the road coming south from Towcester with Dorchester-on-Thames (Frere 1962; 1984; Burnham and Wacher 1990, 117-122), and Neatham (*Onna?*), Hampshire (Millett and Graham 1986). The typicality of these 'small towns' is that they lie on major provincial roads. Limited research has been undertaken in and around them, influenced in the case of Dorchester by the overlying medieval and modern settlement. While the important, early military origins of Alchester have been touched on above, little modern work has been undertaken on the walled settlement to explore its character and history. Aerial photography reveals the potential of the site with a range of buildings, one at least of considerable size, but of uncertain function, flanking the main, east-west street (a spur road from Akeman Street; eg Burnham and Wacher 1990, 99-101; Booth *et al.* 2001, 3). Nationally, the character and function of the 'small' walled towns is very poorly understood, not least why certain settlements merited defence in comparison with others located along the principal roads of the province(s). With two, well preserved, greenfield examples, the sub-region has the potential to begin to address these fundamental questions.

Despite the modern settlement at Dorchester-on-Thames, there is also not only the potential to explore the relationship between the Roman town and the adjacent Iron Age settlement at Dyke Hills, but also to research further the transition into the early medieval period. Recent research, such as on the Queenford Farm cemetery, has focused on late Roman and early Anglo-Saxon period burials and cemeteries outside the town (Harman *et al.* 1978; Chambers 1987). Despite this, much remains to be done to understand the role of the town, which boasts a dedication by a relatively high status Roman official, a *beneficiarius consularis*, and which was also later, in the 7th century, the seat of Bishop Birinus (Blair 1994, 39-41, 58). The Oxford Institute of Archaeology/Oxford Archaeology 'Discovering Dorchester' project considers these issues and one of its foci is the late Roman/ post Roman transition within the walled town.

In addition to what have been described as 'typical' walled towns, there is a further, defended settlement to be considered in the sub-region. *Clausentum*, on the estuary of the Itchen in Hampshire, is an unusual case (Cotton and Gathercole 1958). With evidence of defences from the late 3rd century (contra Johnson 1979), it is regarded by some as a possible Saxon Shore fort, even though its name does not occur in the late 4th/early 5th century *Notitia Dignitatum*. However, with occupation dating from the pre-Flavian periods onwards, it is clearly of significance, presumably as a port (see below), strategically situated at the head of Southampton Water. Though at least partly buried beneath Bitterne, a suburb of Southampton, this remains a key site for research on the coastal communities of Roman Britain and their relations with other regions and provinces of the Empire.

There still remains the issue of the early (pre-Norman) fortification at Carisbrooke Castle and its date. For many years it has been conjectured as a possible component of the late Roman shore-fort system although there is no name in the *Notitia Dignitatum* that could reasonably be attributed to the Island location. Despite the lack of Roman material from Young's recent excavations at Carisbrooke Castle, the early enceinte still remains undated (Young 2000), but a quantity of Roman brick and tile has been recovered from other, earlier excavation at the Castle (Rigold 1969). The circuit is somewhat anomalous in a Saxon context but, against the background of the larger seascape/landscape of the Solent and the Isle of Wight, with late Roman defended sites at *Clausentum* at the head of Southampton Water and Portchester at the head of Portsmouth Harbour (and Chichester), the otherwise apparent absence of equivalent fortification on the Island is puzzling.

In addition to the walled towns, the sub-region boasts a number of undefended roadside settlements, of which only a couple, Asthall and Wilcote in Oxfordshire, have seen modern excavation of note (Booth 1997; Hands 1993; 1998; Hands and Cotswold Archaeology 2004). Given the apparent importance of the roads represented in the sub-region, not least Akeman Street and the Devil's Highway, which provide east-west communications, as well as Watling Street to the north, the incidence, extent and characterisation of the associated

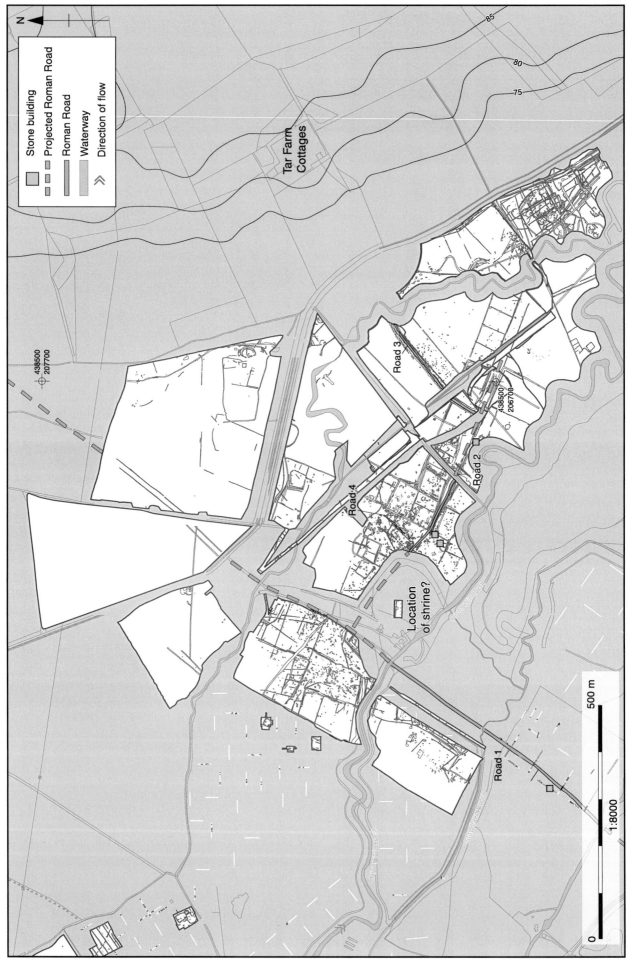

Figure 11.2 Plan of the Romano-British settlement at Gill Mill, Oxfordshire

roadside settlements offer the possibility of beginning to 'fingerprint' the character of different highways. A major question is how variable the settlements are that develop alongside such roads, and what light that variability throws on their relative importance as transport routes. The Oxfordshire research has not yet been matched by work on the comparable, roadside settlements represented in Berkshire and Hampshire, which to a large extent remain undefined. Indeed our ignorance of these settlements, including even their precise location and extent, is highlighted by the difficulty of matching sites with names of settlements with presumed *mansiones* or relays (*mutationes*) for the *cursus publicus* listed in the Antonine Itinerary and Ravenna Cosmography.

Urban economies and industries

Urban centres contain subtly different evidence of food stuffs and activities from the rural sites, but perhaps some of the more conspicuous contrasts, apart from sheer quantities of faunal remains, can be seen in the butchery and processing of domestic animals (eg Maltby 1985; 1989). Significant contributions have been made to our understanding of the role of animals, both domestic and wild, in urban society in both Silchester and Winchester (Grant 2000; Ingrem 2006; 2011; 2012; Maltby 2010). At the same time, at Silchester, a greater understanding has been obtained of the role of plants and plant foods in urban diet and society, including the contribution of imported foods (eg Robinson 2006; 2011; 2012).

Lived-in environments

Urbanisation creates specific environments, which are rarely dealt with. Their appearance and the level of maintenance of buildings have been little explored and environmental evidence might shed some light on these issues as has been attempted using geochemistry and micromorphology at Silchester (eg Banerjea 2011; Cook 2011).

Nucleated settlements

Other nucleated settlements in the sub-region, particularly those whose role in the road network may have been subsidiary to other functions, deserve comment. Outstanding among these is that at Frilford, Oxfordshire where recent excavations have valuably strengthened our knowledge of the settlement, including important religious and ritual aspects (Lock *et al.* 2003; Lock and Gosden 2004; Gosden *et al.* 2005; Kamash *et al.* 2010). Probably not unconnected to the latter, this is one of a very small number of smaller, nucleated settlements in Britain, and the only one so far known in the sub-region, which boasts an amphitheatre. Of the vast majority of the smaller, nucleated settlements in the sub-region we know very little. The potential interest and significance of these sites is sometimes highlighted by metal detectorist finds, such as those of *siliquae* from the ill-understood settlement at Stanford in the Vale, Oxfordshire (Henig and

Booth 2000, 72). Gill Mill in the Windrush valley, however, has provided the opportunity for extensive excavation of a nucleated settlement (Booth and Simmonds 2011; Fig. 11.2).

Unlike the well-preserved chalkland landscapes of the military training area of Salisbury Plain, where complex arrays of earthworks indicate numerous nucleated settlements (McOmish *et al.* 2002; Fulford *et al.* 2006), in our sub-region such sites have been ploughed out, whether on chalkland or other landscape environments. Add to the level of destruction the weakness of our knowledge-base of these sites, and it is not surprising that it is difficult to recognise that our sub-region – as, indeed the larger region as a whole – probably supported numerous nucleated settlements of this kind. This underlines how far we have to go to understand the lesser nucleated settlements of the sub-region and to characterise their social and functional differentiation.

Rural settlement

In contrast to the lesser nucleated settlements, a great deal more is known of single settlements or settlement complexes like villas (Plate 11.3). Partly this is a reflection of the intensity of effort by antiquarians on masonry structures in the countryside which might yield spectacular examples of Roman civilisation, such as mosaics, and also of the effects of aerial photography, revealing the plans and interrelationships of villas and their surroundings (Plate 11.4). It is also partly the result of extensive modern developments, which have required large-scale excavation of single sites. This is true in the context of major, modern urban and other settlement development, such as the development of Milton Keynes, Buckinghamshire and of the expansion of small towns like Abingdon, Oxford. The former provided the context for the extensive excavation of the large villa complexes at Bancroft (Williams and Zeepvat 1994) and Stantonbury as well as smaller farms with Roman-style buildings such as Wymbush (Zeepvat 1988), while the latter led to the excavation and detailed publication of the small villa at Barton Court Farm (Miles 1986).

These development-led excavations associated with full publication have now been complemented by a major, research investment on villa and other settlements that formed the Roman phase of the Danebury Environs Programme on the heavily ploughed chalkland landscape of north-western Hampshire. In several cases this involved re-visiting and re-evaluating villas first investigated in the 19th or earlier 20th century (Cunliffe 1991; 1993; Cunliffe 2008; Cunliffe and Poole 2008a-g). Thus, in the sub-region we have good examples of well researched clusters of rural settlement in three contrasting landscapes: the clay and drift soils of northern Buckinghamshire around Milton Keynes, the gravels of the Upper Thames around Abingdon, Oxfordshire, and the chalklands of north-west Hampshire close to Andover, the latter complementing slightly earlier work undertaken on villas, such as Latimer, Buckinghamshire, in the Chilterns

Plate 11.3   Excavation at Cox Green Roman villa, Berkshire, *copyright M Fulford*

(Branigan 1971). In west Oxfordshire, close to Akeman Street and exploiting light and heavy soils, we also have the example of the extensively researched and published Shakenoak villa (Brodribb *et al.* 1968; 1971; 1972; 1973; 1978), the only site in the sub-region with possible evidence of fish-farming (ibid. 1978, 15-20). Building on the major landscape project at Heathrow in nearby Middlesex (Lewis *et al.* 2010), our knowledge of late Iron Age and Roman settlement in the Middle Thames Valley is also rapidly developing (eg Preston 2003). A recently published example is the settlement at All Souls Farm Quarry, Wexham, north-east of Slough in Buckinghamshire (Preston 2012).

In the first place, the above excavations have provided good chronologies which, for the most part, have shown trajectories of development which go back to the late 1st century BC/early 1st century AD, this really critical period in the expansion of rural settlement in the sub-region. Frequently late Iron Age buildings are found to underlie Roman-style constructions, although not in Oxfordshire. In addition this work has provided enormously important assemblages of both material culture and biological evidence, which, together, have provided the basis for reconstructing their respective agrarian regimes, particularly in the areas of animal and crop husbandry. An extremely valuable aspect of the work undertaken in the context of the development of Milton Keynes was the capture through excavation of a range of settlements (Mynard 1987). By no means comprehensive in its coverage of the landscape, this has nevertheless given a much clearer idea of the diversity of rural settlement across a limited area of the countryside and of the perpetuation from the Iron Age into the Roman period of traditional architectural forms, notably

round houses. Bearing in mind discoveries outside the sub-region, such as at Stansted in Essex (Cooke *et al.* 2008), the latter are clearly more common than has previously thought to be the case. They have also been found, for example, on the clay soils of East Berkshire (eg Roberts 1995).

While excavation of single sites has been the principal methodology of researching rural settlement, extensive landscape survey involving surface collection of material culture has also deployed in the sub-region, as in the East Berkshire and Kennet Valley Surveys (Ford 1987; Lobb and Rose 1996), or the Whittlewood Survey in north Buckinghamshire (R. Jones 2003). The latter have provided important information on the existence and density of settlement of different periods and on soil types where there had been no history of systematic work before. The primary concern of the Maddle Farm Survey (West Berkshire) was the characterisation of the agricultural exploitation of the chalk downland landscape during the Roman period through the systematic analysis of off-site sherd (manuring) scatters. However, sample excavation was also carried out on a limited number of sites to provide, principally, chronological control, as well as stratified samples of material culture and biological data (Gaffney and Tingle 1989). Further, complementary field survey involving surface collection (but without sample excavation) was undertaken below the chalk escarpment of the Berkshire Downs of a sample of the Vale of the White Horse, Oxfordshire (Tingle 1991).

Re-evaluation of surveys already undertaken in a variety of soil and landscape settings in combination with assessment of the evidence of excavated sites have the potential to lead to fresh insight into the question of

Plate 11.4 Aerial photograph of the Yewden villa, Buckinghamshire, *copyright National Monuments Record 4632/16*

population size during the Roman period. A range of figures, with considerable variation in magnitude, have been suggested in the past. Although there is scope for more, targeted survey in under-represented areas in the sub-region, there is the potential now for re-evaluating the data we have already collected for the insights it can provide on population dynamics and its role in economic growth and decline.

The sub-region thus has a formidable resource base upon which to extend the important work on rural settlement and the exploitation of the landscape, whether by extensive survey including geophysical survey and surface collection in those limited areas where considerable excavation has taken place, or by developing excavation (and geophysical survey) programmes to extend understanding of those areas where surveys by surface collection have been undertaken. With this approach two important questions can be addressed: first, the economic and social relationships between individual settlement components of a sample landscape; second, the larger question of the relationship between the rural settlements (including nucleated settlement) of a *civitas* and their *caput*. In this context the accumulation of small-scale work, as for example in the hinterland of Silchester, has provided invaluable data to shed light on town-country relations as reflected by ceramic and faunal assemblages (eg Ingrem 2012; Timby 2012).

If the emphasis up to now has been on the individual settlement, it should not be overlooked that the sub-region has a rich range of resources which provide the basis for understanding the look of the countryside in terms of the location of woodlands and the existence and spread of field systems, as, for example, those on the Berkshire Downs.

Woodland resources and woodland management

Woodland, though less predominant physically in the landscape, and in the level of archaeological enquiry in this period, is nevertheless, still a key resource. The nature and variety of potential woodlands are rarely addressed; though certainly evidence from old and unmanaged, and essentially unused woodlands will be more difficult to recover in the direct (i.e. charcoal and waterlogged wood) record. Nevertheless, woods are still required for pannage, as well as for fuel, for construction (fencing, buildings, bridges, harbours/jetties, boats) and for personal and other objects (bowls, furnishings etc). Thus charcoal and waterlogged wood records are important in the first instance in recognising the presence, if not the location, of managed, coppiced and pollarded woodlands. Analysis of charcoal assemblages from Silchester have contributed to the history of the changing exploitation of wood types and the role of coppicing (Straker 2000; Veal 2012). There is relatively little evidence to date on where the main woodlands were located, although some informed guesses have been made, such as on the steeper slopes of the Chalk and the Chilterns, as well as the Tertiary clays of southern Hampshire and the Isle of Wight.

Field systems and paddocks

The distribution of field systems seems to indicate areas and topographies or geologies that were under less cultivation pressure. Field systems seem to extend from the higher slopes and onto the footslopes, indicating that they may extent into footslope and dry valley locations that have been sealed by hillwash, as at Aston Clinton and Pitstone, Buckinghamshire (Masefield 2008; Wainwright *et al.* 2010; see also Fig. 11.1). Fields for animal husbandry are less likely to have such pronounced lynchets and banks, as pasture does not result in as much erosion as cultivation. Paddocks have been recorded at, for instance Broughton, Milton Keynes (Petchey 1978), and long narrow rectangular fields located elsewhere (eg Berryfield, Aylesbury, Weedon Hill and Pitstone in Buckinghamshire (Dodds 2002; Wakeham *et al.* 2013; Wainwright *et al.* 2010)).

Field systems were studied as part of the Maddle Farm survey (Gaffney and Tingle 1989) and were shown to be both Roman in date and integral to understanding the role of stock-raising in the agricultural economy of that landscape (see also Ford *et al.* 1988). Ideally, if we are going to characterise the totality of settlement and its diversity within a small sample area, we need to know the location and layout of fields and field systems as well as the role of more significant, linear boundaries. The latter include the North and South Oxfordshire Grim's Ditch systems (Copeland 1988; Cromarty *et al.* 2006, 157-200), the linear earthworks around *Calleva* (Silchester), and the earthwork complexes to the east of Winchester around Avington (Crawford 1951). Away from the chalk we still have very little idea of the extent to which the land was parcelled out into fields in the late

Iron Age and Roman periods, rather than given over to woodland or common grazing areas. The writing tablet from London which records the sale of a wood in Kent (Tomlin 1996) reminds us of the detailed mapping and recording of the landscape on the part of the provincial authorities. We are still a very long way from recovering such details of the late Iron Age and Roman landscape of the sub-region.

Specialisation and regionality

In some areas such as the Thames valley hay meadows have been specifically defined, and this has been argued to represent specialisation and supply for the Roman army (Lambrick 1992a, 101-2). Other examples of specialisation may also be identified from environmental assemblages. It is important to examine variation between farmstead types in order to explore the relationship between meat and cereal or dairy and meat production and thereby explore the existence and extent of regional specialisation. We have good insights for the Chalk, for example from the Danebury Environs' settlements (Hammon 2008), and from Maddle Farm, near Lambourn, Berkshire, where there seems to have been a large and flourishing estate combining intensive cereal cultivation with stock-raising (Gaffney & Tingle 1989). Equally, and reflecting the work carried out on settlements on the gravel, important insights have been gained in our understanding of the development of animal husbandry in the Thames Valley from the later Iron Age and through the Roman period (Hesse 2011; but see also Hambleton 1999; Hambleton 2008).

Cattle generally predominate in most faunal assemblages followed by sheep and pig with some domestic fowl present on many sites. However pig are more common than sheep in the third century AD at Latimer in the Chilterns, Buckinghamshire and this may be due to assemblage or site/context biases, or it might indicate some regional variation (Maltby 1985; 2002). The proportion of animals and their age profiles, as represented in the faunal assemblages from rural sites, can assist in characterising and mapping Roman farming in the Thames-Solent corridor. In the Thames Valley research has shed important light on several important issues, such as the influence of major and minor urban centres, the changing – and increasing – exploitation of cattle over time, the extent of dairying and the role of cattle for traction (Hesse 2011; cf Ingrem 2012).

In contrast from the coastal zone, and from a late Roman military context, we have, to date, one important faunal assemblage, that from Portchester Castle (Grant 1975).

In general spelt wheat (*Triticum spelta*) dominated, while other cereals such a free-threshing wheat (*Triticum* sp.) and emmer (*Triticum dicoccum)* and barley (*Hordeum*) are present. Campbell provides an important synthesis of the evidence from the Danebury Environs' sites located on chalk soils (Campbell 2008). The proportions of the different cereals according to site type, geology/soil and over time would also contribute to the mapping of different agricultural regimes. In addition the cultivation of other food plants can also be demonstrated. Fruit and vegetables are less common because the chances of pips and stones becoming charred are less than those of cereal crops. Nevertheless, the preservation of soft fruit and vegetable remains by waterlogging has been recorded in Buckinghamshire at Bancroft (Pearson & Robinson 1994), indicating the high potential value of such deposits. Mineralised, waterlogged and charred assemblages, as well as pollen, have also contributed to the record of fruits and vegetables in an urban environment, as at Silchester, Hampshire (Dark 2011; Robinson 2006; 2011; 2012). This direct palaeo-environmental evidence corroborates field evidence of ditched fields or enclosures, such as at Mantles Green, Buckinghamshire, for instance (Yeoman & Stewart 1992), which may relate to vegetable or herb gardens. Celtic bean, pea and lentil are present on a number of sites. Bean is more evident than cereal remains at Brading Roman villa on the Isle of Wight (Scaife in Trott 1999) possibly indicating specialisation. Flax has been recorded at a number of sites, in particular in Buckinghamshire, Oxfordshire and Berkshire, and a number of other specialised crops are also recorded from the Roman-British period.

Foodstuffs, trade, presence and consumption

The definition of a Romano-British diet should be within the grasp of palaeo-environmental analyses and interpretations. Aiming towards defining this as well as the broader economy would considerably enhance our comprehension of Roman life-styles. Here the presence of table foodstuffs may be provided by charred and waterlogged remains, but also in faecal remains and mineralisation. Interestingly, palaeo-environmental archaeologists have not attempted to recreate, via their accumulated data any menus or meals, yet the potential is there, particularly from mineralised deposits.

Luxury and prestige foods, some meats and fruits became socially exclusive. The range and variety of foodstuffs in the Roman diet increased with the import of foods from Europe and the Mediterranean regions and the presence of imported foods such as figs, olives, walnuts (*Junglans*), grapes (*Vitis*) and vines is recorded (eg Booth *et al.* 2007, 280-3; Robinson 2012).

Processing, parching and butchery

The types of crop processing wastes are often indicative of the use of the grain, that is, whether it is processed to store in spikelet form, as corn, or processed for consumption. The evidence of processing waste provides interpretation to suggest, not only specific activities, but also possibly the role and function of specific features or even sites (cf. Stevens 2003). Corn drying ovens/kilns are widely distributed and common throughout the period, and yet their function still remains enigmatic or multifunctional, including their serving as malting ovens

for the brewing of beer, despite van der Veen's work (1991; cf Campbell 2008, 69-70). *Triticum spelta* (spelt) has also been recorded in corn drying ovens, while other ovens may have been used for parching beans as suggested at Brading Roman villa, Isle of Wight.

The processing of animal carcasses and butchery patterns and practices vary between urban and rural assemblages (eg Maltby 1985; 1989; 2010; Hammon 2008; Ingrem 2012), and similar analytical approaches across sites need to be adopted to enable full inter and intra-site comparisons. These data can feed into many of the broader themes such as native vs villa estates, regional specialisation (see above) and urban and lived-in environments (see below).

The built environment

Much of our knowledge of the architecture of the sub-region is based on antiquarian excavations of rural and urban settlement. Thus our knowledge of the urban, built environment is heavily influenced by the plans of buildings recovered by the Society of Antiquaries' excavations at Silchester. So, too, our knowledge of villa and other buildings in the countryside is still very dependent on early work, which was not sensitive to the chronological development of individual structures (particularly of timber) or of groups of buildings. New work across the sub-region is leading to major changes in perception of the rural built environment, including increasing recognition of the continuation of traditions of later prehistoric roundhouse architecture into the late Roman period. At the same time, as in the very recently published Roman Danebury Environs Programme, re-examination of previously excavated villa buildings, as at Brading on the Isle of Wight (Plate 11.5) has provided important new information on other distinctive building types, such as the aisled hall (Cunliffe 2008).

Equally, excavation in towns like Silchester is beginning to show the complexity of the architectural development underlying both public buildings, such as the amphitheatre and forum basilica, and domestic buildings which make up the Antiquaries' 'Great Plan' completed in 1909 (Plate 11.6). The small sample (<0.3 ha) of late 1st/early 2nd-century (timber) built environment revealed by the continuing excavation of *INSULA IX*, Silchester has no parallel elsewhere, not least because of the dearth of research on the early Roman towns in Britain (Booth 2009, 399-401, Figs 15-16). The extent of our ignorance is reinforced when we look across to the 'small towns' and the evidence of their built environment, as tantalisingly revealed by aerial photography at Alchester and at Sansom's Platt (Winton 2001), Oxfordshire, but not researched through modern excavation. In sum, the sub-region has much to contribute to our knowledge of the architecture and built environment of Roman Britain. To date, however, lower status rural settlements have failed almost totally to provide evidence for structures.

Plate 11.5   Brading Villa, the aisled barn, Isle of Wight 2008, *copyright Isle of Wight Council*

Plate 11.6   Late Roman building on Insula IX at Silchester, Hampshire, *copyright M Fulford*

Industrial settlement and landscape

The sub-region is distinctive in having the major Romano-British pottery industries of the New Forest and Oxfordshire, both of national importance (see below), entirely located within it, while a third, the Alice Holt/-Farnham industry, extends across the county boundary into Surrey (Booth et al. 2007, 308-11; Fulford 1975; Lyne and Jefferies 1979; Young 1977). Much of our knowledge of these industries derives from the kilns themselves while their larger, landscape context, extending in each case over tens of square kilometres, remains poorly studied, partly for reasons of modern urban development (Oxfordshire) and partly because of managed afforestation (Alice Holt and New Forest, Hampshire). Nevertheless, just as the impact of urban communities on rural settlement and the landscape requires further evaluation, so, too, does the impact of rural-based industries in terms of the character and location of the settlements of the pottery manufacturers, the supply of fuel and clay, the degree of specialisation of potting communities, particularly in relation to other agricultural activities, and the extent of take-up of potting among settlements as a whole in the respective areas, and so on. For the impact of the Oxfordshire industry on the woodland environment see Day 1993.

Island settlement and landscape/coastscape

The question of urban-rural relationships is not, of course, relevant to the Isle of Wight, where there is no

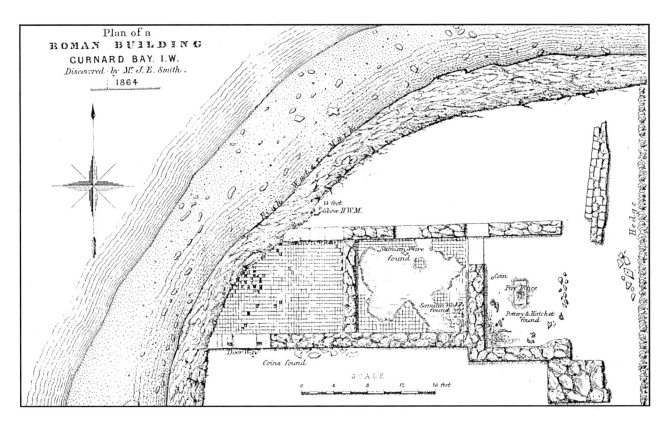

Plate 11.7 Plan of Building at Gurnard Fort, Isle of Wight (19th century excavation)

evidence of *civitas* organisation. This begs the question whether the settlement pattern and agricultural economy of the Island were otherwise significantly different from that of the mainland. The absence of roads has obviously discouraged the development of nucleated settlement. However, the possibility that such settlement did develop needs urgent investigation. In particular, the context of the historic discoveries of the Carisbrooke villa (Spickernell 1859) and other reported Roman buildings in its vicinity towards the centre of the Island requires evaluation to determine whether they represent individual elements of a nucleated settlement.

Early work has shown that villas and Romanised settlement forms have been discovered across the Island, giving the appearance of a landscape little different to that on the mainland (Plate 11.7). There is however a great deal of unpublished research from recent excavations and evaluations of late Iron Age and Roman settlements in a variety of landscape contexts across a range of site types on the Island. Bringing to publication recent work is undoubtedly a priority and would be a very helpful contribution to our knowledge of settlement patterns and diversity on the Island. There is also a strong argument for integrating it with a focused study of a sample of the Island's landscape that combines survey and excavation methodologies. This would provide an enormously valuable comparison with similar mainland projects of the kind described above and, thereby, a powerful contribution to the debate about the nature of urban-rural relations. It would also address the question whether the pattern of Island settlement and acculturation mirrors that of the mainland throughout

the late Iron Age and Roman period, or whether there are periods of greater or lesser integration with the mainland.

The Isle of Wight draws attention to a distinctive aspect of the sub-region's landscape – the Hampshire and Isle of Wight coasts – and the extent to which they supported distinctive, maritime settlements and economy. At present there seem to be two very contrasting types of settlement evidence. On the one hand there is the major settlement at *Clausentum*, defended from the late 3rd century onwards, but about which little is known; on the other there is the material – pottery, coins, animal bone – collected from the intertidal zone at Fishbourne Creek on the Isle of Wight and interpreted as a small emporium (Lyne 2012 a, b, c and d; Tomalin *et al.* 2012). This invaluable collection of material invites us to consider to what extent it might be representative, as a minor and informal trading point, of small ports and harbours more generally along the Solent shores and estuaries of the sub-region. Thus far there is no evidence of more formal port facilities along both Island and mainland coastlines, even though they might reasonably be expected at *Clausentum* and at the late Roman fort at Portchester.

In general, our resources are not particularly helpful in determining the role of the coast and maritime relations in the life of the sub-region during the Roman period. In the later pre-Roman Iron Age imported amphorae, notably the Dressel 1 types of the Roman Republican period, and other imported pottery from Brittany have been recorded from central southern Britain, including the Isle of Wight (eg Fitzpatrick and

Timby 2002; Tomalin 2012a). In contrast, Roman-period artefact distributions do not help us to define either a role for ports in general of the Hampshire and Isle of Wight coast, or of specific ports such as *Clausentum* beyond the notion of the Solent as Ptolemy's *Magnus Portus* (Tomalin 2012b). Biological data, such as oysters suggestive of a south coast origin from Lowbury Hill, Oxon (Somerville 1994), or the presence of marine fish on inland sites such as Silchester (eg Hamilton-Dyer 2000, 482-4; Ingrem 2006, 183), merely beg the question as to their relationship with coastal settlement and the degree of intensity in the exploitation of marine resources. Even where distinctive evidence is recovered, as with the settlements associated with shell middens in the Ventnor area of the south coast of the Isle of Wight (Poole 1929), this may simply reflect local consumption rather than any engagement with mainland markets.

In regard to cross-Channel or Atlantic trade, the evidence from the Isle of Wight is, by comparison, particularly helpful for the late Iron Age/earliest Roman period when distinctive imports of amphorae of Dressel 1 and 2-4 types have been recorded from a large number of island sites. The assumption is that this material derives from direct contact between overseas traders and island communities, rather than through redistribution from mainland ports such as Hengistbury Head (Dorset), which was particularly active in the later Iron Age (Cunliffe 1987; Fitzpatrick 2001; Tomalin 2012a).

Ceremony, ritual and religion

Evidence of temples, shrines and of religious activity more generally is represented in a variety of forms among the settlements of the sub-region. The distribution of built (temple) sites is uneven, with an emphasis to the north of the sub-region with examples in Buckinghamshire (Plate 11.8), Oxfordshire and (east) Berkshire, but fewer known sites in west Berkshire, Hampshire and the Isle of Wight. Albeit poorly understood, temples and shrines represent one component of the urban fabric and are integral with it, while in rural situations they may appear as a distinct element of the landscape, even if, in some cases, settlement may have developed around them. This may be the case with the development of the settlement at Frilford, Oxfordshire from the Iron Age, discussed in the context of nucleated settlement above (but cf Harding 1987, 12-16). Other, nationally important temple sites such as Weycock Hill at Waltham St Lawrence, Berkshire and Woodeaton, Oxfordshire have undergone some modern work, but the discovery, on the one hand, of the great Iron Age coin hoard attributed to Weycock Hill (Burnett 1990; Bean 2000, 253-62) and, on the other, through aerial survey, of further temple buildings at Woodeaton (eg Henig and Booth 2000, 89), remind us how little is known of these two sites and how they relate to local settlement from the late Iron Age onwards. Context is also an important question in relation to the Hayling

Plate 11.8 Reconstruction of the temple at Thornborough, Buckinghamshire, *copyright Buckinghamshire County Council*

Island (Hampshire) temple (Downey *et al*. 1979; King and Soffe 1998), where completion of the publication of this important late Iron Age and Romano-British site would make an important contribution to the archaeology of the sub-region.

While the process of classification draws attention to 'Romano-Celtic' temples and shrines as distinct types of site, deserving of further research in their own right, they should not be divorced from their landscape context. In this context they may be seen, alongside rural settlement with a similar chronology, as part of the appropriation of estates and the development of new patterns of land ownership from the late Iron Age/earliest Roman period. At the same time, the unevenness of distribution noted above suggests that, as with the enigmatic rectangular enclosure – very probably a rural shrine – at Lowbury Hill, Oxfordshire (Fulford and Rippon 1994), the expression of cult and religion in built form takes on different, physical identities in different parts of the sub-region. Chance discoveries of single finds, such as of the altars from Bampton and Bablock Hythe, Oxfordshire (Henig 1993, nos 28, 35) and of the Christian, lead tanks from a well at Caversham, Berkshire (Booth *et al*. 2007, 223) and from close to the villa at Wigginton, Oxfordshire, remind us how little we know, not least of their relationship with settlement and religious practice.

The discovery of single finds, such as the lead tanks, from secondary contexts, draws attention to the potential breadth of ritual behaviour and the increase in recognition of special or structured deposits. These can range from major deposits of metalwork, represented in the sub-region by the celebrated pewter hoards from Appleshaw, Hampshire, Appleford, Oxfordshire and Thatcham, Berkshire (Poulton and Scott 1993), to those of articulated animal remains placed in pits or wells. The work of Hill (1995) for Wessex and of Grant (1984) for the hillfort of Danebury, Hampshire, has shown that structured deposition in the Iron Age of animal remains is well represented in the sub-region, particularly among settlements on the Hampshire chalk. For the Roman period, however, variability in practice across different environments of the sub-region and the landscape at large is not well researched, but the evidence is indicative of strong continuity of practices, particularly in relation to structured deposition, from the Iron Age throughout the Roman period in urban and rural contexts (Fulford 2001; Eckardt 2006; 2011; Maltby 1994; Morris 2011, 66-98; Oliver 1993). A votive explanation for prehistoric finds of metalwork associated with watery contexts is widely invoked and generally accepted, but the equivalent has not been systematically researched for the Roman period. For example, there has been no survey of Roman finds from the Thames (or from any river in the sub-region) in the way that there has been for later prehistoric materials.

Other evidence for religious activity can be found particularly in rural areas; for example, a Taranis shrine was identified at Wavendon Gate, Milton Keynes (Williams *et al*. 1996) and a possible late shrine at Thruxton, Hampshire (Cunliffe and Poole 2008d).

Concentrations of particular types of artefact, identified through PAS records, may also help locate sites.

Cemeteries

Patchiness of the record in regard to the structured deposition of material culture and animal bones corresponds with the uneven quality of the record for the burial of human remains which become archaeologically visible again from the later Iron Age. With cremation the predominant mode of disposal in the 1st and 2nd centuries AD, there have been no extensive excavations of cemeteries, particularly urban, in the sub-region. On the other hand there has been recognition of what seems a regionally important early Roman burial tradition at Alton in Hampshire, one of richly furnished, single and multiple cremation-burials (Millett 1986; 1987). However, there have been modern investigations and publications of one large late Roman inhumation cemetery, that of the extramural cemetery of Lankhills at Winchester, Hampshire in the sub-region (Clarke 1979; Booth *et al*. 2010). The earlier publication did not include a report upon the human remains, but even without this the information upon the disposition of the graves, their cuts, fills and the associated grave goods has proved of immense value in defining late Roman burial practice, and has initiated debate about group identity within and around the late Roman city (eg Baldwin 1985; Evans *et al*. 2006). The more recent excavation of the Lankhills cemetery and analysis of the human remains are adding valuable new perspectives on the earlier work, particularly through isotopic analysis (Eckardt *et al*. 2009; Booth *et al*. 2010, 411-28). Other urban cemeteries are less well researched, though the potential for 'small' towns, as indicated by the Queenford Farm cemetery outside of Dorchester-on-Thames, Oxfordshire (Chambers 1987) and finds of burials outside *Magiovinium*, Buckinghamshire (Neal 1987), all hint at the unrealised potential that more extensive research would generate.

For the countryside the picture is quite limited with very few modern investigations. However, the late Roman inhumation cemetery of some 57 individuals at Radley, near to Barton Court Farm, Oxon and the smaller, late or sub-Roman cemetery at the Thruxton villa provide valuable examples (Chambers and McAdam 2007; Cunliffe and Poole 2008d).

A major question, relevant as much for Roman Britain as a whole as for the sub-region, is how far, if at all, there was significant variation in the demographics – gender, age structure, pathology, etc – between town and country, and in burial traditions? For example, the presence of inhumations among early Roman cemeteries (where cremation is the norm) and the presence of cremations among late Roman burials (where inhumation is the norm) require investigation (eg Chambers and Boyle 2007). The role of distinctive, rectangular enclosure of early Roman cremation cemeteries in the sub-region, as, for example, at Roden Down, Berkshire (Hood and Walton 1948), and as indicated elsewhere through aerial photography, also requires further investigation. Two examples of *bustum* burials have been noted in the region, one at Didcot, Oxfordshire (Cotswold Archaeology 2003) and the other at Denham, Buckinghamshire (Coleman *et al.* 2004; Barber 2011), and this type of practice would merit closer study. In general, and crucial to addressing all these questions is the need for the identification, excavation and full publication of rural cemeteries across the sub-region. Isotopic research on rural populations is needed to compare with that carried out on Roman urban communities.

Communications

In the Solent-Thames area natural communication routes include not only rivers but also the south coast harbours and access to the sea, which also offer the possibility of considering relations with regions beyond the Roman province(s). The sub-region also contains Roman roads that played a significant, strategic role in provincial life, linking the it to the province(s) beyond. One major road led westwards from London to Silchester, then, variously, to the south-west to Dorchester (Dorset) via East Anton (Andover, Hampshire), to the west to Bath, and to the north-west to Cirencester from London through Berkshire and Hampshire. A second, major route ran east-west in the north of our region, probably originating in Colchester and then running westwards through *Verulamium* to Alchester and on to Cirencester. Together with the west-to-east- flow of the Thames, the sub-region thus has a major sample of routes linking east and west, and in particular linking London with the west of Britain, including Wales. The north-south configuration of the counties of our region however also invites us to consider the importance of north-south communications. One such was represented by roads leading south from Towcester, through Alchester and Dorchester to Silchester, and thereafter to Chichester and Winchester. A second north-south road linked Cirencester with Winchester (via, amongst other small towns, East Anton) and beyond, although the onward road connections to ports at *Clausentum* and, later, Portchester are far from clear.

The existence of ports such as Bitterne (*Clausentum*) and Portchester, together with Chichester (West Sussex) to the east, raises the issue of the role that the harbours of the Solent played in facilitating trade and traffic from the south coast to the north and vice versa. There is also the question of how such maritime trade differed from that handled by London and the Thames Estuary? Examining the role and relative importance of different roads and, in particular the relative importance of east-west as opposed to north-south communication, is an issue of provincial-wide importance and one which is appropriate to the resources of the sub-region. As already suggested above, this can be approached through consideration of the size and material contents of the numerous settlements that developed along them (see also above). From the perspective of the written sources, while *Calleva* is listed in a number of itineraries in the Antonine Itinerary, none of these include settlements on the road north to Alchester, perhaps indicating that by the late 2nd century that road was of less importance.

Consideration of the role of the rivers of the sub-region and, particularly, of the role of the Thames and its major tributaries is also of considerable importance. That the Thames was probably of major significance in the late Iron Age and earliest Roman period is indicated by the emergence of centres, such as Abingdon and Dyke Hills, Dorchester-on-Thames, Oxfordshire (eg Allen 2000, 22-27), along its length. Equally, even if its location is not right beside the Loddon, a significant tributary of the Thames, it is hard to account for the rise of *Calleva* unless communication linking to the Thames played a major role in its development (Fulford and Timby 2000, 557-8; Cunliffe 2012). The closest parallels for its late Iron Age and earliest Roman material culture certainly lie to the east, to Essex, Hertfordshire and Kent. By the same token, and paralleling the situation in the Iron Age, the role of the Thames needs to be considered in the context of the early emergence of Anglo-Saxon settlement at and around Dorchester-on-Thames in the 5th century.

It is always assumed that the relatively cheaper water transport offered by seas and rivers would have taken priority over that carried overland, but objective data are seriously lacking. Similarly, fording places, bridges and pontoons must have existed across a number of rivers, streams and brooks which would considerably aid our understanding of the Roman built environment, but also provide us with stratified palaeo-environmental (pollen, sediment and snail) sequences. While the question of the sacred nature of rivers and watery places has been commented upon above, there still remains considerable scope to examine the role of the rivers as a means of communication and as a source of food. While study of Oxfordshire pottery suggested that the Thames may have provided a major role in its distribution, this is hard to prove definitively (Fulford and Hodder 1974; cf Booth *et al.* 2007, 314-5). Much more quantitative data derived from the study of pottery and other types of material culture are required before we can discriminate confidently between the roles of river as opposed to road in the distribution of food, raw materials and manufactured goods. However, preliminary study of the distribution of SE Dorset BB1 into the sub-region strongly suggests that the road network played a leading role (Allen and Fulford 1996).

Riverside settlements are known at several locations along the Thames, but they tend to be obscured by medieval and later development, as at Dorchester, Reading or Henley, for example. Research on Roman material dredged from the Thames might be helpful both in regard to locating further riverside settlement, as well as material transported along it. The question of the extent and scale of river transport is by no means confined to the Thames, but is relevant to other rivers of the sub-region, ranging from the Ouse in Buckinghamshire to the Kennet (Berkshire) and the rivers of the south Hampshire basin.

Like the Zwammerdam craft from the lower Rhine region, the small, Barland's Farm craft recovered from the Wentlooge Level of south-east Wales (Nayling and McGrail 2004) reminds us of the kind of vessel which could have navigated the rivers of the sub-region and the size of cargo that it might have carried. Indeed, Roman material recovered from the Solent is also a reminder of the possibility of recovering the remains of Roman sea-going craft from that part of the sub-region. There is clear evidence of cross-channel links in terms of the Roman population itself and continued trade and the import of food stuffs and wine etc, but little physical evidence of the ports, harbours, quays, jetties or even boats. Examination of coastal and intertidal areas along the Hampshire and Wight margins of the Solent may find evidence of these. Waterlogged timbers should therefore be examined and routinely radiocarbon dated. Furthermore, waterlogged, intertidal, fluvial and alluvial deposits may contain evidence of boat fragments and jetties. Detailed excavations and surveys have to date recovered wooden structures of prehistoric and Saxon date, for example at Testwood Lakes and at Langstone harbour, but not yet any of Roman date. In part little effort has been expended in this direction, and detailed geoarchaeological survey may be required to aid location of eroded, or even *in situ* finds and evidence.

0   50 mm

1:1

Plate 11.9 Shale bracelet from Grave 1070 at Lankhills, Winchester, *copyright OA*

Material culture

Roads, rivers and the sea were critical to the distribution of foodstuffs and consumer goods. While tracking the former is relatively hard except when it is carried in distinctive containers such as amphorae or barrels, distinctive categories of material culture offer the possibility of tracking the production of particular industries, such as shale from the south coast, or particular kinds of object (Plate 11.9). More importantly, and led by provincial-wide studies of lamps and lighting equipment (Eckardt 2002), toilet instruments (Crummy and Eckardt 2003), etc, the study of material culture in general has considerable, untapped potential for addressing questions of acculturation and social identity at a regional and sub- or micro-regional level. Contributing to this debate, well-contextualised assemblages of material culture have been reported from a variety of rural and urban locations in the sub-region (eg Rees *et al*. 2008). The significant level of material recorded by the Portable Antiquities Scheme (PAS) undoubtedly has an important role to play in this area. For example, case studies of the coin finds recorded by the PAS from Hampshire and the Isle of Wight show the potential of this material, not least in establishing local identities of coin circulation and loss (Walton 2012).

Solent-Thames is well placed to examine the relationship between new, Roman or Gallo-Roman material culture and native traditions in the critical period of change during the later 1st century BC and 1st century AD. Much of that direction of change was from the east, the counties bordering the Thames Estuary, but there is also the contribution of the ports of entry of the south coast to be explored (cf Fulford 2007). Beyond that and into the Roman period proper, the 2nd to 4th century, the study of the spread of Roman coinage alongside that of manufactured Roman consumer goods through the *civitates* of the sub-region has much to contribute to our knowledge of the development of urban and rural markets.

Timby's recent study (2012) of late Iron Age and Roman pottery supply to the hinterland of Calleva is very illuminating in this respect. It also demonstrates the value of the contribution that small-scale, development-led interventions can make to the period. Gaining greater insights into differential and changing access to the various types and categories of material culture will contribute to a better understanding of the variable social role that it played through the settlement hierarchy of the sub-region.

Industry

Pottery industries

Reference has already been made to the landscape and settlement context of the larger industries of the sub-region, in particular the potteries of the New Forest (Fulford 1975) and Oxfordshire (Young 1977).

Plate 11.10 Kiln from the Oxfordshire pottery industry, *copyright OA*

Surprisingly little is known about the various components of the process of pottery making other than the final stage of firing, represented by the kilns themselves (Plate 11.10). So, clay extraction and preparation, the acquisition of the fuel (and the management of woodland resources), the workshops and drying sheds are all poorly understood. While the sub-region is dominated by these two industries, and by that of the Alice Holt/Farnham region (Surrey) right on its boundary (Lyne and Jefferies 1979), very little is known about the relationships between them. There is also the Poole Harbour industry (SE Dorset BB1), situated just beyond the south-western boundary of the sub-region, to conside Its wares are well represented in the sub-region (Allen and Fulford 1996). The earliest to begin production, possibly even before the Roman conquest of AD 43, and to make an impact in the sub-region is the Alice Holt industry and its products are well represented in assemblages in London and Silchester by the third quarter of the 1st century AD. The origins of the Oxfordshire industry are less clear, but it was making a significant contribution to pottery assemblages at Silchester by the mid-2nd century AD (Timby 2011). It overtakes the Verulamium-region industries by the later 2nd century and, along with the Alice Holt and New Forest industries, dominates consumption in the sub-region in the 3rd and 4th centuries (Timby 2011; Young 1977).

Unlike the Verulamium-region industry, which was located close to *Verulamium*, and with kilns stretching along Watling Street towards London, where very similar production is also now attested (Seeley and Drummond-Murray 2005), the Oxfordshire kilns are situated alongside the Alchester-Silchester (north-south) route, relatively remote from a major urban agglomeration. This location gives us the basis for exploring the significance of the north-south line of communication in the sub-region, and perhaps also the link with a potential river port at Dorchester-on-Thames giving access to the east-west lines of communication described above.

The origins of the New Forest industry, even more remotely located, are also unclear, but the full repertoire of table and grey wares was certainly established by the late 3rd century (Fulford 1975). There are two major issues to be explored here: one is the possibility of earlier production of grey wares in the 2nd and earlier 3rd centuries, where analysis of independently dated assemblages from Winchester will be of crucial importance. The second is the relationship with the production of BB1 at Poole Harbour nearby, which was supplying distant markets such as the northern frontier and London by the early-to-mid 2nd century. Although the industries did complement each other's repertoires to some extent in the later 3rd and 4th centuries, with colour-coated and parchment/white wares reserved to the New Forest, the manufacture of cooking and domestic wares is common to both industries. How did this relationship work, given that Poole Harbour BB1 remains a major component of pottery assemblages in the sub-region into the first half of the 5th century?

While there has been considerable progress in mapping the distribution of the late colour-coated and 'parchment' wares of the New Forest and Oxfordshire industries, much less is known about the grey and white wares, the former being common to these and the Alice Holt industry. The sub-region offers the possibility of significantly enhancing our understanding of the inter-relationships of these three major industries, not least with regard to the wares and types of vessels all three of them produced. If furthering our knowledge of these three industries addresses topics of national importance, we should not overlook other pottery production in the sub-region, whose study will help inform us both about the movement of ideas, but also of minor networks of marketing and distribution. The late Roman grog-tempered production, for example, thought to be located in the south Hampshire basin, was a significant supplier in the sub-region with a presence as far north as Silchester and south Wiltshire (Lyne 1994). Its relationship with similar, but earlier established production in the nearby Isle of Wight (Vectis Ware; Tomalin 1987, 30-40) demands investigation. Indeed ceramics offers a valuable medium for exploring the relationship between the Island and the mainland (and, across the Channel, to northern France). On the whole it would seem that Vectis ware consumption was very much confined to the Island. The fact of insular production hints at inadequate or irregular supplies of cooking/domestic wares from mainland sources, and the lack of off-Island movement of Vectis Ware reinforces that perception. Nevertheless Island sites still have good representation of the major traded wares represented on settlements across the Solent.

Brick and tile

While pottery industries remain a very important and distinctive resource of the sub-region, we should not overlook brick and tile. On the basis of its bulk, and of the quantities required in any building project, whether urban or rural, it is generally assumed that most production is located close to the point of consumption. Study of fabrics and the dies used to produce relief-patterned flue-tile (Betts *et al.* 1997) has indicated that brick and tile could travel considerable distances (see also Betts and Foot 1994). Indeed, the sub-region is towards the edge of the distribution of tile stamped with distinctive dies produced in the south-eastern counties of Surrey, Sussex and Kent. However, whereas we can assume major tileries were established to serve the major towns like Silchester and Winchester, and possibly also for each of the 'small' towns, we know very little about them, never mind their impact with and beyond the major centres (cf Warry 2012 on the tile production required to serve Silchester). To address this, there needs to be systematic characterisation and comparison of assemblages from different centres and analysis of change over time. It has been suggested, for example, that the production of brick and tile significantly declined in the later Roman period.

Stone exploitation

If production of brick and tile was not exclusive to the sub-region, the exploitation of certain other resources used in building was more regionally focused. Limestone slabs, either from the Purbeck beds just outside the region in south-east Dorset, or from Oxfordshire Jurassic sources such as those around Stonesfield, Oxfordshire were used for roofing slates, typically in the 3rd and 4th centuries. Researching the relative importance within the sub-region of these two sources would make a significant contribution to our knowledge of the development of regional traditions in the building industry through the Roman period. Remoter sources of roofing slate, such as from the Forest of Dean, Gloucestershire, also make a significant contribution to the sub-region, as at Silchester (eg Shaffrey 2006a, 337-8). But how widespread in the sub-region was the consumption of this relatively exotic material?

Freestone from the Jurassic limestone quarries of Bath and the Cotswolds (including those in Oxfordshire) was also used in the sub-region for general building and other specialist, architectural stonework. The dominant lithology of the sub-region was, however, undoubtedly flint quarried from the chalk and used in all the counties on the sub-region. In both cases important work needs to be undertaken to characterise the extent of the use of these materials, particularly in locations away from the source areas, and thus build on Hayward's recent characterisation of freestones and their use in southern England (Hayward 2009). Freestone, like roller-stamp-decorated flue-tile, could travel long distances to be used for architectural or funerary purposes, but (as with ceramic building material) the bulk use of these materials at a distance from the likely source area, needs to be further investigated (eg for Silchester, cf Sellwood 1984; Hayward 2011).

Material from distant sources was also used in the manufacture of mosaic pavements in villas and town houses in southern Britain. To this end in the early Roman period a variety of coloured stone was exported from sources on the Isle of Purbeck in south-east Dorset (Allen and Fulford 2004; Allen *et al.* 2007; Allen and Todd 2010). Certain types of Chalk were also used selectively in mosaic making (Wilkinson *et al.* 2008).

The material requirements to produce querns and millstones were very different to those needed for roofing slate or mosaic materials. In the south of the sub-region a major source of querns in the late Iron Age and early Roman period was Lodsworth, West Sussex (Peacock 1987). Other sources, including of Upper and Lower Greensand, were exploited in the sub-region but have not been researched. In addition, and from outside the sub-region, Old Red Sandstone from the west of England, Millstone Grit from the north and Niedermendig lava imported from Germany were also used, but only the first has received serious study (Shaffrey 2006b). Alongside the provenancing of materials, consideration also needs to be given to change over time. There is certainly evidence for watermills in the sub-region in the later Roman period (Booth *et al.* 2007, 298-9; Cunliffe 2001; Cunliffe and Poole 2008c), but the extent of the use of this technology and other mechanised forms of milling demands further research.

Shale from just west of the region was also an important regional resource for personal adornment in the Roman period, as in the later Iron Age, and would repay study both as an indicator of trade and of cultural affiliations within and beyond the region (see Plate 11.9 above).

Iron-making

Several county contributions also mention iron-making as well as iron-working at a variety of site types. Though we are accustomed to thinking that the major sources of iron in the Roman period, such as the Weald, the Forest of Dean and Northamptonshire, accounted for consumption in the south of Britain, there is increasing evidence for further, localised manufacture of bloomery iron in both urban (eg Silchester: J Allen (2012)) and, potentially, rural contexts. The slag masses point to the continuation of prehistoric techniques using bowl-shaped hearths alongside shaft furnaces. The extent to which the making of iron, as opposed to that of iron artefacts, existed through the settlement hierarchy of the sub-region requires urgent investigation, as does the extent to which local sources provided the ore.

Food production

There is an increasing body of evidence for malting and corn drying on a large scale (eg from the Danebury Environs' sites, summarised in Campbell 2008, 69-70). At Weedon Hill (in Buckinghamshire) an unusually complete malting oven has been excavated (Wakeham, *et al*.2013) and there is also evidence for barley malting associated with corn driers at Bancroft Villa, Milton Keynes (Williams and Zeepvat 1994, 83-6). There are also sites with multiple corn driers, eg among the Danebury Environs sites (Cunliffe and Poole 2008a-g) and at Yewden Villa, Buckinghamshire (Cocks 1921; Eyers 2011; Plate 11.11). This larger scale production may have been linked to supplying particular markets, including overseas, as is evidenced from written sources of the supply of corn to the Rhineland in the mid-fourth century.

The later Roman period

Although there is considerable continuity of settlement between the late 1st/early 2nd century AD and, in some cases certainly, the early 5th century, it is important to consider certain developments that are peculiar to the 3rd – 5th century. The most obvious of these is the provision of new coastal forts in east and south-east Britain. In the case of Solent-Thames, the construction of the fort at Portchester, at the head of Portsmouth Harbour on the Hampshire coast, in the late 3rd century (Cunliffe 1975; Plate 11.12). Although its identification with *Portus Adurni*, one of the forts listed in the late 4th century *Notitia Dignitatum*, is uncertain, it does appear to be a military establishment in origin, even if it did not continue to be garrisoned continuously thereafter. Indeed distinguishing between civil and military occupation in general in the 4th century remains difficult (cf Gardiner 2007). The construction of a new fort at Portchester may be linked programmatically with the building of defences around the existing settlement at *Clausentum* (see above) and there is the still unresolved question of late Roman fortification of Carisbrooke Castle on the Isle of Wight (see above). While not far from the head waters of the tidal River Medina, the location of the fortification is more central to the Island than close to the coast. Portchester seems to be the only completely 'new' foundation, but little is known of its immediate context and impact on surrounding settlement. The, as yet unlocated, cemetery would have enormous potential in advancing our understanding of the inhabitants of this site and change over time.

The question whether or not there is a Roman phase at Carisbrooke reminds us, that while there is some

Plate 11.11 Tuning fork kiln corndrying oven from Yewden villa, *Society of Antiquaries, reproduced courtesy of Surrey Archaeological Society (Rref:PD1114/4) fig. 1.6*

Plate 11.12 Portchester Castle, Hampshire, *copyright P Booth*

knowledge of the mid and late Roman fortification of the larger towns of Silchester (Fulford 1984) and Winchester, and of some of the smaller, such as Alchester (Young 1975), Dorchester-on-Thames (Hogg and Stevens 1937; Frere 1962), and *Magiovinium* on Watling Street, little is otherwise known of the defence of *mansiones* and other stations along the major roads of the sub-region, never mind their character and function in the late Roman period. The evidence from Neatham, Hampshire is important here, providing not only evidence of the nature of occupation from the early 2nd century onwards, but also of defence, in this case apparently short-lived and confined to the 3rd century (Millett and Graham 1986). The extent to which stations along the roads were defended, as they were, for example, along Watling Street, has considerable implications for understanding the strategic organisation of the south of Britain in the 4th century.

There has become increasing interest in the subject of identity and social mobility in Roman Britain and late Roman cemeteries are, potentially, a critically important resource (cf Eckardt 2010). With inhumation burial, the predominant rite in late Roman Britain, the potential for analysing assemblages of grave goods in association with individuals for whom there is information on age and sex is very great. This has been argued in relation to the Lankhills, Winchester, cemetery, where incomers from the upper Danube region have been postulated on the basis of distinctive groups of grave goods (see above). While burials with accompanying grave goods are, perhaps, the exception in southern Britain in the 4th century, techniques of analysis of the bone and teeth can also be of assistance in identifying individuals or groups differentiated by diet or by probable region of origin. Indeed these techniques are important resources for testing hypotheses based, as is the case with Lankhills, principally on the analysis of associated material culture

and its disposition within the grave. As we have seen above, isotopic analysis of human remains from Lankhills does indicate diversity in the Winchester population with an overseas component, but it does question how far reliable conclusions can be drawn on the basis of the study of material culture and grave ritual alone.

Roman to Anglo-Saxon transition

The period of the 5th to 7th century continues to remain a very challenging one for southern Britain in general, as much as for Solent-Thames in particular. With the demise of the widespread introduction of new coin into circulation after the first years of the 5th century and of the production of mass-produced manufactured goods, notably pottery, there is almost no material culture to be associated with the 5th to 7th centuries, other than Anglo-Saxon. On the other hand, there is no evidence for rapid loss of population through noticeable increases in burial beyond the end of the 4th century. If anything, as in the Lankhills (urban) context, the case for population loss could be argued on the basis of a sharp decline in burial in the early 5th century, but our sample size is very small. The assumption is that population levels remained unchanged, but essentially invisible, but more data are needed to confirm or refute this. Only large-scale excavation in both rural and urban contexts, and of both settlements and cemeteries, has the potential of showing change beyond the beginning of the 5th century, as has been demonstrated at Barton Court Farm, Oxfordshire with a history extending to the 6th century (Miles 1986). Sequences can be established either through horizontal or vertical stratigraphy that extend beyond the end of the 4th/beginning of the 5th and include contexts associated with the latest material culture, among which the closely dated coins of the

House of Theodosius are among the most helpful (cf Silchester, Fulford *et al.* 2006, 273-8).

In the absence of datable material culture, testing of postulated post-400 chronologies must rely more on radiocarbon dating (cf Fulford 2000), though this is not without its problems (cf Booth, *et al.* 2010, 448-56). This is not to suggest that we can expect close dating within this time span of two to three centuries, rather a greater or lesser probability of a date belonging before or after the beginning of the fifth century. The application of radiocarbon dating should become routine in the appropriate (Roman to Saxon) context (cf Pollard 2012, 182-5).

With Dorchester-on-Thames and Winchester the sub-region is distinguished in having two urban centres, one a 'small' Roman town, the other a civitas capital, which both play a prominent role in the emergence of Anglo-Saxon Wessex in the seventh century. While our knowledge of the 5th to the 7th centuries in these two centres is still limited, it is clear that both, with their immediate rural hinterlands, have much to contribute to our understanding of the transition from Roman to Saxon. At the same time there is much to learn from the negative – from those urban settlements and their hinterlands, both major and minor, such as Silchester and Alchester, which do not re-emerge as significant centres in Anglo-Saxon England (cf Fulford 2012b). What determined continuity or not; and what do we understand by continuity? We have probably attached too much importance to the rapid demise of Roman material culture without giving sufficient consideration either to the evidence of settlement histories as revealed through vertical and horizontal stratigraphy or to environmental sequences which do not, for example, point to a rapid or widespread regeneration of woodland in the early post-Roman period (Dark 2000b, 140-2; Day 1993).

Chapter 12

The Roman Period: Research Agenda

by Mike Fulford

12.1 Introduction

The Solent-Thames region extends north-south from around the centre of England to the south coast and the Isle of Wight. It is unevenly bisected by a major river, the Thames, and its geology is dominated by the chalk, the gravels of the Thames valley and the heaths and claylands of south Hampshire including the Hampshire Basin. *The Research Agenda*, sketched out below, focus on aspects and attributes of the region which are distinctive to it, and which could contribute to a larger, national research agenda. In other words, these agenda indicate Solent-Thames' particular potential contribution to our knowledge and understanding of Roman Britain. The definition of 'Roman' extends from the late Iron Age, the later first century BC to the fifth/sixth century AD.

12.2 Inheritance

There are no clear boundaries between Iron Age and Roman in this region although it is clear that the during the 1st century BC to early 2nd century AD there was a period of major change in the countryside. To assist in understanding this,

12.2.1 Sites with well-preserved deposits of both late Iron Age and Roman date should be given careful attention in order to investigate continuity of local tradition at these sites. Sampling strategies should ensure that as wide a range of contexts are sampled as possible. Excavations of deep, well-sealed features are required (as opposed to buildings).

12.2.2 Radiocarbon dating should be used more widely and systematically to help understand change between the late Iron Age and early Roman period.

12.3 Environmental evidence

Detailed examination of the fields (lynchets, sediment analysis of colluvium, proxy palaeo-environmental evidence for the use of the field), may start to help define how field and field systems operated (cf. Allen 2008a). It is important to define the composition of the farmed resources (i.e. cereal types and proportions of livestock) between the main groups of farms to define how they are feeding themselves and/or supporting the wider Roman economy.

Changing farming methods (i.e. from ard to mouldboard plough) increases soil disturbances and consequently may be represented in increased ploughwash and the nature of build-up in lynchets or valley bottoms, and ultimately in alluviation of floodplains. The use of a mouldboard plough, not an ard may be detectable in the nature or erosion products and presence of B horizon or B/C horizon material in lynchets and ploughwash deposits. Soil micromorphology may be able to address this in combination with geoarchaeological field records and other analyses (eg soil magnetic susceptibility). The following recommendations are suggested:

12.3.1 Environmental evidence should be collected and analysed to help identify how field systems operated and developed.

12.3.2 Variation in resources and agricultural regimes from different scales of farm needs to be investigated.

12.3.3 Attempts should be made to identify any changes in farming methods from field, farm and valley environments.

12.3.4 Evidence for a Roman cultivation signature in the alluvial sequences of, for instance, the Thames Valley should be sought.

12.4 Landscape and land use

There have been extensive programmes investigating exploitation of the chalk downland and river valleys, but less of the claylands for example. This imbalance needs to be addressed so that an overall pattern across the region can be developed for the existence and spread of fields, stock raising and woodland. The importance of the full range of palaeo-environmental evidence in this respect must be emphasised. The following areas of research have been highlighted:

12.4.1 'The time is ripe for an extended programme of sampling across as wide a range of urban and rural site as possible' (Burnham *et al.* 2001, 70). Studies of different types of site within a local area should be given high priority, in order to build up a picture of supply and demand eg urban sites and those in their hinterland.

12.4.2   Corn dryers should be studied, both in terms of their archaeobotany and possible multiple functions, and their archaeological context. Since the majority appear to be of late Roman date, particular attention should be given to early Roman corn dryers wherever they are identified.

12.4.3   Spelt wheat was using for brewing throughout the Roman period, though there is some evidence that barely or a mixture of wheat and barley may have been used towards the end of this period. Samples that contain sprouted barley grain, believed to represent grain prepared as malt, should be radio-carbon dated. The material itself should be used for this purpose and a minimum of two dates from a given assemblage should be obtained.

12.4.4   The retrieval of information regarding the development of synanthropic fauna, pests and disease, especially in rural settlements.

12.4.5   The development of horticulture and the access of the rural population to 'exotic' foods.

12.4.6   Detection of evidence for viticulture to compare with that found in the Midlands.

12.4.7   Investigation of Roman urban deposits for insects.

12.4.8   Diet, including evidence from mineralised deposits from latrines and other sources of cess.

12.4.9   The location of woodland, and if and how it was managed.

12.4.10   The exploitation of woodland for construction and use as fuel needs to be investigated throughout the settlement heirarchy, and in domestic, religious and industrial contexts.

12.4.11   The exploitation of fish and shellfish on Roman sites, including the identification of further evidence for (freshwater) fish farming. This research has the potential to help us understand the connections between coastal and inland settlements.

12.4.12   Breed improvement for cattle and sheep, and variation in the proportions of the principal domestic animals in relation to the socio-economic status of the producer.

12.4.13   Information about 'exotic' species, such as the north Buckinghamshire chestnuts should be sought within pollen sequences.

12.5   Social organisation

To go beyond the familiar catechism of settlement heirarchies for Roman Britain: of large town, small town, other nucleated settlement, villa, other rural settlement, etc., in order to gain a better knowledge and understanding of social organisation requires focused and extensive work on each category of nucleated settlement ans well as the careful sampling of rural landscapes and their constituent settlements across the sub-region through survey and excavation. The careful excavation of burials and cemeteries in association with their parent towns and settlements can also shed important light on social organisation. Possible approaches are identified in the sections which follow.

12.6   Settlement

Characterisation of settlement and economy

Our knowledge of settlement types and distributions is heavily biased towards the chalk and the river gravels of the upper Ouse, and the middle and upper Thames, even if we still know little of non-villa settlement, settlement hierarchies and site economies in these areas. Barton Court Farm villa (Abingdon, Oxfordshire) and Bancroft villa (Milton Keynes, Buckinghamshire) remain exceptional for the contribution that they have made to our understanding of modest villas on the gravels and the workings of their associated, assumed estates. While the Thames Valley gravels have seen a very considerable amount of modern archaeology in advance of gravel extraction, there has not been a comparable focus on the settlement of the chalk, where we are still very largely reliant on the results of antiquarian or pre-modern fieldwork, the exceptions being the Danebury Environs (north Hampshire) and the Maddle Farm (Berkshire) projects. An ambition would be to reach the point, on the basis of comparable data from different environments, of being able to offer characterisations of the settlement and agricultural economies of these sub-regions. For the Chalk,

12.6.1   a comparative, landscape approach to 'blocks' of chalkland, such as the Berkshire Downs, the Chiltern Hills, the central or eastern Hampshire chalk and the Isle of Wight might address questions relating to:

A – Non-villa settlement and burial practice

B – Nucleated settlement and burial practice

C – Settlement economies

D – Temples and religious sites

E – The relationship of the above to the mid and late Iron Age background.

12.6.2   Equally important is the need to gain an understanding of settlement, its density and variability as well as economy in other environments, such as claylands and heathlands. This is crucial not only to our understanding of population density and its fluctuation over time, but also to determining the extent of woodland in the region and its change through time. For the claylands and heathlands, we particularly need a much better characterisation of settlement patterns in:

A – East Berkshire

B – The Vale of Aylesbury, Buckinghamshire

C – The Hampshire Basin

D – The New Forest

E – The claylands of the Isle of Wight

F – North-east Oxfordshire claylands

G – The Vale of the White Horse.

12.6.3   The PAS records show concentrations of reported finds on a landscape scale which do not map onto existing HER records. These require further investigation through geophysical survey and systematic surface collection.

Patterns of development and abandonment

The (differential) development of 'villas', representing a concentration of resources in the countryside, suggests an associated re-organisation of settlement and the wider, associated (managed) landscape. Preliminary survey of the evidence on the Chalk and on the river gravels suggests that the first centuries BC and AD were a period of increased rural settlement, but that this was followed by settlement desertion in the first/second century AD. At the end of the Roman period the lack of dated material culture has lead to the assumption of widespread settlement desertion after the early fifth century AD. To address this,

12.6.4   the evidence for major change in settlement occupation across the diverse landscapes of the region between the late Iron Age and the early medieval period needs to be collated.

12.6.5   the relationship of such change to the development and decline of 'villas' and associated reorganisation of the rural landscape should be investigated.

12.7   Civitas capitals and other towns

Our region includes two *civitas* capitals, and several 'small towns', both defended and undefended. While much has been learnt recently of the origins and early history of *Calleva*, the context for the particular choice of locations at Silchester and Winchester and the subsequent development of both towns is poorly understood. Whereas later it is unexceptional for the 'small' towns of Roman Britain, including those of Solent-Thames, not to develop in the post-Roman period, the abandonment of a major town in southern Britain, such as *Calleva Atrebatum* (Silchester), is exceptional. While exploring the context and the reasons for abandonment may be a priority for the early medievalists, the fact is that it has resulted not only in a well preserved late Iron Age and Roman town, but also, coincidentally, in a relatively well preserved immediate hinterland, devoid of intensive modern development. A particularly unusual feature of *Calleva* is the scale of nucleation in the late Iron Age.

Despite some major research programmes, such as the Wroxeter Hinterland project, we still know very little of the impact of towns on their immediate hinterlands and of relationships between town and country. The former can be addressed by non-intrusive survey; the latter by comparative analysis of assemblages of material culture and biological remains.

Beyond a limited understanding of their morphologies and plans, little is known about what urban settlements were really like. Attempting to address this issue is a challenge, but palaeo-environmental science is best placed to do so. It requires the combination and integration of variety of disciplines such as pollen, soil micromorphology, soil chemistry, plant and faunal remains, and perhaps too land snails. Similarly palaeo-environmental evidence can be used to explore the differences between urban and rural settlement in terms of food processing for example, and its development over time. Key to these issues are the following:

12.7.1   Our knowledge of towns and their histories of origin, development and change at all levels of the urban heirarchy is very limited. Opportunities to improve our knowledge, particularly through large-scale area-excavation, should be seized whenever possible.

12.7.2   The hinterland settlement and mortuary landscape of both 'large' and 'small' towns requires further research. Examples with hinterlands relatively untouched by modern development offer major opportunities for research.

12.7.3   Researching the hinterlands and mortuary landscapes of smaller nucleated settlements.

12.7.4   Researching settlement nucleation away from the road network to understand its context, character and later history.

12.7.5   Researching the settlement heirarchy and possible existence of nucleated settlement on the Isle of Wight.

12.7.6   The character of urban environments and their change over time.

12.7.7   Characterisation of economic activity through the various levels of the urban heirarchy.

12.8   Ceremony, ritual and religion

Although several temples and shrines have been identified, there has been little modern research in the sub-region. Evidence shows that the range of ritual activity was wide, both within settlements and in rivers and other watery places. Cemeteries need much more study to identify variations in burial practice, gender, age profile, pathology etc., as well as in the diet and possible origins of their populations. The following are priorities:

12.8.1   Sampling for biological remains from deposits associated with temples and shrines, and from cremation cemeteries, in order to widen our understanding of the use of plants and animals in religion and ritual.

12.8.2   Stable isotope analysis of cemetery populations.

12.8.3   Radiocarbon dating of burials potentially post-dating AD 400.

12.8.4   Researching the contexts of metal-detected major finds, including hoards

12.8.5   Patterns in the location and distribution of temples need to be explored.

12.9   Warfare, defences and military installations

Recent work at Alchester has shown that the military impact of the conquest is not as well understood as previously thought. We need to be alert to the possibility of further discoveries that will shed light on the progress of the conquest of the region. The construction of town and coastal forts in the later Roman period raises questions about the permanency or periodicity of garrisons and militias. PAS records show military equipment in the landscape at all periods. Research directions include the following:

12.9.1   Research on the context of Roman military equipment of all phases, with particular reference to PAS material, in the sub-region.

12.10   Material culture

Material culture has considerable potential for addressing questions of acculturation and social identity.

Distribution of objects and styles, including coinage, can provide information about development of markets and settlement hierarchies. Well-dated assemblages are however rare. In particular, the sub-region needs

12.10.1   The publication of well-dated assemblages of material culture of all types.

12.10.2   The development of regional pottery fabric series to complement the national series, in conjunction with the publication of as yet unpublished pottery assemblages from kilns.

12.10.2   The resources of the PAS to be exploited to understand more clearly variations in the characteristics of the material culture of the sub-region.

12.11   Crafts, trades and industries

Pottery

Solent-Thames is distinctive in having two major Roman pottery industries, the New Forest and Oxfordshire industries, while a third, the Alice Holt industry, straddles the border with Surrey. The New Forest and Oxfordshire kilns spread across extensive territories and we lack knowledge of the landscape and settlement context in which these industries developed and operated and their impact on woodland and its management. Research should aim to:

12.11.1   Increase knowledge of the Roman landscape and settlement context of the Alice Holt, New Forest and Oxfordshire industries.

12.11.2   Explore the relationship between kilns, workshops and settlements.

12.11.3   Increase knowledge of the exploitation and management of associated woodlands through the study of pollen sequences and wood charcoal assemblages from the pottery production sites.

12.11.4   Develop a methodology for distinguishing between the `grey ware' products of the Alice Holt and New Forest industries in hand specimen and apply it to dated pottery assemblages to determine the respective markets of the two industries in these wares.

12.11.5   Collect the evidence of localised pottery manufacture and publish the pottery associated with the kilns with appropriate description/characterisation of fabrics.

Iron-making

Solent-Thames lies between the major centres/regions of iron production: the Forest of Dean, the Weald and Northamptonshire. Sites across the region (eg Isle of Wight, Buckinghamshire) attest small-scale iron-making, including the continuation of prehistoric traditions alongside shaft furnaces, as well as iron-working. Recommendations for research include:

12.11.6   Characterisation, including chemical analysis, and quantification of iron slag assemblages to ensure correct identification of both iron-making and iron-working residues.

12.11.7   In the absence of good material culture evidence, dating slag assemblages may require radiocarbon dating to establish a chronology of local traditions.

12.11.8   Characterisation and quantification of the wood charcoal used in this industry.

Stone

The region exploits flint extensively, but is heavily dependent on extra-regional sources for freestone. Within the region, however, there is exploitation, notably of greensands and limestones, particularly for the manufacture of querns and roofing slates, but the Solent-Thames region also receives material of similar, geological character from other regions, notably the Isle of Purbeck (slates) and Lodsworth, West Sussex (querns). Specific issues that merit attention include:

12.11.9   The development of methodologies based on petrographic analyis to differentiate in hand specimen between Solent-Thames and extra-regional stone sources.

12.11.10   The characterisation, including by petrographic methods, and quantification of non-local building materials, including unworked material from settlement excavations.

12.11.11   The distribution of Stonesfield (Oxon) slate, vis à vis other sources of roofing slate.

12.11.12   The sources and distributions of Solent-Thames-produced querns (and millstones).

12.11.13   The identification of quarries.

Ceramic building material

There has been little systematic research of ceramic building materials in the region. Priorities for research include:

12.11.14   Characterisation and quantification of settlement assemblages by type of material.

12.11.15 The extent of trade in these materials through research of type and fabric

Marine resources

The exploitation and consumption of marine resources in the sub-region is ill-understood. Research needs to:

12.11.16   Sample coastal sites appropriately for the recovery of evidence of fishing, shellfish harvesting and salt-making.

12.11.17   Sample appropriately inland settlements, both urban and rural, to recover and quantify fish remains if they are present.

12.11.18   Research shellfish assemblages to recover evidence of origin and to quantify relative abundance across the sub-region.

12.12   Communications and trade

The inclusion of a substantial tract of the south coast of England from the Avon to the major natural harbours of the eastern Solent reminds us how little we know of Atlantic and Channel trade and communication from the late Iron Age after the *floruit* of Hengistbury Head. The same is true throughout the Roman period and into the early Anglo-Saxon period. At the same time we also know very little of the coastal infrastructure of seaborne trade. The following are some of the priorities for research:

12.12.1   The use of the Solent and its harbours for trade and communication during the Roman period.

12.12.2   The remains of harbours, jetties (including waterlogged structures), boats etc.

12.12.3   The extent of trade and traffic along the south coast of Britain.

12.12.4   Distinguishing between south-coast generated overseas trade and traffic from that connected with London and the Thames Estuary.

12.12.5   The development of *Clausentum* and potential associated port facilities.

Consideration of the relationship between Solent-Thames and the south coast of England, to west and east of the Hampshire and Isle of Wight coasts, and the larger Roman world of Gaul and beyond, in turn raises further issues connected with trade, traffic and communications in general.

The Thames, for example, is a major river of England and of the region, apparently with little evidence of its use for communication/transport after the Late Iron Age. However, the river itself has only recently been the subject of focused research. To improve our understanding,

12.12.6   The use of the Thames and its tributaries for the movement of goods and people requires investigation.

12.12.7   The location of river crossing-points needs to be sought.

12.12.8   The location and extent of Roman-period deposition in the river needs further research.

12.12.9   The influence of the Thames on the development of riverine settlements needs to be explored.

Our region is also bisected by the principal Roman road leading west from London, and all traffic and communications between it, central southern England and the south-west (as well as south Wales) would have passed along it. Research priorities include the following:

12.12.10   Assessment of the importance of communication and trade using this east-west road communication in comparison with use of the river(s), particularly the Thames and its major tributaries, such as the Kennet and the Thame.

12.12.11   Assessment of the importance of the east-west road route originating from London compared with the Corinium – Alchester – Verulamium road, which runs across the north of the region.

12.12.12   Assessment of the relative importance of north-south routes in the sub-region.

12.12.13   The influence of the major roads on the development of roadside settlement should be investigated.

12.12.14   Assessment of changes in the relative importance of the major roads that cross the region over time.

12.13 The Isle of Wight

The Isle of Wight is, arguably, the most distinctive topographic entity of our region. It is unique in England (Britain) in the sense that it is both a sizeable island and it has produced extensive evidence of Romanisation, comparable to that of the adjacent mainland. The Island invites the following questions:

12.13.1   What are the differences (or similarities) of the island to the mainland in terms of settlements, patterns of settlement, exploitation of resources, etc.?

12.13.2   How can we define the relations between the Island and mainland (and the Island and overseas) through the Roman period more closely?

Chapter 13

The Early Medieval Period: Resource Assessment

by Anne Dodd

with contributions by Sally Crawford and Michael Allen and incorporating the county assessments by Steve Clark (Berkshire), Michael Farley (Buckinghamshire), David Hinton (Hampshire) and Ruth Waller (Isle of Wight)

Introduction

A preliminary draft of this chapter was prepared by Sally Crawford, and was expanded and updated by the present author. The Introduction, and the sections on Inheritance and Social Organisation, are largely by Sally Crawford, the remainder largely by the present author, drawing on and incorporating material from the county assessments available online (referenced here as Clark 2007; Farley 2008; Hinton 2007; Waller 2006). Only selected references are given here; full references for works cited by the county contributors can be found in their bibliographies online. We are very grateful to John Blair, Derek Keene, Stephanie Ratkai and Michael Shapland for providing information about currently unpublished sites and research, and for allowing us to refer to this in advance of their own publications. Responsibility for any errors or omissions lies with the present author.

Nature of the evidence

The early medieval period is one of important social, political, economic, cultural and ethnic change. Study of the period is supported by some documentary sources and by archaeology, but the interpretation of both is complex and controversial. Some of the key developments in this period, such as the extent of continuity of late Romano-British society, culture and economy; the date and nature of the arrival of Anglo-Saxon culture and its associated Germanic incomers; settlement of the land; the transition from paganism to Christianity; the development of kingdoms; the emergence of urbanisation; land division and use; and the development of minsters, estates and manors, are all open to intense debate.

What is certain is that seismic shifts in culture, religion, economy and, to an arguable extent, population, took place, and it is in this period that many of the administrative structures were created that underpinned later medieval society, and indeed persist to the present day. Archaeological evidence, traditionally given second place in terms of authority to documentary evidence, is being given increasing precedence in efforts to resolve the difficulties of the early medieval period. Archaeological exploration in the Solent-Thames area has been, and will

continue to be, central to exploring the issues and establishing a framework for interpreting the early medieval past. Early medieval material culture is, however, relatively sparse in comparison to the preceding and following periods, which in itself raises a number of problems for interpretation. As Steve Clark noted for Berkshire, the majority of Anglo-Saxon pottery, handmade and fired at relatively low temperatures, is very rarely found in fieldwalking exercises, even where Anglo-Saxon settlements have been identified. Coins circulate only from the mid-Saxon period: secular settlement consisted of timber-framed buildings and sunken-featured buildings (SFBs), structures that do not survive well in the archaeological record, and successful Anglo-Saxon urban settlements lie beneath modern towns, where they are only rarely accessible and much has been destroyed by later development. This is a difficult period to detect and find in fieldwork and evaluation exercises (Hey and Lacey 2001).

Early Anglo-Saxon furnished cemeteries, with their wealth of material culture, offer the most 'visible' aspect of early medieval archaeology. The visibility of such burial places, however, led to considerable antiquarian interest in them; as a consequence, some of the more important early Anglo-Saxon furnished cemeteries in the Solent-Thames area were excavated in the 19th and early 20th centuries, with inevitable loss of archaeological information. Nonetheless, the material evidence indicates that this region is particularly interesting, as it exhibits a rapid spread of Anglo-Saxon culture in areas where we might arguably least expect it, for example on the Hampshire downs.

For the early and middle part of the Anglo-Saxon period (*c* 450-850), the boundaries of the modern counties which make up the Solent-Thames area, with the probable exception of the Isle of Wight, have only a broad relationship with any putative Anglo-Saxon territorial boundaries. David Hinton has drawn attention, for example, to the various place-names straddling the borders of modern Hampshire, such as North Tidworth in Wiltshire and South Tidworth in Hampshire, which offer convincing evidence of earlier territorial units now cut by modern boundaries (Hinton 2007). By the later Anglo-Saxon period, however, the territorial boundaries

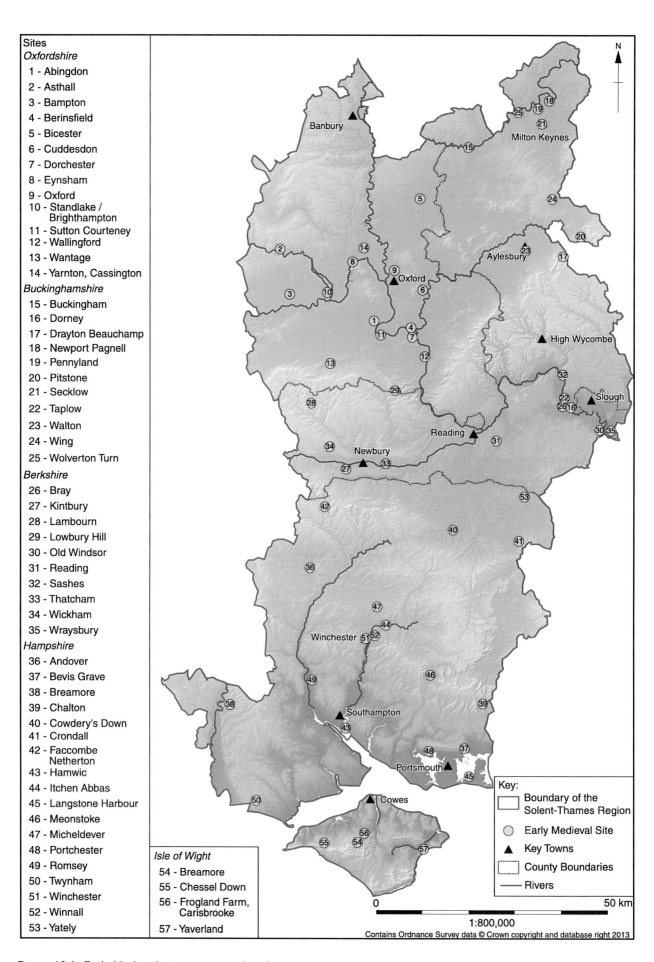

Sites
Oxfordshire
1 - Abingdon
2 - Asthall
3 - Bampton
4 - Berinsfield
5 - Bicester
6 - Cuddesdon
7 - Dorchester
8 - Eynsham
9 - Oxford
10 - Standlake /
     Brighthampton
11 - Sutton Courteney
12 - Wallingford
13 - Wantage
14 - Yarnton, Cassington

Buckinghamshire
15 - Buckingham
16 - Dorney
17 - Drayton Beauchamp
18 - Newport Pagnell
19 - Pennyland
20 - Pitstone
21 - Secklow
22 - Taplow
23 - Walton
24 - Wing
25 - Wolverton Turn

Berkshire
26 - Bray
27 - Kintbury
28 - Lambourn
29 - Lowbury Hill
30 - Old Windsor
31 - Reading
32 - Sashes
33 - Thatcham
34 - Wickham
35 - Wraysbury

Hampshire
36 - Andover
37 - Bevis Grave
38 - Breamore
39 - Chalton
40 - Cowdery's Down
41 - Crondall
42 - Faccombe
     Netherton
43 - Hamwic
44 - Itchen Abbas
45 - Langstone Harbour
46 - Meonstoke
47 - Micheldever
48 - Portchester
49 - Romsey
50 - Twynham
51 - Winchester
52 - Winnall
53 - Yately

Isle of Wight
54 - Breamore
55 - Chessel Down
56 - Frogland Farm,
     Carisbrooke
57 - Yaverland

Key:
◻ Boundary of the
   Solent-Thames Region
◯ Early Medieval Site
▲ Key Towns
▢ County Boundaries
— Rivers

0   50 km
1:800,000
Contains Ordnance Survey data © Crown copyright and database right 2013

Figure 13.1 Early Medieval sites mentioned in the text

which still provide the framework for modern county boundaries were established (at least until the boundary revisions of the historic counties from 1974), so that it is no surprise to find some real overlap between the Solent-Thames counties and Anglo-Saxon territorial divisions. The straight boundary sections between Surrey and Berkshire, for example, were established by the 9th century (Clark 2007: Gelling 1976, 844), and the shire itself was first referred to in AD 860.

History of research

The Solent-Thames resource assessment brings together four counties that are not usually considered as a group, and there are therefore no earlier overviews taking in the specific region under discussion. The history of research into this period has been reviewed for each county by the county contributors. This information is summarised below and can be found in more detail in the individual county assessments. In addition, the current Thames through Time project provides a detailed review of the evidence for our period from the Buckinghamshire, Oxfordshire and Berkshire Thames Valley (Booth *et al.* 2007).

All counties in this region have provided important sites for interpreting the Anglo-Saxon past (Figure 13.1), and all still have the potential to address the significant questions of the period through their surviving early medieval archaeology. Previous excavation and research has been of variable quality and intensity. Here, as elsewhere, 19th- and 20th-century development led to many (often spectacular) discoveries, but also to the irrecoverable destruction of archaeological evidence. One of the key points to emerge from the present resource assessment, however, is the extent to which our knowledge of the early medieval resource is skewed; by the impact of modern development that focuses research in limited areas; by the presence of 'honeypot' sites that dominate the archaeological story of our region; and by the effect of modern administrative boundary changes that have removed significant areas of the region's archaeology from their historic context. The early medieval archaeology of Berkshire has perhaps suffered most, since the intensively researched Upper Thames Valley sites of North Berkshire lay within the area transferred to Oxfordshire in 1974, creating a completely artificial imbalance of resources between the two. A similar dislocation has resulted from the transfer of Thames-side parishes between Berkshire, Buckinghamshire and a series of new unitary authorities.

In Buckinghamshire there was little systematic research into the early medieval archaeology of the county before the 1970s. Since then, however, there has been an explosion of information, largely as a result of increasing development pressures, although much of this has been focused on the areas around the county's historic towns and villages. The work of the Milton Keynes Archaeological Unit, between 1971 and 1994, has provided a particularly important resource. The rural archaeology of the county has benefited from the recent Whittlewood Project, led by the University of Leicester,

which studied village development in the north-west of the county.

The presence of the university at Oxford meant that the surrounding area saw an unusually high level of early investigations, and the archaeology of the early medieval period has benefited from the work of researchers such as Stephen Stone at Standlake in the 19th century, and E T Leeds at Sutton Courtenay, Abingdon and elsewhere in the early 20th century. The threat to the archaeology of the Thames gravel terraces from intensive quarrying was identified in Don Benson and David Miles's influential study of the cropmarks of the Upper Thames Valley (1974). During the later 20th century, pressure for development and ongoing quarrying of the gravel terraces of the Upper Thames has underpinned continuing excavation and research in parts of the county, although areas further away from Oxford and the Thames have been less explored.

In Berkshire, as elsewhere, the pattern of archaeological activity in the 19th and early 20th centuries was largely influenced by antiquarian interest in visible monuments such as barrows, and chance discoveries arising from quarrying and railway development. In the post-war period the pressure for housing and gravel extraction continued to drive patterns of archaeological work, and major town centre redevelopments took place from the 1970s on. At that time a series of large-scale surveys across much of the county revealed a dearth of Anglo-Saxon material in the interior of East Berkshire, to the south of Reading, and in the Kennet Valley. More recently, the Lambourn Valley has begun to produce significant evidence for early-mid Anglo-Saxon activity, and finds from recent excavations at Lambourn, Kintbury and Thatcham are beginning to confirm long-held suspicions about the antiquity of these settlements.

The onset of sustained archaeological research into Anglo-Saxon Hampshire is largely datable to the period from the 1960s on, with a number of important early to mid Saxon cemetery excavations, systematic investigations at *Hamwic*, the campaigns of the Winchester Research Unit led by Martin Biddle, and the investigation of rural settlement at sites such as Chalton, Cowdery's Down and Faccombe Netherton. By contrast, the Isle of Wight, lacking a university, not subject to major modern developments, and without funding or individual resource to promote early Anglo-Saxon archaeology, has been poorly served by excavation, although its potential for answering a number of key questions about the period, particularly about early ethnicity and the nature of Anglo-Saxon early settlement, is great. There is a real need for systematic archaeological survey to identify and investigate Anglo-Saxon sites and for a re-assessment of the island's metal-detected evidence.

Inheritance

The question of the date of transition from Romano-British to Anglo-Saxon used to be phrased in terms of movements of people. Now, however, the transition is usually more cautiously framed in terms of the abandonment of late Romano-British culture (in itself notoriously difficult to pinpoint in the archaeological record) and the beginnings of very visible Anglo-Saxon culture use. It is suspected that the people using Anglo-Saxon culture – and speaking Old English – were probably, though not absolutely necessarily, of different ethnic origin from the native Romano-British. Some of the Romano-British may have adopted an Anglo-Saxon way of life, becoming 'Anglo-Saxon' in the archaeological record. DNA and other analysis of skeletal material may yet answer the question of how many of those buried in Anglo-Saxon cemeteries were descended from continental Germanic migrants, and how many were the native '*wealh*' who had adopted a new lifestyle. Whether Romano-British people who adopted Anglo-Saxon culture, if indeed any did, regarded themselves as Anglo-Saxons will however remain contentious. The issue of transition, then, must focus in the present state of technology on when people living in the region adopted Anglo-Saxon ways of living and of burying their dead, rather than on whether those people were native Romano-British or new Germanic incomers.

The Roman small town of Dorchester-on-Thames and its surrounding region have produced some of the most important archaeological evidence for this process of transition. Burials from the town were interpreted many years ago as evidence for the presence of Anglo-Saxon *foederati* warriors supporting the rule of a local Romano-British tyrant, exactly the mechanism described by Gildas and Bede by which Anglo-Saxon warriors were introduced into England in the first place (Hawkes and Dunning 1961). Recent work has added to the evidence for a high-status late Roman presence in the town (Plate 13.1), and has demonstrated that at least one burial in the Anglo-Saxon cemetery nearby at Wally Corner, Berinsfield is of the early to mid 5th-century, and therefore earlier than published (Booth *et al.* 2012, 22-23; Hills and O'Connell 2009). This has led to renewed interest in the possibility that the earliest Anglo-Saxons in the region were involved with the protection of Dorchester, located on the eastern boundary of the late Roman province of *Britannia Prima*.

Evidence for the continuation of a Romano-British way of life, or even for any continuity or contiguity between 'Romano-British' and 'Anglo-Saxon' people, is elusive. Settlement reorganisation can have many causes and evidence needs to be considered carefully. In Oxfordshire, important excavations at Barton Court Farm, Abingdon, demonstrated early Anglo-Saxon settlement in close proximity to the villa, but no evidence for the continued use of the buildings – until bodies were inserted into them in the 6th century (Miles 1986). The presence of Anglo-Saxon buildings on the site is also unlikely to be evidence for native Romano-British inhabitants adopting Anglo-Saxon building styles, because the settlement does not respect earlier Romano-British boundary ditches, indicating a significant break with the Romano-British use and partitioning

Plate 13.1 Late Roman belt-buckle, Dyke Hills, Dorchester-on-Thames, *copyright Ashmolean Museum, University of Oxford*

of the land. At Bierton, north-east of Aylesbury, Farley draws attention to substantial quantities of early to mid Saxon pottery near to a Roman villa that succeeded a high-status late Iron Age settlement, and to the evidence from Walton by Aylesbury, where both late Roman and early Saxon occupation is present.

The coastal part of this region, where some continued contact with Rome and Gaul might be expected, provides little evidence for continuity. In Hampshire, no finds have been made of imported pottery in the 5th century. The *civitas* capitals, Winchester and Silchester, show no signs of continued urbanisation into the 5th century, and the evidence for continuity at Portchester is ambiguous. Hinton suggests that only the Otterbourne hoards hint at continuing Romano-British authority and contact with Gaul, but there is scant evidence in Hampshire for continuity of estates, forts or urban centres, or for the presence of any *laeti*, *foederati* or mercenary soldiers. As elsewhere, however, there are a number of cases where early Saxon settlement is found on or near to the sites of Roman villas, as in the Meonstoke area, for example, and at Northbrook, Micheldever north of Winchester. In both cases sunken featured buildings, and Anglo-Saxon finds including 5th-century brooch types, are reported from nearby.

In Berkshire, identifying the decline of Roman activity is hampered by lack of robust dating evidence, so that, for example, the date of abandonment of the Roman rectilinear field systems of the Berkshire Downs by an aceramic population cannot be identified (Bowden *et al.* 1993, 111).

A very few cemeteries provide tantalising glimpses of evidence for continuity or at least cross-cultural links. The lack of continuity may be in itself an interesting indicator of contemporary attitudes. Burials continued at the Roman cemetery at Frilford (Oxfordshire) into the early 5th century and early Saxon burials were found adjacent and superimposed on different alignments (see Fig. 11.1 for location). The cemetery at Itchen Abbas (Hampshire) is reported to include a male burial with hob-nailed footwear amongst several hundred graves, including cremations, and objects datable to the mid to late 5th century. Another candidate, although poorly understood, is the Roman mixed-rite cemetery at Hoveringham Gravel Pit near Bray, Berkshire, where there was evidence for early 5th-century metalworking and an 'early Saxon floor surface' cut by later burials.

Also ripe for review is the extent to which Romano-British estate boundaries continued in use into the Anglo-Saxon period. David Hinton has raised the possibility of some plausible continuity of boundaries around the villa at Rockbourne, Hampshire. David Tomalin has suggested pre-Anglo-Saxon origins for some of the estates in the Isle of Wight, and similar evidence of Roman estates surviving into the Anglo-Saxon period has been discussed by Mike Farley for Buckinghamshire.

Deliberate re-use of earlier monuments by Anglo-Saxons, perhaps to legitimise Anglo-Saxon rule, or to appropriate cultural markers, is indicated by the re-use of the Roman temple site at Lowbury Hill (Fig. 11.1), the Iron Age hillfort at Taplow, and prehistoric earthworks at Oliver's Battery, Winchester, for princely burials in the 7th century. The re-use of Bronze Age barrows for Anglo-Saxon graves in communal cemeteries is a widespread feature in the region, and is particularly marked in the 7th century. Examples include cemeteries at Stanton Harcourt (Fig. 7.1) and Standlake (Oxfordshire), Field Farm, Burghfield (Berkshire) (Fig. 9.1), and Bargates, Christchurch and Portway East (Hampshire). Iron Age hillforts, Bronze Age barrows and other prehistoric monuments crop up frequently as boundary markers in Anglo-Saxon charters, suggesting that these monuments influenced the route of boundaries.

Plate 13.2 Photograph of mass Viking burial in the henge ditch at Oxford, copyright TVAS

Post-Conversion use of earlier monuments included their use as execution cemeteries. Examples from this region include burials at Bronze Age barrows (Stockbridge Down, Hampshire) and prehistoric earthworks (Ave's Dyke, Oxfordshire). Probable examples occur in other counties, and a review of undated excavated inhumations without grave-goods in these contexts across the region would probably yield further cases of execution cemeteries; such has already been the case for the Harestock cemetery, excavated in the 1980s. The majority of burials at this cemetery, located on the boundary of Anglo-Saxon Winchester, were young males, some decapitated before burial. Radiocarbon dating of the skeletons has established a 9th- to 11th-century date, confirming the likelihood that this is the site of execution burials (data from Winchester City Council Museums Service). The silted-up ditch of a henge at Oxford was chosen for the burial of a group of men now interpreted as a probable Viking raiding party executed in the late 10th century (Pollard *et al.* 2012; Plate 13.2). Other burials at re-used monuments may not necessarily be deviant. Annia Cherryson's radiocarbon dating programme has also revealed a rare example of 9th- to 10th-century burials in a barrow at Bevis's Grave, Portsdown, Hampshire (Blair 2005, 244). John Blair has posited that the very late use of primary and secondary barrows may be a phenomenon relating to the south coast, noting further examples in Sussex and Wiltshire (ibid.; now see also Semple 2013).

Some evidence exists for the use of earlier monuments as sites for churches. The important minster church at Bampton (Oxfordshire) appears to have been located on the site of Bronze Age barrows (*South Midlands Archaeology* 28, 47–9), while recent investigative work at Abingdon in Oxfordshire and Aylesbury in Buckinghamshire has demonstrated that the Anglo-Saxon settlements, both of which are characterised by early religious foundations, were situated within an Iron Age defensive structure (Allen 2011; Farley 2012). The association between hillforts and churches in Buckinghamshire has been reviewed by Kidd (2004). The re-use of old Roman towns for the establishment of bishops' seats is evidenced in the region at Winchester and Dorchester, and it seems likely that Romsey Abbey was built on the site of a former Roman villa.

Chronology

Anglo-Saxon sites in the region have traditionally relied heavily on artefact dating, and for many years this provided answers that were adequate for the broad characterisation of the region's archaeology as 'early', 'middle' or 'late' Anglo-Saxon. More accurate chronologies are now however needed to make progress with key questions such as change in settlement and burial organisation in the region over time, and this will require better dating of key artefact types.

Here, as elsewhere, pottery has always been widely used to date sites (see also Material Culture, below). The early Anglo-Saxon pottery is not however particularly

helpful for dating, and the most consistent chronological marker is the disappearance of decoration, generally dated to the 7th century. The persistence of the common organic-tempered tradition throughout the mid Saxon period, with no obvious change in form, style or technique, makes the recognition of the transition from early to mid Saxon exceptionally difficult. At *Hamwic*, Jane Timby has identified a broad evolution of fabric types through the mid Saxon period (Andrews 1997), but it is unclear how far this can be applied outside the local context. Elsewhere there is no distinctive local mid Saxon pottery tradition, and ceramic dating often relies on the presence of occasional sherds of imported wares. Maxey-type ware is found in northern Buckinghamshire, but not elsewhere in the region. Ipswich ware occurs sporadically and in small quantities across the region and can be a valuable chronological indicator. Continental imported pottery occurs at *Hamwic*, and occasionally elsewhere in very small quantities. Late Saxon pottery is more readily datable and identifiable, with a number of distinctive local traditions, and significant levels of identifiable regional imports such as St Neot's type ware. Type series have been developed for major urban centres including Oxford, Winchester and Southampton, although there remain considerable uncertainties about the dates at which different industries originate, first arrive in the region, and go into decline.

Late Roman coins and pottery have been used to date the final phase of occupation at a number of Romano-British sites, although it is acknowledged that sites could have continued in use after Roman coinage ceased to be imported and late Roman pottery ceased to be produced. Although the use of coins was revived amongst the Anglo-Saxons from the mid 7th century onwards, and silver *sceattas* were apparently minted in very large numbers, coins are never as abundant as in the Roman period, and remain relatively rare finds on most sites in the region.

Dating based on other artefact types has been particularly valuable in the dating of cemeteries of the 5th to 7th centuries, with detailed study of the evolution of decorative styles on brooches by Tania Dickinson, John Hines and others. Other researchers have enhanced our understanding of the dating of beads and pendants, buckles, pins, spears and shield bosses, although these are rarely datable to within less than half a century. It is likely that this will be significantly enhanced by the results of a major new study of the chronology of Anglo-Saxon graves and grave goods of this period, and the implications of this for understanding the chronology of early Anglo-Saxon burial in the region will need careful consideration (see now Bayliss *et al.* 2013). Artefact dating has its own problems, however, and even when artefacts are part of a mortuary assemblage, the question of their age when buried is still an issue.

The dating of burials from the evidence of grave goods has also, inevitably, led to an almost exclusive focus on the study of accompanied burials from cemetery sites in the region.; the dating of unaccompanied burials is usually only inferred from indicators such as alignment, orientation and rare direct stratigraphic relationships between graves. This is perhaps a particularly serious shortcoming in terms of our understanding of the later phases of cemetery use, when unaccompanied burials may have been more numerous. Artefacts are not generally very informative for the dating of rural settlement sites in the region, which are much poorer in surviving material culture than contemporary sites in eastern England, particularly during the mid Saxon period. Many sites have been dated on little more evidence than an absence of decorated early Saxon pottery, and the presence of organic-tempered wares. Pottery is the most common chronological indicator for urban sites although other datable artefact types such as strap ends, hooked tags, pins and brooches occur occasionally.

Until the last ten years or so, scientific dating methods were not often used for sites of this period in the region, typically being confined to excavations with a major component of environmental and geoarchaeological research, or to isolated human burials. An early exception was Cowdery's Down, where radiocarbon dates were obtained for the settlement in the absence of datable artefacts. A series of radiocarbon dates was also obtained for the unusual mid Saxon trading or meeting site at Dorney. Elsewhere, the use of scientific dating was sporadic, and there was a widespread belief that the nature of the radiocarbon calibration curve meant that radiocarbon was unlikely to add much to what was known from pottery and other artefacts. As dating techniques have improved, however, scientific dating methods have been much more systematically employed, and have been very influential in promoting reconsideration of conventional models. A major radiocarbon dating programme at Yarnton, for example, revealed that what was thought to be a conventional early Saxon settlement of SFBs and post-built halls was in fact largely datable to the 8th and 9th centuries (Hey 2004), and radiocarbon dating has been important in identifying mid Saxon re-use of the hillforts at Aylesbury and Taplow.

Wherever possible, radiocarbon dating should be based on sequences of samples from well-stratified deposits, to support the use of Bayesian modelling; this allows estimates to be calculated for events that are not directly dated, and may be of great value in re-assessing conventional chronological models in the future. Some re-visiting of archival material from earlier sites may also be of value, together with recalibration of old dates that are often quoted in publications in ways that are difficult to use today. The use of other scientific techniques such as dendrochronology and archaeomagnetic dating is less widespread, although useful results have been obtained where suitable samples were available; for example, dendrochronology was used to date 10th-century waterfront revetment timbers at St Aldate's in Oxford.

Landscape and land use

The region has a wide range of landscape types, which makes a simple summary of landscape and land use in the area difficult. Historic Landscape Characterisation studies have been completed for Buckinghamshire, West Berkshire and Hampshire, but our period lies largely beyond their chronological reach. For the end of our period, Domesday Book can provide a general overview of the resources of the region, but such generalisations inevitably simplify almost immeasurable diversity at a local level. The *Domesday Geography of South-East England* (Darby and Campbell 1962) reviews the evidence for each county, followed by a general summary for the region. The mapping of ploughteams suggests a much heavier emphasis on arable farming in Buckinghamshire north of the Chilterns, Oxfordshire and North Berkshire than in north-east and Chiltern Buckinghamshire, east Berkshire, and much of Hampshire (ibid., fig. 170). Conversely, high woodland values are recorded across the Chilterns and east Berkshire, into north-east Hampshire, and along the Avon valley at the western edge of the New Forest (ibid., fig. 174). The greatest values of meadowland, unsurprisingly, are concentrated in the river valleys, principally along the Thames and its tributaries, notably the Ock and the Kennet, but also along the Rivers Avon, Test and Itchen in Hampshire, and substantial quantities of meadowland are also recorded from the claylands of north Buckinghamshire (ibid. fig. 176). In an age when we assume most people were largely self-sufficient in basic agricultural produce, however, it is clear that they needed access to a range of resources, and the record of estate holdings and settlement centres does not necessarily provide an accurate guide to the location of these within the landscape.

One notable characteristic of the region is the existence of long, thin 'strip' estates on the slopes of the Chilterns and Berkshire Downs, which provided their occupants with access to a full range of resources. In her study of a group of parishes in the Vale of the White Horse, on the downs in North Berkshire (and now largely transferred to Oxfordshire), Della Hooke shows from the evidence of charters how long, thin 10th-century estates had access to meadow, watermeadow, pasture and marsh in the Vale, with arable (and the settlement nuclei) in a wide band around the springs and streams of the scarp foot at the 100m contour, and open downland pasture on the higher ground to the south (1987). A similar group of parishes can be found between Taplow and Eton on the north bank of the Thames in south Buckinghamshire (Plate 13.3). These estates extend from meadow and fisheries on the Thames floodplain up to woods and commons on the infertile gravels of the Burnham plateau to the north, with the villages located roughly halfway between on the 45m contour (Julian Munby in Foreman *et al.* 2002). In other cases, estates would have rights in resources at some distance from the main settlement; the woodland rights of Oxfordshire medieval manors in Wychwood, for example, were studied by Beryl Schumer (1984).

Charters and place names can be a rich source of information about landscape and land use in our period. In the present study region both have perhaps tended to

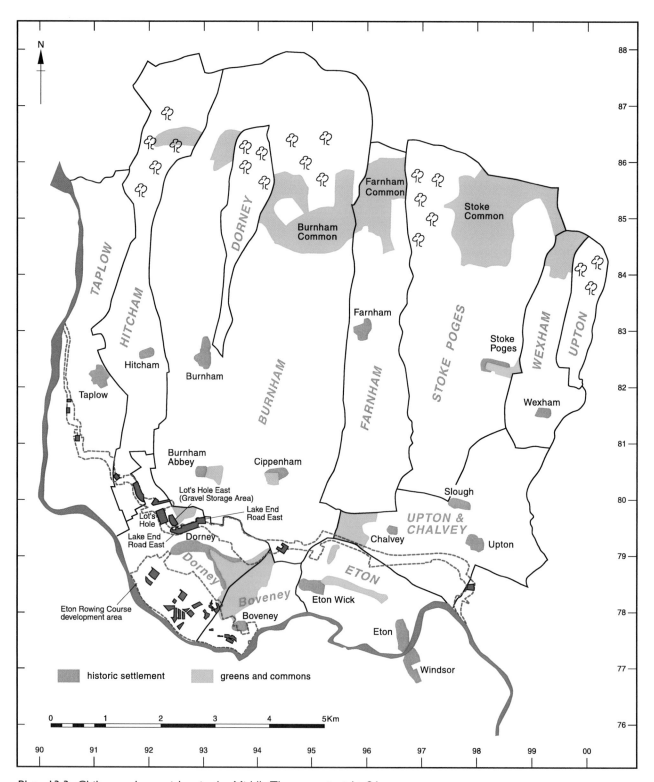

Plate 13.3 Chiltern-edge parishes in the Middle Thames, *copyright OA*

be under-exploited, although an important study of contrasting Berkshire landscapes by Della Hooke illustrates how informative these sources can be (1987; 1988). In recent years increasing interest in landscape archaeology and landscape studies is encouraging researchers to look anew at the potential of place names (see, for example Clark 2007; Cole 2010). Here we can see how names reflect places chosen for settlement, the *denu* and *comb* names of Chiltern valley settlements, *mere* settlements which drew water from ponds, *welle* names

recording the springs of the scarp-foot springlines, *dun* names for sites on well-drained whaleback-shaped hills, eg settlements on dry ground within marsh, *broc* settlements with muddy streams, and moors and marshes preserved in *mor, fenn* and *mersc* (Cole 2010, 22). The abundant placenames in *leah* and *feld* across the region record woodland pasture and clearings, and some places record farm crops and livestock: Wheatley, Rycote, Pishill, Swinbrook, Shiplake and Shipton, Oxford, Horspath and, perhaps surprisingly, watercress at Cassington (ibid., 24).

The recovery of plant remains and animal bone in excavations provides the main resource for understanding agricultural practice during the Anglo-Saxon period. Much of this remains very site-specific, but for a recent regional review see Mark Robinson's discussion of the evidence from the Upper and Middle Thames Valley (Booth *et al.* 2007). Some of the key published assemblages are also noted below. At the start of our period, the extent to which Roman arable reverted to grassland is not clear: evidence from different parts of the region does not offer one coherent picture, and it is likely that in this, as in the process of Anglo-Saxon settlement, the story is complex and there were local and regional variations. In the Thames Valley, Robinson suggests there was a decline in the intensity of agricultural exploitation, but that the lack of evidence for substantial regeneration of scrub and woodland means that cultivation and grazing were continuing, albeit at a reduced level (ibid., 29-30). The early Saxon period also sees a significant change in cereal production, with the widespread adoption in the Upper Thames Valley of free-threshing wheat (*Triticum aestivum*) in place of the spelt (*T. spelta*) generally cultivated in the region during the Roman period (ibid., 317-20). It is less clear how quickly this change took place in the Middle Thames Valley. Barley was also a major crop at early Saxon sites in the region; the evidence for cultivation of oats is ambiguous, but oats were probably deliberately grown, along with beans, peas and flax. There is little evidence for the cultivation of rye in the Thames Valley.

An extensive campaign of environmental research during the Yarnton excavations has provided very important evidence for intensification of agriculture from the 8th century onwards (ibid., 331-4; Hey 2004). Changes in the weed assemblages at this time provide evidence for more intensive ploughing and the spread of cultivation onto heavier clay soils; over the same period, former grass pasture was converted to hay meadow, and a wider variety of plants were being grown. Rye and lentils appear, albeit in small quantities, alongside wheat, barley, oats, flax, beans and peas, with grape and plum pointing to a resumption of horticulture. The quantities of charred cereals found begin to increase again, after a marked decline in the post-Roman period. Evidence for horticulture also comes from late Saxon deposits in a channel of the Thames at Oxford, where seeds of celery, plum, apple and summer savory were found.

The region has not yet produced much evidence for the origins of open field farming, although occasional references in charters may hint at this. The limited evidence is discussed by the county contributors. For Buckinghamshire, Michael Farley notes that although the county north of the Chilterns is a land of ridge and furrow there is as yet no good evidence from the county for the date at which this originated. In her study of the late Saxon estates of the Vale of the White Horse, Della Hooke identifies a number of features such as headlands, furrows and acres mentioned in charter bounds that imply some form of open field agriculture (1987, 138-9). Steve Clark also notes a charter reference to open field features on the boundary between Chievely and Winterbourne (2007). For Hampshire, David Hinton notes occasional references to 'acres' in 10th- and 11th-century charters, but comments that the soils of Hampshire did not lend themselves to the creation of ridged strips with deep furrows. Although an extension of cereal cultivation in Hampshire over the Saxon period is likely, it is difficult to prove.

Animal bone evidence from sites in the region is not easy to interpret, as assemblages are affected by factors of preservation and disposal practices. However, pigs and sheep/goats appear to have been more important in the agricultural economy of the Thames Valley than during the late Roman period, and poultry were distinctly more common; at Barton Court Farm, the evidence suggested a meat diet dominated by beef in the Roman period, giving way to one with a greater emphasis on mutton, pork, poultry and fish in the early Saxon period (Booth *et al.* 2007, 320-21). By the mid Saxon period, if not before, there is some evidence for specialisation. An increasing emphasis on the keeping of sheep for wool is suggested from Eynsham (Jacqui Mulville, in Hardy *et al.* 2003); similar evidence is reported from nearby New Wintles Farm and Shakenoak (Blair 1994, 20, 22; Hawkes 1986). At mid Saxon

Plate 13.4 Pigs in woodland, Winchester calendar, *copyright The British Library Board, 002482 Cotton Tiberius B.V. Part 1, f.7*

Wolverton Turn, Milton Keynes, horse bone reached an unusual 11% of the main domestic NISP at the site, with both young and old animals present, and Naomi Sykes has suggested this could be compatible with an emphasis on horse breeding (The animal bone, in Preston 2007). Polecat and wild boar were also identified from this site. At Wraysbury, a high ratio of pigs, the presence of young animals, and the Domesday evidence for abundant woodland resources suggested that the rearing of pigs may have played a major part in the economy of late Saxon estates here and nearby (Clark 2007; Booth *et al.* 2007, 320-21; Plate 13.4).

Very large assemblages of animal bone from *Hamwic* have been studied over a number of years, but few have been published in full. An overview was recently published by Sheila Hamilton-Dyer in the context of the analysis of a further 9000 bones from the St Mary's Stadium site (Birbeck 2005, 140-54). The animal economy of the town was overwhelmingly based on the three main domesticates, cattle, sheep and pig, and largely drawn from older cattle and sheep that had already been used for other purposes. Some pigs and poultry may have been raised in the town, and some fish and shellfish was eaten, although fish does not appear to have formed a major component of the diet. The biometrical data that have now been collected on a very large scale for *Hamwic* animals show that the town's meat resources were drawn from a single group of closely related animals, probably from the immediate hinterland, and this has been interpreted as a sign of the central organisation of provisioning and communal use of rubbish pits for domestic and industrial waste (ibid., 153-4).

The St Mary's Stadium project was also the opportunity for the first major programme of environmental sampling and analysis to be undertaken for *Hamwic*, and provided important results. A study of mineralised plant remains by Wendy Carruthers (ibid., 157-63) suggested that cereals formed the major part of the diet, with peas and beans also being consumed on a regular basis; the range of other foods consumed was fairly limited, including native hedgerow fruits, apples and pear or quince, plums, a few grapes, and plants used for flavourings, including mustard and the non-native species

fennel, coriander and dill. Charred plant remains were studied by Kath Hunter (ibid., 163-73). Interestingly, wheat was very under-represented in the assemblage, which may reflect the supply of ready-milled flour or even ready-baked loaves to *Hamwic* from elsewhere. More barley chaff was present, and it was notable that barley and oats often occurred together; it is suggested this mixed crop or drage was supplied to the settlement for animal fodder.

The waterlogged plant remains were studied by Alan Clapham (ibid., 173-81). In addition to the species identified amongst the mineralised remains, this analysis also identified lentils, a possible gooseberry seed, sloe, dog rose and opium poppy. It is suggested that hazelnuts and wild strawberries could have been grown in gardens or orchards in the settlement and catnip (*Nepeta cataria*) could have been a medicinal herbal tea. Hemp and flax were probably grown for their fibres, used in the manufacture of ropes and cloth; however, the seeds of both species can be used to make oils. An interesting group of seeds were from taxa of coastal or marine habitats, including sea-beet, samphire and carrot, which may have been used as vegetables; a single parsnip seed, if of the cultivated type, could also have been grown in a local garden. The remains of at least five or six honey bees were also identified, and suggest that bees were kept nearby (Mark Robinson in ibid., 181-3).

For the late Saxon period, good assemblages of animal, fish and plant remains have been published from Eynsham Abbey (Hardy *et al.* 2003), Oxford (Dodd 2003) and Southampton French Quarter (Brown and Hardy 2011). An important reference for the region is now provided by the recently published studies from Winchester, both from the intramural Northgate House/Discovery Centre site and from the suburbs (Ford and Teague 2011; Serjeantson and Rees (eds) 2009). At Northgate House/Discovery Centre, sheep were the predominant species represented, which contrasts with the evidence from both *Hamwic* and the Winchester suburbs, and may indicate some socio-economic difference in diet. Sheep become more numerous in the suburban assemblages, at the expense of cattle, during the Saxo-Norman period, though as this

Plate 13.5 Hunting, Winchester calendar, *copyright The British Library Board, 068370 Cotton Tiberius B.V. Part I, f.7*

encompasses the late 10th to 12th centuries, and therefore overlaps with the Northgate House/Discovery Centre late Saxon phase, this difference may be more apparent than real. The slaughter pattern suggested a mixed sheep economy, with some younger animals killed early for meat, while others were kept longer for their secondary products and breeding. The same pattern was observed with cattle bone, with both young animals and older breeding cows and draught oxen present. Some neonatal pig bone would be consistent with the rearing of pigs in urban backyards.

Unusual remains included a badger humerus with cut marks consistent with dismemberment of a carcass for meat or fat, and a mustelid metatarsal, possibly from a pine marten skinned for its fur. Domestic fowl were kept for both meat and eggs. Charred wheat, barley, oats and a little rye were present, and the low incidence of chaff indicates that grain, at least for human consumption, was supplied to the town ready processed as flour. Pulses such as peas and beans also continued to form a significant part of the diet, and the same range of fruits was identified as at *Hamwic*, although some of the more unusual herbs such as coriander, caraway, lovage and dill were absent. Interestingly, wild turnip (cf. *Brassica rapa*) seeds were common and could have been from plants used as a root or leaf vegetable.

The Anglo-Saxon elite were keen hunters, though game never represents more than a small proportion at any site (Plate 13.5). David Hinton notes a higher proportion of venison at Faccombe Netherton and Portchester than at other sites, and Portchester also produced evidence for the hunting of wild birds, including falconry (Hinton 2007). The evidence for hunting in the Thames Valley was reviewed by Booth *et al.* (2007, 340). In her study of different landscape types in Berkshire, Della Hooke concluded that east Berkshire, much of which was later taken into Windsor Forest, was sparsely populated and heavily wooded. She notes possible charter evidence for *haga* features, substantial fences or enclosures already demarcating woodland set aside for hunting in the late Saxon period. Three parks are also mentioned: *bogeles pearroc* in Winkfield parish, and *godan pearroc* and *hwitan pearroc* in Waltham St Lawrence, which may already have denoted private hunting grounds (1988, 148, fig. 6.10).

Palaeo-environmental data also have great potential significance as indicators of change in climate, hydrology, ecology and farming practices over time, and over a wider area than single sites. Mike Allen notes good examples of stratified sequences that relate to the wider landscape such as the palynological record from the alluvium in the Itchen valley at Winnal Moors, Winchester (Waton 1982; 1986 – but see Allen 2000b for some caution in interpretation) and from colluvial records at sites such as Chalton, Hampshire (Bell 1983) and Duxmore, Newbarn Combe and Redcliffe, Isle of Wight (Allen 1992). Local proxy palaeo-environmental data have been obtained as short pollen sequences from Cowdery's Down, Hampshire (Waton 1983a), and snail and other data from across the region, and in rare instances waterlogged plant remains (Scaife 1996). The combination of on-site and off-site data such as could potentially be achieved at the Chalton ridge (Champion 1977) and from colluvial valley bottom studies (Bell 1983), should be seen as one of the major ways forward in mapping early medieval landscapes and land-use. Saxon fields and field systems, though they exist, have largely been neglected in palaeo-environmental, geoarchaeological and archaeological studies, with rare exceptions (Bowden *et al.* 1993). This clearly needs to be rectified, especially as there are limited documentary sources to aid this work.

Rivers, intertidal and coastal

The palaeohydrology of the River Thames and the changing environment of its floodplain have been studied in detail by Mark Robinson; at Oxford, the evolution of a series of channels of the Thames and the islands between that supported the river crossing has been the subject of a long-running programme of research (Booth *et al.* 2007; Dodd 2003).

It is clear, not least from the evidence of Domesday Book, that fisheries were widespread on the rivers of the region, particularly on the Thames, and eels were probably the main catch. Fish traps and eel baskets have been recorded on the Kennet at Anslows Cottages south of Reading and at Wickhams Field, and potentially exist in the Ouse, Buckinghamshire (Butterworth and Lobb 1992; Crockett 1996; Plate 13.6). The evidence for river fishing along the Thames Valley was reviewed by Booth

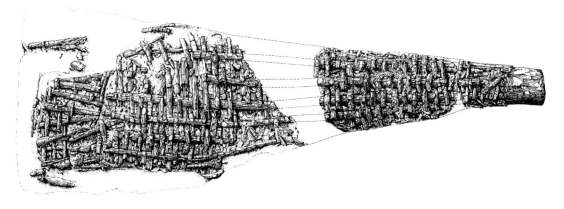

Plate 13.6 Eel-trap at Burghfield, Berkshire, *copyright Wessex Archaeology*

et al (2007, 340-41), and a particularly large and diverse assemblage of fish was found at Wraysbury (Coy, in Astill and Lobb 1989, 111-24). The region's rivers and watery habitats clearly also provided an important resource for the trapping and hunting of wading and water birds, and geese were kept on the floodplains (Booth *et al.* 2007, 340). Timbers found at Anslow's Cottages may be related to the management of water meadows (Butterworth and Lobb 1992, 176). Mike Allen comments that apart from rivers, the intertidal zone also provides evidence for fishing, fishtraps etc. Within the Solent-Thames corridor, only two projects have systematically examined these areas for such data: Langstone, Hampshire (Allen and Gardiner 2000), and Wootton-Quarr, Isle of Wight (Tomalin *et al.* 2012; see Fig. 7.1 for location). Other such locations also probably exist, especially on the Isle of Wight (for example Shalfleet, Yar and Newtown).

The remains of marine fish and shellfish are found in increasing numbers as excavators routinely sieve samples for the recovery of small bones. At the Northgate House/Discovery Centre site, Winchester, some 4800 identifiable bones were analysed from late Saxon deposits, with herring representing some 60% and eel some 30% of the groups (Nicholson, Fish Remains, in Ford and Teague 2011). The remainder comprised flatfish, particularly plaice, small cod, whiting and hake, and a mixture of sea fish such as bass, sea bream, conger eel and grey mullet and river fish such as trout, pike, dace, gudgeon and stickleback. Shellfish were also consumed, including oysters and carpet shells, and some cockles and mussels. The evidence for traded marine fish and shellfish far inland in the Upper and Middle Thames Valley is reviewed by Booth *et al.* (2007, 340-41).

By the time of Domesday Book, mills were widespread across the region. The re-introduction of water-powered milling in the Anglo-Saxon period seems, on present evidence, to date from the mid Saxon period, but the only excavated site in the region, at Old Windsor, remains unpublished. Here, dendrochronological and radiocarbon evidence suggests the mill was in operation in the early 8th century (Keene, forthcoming). A small millstone, possibly imported from Germany, was found at the mid Saxon site at Dorney (Foreman *et al.* 2002, 37), and Della Hooke notes charter evidence that there was a mill on a mill stream at Woolstone by the 10th century, which suggests that mills were being established on the estates in the Vale of White Horse at least by this time (1987, 138).

Social organisation

The region has early links with several different ethnic or tribal groups which may be broadly equated, according to the documentary sources, with the Jutes, the West Saxons, and the Anglian Mercians. Over much of the region, including the Thames Valley and probably northern Hampshire and western Buckinghamshire, the material culture of the 5th and 6th centuries is predom-

inantly identified as Saxon, and identifiable with people Bede refers to as the Gewisse. There is also a marked element of Kentish influence in the material culture of this region, most notably in the grave goods at Taplow, and this may reflect the power of the kings of Kent in southern England in the late 6th and early 7th century. The extent of Anglian influence in eastern Buckinghamshire is unclear, while recent work by Nick Stoodley is providing archaeological support for Bede's assertion that the people of southern Hampshire and the Isle of Wight were Jutes.

By the middle of the 7th century, Mercian expansion into the Thames Valley was pushing the rulers of the Gewisse southwards into Hampshire, and their takeover of former Jutish territory may be reflected in the establishment of their bishopric at Winchester and the emporium of *Hamwic* on the south coast. The Thames Valley remained disputed territory for two hundred years, although for much of the time it was under the control of the Mercians. Grave goods of the 7th century no longer reflect such tribal identities, and the Mercians are not distinctive in the archaeological record, except perhaps for the high-status cremation at Asthall. Documentary sources show that the kings of Mercia had residences at Thame and Benson at the foot of the Chilterns, and they presumably controlled the whole of Buckinghamshire. Hampshire lay within the kingdom of Wessex. By the middle of the 9th century, the kingdom of Wessex had re-established control of the region south of the Thames, while Oxfordshire and Buckinghamshire remained Mercian.

It is clear from historical sources that the people of Wessex and Mercia retained a strong sense of their distinctive identities throughout the late Saxon period, and old rivalries continued to resurface in dynastic disputes well into the 11th century. At the same time, however, the rulers of Wessex emerged from the Viking wars of the 9th century as the leading power in England, and were ultimately to extend their control over the whole country. Throughout the period of the Viking wars and the creation of the Danelaw in the north and east, the Solent-Thames region remained almost entirely within English-controlled territory, with the possibly temporary exception of a small portion of north-east Buckinghamshire.

Evidence for early power centres, perhaps as transfers of power from Roman authority to petty kings, is rare – there is nothing in the Roman centres of Portchester, Winchester or Silchester in Hampshire to suggest any such system. Equally in Berkshire there is no evidence of re-use of Iron Age hillforts for defence in the sub-Roman period, such as has been identified further west in the country, while in Buckinghamshire the re-occupation of hill forts at Aylesbury and Taplow appears to date from the mid Saxon period. In Oxfordshire, however, the evidence of a high-status late Roman presence at Dorchester, together with very early Anglo-Saxon burials, has led to the suggestion that Germanic mercenaries may have been brought here to defend the late Roman town.

Much analysis has taken place on the significant

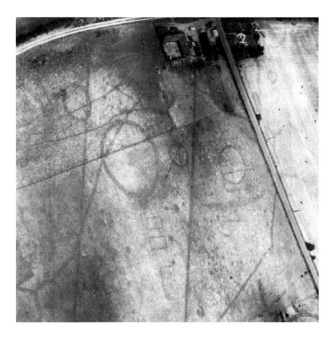

Plate 13.7 Cropmarks of Saxon halls at Sutton Courtenay, Oxfordshire, *copyright Cambridge University Committee for Aerial Photography (AFT91, 25th June 1962)*

number of furnished inhumation cemeteries in the region, which indicate that these represent the families of the early Anglo-Saxon settlers. Discussion continues as to the meaning of the uneven distribution of grave-goods amongst the buried population. Not until the 7th century is there clearer evidence for the emergence of an elite, in the form of the rich barrow burials at Taplow, Buckinghamshire, and at Cuddesdon, Asthall and Lowbury Hill, Oxfordshire, of which Taplow is significantly the most complete, excavated and spectacular example (see Plate 13.8 below). It is also at this period that there is evidence for visibly 'higher status' buildings appearing, though excavated examples are scarce in this region. A complex of buildings comparable in scale to the excavated palace at Yeavering in Northumberland has been identified south of the Thames at Sutton Courtenay, and may have been a power base of the Gewisse (Plate 13.7). It is located not far from the Milton II cemetery where 7th-century Kentish gold and garnet composite brooches were discovered in the 19th century, and is close to Dorchester, where the first bishopric of the West Saxons was established around 635. The elaborate complex of buildings at Cowdery's Down in Hampshire is also interpreted as an elite residence, although there is little evidence to suggest who the owners were. The establishment of the 'wic' settlement at *Hamwic* shows strong central control, with evidence for regulated street patterns and centralised supply of food and possibly raw materials.

The development of large 'multiple estates' in the Anglo-Saxon period is attested in the documentary evidence but is harder to see in the archaeological evidence, though the case has been made for the large parishes around Carisbrooke on the Isle of Wight having their origin in early Anglo-Saxon estates (Hase 1994). Minster churches are likely to have been established in many places across the region during the late 7th and early 8th centuries, and the documentary evidence associated with some of them suggests that they were originally endowed with huge estates running to hundreds of hides. The later break-up of these large holdings into smaller estates is recorded in documentary sources throughout the region. It is possible that the three reorganisations of the settlement at Yarnton, Oxfordshire between the 8th and the 10th centuries may be reflecting changing patterns of land holding. The small estates of the late Saxon period were the precursors of the manors and parishes of the medieval period, and the archaeology of the present study region has some evidence for the development of estate centres, such as Faccombe Netherton.

Berkshire and Hampshire are both mentioned in the *Anglo-Saxon Chronicle* by the late 9th century, but the definition of Oxfordshire and Buckinghamshire is thought to date from the early years of the 11th century. The development of later Anglo-Saxon systems of government and justice, including shire and hundred courts, is visible in the form of the shire towns themselves, and shire meeting places, such as Scutchamer Knob in Oxfordshire, the excavated hundred mound of Secklow in modern Milton Keynes (Adkins and Petchey 1984), and Gallibury Hump on the Isle of Wight. It is also graphically evident in the execution burials increasingly being recognised prominently located in the landscape on boundaries, meeting places, routeways, old monuments and hilltops.

Although society remained overwhelmingly rurally based, the first towns in the region develop from the late 9th century onwards. Some towns in the region – Winchester prominent amongst them – were already important ecclesiastical and probably royal centres before the later Anglo-Saxon period. Winchester, Oxford and Wallingford were fortified as part of the network of defended *burhs* established in response to the Viking threat, and were to develop into important centres of administration as county towns. Alongside these, smaller towns appear to have been developing, though only identifiable as places with a market or traders mentioned in Domesday Book. John Blair has drawn attention to the number of places of this kind that had a minster site at their core, and the presence of a resident high-status ecclesiastical community may have provided a stimulus for craftworking and trade.

Settlement

Early Saxon settlement

The region has a number of well-excavated Anglo-Saxon settlement sites supported by good environmental evidence, though these are not evenly distributed across the counties. Early Anglo-Saxon settlement generally conforms to the national pattern of small, non-hierarchical and unenclosed rural settlements consisting of a few timber halls and ancillary sunken-featured buildings.

Although early Saxon settlements nationally clearly varied considerably in size, it has been estimated that most might have been home to communities of perhaps 30-50 people (Hamerow 2012, 71).

The largest number of known early Saxon settlement sites in the Solent-Thames region are in the Oxfordshire Thames Valley; these were reviewed recently for the *Thames through Time* series, where a full summary can be found (Booth *et al.* 2007, 88-98). The most extensive early Saxon settlement excavation in the region took place here, at the contiguous sites of Barton Court Farm/Radley Barrow Hills near Abingdon (Miles 1986; Chambers and McAdam 2007). At Barton Court Farm, a group of seven SFBs and several post-built structures were found on the site of a modest late Roman villa. Pottery dating from perhaps as early as the mid 5th century was recovered from the main Roman ditches, suggesting little or no lapse between occupation periods. This may have been an outlying part of the larger settlement focus at Radley Barrow Hills, some 300 m to the north-east. Here, a total of 45 SFBs were found, but only 7 rectangular post-built structures could be identified, with varying degrees of confidence, among a mass of postholes. Some smaller post-built ancillary structures were suggested, and numerous fencelines. One of the most interesting aspects of the site was the clear presence of a central group of buildings apparently arranged around three sides of an open space. Both sites were dated to the 5th to 6th centuries.

The remains of other important settlement sites were the subject of earlier salvage recording at Sutton Courtenay and Cassington. During the 1920s and 1930s E T Leeds recorded the remains of the first Anglo-Saxon settlement to be recognised in this country, comprising an area of at least 33 SFBs near the village of Sutton Courtenay (Leeds 1923; 1927b; 1947). However, much of the site was lost to gravel quarrying. At least three areas of settlement remains and two areas of burials accompanied by characteristic early Saxon grave goods were found within an area roughly 2km west and north of the village of Cassington during gravel quarrying in the 1930s and 1940s, and it is likely that an extensive area of early Saxon settlement of considerable interest has been largely lost here (summarised in Hardy *et al.* 2003, appendix 6). More recently, 10-12 SFBs were found at Oxford Science Park, Littlemore; evidence for other buildings at this site may have been destroyed by ploughing and the full extent of the settlement may not have been recovered within the excavated area (Moore 2001a).

More commonly within the Oxfordshire Thames Valley, SFBs are found singly or in small numbers in restricted investigation areas (Booth *et al.* 2007, 88-98). While the accumulation of this kind of evidence in places such as Eynsham and Abingdon is valuable, it does not provide the opportunity to study these buildings as part of their wider contemporary settlement landscape. Cropmark evidence suggests that these kinds of buildings could be widely spread, and the region has produced evidence for the noted Anglo-Saxon phenomenon of 'shifting settlement'. Away from the Thames gravels there

is currently much less excavated evidence of Anglo-Saxon settlements in Oxfordshire, although occupation of this period is indicated by substantial numbers of burials and pottery scatters. Finds associated with early to mid Saxon settlement were excavated at the disused Roman villa at Shakenoak (see Fig. 11.1 for location), and elsewhere features of Anglo-Saxon type and date have been found at Wootton near Woodstock, Churchill near Chipping Norton, Kirtlington, Bicester, Wantage and possibly from Cogges near Witney (HER data; Harding and Andrews 2002; see also Dodd 2010).

Evidence for early Saxon settlement in Buckinghamshire has been accumulating quite rapidly since the 1970s. Until the incidental discovery of the settlement at Walton, Aylesbury, in 1973-4 (Farley 1976, and later Dalwood 1989) no early Saxon occupation site was known in the county (for this important multi-period site see also below). Shortly afterwards Hartigan's and Pennyland were discovered (Williams 1993), then a single SFB at Bancroft (Williams and Zeepvat 1994), all in the Milton Keynes area, followed by sites in Bierton at The Vicarage (Allen 1986) and Church Farm (SMR data). The site at Pitstone was first discovered by fieldwalking (Bull 1978) then by excavation (Phillips 2005). Others are known at Fenny Lock (Ford and Taylor 2001), Aston Clinton (SMR data) and at Taplow (Allen *et al.* 2009), and recent excavations at Brooklands, Milton Keynes, have located a small number of SFBs and pits (OA forthcoming). The most important early-middle Saxon site probably remains Pennyland in Milton Keynes (Williams 1993), which was not in the immediate vicinity of a village but approximately 1km distant from Great Linford. It was sited on and around the enclosures of a levelled Iron Age site. Pennyland produced 13 SFBs and 2 post-built halls. The earliest phase comprised a scatter of unenclosed SFBs, and may have extended beyond the area of excavation. The appearance of enclosures at the site in the 7th century is discussed further below. An unusual find here was of a wattle-revetted well/ waterhole with parts of a ladder; another ladder was found at Hartigans with a single SFB in the vicinity (Williams 1993).

The direct archaeological evidence for rural settlement in (new) Berkshire is sparse and somewhat fragmentary, usually consisting of SFBs and assemblages of pottery associated with ditches, pits or postholes. SFBs have been found at three rural sites and are thought to be representative of earlier Anglo-Saxon settlement. The SFB at Wellands Nursery, Wraysbury contained 171 sherds of 5th-century pottery, a hearth fragment, a spindlewhorl, animal bones and a quern fragment (Pine 2003a, 123). At Ufton Nervet near Newbury the SFB contained a whetstone, an iron ring and 280 sherds of pottery including 10 decorated sherds which placed the site in the 6th century (Manning 1974, 49-54). At Charnham Lane, Hungerford the truncated remains of an SFB contained early organic-tempered and sandy ware pottery, animal bones including a cow skull, and charcoal (Ford 2002, 27). The first two of these SFBs were found on the sites of Roman enclosures, but what all three sites have in common is that they were found positioned within relatively large areas of excavation and yet lack other contemporary buildings.

In contrast, a recently excavated site at Wexham, Slough, has revealed two early Anglo-Saxon timber halls without any accompanying SFBs (Preston 2012; Plate 13.8), one of which may have been deliberately located within an Iron Age enclosure. The lack of co-occurrence of these two building types may perhaps be a local peculiarity, but post-built halls can be hard to detect during excavations, and may simply not have survived on other sites. Alternatively, the SFBs may be isolated buildings on the periphery of settlements, or evidence of highly dispersed settlement (Ford 2002, 81), as at Stanton Harcourt, Gravelly Guy, Oxfordshire (see Fig. 9.1 for location). The finds within the Berkshire SFBs do not offer much clue to their function, but it is generally thought that weaving or some other industrial use is likely.

A gazetteer of early Saxon sites in Hampshire and the Isle of Wight datable to the 5th to 7th centuries was completed around 1990 by Sonia Hawkes (Hawkes 2003, 201-207). More recent work, and new discoveries, were reviewed by Russel (2002) and by Hinton for this resource assessment (2007), and further reports have subsequently appeared in *Hampshire Studies*. Early sites have been identified in the valley of the River Anton at Andover, reviewed in the context of work at Goch Way, near Charlton (Wright 2004). Here, SFBs found at Goch Way and Old Down Farm are thought to form part of a wide area of dispersed settlement of the 5th to 7th centuries either side of the river, probably to be linked

with the contemporary cemetery at Portway, some 1.4km to the west. At Micheldever two SFBs were found at Northbrook, on the site of what was probably a modest Roman villa, and early Saxon finds from metal-detecting suggest there was a cemetery nearby (Johnson 1998). Five SFBs and 12 pits were found at Abbots Worthy, near Winchester, downhill of the nearby cemetery at Worthy Park (Fasham and Whinney 1991). A focus of activity at Shavards Farm, Meonstoke has been the subject of numerous investigations; here a combination of chance finds, metal-detecting, purposive excavation, field walking and geophysical survey has identified pits, SFBs and post-built structures along with more than 13 burials of 6th- and probable 7th-century date (Russel 2002; Entwistle *et al.* 2005). At Portchester, excavations within the Roman fort identified a phase of occupation datable to the 5th to 7th centuries. Within the excavated area were four SFBs, 2 irregular post-built structures and a well, along with evidence of ploughing; the excavator suggested this could have formed part of a sequence of shifting settlement and cultivation throughout this period (Cunliffe 1976, 121). Despite evidence for numerous cemeteries, neither Hawkes nor Waller (2006) was able to report any excavated settlement remains of this period on the Isle of Wight.

Mid Saxon settlement

The mid Saxon period saw important changes in the settlement pattern. The Solent-Thames region contains an impressive range of good examples of increasingly

Plate 13.8 Excavations of a 6th century hall-house, Wexham, Berkshire, *copyright TVAS*

specialised site types; of the expression of social status and ownership through the appropriation of significant sites and the construction of more elaborate buildings; and of the control of access to space, and closer control of livestock and crops, by the widespread creation of enclosures within settlement sites. Yet, as examples accumulate, the difficulties of interpreting mid Saxon sites are becoming more apparent. The overlapping archaeological signatures of high-status secular and minster sites, and the likelihood that such places saw mixed and changing use over time, can complicate issues of interpretation (see, for example, Thomas 2012, 52; Hamerow 2012, 98-101). Helena Hamerow asks why it is that the archaeological record of the mid and late Saxon periods seems to be so dominated by 'high-status' settlements (Hamerow 2012, 164). She suggests this is a problem that requires not just further research but 'a new conceptual approach' to understanding why we find the farms and dwellings of ordinary farmers (who must, after all, have made up the vast majority of the population) so difficult to identify.

It is also becoming increasingly clear that there may have been significant regional variations in the way in which rural settlements developed in the mid Saxon period (Thomas 2012, 46-7). This question has recently been addressed by John Blair, on the basis of data collected during an ongoing investigation of the results of development-led excavation for this period (Blair 2013). He suggests that there are genuine and very substantial disparities in the evidence for mid Saxon settlement (*c*. 650-850), with a concentration of abundant evidence in the East Midlands, Norfolk and the Wash catchment, and a marked scarcity of settlement evidence elsewhere. Over much of England the building and everyday material culture of this period may be 'below the horizon of archaeological visibility'. It is possible that this reflects a continuing, or renewed, influence from British culture across much of the country, which had less impact in those parts of eastern England where contact with north-west Europe and southern Scandinavia remained strongest (ibid.). The true range of mid Saxon settlements in the present region may therefore only become apparent through the systematic use of scientific dating techniques, and an over-reliance on artefact dating in the past may have prevented us from recognising mid Saxon elements on sites interpreted as entirely early Saxon.

The re-use of prehistoric hillforts as a focus for high-status activity in the mid Saxon period is gradually emerging from recent work in Buckinghamshire. Aylesbury, first mentioned as a place in AD 571, probably contained a royal residence (place name 'Kingsbury') and certainly a minster. It lay within an Iron Age hillfort (Farley 1986) and excavation revealed that the Iron Age ditch had been re-cut in the mid Saxon period. It is clear that a large minster cemetery of mid to late Saxon date lies beneath the town centre (see below; Farley 2012). The exceptionally rich barrow burial overlooking the Thames at Taplow was located adjacent to another late prehistoric hillfort that was reoccupied during the early

to mid Saxon period. The evidence available from limited excavation for the re-use of the site suggests that this included both burial and domestic occupation; a high proportion of deer bone amongst the faunal remains and the presence of a sherd of imported east Mediterranean pottery would be consistent with high-status occupation, although very little structural evidence was recovered (Allen *et al.* 2009). There is now growing evidence for the re-use of fortifications of this kind by the kings of Mercia, and place-name evidence suggests that they may have formed part of a wider system of specialised satellite settlements in their vicinity (this is discussed, for example, in Blair 2013 and in Baker and Brookes 2013).

The evidence from Taplow can be associated with another unusual site found at Lake End Road West, Dorney, roughly 4km downriver on the Thames terraces. Here, finds from over 100 mid Saxon pits included one of the largest assemblages of imported finds and pottery yet known from outside the *wics* (Foreman *et al.* 2002). No evidence for contemporary buildings was found in the area, and it was suggested that this could have been the site of a market or fair, or even (given the absence of coins) of meetings or councils. The dating of the imported finds suggests that the site could have been in use in the period *c*. 740-80.

The site at Pennyland was reorganised in the 7th century into a more regular layout with a trackway and enclosures defining two house plots and paddocks. By the mid 8th century occupation seems to have shifted elsewhere, and the excavated site contained only four SFBs, a well and several probable granaries (Hamerow 2012, 80-81). At Aylesbury, numerous excavations over many years have gradually revealed a long sequence of occupation within the suburb of Walton (Ford and Howell 2004; see also Stone 2011 for the most recent work, with a summary of previous discoveries). A good argument can be made here for continuity of occupation from the early Saxon period (and possibly earlier) through to the present day, pretty well on the same location. Some 10 SFBs are distributed across a distance of at least 400m (one of them burnt down; Farley 2008) and there is an early cemetery nearby. There are also now known to be at least 11 post and post-in-trench type structures, some certainly small 'halls'; finds include *sceattas* and Ipswich ware and there is a substantial boundary of 10th- to 11th-century date associated with a manorial site which was itself enclosed within a later earthwork. There is also evidence to suggest that Walton Street, which runs through the hamlet into Aylesbury was established by the 10th century.

Part of a mid Saxon settlement has also been excavated at Water Eaton, Bletchley; here, parts of two ditched enclosures and a trackway were identified, with a single SFB inside one of the enclosures (Hancock 2010). A sherd of Ipswich ware and 14 sherds of Maxey ware were also recovered. Michael Farley comments that the most coherent evidence for a site whose dominant occupation period was middle Saxon is that at Wolverton Turn within Milton Keynes (Preston 2007). Although much damaged (and much excavated) the site appears to consist of a substantial ditched enclosure of mid Saxon date, so far unique in the county. There are associated radiocarbon dates of cal AD 690–890 and the site produced both Ipswich and Maxey ware. It contained one identified rectangular post-built structure and an SFB lay nearby. Others have subsequently been found here (Thorne 2005).

Andrew Reynolds (2003) and Helena Hamerow (2012, 102-5) have drawn attention to the appearance of large buildings, enclosures and regular axial or 'courtyard' layouts as probable markers of high status settlements from the first half of the 7th century onwards. There is increasing evidence that a royal centre approaching the scale of the excavated palace at Yeavering (Northumberland) was located south of the Thames, between the villages of Drayton and Sutton Courtenay (Oxon). The site was first identified from cropmarks visible in aerial photographs (reproduced in Booth *et al.* 2007, fig 3.26; see Plate 13.7). Subsequent exploratory excavations have confirmed the presence of a complex of halls apparently arranged in an L-shaped group, the largest of which is now known to measure in excess of 30x10m (Hamerow *et al.* 2007; Wessex ArchaeologyTime Team 2010). A number of reported metal-detected finds include a fragment of a gold disc brooch, gold droplets and copper alloy horse harness mounts with Style II decoration; these support the view of a high status site here in the late 6th and early 7th century (Hamerow *et al.* 2007, 170-79, 185-6). Fourteen *sceattas* datable to the period 700-730 suggest the site retained a role as a recognised meeting place for trade into the 8th century (D M Metcalf in Hamerow *et al.* 2007, 180-83). A second group of halls has been identified on aerial photographs at Long Wittenham, some 6km to the east. The date of these is unknown, but the largest has been estimated as measuring some 21x10m, which suggests the possibility of another significant complex here.

The late Saxon monarchs held many estates within (modern) Oxfordshire, including Faringdon, Wantage, Bampton, Shipton-under-Wychwood, Wootton, Kirtlington, Headington, Benson and Cholsey; other royal residences known from documentary evidence include Woodstock and Islip, and possibly Hook Norton (see Blair 1994, 109 and fig. 62). However, only a couple of places can be identified as mid Saxon royal vills; a significant proportion of late Saxon royal estate centres and residences lay in or near country which offered good hunting, and seem likely to have been quite late and associated with the increasing development of royal hunting grounds in the region. Wulfhere of Mercia ratified a charter for the minster at Chertsey in 672-4 'in the residence which is called Thame' (ibid., 49). The outlines of two large oval enclosures are preserved in the street plan of the town, one of them containing the parish church, and these may be the sites of early ecclesiastical and secular centres; this has so far not been confirmed by excavation. The location of the royal residence at Wantage where King Alfred was reputedly

born in 849 is also unknown. The first reliable reference to the royal vill at Benson occurs in the witness list to a purported grant to the minster at Abingdon by Aethelbald of Mercia in the period 727-36. It must subsequently have been taken by the West Saxons, as Offa is recorded as recapturing it from Cynewulf of Wessex in 779. Recent excavations uncovered some early Saxon remains, but nothing of the mid Saxon royal residence has yet been identified (Kelly 2000, 22-7 no. 5; Blair 1994, 55; Pine and Ford 2003).

Excavations in Banbury in 1997-9 investigated the north-east corner of a previously unsuspected ditched enclosure of mid Saxon date on the site of the later castle of the bishops of Lincoln. The ditch may have been waterfilled, and a single small building was present within the excavated area. A sherd of Ipswich ware occured with other mid Saxon pottery, and three coins were found fused together, two of them coins of Burgred of Mercia datable to the period 871-4 (the middle one being unidentifiable). The only other coin is one of Cnut. Other Anglo-Saxon finds included horse furniture, a copper alloy toilet implement, a bun-shaped loomweight, lava quern fragments, a purple phyllite whetstone and a gaming piece made from a horse tooth. The site continued in use after the mid Saxon period, but the remains were ephemeral and not closely datable; possible evidence for stone structures was noted but the exact nature of occupation is uncertain. The site was subsequently developed as a palace of Alexander, bishop of Lincoln in the early 12th century. At the time of writing, a report on the excavations is in preparation (Hewitson *et al.* forthcoming), and we are grateful to Stephanie Rátkai for the opportunity to include this information in advance of publication.

At Yarnton (Hey 2004), a wide-ranging investigation showed a decisive change in the form of rural settlement during the 8th century, which then persisted into the 9th. During the 8th century what seems previously to have been an area of dispersed and shifting settlement was reorganised into an ordered settlement, with paddocks, a droveway, and buildings set out within enclosures. Amongst these were a granary and a possible fowlhouse as well as at least one hall and a number of SFBs (Plate 13.9). During the 9th century a second hall was built within a new enclosure, and a small cemetery was present on the site. An extensive programme of environmental research showed that the reorganisation of the settlement was associated with the intensification of arable farming, the resumption of hay cultivation and the expansion of the area under crops to include heavier clay soils. Perhaps most significant of all, two very similar sites that are likely to be contemporary with Yarnton were found nearby at Cresswell Field and Worton, both comprising hall-type and ancillary buildings with trackways, enclosures and probable associated SFBs. It is possible that 8th-century Yarnton and its neighbours formed part of the endowment of the minster at nearby Eynsham. If so, might these self-contained, enclosed and organised farmsteads be the holdings of free tenants of the minster at this time?

Plate 13.9 Reconstruction of Middle Saxon buildings at Yarnton, *copyright OA, drawn by Peter Lorimer*

Another glimpse of a 7th- to early 8th-century settlement may come from the site at New Wintles Farm near Eynsham. This site has never been fully published, but seems to have remained essentially small scale and unenclosed throughout (Hawkes 1986; Booth *et al.* 2007 108-9 and fig. 3.32; Hamerow 2012, 83). The contrast with Yarnton is striking, and the site perhaps bears comparison with that excavated recently at Riverdene near Basingstoke, Hants (below).

Astill (1984) identified a number of sites in Berkshire that appear to have been 'central places' of higher importance, often at the centre of secular or church administrative units. Settlements with characteristics of higher status centres in the mid and/or late Anglo-Saxon period include Aldermaston, Bucklebury, Compton, Cookham, Kintbury, Lambourn, Reading, Old Windsor and Thatcham. Archaeological evidence from Reading, Thatcham and Old Windsor is beginning to confirm the existence of higher status settlements at this time, based partly on the discovery of Ipswich ware. Perhaps the most important is Old Windsor. The excavations of 1952-58 remain unpublished and only outline details have so far been available, but a new review of the evidence is due for publication in 2014, and we are very grateful to Derek Keene for permission to use this information here (Keene forthcoming). What seems initially to have been an ordinary riverside settlement was developed, probably from the early 8th century, into an elite centre with a mill, a sequence of timber halls and a building possibly constructed using stone, tile and window glass, but apparently identified only from rubble. Finds assemblages that include Ipswich ware, Tating ware and decorative metalwork suggest a high-status place

integrated into the trading networks of the 8th century, and probably one that was used intermittently by the royal court. The mill and other buildings were destroyed by fire in the late 9th or early 10th century, prompting suggestions of a devastating Viking raid. Use of the site seems to have been revived towards the middle of the 11th century, with timber halls laid out to the west of the earlier focus; this can be associated with evidence for Edward the Confessor's interest in Windsor during the latter part of his reign, and a number of royal councils were held there. Royal interest in the site persisted into the middle of the 12th century, although increasingly as an adjunct to the new riverside castle.

Reading was described in Asser's Life of King Alfred as a royal estate in 870, when the Vikings arrived to set up an encampment, perhaps to the east of the town, between the Thames and Kennet. The late 9th century also saw the burial of a coin hoard alongside a coffin and inhumation in St Mary's churchyard, suggesting that the minster may have been in existence by this stage. Pottery of early to mid Saxon date has been found in numerous excavations in the centre of Reading, but no structural evidence has been recovered.

Both Old Windsor and Reading have produced sherds of Ipswich ware, a distinctive type of mid Saxon pottery which may indicate high status sites, especially when found towards the outer limit of its distribution range, such as the Thames Valley (Plate 13.10). Excavations at 12 Church Gate, Thatcham, have found two sherds of this pottery in a ditch (Wallis 2005). St Mary's Church at Thatcham has long been suspected as an early and important mother church (Kemp 1968) and Thatcham itself was a royal estate and the centre of a hundred in

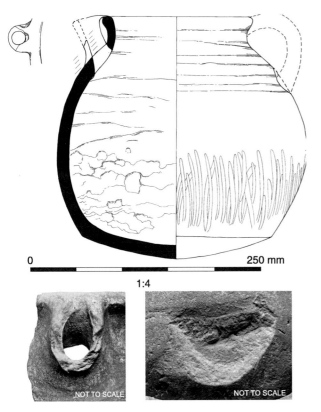

0   250 mm

1:4

NOT TO SCALE   NOT TO SCALE

Plate 13.10 Ipswich Ware vessel, *copyright OA and Wessex Archaeology*

Domesday Book. Further excavations at this site also produced organic- and limestone-tempered pottery consistent with a middle Saxon settlement. Whilst there is no suggestion that settlement started any earlier, Thatcham's location close to the line of a Roman road and a small Roman town has been remarked upon (Lobb and Rose 1996, 94).

Lambourn was mentioned in King Alfred's will. It has been assumed that the Anglo-Saxon royal core of this settlement lay within the small oval marked out by a pattern of lanes, with the church at the southern edge and settlement perhaps extending slightly to the south of it (Astill 1984, 70-71). Archaeological evaluations at the Red Lion Hotel, just outside the oval but within Astill's predicted area of Saxon settlement, produced ditches and 'negative features' associated with Anglo-Saxon pottery. This includes 2 decorated sherds which may be from a bossed urn of 5th- or early 6th-century type and other organic tempered and sandy wares thought to be 'early' Anglo-Saxon. The subsequent watching brief at this site produced evidence for postholes and flint surfaces, associated with less chronologically diagnostic early-middle Saxon pottery, which taken together suggests 'substantial and long lasting settlement' (Foundation Archaeology 1999a and b).

Excavations at Wraysbury, on the opposite bank of the Thames from Old Windsor, found an area of late Saxon settlement to the north of St Andrew's church (see below). Excavation 100m to the west of the church, however, found considerable quantities of material of mid to late Saxon date, including pottery, two glass beads, iron objects and five coins comprising two *sceattas*,

two pennies of Offa and one of Coenwulf (Astill and Lobb 1989, 68). No contemporary structural remains were found, so the nature of this site remains uncertain.

At Portchester, the early Saxon huts were replaced by what appeared to be two groups of structures separated by an open space, each consisting of at least two buildings with associated wells and pits; one of the buildings had an adjacent enclosure defined by a fence. This phase of occupation appears to have lasted from the 7th century through the 8th and 9th centuries. Ninth-century artefacts, notably coins including a Carolingian gold import, decorative metalwork and imported east Mediterranean glass, seem to suggest higher status than most settlements, though the recognition since the 1970s of mid Saxon 'prolific sites', apparently trading-places rather than residences, raises the likelihood that the old fort was a landing-place and perhaps a mart (Cunliffe 1975 for the excavations; Ulmschneider 2003 for *sceattas* and 'prolific sites'). Perhaps in some ways comparable is the mid Saxon settlement evidence from Yaverland on the Isle of Wight (unpublished; see Waller 2006). This site, partially excavated by *Time Team* in 2001, had at least two post-built houses located at an area of former Roman occupation within the earthworks of a former Iron Age hillfort. Waller comments that this site overlooks the navigable Brading Haven, a natural harbour known to have been used for trade during the Roman period.

Hampshire also has two well known and well preserved sites of this period that have been very influential in the study of Anglo-Saxon timber building technology and in the development of ideas about the expression of status in settlement organisation noted above (Reynolds 2003; Hamerow 2012). The excavations at Church Down, Chalton, and particularly at Cowdery's Down, Basingstoke, revealed rural settlement sites that showed elaboration of buildings and control of space and access by the use of enclosures (Addyman and Leigh 1972; 1973; Millett 1983). At Chalton, there is a two-phase sequence of enclosures and buildings, with numerous lesser buildings, including some grouped around a square; the excavators considered it likely that these represented the homesteads of different families. Millett has subsequently suggested the layout might suggest a 'chief' with dependents and labour force (Millett 1983, 247-9). At Cowdery's Down two successive phases of the layout of the site incorporated large and elaborately built structures associated with fenced enclosures. These were superseded by the remodelling of the site into a single compound, with new buildings, in the third phase. By then, however, the settlement as a whole was expanding, with even larger buildings. David Hinton (2007) comments that the interpretation of the site as one always of high status but also showing increasing ostentation in its buildings still seems valid. Both sites are considered to be of 6th- to 7th-century date, although the quantities of finds recovered from both were very small and the pottery undiagnostic. An enamelled mount and ring from a hanging bowl were found in a pit outside one of the larger post-built halls at Chalton.

A further site of this period was discovered in 1995 at Riverdene, Basingstoke, only 1km from Cowdery's Down (Hall-Torrance and Weaver 2003). Riverdene is thought to be slightly later than Cowdery's Down, with a single radiocarbon date obtained on animal bone giving a range of cal AD 610–890 at 95% probability, or cal AD 650–780 at 68%. A total of 8 possible post-built structures and up to 11 SFBs were identified, although many of these were not very well preserved or particularly coherent in plan. They are thought to represent elements of a settlement dispersed over a wide area. Although there was no certain evidence for any enclosures or trackways within the excavated areas, the excavators suggested that the site may have been divided into different land-use zones, with evidence for some grouping of SFBs and post-built structures. Some 4km to the north-west of the Cowdery's Down settlement, excavations in 1995 at Monk Sherborne found the remnants of a rectangular post-built building within an enclosure system, a short distance from the remains of a substantial Roman winged corridor villa. A Roman pit adjacent to the post-built building had slumped or been re-cut in the Anglo-Saxon period, and within it were found an iron belt buckle and belt fitting with silver wire inlay and plating. Both are likely to be Frankish imports dating from the early 7th century. Metalworking debris was present within the post-built building and elsewhere on the site, although there was insufficient evidence to prove that it was of Anglo-Saxon date (Teague 2005).

Late Saxon settlement

Examples of excavated late Saxon rural settlements are rare in the region, and investigation has depended to a much greater extent on the accumulation of information from a wider variety of sources, including fieldwalking, survey, small-scale test pitting and 'keyhole' excavations within the built-up areas of modern villages. In recent years the most systematic investigations of rural settlements have been undertaken in Buckinghamshire. A number of areas of village shrinkage and 'deserted' settlements within or close to existing villages have been explored in Milton Keynes (Great Linford, Loughton, Tattenhoe, Shenley Brook End, Caldecotte etc.). Michael Farley notes that these investigations have not generally produced evidence of continuity from the early Saxon period and only sparse middle Saxon evidence. Two exceptions may be Westbury (Ivens *et al.* 1995), which produced a couple of wells with surviving ladders and a small inhumation cemetery, and Walton, Aylesbury, where small ditched plots or enclosures were laid out in the late Saxon period, and were probably used as paddocks or pasture for livestock (Stone 2011; see above for early and mid Saxon occupation at this site). In both cases there was no certainly associated settlement.

At Bradwell Bury in Milton Keynes quite a substantial enclosure, probably of late Saxon date and unusual for the period in Buckinghamshire, was succeeded by a medieval earthwork (Mynard 1992). A number of irregular post-built structures were also recorded here

(Mynard 1994). Elsewhere at the Milton Keynes sites and others (Walton, Bedgrove, Bradwell Bury (Mynard 1994), Great Linford (Mynard 1992), Weston Underwood (Enright and Parkhouse 1996) and Loughton (Pine 2003b)) evidence for late Saxon occupation comes in the form of the readily distinguishable St Neot's ware pottery. South of the Chilterns, the excavations at Lot's Hole, Dorney found evidence for a large enclosure bounded by a trackway on the south, and containing a post-built structure that could represent one or two phases of a 'hall' type building (Foreman *et al.* 2002).

The recent Whittlewood project studied a block of 12 parishes crossing the Buckinghamshire/Northamptonshire border. Here, both nucleated and dispersed settlements exist in what was formerly part of Whittlewood Forest. The authors of the report suggest that the character of the area might owe much to its deliberate preservation by the Crown as an area of woodland, pasture and hunting grounds, in which the expansion of arable cultivation was discouraged and prevented, leading to 'the creation and survival of an alternative midland landscape' (Jones and Page 2006, 223-6). The Whittlewood project showed that a landscape of dispersed farmsteads existed in the area before 850. Some of these, termed 'pre-village nuclei', underlie both later nucleated and later dispersed villages; others were abandoned and subsumed into the open fields (ibid., 234-5). In other cases, both nucleated and dispersed, the 'pre-village nucleus' appears to date from the period between 850 and 1000. In the authors' words, 'Whether a single pre-village nucleus or many nuclei developed into a nucleation or a multi-nodal village, a hamlet or farmstead, seems to rest in the critical phase of transition which has become known as the 'village moment'' (ibid., 235). The villages of Whittlewood, both nucleated and dispersed, seem to have developed by a process of slow growth outwards from earlier settlement foci, but the authors note that this might be in contrast to other parts of the midlands (ibid., 236).

What appears to be emerging is a picture of increasing complexity at a regional and 'micro-regional' level, where different chronologies and processes might lie behind superficially similar end results. In Gabor Thomas's words, 'grandiose theories on village origins are becoming increasingly untenable' (2012, 45), and the substantial dataset collected by John Blair for the period tends in the same direction (see above and Blair 2013). There would seem to be an excellent case for renewed investigation of this topic across the varying landscapes of the Solent-Thames region. John Blair (pers. comm.) suggests that we should see Buckinghamshire as part of the eastern zone of building culture, where settlements of the mid to late Saxon period are relatively abundant and visible. The culture of building and everyday settlement in the rest of the region may have been subject to different influences, resulting in much lower levels of archaeological visibility.

In Oxfordshire, traces of possible Anglo-Saxon predecessors to post-Conquest manorial centres have been identified in excavations at Cogges, near Witney, where the post-trenches of timber structures were

Plate 13.11 Bow-sided late Saxon building at Bicester, *copyright Wessex Archaeology*

overlain by the buildings of the priory founded around 1100, and at Deddington and Middleton Stoney castles (Blair 1994, 135-6). The most impressive group of buildings of this period yet known in the county were excavated at Chapel Street, Bicester (Harding and Andrews 2002; Plate 13.11). Here, five substantial timber buildings associated with ditches, pits and a probable 6-post granary were excavated along the east bank of the River Bure, opposite the parish church which has been identified as a probable Anglo-Saxon minster housing the relics of St Eadburh. The settlement site is likely to have been occupied between the later 10th century and the 12th century. The largest building, which probably dates from the 11th century, was bow-sided and measured 23m in length and up to 6.25m in width. The nature of this settlement is unclear, but John Blair notes that the area is known as Bury End, which could imply some kind of defended site here before the reordering of the 12th-century planned town around the market place to the north (Blair 2002, 139-40).

The 10th century saw another significant change at Yarnton, with the abandonment of the mid Saxon farmstead and the probable relocation of the estate centre towards the medieval manor house and church to the north-east. Excavation and survey revealed that much of the intervening area had been laid out in a series of small, rectilinear plots, some of which were cultivated, while others were probably individual farmstead tofts (Hey 2004). Another group of small enclosures, laid out around a waterhole, was excavated at Manor Farm, Drayton (Challinor *et al.* 2003), not far from Sutton Courtenay, and a ditched enclosure containing a probable house and dating from the 10th to the 12th centuries was found in a small excavation in the heart of

the village of Brighthampton (Ford and Preston 2002).

Wraysbury remains the best-known excavation of a late Saxon rural settlement in Berkshire. Here two late Saxon ditched enclosures were found, and two buildings were partially excavated; a third building was inferred from a large deposit of well-preserved daub, some with plaster attached (Astill and Lobb 1989). Substantial collections of bird, animal and fish bone are thought to be kitchen waste and discussed above. Small scale evidence has come from Hungerford and Ufton Nervet.

David Hinton's review of late Saxon settlement evidence from Hampshire notes a number of small-scale investigations but nothing that has yet revealed much of the form of rural settlement of the period in the county. Hampshire does have two well-known excavated high-status settlements. At Portchester, following a phase of rubbish dumping (see below), a new complex of buildings was laid out in the 10th century comprising a substantial hall, a separate post-built building that may have been a store, and a third buttressed hall with an internal subdivision that the excavator suggests was possibly domestic in function (Cunliffe 1976). A second 10th-century phase of building saw the main hall replaced, and a new building added, followed, around the beginning of the 11th century, by the construction of a tower on stone foundations. The description of the attributes of the thegnly residence in the 11th-century text *Geþyncðo*, the church, kitchen, bell-house and enclosure gate, suggested the possibility that this structure may have been a bell tower. A small cemetery of some 21-22 burials developed next to the tower in the middle of the 11th century.

The estate at Faccombe Netherton was first mentioned in a charter of 863. Slight remains on the site suggest the presence of a settlement here before the middle of the 9th century, but the earliest substantial excavated buildings are dated to the period c. 850-925 and comprised an aisled timber hall and a building constructed using flint for at least its lower walls, interpreted as the private apartments. By the middle decades of the 10th century, c 940-980, the complex comprised the retained and repaired hall, a new building interpreted as private accommodation with a latrine, a kitchen (occasionally used as a smithy) set to the south, and possible domestic or agricultural buildings. By around the year 1000, the complex had been surrounded by a bank and ditch. A group of new regularly aligned domestic buildings comprised a large hall with private apartments set immediately to the south and a possible small kitchen beyond, and a further post-built building of unknown function set at right-angles to the north end of the hall. The excavator suggests that the church of St Michael, set some 50m south-east of the domestic buildings, was probably in existence by the same time (Fairbrother 1990).

Urban settlement

The region contains the important middle Saxon *wic* settlement of *Hamwic*. Modern excavations in the area began in 1946 with redevelopment following wartime destruction and it is now estimated that *Hamwic* spread over an area of some 47ha, of which some 4.5% had been investigated by 2005 (Birbeck 2005, 4, 196). Excavations up to 1983 were reported and synthesised by Morton (1992), followed in 1997 by the publication of the important Six Dials site (Andrews 1997), the St Mary's Stadium site (Birbeck 2005) and most recently, reports on the Deanery School site near to St Mary's Church towards the southern edge of the settlement (reported in *Hampshire Studies* 67 (II) for 2012). Three

0 _____ 40 mm
2:1

Plate 13.12 Gold pendant from St Mary's, Southampton, *copyright Wessex Archaeology*

possible early nuclei have been suggested, a minster or mixed secular/ecclesiastical high status enclave around St Mary's Church (Plate 13.12), later the mother church of Southampton; the waterfront; and the Six Dials area. Current evidence suggests the densest settlement may have been focused along the NW-SE axis represented by Six Dials and the Chapel Road area, with less dense settlement towards the river, and around St Mary's (Morton in Birbeck 2005, 197-8). Evidence from the Stadium excavations supports the dating of *Hamwic* to the period from the later 7th century to the middle of the 9th century, although some occupation continued thereafter at a much reduced scale. Other trading settlements probably existed, associated with other river valleys in Hampshire (Birbeck 2005, 190), but the scale of *Hamwic* is currently exceptional. It was a place of intensive craft working, but without evidence for large-scale zoning; instead, the impression is of a 'patchwork' of different crafts, probably interdependent for tools and materials, carried on in individual houses side by side (Andrews 1997, 205; Birbeck 2005, 204). Its population at its maximum extent might be estimated at somewhere around 2000-3000 people, amongst whom there may have been significantly more men than women (Andrews 1997, 253). Series H (Type 49) *sceattas* were minted at *Hamwic*, and there is clear evidence for international trade although it is now suggested that this might have been on a smaller scale than previously supposed (Birbeck 2005, 203). The recent excavations at St Mary's Stadium and the Deanery, in contrast to earlier work, have included substantial environmental research.

The Solent-Thames region has a large variety of places where late Saxon urbanism can be investigated, and some where a considerable amount of important work has already been carried out.

No Buckinghamshire towns were larger than market towns and the only towns directly mentioned in the late Saxon period are Newport Pagnell, Buckingham and Aylesbury, all of which were briefly mint towns. Newport, on the Ouse, had burgesses and was an unusual borough in that it was not in royal hands (Darby 1962). It has been suggested that it was founded in the 870/880s by the Danes as a combined trading and frontier post (Baines 1986). There is little archaeological evidence available of its extent or character, and only sparse finds (Beamish 1993).

Buckingham was noted both in the Burghal Hidage and the *Anglo-Saxon Chronicle* (AD 914) and also had burgesses. For a discussion of its foundation see Baines (1984; 1985). There have been various, so far unsuccessful, attempts to predict the line of its Saxon defences and of its twin – the Chronicle notes 'both of its fortifications'. The loop of the Ouse that contains the high ground on which the town's castle was subsequently built must be one element of the site, but a small scale excavation here produced only a few sherds of St Neot's ware and a mid-Saxon pin (Hall 1975).

The re-occupation of an Iron Age hillfort at Aylesbury during the mid Saxon period has been noted above, and there is evidence for both a minster here (see below) and a royal residence (from the place name Kingsbury). By the time of Domesday Book Aylesbury, a king's town, had dominion over several hundreds around and considerable revenue from its market. Briefly becoming a mint town, Aylesbury was to become a classic small market town initially contained within the defences of the preceding Iron Age hillfort but with a large market area developing beyond the defences which in the medieval period itself became enclosed by buildings. Brill is known as the site of a house of Edward the Confessor. It acquired an earthwork castle post-Conquest, but it is unclear whether there was any proto-urban development here.

Modern Oxfordshire contains two important Burghal Hidage sites, Oxford and Wallingford, both probably selected for fortification as part of a chain of *burhs* guarding important Thames crossings (the others being Cricklade, Wilts, and Sashes Island near Cookham, Berks). Oxford is the only one of the group to lie on the Mercian bank of the river, and the record in the *Anglo-Saxon Chronicle* that Edward the Elder took control of it in 911-12, along with London, lends support to the idea that it may initially have been a Mercian rather than a West Saxon foundation (see Haslam 2010 for an alternative interpretation). Oxford has been the subject of extensive archaeological investigations since the 1960s (see Dodd 2003 for a synthesis of work up to the turn of the 21st century). The late Saxon defensive rampart and its facing stone wall have been revealed in numerous

excavations and its course is generally well understood, although uncertainties remain about the extent of the original defended area and the chronology of possible later extensions. A distinctive late Saxon street surface has been identified under most of the streets in the city centre, suggesting that they originated as part of a formal gridded plan, as at Winchester.

Investigations along the line of the later Thames Crossing at the south of the medieval town have shown that there was a developed crossing in place by the mid Saxon period, and accumulating evidence for a large mid to late Saxon cemetery around Oxford Cathedral supports the suggestion that the minster church of St Frideswide was located here. The nature of occupation within the *burh* during the 10th century is not currently well understood, but Oxford seems to have developed rapidly in or by the early 11th century, when its central street frontages appear to have been quite densely built-up. Finds assemblages comprising pottery, metalwork, bone, leather, stone and some wooden objects have been recovered and studied, although these are not on the scale of assemblages from contemporary Winchester. The town has benefited from detailed environmental and geoarchaeological studies for this period and programmes of dendrochronological and radiocarbon dating.

The *burh* of Wallingford had a hidage assessment of 2400 hides, equivalent to Winchester (Plate 13.13). Eclipsed by Oxford and Reading from the 13th century

Plate 13.13 Aerial view of Wallingford burh, *copyright Environment Agency Jan 2003*

onwards, it eventually declined into a small market town. As a result, it retains good potential for investigation of its late Saxon and medieval archaeology, and stretches of the defensive rampart remain upstanding. Limited investigations of the rampart have shown it to be constructed of earth and turves, with evidence for a timber revetment; it was subsequently heightened, and fronted or capped by a stone wall. Excavation in the 1980s revealed a late 10th- or early 11th-century timber-lined cellar at Nos 9-11 St Martin's St in the centre of the town, and more recently a mortar mixer and a large number of burials dating from the late Saxon period and later have been excavated, associated with the lost town centre church of St Martin (Booth *et al.* 2007, 276 and fig. 5.38). Opportunities for excavation have, however, been more limited than at Oxford, and the Wallingford *Burh* to Borough Project, initiated in 2001, has provided an important stimulus for renewed research into the origins and development of the town. Oxoniensia contains a number of interim reports (eg. Christie *et al.* 2010), and the project monograph has recently been published (Christie and Creighton 2013). This also publishes earlier excavations, including the important work carried out at Wallingford Castle in the 1960s.)

The project has provided the opportunity to investigate a number of important questions relating to the form and function of *burhs*. The reason why Wallingford was chosen for fortification remains unclear, and the project is investigating both possible early and mid Saxon predecessors and the evidence for reworking of the surrounding landscape, redirection of routeways, water supply and the river crossing. Wallingford also represents a valuable case study for the way in which *burhs* were organised, and the chronology of urban development. Christie *et al.* suggest a model that would see late Saxon Wallingford as a defended area that was used in a number of different ways: open space for grazing, storage, temporary refuge and the holding of fairs, thegnly residences focused on early churches, a high-status residence on the site of the later castle, and 'urban' occupation essentially limited to the street grid in the south-east quarter of the town (2010, 46).

Elsewhere in Oxfordshire, Bampton was the site of an important minster and a royal manor, and is recorded in Domesday Book as having a market. John Blair has suggested that the early market was located to the south of the minster precinct, and a sunken-floored building of probable 11th-century date has been excavated here (Mayes *et al.* 2000). Abingdon is likely to have been another early minster settlement, and was the location of an important abbey of the Benedictine reform. Domesday Book records the presence of 10 merchants living in front of the church gate, suggesting that a small urban community was becoming established here. Although very little is known of the town at this period, it has recently been shown that its medieval boundaries still followed the line of the defensive ditch of the Iron Age oppidum that once occupied the area (Allen 1997; Brady *et al.* 2007).

Although now in Oxfordshire, the *burh* of Wallingford was the principal town of late Saxon Berkshire, with 512 house plots recorded in Domesday Book. The second place in the county recorded in the Burghal Hidage is *Sceaftesege*, which has been identified with Sashes Island in the Thames at Cookham, the site of a mid Saxon minster church and a late Saxon royal estate. Nothing of the burghal fortification has yet been discovered. Reading is described as a borough in Domesday Book, with 59 houses shared between the royal manor and the estate of the minster church; a mint operated at Reading during the reign of Edward the Confessor. Astill (1984) suggested that the early town was probably located around the church of St Mary, but very little evidence for it has yet been recovered. By the time of Domesday Book, Old Windsor is described as having 95 *hagae* and occupation evidence of this period appears to have been recovered during Hope-Taylor's excavations. On a very much smaller scale, Domesday Book records 7 *hagae* at Aldermaston, 9 at Faringdon (now in Oxfordshire but formerly in Berkshire) and 12 at Thatcham, all three royal estates and minster centres (Astill 1984; Blair 1994, 119). At Aldermaston and Thatcham Astill suggests this early settlement is likely to be found in the area near to the church (1984). Whether such small numbers of properties can be considered to be 'urban' in any meaningful sense is perhaps doubtful, but the numbers are comparable with the numbers of merchants recorded at Abingdon.

At Southampton, *Hamwic* appears to have been in decline by the middle of the 9th century. The location of the Burghal Hidage fortification has not been certainly identified, although it has been suggested that this was the former Roman small town/port known as Clausentum on the east side of the Itchen estuary. By the 10th century, if not before, occupation seems to have been firmly established on the site of the later medieval town of Southampton to the west. Evidence has been found in a number of excavations for the existence of a defensive ditch enclosing an area smaller than the later medieval walled town, although this may have been a short-lived feature. A review of late Saxon pottery in Southampton identified numerous sites within this proposed enclosure and on the line of the proposed enclosure ditch pottery of this date (Brown 1994 fig. 5, table 1). However, more than half the assemblage had come from excavations outside the proposed enclosure, to the north of the medieval walled circuit (ibid., 150, table 7), and amongst this the pottery from Bargate St (SOU 142) contained 'superb' imported vessels. More recently, investigations on the Lower High Street (SOU 266), within the 'enclosed area', found remains of late Saxon timber-framed buildings with hearths and rubbish pits, and excavations slightly to the north, on the west side of the High St, found numerous late Saxon pits and evidence for boundary ditches at right-angles to the street alignment (Brown and Hardy 2011).

Further substantial evidence of mid to late Saxon occupation has also been recovered beyond the area of the proposed enclosure. Excavations at the West Quay Shopping Centre found mid Saxon pottery and glass, an

8th-century *sceat* and a coin of Ceolwulf of Mercia, dating from 821-23. Substantial late Saxon evidence was also found at the site, comprising the remains of larger and smaller post-built buildings with wattle and daub walls, and evidence for copper alloy and iron working, textile manufacturing and the making of combs, knife handles and ice skates from animal bone (Southampton City Council). Hinton (2007) suggests, additionally, that the reporting of a 'post-in-trench' hall from beneath the medieval castle (Oxley ed. 1988, 47) may suggest that there was an aristocratic nucleus in use from the mid Saxon period onwards, and the town may have expanded around it. The quantity of imported pottery noted by Brown, largely from Northern France, provides archaeological evidence that the late Saxon settlement here was functioning as a port (1994, 147), and he notes Rumble's suggestion that *Hamtun* may have been 'an estate within which there were several centres of activity rather than a single occupied site' (ibid. 128).

Winchester was the capital of the late Saxon kings of Wessex, and the largest *burh*. Its pre-eminence in the study of late Saxon urbanism in southern England was established by the work of the Winchester Excavations Committee, under the leadership of Martin Biddle, which carried out 4 major and 20 smaller excavations in the city over the period 1961-72. Sites investigated included the mid to late Saxon cathedral, the medieval bishops' palace at Wolvesey, the Norman castle and underlying late Saxon evidence, and late Saxon and medieval houses on the west side of Lower Brook Street (medieval Tanner Street). The Winchester Research Unit, founded in 1968, carried on the work of post-excavation analysis, historical research and publication. The Unit's publications to date include major surveys of the early medieval and medieval city that incorporate the important early documentary evidence surviving for Winchester (Biddle 1976; Keene 1985), the Winchester mint and its output (Biddle 2012) and the extensive collections of small finds recovered from the Unit's excavations (Biddle 1990). Interim reports of the excavations appeared in the *Antiquaries Journal* between 1964 and 1975 but the final reports have not yet been published.

A campaign of excavation targeting sites on the defences and in the suburbs was subsequently undertaken under the auspices of Winchester Museums; publication of the results is currently underway (Rees *et al*. 2008; Serjeantson and Rees 2009). Large-scale excavations were also conducted by the Museums Service in advance of the construction of the Brooks Shopping Centre in the heart of the historic city (Scobie *et al*. 1991). Excavations in advance of development in the north-west corner of the historic city, undertaken by Oxford Archaeology, have recently been published (Ford and Teague 2011). Here, a programme of scientific dating suggested that the late Saxon street seen in the excavations had been established in the period 840-880. This was soon followed by the establishment of occupation along the street frontage, and there was substantial evidence for craftworking including dyeing, metal

working and bone working (ibid. 189-90; Plate 13.14). The *burh* at Winchester is understood to have been established as a response to the Viking threat in the late 9th century, and was protected by the reinstatement of its Roman walls. Biddle and Hill (1971) proposed that a grid of surfaced streets formed part of the initial plan of the *burh*, and that it had been designed from the outset to function as a defended town. The south-east area of the city contained the ecclesiastical enclave of the Old, New and Nunnaminsters, along with the late Saxon royal palace, which has yet to be securely located by excavation. Parts of the town were densely built up by the early 11th century, and the evidence from the Oxford Archaeology excavations (and the still unpublished Staple Gardens cemetery) suggests that this may have begun in the north-west quarter of the town more than a century earlier (Ford and Teague 2011). It is possible that this could represent relocation of some of the functions of *Hamwic* to the safer environment of the walled city.

Plate 13.14 Bone spoon from Winchester, Hampshire, *copyright OA*

Winchester has evidence for pre-Conquest urban churches, for domestic housing and for craftworking, as well as abundant evidence for material culture, diet and lifestyle. It is to be hoped that the eventual full publication of Winchester's key sites will make more widely available a very substantial resource for the future study of late Saxon urbanism. At the time of writing, Tom Beaumont James's *English Heritage Book of Winchester* (2007) provides an accessible overview of the city's archaeology and history. Work is also underway once more to finalise and publish the city's Urban Archaeological Assessment, and Historic Towns Atlas.

Hinton (2007) notes that the *burh* of Twynham (now Christchurch) was, like Southampton, a small one. It used to be assumed that it was chosen solely because of the minster, but the Bargates excavation shows that the river-mouth was attracting attention earlier than the foundation of the church. Excavation within the town has traced the defences, but has also shown that it was slow to develop; the market may have come at the time of the defences, and the gate leading out from it could perhaps be late Anglo-Saxon, but pottery, coins and other data do not demonstrate significant urban life.

Domesday Book records markets at three other places, and the clusters of sites around Andover and Basingstoke suggest that those were places where local and regional trading was likely to have happened well before the end of the 11th century.

At Portchester, a distinct break in the sequence was identifiable at around the time (904) that the site is recorded as passing into the king's hands. The earlier buildings went out of use and the site was used for the tipping of large quantities of food refuse, particularly animal bone, oysters and shellfish. Barry Cunliffe suggests this could be associated with the recorded Burghal Hidage fortification of Portchester in the early 10th century (1976, 303).

Elsewhere, work at Romsey has identified elements of late Saxon occupation around the abbey (Scott 2001, 155-7). It is suggested that the three main streets of the historic town, which meet at the market place outside the abbey gate, may have been in existence at this time. The remains of three late Saxon buildings and elements of potential property boundary ditches have been identified in excavations. The evidence suggests that at this stage the growing settlement comprised a series of relatively wide plots laid out alongside the roads, and within them the buildings were well spaced out and not aligned on the street frontage.

The built environment

Buildings associated with rural settlement in the region are generally considered to consist of either timber 'halls' or sunken-featured buildings. However, in the light of current research and evolving views about the nature of mid Saxon settlement in the region (see above), we need to look more closely for evidence of ephemeral types of buildings that may not conform to traditional expectations. In this context, the evidence from late Saxon towns for buildings with cob and post-and-mud walls (see below) may be particularly relevant, if we assume that early town buildings are likely to have followed rural practice.

The impressive range of well-preserved timber 'halls' from Church Down, Chalton and Cowdery's Down made a substantial contribution to the study of Saxon building techniques (Addyman and Leigh 1972; Millett 1983). A range of well-preserved buildings were also recorded and considered in detail at Faccombe Netherton (Fairbrother 1990). The buildings from these sites still remain among the key examples cited by Hamerow in her recent updated survey of building techniques (2012, 17-66). Elsewhere in the region, however, buildings are rarely well-preserved. Among the few exceptions are the mid Saxon buildings from Yarnton, the mid and late Saxon buildings at Portchester and the late Saxon buildings at Bicester, which display both post-in-posthole and post-in-trench techniques. The apparent simple functionality of buildings constructed with posts in individual postholes may belie a much more elaborate superstructure; at Eynsham, for example, part of a collapsed wall from a 10th-century post-built hall had survived in the fill of a pit. Here it was apparent that the wall had been constructed of vertical timber studs alternating with panels of plaster set on wattle frames (Blair and Hamerow 2003).

Few excavations have revealed much of the internal features of 'halls', although evidence for partitions, hearths and internal posts and slots possibly from benches sometimes survives. It is very likely that some buildings had upper storeys, and internal post settings are sometimes interpreted as supporting a loft. The poor survival of internal features in these buildings makes their function difficult to interpret, and this is usually compounded by a general lack of associated finds and environmental remains. However, some evidence for a greater diversity of building types is gradually emerging, and the appearance of more specialised buildings is generally seen as a mid to late Saxon development. Within the present study region, buildings at Yarnton were interpreted as a granary and a fowlhouse, and a granary was identified at Pennyland; a building containing an oven built with re-used Roman tile at Portchester may have been a kitchen or bakehouse, and latrines were identified at Eynsham and Faccombe Netherton. Evidence for very large outdoor hearths from mid Saxon Eynsham implies that cooking was also undertaken in the open air.

The region in general has not featured greatly in the typological and functional study of SFBs. Considerable numbers have been excavated at the settlement sites noted in the preceding section of this chapter, the largest sample coming from Radley Barrow Hills, and largely replicate what has been observed elsewhere (Hamerow 2012; Tipper 2004). Although SFBs seem to become less common over time, the evidence from Yarnton shows that they continued to be used through the mid Saxon period, and one, dated by radiocarbon, could have been backfilled as late as the late 9th century (Hey

2004, 65). Although two-post SFBs predominate in the regional sample, other types of construction are known and the region has good examples of a range of more unusual SFB features. At Oxford Science Park, Littlemore, for example, three fully excavated SFBs had no evidence for postholes, and five had stakeholes in the base, with at least 146 counted in SFB1, and a marked concentration of stakeholes around the edges of SFB9 (Moore 2001a, 168-176). Convincing evidence for stakeholes in the base of SFBs occurs at many sites in the region, including Yarnton, Radley Barrow Hills, Micheldever Northbrook, and Basingstoke Riverdene. SFB1 at Littlemore and SFB28 at Radley Barrow Hills are described as containing centrally placed hearths, and central deposits of ash and charcoal were found in SFB38 at Didcot (Boyle *et al.* 1995) and SFB21 at Yarnton Worton. Several sites in the region have examples of repair and replacement of structures in the same position, and at Barrow Hills it was estimated that around 50% of the SFBs were refurbished or replaced in or near the same location (Chambers and McAdam 2007, 80-81).

There is currently little certain evidence for the use of stone in secular buildings, and in most cases it seems to be associated with high-status and urban sites. At Faccombe Netherton, flint was used for the lower walls of a structure interpreted as private apartments, datable to the late 9th or early 10th century (Fairbrother 1990), and the presence of a stone building at Old Windsor in the 8th and early 9th century, possibly with a tiled roof and glazed windows, was inferred from a deposit of rubble (see above). A stone building associated with gold working dating from the later mid Saxon period underlay the nave of the later St Mary's Church in Lower Brook Street, Winchester, and it has been suggested that this may have formed part of a high status settlement in the area (see Biddle 1975b, 305-10). Mid Saxon buildings using possible limestone sills for cob walls were found in excavations at Beech House Hotel, Dorchester (Rowley and Brown 1981, 13); a coin of Burgred of Mercia (852-74) was recovered from the wall of the latest of these buildings. At Portchester, a structure interpreted as a possible stone or stone-founded tower was constructed at the beginning of the 11th century (Cunliffe 1976). Surviving stonework in the region's churches is considered below.

The buildings found at *Hamwic* were essentially in the same style as those on rural settlements (Morton 1992, 42). They were rectangular, were constructed of timber with wattle and daub infill, and had either thatched or shingle roofs, earth floors possibly strewn with straw, bracken and reeds, and often centrally placed hearths (Birbeck 2005, 199). The evidence from Six Dials suggests that, at least in the more densely occupied parts of *Hamwic*, the buildings were set quite close together within plots aligned along the streets.

Excavations in the region usually recover an incomplete record of late Saxon urban buildings, which have often suffered considerable truncation from intensive later activity, and are only partially revealed in

small town-centre excavations. There is very little evidence for the form of 10th-century buildings in Oxford, although it is likely that these were essentially of the same form as rural post-built 'halls', and some may have been constructed with cob or post-and-mud walls (Dodd 2003, 35-41). The appearance of cellar pits in the town in the early 11th century may be a sign of increasing pressure on central space, and numerous examples have been excavated. Oxford also provides evidence for the development of a distinctive form of urban plot in the early 11th century, with small street frontage structures interpreted as stalls, larger workshop buildings behind, and the largest buildings, with cellared storage, at the rear (ibid.). The late 9th- and early 10th-century buildings identified in recent excavations in the north-west quarter of Winchester were set close to the street frontage, and were constructed on surface-based sill beams, with walls of wattle and daub or cob (Ford and Teague 2011, 194-5). Cellar pits appeared during the late 10th and early 11th century, along with the introduction of structures built with large rectangular-sectioned posts set into the ends of deep elongated pits. This more substantial building technique has been associated with houses of higher rank in 11th- and 12th-century Winchester. However, our understanding of urban buildings in Winchester and elsewhere in the region is currently limited by incomplete publication of many earlier excavations. Oxford, Winchester and Wallingford had defences of stone or stone-facing during the late Saxon period, and Oxford and Winchester had metalled streets.

Ceremony, ritual and religion

Early Anglo-Saxon cemeteries

The early Anglo-Saxon cemeteries of the Upper Thames Valley (covering much of Buckinghamshire, Berkshire and Oxfordshire) were studied by Tania Dickinson (1976). Her distribution plan, updated with more recent discoveries, was published with a table summarising key features and publication references by Booth *et al.* (2007, 418-29). For Hampshire, information has come from a number of different sources, discussed below. Overall across the region the quality and quantity of evidence is variable, and it is unclear whether this is due to uneven archaeological investigation or an uneven presence of sites. Most known sites in (new) Berkshire, for example, were excavated in the 19th and early 20th centuries, and evidence was poorly recorded. In contrast Oxfordshire has been particularly well served by excavations, so that Oxfordshire inhumation cemeteries at Abingdon and Berinsfield (Leeds and Harden 1936; Boyle *et al.* 1995) have a national importance in defining and interpreting early Anglo-Saxon furnished inhumation ritual. Cremations across the region have been less well studied, though both cremation and inhumation were standard rites with cremation the minority ritual; the opportunity for studying cremation and inhumation as concurrent practices by one population has not yet been exploited. At the time of writing, the implications for the region of the recent dating project for Anglo-Saxon grave goods remain to be assessed (Bayliss *et al.* 2013).

Michael Farley comments that the evidence from Buckinghamshire is not extensive; apart from the rich finds from Taplow, the only adequately recorded cemeteries prior to the 1980s were at Dinton, Bishopstone, and Tickford near Newport Pagnell. These early discoveries indicated that Buckinghamshire cemeteries were relatively small and that they largely comprise inhumations. The number of known urned cremation burials from the county is probably in single figures. Lists of known cemeteries were compiled by Jack Head in 1946, and by Michael Farley in 1994 (Hunn *et al.* 1994). Since that time further cemeteries and single burials have come to light (see Farley 2008 for complete list). Most recently a large inhumation cemetery has been discovered near Wolverton (Zeepvat pers. com.). Recent finds slightly redress bias of earlier discoveries, but still leave a substantial gap in the Chilterns and south. Here, a single isolated 7th-century female burial with an amethyst pendant and a silver ring was found during the Eton Rowing Course excavations near Boveney; her grave was some 80m from two prehistoric barrows, but apparently isolated from any other Saxon activity (Foreman *et al.* 2002, 28-34).

Of the recent discoveries, three have been relatively extensive by Buckinghamshire standards: Dinton near Aylesbury (Hunn *et al.* 1994), Westbury, Shenley (Ivens 1995) and Drayton Beauchamp (Masefield 2006). Dinton was a mixed inhumation cemetery of 20 graves, 16 of which had grave goods, and probably dated from the late 5th to 6th centuries. The excavation was on the periphery of an 18th-century discovery. It appeared to have a two-family centred grouping and its location may have been related to a pre-existing field boundary. At Westbury (Ivens *et al.* 1995) a small aligned cemetery of 7 inhumations was discovered, 3 having grave goods; the most striking burial was prone and accompanied by a gold pendant. At Drayton Beauchamp an 18-grave inhumation cemetery (several furnished), was recently discovered during road construction; it included a female grave with jewellery. All modern cemetery investigations include an appraisal of the age and sex of those buried, and the more recent reports consider pathologies.

These recent discoveries have all come from flat cemeteries with no indication of surmounting barrows. Apart from Taplow, only one barrow, the Cop at Bledlow, has been considered to be a Saxon, rather than an earlier, barrow, and that only following a re-interpretation of the evidence. However, there are a number of *low* names in the county, some of which are recorded in a note on Buckslow (?an eponymous name) near Buckingham; many of these may record the sites of levelled barrows. There are also the well-studied 'heathen burial' references in charters, one of which at Ashendon, where there has also been a brooch find, may

indeed record a 'pagan' grave. Two finds of hanging bowl escutcheons, from Oving and Brill, may hint at the presence of other graves of status in mid-Buckinghamshire.

The largest numbers of known early Saxon cemeteries in the region are within modern Oxfordshire (Booth *et al.* 2007, 419), although as elsewhere many sites were discovered during the 19th or early 20th century and are essentially only known from the grave goods retained in museum collections. Large cemeteries (for the region) containing in excess of 100 burials are known from Abingdon, Berinsfield, Long Wittenham and Standlake Down, and cemeteries with around 70 known burials, or more, were discovered at Brighthampton, Lockinge and Wheatley. Some 54 burials were excavated from a cemetery at Watchfield. Although the distribution of Oxfordshire cemeteries has a strong bias towards the Thames gravels and particularly the area between Abingdon and Dorchester, known sites spread far up the Cherwell Valley and onto the Berkshire Downs. Most of the sites have been dated on the basis of grave goods, including many studied by Dickinson in museum collections. On this basis the cemeteries are broadly divided between those of the 5th to 6th centuries, and those of the 7th century, this latter group showing a marked expansion along the valleys of the Windrush and Evenlode into West Oxfordshire.

Two cemeteries in the county show clear evidence for continuing use of late Roman burial grounds well into the 5th century. At Frilford (see Fig. 9.1 for location) one cemetery contained both late Roman and up to 28 early Saxon burials (see Booth *et al.* 2007, 168), while recent excavations 3km away at Tubney Wood have identified a small cemetery where unaccompanied burials of Romano-British type have been radiocarbon dated to the 5th to early 6th century (Simmonds *et al.* 2011). Recent radiocarbon dating of burials from Shakenoak Villa, North Leigh (see Fig. 11.1) has also demonstrated the presence of burials of this date (ibid.), while radiocarbon dating of skeletons from the Berinsfield cemetery has identified at least one individual who is likely to have been buried before AD 466 (Hills and O'Connell 2009). Systematic radiocarbon dating of skeletons from late Roman and suspected early Saxon burial sites is clearly called for in future, and has the potential to challenge many current assumptions.

The 5th- and 6th-century cemeteries in the county show the same range of burial practice as is found elsewhere in the country; weapons are found with between a half and two thirds of male burials, and characteristic round saucer and disc brooches and amber beads with female burials. Booth *et al.* 2007 figs 4.25 and 4.26 show a range of typical grave goods for the region. The brooch styles are considered to have predominantly 'Saxon' affinities, and small-long and square-headed brooches are only present in relatively small numbers.

While cremation appears to have been less common than inhumation, significant numbers of cremations are known from some cemeteries, most strikingly from Abingdon where 99 cremations were identified alongside 128 inhumations, Long Wittenham (more than 51 cremations with 196 excavated inhumations), 13 cremations at Frilford, and more than 12 alongside 67+ inhumations at Brighthampton (ibid., 420-27). The Oxfordshire evidence suggests that there was a marked shift in burial grounds during the 7th century, although the scarcity of datable grave goods in the early 7th century, and the paucity of associated radiocarbon dates, makes it difficult to be more precise about the date at which these changes took place. The county contains good examples of the re-use of Bronze Age barrows for new cemeteries in the 7th century (notably at Standlake and Stanton Harcourt), the appearance of small new possible 'family' burial grounds (as at Didcot Power Station) and of high status 'princely' burials in individual barrows (as at Asthall) (see also Booth et al. 2007, 185-93).

Steve Clark has reviewed the evidence from modern Berkshire, where the majority of known early Saxon burial sites consist of single burials or small groups, many of which were investigated before the advent of modern excavations and recording standards. Of the 35 Anglo-Saxon burial sites on the Sites and Monuments Records for Berkshire 16 were first investigated in the 19th century or before, whilst another eight were excavated before 1945. Three of the most significant, and possibly earliest, Anglo-Saxon burial sites are among those excavated long ago. The East Shefford cemetery (north of Wickham) consisted of at least 71 graves and may have been in use from as early as the 5th century until the late 6th century. The first excavations covering the bulk of the cemetery were not properly recorded, and the site suffered from looting according to Harold Peake, who excavated 27 remaining undisturbed graves in 1912. Pottery found with these burials suggested a Frankish influence at the site (Peake 1931, 129-30). Although the cemetery appears to have been dominated by inhumations, one or possibly two funerary urns may also be attributable to the site.

The early burial evidence from Reading now mainly consists of the mixed cemetery from the Broken Bow/Dreadnought site near Earley, discovered (as at East Shefford) in the course of railway works. The site contained 5 inhumations and 9 cremations and was attributed by its excavator to the 'late pagan' period (Stevens 1894), although one of the burials is thought to display 'sub-Roman' characteristics (Lobb and Rose 1996, 92). Further down the Thames a confused set of records suggests a number of early burials at Aston Remenham, although Dickinson dates the site to the 6th century. It is possible that three or more burials have been found, one accompanied by many weapons. There are other potentially early – but poorly recorded – burial sites in the Reading area (for example at Pangbourne, Purley and the Oxford Road, Reading) and in the Lambourn Valley (a single inhumation between Eastbury and East Garston, and a possible site in the valley brought to light by metal-detector finds). A cremation of possible late 5th-century date was found at Beenham in 1992 (although the SMR also lists it as Bronze Age).

The expansion of Anglo-Saxon settlement is probably reflected in the wider distribution of 'pagan' burials and cemeteries, which in the main most likely date to the 6th century onwards. The only other large furnished cemetery found to date in new Berkshire is the final phase (probably 7th century) site at Field Farm, Burghfield, south of the Kennet and Reading, consisting of at least 50 inhumations in and around a Bronze Age barrow. Although this is the only large cemetery recorded to modern standards the acid soil conditions mean that skeletal remains survived in only a couple of the graves (Butterworth and Lobb 1992). The Field Farm site is perhaps a rare example of a pre-churchyard burial ground where we can also identify the likely contemporary settlement site, in this case Wickhams Field, although this is only evidenced by two wells and a number of pits (Crockett 1996). The burial at Lowbury Hill represents the best example in Berkshire of the high status barrow burials of the period (see Booth et al. 2007, 390 for a summary); a second barrow burial at Cock Marsh, Cookham is less well understood.

A map and gazetteer of early Anglo-Saxon sites in Hampshire, including the Isle of Wight, was prepared by Sonia Hawkes to accompany the publication of the cemetery at Worthy Park, Kingsworthy, north of Winchester, and was published posthumously (2003, 201-7, figs 1.1 and 1.2). This listed sites of more and less well preserved cemeteries and numerous finds of burials and probable grave goods. More recent developments, including publications of older sites, were reviewed by Russel (2002), and by Stoodley (2006). David Hinton discusses the evidence in some detail in the Hampshire county survey for this assessment (2007), where he considers its implications for our understanding of late Roman to early Saxon continuity, cultural affiliations and social status. Hampshire has a number of cemeteries that have contributed important data for the study of the period, and David Hinton draws attention to the evidence for change in burial practice from the 5th/6th centuries into the Final Phase cemeteries of the 7th to 8th centuries, seen, for example, in the two Winnall cemeteries near Winchester, and the Portway East and West cemeteries at Andover. Significant sites include those associated with *Hamwic* (Birbeck 2005; Cherryson 2010), and a notable group in the vicinity of Winchester. The latter include Winnall I and II (Meaney and Hawkes 1970), Worthy Park, Kingsworthy (Hawkes 2003), Itchen Abbas, a poorly understood mixed cremation /inhumation cemetery 1.5km east of Worthy Park, and the recently discovered site at Twyford south of Winchester, where 18 burials have been excavated from a much larger cemetery (Dinwiddy 2011).

The re-use of prehistoric barrows and other earthworks for Saxon burials is evident at numerous sites in the county, including Bevis's Grave at Bedhampton on the Portsdown Ridge and Oliver's Battery, Winchester. Elsewhere in the county, notable cemeteries, often with substantial numbers of both inhumations and cremations, are known at Alton, Mount Pleasant (Evison 1988), Andover, Portway East (Cook and Dacre 1985) and Portway West (7th- to early 8th-century; Stoodley 2006), Christchurch Bargates (Jarvis 1983), Horndean Snell's Corner (Knocker 1956). Also in this group are sites such as Micheldever and Meonstoke, where evidence suggests cemeteries have been considerably disturbed (see above). The cemetery at Breamore, discovered as a result of metal-detecting, appears to have had an unusual number of weapon burials, and an absence of cremations. David Hinton comments that it is also unusual in being located on the valley floor by the River Avon, which invites comparison with the cemetery at Christchurch Bargates, which also had more weapons than usual, and was located at the mouth of the river. These two cemeteries appear different from those elsewhere in the county.

For the Isle of Wight, Hawkes noted 13 sites, of which the most significant is the large mixed cremation and inhumation cemetery at Chessel Down, which contained some exceptional grave goods (see also Waller 2006). The cemetery evidence from the Isle of Wight was previously reviewed in detail by Arnold (1982).

The region contains a number of sites that provide good evidence for burial practice in the mid to late Saxon period. Burials have been found apparently in isolation, in small numbers at settlement sites, in larger numbers in open 'field' cemeteries that may have been under church control, and in graveyards at minster sites themselves. The evidence from the Thames Valley was reviewed by Booth *et al.* (2007, 263-73). Elsewhere, around 100 burials were excavated from a large cemetery in Milton Keynes Village (Parkhouse *et al.* 1996). Two burials here were radiocarbon dated to the 10th to 11th centuries, but seven sherds of Ipswich ware and one of Maxey ware were also found and the excavators suggest the cemetery may have been in use from the mid Saxon period into the post-Conquest period. The cemetery lies some 200m from the church of All Saints, and the excavators suggest there could have been an earlier church on the cemetery site, preserved in the place name Chapel Yard.

In a recent study of burials from *Hamwic*, Cherryson (2010) notes 8 unfurnished burials of the late 8th century from St Mary's Stadium (II), possibly a small family burial ground, and at least 19 individuals from a late 9th-century burial ground at Six Dials, which she suggests may have been under church control. At Marine Parade (SOU13), some 80 burials of men, women and children were found north and south of a double-celled timber church; radiocarbon dates suggest the church and its cemetery were in use from the 8th century into the 9th century. With the minster church of St Mary's located only some 300m to the south-west, it is likely that this site was under the minster's control, and Cherryson suggests that its eventual disuse might reflect increased access for ordinary people to St Mary's itself. The evidence invites comparison with, for example, the crowded cemetery of hundreds of late Saxon burials excavated at Staple Gardens, Winchester (S Teague pers. comm.), or the late Saxon burials found beneath St Aldate's Church in Oxford (Tyler 2001). The evidence for churchyard burials is reviewed below.

Pre-Christian ritual sites

The identification of pre-Christian ritual sites is problematic in the present study area, as elsewhere. There may be little if any surviving evidence of sacred springs, groves, trees and mounds, and the pagan shrines referred to in contemporary written accounts have proved elusive archaeologically. Possible examples have been suggested in the study area at New Wintles Farm near Eynsham and Cowdery's Down (Blair 1995), and more recently at Black Bourton, Oxfordshire (Gilbert 2008). Excavations at Weedon Hill, Buckinghamshire, a site with a 'weoh' (temple/shrine) place-name element, have not produced any evidence (Farley 2008). 'Special' or 'placed' deposits are increasingly being suggested at settlement sites (for a recent discussion of the evidence, see Hamerow 2012, 130-40). These are most commonly whole or partial animal burials, with cattle skulls particularly strongly represented. Unusual human burials from the early Saxon settlement at Sutton Courtenay are noted by Hamerow (2012, 133), and a young adult found in a pit at Oxford Science Park Littlemore may have been buried in a crouched position or simply thrown in (Moore 2001a, 176).

Other notable deposits in the region include a dog burial from the base of SFB118 at Audlett Drive, Abingdon (Keevill 1992), while at Yarnton an uncooked goose had been deposited intact in the top of a pit, and the skulls and jaws of cattle and horses had been deposited in SFBs (see Booth *et al.* 2007, fig. 5.24). A semi-complete and deliberately perforated jar had been placed on the base of an SFB at Brooklands, Milton Keynes, which also contained piglets and ten pike heads (OA forthcoming). David Hinton (2007) notes further evidence from Cowdery's Down, where a complete cow had been buried in a pit that showed evidence for distinct and deliberately placed layers in it, with part of a pig's jaw near the base. He also notes Stoodley's identification of a possible shrine at the cemetery of Portway East, and reminds us that the objects people carried and wore, and their decorative motifs, should also be seen as evidence for their beliefs.

More attention has also been paid in recent years to the possibility that weapons found in the River Thames might represent votive offerings, rather than simply casual losses. Substantial numbers of swords, seaxes and spearheads have been recovered from the river, and a review of the evidence was published by Booth *et al.* (2007, 231-4). So far, similar concentrations of weapons have not been found in other rivers in the region, although a 6th-century spearhead found in a minor channel of the River Windrush close to a Roman ford may fall into this category (Allen and Robinson 1979; Allen pers. comm.).

Churches, minsters and parishes

The conversion of the Anglo-Saxons to Christianity saw the re-adoption of disused Roman towns in the region as the seats of West Saxon bishops, firstly at Dorchester on Thames, around 635, and secondly at Winchester, which became the seat of the West Saxon bishop around 660. The Old Minster at Winchester is discussed further below. The mid Saxon bishopric at Dorchester was short-lived, and the area was subsequently absorbed into the Mercian sees of Lichfield, and then Leicester; the bishopric of Dorchester was re-established in the late 9th century following the Viking occupation of Leicester, surviving until its transfer to Lincoln in 1072. Evidence for Anglo-Saxon occupation in Dorchester and its immediate vicinity has been recovered in a number of excavations. Perhaps the most striking results were from the Beech House Hotel excavations, which uncovered two successive phases of small rectangular buildings on stone foundations, the later phase potentially dated to the middle of the 9th century by a coin of Burgred of Mercia (Rowley and Brown 1981).

In a recent detailed study of Dorchester Abbey, Warwick Rodwell has argued that the most likely location for the mid Saxon cathedral of St Birinus is on the site of the later (and present) abbey church. Given the practice of the time, it is possible that there was more than one building here, but he suggests that the principal structure may have been a relatively small transeptal church like the contemporary Old Minster at Winchester (2009, 26-7). No upstanding remains survive, and excavations to date have found no conclusive evidence of a church from this period. There does, however, appear to be an area of probable surviving late Anglo-Saxon masonry in the north wall of the present church, suggesting the former existence of a large arch leading into a *porticus*. Burials excavated at the site in 2001 include some that are likely to be of Anglo-Saxon date, which would imply a pre-monastic cemetery to the north of the present church (ibid., 29-31).

The establishment of bishoprics was followed in the late 7th and early 8th century by the foundation of minster churches across much of England. No upstanding remains survive for any of these within the region, and their existence has been proposed from a combination of: limited contemporary documentary evidence, dedications and traditions linking them with otherwise obscure local Anglo-Saxon saints, later evidence for unusual importance and residual authority beyond the immediate parish, and topographical factors. In many cases, archaeological research is now beginning to provide solid support, most often from the discovery of mid and late Saxon burials across relatively wide areas, implying the existence of substantial cemeteries. Within the present study area, the Thames Valley was the location of an exceptional number of important minster churches, and these were reviewed by Blair (1996; see also Booth *et al.* (2007, 247-58); for Buckinghamshire see Bailey (2003) and for Hampshire, see Hase (1988)). The fortunes of minster churches varied. A number were

refounded during the Benedictine reform of the 10th to early 11th century, while others appear to have continued to serve their local regions, but at a reduced level, having been deprived of the greater part of their original landed endowments. During the late Saxon period, private estate churches built for thegnly and aristocratic residences, both in the countryside and in towns, are thought to represent the origins of many later parish churches. In most cases in the region the commonest surviving elements are towers, and these are included in Michael Shapland's detailed study of Anglo-Saxon Tower-Nave churches (Shapland 2012); we are very grateful for access to this information in advance of publication. A comprehensive review of the Anglo-Saxon church has been published by John Blair (2005).

Churches were rarely noted in the Buckinghamshire Domesday and Michael Farley comments that only four can be directly inferred, namely Buckingham, Aylesbury, Haddenham and the 'monastery' of North Crawley, although several priests held land elsewhere. The place name Whitchurch leaves little doubt of its origin. Of these the first three could be considered 'minsters', that is founder churches with rights over lesser churches subsequently established in their territories. Of this group only Aylesbury has a little related archaeological information derived from investigations within the town and a watching brief within the church. Dealing with the latter first, Durham (1978) recorded traces of an early nave and a possible later west tower, both preceding the present medieval structure. Michael Farley (1979) plotted past discoveries of burials, which are widely spread across the old town core and support the idea of an extensive minster churchyard. This was later confirmed in excavations at George Street (Allen 1983) with four radiocarbon dates of cal AD 830–920. Subsequently, excavations at the Prebendal demonstrated the existence of a hillfort within which the town had been sited and that its ditch had been re-cut in the Middle Saxon period (Farley 2012). Aylesbury is linked with St Osyth who was allegedly born at nearby Quarrendon. An association between hillforts and churches has been locally noted by Kidd (2004).

Another group that can be added to the list of known pre-Conquest churches in Buckinghamshire are those containing fabric demonstrably of the period. None of them, with the possible exception of Wing, coincides directly with any form of documentary evidence. The church of All Saints, Wing, dating from at least the 9th and possibly from the 8th century, has the most extensive surviving remains. These comprise part of the fabric of the nave and its north and south aisles, together with a polygonal apse over a vaulted crypt at the east end of the chancel, (Plate 13.15). Excavation on an adjacent development site recovered 77 burials from what would appear to be a large Saxon and medieval cemetery contained by a substantial boundary ditch, indicative of a church of some status (Holmes and Chapman 2008). The graves in the excavated area were laid out in closely packed rows; one was radiocarbon dated to the period cal AD 660–890, and two others gave mid to late Saxon

Plate 13.15 The church at Wing, Buckinghamshire, *copyright Buckinghamshire County Council*

radiocarbon dates. The cemetery continued in use into the post-Conquest period. Elsewhere, Taylor (1980–4) also notes Saxon fabric at Hardwick, Iver, Lavendon, and Little Missenden. In addition (post-Taylor) it is reasonably claimed that the demolished St Nicholas, whose churchyard contains the Taplow barrow, is of Saxon origin (Stocker and Went 1995).

For Berkshire and Oxfordshire, probable and possible minster sites are mapped and discussed by John Blair in the historical atlases published for both counties (1998a; 2010a). The evidence for Abingdon is also discussed in the recent edition of the abbey's Anglo-Saxon charters (Kelly 2000). The most extensive archaeological investigations to date have taken place at Eynsham (Hardy *et al.* 2003). Here, evidence was found for high-status occupation in the early 8th century, associated with the establishment of enclosures containing post-built halls. The evidence for continuing, uninterrupted occupation at the site through the 9th century suggests that this can all be linked with the minster that is identifiable from documentary sources at that time. A 10th-century phase of reconstruction of the enclosures and buildings was followed in the early 11th century by the construction of the reformed Benedictine abbey (Plate 13.16). The excavations recovered important evidence that the abbey was built on a formal claustral layout. Elsewhere, work has been carried out at Bampton, where evidence suggests the minster was laid out in relation to Bronze Age barrows and within a large oval enclosure; Bicester and Oxford, where excavations have recovered evidence for mid to late Saxon cemeteries that can be associated with probable minster churches; and at Abingdon, where limited investigations have suggested the form of the late

Saxon Benedictine abbey church (Blair 2002 for Bicester; Booth *et al.* 2007, 248-55; Allen 2011).

The evidence for minsters in Berkshire comes largely from documentary sources which indicate that Bradfield was established by the 670s as a Mercian foundation (Kelly 2000, 3-7) and Cookham was in existence by *c.*750, with a charter of 798 recording a long tussle between the Mercian and West Saxon royal houses for control of the site. Sonning is recorded in 964 as a second seat of the Bishop of Ramsbury, suggesting an important church to go with the large landholdings attached to this estate. Domesday Book provides late evidence for the likely minster status of churches at Aldermaston, Bray, Compton, Bucklebury, Lambourn, Reading, Streatley and Thatcham. Some of these churches may have been in existence from the late 7th, 8th or 9th centuries, but others could be the result of later foundations and reorganisations (Blair 1998a). The majority of these churches retained large medieval parishes, although presumably still much shrunken from their original areas of pastoral responsibility. It also seems likely that the foundation of a minster church was a catalyst that encouraged the emergence of significant settlements at many of these sites, and the concentration of minsters close to the important 'highway' of the Thames was no coincidence (Blair 1996).

Churchyard burials positively dated to the Anglo-Saxon period are rare in Berkshire, and tend to depend on finds such the late 9th-century coin hoard which accompanied a burial in St Mary's churchyard Reading, which has been interpreted as a Viking (and presumably therefore not necessarily Christian) interment (Blair 1998a). A collection of 10th-century coins was found with a skull in Kintbury Churchyard in 1762. Burials in the vicinity of this churchyard have been reported on at least six subsequent occasions, although all without grave goods and therefore not strictly datable (Meaney 1964, 48). Nevertheless the suspicion is that these finds point to a late Anglo-Saxon churchyard, which may have extended beyond the current limits. Despite the lack of written evidence it is possible that Kintbury possessed a church of minster status, given the size of its medieval parish and its status as the centre of a Domesday hundred. An undated burial, suspected to be 'Saxon or earlier', has also been found outside the modern churchyard at Aldermaston, prompting suggestions that either the churchyard has shrunk or it was preceded by a pre-Christian burial ground (Chadwick 1985, 84).

Evidence for late Saxon private churches, and for surviving fabric of this period, is limited in both counties. John Blair has suggested that, rather than simply being an accident of survival, this may reflect a relatively slow development of local churches in the area compared with elsewhere in England (Blair 2005, 421). Excavations at Woodeaton in Oxfordshire revealed the remains of a timber church of the early to mid 11th century underlying the present building, and excavations in Wallingford have revealed a mortar mixer and a long sequence of burials associated with the lost urban church of St Martin (Blair 1998b; Booth *et al.* 2007, 267 and fig.

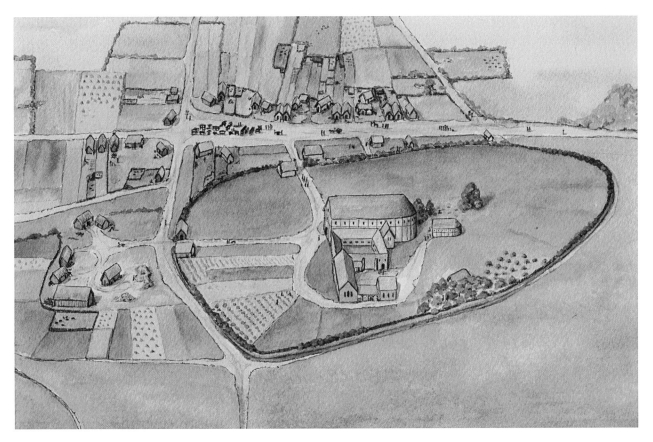

Plate 13.16 Reconstruction of Late Saxon Eynsham, *copyright OA, drawn by Ros Smith*

5.38). The most substantial surviving pre-Conquest remains are those of the tower of St Michael at the Northgate in Oxford, which has been dated by John Blair to the period 1010-1060 on architectural grounds (Dodd 2003). Recent excavations at Oxford Castle have provided further support for the view that the standing St George's Tower may also be of Anglo-Saxon date, and possibly associated with another pre-Conquest gate church (see Plate 1.6). Other pre-Conquest churches in the town are known from documentary references. Outside Oxford the most impressive surviving remains of Saxon church architecture in the county are to be found at St Matthew's, Langford, where the early post-Conquest tower shows a mixture of Norman and Anglo-Saxon features (Shapland 2012, 575-92). The church is also notable for its surviving sculpture, comprising two crucifixion scenes and a sundial. The architectural style of the tower dates it to the period when Aelfsige of Faringdon held the estate, a surviving Anglo-Saxon landowner who was evidently prospering under the Normans. Elsewhere, Saxon fabric survives at Cholsey, Caversfield, North Leigh, Swalcliffe and Waterperry.

New Berkshire has only one clear example of a surviving Anglo-Saxon building, the church tower at St Swithun's, Wickham, which (excepting the uppermost levels) dates from the late 10th or early 11th century (Shapland 2012, 724). The place-name Wickham suggests Anglo-Saxon consciousness of a nearby Roman settlement and the church is situated on a Roman road and re-uses Roman tiles and ballisters in its fabric. Michael Shapland suggests that this was a place that had

long held significance in the local landscape, and the tower may have been constructed at an estate centre of Ealdorman Aelfhere of Mercia (ibid., 728). Claims have been made that various other churches in Berkshire incorporate Anglo-Saxon work in their later fabrics, including Boxford, Bucklebury, Cookham, Speen (said to be '11th century') and Stanford Dingley. At Hurley Priory excavations in the 1930s uncovered stone footings said to be from an Anglo-Saxon church underneath the early Norman priory, in addition to possible Anglo-Saxon work surviving in the nave (Rivers-Moore 1939, 24-25).

The Christian archaeology of Hampshire has been relatively well served. Churches have been excavated in Winchester: the Old and New Minsters (at the time of writing only interim reports are available (Biddle 1970; 1972; 1975a), the west end of the Nunnaminster (Winchester Museums Service 1993, unpaginated) and two lesser urban parish churches in the Brooks, revealing development sequences from the Anglo-Saxon period onwards at St Mary's and St Pancras (Biddle 1975b, 312-21). The Winchester Excavations Committee's investigations of the Old Minster revealed the remarkable development of an elaborate church, now totally lost above ground. In its earliest phase, the minster church was a small cruciform structure built entirely of re-used Roman materials, with a building interpreted as the tower of St Martin to the west (Biddle 1970, 314-321, fig. 13). The growing cult of St Swithun was probably the reason why the space between these buildings, where the saint's grave was located, was subsequently enclosed in an elaborate link building with side apses, itself then enlarged with the addition of an elaborate west-work. Finally, the east end of the church was rebuilt with the addition of an elongated apsidal chancel over a crypt, with lateral apses to north and south. In the interim report, the western and eastern developments of the church are suggested to date from the 970s to the 990s. The south wall of the adjacent New Minster and what appears to have been the south range of its associated cloister were also identified. A third small Winchester church excavated is extra-mural St Maurice (Qualmann 1978).

Romsey Abbey is traditionally considered to have been founded by Edward the Elder in 907. The footings of the late Saxon abbey still survive, beneath Norman rebuilding, and the piecemeal investigation of this important site was drawn together by Scott (1996). Excavations have revealed evidence for timber-built structures and floors beneath the late Saxon abbey, substantial quantities of animal bone that included high-status elements such as bird and deer, and quantities of slag from iron smelting (Scott 2001). It seems likely that this derives from high-status occupation on the site during the mid Saxon period, which may have been a royal estate centre or possibly a minster church (ibid.; Hase 1988). Scott suggests that the iron produced at Romsey may well have been taken to *Hamwic* to be finished and worked into objects (2001, 155). A number of charcoal burials have also been recorded and are likely to be associated with the late Saxon abbey. Geophysical survey at Wherwell hints that the first, late 10th-century phase there included an eastern apse (K. Clark in Roberts 1998, 152).

Some investigations have also taken place in lesser churches. Excavations at Yateley revealed the small nave that was the original Anglo-Saxon element there (Hinton 1983). A similar-sized nave was also excavated at Hatch Warren (Fasham and Keevil 1995, 76-83), while at Little Somborne the nave had been reduced in length at the west end (Webster and Cherry 1976, 182). Yateley was not a parish church in the Middle Ages, but was dependent upon Crondall, where recent work has shown that there too the south aisle arcade was on a mortared flint wall, possibly also part of an Anglo-Saxon structure. Absence of direct dating evidence from such work is typical, as also at Otterbourne, where the footings could as well be Anglo-Saxon as Norman or later (Hinton 2007). The late Saxon period must have been the period when many parish churches and private chapels were built, encroaching on the prerogatives of the 'minsters' (Hase 1988), many probably being timber predecessors of later medieval stone buildings. The stone foundations at Portchester that may have supported a timber tower have been noted above, and the burials around it suggest the bell tower appropriate for a thegn's residence, implying ecclesiastical use, even if as a private chapel not a parish church (Cunliffe 1976, 49-52, 303). Many churches may have started as single-cell structures, with chancels added later, though only St Mary's, Winchester, can be cited, and that may not have

had ecclesiastical use before its enlargement (Biddle 1975b, 313). Unfortunately, the chancel at Yateley was not available for excavation (Hinton 1983).

There are no surviving Anglo-Saxon churches on the Isle of Wight, although two are thought to contain Saxon remains, with a possible 2-cell church within the 12th-century nave at Freshwater, and the possible sundial and north wall of the chancel at St George's Church, Arreton (Waller 2006).

Transport and communications

The fact that none of the country contributors to this resource assessment was able to make much comment on this topic suggests that it remains under-researched in the region. There is little direct archaeological evidence for Anglo-Saxon routeways (although late Saxon street surfaces have been recorded within central Oxford), or for boats or installations associated with the use of the region's rivers and coastal waters for navigation. A number of studies, however, suggest that there is considerable potential for investigating these topics by drawing on a wider range of sources. These include known Roman roads that may have remained partially in use, documentary references to routeways of different kinds, placenames, the distribution of coins, hoards and traded goods, the location of settlements, bridges and fords, and topography. The evidence for Anglo-Saxon Oxfordshire and the Upper Thames has been reviewed by John Blair (1994; 2007; 2010b; for placenames see also Cole 2010) and the topic has also been considered by John Baker and Stuart Brookes, whose recent study of the landscape of civil defence during the Viking Wars incorporates a detailed assessment of placename evidence for routeways, river crossings and landing places in Wessex, with a detailed case study of the Thames Valley (2013).

Evidence for trade routes such as saltways from Droitwich to the Thames survives in documentary references and place names, and a cluster of *sceatta* finds including the Aston Rowant hoard along the scarp slope of the Chilterns suggest the existence of a significant trade route on the line of the reputed Icknield Way. Although doubts have been raised about the reality of the Icknield Way, Michael Farley notes that the name *icenhylte* appears in a late Saxon charter for Risborough, through which it should pass (2008), and Della Hooke notes references to both *ikenilde stret* and the Ridgeway (*hrycwaeg*) in her study of the charter evidence for the late Saxon estates in the Vale of the White Horse (1987, 139, fig. 3). In Hampshire, research has shown that some Roman roads remained partly in use, and David Hinton notes that the obligation to carry out bridgework in the mid and late Saxon period implies road maintenance, even if the king's authority would have been needed to enforce it (2007). He also suggests that the proliferation of horsegear among finds of the late Saxon period shows that riding had spread beyond the ranks of the aristocracy by the 11th century.

Rivers are also thought to have been key to transport and communication, though the extent to which the region's rivers were navigable by boat is not certain. In the absence of direct archaeological evidence for river navigation in the form of wharves and landing places, much must still be inferred from the evidence of settlement and cemetery locations, the distribution of traded goods, placenames and documentary references. The distribution of early Saxon cemeteries in the region shows a marked bias towards river valleys, particularly along the Upper Thames, which has long been proposed as a corridor for the movement of incomers into the interior of the country. However, it is also true that many of the region's cemeteries have been discovered in the course of quarrying on river gravel terraces, and the spread of settlement by other routes may still be significantly underrepresented in the archaeological record. The likelihood that river valleys did play a significant role in early communication systems is reinforced, however, by the marked clustering of important sites around the confluences of the Thames and its tributaries.

The control and exploitation of rivers and estuaries can also be seen in the archaeology of Hampshire. David Hinton has noted the rich finds and profusion of weaponry at the recently excavated cemetery at Breamore, by the River Avon, and the relatively weapon-rich cemetery at Christchurch Bargates, at the Avon estuary. Rich and exotic grave goods were revealed at the 5th- to 6th-century Chessell Down cemetery on the Isle of Wight, and recent metal-detected finds suggest the existence of other cemeteries of comparable wealth elsewhere on the Island (Waller 2006). This is clear evidence for seaborne communications along the Channel in the early Saxon period, thought to have been under the control of the Jutes. David Hinton notes the rare find of a simple log-boat dated to around the year 500, which has been raised from Portsmouth Harbour and may have been used in local coastal trade.

The establishment of *Hamwic* may mark the displacement of the south coast Jutes by the West Saxons, and the continuing seaborne trade evidenced by imports at *Hamwic* itself, on the Isle of Wight, and at Portchester had presumably passed under their control. Continuing use of a long-lived trading site overlooking the natural harbour of Brading Haven into the mid Saxon period is noted by Ruth Waller (2006). Here, two post-built houses formed part of a sequence of Saxon occupation established at the site of an Iron Age hillfort and village, and a Roman harbour. Mid Saxon use of rivers for inland travel and trade is implied by the presence of large assemblages of finds, including imported goods and luxury items such as glass, at the Middle Thames sites at Old Windsor, Wraysbury and Dorney. Much of this material may have been imported via the port at *Lundenwic*. In their review of placename evidence for the Thames Valley, Baker and Brookes (2013, 283-6 and fig. 56) observe that the Upper Thames has abundant placenames referring to river crossings such as fords and bridges, but little evidence for places where boats landed, while below Goring there are only a few places

where the river could be crossed, but placenames associated with landing places for boats are common.

Evidence suggests that substantial river works were carried out in the late Saxon period in order to improve navigability and trade. Several stretches of possible bypass and tributary canals of the 10th to 12th centuries have been recognised on the Upper Thames at Radcot, Bampton and Wallingford, and the 12th-century Chronicle of Abingdon Abbey records that the late Saxon monks constructed a new navigation cut on the Thames (Blair 2007). The Oxford boatmen using Abingdon Abbey's new navigation cut paid their tolls in herrings, presumably brought upriver on return journeys from London. For Hampshire, Christopher Currie has discussed new evidence for the improvement of navigation on the lower Itchen (2007). Trading networks are most clearly visible in the archaeological record in the form of non-local goods and materials such as marine fish and shellfish, architectural stone, querns, millstones, whetstones and pottery. Evidence for these in the region increases significantly in the late Saxon period. The potential of architectural stone as an indicator of regional resource and transport networks was identified by Jope (1956), and the distribution of mid to late Saxon pottery types in the Oxford region was illustrated by Maureen Mellor (1994, fig. 7). Such distributions must reflect the possibilities of the contemporary transport and communication networks, even if they also reflect other factors such as ownership and control of resources and markets. With the enormous increase in data now available from two decades of development-led excavation, an updated review of the quantity and distribution of non-local goods in the region could make a significant contribution to the renewed research interest in transport and communications.

Material culture, crafts, trades and industries

Early Saxon

Our evidence for the material culture of the region during the early Saxon period derives largely from two sources, grave goods in cemeteries and finds from settlement sites. The county reviews also note the increasing contribution of finds reported to the Portable Antiquities Scheme. Grave goods from cemeteries in Buckinghamshire, Berkshire and Oxfordshire were catalogued by Tania Dickinson (1976) and her work remains the most detailed and comprehensive overview of this class of material in the region. The range of objects surviving from graves are broadly typical of those across the country, and, as elsewhere, textiles, leather and wood are underrepresented in the surviving record. Spears and shields, more rarely seaxes and swords, are the characteristic of male graves, with jewellery most characteristic from female graves, usually brooches and beads, quite commonly pins, and rarely rings and bracelets. Belt and strap buckles in copper alloy and iron occur with both male and female graves. Many graves contain knives, suggesting that these were common personal possessions and some graves (almost all female) contain combs and toilet implements (tweezers, picks, scoops, brush holders and scrapers). A symbolic significance for these types of objects, associated with personal appearance, is suggested by their occurrence in miniature form with cremations. Women's graves commonly contain objects that were probably suspended from a belt; these are typically iron or copper

alloy rings, iron rods often interpreted as keys (symbolic or functional), and occasionally bags or purses evidenced by surviving 'bag rings' of ivory or iron, 'strike-a-lights', now generally considered to be purse mounts, and collections of rings and broken objects (often Roman or earlier).

Vessels occur in a number of graves in the region. The commonest type are wooden stave 'buckets' with copper-alloy or iron bindings. Metal vessels of cast or sheet bronze

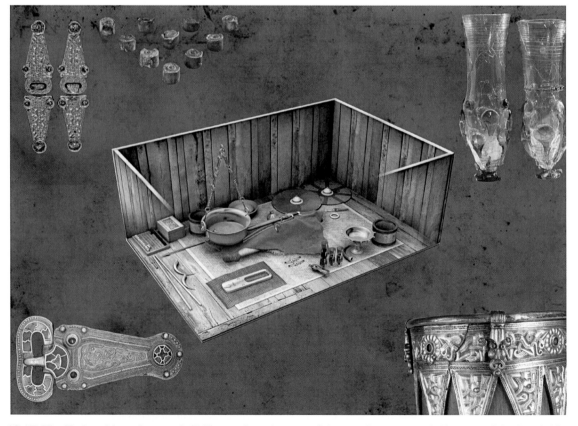

Plate 13.17 The Taplow Mound, *copyright T Allen*, and a selection of the artefacts, *copyright Trustees of the British Museum*

are rarer and their association in the region with high-status male burials suggests that they were prestige items. Glass vessels are even rarer and known from only a few graves. Both plain and decorated pottery urns were used for cremations, and pottery vessels were also occasionally deposited in inhumation graves. Some of the more distinctive objects, particularly brooches and pottery, suggest an early association between the Thames Valley and 'Saxon' continental regions. The grave goods of this region can be contrasted with those of northern and eastern England, traditionally considered 'Anglian', where different brooch styles occur along with wrist-clasps and girdle hangers, both absent here. A few examples of elaborate Kentish-style garnet-inlaid disc brooches occur, though in general grave assemblages in the region are more modest than those found in eastern Kent. The richest surviving burial from this period, and the only one to rival finds at Sutton Hoo, remains the 'princely' burial at Taplow, Buckinghamshire, with its extensive weaponry, feasting equipment, a lyre, gaming pieces, clothing artefacts, gold metalwork, and imported artefacts (Plate 13.17). This and other princely graves from the Upper Thames Valley region are discussed further by Booth et al. (2007).

The material culture of Hampshire cemeteries in the 5th and 6th centuries is superficially similar. Stoodley has noted, however, that women buried in the cemeteries in the north of the county, such as Alton and Andover, wore pairs of brooches pinned at the shoulder, in the style of the Saxon 'peplos' dress, while those in the south of the county, at Droxford and Worthy Park, and possibly on the Isle of Wight, appear to have been wearing a single pin or brooch, indicating a different style of costume. He suggests that the single pin or brooch is comparable with contemporary burials from northern Jutland, and that archaeology may be providing support for Bede's observation that the people of southern Hampshire and the Isle of Wight were part of a Jutish enclave connected with Kent. By contrast, those in the north of the county can be more readily associated with the Saxon culture of the Thames Valley (Birbeck 2005, 190-92).

Pottery is usually recovered at early Saxon settlement sites in the region, although assemblage sizes can vary considerably. In his discussion of the small assemblage from Yarnton (117 sherds), Paul Blinkhorn noted evidence from Pennylands and West Stow that different SFB backfills contained very different quantities of pottery, ranging from none at all to hundreds of sherds (Pottery report in Hey 2004, 271). He suggested these differences could reflect site use and disposal practices, with the implication that the area investigated at Yarnton may have been one where little pottery was used or disposed of. Two of the largest assemblages from the region were studied by Blinkhorn from Radley Barrow Hills (9131 sherds; Chambers and MacAdam 2007) and Eynsham Abbey (6248 sherds; Hardy et al. 2003). The assemblages comprised handmade jars and bowls in quartz-, chaff- and calcareous/limestone-tempered fabrics. Only 3-4% of the pottery was decorated, a proportion consistent with

other assemblages elsewhere, with decoration comprising stamps, bosses and incised patterns.

Pottery aside, the range of other finds from Barrow Hills is typical of the relatively limited surviving material culture of early Saxon settlement sites in the region. The assemblage comprises a few brooches, buckles, toilet items and pins of types also found as grave goods, a rather larger number of combs, parts from a small number of locks and keys, an arrowhead and two ferrules, a few iron tools, nails and knives, parts from a possible snaffle bit, metal bucket fittings, spindlewhorls, loomweights, pin beaters and numerous bone pins or needles (Chambers and MacAdam 2007). More unusual were two objects interpreted as razors. Many of the objects used at the site must have been made of organic materials such as wood, wool and leather, evidence for which is rarely recovered.

How people obtained these possessions remains obscure. Simple bone, wooden, leather and iron objects were presumably made at the settlements themselves, but there is little evidence in the Solent-Thames region to clarify how iron was obtained, or how the women of the region acquired the amber beads that are so characteristic of 6th-century grave assemblages. Rare evidence for the casting of an elaborate bronze brooch was found at the settlement site at Purwell Farm, Cassington (Arthur and Jope 1962-3, 3). Many of the more prestigious objects are likely to have been gifts, and the obligation of leaders to reward their followers with generous gifts in return for service and loyalty is a strong theme in surviving Anglo-Saxon literature. In the absence of a coin economy, we can only assume that some goods would have been obtained in exchange for agricultural produce, through a process of more or less formal barter and marketing. Pottery production is assumed to have been largely local in scale, but some may have been obtained from some distance (Booth et al. 2007, 323-4).

Mid Saxon

Our evidence for material culture over much of the region becomes sparser through the mid Saxon period, as the practice of burial with grave goods declined. A marked change in the types and use of grave goods in the 7th century is evident across the country, and reflected also in the present study area. Not only do the styles of the objects change, but there is increasing evidence for social polarisation, with a smaller number of furnished graves containing richer objects, and a larger number of graves containing little or nothing. Whether this reflects changing access to portable wealth in life as well as changing attitudes to burial of the dead is an important question. The richest cemetery of this period in the Upper Thames Valley, Lechlade Butler's Field, lies just outside the present study area, in Gloucestershire (Boyle et al. 1998; 2011). Nothing on this scale is known elsewhere in the Thames Valley, although 7th- to early 8th-century types of grave goods are recorded from numerous places, with a notable concentration in West Oxfordshire (see Booth et al. 2007, 418-29). The largest known cemetery of this date in the Thames Valley is Standlake Down, discovered in 1825, where up to 100 graves seem to have been present, including at least one identifiable rich female burial with gold pendants and a silvered bronze foil cross (Dickinson 1976 v ii, 202-7).

In Buckinghamshire, a small group of 5 burials from Bottledump Corner, Tattenhoe, Milton Keynes included one with knotted silver wire rings, beads of glass and amethyst and a silver pin probably from a linked pin and chain set (Parkhouse and Smith 1994). In Hampshire, the cemetery known as Winnall II, near Winchester, was one of the early type-sites for the material culture of Final Phase cemeteries. Comparing it with other sites known at the time, Meaney and Hawkes (1970, 45-6) suggested that late cemeteries appeared to be characterised by a high proportion of unfurnished graves and graves with only a simple buckle or knife, a decline in weapon burial and the appearance of new weapon types. There were also new types of object such as wooden caskets and cylindrical sheet-bronze thread boxes with female graves, and new, simpler types of jewellery including silver linked pin and chain sets, plain glass beads on silver wire rings, pendants of gold, silver and garnets, and buckles for narrow belts. The evidence from Hampshire is providing important contextual information about some of the more conspicuous cemeteries of the 7th century, particularly those with an unusual emphasis on weapon burial at *Hamwic* and Bargates (Stoodley in Birbeck 2005; Hinton 2007). Other cemeteries with notable 7th-century grave goods have been reviewed by Hinton (2007) and Stoodley (2006).

The mid Saxon period saw a great expansion in trade and the processing of agricultural surplus into tradeable goods. The minting and use of coins began again, in the form of the *sceatta* coinage, apparently produced in great quantities during the later 7th and early 8th centuries. Over 150 *sceattas* are known from *Hamwic*, some of them probably brought from abroad, and many probably minted at *Hamwic* itself and nearby. It is clear that *sceatta* coins were being brought into the Upper Thames and Thame valleys, where distribution maps show notable concentrations. The region's finds include a number of coin hoards: a 7th-century hoard of nearly one hundred coins and gold and garnet clasps from Crondall in north Hampshire, an 8th-century hoard from Aston Rowant, Oxfordshire, late 9th-century hoards from Pitstone in Buckinghamshire (AD 874-9) and Hook Norton in Oxfordshire, 9th-century hoards associated with a coffin and burial in St Mary's churchyard, Reading, and in Kintbury churchyard, Berkshire.

By the standards of the region, the trading and manufacturing centre at *Hamwic* provides the most substantial insight into material culture at this time. A useful overview of the evidence was published with the Six Dials excavation report and reports on some of the finds have been published (Andrews 1997; Andrews 1988; Hinton 1996; Hunter and Heyworth 1998). Its occupants were engaged in the production of a range of goods that were presumably destined for home consumption as well as export. Even if the scale of production was unusual,

and despite some evidence for gold-working and gilding, the output seems to have been relatively mundane. Textile production was a major activity at *Hamwic*, judging by the common occurrence of spindlewhorls, loomweights and thread pickers at most excavated sites, although it is not clear whether this was a specialised activity in certain households, or a widespread secondary or part-time activity undertaken in many. There is also a strong signature for metalworking, including some technologically accomplished work. Copper alloy products included pins, buckles and fittings for straps and belts, finger rings, hooked tags and brooches, fittings for boxes and chests, tweezers, spoons, rings and loops. Ironwork included technically accomplished knives, a variety of iron tools, wool-comb teeth, building and household ironwork, buckles and strap-ends, bucket handles, bells, a spur and a sword pommel. The main products of *Hamwic* bone and antler workers seem to have been combs and textile tools (spindlewhorls, needles and threadpickers). The preparation of hides and working of leather is evident from structural remains and waste, although direct evidence for leather goods is lacking. The glass assemblage from *Hamwic* suggests that vessels were present in some numbers, but it is considered unlikely that glass was made at the site, and much of the assemblage is likely to represent cullet traded for re-use in beads and jewellery.

The commonest mid Saxon dress items found in the region are pins with biconical, globular and decorated heads, and strap ends; these are, however, found in much smaller quantities than on contemporary sites in eastern England. There are relatively few brooches from this period, but an unusual metal-detected example of an equal-armed bow brooch from Yarnton is exactly paralleled at the Frisian trading settlement at Domburg (Hey 2004, 286-8, plate 15.1 (b)). A fine iron disc overlaid with embossed silver sheets forming a cross with interlace was found at Wraysbury and is of late 7th- or 8th-century date (Astill and Lobb 1989, 90-94). As Christianity spread through the region in the late 7th and early 8th century literacy and the use of books will have spread with it, but evidence for this remains very slight. Despite the rich material culture of monastic sites in eastern England, there were relatively few finds from mid Saxon Eynsham, although these did include two styli, three *sceattas* and eight sherds of Ipswich Ware.

In general, our understanding of trade, processing and manufacturing activities in the mid Saxon period is very limited outside *Hamwic*. Evidence from the Thames Valley was reviewed by Booth *et al.* (2007), but elsewhere the county assessments suggest little has been found. Some evidence that traded goods were moving along the Thames comes from the mid 8th-century trading or marketing site at Dorney (Foreman *et al.* 2002), where finds included Niedermendig lava quernstones, a millstone that may have come from Germany, possibly imported whetstones, and fragments of three glass vessels, found in association with North French and Tating-ware pottery. Tating ware is also reported from Old Windsor. Possible inland marketing sites are increasingly being recognised from concentrations of metal-detected finds. Mid Saxon finds from Froglands Farm to the south-west of Carisbrooke Castle on the Isle of Wight suggest a market at this site, for example; similar possible sites need to be identified to further a research-based programme of excavation (Ulmschneider 2003).

The likelihood that an inland market existed close to the high status complex at Drayton/Sutton Courtenay, where 14 *sceattas* have now been found, has been noted above. The recovery of fragments of gold and gold/copper solder at this site suggests that luxury metalwork may have been produced there for an elite early 7th-century settlement (see above), and there is also evidence for gold-working associated with a possible high-status enclave around the minster at mid Saxon Winchester. Large deposits of iron smelting slag were found at Romsey, and it is suggested that iron was smelted there and supplied to *Hamwic* for finishing and working (see above).

Plain handmade pottery in quartz-, chaff- and limestone-tempered fabrics continued to be used in Oxfordshire into the 8th century and possibly even later, and is indistinguishable from undecorated pottery of the early Saxon period. This has led to considerable difficulties in understanding the chronology of sites of the period (see above); indeed, so little identifiable material of later 8th- and 9th-century date was present at Yarnton and Eynsham Abbey that Paul Blinkhorn has suggested there may have been a complete hiatus in pottery use in western Oxfordshire at this time (Hardy *et al.* 2003, 172-4). Often the only recognisably mid Saxon pottery on sites in the area is Ipswich Ware, which has been found in small quantities at an increasing number of sites in Buckinghamshire, Oxfordshire and Berkshire. At *Hamwic*, some 18% of the total pottery assemblage is made up of imported pottery from northern France and Belgium in fine fabrics made on a fast wheel (J Timby and P Andrews, in Andrews 1997). Of the remainder, Jane Timby notes that organic-tempered wares dominate the local assemblages in the first half of the 8th century, and appear to carry on early Saxon traditions. Around the middle of the 8th century sand-tempered wares become the dominant form, with some chalk-tempered ware also present. From the late 8th century through the first half of the 9th century the composition of the local assemblages changes again, with mixed-grit wares becoming dominant, accompanied by small quantities of shell-tempered and flint-tempered wares. The great majority of vessels were simple cooking pots, and these could have been very locally made, although no kiln sites have yet been identified.

Late Saxon

The production of coin expanded again in the late Saxon period, with mints operating from the growing network of towns. There is evidence for two Hampshire mints, Southampton (until the 1020s) and Winchester; a major study of the Winchester mint has recently been published (Biddle (ed.) 2012). Berkshire had two, one at Wallingford, now in Oxfordshire, and a short-lived one

at Reading that operated during the reign of Edward the Confessor. The mint at Oxford was probably established in the reign of Alfred, and continued in operation throughout the late Saxon period. Mints appear to have operated for brief periods at the three Buckinghamshire towns of Newport Pagnell, Buckingham and Aylesbury.

The most substantial study of material culture of the late Saxon period from the region is the two-volume publication of the Winchester small finds, which considers both the objects themselves, and the way in which they were produced (Biddle 1990). This has since been supplemented for the suburbs and defences (Rees *et al.* 2008), and by the report upon Northgate House/ Discovery Centre (Ford and Teague 2011). At Northgate House/Discovery Centre evidence was found for a variety of crafts, including the working of metals, bone and textiles. Typically, however, this appears to have been small-scale and mixed, and suggests a style of industrial activity not unlike that suggested for *Hamwic* (above), in which households may have made a variety of different products in limited quantities. A large number of potsherds stained with the dye madder were found at the Northgate House/Discovery Centre site, and suggest that households were carrying out small-scale spinning followed by the dyeing of yarn in ordinary cooking pots. A review of the evidence from Oxford includes wooden objects, shoes and other leather items from waterlogged deposits around the Thames channels on the south side of the town (Dodd 2003), and evidence from the Thames Valley as a whole has been considered by Booth *et al.* (2007). As in the mid Saxon period, there is widespread, if small-scale, evidence for tools, products and waste, but little that identifies any substantial production sites, although the smelting of iron from bog ore was noted at late Saxon Wraysbury (Astill and Lobb 1989).

The spread of Viking styles of metalwork across the country in the late Saxon period is signalled by a fine buckle plate of late 9th-century date from Eynsham (Hardy *et al.* 2003, 251-4, plate 9.2). This is associated with the increasing prominence of horsegear in finds assemblages of the time, and notable Upper Thames Valley examples are reviewed by Booth *et al.* (2007, 341-3). Other metal items are rare, but the PAS is bringing more to light, such as the skillet ornamented with a cross from the Isle of Wight (Plate 13.18). This was probably owned by the clergy and used in baptismal rites.

Maureen Mellor's study of the pottery of the Oxford Region remains the primary source for late Saxon ceramic traditions in the Upper Thames Valley (1994). The largest quantities of late Saxon pottery here are from Oxford itself, where three fabric traditions dominated the supply of the utilitarian cooking and storage pots used in the town: a handmade and possibly quite local shelly ware (Mellor's Fabric OXB); St Neot's-type ware (Mellor's Fabric OXR) supplying fine-walled wheel-thrown vessels; and a long-lived oolitic limestone-tempered handmade ware now usually known as Cotswold-type Ware (Mellor's Fabric OXAC). The introduction of decorative tableware in the form of

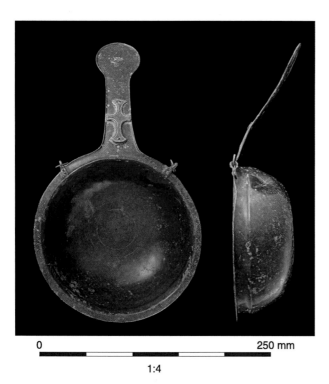

0   250 mm

1:4

Plate 13.18 An Early-Medieval sheet copper alloy skillet of seventh to eighth century date, Isle of Wight (PAS IOW-0D5540), *copyright Frank Basford*

tripod pitchers in quartz-tempered Medieval Oxford Ware (Mellor's Fabric OXY) is probably datable to the Norman period.

Much of the pottery from excavations at Winchester has not been published; the 8,000 odd sherds of late Saxon pottery from the Northgate House/Discovery Centre site is the largest published assemblage, and was analysed by John Cotter (Ford and Teague 2011). Here the pottery was dominated by chalk-tempered coarse-ware traditions. Wheelthrown sandy Michelmersh-type wares were also in use, although much less common, and all these wares may have been produced at the nearby Michelmersh kilns (Mepham and Brown 2007). Winchester ware (MWW), probably introduced *c.* 950, was a high quality wheel-thrown glazed sandy ware that is quite exceptional in the region at this date and was presumably used for decorative tableware, including spouted pitchers. As elsewhere, pottery in late Saxon Winchester seems primarily to have been used for storage jars and cooking pots; the Northgate House/Discovery Centre assemblage also included limited numbers of bowls, cresset lamps and crucibles.

Late Saxon pottery from Southampton was discussed by Duncan Brown (1994), who also studied the pottery assemblage for the recently published French Quarter excavations (Brown and Hardy 2011). Here, the assemblage was dominated by flint-tempered coarse-ware, with much smaller amounts of sandy and organic-tempered sandy wares. The great majority of the assemblage comprised jars/cooking pots, with a few jugs or pitchers, a very few bowls and a single shell lamp. Some regionally imported pottery is represented by Michelmersh-type ware and probable Winchester ware;

Brown comments that the quantities of continental pottery are lower than on other sites, but the usual range of North French types is represented.

Understanding of late Saxon material culture in the region is dominated by assemblages from urban sites. This undoubtedly results in part from the lack of excavated rural settlements of the period in the region, and opportunities are needed to redress this imbalance.

The material culture of late Saxon rural settlements, however, may also have much to tell us about the relationship between town and country, and whether goods were really moving into and out of towns via developing marketing networks. Clearly, the owners of rural estates had access to facilities of their own. At the top of the range, the aristocratic and well-connected late Saxon owners of Faccombe Netherton had a smith working on site, casting gold and copper alloy, gilding with mercury and possibly inlaying with silver (Fairbrother 1990, 62). Ivory carving was carried out at the reformed Benedictine abbey at Eynsham in the early 11th century; two fragments of carved ivory were found, one on walrus ivory and the other on probable elephant ivory. One was clearly unfinished, providing evidence for on-site manufacture (Hardy *et al.* 2003, 267-70). At the other end of the range, a small smithy was present at 10th-century Yarnton; it was probably a small-scale forge used for occasional repairs to estate ironwork, and a number of objects found nearby may have been scrap collected for melting down (Hey 2004, 79).

Pottery seems to have been 'bought in' at all the settlement sites, however. The same fabrics as are evident at Oxford were in use at late Saxon Yarnton, Eynsham and Bicester. The late Saxon pottery assemblages at Manor Farm Drayton, and The Orchard, Brighthampton were smaller, but included the same local types. Unusually the pottery at Drayton also included 6 sherds of Ipswich-Thetford type ware, which is very rare for the region. Also found at the same site was a fine zoomorphic strap-end with silver wire and niello decoration, which is most likely to date from the later 9th century. At Faccombe Netherton the cooking pots were in a range of handmade coarsewares that were presumably obtained from elsewhere, as were the small numbers of identified vessels in Winchester ware and Stamford ware.

Warfare, defences and military installations

There is no doubt that the region in the Anglo-Saxon period was directly involved in the many conflicts of the age. Before we have any written record of the inhabitants of the region, the important finds from Dorchester-on-Thames and Berinsfield (see above) may reflect the presence of Germanic mercenaries and their families brought in to defend the Romano-British town and its community. But for much of the Anglo-Saxon period, at least up to the Viking wars of the 9th century, there is little in the archaeological record that reflects the *Anglo-Saxon Chronicle* accounts of battles and conquests. No excavated settlements of the period show any sign of defences, and no battlefields or battlefield cemeteries have been certainly identified.

A number of linear earthworks in the region have sometimes been tentatively ascribed to the post-Roman, pre-Conquest period, but many of these, including Grim's Bank around Silchester, the North Oxfordshire and South Oxfordshire Grim's Ditch earthworks, and Grim's Dyke running west from the Thames at Streatley are now considered likely to be late Iron Age or Roman in origin (Clark 2007; Booth *et al.* 2007, 369-70). The series of parallel earthworks on Greenham and Crookham Commons are of uncertain date, as are linear earthworks to the west of Reading running south from the Thames (see Clark 2007). For Hampshire, David Hinton also notes the ambiguous evidence for re-use of prehistoric earthworks such as the Devil's Ditch earthwork across the Portway road east of Andover, Bokerley Dyke, which still forms part of the boundary between Dorset and Hampshire, and another Devil's Dyke west of North Tidworth. Unusually for the region, David Hinton notes some scattered evidence for post-Roman re-use of the hillfort of Whitsbury Camp (Ellison and Rahtz 1987). The late Bronze Age/early Iron Age hillfort at Taplow was reoccupied in the early to mid Saxon period, although there is currently only limited evidence for the way in which it was being used; the reoccupation of the hillfort at Aylesbury is likely to date to the mid Saxon period and to be associated with the foundation of a minster church there (see above).

The Viking wars and the Anglo-Saxon response are more clearly visible in the archaeological record of the region, which contains important evidence for the study of these events. The establishment of the region's larger *burhs* (later towns) has been discussed above. One of the best examples in the region of a temporary fortification is the *burh* of *Sceaftesige*, assumed on etymological grounds to have been located at Sashes Island, a site in the loop of the Thames adjacent to Cookham (Gelling 1973, 81). A map of the area dated to 1560 shows a bank called the 'warborow' blocking off the river channel closest to the Berkshire bank, which could conceivably have survived from the Anglo-Saxon period (Bootle and Bootle 1990, 10-13). The Danish army overwintered at Reading in 871, and Asser tells us they constructed a fortification between the Thames and Kennet at Reading. Astill (1984, 73) suggests that the most likely site for the camp is the area later occupied by Reading Abbey, with a defensive line running along what was to become the western Abbey Precinct wall as far as the 'Vastern' or 'stronghold'. Two probable Viking burial sites are known in the area, a single individual with a horse and sword found near Reading in 1831, and two men with weapons found at Play Hatch, Sonning in 1966 (Evison 1969).

Following the peace treaty concluded between Alfred and Guthrum, the boundary between English territory and the Danelaw probably ran across the north-eastern corner of Buckinghamshire, and it has been suggested that Newport Pagnell may have been founded as a Danish frontier and trading post (Baines 1986).

Ruth Waller notes that excavations at Carisbrooke Castle on the Isle of Wight have revealed Anglo-Saxon occupation at the site of the Norman fortified stronghold. It has been suggested, given the strategic importance of the site, that timber buildings found within the lower enclosure of the castle may have been part of a late Saxon *burh* (Young 2000). Although Viking raids on the Island are recorded in the *Anglo-Saxon Chronicle* there is no direct archaeological evidence.

Since the completion of the county contributions for this resource assessment, a new study of the evidence for the Viking wars has been published by John Baker and Stuart Brookes (2013), which focuses on southern England and the kingdom of Wessex and contains a detailed discussion of the Thames Valley. Although Baker and Brookes review the evidence for the well-known major fortified sites, their main concern is to understand how these places functioned within their landscape context, and what this can tell us about the strategy and reality of warfare at the time. A detailed case study of the Thames Valley discusses the location of beacons and look-out sites and the way in which they formed integral links in the communication lines from one stronghold to another. Baker and Brookes also argue that we should not see the civil defence network revealed by the Burghal Hidage as 'the result of a single moment of inspiration', but rather as a stage in the evolution of strategic systems, an evolution that had been underway from the 7th century and was to continue through the 10th century and into the second Viking wars of the reign of Aethelred. The range of different types of stronghold evident in the Burghal Hidage, and the way in which some were replaced, and the burghal system was expanded, suggests to Baker and Brookes a system that incorporated old and new resources, which were adapted, augmented or abandoned as circumstances changed.

While the first Viking wars are the most strongly marked in the archaeological record of the region, the renewed conflict of the late 10th and early 11th century is also being recognised, particularly in some very recent work at Oxford. At Oxford Castle, excavations have revealed evidence comparable to that at Cricklade and elsewhere for the heightening and strengthening of the original rampart (Oxford Archaeology 2006a; in prep). Most recently, the skeletons of up to 37 young males have been found buried in the silted-up ditch of a henge just north of the late Saxon town (see Plate 13.2). The results from radiocarbon dating and isotopic and osteological analysis of these individuals suggest that they were most probably a group of professional soldiers, quite possibly a Viking raiding party, who had been executed in the later 10th century (Pollard *et al.* 2012). Contrary to earlier interpretations, the radiocarbon dating does not support identification of the group as victims of the notorious St Brice's Day massacre in 1002.

Legacy

There are few physical remains of the period in the region. The cathedrals, abbeys and minster churches of the Anglo-Saxons were demolished and rebuilt under the Normans. Elsewhere, with a building tradition based largely on timber, very little survives. Only a few examples of Anglo-Saxon architecture remain in the region, most notably the towers of St Michael's and probably St George's at Oxford, the crypt and apse at All Saints Church, Wing, and the towers at St Swithun's Church at Wickham and St Matthew's Church at Langford. Parts of the late Saxon rampart at Wallingford remain upstanding, and sections of the city wall can still be seen above ground at Winchester, some of it thought to survive from the Roman period although nothing is specifically attributed to the Anglo-Saxons. The Saxon rampart and wall are completely lost above ground at Oxford, although a section of the wall and rampart found in excavation has been preserved *in situ* in a display at Oxford Castle. A number of known burial mounds survive, including Taplow and Asthall, and the prehistoric mound used as a meeting place now known as Scutchamer Knob at East Hendred, near Wantage. Finds from excavations form an important resource in the county and city museum services of the region, and exceptional collections are held at Winchester, Southampton, the Ashmolean at Oxford and the British Museum.

The true legacy of the Anglo-Saxon period lies in its enduring impact on language and culture, settlement, landscape organisation and administration. Place names across the region derive in very great part from the way in which the Anglo-Saxons described the landscape around them and the way in which it was used. The names and identities of the county administrative units and dioceses that form the basis of much of our local and church administration today derive from the Anglo-Saxon period. So too does much of the settlement network. Major towns such as Oxford, Winchester, Southampton, Aylesbury and Reading originated in the mid to late Anglo-Saxon period; Buckingham and Wallingford, although much declined today, were also important places at the time, while many of the region's market towns developed from places that were Anglo-Saxon minsters and royal estate centres. Although displaced from its original Anglo-Saxon site, Windsor remains a major royal residence even today. Across the region, much of the rural settlement framework of parishes, villages and hamlets may have its origins in the estates of the late Saxon period, although the dating of village plans cannot yet be carried back this far in the region. The street plans of towns, however, often preserve considerable elements of the late Saxon layout, with the line of defences often clearly legible even when upstanding elements have disappeared; bridges, fords, streets and market places often remain where they were a thousand years ago, and many churches and their accompanying graveyards still occupy their Anglo-Saxon sites.

Chapter 14

The Early Medieval Period: Research Agenda

by Anne Dodd and Sally Crawford with contributions from Michael Allen

14.1 Nature of the evidence

The Solent-Thames area represents a disparate group of counties, covering a range of geographical and geological areas, and with variable links to historically attested administrative and political territories (see Chapter 13). Different counties have traditionally had different levels of significance in wider Anglo-Saxon studies, with Winchester and *Hamwic* perhaps the best known of all sites in the region. In this respect, development-led archaeology has been a useful counterweight over the last twenty years or so to the tendency of academic research to focus on places perceived as particularly important. Even so, coverage remains partial and development is concentrated in the most economically active and urbanised areas. The surveys carried out from the 1970s to the 1990s provide a valuable baseline for understanding some of the less explored and more rural parts of the region, and the increasing interest in landscape archaeology may also contribute to a more even coverage. Much progress has been made in the publication of archaeological reports in the region, but numerous outstandingly important excavations remain unpublished; as a consequence, the development of the research agenda for the region is constrained by our inability to integrate some of its most significant archaeological data.

Regionally, the borders of the Solent-Thames region present particular problems. The Thames represents an exceptional corridor which cannot be fully explored in this study, though the publication of the Thames Through Time volume dealing with the Roman and Early Medieval periods mitigates this issue (Booth *et al.* 2007). The Ouse, by contrast, is split between three separate English Heritage regions. Equally, the extent to which London had an impact on the relevant counties in this region cannot be explored within the Thames Solent boundaries, and the important coastal archaeological resource of Hampshire and the Isle of Wight is cut off from its neighbours to the east and west. There clearly remains much scope for continuing cross-boundary studies. Nevertheless, it is also true for this period, as for others, that the drawing together of what are, geographically and territorially, disparate counties offers interesting research opportunities.

There is a relatively low level of data from the early medieval period, which makes direct comparison with earlier and later periods difficult. The remains of this period may be particularly ephemeral and hard to predict, and the exploration of sites and landscapes of this period should continue to be a high priority when opportunities arise. This should include the gathering of palaeo-environmental and palaeo-economic data to support consideration of the significant inter-regional variation. Palaeo-environmental scientists, archaeologists and documentary historians need to pool information rather than work in isolation, and compare and contrast interpretations derived from proxy palaeo-environmental data, landscape archaeology and documentary sources.

Nevertheless, the drawing together of what are, geographically and territorially, disparate counties offers a number of specific research opportunities, as listed below:

14.1.1   This is an area made up of regions normally kept separate in geographical and regional studies, providing an opportunity to compare data across these regional boundaries.

14.1.2   This is a period that remains relatively under-represented and poorly understood in the archaeological record across much of the region, and remains a high priority for investigation when opportunities arise.

14.1.3   The region offers a good opportunity to compare land-based and water-based transport in the early medieval period.

14.1.4   There are significant differences in the levels of research and data collection across the region, making research in those areas that have been least-well served a high priority for further research.

14.2 Inheritance

The ending of Roman Britain is viewed as a significant break in British history, but the archaeological evidence from this area suggests that the Romano-British way of life did not come to an abrupt halt. Documentary sources offer a picture of aggressive Anglo-Saxon conquest of the area, and several excavated sites in the region are key in elucidating the evidence. The Solent-Thames region has played a significant part in framing our interpretation of the ending of Roman Britain, and here, as elsewhere, continuing exploration of the Roman/Anglo-Saxon interface remains a priority. Issues to be addressed include:

14.2.1   Establishing the identity of the group using the new culture, building on current work on isotope evidence and DNA analyses, and with particular attention to extending studies to include Roman-period skeletons

14.2.2   Establishing if, when and how villa estates ceased to function

14.2.3   The use of environmental evidence to identify possible change from specialised farming to a generalised approach.

14.2.4   The identification of the extent to which there was continuity of use between Romano-British sites and Anglo-Saxon

14.2.5   Identifying and exploring the extent to which Romano-British agricultural practices persisted into the Anglo-Saxon period

14.2.6   Arriving at a better understanding of the relationship – economic, political, social – between incoming Anglo-Saxons and surviving Romano-British communities across the region.

14.2.7   Carrying out detailed comparison of the settlement patterns and of the chronology of change in different activities between the Roman and early Anglo-Saxon periods

14.2.8   A review of existing evidence to identify areas with material culture overlap and areas without, with particular reference to the reasons for the abandonment of Silchester

14.3 Chronology

There are a number of key chronological research questions relating to the early medieval period in the Solent-Thames region in particular. Recent initiatives to carry out systematic radiocarbon dating programmes on burials both nationally and locally will contribute much-needed new insights, but at the time of writing the significance of this work for the regional archaeological resource remains to be assessed. The traditional reliance on pottery for dating is problematic for this period, and the difficulties of identifying mid Saxon sites in particular from artefactual evidence have been highlighted in Chapter 13. The refinement of existing artefact-based chronologies remains a high priority for the region, supported by the systematic use of scientific dating techniques, in order to test and refine existing chronological models. Single radiocarbon dates are much less

useful than sequences of samples that permit the use of Bayesian modelling, and the advice of specialists should be sought on sampling strategies. Areas to priorities include:

14.3.1   The date of earliest Anglo-Saxon settlement and the degree of overlap with Romano-British culture.

14.3.2   The development of better definition of chronologies within Anglo-Saxon cemeteries

14.3.3   Better definition and dating of pottery sequences in the region.

14.3.4   A review of the current radiocarbon dating evidence, particularly from sites radiocarbon dated before the early 1990s.

14.3.5   The identification of mid and late Saxon rural settlement

14.4 Landscape and land use

The region has a wide range of different landscape types, from the heathlands of East Berkshire to the woodlands of the Chilterns, the Berkshire and Hampshire downs, the gravels and riverside meadows of the Thames Valley, and the coastal environments of Hampshire and the Isle of Wight. These supported a range of different activities, associated with contrasts in settlement patterns, and land use will have varied both from place to place, depending on the key resources available, and over time, with evidence for a return to mixed subsistence-level farming in the early Anglo-Saxon period, and increasing intensification and specialisation thereafter.

The region has a number of well-excavated sites with good environmental evidence, but the presence of early medieval economic evidence is highly variable and disparate both across the Thames-Solent corridor and within it, and many studies remain site-specific. Many Saxon rural settlement sites contain relatively few good contexts from which to sample, and these may be biased by the specific nature of activities associated with them, for example sunken-featured buildings. Concerted attempts should be made both to improve the available sample of this type of evidence, and to provide syntheses on a regional or sub-regional basis to inform research aims for the future. It is also clear that much can be learned by incorporating other sources of information such as evidence for field systems, trackways, enclosures and ridge and furrow, place-names, manorial and parish boundaries, charters and the records of estate rights and resources. Where opportunities arise it is clearly of great value to attempt to consider environmental data in this wider landscape context. The link between changing agricultural practice and estate structure in the mid and late Anglo-Saxon period is a particularly important area for enhanced research, and there is currently little known about the chronology and context of the development of open field agriculture in the region.

One key theme to address is agricultural change, in all its forms, after the end of the Romano-British period. Tied in with this is the examination of changing regional specialisation in herds and in crop vs herd proportions. As with other periods, the opportunity to look at regional variation in stock composition and potentially in breeds should be objectives, possibly using isotope analysis (Sykes *et al.* 2006).

The quantity of woodland is recorded in Domesday and was clearly a major managed resource for timber, wattle, browse, pig pannage and orchards. It remained a key resource for timber for construction, the manufacture of artefacts and probably more importantly as fuel for domestic fires and furnaces. Palaeo-environmental evidence (pollen, charcoals etc) should help define the presence and location of such resources.

As in prehistory, colluvium and alluvium may mask early medieval sites and evidence, but can also contain significant evidence of the local and wider land-use via contained palaeo-environmental data. Thus site-based studies of colluvium, alluvium and riversides are integral to studying both early medieval sites and the landscape in which they reside. Economies may exploit ridges and valley bottoms differently, with possibly better pasture developing in the dry valleys upon the lush vegetation of the deeper soils. Changing agricultural practices and the management of rivers and riversides for mills and fish traps, potentially increases and changes colluviation and alluviation patterns. As the site- and activity-specific level of interpretations is often greater in more recent periods, the precise level of site taphonomy and sedimentation is often directly related to those activities. As such, detailed but targeted geo-archaeological description of basic sedimentary sequences (eg ditches and infills) can elucidate, inform and answer questions not readily addressed using basic context records and artefacts assemblages.

Given the frequency of mills and fisheries recorded in Domesday, archaeological evidence of these should be sought (eg by sieving for fish bones). Established ports such as Southampton and Porchester would have had relatively major quays (as at Poole, Dorset), and the opportunity of examining these, and the waterlogged deposits and ecofacts that might be associated, should be seen as a priority. To date no comparable sites have been highlighted on the Isle of Wight. Specific research aims should include:

14.4.1   The collection of more extensive environmental samples to allow detailed analysis of particular sites, and consequently to inform comparisons of environmental data across the region.

14.4.2   Building upon and adding to existing environmental information to identify when and where changes in agriculture and land use took place, for example evidence of

possible woodland regeneration or the introduction of new crop species.

14.4.3   Better understanding of the process of agricultural intensification in the mid to late Saxon period and the origins of open field systems

14.4.4   The significance of environmental data and information from other sources such as place names for understanding the way in which estates were structured in the mid and late Anglo-Saxon period

14.4.5   The use of palaeo-environmental data and enquiry to further the identification of the location and nature of woodland, including the regrowth of more extensive woodlands such as on the slopes of the Chilterns

14.4.6   A review of rural field systems to promote their preservation, particularly in the light of more intense pressure on land from modern agricultural practice.

14.4.7   Geoarchaeological studies to identify activities occurring at particular sites and site types.

14.5 Settlement

The region has a reasonable number of excavated settlement sites, from the early to the late period, and is particularly notable for the range of urban settlements that have been studied within it. Despite an ever-increasing dataset, however, our understanding of how settlements were organised, the way in which they functioned, and their interrelationship with other sites in their contemporary landscape context, remains limited. In this respect, the uneven distribution of archaeological research in the region remains a significant handicap, and opportunities to investigate currently poorly understood areas should be a high priority. The recording and interpretation of settlement sites needs to move beyond the simple cataloguing of relatively well understood building types to consider how evidence for other types of structures, settlement organisation and function might be recovered.

Important examples of increasingly specialised site types over the mid Saxon period have come from this region. The question of changing settlement form at this time should now be pursued in the light of recent reassessments of the nature of this transformation (see Chapter 13), and the possibility of very significant levels of regional variation. In particular, we should be aware that settlements of the mid and late Anglo-Saxon period may not have the clearly visible and diagnostic buildings characteristic of the early Saxon period. Late Saxon rural settlement and agricultural change is particularly poorly understood in the region compared with other parts of the country.

The region has good preservation of late Saxon remains in numerous urban centres, both large and small, which represents a nationally-important resource for the continuing study of the origins and development of towns into the medieval period. As with rural settlement, recent trends in academic thinking in this area are tending to emphasise the complexity of urban development, as the functions of towns diversified and their economic relevance, at least in our region, only slowly increased. The archaeology of small towns remains under-researched in the region and more work is needed to understand how they developed alongside their better-documented and larger contemporaries.

For all settlement types, at all stages in the early medieval period, there is a clear need for better dating information to enable us to understand the chronology and processes of change. As has been noted above, the systematic recovery of samples for programmes of radiocarbon dating using Bayesian modelling should be pursued where opportunities arise, and more work is needed to refine our understanding of the dating of artefacts.

A number of these research priorities can be addressed in part through the enhanced study of environmental remains. Study of waterlogged plant assemblages should be conducted in urban Saxon centres throughout the Solent-Thames region. Even evidence recorded in small interventions, provided site recording is of an adequate standard and environmental assessment and analysis is thorough, has the potential to contribute to wider issues of interpretation. These include better definition of the character and diversity of urban centres, of larger trade markets and of economic networks.

The importance of defining both urban and rural economies is that they are clearly directly interrelated, and studying the detail of town economies cannot be completed without a good comprehension of the rural economies that supply them. With rare exceptions, little use has been made of palaeo-environmental and palaeo-economic data to investigate these questions. Key themes for future research have been identified as follows:

14.5.1   A review of settlement patterns and land use is needed, particularly as regards the apparent concentration of settlement on gravel terraces in the Thames Valley

14.5.2   There is a need for more detailed studies of landscapes at a scale comparable to the Whittlewood research project, and a search for appropriate areas should be undertaken. This would also allow for regional comparisons of settlements.

14.5.3   More work is needed on the dating of settlements, using scientific dating methods where suitable samples are available

14.5.4   More work is needed on the way in which

Anglo-Saxon settlements were organised and functioned

14.5.5   More information on settlement change and village formation in the mid to late Saxon period in particular is required to test existing possible models.

14.5.6   Pollen analysis and environmental analysis needs to be carried out as a routine part of site excavation, to look at changes in diet for example.

14.5.7   The region's archaeological resource is important for the study of urban origins and development, and this should remain a regional priority

14.5.8   Settlement patterns require further study in areas of dispersed settlement such as the Chilterns. There is currently only limited information available about the region's upland areas in general.

14.5.9   More emphasis is needed on comparison of patterns of production and consumption to shed light on the relationships between rural, specialised and urban sites

14.6 Social organisation, economy and subsistence

Anglo-Saxon settlement sites, particularly those without the more readily identifiable sunken-featured buildings, are ephemeral, and settlement morphology, particularly for the middle and later Anglo-Saxon periods, is still under dispute. Problems of identifying sites are exacerbated by lack of dating evidence. Among the avenues of study that require attention are the following:

14.6.1   There is an increasing awareness that so-called 'productive sites' need further study and investigation: our limited knowledge of these is evidence that our current understanding of economy and exchange in the middle Anglo-Saxon period is inadequate. The Thames-Solent area has a significant part to play in understanding middle Anglo-Saxon economy and exchange, through looking at the distribution of sceattas and the centrality of the upper Thames as a magnet. For this we can compare the recent work by John Maddicott on links between Droitwich and London and the rise of the kingdom of Mercia (Maddicott 2005)). The visible patterns of travel and exchange between the Cotswolds and the Thames, and the direct link for continental trade northwards through Hamwic to the Thames

Valley, are important phenomena that need studying.

14.6.2 The distribution of all artefact types needs to be examined in relation to these axes of exchange, in order to determine which (if any) were moved along them, and by what means and mechanisms

14.6.3 In view of the increasingly important role played by cemeteries in identifying population movement, health, and ethnicity, scientific investigation of skeletal material, and in particular dating, stable isotope and DNA investigation, should be prioritised for both previously excavated and new skeletal material.

14.6.4 Investigation should include that of evidence for origins and diet through stable isotope analysis.

14.6.5 Evidence is needed to allow recognition of estate centres (consumption) and specialist production sites, both of which would be expected within a 'multiple estate' model.

14.6.6 Domesday records many watermills. Their date of establishment and, in particular, the number of mid-Saxon examples, needs to be determined.

14.6.7 The possible relationship of these dates to the intensification of agriculture and the establishment of open fields should be considered.

14.6.8 Archaeological evidence for specialised production (eg vineyards recorded in Domesday) should be sought.

14.7 Ceremony, ritual and religion

The Solent-Thames region has been of major importance in the study of burial practice for this period, including the transition to Christian rites. However, the evidence from cremations has not been studied as carefully as that from inhumation graves, and the purpose and meaning of the late Anglo-Saxon charcoal burials remains uncertain. No substantive evidence for pre-Christian ritual sites has been found. This period saw the reintroduction of Christianity and the establishment of minsters and a parochial system. While there has been much work on minsters, few churches have been proved to have a pre-Conquest foundation date and the number of standing structures is limited, although Wing is a splendid example. There are many issues that would benefit from further work:

14.7.1 Recent excavations and better understanding of Anglo-Saxon burial patterns, especially

those associated with the post-Conversion period, means that there is a real need to date known unaccompanied burials, which may well be Anglo-Saxon. It is possible that there are many more excavated unfurnished Anglo-Saxon cemeteries than are currently recognised.

14.7.2 There is a serious research need for a radio-carbon dating project on skeletal material from this region on the lines of Dawn Hadley's dating project for the Northern Danelaw.

The bulk of the region's churches will have had pre-Conquest origins, though this is not reflected either in surviving fabric or in Domesday entries. A co-ordinated framework for identifying opportunities for archaeological work at church sites (groundworks, maintenance, installation of heating etc) is important, so that no opportunity to investigate sites is missed.

14.7.3 Clarification of the demise or survival of late Roman Christianity and paganism into the 5/6th centuries should be sought.

14.7.4 Understanding of the significance and cultural context for the re-use of earlier sites for burial and other ritual activity needs to be improved.

14.7.5 Evidence for Anglo-Saxon pagan religious practice other than in burials eg 'shrines', ritual embedded in daily life (as often suggested for later prehistory) needs to be identified.

14.7.6 The nature of middle-late Saxon religious sites, including better identification and understanding of the characteristics of early minsters and monasteries, requires further work.

14.8 Transport and communications

The location of Anglo-Saxon settlements on or close to the known lines of Roman roads suggests that many, although not all, of these continued to play an important role in transport and communication in the later period. Waterways were also important lines of communication, although not enough is known about this in a cross-channel and coastal context. The extent to which rivers were navigable is also unclear, although evidence for alterations to channels, waterfront activity and structures has been found in a few areas. More work remains to be done for all of these topics, as follows:

14.8.1 There is very little evidence for early medieval activities along the Thames waterfront, though recent open area excavations at

Dorney in Buckinghamshire hint at the possible importance of the waterfront in the Middle Saxon period, away from the main known areas of dense settlement. There is a need to focus on gathering evidence from the Thames waterfront.

14.8.2   Further work is needed on understanding the fate of Roman roads in the early medieval period.

14.8.3   Cross-channel and coastal communications along the south coast require investigation.

14.8.4   Whether the Upper Ouse was navigable prior to the construction of mills along it needs to be determined. This of necessity requires more research on riverine vessels of the Anglo-Saxon period.

14.8.5   If possible the late Saxon road network should be reconstructed.

14.9 Material culture

A number of coin hoards have been found across the region and finds from metal detecting are adding coins and other metal artefacts to the record, particularly for Hampshire and the Isle of Wight. Goods found in inhumation cemeteries have demonstrated that during the early part of the period the population was in general relatively wealthy, with access to luxury imported goods such as Rhineland pottery. The princely burial at Taplow was exceptional, but it is possible that other rich burials may still be found. For the later period the main evidence for material culture comes from excavations of urban sites, particularly Oxford and Winchester where there have been extensive excavations over many years. There is much more than can be learnt about material culture in relation to society and as a possible dating tool. Key avenues of enquiry include:

14.9.1   The systematic classification and dating of artefacts, in particular to help understand Middle Anglo-Saxon patterns of trade, travel and economy.

14.9.2   Rectifying the current uneven implementation of Archaeology Inventory Projects.

14.9.3   Further ceramic studies to identify and understand patterns of variation within the Solent-Thames region.

14.10 The built environment

Understanding of urban development in the region has been based on piecemeal excavations, and there is a need for a proactive approach to urban research. In the same way, a regional understanding of late Anglo-Saxon domestic settlement is lacking. There are precious few examples of excavated late Anglo-Saxon rural houses across the region. These issues can be addressed through:

14.10.1   Reassessment of the current evidence for Anglo-Saxon towns in the region to identify further research priorities.

14.10.2   More research into what late Anglo-Saxon domestic buildings looked like.

14.10.3   The identification of regional variations in domestic buildings.

14.10.4   The prioritisation of evidence for Anglo-Saxon occupation on medieval sites with documented Saxon antecedents. Where such evidence appears to be lacking, the reasons for this also require fuller investigation.

14.11 Warfare, defences and military installations

Important new work on later Anglo-Saxon defences is taking place at Wallingford. The Wallingford project emphasises the previous lack of coherent study of later Anglo-Saxon burhs and their defences. The region has a number of important later Anglo-Saxon defensive structures, in particular the *burh* of Sashes, still presumably preserved under spoil. Research themes include:

14.11.1   Further research on other early medieval defensive structures in the region, following the Wallingford project model.

14.11.2   A review of the linear earthworks in the region.

14.11.3   Further consideration of roads and herepaths from both documentary and archaeological evidence.

14.11.4   The identification of pre-Viking Age defensive sites.

14.11.5   The exploration of the impact of the establishment of burhs on their hinterland, and their possible role as drivers for the re-organisation of estates or intensification of production.

14.11.6   Investigation of undocumented burh-like fortifications (eg Newport Pagnell?).

14.11.7   Detailed recording of evidence for defensive networks of beacons, lookouts, strongpoints etc recognisable around burhs.

14.12 Legacy

The Conquest provides a clearly dated political event to mark the division between the Early and Later Medieval periods, but in terms of settlement, landscape and administration there was no significant change. The majority of settlements and parishes were already in existence by the end of the Anglo-Saxon period, and the large administrative units created survived into the later 20th century. The development of these structures during the Early Medieval period requires more systematic study.

14.12.1 The extent to which the processes of nucleation of villages, formation of open fields, development of a system of local churches began in this period needs more investigation.

14.14.2 A more thorough search is needed for evidence of Anglo-Saxon occupation on `medieval' sites without documented Anglo-Saxon antecedents.

14.13 Specific problems in the region and particularly the Isle of Wight

There are a number of specific problems in this region, relating to publication and the identification and protection of sites, for which a strategy is required. The Isle of Wight remains an under-studied resource, which should be addressed by:

14.13.1 Further study of the status of the Island and its relationship with the South coast in this period.

14.13.2 Investigation of the use of the coastal inlets on the Isle of Wight in comparison with those of the Hampshire coast.

14.13.3 Further investigation of estate links between Hampshire and the Isle of Wight.

Chapter 15

The Later Medieval Period: Resource Assessment

by Julian Munby

(County contributions by Grenville Astill, Vicky Basford, Chris Dyer, Bob Edwards, Julian Munby and Kim Taylor-Moore; palaeoenvironmental contribution by Mike Allen)

Introduction

The overall environmental setting of the region is well understood, and as in previous eras this has been an important factor in determining the possibilities for settlement and land-use. The region comprises a cross-section though the geology of southern England:

A. the Jurassic ridge of the Cotswolds;

B. the Buckinghamshire clay vale leading down into the vale of White Horse;

C. the Chilterns and then the Berkshire Downs;

D. the west end of the London Basin in north Hampshire and east Berkshire

E. the Hampshire downs

F. the Hampshire basin

G. the Isle of Wight.

These major divisions of the region include a varied cross-section of southern land forms:

Downland scarp fronts/wooded backs

Clay vales/gravelled river valleys: champion land

Forested areas on clays/sands

Sandy/clay heaths and wastes

Maritime fringe of drowned harbourlands.

Within this framework there was a large proportion of 'Midland England' parishes of manor or manors coterminous with the parishes, nucleated villages and common field systems. But there were also a great number of distinctive local *pays* – eg Banburyshire, Otmoor, New Forest and the Forests of Bere, Windsor, Wychwood and Whittlewood, and even the relatively compact area of the Isle of Wight has great variety of landscape character.

The area, as with so much of south-east England, can be said to fall within the greater London region, traversed by road and river routes centred on London, and favoured by the annual travels of a peripatetic monarchy based on Windsor. In terms of more local cultural provinces, Oxfordshire Buckinghamshire and Berkshire occupy the western half of Phythian-Adams' *Thames* Province (7), while Hampshire lies at the centre of the *'French' channel* Province (6) – (Phythian-Adams 1993, fig. I).

The nature of the evidence

Within the setting provided by geography, soils and vegetation, the material culture of the medieval period is abundantly represented by extant, ruined, and buried remains of all kinds (see Figure 15.1 for selected key sites), by visual representations in art (glass, painting, sculpture), and by description or indication in large numbers of written sources (charters, surveys, accounts, narratives). There is enormous potential in all these areas for further research and discovery. On the environmental side, by the later medieval period the main research focuses more fully upon the economic aspects such as foodstuffs, and farmed produce. Most attention is traditionally paid to context, feature and site-specific

Table 15.1 Rough quantification of medieval 'structural' elements by county

	Parishes	*Markets*	*Castles*	*Abbeys, etc.*
Berkshire	193	37	17	<40
Buckinghamshire	202	41	25	<30
Hampshire/Isle of Wight	349	61	35	<70
Oxfordshire	280	35	21	<50
Total	1024	174	98	<190

Sources: Lewis, *Topographical Dictionary*, etc,; Letters et al., *Gazetteer of Markets and Fairs in England and Wales to 1516* (L&I Soc. 2003) not in biblio; King, *Castellarium Anglicanum*, OS *Map of Monastic Britain* (visual inspection)

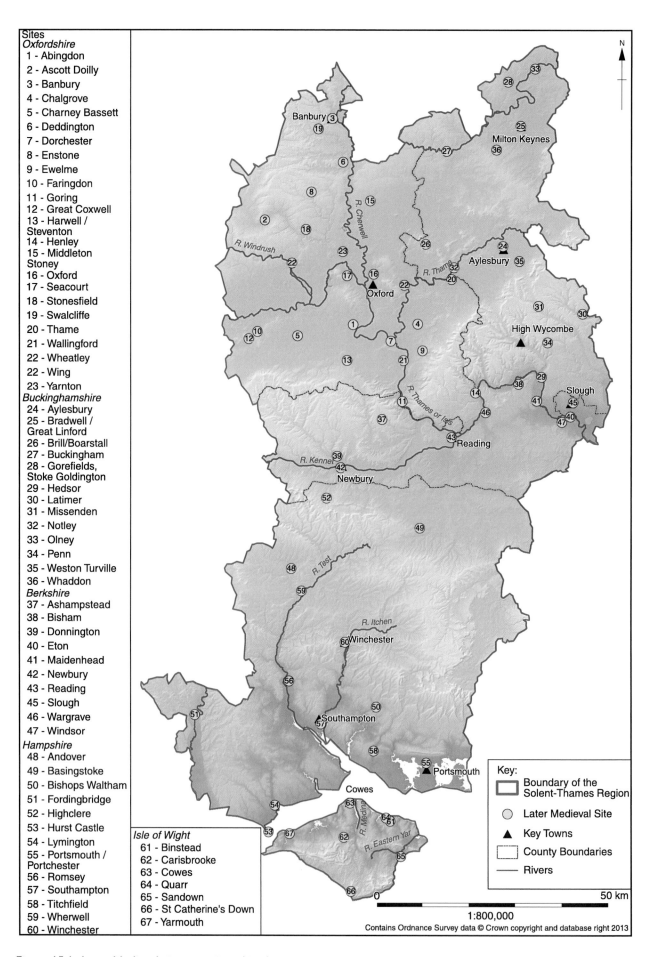

Sites

Oxfordshire
1 - Abingdon
2 - Ascott Doilly
3 - Banbury
4 - Chalgrove
5 - Charney Bassett
6 - Deddington
7 - Dorchester
8 - Enstone
9 - Ewelme
10 - Faringdon
11 - Goring
12 - Great Coxwell
13 - Harwell / Steventon
14 - Henley
15 - Middleton Stoney
16 - Oxford
17 - Seacourt
18 - Stonesfield
19 - Swalcliffe
20 - Thame
21 - Wallingford
22 - Wheatley
22 - Wing
23 - Yarnton
Buckinghamshire
24 - Aylesbury
25 - Bradwell / Great Linford
26 - Brill/Boarstall
27 - Buckingham
28 - Gorefields, Stoke Goldington
29 - Hedsor
30 - Latimer
31 - Missenden
32 - Notley
33 - Olney
34 - Penn
35 - Weston Turville
36 - Whaddon
Berkshire
37 - Ashampstead
38 - Bisham
39 - Donnington
40 - Eton
41 - Maidenhead
42 - Newbury
43 - Reading
45 - Slough
46 - Wargrave
47 - Windsor
Hampshire
48 - Andover
49 - Basingstoke
50 - Bishops Waltham
51 - Fordingbridge
52 - Highclere
53 - Hurst Castle
54 - Lymington
55 - Portsmouth / Portchester
56 - Romsey
57 - Southampton
58 - Titchfield
59 - Wherwell
60 - Winchester

Isle of Wight
61 - Binstead
62 - Carisbrooke
63 - Cowes
64 - Quarr
65 - Sandown
66 - St Catherine's Down
67 - Yarmouth

Key:
Boundary of the Solent-Thames Region
○ Later Medieval Site
▲ Key Towns
County Boundaries
— Rivers

0   50 km
1:800,000
Contains Ordnance Survey data © Crown copyright and database right 2013

Figure 15.1 Later Medieval sites mentioned in the text

activities and events that can be determined via environmental scientific enquiry.

To obtain a rough quantification of the 'structural' aspects of the medieval heritage, the area contains the following (Table 15.1).

The medieval antiquities of these counties have been the object of systematic study since the 17th century, with an increasing body of visual evidence being created in the 18th and 19th centuries. Whereas an interest in ecclesiastical remains was predominant in the 19th century, a growing interest in secular and domestic buildings developed in the 20th. Archaeological excavations on medieval sites began with investigation of monastic sites and later turned to castles and other monuments. There is a considerable body of literature on the study of medieval antiquities from before the mid-20th century, whether glass, heraldry and monumental brasses, or architectural remains.

The development of archaeological excavation for research purposes, and then increasingly for rescuing threatened sites, grew in the first half of the 20th century, and then became one of the principal activities of archaeological endeavour. Other developments from the mid-century were an interest in the landscape and in vernacular buildings, which have resulted in a wide variety of fieldwork and discovery. Together these enterprises have produced a wealth of information, some published in journals, monographs, the rest as 'grey literature', which is largely reflected in the county Historic Environment Records. The most recent development has been the systematic recovery of information from collectors of portable antiquities (usually by metal-detecting), which has brought some surprising data into the public domain.

Many lines of palaeo-environmental enquiry have been carried out at the context- and feature-specific level to determine the activities related to excavated evidence. These enquires provide specific information, but have not been used sufficiently to inform the wider context of which the feature, the activities and the site form a small but important part (in addition to external factors such as significant changes in climate within the medieval period). Key deposits remain garderobe deposits, waste and refuse pits and deposits, which are often rich in charred, mineralised and sometimes waterlogged remains, and may require multiple sampling and subsampling.

The nature of the evidence base thus consists of a large number of field monuments, landscape features and environmental evidence, a growing body of literature describing excavations and fieldwork, and an ever-increasing amount of objects in museum collections. And there is of course an abundance of documentary sources (as there are buildings and art-works) waiting the attention of those who take the trouble to find them.

Chronology

The political and social shock of the Norman Conquest provides a firm enough date for the commencement of the later medieval period in England, if a slightly fuzzy one for significant change in material culture. No entirely new kind of material evidence appeared in 1066, and the shock of governmental change did not rupture the continuity of eg coinage or pottery production. Even in specific areas associated with Norman rule and culture: the castle and Romanesque church architecture, both have pre-conquest flags of forthcoming changes.

Likewise for the end of the period, in the mid-16th century, the political and social shock of the 'age of plunder' has long been believed to inaugurate a profound economic reorganisation of land and resources. This can be recognised in changes in housing (the end of the hall house), and some other developments in material culture, whether pottery or the introduction of renaissance decoration, but there was no immediate or very distinctive change. Indeed, taking a broader view (and disregarding for a moment the rise and fall of feudalism, and the elimination of the small landowner and monasteries), the cultural milieu of the English countryside (manor and church; ox- and, from the 13th century, horse-drawn ploughs and manual haymaking) may be seen as an unbroken continuum, established before and after the Norman Conquest, changed by the age of 'improvement' but finally fractured only by the First World War.

Within the broad continuum there were of course major political events: invasion, French and civil wars, demographic events: population growth and post-plague collapse, and economic change. Archaeology will produce its own indicators of cultural change and chronological distinctiveness that have their own validity, and as always the interesting issue is how a single narrative may derive from such disparate areas of investigation (Pantin 1958).

Pottery remains the most important indicator for assembling medieval chronologies, while the development of scientific methods of dating (especially dendrochronology) have been important in providing some areas of certainty in the chronology of building practice.

Landscape and land use: environmental evidence

Medieval land-use has a clear relation to the landscape, while modified by general considerations of location (proximity to rivers and routeways) and land ownership. With the exception of the Chilterns the entire area falls within the open field zone mapped by Gray (1915) almost a century ago. Long and narrow scarp-foot parishes occur from Lincolnshire to West Berkshire and are able to exploit the resources of hilltop and vale. In chalk downland the parishes often extend up to where there are extensive areas of common pasture. In vales and valleys large parishes typically have nucleated villages. In the more wooded or heathland areas scattered settlement are prevalent, such as the Chiltern region of 'woodland landscape of hamlets, farmsteads, irregular open field and much enclosed land'. Some of the more marginal land was used for forest (though it is always necessary to understand the physical forest bounds as opposed to the much wider legal boundaries, and recognise the significance of private forests (chases) and nearby parks. Beyond the regional generalisation there are of course distinct local areas like Otmoor or the New Forest and the Hampshire/Berkshire heaths where the soils and drainage produced special local conditions, or the Isle of Wight with great complexity in a small area.

The general impression from landscape studies is of an ordered (if not actually a peaceful or unchanging) landscape, with clear transitions from arable fields to pastures or commons, from wastes and woodlands to forests, that were apparent and understood by all. Important resources were shared (post-harvest grazing in open fields, access to valuable hay meadow or firewood), and demesne resources such as woodlands, warrens, and fishponds carefully conserved and controlled through courts and custom. Water was organised, its energy harvested, as it was channelled, bridged or used for travel and movement of goods. Lords, communities and lowly individuals knew the ownership and value of land, and national surveys from Domesday (1086) to the Hundred Rolls (1279) and numerous episodes of taxation made this a matter of record. Above all, the ordered flow of rural and urban products into local markets and beyond, by road and river, gave the land a continuing function in supplying the county's population, the capital's needs for food and fuel, and international needs for wool or cloth.

There is an overall major shift in some areas, and particularly on the chalk downlands, from arable to sheep pasture (more pronounced in the post-medieval period) and creation of warrens, which essentially created the downland landscape we see today. There are clear economic reasons for this related to wool production, but the change may also be related to soil degradation over the previous three to four millennia, evident from field systems of the later prehistoric and Roman periods. According to Allen, arable cultivation led to decreasing soil fertility due to erosion, soil depletion and degradation, such that these soils were not agriculturally viable using medieval technologies, and thus were laid down to pasture, a position only reversed in the 20th century with mechanisation and enhanced fertilisation (Allen 1988). More environmental evidence is still needed to clarify this issue.

Coupled with this is evidence of subtle shifts in the location of farmsteads and fields; farmsteads and fields shifted towards the edges of valleys and slopes, and fields were often concentrated in the dry valleys where soils are thicker. Although important work has been carried out on the alluviation of the Upper Thames Valley (Robinson and Lambrick 1984; Lambrick 1992b; Robinson 1992a and b), full understanding of medieval land use of some of the larger valleys (eg Middle Thames, Kennet, Itchen, Test etc) awaits further study of their hydrology. Other changes to the rural landscape arose through assarting, small-scale clearances around the edges of woodland and forest that cumulatively resulted in extensive change.

Regional variation and style of rural farmsteads

A number of crop introductions and changes occurred within the later medieval period, although their dating and spread within this region has not been studied in detail. The introduction of rivet wheat (*Triticum turgidum*) was one such, pulses such as peas and beans another, and maslin (mixed) crops such as two-row barley and oats a third. There is considerable potential here to link environmental data with information from manorial and other documentary records.

There is evidence of crop infestation during the later medieval period, and this should be examined on a regional scale to define if there are intra-regional patterns, if these are just isolated outbreaks or if they belong to an epidemic. Are some of the changes in crops, and introductions of new crops, related to this? In tandem with this is the start of an increase in the size of livestock, and the emergence of regional breeds. Can these be detected and defined in the animal bone record?

Across the region there is a clear diversity of the scale of rural farmsteads, but there may be some larger patterns based on intra-regional specialisation – and regionalisation. Certainly the nature and composition of the farm economy (crops vs livestock) varies between the Chilterns and the clay vales, each having distinctive scales of farming and livestock / crop balance. The variation in the style and scale of farming operations is obviously defined in part by the local soils and landscape, but may also be affected by economic aims, for example the balance between self-sufficiency and involvement within the wider economic market and rent/surplus extraction. The examination of crops, crop-processing and storage regimes (including buildings), and of patterns of animal husbandry (including changes in animal sizes) and butchery may help in defining these in the future.

Animal husbandry (pasturage, corralling and stabling), stock composition and animal size

There is clear evidence in the archaeological and building records of barns, byres and outbuildings, but there has been little engagement with archaeological science to aid in defining or confirming either their specific function or to define animal husbandry regimes. This may include pasturage, corralling, stabling (resulting in trampling and increased phosphates etc., from dung), and fodder. The identification of ditched enclosures as paddocks, rather than fields or garden plots, via examination of soil profiles (where buried), soil chemistry and palynological evidence, is important in determining the character of farming regimes. The size of animal bone assemblages need not relate to herd size, though establishing the latter (like human population size) is a huge challenge and some estimates could perhaps be advanced.

Plate 15.1 Felling woodland for timber, Winchester calendar, *copyright The British Library Board, 002515 Cotton Tiberius B.V. Part 1, f.6*

Changes in animal husbandry between the early medieval and later medieval periods are important in characterising 'medieval animal husbandry'. Beyond that changes within the later medieval period, and variation across the regional can only be determined by the acquisition of good, reliably-dated datasets with similar recording attributes to enable extra-site comparisons.

Woodlands and woodland management

There is much documentary evidence for woodland (Plate 15.1), and indeed environmental evidence (charcoal, pollen) for managed woodlands, but we have less understanding of their relationship to present woodland cover, and this is an area that should be addressed. Once again the combination and integration of environmental science with documentary evidence may be valuable.

Fields, field boundaries and hedges

Fields and paddocks are bounded, fenced and hedged, and environmental evidence (soil, pollen, snails) may help define these specific local environments. Land snail evidence is not widely deployed on medieval contexts but this is an area to which it might usefully contribute.

Social organisation

Documentary evidence is the major source of information about social organisation during this period, and necessarily provides the descriptive background against which the material culture and lifestyle can be reconstructed.

The Crown is represented by royal castles and manors, and a landscape organised to provide leisure activities of hunting (and jousting), and to provide timber, food and firewood, or horse breeding. Secular aristocrats and church magnates participated in this lifestyle and replicated similar facilities in greater or lesser degree.

For those in the church, the religious life encompassed a wide ranged experience: of communal life for those in orders (whether enclosed or more open orders), for secular priests living alone or in a collegiate existence, communities of women in nunneries, and solitary hermits or anchorites

Manorial lords were distinct in their landholding and access to control over rural communities, while middling landholders and freeholders might acquire considerable amounts of land outside of manorial control, or with minimal obligations to any notional superior. Small landholders, peasant farmers and the slaves so prevalent in Domesday Book had a clear ranking that came to mean less and less in the later medieval period, as the open land market and declining call on services allowed them to achieve what they could by way of advancement.

Townsmen had for long been largely free of any service due to others, though the stratification of greater and lesser burgages can easily be imagined, and surfaces in occasional disputes. It is in towns that social conflict can best be observed, whether between secular population and ecclesiastical authorities, or racial and ethnic groups.

This basic social organisation of medieval society is a backdrop against which the archaeology will always be considered. Domestic space, organisation of property, the quality of material culture and food preferences can all be investigated archaeologically and lead to consideration of differences between all ranks of society. Some aspects of life, such as migration patterns and diet, can be informed by modern scientific approaches to human and food remains. Faunal remains help to identify variation in diet.

Women and children are not absent from the documentation, but the archaeological aspects of their role and spatial activity is less clearly understood. The location of social outcasts such as lepers and the inhabitants of hospitals are often identified from historical evidence and lend themselves to studies of their homes and burial places.

Settlement

Rural settlement

Settlement types and patterns are being studied at regional level (eg Lewis *et al.* 1997) and nationally (eg Roberts and Wrathmell 2000), which is beginning to establish the necessary framework that crosses county boundaries. It is as well to remember earlier multi-volume syntheses such as the *Domesday Geography* and the *Cambridge Agrarian History of England* which abound with useful information (Darby 1986; Hallam 1988, and Miller 1991). Despite much attention being paid to rural settlement (especially on favoured topics such as moats and deserted medieval villages) much remains to be done. The region has seen important excavations of deserted sites (Seacourt – Biddle 1961/2), moated sites (Chalgrove – Page *et al.* 2005), villages (Great Linford – Mynard 1991), and extensive areas that have included village edges and origins (Yarnton – Hey 2004). The connection between the excavated sites and the present day villages as existing or recorded in maps and documents remains the key problem. The increasing amount of data from evaluation and the recovery of portable antiquities will be important once analysed, but the emerging picture is likely to be a fluid one of shifting extent and focus of rural settlement, as has been suggested in Buckinghamshire.

Village origins (likely to be related to the organisation and exploitation of field systems) may belong to the increasing organisation of rural life along with the formation of parishes and hundreds in the 9th-10th centuries, but there is ample evidence of earlier village nuclei in and around later village centres. Village expansion, whether or not 'planned', is also evident and should be expected from the conventional history of a rising population until the 14th century. Decline and abandonment of settlements can now be seen as a complex process arising from a number of causes, such as re-settlement, economic decline, and decisions of the manorial lord, in addition to population decline from plague (Steane 2001). Archaeological evidence of shrinkage rather than abandonment has been found on sites in Buckinghamshire. In Berkshire the late medieval rise of the cloth trade in Newbury may have encouraged population movement from village to town, though this will not have been a new phenomenon (M Yates 2007).

Manorial sites

The region is rich in standing remains of manorial sites, in the occupied manor houses that have been the subject of architectural investigation for 150 years, and abandoned sites surviving as earthworks or buried and unlocated. Documentation is abundant for seigniorial sites (whether lay or ecclesiastical) and the numerous royal houses in the Thames valley, both large and small are well known. Excavated sites include Whaddon, Buckinghamshire and Chalgrove, Oxfordshire where the quality and complexity of the sites is in stark contrast with peasant housing (Page *et al.* 2005). Episcopal houses at Witney, Bishop's Waltham and Winchester have been extensively explored and are appropriately more palatial (Allen with Hiller 2002, Hare 1988, Biddle

Plate 15.2 Aston Clinton moat, aerial view, *copyright Buckinghamshire County Council*

1986). Apart from Windsor many royal sites await investigation (or even location). Monastic granges such as Dean Court, Cumnor, just west of Oxford (Allen 1994) have provided insights on the monastic economy, as has the exploration of the Faringdon grange at Wyke (now a Scheduled Monument).

Moated sites have been the subject of much interest, and their distribution carefully studied; their owners ranged in status from minor landowners building defended homes to smaller and larger manorial lords, and excavations have shown that they often contained buildings of manorial status (Plate 15.2).

The manorial control of food resources is demonstrated by the presence of fishponds, rabbit warrens and parks. A Buckinghamshire survey has identified 183 fishponds, mostly manorial and some monastic (Croft and Pike 1988). They may relate to moats and other managed water systems, but across the region the presence of fresh-water fisheries was important and widespread. Parks provided an open-air larder for venison and the possibility of a contained hunting ground. The importance of hunting as a quasi-military form of popular recreation cannot be overstated, and this accounts for the prevalence of parks in the landscape (and as likely to be ecclesiastical – as at the Cistercian Thame Park – as secular). Their enclosing features can often be traced in current landscapes, while many survived to become amenity parks subject to decorative 'landscaping' in later centuries.

Towns

The urban hierarchy is well understood, with a prevailing network of rural market towns and larger centres distributed (unevenly) as a result of chance and history. The county centres were relatively small (Buckingham) or multiple (Abingdon/Reading) and both Oxford and Winchester owe much of their prominence to their role as centres of the church and learning. The importance of Southampton as a trading port, partly outgrown by the 12th-century newcomer at Portsmouth by the end of this period, derived from its location. Perhaps more typical of the region are what have been called 'the Banburys of England' (Everitt 1974, 1985), which would include primary centres such as Newbury, Berkshire, Aylesbury, Buckinghamshire and Basingstoke, Hampshire.

Urban excavations in this region have included pioneering work in Oxford, Winchester, and Southampton, and a considerable quantity of excavations in recent decades (see Plates 1.5 and 1.6), with much published but still not all. Small town surveys in the 1970s promoted hopeful agendas for action that have not borne fruit, and the successor surveys of the 21st century are more colourful but perhaps no more informative, while the questions remain. Such exploration as there has been in the smaller market towns has demonstrated the variable amount of archaeology that can be expected to survive, and shown that it is rather the deep stratigraphy of larger centres that is exceptional. The distribution of

archaeological exploration has been uneven: Aylesbury has been investigated but not Buckingham, Southampton much more than Portsmouth. The extensive excavations in Southampton, Oxford, Reading and Winchester have provided large amounts of data on all aspects of urban life, from origins and development to industry, diet and environment. Urban buildings range from urban castles and defences (Banbury, Oxford, Winchester, Southampton) to churches and monastic sites, friaries (Oxford), intra- and extra- mural hospitals (Winchester) and numerous domestic buildings (Reading, Newbury and elsewhere).

The study of urban topography has flourished in places with unusual quantities of written documentation (Oxford, Southampton and Winchester). This compelling body of evidence both points up comparisons and contrasts in the archaeological record. The easy assumptions of historical map analysis have to be subjected to archaeological scrutiny, especially in the matter of 'planned' layouts and extensions. Towns within Hampshire have been subject to plan analysis (Lilley 1999). Recently, a case based on both map and archaeological evidence has been made for a planned extension on the north at Abingdon (Thomas 2010, 51-4)

The urban environment

Palaeo-environmental evidence can aid in determining the nature of local lived-in environments in urban centres. How clean were these? Were animals (other than horses) corralled and penned in towns, is there evidence of cess pits and waste in the lived-in environment? Were streets clean, cobbled and paved areas, or were they weedy environments with herbaceous plants growing along street margins?

The presence of stratified organic deposits is seen certainly in Winchester, Southampton, Oxford and other large medieval centres. These provide the opportunity of examining the nature of medieval urban life and of the medieval urban environment.

Localised and specialist deposits of animal bones, fish bones, shellfish (Mollusca) or plant remains may represent specialist activities such as tanning, bone-working etc, or markets (eg fish markets in Southampton). Although a systematic approach to sampling such deposits has already been employed on some sites, this needs to be made universal if we are to understand the distribution and significance of these deposits, as well as their nature and manner of accumulations.

Butchery practices may vary in urban compared to rural environments, but also on the scale of meat and food production (see comments on the *Mary Rose* below). Butchery itself provides information about local compared to wider consumption and the scale of preparation for sale or consumption.

Rural and urban economies

It is important to define the economies of both rural farmsteads and of towns to provide the basis for identi-

Plate 15.3 Great Coxwell Barn, Oxfordshire, *copyright Lucy Lawrence*

fying patterns of trade and commerce. The interpretation and integration of a whole variety of palaeo-environmental analyses (animal bone, charred seeds, insects, soil science etc) should be aimed at defining site-based practices, and providing data to aid in interpreting and understanding the regional medieval economic market and market place. As the medieval period progresses, there is also an increase in the trading economy that supplies the growing towns, from which there is now an increasing palaeo-environmental database (for example Oxford, Winchester and Southampton; eg Green 1979).

It is also clear from documentary records, particularly ecclesiastical records, that transhumance (for summer uplands grazing) and the large-scale movements of herds are seen across the region. This raises further questions about the influences of this seasonal activity upon settlements along these routes.

The built environment

The study of medieval buildings has, more than most areas, involved excavation, the study of standing buildings, and the documentary background. Moreover, the study of vernacular (traditional) architecture has been a remarkable instance of a popular academic endeavour over the last half century, largely achieved in the absence of any organised research framework as a self-supporting empirical activity, and producing a huge increase in knowledge and understanding through the emerging synthetic accounts. The more recent addition of widespread dendrochronological dating and more systematic research projects on specific topics have sharpened the edge of our understanding.

Rural building

The pioneering excavations at the deserted village of Seacourt, Oxfordshire revealed what has since become well understood from many sites about the impermanence of some domestic structures, and the tendency (particularly revealed by archaeology) for constant cycles of rebuilding. By contrast, Currie's extensive study of peasant housing in Oxfordshire (1992), and the work of Roberts in Hampshire (E Roberts 2003) have shown just how many peasant houses of the 13th and 14th century do survive, and as substantial buildings rather than the 'flimsy' and impermanent structure once assumed.

Fieldwork in Hampshire has identified hall houses with early roofs, and examined the 'cruck boundary', the eastern edge of the distribution map of cruck buildings that runs through the county (and perhaps the western edge of the common use of crown-post roofs). Timber-framed houses of the 13th century are rare, 14th-century examples more common, and most date to the 15th-17th century, especially because of farm leasing, for example by the Bishop of Winchester.

The significance of the age and survival of houses is not yet fully understood. The quantity of early buildings surviving at Harwell and Steventon, Oxfordshire, for example, is striking, and the number of 14th-15th-century hall-houses in Wargrave (a borough of the Bishop of Winchester) is also notable. Whether these relate to lordship, to the contemporary economy, or to a lack of later prosperity, is however uncertain.

Farm buildings have attracted much interest, and major early barns such as Great Coxwell of c.1300 (Plate 15.3), or the even larger late medieval example at Cholsey south of Wallingford (now lost), represent a

Plate 15.4 Long Crendon Courthouse, Buckinghamshire, *copyright Jill Hind*

body of large farm buildings of various sizes that represent significant monastic or institutional investment on farming. As long ago as 1979 James Bond commented on the small size of those surviving on the Abingdon Abbey estates in relation to those of other Benedictine abbeys, and how these might reflect differing management practices (Bond 1979, 64-5). This remains a fruitful area for future study. Examples such as those at Swalcliffe and Enstone (Oxfordshire) demonstrate the quality of such buildings in their masonry or carpentry (Munby and Steane 1995). It is probable that many more remain to be discovered.

Manor houses from castles to bishop's palaces and modest moated houses have been studied as long as medieval archaeology has been a matter of interest. They can present bewildering complexity (Windsor Castle and Broughton Castle near Banbury), surprising sophistication (Upton Court, Slough) and aesthetic interest (Sutton Courtenay 'Abbey') (Thornes 1988; Currie 1992). The excavations at the Bishop of Winchester's palaces has been mentioned above.

Urban building

As with rural vernacular, town houses and other buildings have benefited from a generation of close study, and much more is known, but more remains to be found. In Oxford a succession of domestic buildings has been recognised, from late-Saxon houses with sunken floors (similar to York's Coppergate houses), through stone houses of the 12th century, and to later stone halls with timber-framed fronts. The appearance of jettied and storeyed buildings is general from the 13th century across the region, with a difference in scale from larger towns (eg Oxford) and

smaller (Thame). The appearance of 'wealden' houses in towns and market centres in Oxfordshire, Berkshire and Hampshire may represent a fashion or a particular use (as inns for example). The varieties of style and planning can be seen in the increasing number of hall houses being recognised in Hampshire; these are of course easier to discover when timber-framed, and there may be many more medieval stone houses awaiting recognition. Typical later medieval survivals include inns (Aylesbury, King's Head; Oxford, New Inn) and town houses of prominent families (Buckingham, Castle House). In Oxford there are distinctive academic 'halls' in which students lived, but little different from other house types. Guildhalls and court houses such as those at Aylesbury and Long Crendon north of Thame (Plate 15.4) are modified for use of large public rooms, while colleges and almshouses are adapted for individual use (more like retainer's lodgings in large domestic establishments). In Oxford as elsewhere the survival of cross-vaulted cellars can be linked to the known sites of wine taverns. The Undercroft, Southampton is cross-ribbed. Inns may be distinguished from large storage cellars, several of which were identified in the survey of Southampton, by the presence of fireplaces (Faulkner 1975).

The quantum of survival is an interesting and largely unexplored topic, which depends on many factors such as destructive urban fires and the later economic history of the town. There are more medieval houses in Winchester, few in Oxford, more in Abingdon than many equivalent places, though fieldwork in Hampshire is constantly producing new examples. In Oxford more houses are known from documentary sources or from their representation on topographical drawings than exist now (and this is particularly notable with the evidence for early stone houses). Medieval cob-walled buildings do not survive in the region's towns, but excavation has shown that these were an important element of the townscape in the suburb of St Thomas at Oxford (Roberts 1996; Hardy 1996; Cook 1999), and a particularly well-preserved example was found under one of the castle ramparts at Wallingford (Dewey and Dewey 1977, 36 and 38; Christie and Creighton 2013, Plates 5.21-26).

Ceremony, ritual and religion

Monastic houses

Like castles, monasteries have attracted much archaeological attention, but continue to produce new aspects for study in addition to supplying answers to old questions. Many sites remain little known with much uncertainty as to the location of the churches or monastic buildings.

The ancient monastic centres were at Abingdon, Dorchester and Winchester, the last two being cathedrals. Concentrations of urban houses were to be found at Oxford, Reading, Winchester and Southampton (including friaries), and of others in the Thames valley and along the south coast, with a scattering of all sorts in the countryside (especially nunneries). Reading was favoured by royal travellers moving west from Windsor, and Oxford was a centre of monastic as much as secular learning. Winchester was the centre of a Diocese reaching as far as Southwark

(though much of Berkshire was in the Diocese of Salisbury), and the Lincoln Diocese encompassed both Oxfordshire and Buckinghamshire, having moved from Dorchester after the Conquest. While the most impressive (if poorly known) ruins are to be found at Reading (Plate 15.5), re-used churches survive at Romsey, Dorchester and Oxford, the last a minor Augustinian priory (St Frideswide) resurrected as a cathedral. At Notley, Thame and Titchfield, significant portions of the more usable buildings were incorporated in 16th century houses. Archaeological work has been uneven. Geophysical survey has been used on the abbey church and cloister at Abingdon (Allen 2011), exploratory work with geophysics (and dendrochronological dating) has located buildings at Wherwell, Hampshire, and a series of rescue observations were employed to recover the plan at Bicester, Oxfordshire (Hinton 1968, 1969; see Fig. 13.1 for location). Major excavations have been carried out at Reading Abbey, Winchester Old Minster and Hyde Abbey, the Greyfriars and Blackfriars in Oxford, Missenden and Bradwell Abbey, Buckinghamshire (Lambrick 1985b; Bucks County Museum 1984-5). Older excavations and observations, eg at Goring, Oxfordshire and Burnham, north-west of Slough, Buckinghamshire, are also valuable.

Subsidiary monastic buildings in precincts and in rural granges have been studied at Gorefields, Buckinghamshire, where a monastic grange had apparently originated as a nunnery, at Faringdon Wyck, Oxfordshire, where the Beaulieu Abbey grange had a group of barns as large as the surviving example at Great

Plate 15.5   Reading Abbey dormitory, Berkshire, *copyright Jill Hind*

Coxwell, and at Dean Court, Cumnor, west of Oxford, where the economy of a small grange of Abingdon Abbey could be explored (Allen 1994). At Dean Court and at Charney Bassett only one wing of the 14th century granges still survives, but more intact survivals include the Abingdon Abbey range of domestic and service buildings, the 'Pilgrim's Hall' at Winchester (Crook 1991), and the small remnant of Oseney Abbey (Oxford).

Hospitals

The lowest common denominator of religious foundations was the Hospital, present in most towns or on travel routes, and besides there were hermitages and occasional anchorites.

While major medieval hospital buildings still exist in use at St Cross, Winchester, the character of most smaller hospitals is imperfectly understood, though parts of the infirmary hall and subsidiary buildings were excavated at the Hospital of St John, Oxford (now Magdalen College) (Durham 1991). The survival of the 15th century church, almshouse and school at Ewelme, Oxfordshire is unusual.

Numerous collegiate buildings of a quasi-monastic plan continue in use at Eton College, Berkshire, Winchester School, and in the University of Oxford.

Parish churches

The parish church has for long been the subject of study, from the early interest in tombs and heraldic memorials, to the rebirth of medieval archaeology in the early 19th century, when the art and architecture of the parish church and its numerous fittings became the object of intense investigation and record. Some key aspects of this study took place in this region as a result of the interest in Gothic architecture promoted by the Oxford Society and J. H. Parker's publications, as a result of which there are copious drawings and photographs of churches throughout the region. Publications on wall paintings, stained glass, church plate and bells have continued from the 19th to 20th centuries. Only Buckinghamshire and Oxford city benefited from RCHM inventories with systematic descriptions of all churches, while the complete *Victoria County History* accounts of *Berkshire, Buckinghamshire* and *Hampshire*, and the 14 volumes of Oxfordshire contain substantial church histories and descriptions. Pevsner's *Buildings of England* series, with second editions for *Buckinghamshire, Berkshire* and *Hampshire* provide more recent accounts.

The much more recent interest in the (below-ground) archaeology of churches has added much to our understanding of their potential, and yet there is enormous scope for further work. Very few aspects of the church as a cultural indicator have been mapped or studied in regional terms, even though church types (such as the 'wool' church, steeples, or the early two-cell parish church) are well known.

The place of the church in relation to the parish and village plan has been a matter of interest as has origins in relation to the history of the manor and parish. The existence of a vicarage, rectory or rectory farm and other parochial buildings may be significant aspects, as is the patronage of Religious or lay rectors in building works. The existence of private chapels in houses is another aspect of personal devotion that can be also be seen in the proliferation of manuscript Books of Hours and devotional objects.

Cemeteries

The thousands of burials in parish, monastic and cathedral churchyards are an important resource for human anatomy and anthropology. Burial groups are divided between the religious and the laity, and among the latter the rich are often buried in separate, more prestigious locations than the rest. Despite the large numbers of medieval abbeys and churches, there are very few large cemetery groups excavated in the region, and less that are published. Of the towns, Winchester is best served, and here a group of more than 1000 individuals was excavated at St Swithun's cathedral priory (Kjølbye-Biddle 1992). Other smaller groups have been excavated but not yet published, from the Benedictine nunnery of St Mary Nunnaminster and from Hyde Abbey (Scobie in prep).

A number of groups, mainly of the religious, has been excavated and published from the cathedral and the friaries at Oxford, of which the largest (c.100) was at the Oxford Blackfriars (Lambrick 1985b). An assemblage of approaching 100 medieval bodies of lay people was found at the church of St Peter-le-Bailey (Webb and Norton 2009), and there is also a group from the chapel of St George at Oxford Castle. One of the largest groups in Oxfordshire is that of approaching 1000 bodies from the lay cemetery at Abingdon Abbey (Plate 15.6), but although specific studies have been carried out (eg Wakely 1993; Duncan 2000), this is still not fully published.

There are no large cemetery excavations published from Buckinghamshire, although the Anglo-Saxon cemetery at Wing continued into the 12th century (Holmes and Chapman 2008). Outside Winchester, one of the largest studies in Hampshire has been the cemetery of more than 250 individuals associated with the church of the lost settlement at Hatch Warren, Basingstoke (Fasham *et al.* 1995). On the Isle of Wight only one medieval cemetery, that at Flowers Brook, Steephill, has been excavated. About 40 individuals were recovered, but this is not published.

Burials from medieval hospitals are a significant source of information about disease, poverty and other social issues. Studies from the region include a group from the Litten cemetery, Newbury, Hampshire (Clough 2006), and the very recent excavation of the cemetery of the Hospital of St John at Oxford. Other, more specialist groups include the cemeteries of leper houses, but none of these has been comprehensively

Plate 15.6 Excavation in the lay cemetery of Abingdon Abbey, Oxfordshire, *copyright OA*

investigated. A small group has been examined from the leper hospital of St Margaret at High Wycombe (Farley and Manchester 1989).

There were few racial minorities in the region in the medieval period, the most notable being the Jewish community. A Jewish cemetery of 88 individuals, mostly subadults, was excavated at Mews Lane, Winchester (Winchester Archaeology Service 1995 archive). The approximate location of the cemetery of the medieval Jewish community in Oxford is known, but no bodies have yet been found. Much remains to be learnt about the diet, lifestyle and life expectancy of Jewish people in medieval England, and in the Solent-Thames region.

Religious practice and pilgrimage

Places of veneration, including shrines and holy wells are numerous. In this class may be included preaching and market crosses, and features found in and around parish churches. Portable objects of veneration, such as pilgrim's badges and religious souvenirs (eg lead ampullae for holy water) are not infrequent finds and have often been recorded under the Portable Antiquities Scheme.

Warfare, defences and military installations

The early defences of the pre-conquest *burhs* were the origin of later town walls at Oxford, Wallingford and Winchester, which were maintained and refurbished perhaps largely for reasons of status. Later walled towns include Southampton and Portsmouth (very late), both necessary for their coastal setting, but apparently no other towns in Berkshire or Buckinghamshire thought provision of defences worth the expense. Although defended towns are few their standing remains have perhaps received less attention than buried sections; the Southampton defences have been the subject of a study, but the standing remains in Oxford have been less investigated than the remains of the outer part of the double wall in the north-east sector. The castles of the region are varied in character (Table 15.2); the larger numbers of them in Oxfordshire and Buckinghamshire perhaps reflects seigniorial choices in providing fortified homes, and the prevalence of early castles of the Anarchy in the mid 12th century, most of which are earthwork castles.

Much remains to be learnt from castles, which range from early earthwork constructions to royal and seigniorial centres such as Windsor. The survival of above-ground evidence is remarkable at Windsor but is paralleled elsewhere in less exalted form. On the other hand, castles' level of survival particularly in urban environments is not good, and the loss of Banbury Castle in several phases of development has been unfortunate, while the discoveries at Oxford Castle have shown how much of the medieval castle had been lost to the prison phase (while late-Saxon material had survived).

Excavations at castles such as Wallingford, Windsor, Winchester, Portchester, Southampton, Carisbrooke, Banbury and Oxford have produced important results (Plate 15.7) showing the complexity of development (Windsor and Portchester) and of origins (Carisbrooke), including the pre-castle phase at Oxford. At Portchester, Oxford, Winchester and Windsor excavations have been undertaken alongside studies of standing fabric and

Table 15.2 Numbers of castles by county

Type	Berkshire	Buckinghamshire	Hampshire	Isle of Wight	Oxfordshire
Masonry	3	1	10 (7+3)	3	7
Earth	11	23	12	–	9
Unknown	3	1			

documentary sources. Less work has been undertaken on minor and earthwork castles: Jope undertook pioneering excavations eg at Ascott Doilly and Deddington (Jope and Threlfall 1959; Ivens 1984), and mottes have been investigated at Middleton Stoney, Oxfordshire (Rahtz and Rowley 1984), and Weston Turville, Buckinghamshire. Windsor and Portchester are the principal extant castles, with significant remains to be seen at Winchester and Oxford and individual

structures at Donnington (Plate 15.8), Berkshire and Boarstall, Buckinghamshire; the very impressive medieval mansion at Broughton Castle, Oxfordshire has perhaps less claims to 'castle' status.

The current interest in the concept and status of the castle is producing a burgeoning literature, though a wish to discount the defensive aspects of castles is given the lie by the repeated upgrading of coastal defences in the light of invasion threats and actual attacks (eg at

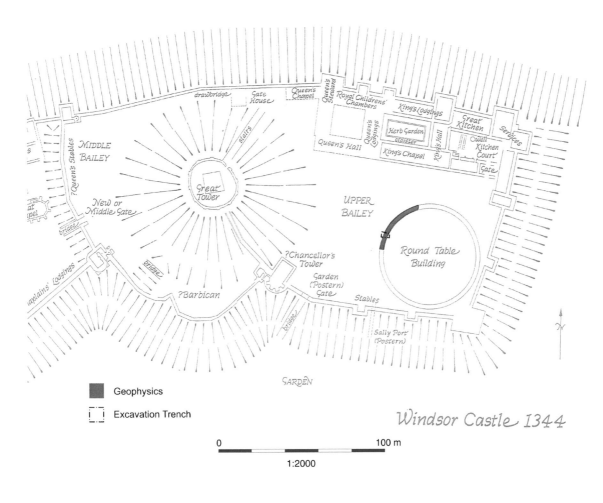

Geophysics

Excavation Trench

Windsor Castle 1344

0   100 m

1:2000

Plate 15.7 Excavation at The Round Table, Windsor, Berkshire and reconstruction: *upper part copyright T Tatton-Brown, drawn by Jill Atherton with additions; lower part copyright OA*

Plate 15.8 Aerial view of Donnington Castle, *copyright Cambridge University Committee for Aerial Photography*

Southampton, Portchester/Portsmouth, and Isle of Wight). Increased risk on the south coast meant that in the early 16th century Henrician castles or defences were provided at Portsmouth, Hurst Castle and the Isle of Wight (East and West Cowes, Sandown and Yarmouth). Other and possibly more productive areas of concern include castles and their landscape setting as manors with adjacent villages and fields, parks and forests (eg Portchester), and the relationship of castles to major seigniorial establishments, such as the king's houses and the 'palaces' of bishops and magnates, and the relationship to landholding and household mobility. At a lower level, concerns for security play a part in the prevalence of moated homes.

Material culture

The indicators of material culture range from the size and status of buildings (whether churches or domestic buildings) to the assemblages of finds from different types of sites indicative of life style and status, personal adornment, and diet. Differing rates of survival make it hard to compare the building stock, but notable instances such as the prevalence of cruck houses in Long Crendon, Buckinghamshire and the quality of early housing in Harwell and Steventon, Oxfordshire are important reminders of the level of sophistication that medieval 'vernacular' building could reach. How these buildings

were used, and what they contained, is less well understood than their structure, while their furnishing and decoration only become better known in the 16th century from the evidence of probate inventories.

With personal adornment and domestic objects the evidence is overwhelming, and small finds can be seen as important indicators of consumer activity and purchasing power in rural and urban households.

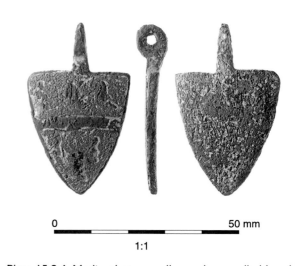

0   50 mm

1:1

Plate 15.9 A Medieval copper-alloy and enamelled heraldic harness pendant (PAS IOW-3594A1). The arms of this pendant were borne by Sir Walter de Beauchamp Knt., of Alcester, lived *c.* 1255–1303, *copyright Frank Basford*

Perhaps the most interesting recent development has been the results of the Portable Antiquities Scheme, and the realisation of the quantity of small metal objects that have been found, eg from the Isle of Wight over 600 new items including 'coins, seal matrices, buckles, harness pendants, brooches, purse bars, strap fittings, tokens, padlocks, cloth seals, keys and steelyard weights' (Plate 15.9). Much remains to be done, even at a basic comparative level of, say, the published finds from rural Buckinghamshire (at Milton Keynes) and a major urban centre (Winchester). Comparison of material culture can also be made by consideration of the differences between monastic and military sites, as the analysis of finds from Carisbrooke Castle has shown (Young 2000). Pottery dominates the excavated finds, and allows continuing study of the varieties and quality of pottery usage, with implications for activity and status (and an increasing understanding of production and marketing).

Trade and industry

Building materials

The bulk production and distribution of building materials will always have been a major enterprise.

Stone

Stone quarrying is important in the Jurassic belt for fine limestone and stone slates, as also in chalk areas for chalk rubble and clunch. From the 11th century at least these have been carried by road and river along the Thames Valley, while materials from Dorset, Devon and Cornwall and the Isle of Wight have been delivered by sea.

Cotswold building stones from the Burford/ Taynton area of Oxfordshire have been exploited from before the Conquest for fine quality building and sculptural stone, and the quarries around Oxford (Headington and Wheatley) were also well used in the later medieval period, and convenient of access for local use and export to Windsor and London. Although large areas of extant quarries (eg Taynton and Headington) are well known and easily identified, many other local sources were used whose existence is less obvious unless large stone pits are recognised (eg in Wytham, Oxfordshire). The identification of stone types in buildings is important in this respect (eg Berkshire churches). The Isle of Wight had important resources of stone (limestone and Greensand) at, for example, Quarr and Binstead, that readily leant themselves to coastal distribution in Hampshire and Sussex and are found in several cathedrals, churches and castles. The winning of stone slates was a specialised industry, which came to be centred at Stonesfield, Oxfordshire where the quarry pits are still extant.

Chalk digging in Buckinghamshire and Berkshire would always have been a more local process at any point where the material could be easily reached, and with more prominent sites like that at Bisham (used for Windsor) close to river transport.

Brick and tile

Clay resources were widely available throughout the region, and exploited for the production of bricks and tiles. Brick was increasingly important in the medieval period, with important early examples of the use of brick from the 15th century (Windsor, Berkshire, Eton, Buckinghamshire and Ewelme, Oxfordshire). However, the means and location of production is poorly understood, though it may be that as at Eton College the workshop for production and firing of bricks was specially established for the project. There are documentary references to production of bricks at Slough, Brill and Tingewick west of Buckingham, but these are not otherwise verified.

The allied trade of floor tile production is well-known from long study of the distribution of products in churches and major secular buildings of the region, but production is less well understood, with the exception of the Penn industry in Buckinghamshire. A recent study (Keen 2002) has emphasised the prominence of the Penn tiles industry, with an extensive distribution in south-east England including prominent royal sites at Windsor, Westminster and the Tower of London. In Hampshire tile kilns are recorded at Highclere and have been excavated at Andover. The production of roofing tiles may have been more closely related to pottery, as at Olney and Latimer in Buckinghamshire where both were produced in succession on one site (Mynard 1984).

Timber

The region was well-supplied with timber, in forests, woods and hedgerows, and its exploitation for construction is well attested in documentary sources and in surviving buildings. It is also known that timber was imported from outside the region, as with the acquisition of an entire wood from Cakeham in West Sussex for Windsor Castle in the 1350s, while the importation of oak and softwood planks from overseas (especially the Baltic) for doors, shutters and panels was a substantial trade throughout the later medieval period. The surviving timber elements of buildings are an important resource for documenting the origins and conversion of the material, to complement the information on supply and transport gained from building accounts. Accounts also emphasise the use of wood products (eg bark and branches for tanning).

A major wood product was firewood, required for heating and cooking in town and country throughout the region. Best documented is London's timber trade, which encompassed wood from the Chilterns that was carried down river from Henley to London, but supplies to towns like Winchester and Oxford can only have been possible with a widespread and ordered management of woodland resources. Wood products on a domestic level must have been a considerable industry in aggregate, if largely evidenced by the survival of carved and turned items in waterlogged deposits. A carpenter's workshop of the 14th century excavated at Whaddon, Buckinghamshire contained remains of turned bowls illustrating all stages of the process (Griffiths 1979).

An increase in industrial activities, in both the urban and rural context, requires increasing and sometimes specialised fuel. The examination of charred plant remains, and of charcoals in particular, will help to define the nature of the fuel and tinder, and the presence of managed woods, pollarding and coppicing.

Productive industries

Pottery

Pottery production sites remains somewhat elusive. Discoveries suggest that the pottery industry involved both large and small-scale production. The industry at Brill, Buckinghamshire is well documented and partly excavated (Mellor 1994), while suspected locations at Nettlebed in the Chilterns and sites near Leafield in Wychwood remain to be located. A site in Berkshire has been discovered at Ashhampstead Common (Mepham and Heaton 1995), and another at Camley Gardens, Maidenhead (Pike 1965), while 'imports' from nearby industries in Wiltshire and Surrey were not infrequent. Exotic imports occur mostly in relation to port sites as at Southampton, while late medieval imports of for example German stoneware became widespread across the region.

Cloth

Cloth production was perhaps a major element in town economies in earlier centuries, and re-emerged in small towns and rural areas in later centuries, but its archaeology is hard to identify beyond the records of dyeing, fulling (mills) or tenter fields, most notably recorded in the Brooks Street excavation in Winchester. Cloth industries were also a favoured enterprise in the 16th century for re-using monastic sites.

Leather

Tanning was another major urban activity of which relatively few traces have been reported despite being a reasonably well documented trade (as was the more specialised parchment making trade recorded in Oxford and Winchester). Tanneries have been excavated at several places in the region, for example the late medieval example at Fordingbridge, Hampshire, at Reading, Berkshire (Ford *et al.* 2013; Plate 15.10) and at Abingdon, Oxfordshire (Pine and Taylor 2006)

Iron and metalworking

Despite good documentation and a wide assemblage of artefacts, the production sites and technology associated with these industries are not well understood, though traces of bloomeries and iron-working are occasionally encountered, as at Olney, Buckinghamshire. Much of the production may have been small-scale, and village blacksmiths were in all probability ubiquitous throughout the region as well as urban smiths, making nails, horseshoes, and iron parts for wooden machinery (eg mills and wheels).

Salt

Salt carried from the Droitwich brine wells along the numerous 'salt ways' will have served much of the northern end of the region, but the south coast and Isle of Wight was a major production area for salt from coastal evaporation pans, especially around Portsmouth

Plate 15.10 Tanning pits at Reading Oracle, *copyright OA*

harbour, and is well-documented at Portchester. The industry is documented from Domesday, and survived long enough to appear on 18th century maps, eg at Lymington (Keen 1989). Salt-making becomes a relatively major industry and sites on the Solent coastline at locations such as Pennington provide the opportunity to examine the nature of the estuary fringes (the physical environment), the modifications made to harness salt water and brine, and the technology and fuel (charcoal) required to help in any of the evaporation processes. These activities may be conducted during periods of increased salinity of the local soils, or can themselves result in such increases, changing their nature and fertility.

Processing

Milling

Mills, that is watermills, were very numerous by the time of Domesday Book (1086) throughout the region (except where water was lacking), and must be accounted one of the great achievements of Anglo-Saxon technology, together with the re-routing of water sources to reach them. Many of these will have been on the site of later mills, whose ponds and leats may be much older than the present structures. There may have been a change from horizontal to vertical-driven wheels in the late-Saxon period. Excavations at High Wycombe and Reading have revealed traces of early mills (Ford *et al.* 2013). Oxford castle mill was observed in 1930 and more recently destroyed without record. On the south coast there were tidal mills (eg at Portchester), though their documented use was interrupted by changing tidal conditions in the 14th century.

Windmills are as likely to have appeared first in this region as anywhere in England, when they came into use in the late 12th century (eg at Dinton, Buckinghamshire, *c.* 1180). Much can be learned of their character from a study of the earlier post-medieval survivals (as at Brill), while mill footprints are a not unusual find (eg Great Linford, Buckinghamshire)

Fulling mills operated in areas of cloth production (eg on Hampshire rivers and on the Kennet in Berkshire) but there is little evidence of the physical remains, even where sites have continued in use, though much of their may have been similar to those of corn-mills.

Water environments

There is an increase in mills on rivers, and of management of rivers (leats etc) for milling and other industrial purposes. In addition there may be management of waterways, and cutting of, for example, *Ranunculus* to promote water flow to aid fishing. Thus there is the direct evidence of changing nature of watercourses, water flow, and the river-bed and river-side environments, but also there is the potential that this may have a wider impact on the floodplain. Thus the development of rivers, river systems and management of watercourses

and their implications and impact upon flooding regions and the nature of floodplains, should be considered a theme that requires addressing.

Transport and communications

River

The River Thames was a significant transport route, but its navigability can be hard to demonstrate: for example, the use of Taynton stone in the White Tower does not prove use of the full length of the Thames for stone transport. Weirs and mills were certainly a hazard to navigation (and so mentioned in Magna Carta), and the difficulty of navigation between Oxford and Reading is thought to have led to the increased importance of Henley as the transhipment port for the cereal grown in the south midlands and destined for London. Henley and other local ports (Marlow and Hedsor) were used for exporting Chiltern products such as firewood and tiles, while the restricted upstream distribution of middle Thames Berkshire pottery of the 12th to 13th centuries suggests less was travelling upstream. The use of smaller rivers such as the Kennet in Berkshire and Great Ouse in *Buckinghamshire* is poorly understood, though the former had wharfage in Reading near its Thames confluence, and documentary evidence has demonstrated the supply of large amounts of cloth from Newbury to London in the late medieval period (M Yates 2007).

Roads

Road transport was always more important than is allowed, whether by pedlar, packhorse or two-wheeled cart. The medieval road network will have been well established with the development of the urban and market system, and is attested by eg routes followed by royal progresses in the Thames valley. Changes in the importance of routes include the creation or upgrading of the route to the newly created Portsmouth in the late 12th century (A3), and the development of long-distance routes such as Southampton to the midlands and London to Coventry (A5). Roads are poorly understood archaeologically, especially where they have remained in use, though surviving earthwork evidence of local roads and tracks may be obvious in deserted or shrunken settlements. The most obvious surviving evidence for medieval main roads is in related structures such as bridges, and their associated hospitals, chapels or hermitages. Thames bridges are necessarily sparse, though more abundant upstream. The sequence of fords and bridges at Oxford has been well studied, and its situation has always required long causeways associated with narrower bridging points. In Buckinghamshire there was a series of bridges along the Great Ouse (some 14 by AD1350), and a series of causeways from Aylesbury to Wendover. A hospital was founded on the bridge at Stony Stratford in Milton Keynes, and there was a bridge hermit on Oxford's Grandpont.

Sea and coast

The south coast of Hampshire/Isle of Wight has always been important for overseas trade, coastal trading, and for cross-channel shipping routes to Normandy and beyond. Interest has concentrated on medieval Southampton, which has abundant archaeological evidence for the receiving and storage of goods, much exotic pottery, and a richly documented participation in international trade. The predominance of the main accounting port should not draw away from other nearby places the possibility that they were also engaged in trade. On the Isle of Wight quays have been identified both from remains and documentary sources. Environmental evidence of trade and imports can be recognised where there is evidence of exotics in the form of spices, but not in other areas, eg imported livestock, the recognition, origin and dating of which is important in characterising the medieval economy of the region.

Use of the south coast ports for overseas trade is an obvious topic, but the coastal trade may have been a greater bulk (demonstrated by the distribution of objects such as Purbeck marble mortars), and will have involved many small landing places as well as large ports.

Marine and maritime environment

The development of harbours provide the potential for examining waterlogged contexts relating to the maritime environment, but may also contain materials from the dryland docks. The sediments may provide long pollen

Plate 15.11 Pepperpot lighthouse, Isle of Wight, *copyright Isle of Wight Museum*

Plate 15.12 Mary Rose undergoing conservation, Portsmouth, *copyright Mary Rose Trust*

records relating to the land-use and vegetation history in and around the docks and their interfluves, as well as waterlogged structural timbers and plant remains.

The maritime link obviously provided the landing point for imports, but also for marine fishing which is well-known at this time as evidenced from Southampton. Studies of fish bones from harbour sites where immediate preparation may occur, or of market sites (eg Southampton) provide important information about local and regional economies, and also provide data about national fishing strategies and economy at this time (Barrett *et. al.* 2004).

Ships and boats

One medieval lighthouse survives on St Catherine's Down, Isle of Wight (Plate 15.11). Wrecks are known from the coasts of the Isle of Wight, but mostly from documentary sources. Existing wrecks of importance include the *Harry Grace-Dieu* in the Hamble, and the *Mary Rose*, now the object of detailed study, and on display in its own museum. By contrast, the development of river boats from the medieval Thames 'shouts' to the post-medieval 'western barges' and punts is not well understood, though it is believed that the 'Blackfriars 3' boat from the London Thames is a shout. A medieval logboat is displayed in the River and Rowing Museum at Henley. Ship-building was carried out on the Hampshire coast, and a dry dock is recorded at Portsmouth in King John's reign.

The *Mary Rose* provided significant understanding about Tudor land-based economies for the provisioning of the ships, via detailed studies of the animal bone (butchery, preparation and packaging of salt beef etc), fish bones (preparation of salt cod), and other food stuffs (waterlogged plant remains of apples, plums, pepper corns etc). The possibility exists via DNA and other studies to start to examine specific crop genetics and species types and development, eg the choice of apples and plums chosen to provision the vessel. Waterlogged plant remains provided details of the clothing, hay and straw stuffing for of shoes and bedding, and the pollen giving evidence of the land-based environment as well as the defining the vegetative nature of the sail fabric (hemp/nettle).

Information from naval vessels indicates the industrial scale of food production and preparation to provision and victual these vessels and fleets, telling us more about the land-based economy needed to supply them, than about the vessels themselves (Allen 2005).

The potential for medieval and post-medieval boats is high, and the *Mary Rose* provides an exemplar (Plate 15.12), but other recent investigations have sadly not engaged with archaeological science, to the detriment of the comprehension of the vessel itself, but more importantly the key crucial and rare insights to the land-based economy and material provisioning the vessels.

Chapter 16

The Later Medieval Period: Research Agenda

by Julian Munby, with contributions by Michael Allen

16.1 Introduction

The major geographical divisions of the region have been well described, and necessarily include a varied cross-section of southern English geology, soils and land forms:

Downland scarp fronts/wooded backs

Clay vales/gravelled river valleys: champion land

Forested areas on clays/sands

Sandy/clay heaths and wastes.

16.1.1 Environmental determinism is unfashionable but at some level is foolish to ignore where so often land-use reflects the soils, topography and situation. These factors need to be considered more explicitly in future research. Political and economic factors of land-ownership also have an important role in this period, and there is often historical evidence allowing them to be better understood.

16.1.2 From large-scale regional considerations there is also a need for better understanding and definition of the local *pays* – eg Banburyshire, Otmoor, the Forest of Bere, the east Berkshire or Whittlewood, and of the extent to which human land-use and zones of activity occupy or traverse the margins of topographic divisions such as scarp slopes and the boundaries of forests and wastes. Even such a relatively compact area as the Isle of Wight has great variety of landscape types.

16.1.3 The historic landscape character of these *pays* needs to be studied, but in greater depth than the contemporary HLC mapping, and with inputs from archaeology and landscape history, and the large quantity of post-medieval data for the early modern landscape. From this can arise an understanding of whether there were in reality typical settlement/landuse types for these areas, or if they were just as often variable and changing over time.

16.2 The nature of the evidence

Within the setting provided by geography, soils and vegetation, the material culture of the medieval period is represented by extant, ruined, and buried remains; by visual representations in art (glass, painting, sculpture); and by description or indication in written sources (charters, surveys, accounts, narratives). Environmental and scientific studies add another dimension.

None of these uniquely explains what happened, but while a combination of evidence may make a rounded story, it is still the case that any one type of evidence may provide a unique witness of an event. It would seem unwise to promote an 'archaeological' research programme based solely on buried evidence for material culture, without considering the desirability of documentary and archaeological/art-historical/architectural studies.

There is an abundance of documentary sources, as there are buildings and art-works, waiting the attention of those who take the trouble to find them. For all future research projects in this period,

16.2.1 Evidence from documentary sources needs to be integrated with the physical evidence, and each allowed to challenge the other.

16.2.2 Consideration of art and art-historical studies should be included.

16.3 Chronology

The political and social shock of the Norman Conquest provides a firm enough date for the commencement of the later medieval period in England, if a slightly fuzzy one for significant change in material culture. Likewise for the end in the mid-16th century, the political and social shock of the 'age of plunder' (Hoskins) was accompanied by a profound economic reorganisation of land and resources, which approximates to changes in housing (the end of the hall house).

In the bigger picture, however, and disregarding the rise and fall of feudalism, and the elimination of the small landowner, the cultural milieu of the English countryside (manor and church, beast-drawn ploughs and manual haymaking) may be seen as a continuum, established before and after the Norman Conquest, but broken only by the First World War. To aid the chronological definition of research in the late medieval period, therefore,

16.3.1   Milestones for the region within the continuum of economic and social development need to be identified.

16.4 Landscape and land use

Field survey, excavation and collection of environmental data remain the most obvious approaches, though making use of the wealth of documentary sources is a necessary adjunct. For river valleys, a prerequisite of effective research may be to define the precise nature of groundwater conditions and flooding. This will make it possible to define areas that were suitable for permanent settlement, for seasonal settlement or for grazing, or areas where evidence of medieval archaeology is sealed below alluvium, making it invisible by normal archaeological reconnaissance methods. It will also allow us to chart the changing extent of land of these different types across time within this period. The following require further investigation:

16.4.1   The chronology of development and character of field systems and their relationship to settlement across the region needs to be further explored.

16.4.2   The character and organisation of ridge and furrow; field drainage.

16.4.3   The relation of surviving ridge and furrow to early field maps.

16.4.4   Identification of 'lost' ridge and furrow from old APs and LIDAR survey.

16.4.5   Evidence needs to be gathered for the extension of arable into forests and onto downland; assarts and early enclosure; hedge dates and types.

16.4.6   The management of water resources: water meadows and leats for mills.

16.4.7   The location of fishponds and fisheries; their relation to weirs and mills/ bridges.

16.4.8   Canals and artificial water bodies.

16.4.9   Sea fishing and coastal fish weirs/traps.

16.4.10 Deer farming and parks; deer leaps and traps; stud farms; rabbit warrens.

16.4.11 Forests and chases; the bounds of the true (as well as the legal) forests; their topography and service buildings.

16.4.12 Timber cultivation and transportation; woodland banks and divisions.

16.4.13 Provision and marketing of firewood and charcoal.

16.4.14 Use of different cereal grains; introduction of rivet wheat; brewing.

16.4.15 The production of fodder such as the cultivation of common vetch and the importance of oats require further consideration

16.4.16 The growth of horticulture; the development of trade in herbs and spices for both culinary and medicinal use.

16.4.17 Rural settlements with anoxic conditions are rare – samples from these should be targeted, and analysed with particular attention to site formation processes.

16.4.18 Changes in fauna of major rivers in relation to pollution and habitat loss should be investigated.

16.5 Social organisation

Documentary evidence is the major source of information about social organisation during this period, but it is seldom possible to rely on this to develop a picture of everyday life, particularly for the lower ranks in society. Integration of archaeology and records is essential. Some aspects of life, such as migration patterns and diet, can be informed by modern scientific approaches, which will include the following:

16.5.1   Stable isotope analysis of burials to investigate origins and diet may provide information of migration patterns and immigration from overseas.

16.5.2   Variations in diet may also reflect differences in social status and location in town/country.

16.5.3   The study of faunal remains, both by quantitive analysis and through analyses such as deficiencies evident in teeth or bones, should be routinely pursued for an indication of diet.

16.6 Settlement

Rural settlement

National and regional studies of settlement types and patterns are beginning to appear, especially valuable where they cross county boundaries, while it is as well to remember earlier multi-volume syntheses such as the *Domesday Geography* and the *Cambridge Agrarian History of England* which abound with useful information.

Topics and questions remain familiar from those raised long ago by Maitland (1897), Seebohm (1913), Gray (1915) and Hoskins (1955), though the data (on early field systems for example) has greatly increased. These include:

16.6.1 The origins and nature of nucleated village settlement.

16.6.2 The need to extend village morphology studies from Buckinghamshire to other areas.

16.6.3 The origins/continuation of dispersed settlement.

16.6.4 Continuity and contrast between Chiltern and Berkshire downs (fringe settlements on scarp edges).

16.6.5 Types of settlement on forest edges and commons.

16.6.6 The nature of dispersed settlement as farms/granges/moats/hamlets.

16.6.7 The character, distribution and chronology of moats.

16.6.8 Village shrinkage and abandonment; change from hamlets to farmsteads.

16.6.9 Evolution of 'farming counties', possibly origination before the Black Death.

Manorial sites

Manorial sites have attracted attention because of their prominence, but fundamental questions remain. These comprise:

16.6.10 The origins of manorial sites, their chronology and their relation to village formation.

16.6.11 Reasons for the abandonment of manorial sites.

16.6.12 The character of manorial sites (moated, relation to village plan).

16.6.13 Better definition of special types (eg royal manors, castles, ecclesiastical granges etc).

16.6.14 The character of peripheral settlements attracted to moated sites, granges, etc.

16.6.15 The character and status of manorial/gentry buildings.

Towns

This region has seen a significant quantity of excavations in large towns, some exemplary but still not all published. Small town surveys in the 1970s promoted agendas for action that have often been disregarded, and the successor surveys are more colourful but perhaps no more informative, while the questions remain. Key among these are the following.

16.6.16 What were the reasons for the survival and persistence of urban sites from the early medieval period?

16.6.17 What factors influenced the origins and growth of the principal towns?

16.6.18 How did the hierarchy of large and small towns, markets and ecclesiastical centres (former Minster towns) develop?

16.6.19 What was the distribution of markets and fairs, and why?

16.6.20 How does the topography and plan form of towns differ, and what are the key differences between small and large towns?

16.6.21 How did tenement patterns develop, and what was their relation to field patterns?

16.6.22 Where were the town fields and commons? How did they relate to liberty and parish boundaries?

16.6.23 What were the drivers for the formation of new towns, and for town extensions and retractions?

16.6.24 How does the survival of deposits vary within and between towns? How did the size of a town affect the management and disposal of waste?

16.6.25 Were there differences in the living conditions between small towns and larger conurbations, and if so, in what did these consist?

16.7 The built environment

Rural building

The study of vernacular architecture has been a remarkable instance of a popular academic endeavour over the last half century, achieved in the absence of any organised research framework as a self-supporting empirical activity and producing a huge increase in knowledge and understanding. The more recent addition of widespread dendrochronological dating and more systematic research projects on specific topics has sharpened the edge of our understanding. More research is however needed on the following topics:

16.7.1 The quality of buildings, framing/roof types as indications of class/status.

16.7.2 Rebuilding as reflecting wealth/agricultural change.

16.7.3 Changing building techniques in timber, stone and brick, and the chronology and distribution of use of different materials.

16.7.4 Crucks and box frames, and in particular, the chronology and distribution of framing types.

16.7.5 The chronology of the end of the construction of open halls, and of the start of the construction of continuous jetties.

16.7.6 Chronology and distribution of roof types, and in particular the change from crown-post to queen-post roofs.

16.7.7 Dating of buildings in local areas/regions as a guide to the chronology of change (eg recovery from Black Death).

16.7.8 Understanding regional differences in survival rates (eg extant stock of early peasant houses in Harwell and the Vale of White Horse, and of hall houses around Winchester).

16.7.9 The plan forms of farmsteads and the nature of subsidiary buildings, especially barns associated with monastic/institutional landlords.

16.7.10 The identification of 'squatter dwellings' on ?commons and wastes.

16.7.11 Buildings identified in written and pictorial sources.

Urban building

As with rural vernacular, town houses and other buildings have benefited from a generation of close study, and much more is known, but more remains to be found. Topics that need further study include:

16.7.12 The origins and development of urban housing types (plan, gables and ridges in relation to streets).

16.7.13 Character and ranking of town houses.

16.7.14 Warehouses and storage cellars.

16.7.15 Origins of inns (wealdens used as); taverns in special cellars.

16.7.16 Halls of gilds and buildings of institutions.

16.7.17 Hospitals, colleges and almshouses. The association of hospitals with urban settlement in particular is currently insufficiently appreciated.

16.7.18 Location and character of parish churches and friaries.

16.7.19 Lost buildings identified in written and pictorial sources.

16.7.20 The development of specific building types using different materials in particular areas of towns and cities, and their relationship to social identity and status

16.10 Ceremony, ritual and religion

Monastic houses

Like castles, monasteries have attracted much archaeological attention, but continue to produce new aspects for study. Fundamental elements that still require study include:

16.10.1 The relation of pre-conquest churches to later churches and claustral buildings.

16.10.2 The character and chronology of major buildings.

16.10.3 Better understanding of subsidiary buildings, economic activities, water management and gardens.

16.10.4 Monastic life, diet, health and death.

16.10.5 Minor monastic and related sites (moated monastic sites).

16.10.6 Barns and granges.

16.10.7 Failed or temporary monastic houses.

Parish churches

The parish church stands at the fountainhead of modern archaeology, and yet even after 150 years of study has much to reveal. Very few aspects of the church as a cultural indicator have been mapped or studied in regional terms, even though church types (such as the 'wool' church, steeples, or the early two-cell parish church) are well known. The study of the spatial distribution of these and other patterns of church types, together with the chronology of church building and rebuilding, the regional patterns of masonry and carpentry, of decoration, tracery and sculpture would be worthwhile.

Aspects that require particular attention include:

16.10.8   The chronology of church building/rebuilding and its relationship to the evolving liturgy.

16.10.9   Study of patrons and rectorial works to fabric.

16.10.10   Regional patterns of church types and chronology.

16.10.11   Location of church in village/parish plan.

16.10.12   Change from parochia to parish, and the role of chapels.

16.10.13   Regional patterns of masonry, decoration, windows, sculpture.

16.10.14   Chronology and types of roof, screens and seating.

16.10.15   Church monuments, plate, bells and windows.

16.10.16   Churchyards and their features; burials.

16.10.17   Rectory and Rectory farms; vicarages.

16.12 Warfare, defences and military installations

The early defences of the pre-conquest *burhs* were often the origin of later town walls, and though defended towns are few their standing remains have perhaps received less attention than buried sections.

Similarly much remains to be learnt from castles, which range from early earthwork constructions to royal and seigniorial centres such as Windsor. Their level of survival particularly in urban environments is not good. The modern fashion for discounting the defensive aspects of castles is given the lie by the upgrading of coastal defences in the light of invasion threats (eg Southampton, Portchester/Portsmouth, and the Isle of Wight). The following measures should be prioritised:

16.12.1   Surviving sections of town defences need to be recorded.

16.12.2   Reconsideration of castle remains and sites, particularly in towns across the region, is needed.

16.12.3   The measures taken to upgrade medieval (and earlier) defensive sites, particularly on the coast, during the later medieval period, should be further studied in relation to contemporary events in political relations with the continent.

16.12.4   Given the importance of royalty in the region, castles should be considered in relation to major seigniorial establishments, such as the king's houses and the 'palaces' of bishops and magnates.

16.12.5   More investigation should be made of the relationship of castles and their landscape setting as manors with adjacent villages and fields, parks and forests (eg Portchester).

16.13 Material culture

Perhaps the most interesting recent development has been the results of the Portable Antiquities Scheme, and the realisation of the quantity of small metal objects that have been found. Pottery dominates the finds from excavations.

16.13.1   There is still a need for further study of the varieties and quality of pottery usage.

16.13.2   Small finds can be seen as important indicators of consumer activity in rural and urban households, and evidence for the influence of overseas trade and proximity to London may be identifiable. They may also indicate the presence and movement of noblemen and their retinues within and beyond the region. These lines of enquiry should be pursued.

16.13.3   Whether these influences also affected changes in use and status of pottery or whether they were the result of wider economic and social change should be investigated.

16.14 Trade and industry

Discoveries suggest that the pottery industry involved both large and small-scale production. There are important early examples of the use of brick (Eton and Windsor; Ewelme) and likewise floor tiles are very prevalent in institutional buildings. Stone quarrying is important in the Jurassic belt for fine limestone and stone slates, as also in chalk areas for chalk rubble and clunch. Stone types have been identified in some areas (eg Berkshire churches).

Cloth production was a major element in town economies and later in rural areas, but its archaeology is hard to identify, whether in relation to dyeing, fulling (mills) or tenter fields. Tanning was another major urban activity and in some places parchment was produced. Milling is widespread, and mills are best known from mill leats and post-medieval windmills.

Other products include coastal salt, iron and woodworking, from small domestic objects to ships. Despite good documentation and a wide assemblage of artefacts, the production sites and technology associated with these industries are not well understood. The following should be actively sought:

16.14.1   Means and location of manufacture of small metal objects.

16.14.2   Patterns of marketing of small metal objects.

16.14.3   The location of the more persistent and the temporary production sites for pottery.

16.14.4   The means and places of production of brick and floor tiles.

16.14.5   Distribution of structures using brick and floor tiles should be examined for evidence of the sources of the materials, and the distance that these materials were transported ie the range of each industry.

16.14.6   Identification of quarry locations.

16.14.7   The means of transport (coastal, river and road) for stone.

16.14.8   Urban tanning sites and production of parchment.

16.14.9   Origins of fibre production.

16.14.10 Evidence for the survival of horizontal mills.

16.14.11 Distribution of coastal tidemills.

16.14.12 Salt production sites and the technology that they employed.

16.14.13 Identification of ironworking sites.

16.14.14 Production sites for wooden objects, including ships.

16.14.15 Study of the markings on casks as a means to identify their origins, and thus inform patterns of trade.

16.14.16 Identification and study of shipwrecks and their cargoes.

16.14.17 Mason's marks should be studied, not only to assist in understanding the orgainsiation

of labour on major building projects, but also to investigate the movement of craftsmen and decorative styles.

16.15   Transport and communications

Use of the south coast ports for overseas trade is an obvious topic, but the coastal trade may have carried a greater bulk of materials (demonstrated by the distribution of objects such as Purbeck marble mortars). Use of the Thames is harder to demonstrate, and the use of Taynton stone in the White Tower does not prove use of the Thames for stone transport. Weirs and mills were certainly a hazard to navigation (and so mentioned in Magna Carta). The difficulty of navigation between Oxford and Reading is thought to have led to the increased importance of Henley as the transhipment port for the cereal grown in the south midlands and destined for London, just as it was anyway for exporting Chiltern products such as firewood. Although it had wharfage in Reading, and despite documentary information showingthe links between Newbury and London for the cloth trade in the later medieval period, the use of the Kennet, and of other smaller rivers within the region, is poorly understood.

Road transport was always more important than is allowed, whether by pedlar, packhorse or two-wheeled cart. The following should be research priorities:

16.15.1   Evidence for coastal and overseas trading ports, which will inform patterns of exchange within Britain and with the continent.

16.15.2   Wharves and other evidence for river transport should be investigated wherever possible to demonstrate how the major rivers of the region functioned

16.15.3   River craft from this period are not well recorded and evidence for Thames barges, 'shouts', punts etc. should be more actively sought.

16.15.4   Evidence for the creation, diversion and maintenance of waterways and for industries such as milling and fisheries is needed.

16.15.5   The extent of road transport and bridges in the region needs further investigation, including evidence from documentary records.

Chapter 17

The Post-Medieval and Modern Period (AD 1540 onwards): Resource Assessment

by Jill Hind

Introduction

The period from 1540 to the present encompasses a vast amount of change to society, stretching as it does from the end of the feudal medieval system to a multicultural, globally oriented state, which increasingly depends on the use of Information Technology. This transition has been punctuated by the protestant reformation of the 16th century, conflicts over religion and power structure, including regicide in the 17th century, the Industrial and Agricultural revolutions of the 18th and early 19th century and a series of major wars. Although land battles have not taken place on British soil since the 18th century, setting aside terrorism, civilians have become increasingly involved in these wars.

The period has also seen the development of capitalism, with Britain leading the Industrial Revolution and becoming a major trading nation. Trade was followed by colonisation and by the second half of the 19th century the British Empire included vast areas across the world, despite the independence of the United States in 1783. The second half of the 20th century saw the end of imperialism. London became a centre of global importance as a result of trade and empire, but has maintained its status as a financial centre.

The Solent-Thames region generally is prosperous, benefiting from relative proximity to London and good communications routes. The Isle of Wight has its own particular issues, but has never been completely isolated from major events. The historic counties of Oxfordshire, Berkshire, Buckinghamshire, Hampshire and the Isle of Wight were already long established political units by the start of the period, although the Isle of Wight was officially part of Hampshire from the late 19th century until 1974. The boundaries of the other counties also remained essentially unaltered until the second half of the 20th century.

Since then the biggest changes have taken place in Berkshire. In the 1974 local government reorganisation a large area of land in the Vale of the White Horse was transferred to Oxfordshire, and at the same time the Slough area was transferred to Berkshire from Buckinghamshire. At this point Bournemouth was also transferred from Hampshire to Dorset. In 1998 Berkshire was split into six Unitary Authorities, Bracknell Forest, Reading, Slough, West Berkshire, Windsor and Maidenhead and Wokingham (Fig. 1.1). Bucking-

hamshire too was changed by the creation of the Milton Keynes Unitary Authority. Portsmouth and Southampton are also now Unitary Authorities.

Inheritance

This period begins in *c.* 1540 when Henry VIII was carrying out his reformation of the Church of England and following the dissolution of the monasteries in 1536-39. The Church had been a major landowner in the Solent-Thames region. The change to secular ownership initially had little impact on the pattern of settlement and land use that existed in the mid 16th century, although those areas that had been directly farmed as part of monastic estates naturally saw some change as a result.

A bigger change was the deliberate slighting of former monastic buildings, many of which were plundered for their materials or converted to new (usually domestic) uses. Hampshire in particular contains some fine examples of former monastic buildings transformed into fine country houses, examples including Mottisfont, Netley and Titchfield. Further changes occurred with the dissolution of chantries and hospitals after 1547, several of which found new uses in endowing new or existing almshouses and hospitals.

There were a number of thriving market towns in all the counties by this period, some such as Burford, Oxfordshire and Newbury, Berkshire, made prosperous by the wool trade. Larger urban settlements existed at the ports of Southampton and Portsmouth, at the historic centres of Winchester, Reading and Oxford, the last boosted by the growth of the University in the 16th century.

A number of forests survived across the area, including the New Forest and those in the hands of the three principal landowners: the crown, monastic houses and the Bishop of Winchester, whose estates extended well beyond Hampshire itself. Within these forests there were still extensive areas of woodland. Across most of the area there was a mixture of open fields, common grazing lands and water meadows.

The majority of the population still lived in the countryside at the beginning of this period, governed by the manorial system. This feudal way of life gradually broke down, but some elements of its influence persisted into the 19th and even 20th centuries.

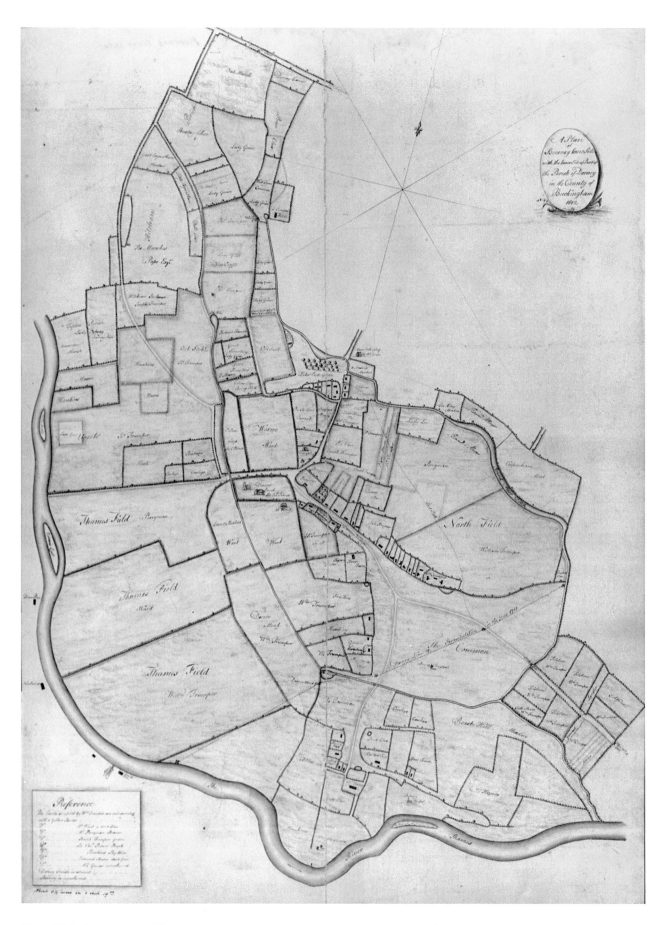

Plate 17.1 Estate map of Dorney, Buckinghamshire, *copyright Buckinghamshire County Record Office, Buckinghamshire County Council*

Nature of the evidence

The amount of historical source material for the post-medieval and modern periods is enormous. Rocque, surveyor to Henry VIII, made detailed surveys of Abingdon, Newbury and Reading at the time of the Dissolution. Antiquaries, starting with Leland, wrote about visits and journeys and many published their surveys of particular counties (Sweet 2004). For the Solent-Thames region the picture is mixed: for Buckinghamshire there are Browne Willis in the 18th century, Lipscomb (1847) and Sheahan (1861); for Oxfordshire Plot (1677) and Wood in Oxford itself (1674); for Hampshire and the Isle of Wight Woodward (1861-9); for Berkshire King (1887). Speed's 18th-century history of Southampton was published by Davies (1883). Local societies have long existed and their archives and the journals they established and continue to publish remain an important resource. Maps are another valuable resource, mainly of 17th century or later date, although Agas produced his map of Oxford in 1578. Tithe maps, enclosure maps, estate maps and county maps all predate the Ordnance Survey, whose tremendous coverage began in the early 19th century (Plate 17.1).

One of the most useful published sources is the Victoria County Histories, which provide an overview on a parish by parish basis. Unfortunately, those for much of the region were produced at a fairly early stage when the scope was generally limited to manorial and church history. For Oxfordshire there is almost the opposite problem, as here coverage is very broad but the series is still incomplete. Buckinghamshire and Oxfordshire were also included in The Landscape of Britain series (Reed 1979, Emery 1974).

For the built environment there are Pevsner's Buildings of England (those for Hampshire and the Isle of Wight are currently being revised) and for Buckinghamshire and Oxford City the RCHME Inventory volumes.

During the 20th and 21st centuries there have been numerous publications of county, parish and thematic histories, for example The Story of Victorian Shanklin (Parker 1977) and the many 'Books of' various towns published by Phillimore. Some care is needed with some of these recent local histories, as there is often an emphasis on photographs, spiced with personal reminiscences, rather than serious and impartial research.

In addition to these documentary sources there have been a number of research initiatives in recent years, the results from several of which are presented as electronic resources. GIS has been used to generate mapping and some is available to the general public through interactive websites. Urban surveys were carried out for Oxfordshire, Berkshire and Hampshire in the 1970s. The English Heritage funded programme of urban survey begun in the 1990s is updating these surveys with GIS components, and extends into previously unsurveyed areas. Work on the small towns of Hampshire and the Isle of Wight is complete and Oxfordshire and Buckinghamshire are underway. The parallel programme of more intensive studies of larger towns and cities has covered Oxford, Winchester and Southampton, for the first two of which an Urban Archaeological Database (UAD) is available, complementing the HER.

Another relevant research programme is Historic Landscape Characterisation (HLC). This has been carried out for Hampshire, West Berkshire, Buckinghamshire and the Chilterns (the last extending to areas beyond the Solent-Thames Region). There has also been the Hampshire Villages survey and the Whittlewood Project, which covers parts of Buckinghamshire.

The Defence of Britain Survey was a national initiative to record military remains, ranging in scale from anti-tank trenches to airfields. This huge database is a valuable resource, although not in fact covering the Isle of Wight, and the project has generated a number of published syntheses. A new project to extend the scope of the defence record, now including air raid shelters and other civilian facilities, was launched in 2007. The area has also featured in a number of the thematic syntheses produced by English Heritage, eg Dangerous Energy (Cocroft 2000) and Cold War (Cocroft and Thomas 2003) as well as non-military themes such as Hospitals (RCHME 1998).

Individuals and local groups have also carried out research projects. A Historical Atlas of Berkshire was compiled by Joan Dils (Dils ed. 1998), one for Oxfordshire by Tiller and Darkes (2010), and a study of Buckinghamshire mills was masterminded by Mike Farley (Farley 2007).

The weakest aspect of evidence is almost certainly that from archaeological excavations and surveys. Building studies are becoming more common, but there have only been a limited number of major excavation programmes on sites from this period, such as the Newbury Wharf area, and most are in urban contexts. Excavations of post-medieval manor houses, like that at The Beeches, Wokingham, Berkshire, have been few (Plate 17.2). The bulk of post-medieval work has been on industrial sites.

Although the contribution of environmental archaeology and geo-archaeology is significantly less for this period than earlier ones, there is still knowledge to be gained. In addition to changes in the landscape, industries and the economic marketplace environmental evidence may shed light on climate changes, such as the Little Ice Age, and an increasing use of exotic, imported substances, such as spices. The impact of the agricultural revolution may also be detected in the record.

The sheer quantity and variety of available evidence for this period indicates strongly the need for co-ordination and co-operation across a range of stakeholders. A combination of efforts from archaeologists, architectural historians, conservation officers, national and local historians (across both the professional and 'voluntary' sectors) is essential. Selected key sites are shown on Figure 17.1.

Plate 17.2 Excavation of the 17th century Beeches manor house, Wokingham, Berkshire, *copyright TVAS*

Chronology

Determination of the dividing line between the medieval and post-medieval periods has traditionally been a matter of debate, but the Protestant Reformation under Henry VIII represented a point of radical change to the structure of society in England and Wales, suggesting that AD1540 is a suitable point to place the division. However, the changes in beliefs and attitudes which underlay this event date from a much earlier period and continued well into the later 16th century and beyond.

The division between the post-medieval and modern periods is even more subjective, although the MIDAS Data Standard uses 1901. It is probably more useful to regard the two as a continuum, within which there are a number of possible subdivisions relating to major events or periods of development, eg the Civil War or the Industrial Revolution. No end date is proposed for this period. The rate at which the world changes continues to increase rapidly so that features constructed during the later 20th century have already reached the end of their useful life, and their possible preservation and level of recording are matters for immediate concern.

Within this period the detailed chronology of change is an important issue. The rate at which the impact of events is visible within the broader social and economic context, and whether there are regional variations in this time-scale, may also be significant.

While documentary sources can be used to date events or the construction of some buildings, it is still necessary to look at typology and chronological sequences of for example pottery. Absolute dating is available from dendro-chronology, which does not always support accepted interpretations. As an example, though not from the region, roof beams in the South Lodge at Ashdown Park had felling dates of 1767, although the lodges existed by 1716 and no alteration had been recorded (http://www.dendrochronology.net/oxfordshire.asp).

Landscape and land use

During the post-medieval period the pattern of mixed arable and pastoral farming across the region was changed by enclosure. This was carried out in order to promote grazing, to consolidate small farms into larger units and later for emparkment. Some areas had already been enclosed in the medieval period, for example where large areas of land were under Church control. Until the early 18th century enclosure was usually, but not always carried out by agreement: the Stonors and Rice Griffin caused riots by their enclosures in Didcot in 1539 and 1597 (Lingham 1979). The pace of land change accelerated when enclosure by parliamentary act became common practice. Between 1761 and 1860 most of north Buckinghamshire (including what is now Milton Keynes) was enclosed (Turner 1973a, b, Turner 1977); Oxfordshire maintained large areas of unenclosed land up to the late 18th century (Emery 1974). Enclosure was a gradual process in Hampshire and Berkshire (Wordie 1984). The

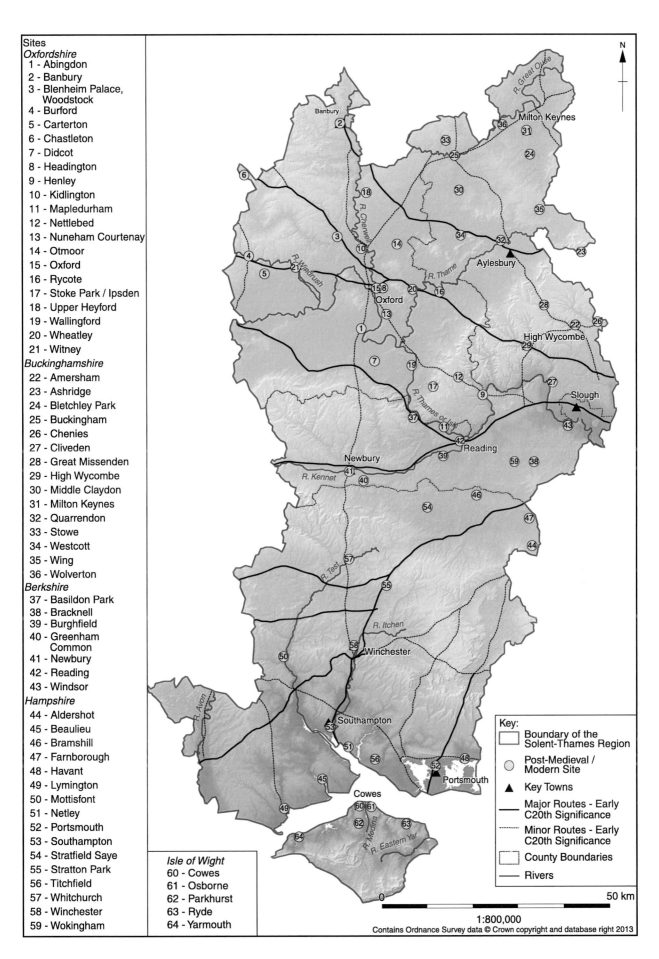

Sites

Oxfordshire
1 - Abingdon
2 - Banbury
3 - Blenheim Palace, Woodstock
4 - Burford
5 - Carterton
6 - Chastleton
7 - Didcot
8 - Headington
9 - Henley
10 - Kidlington
11 - Mapledurham
12 - Nettlebed
13 - Nuneham Courtenay
14 - Otmoor
15 - Oxford
16 - Rycote
17 - Stoke Park / Ipsden
18 - Upper Heyford
19 - Wallingford
20 - Wheatley
21 - Witney

Buckinghamshire
22 - Amersham
23 - Ashridge
24 - Bletchley Park
25 - Buckingham
26 - Chenies
27 - Cliveden
28 - Great Missenden
29 - High Wycombe
30 - Middle Claydon
31 - Milton Keynes
32 - Quarrendon
33 - Stowe
34 - Westcott
35 - Wing
36 - Wolverton

Berkshire
37 - Basildon Park
38 - Bracknell
39 - Burghfield
40 - Greenham Common
41 - Newbury
42 - Reading
43 - Windsor

Hampshire
44 - Aldershot
45 - Beaulieu
46 - Bramshill
47 - Farnborough
48 - Havant
49 - Lymington
50 - Mottisfont
51 - Netley
52 - Portsmouth
53 - Southampton
54 - Stratfield Saye
55 - Stratton Park
56 - Titchfield
57 - Whitchurch
58 - Winchester
59 - Wokingham

Isle of Wight
60 - Cowes
61 - Osborne
62 - Parkhurst
63 - Ryde
64 - Yarmouth

Key:
▢ Boundary of the Solent-Thames Region
◯ Post-Medieval / Modern Site
▲ Key Towns
── Major Routes - Early C20th Significance
---- Minor Routes - Early C20th Significance
▢ County Boundaries
── Rivers

0   50 km

1:800,000
Contains Ordnance Survey data © Crown copyright and database right 2013

Figure 17.1 Post-medieval and Modern sites and roads mentioned in the text

traditional pattern of sheep grazing on the open downland declined and more arable production was introduced, stimulated by military need and by nearness to London. Later diversification into market gardening and dairy production helped offset decline in grain prices.

Again the pattern for the Isle of Wight is different. Here there were many absentee landlords until the 19th century and the overall picture was of small farms. Large sheep runs were a feature, one such estate being at Swainston in the 17th century (M J Jones 2003). In Freshwater some piecemeal enclosure of open strips was taking place in 19th century. Large landowners became more actively engaged in agriculture during the 19th

century, for example the Seeley, Ward and Northcourt estates, as well as the royal estate at Osborne, where Prince Albert established a number of model farms.

Model farms were also built in other parts of the region, such as Coleshill, Oxfordshire and in Hampshire some were even equipped with narrow gauge railways, for example at Tidmarsh (Wade Martins 2002). A particularly elaborate industrialisation of an estate was established at Buscot, Oxfordshire (Parkinson 1993).

One of the best ways to study the changing pattern of the landscape during this period is through cartographic sources, particularly where enclosure maps survive. The HLC studies, completed for Buckinghamshire, Hampshire (although excluding Southampton) and West

Plate 17.3 Aerial view of Blenheim Palace, *copyright Oxfordshire County Council*

Berkshire, are another good source. The changes to the settlements resulting from enclosure are discussed below.

During this period most of the former medieval hunting forests were disafforested. In Buckinghamshire this included Salcey (1825), and Whaddon (1841), and for Oxfordshire Bernwood, (1632), Shotover (1660) and Wychwood (1857), this last not converted to farmland until the 1850s. Forests have not been well studied apart from Bernwood (Broad & Hoyle 1997), and Wychwood (Schumer 1984). Much of the eastern part of Berkshire lay within the royal Windsor Great Forest, where some land was sold off during the 17th century to help Parliament pay for Cromwell's army (Roberts 1997).

After the Windsor Forest Enclosure Act was passed in 1813 the Crown retained a large portion (now Windsor Great Park) for its private use, and ownership of other larger areas. Managed pine forests were established on the heathland after WWI to replace timber used in the war effort (Bracknell Forest Borough Council 2000). In the south of Hampshire is the New Forest, another former royal forest, and now a National Park. Forest Law had undergone some reforms over time but was only formally ended in the later 20th century.

The Chilterns area also retains significant amounts of (primarily beech) woodland. It was particularly important for its post-medieval industries, such as the local furniture industry (Hepple & Doggett 1992; 1994). Thinner wood was useful as a supply of firewood, a significant export from the region to London, as well as fencing, furniture or brooms for example. Thicker branches would be used in construction. These practices continued in the Chiltern region until the canals and railways facilitated a move to coal as a fuel in London. The growth of the city in the 16th and 17th centuries had produced a great demand for wood and development of many small wharves (Hepple & Doggett 1994).

Corn was an even more important product and woodland was cleared to increase the area of land available for agriculture. Some of the grain produced was converted to malt and supplied to brewers, including some in London. London provided a huge market for grain and animals, the latter fattened if not bred in the region. Milk was also shipped to the capital particularly from Berkshire after the railways facilitated its swift movement. Close to the capital market gardens were established, some with orchards, such as Veitch of Langley Marish who from c. 1880 was producing apples, pears and roses. The earliest recorded nurseries were the Royal Nurseries in Slough, established by Thomas Brown in 1774 (VCH Buckinghamshire III 1925).

Similar diversification of production can be seen in the hinterland around Southampton, probably to serve that town but possibly also supplying London by rail.

Designed landscapes are a very common feature across the region, many included within the EH Register of Parks and Gardens. Some have been studied in detail: Ashridge (Wainwright 1989) and Blenheim, Oxfordshire (Bond & Tiller 1997; Plate 17.3). The assemblage includes examples by some of the greatest names in landscape design including William Kent, Humphry Repton, Lancelot (Capability) Brown and Gertrude Jekyll. Not all of the landscapes of interest are associated with great houses and there are many smaller properties along the Thames of interest. Public landscapes should not be forgotten, both public parks and (from the mid-19th century) the municipal cemeteries, such as the well-preserved example at Henley-on-Thames (see Fig. 15.1). In Oxford many of the colleges have fine grounds (Batey 1982). The common fields and common of Southampton were retained as public parkland.

Several of the large estates have changed their uses and the associated parkland is often at risk from the need to provide a range of recreational facilities such as golf courses, as at Mapledurham, Oxfordshire. Built structures, including ice houses, bridges, grottoes and bridges, as well as statues and monuments are a vital part of designed landscapes and need to be recorded and preserved. The duck-decoy at Boarstall in Buckinghamshire is another estate survival, now fortunately owned by the National Trust (Plate 17.4; see Fig. 15.1 for location).

Water meadows do not survive well across the region generally, but the chalk valley bottoms of the Kennet Valley, Berkshire and most particularly of Hampshire are important (OAU 2000c). Some commons, heaths and wastes have survived, notably in the southern parts of Buckinghamshire and the Chilterns. These form an almost continuous band on the north bank of the

Plate 17.4 Duck Decoy at Boarstall, Buckinghamshire, *copyright Jill Hind*

Thames, and it is possible that they formed a route for transfer of cattle to London (Morris 2009, 18).

Evidence for land reclamation is also limited, although there has been work done on former gravel pits in Berkshire and Oxfordshire. Bembridge Haven and Newton Marsh in the Isle of Wight were drained in the 1880s and the 17th century respectively. Plans to drain Otmoor in Oxfordshire were halted after protests from local people in 1829 (Hobson & Price, 1961) and it was again spared from a plan to drive the M40 across it in the 1980s (Waite 2011).

Rivers across the region have obviously played their part in flood control and irrigation, often managed by dams and weirs. Flood meadows are still maintained along the Thames. Diversion of water for agriculture allowed the watercress beds on the Chess and Misbourne rivers in Buckinghamshire to thrive in the 19th century (Reed 1979), with other examples found at Ewelme, Oxfordshire and in the Itchen valley in Hampshire. One of the most important improvements to farm land came through the laying of land drains, networks of clay pipework. These were of particular benefit on clay soils, such as can be found in many parts of the Thames Valley. The Verneys employed this improvement technique on their lands around the Claydons, Buckinghamshire (Broad 2004). Evidence for land drains is commonly seen on aerial photographs. Much marshland was also drained, including Otmoor, north of Oxford.

Apart from the effect of enclosure and changes to the balance between arable and pastoral farming, the use of land has not been well-researched. As the small number of references in the text for this section suggests, there are many questions still to be answered.

Social organisation

Throughout the post-medieval and modern periods there was a change in the level of control over society, reducing the importance of the manorial system in favour of larger landowners in rural areas. In the towns the medieval guilds were either disbanded or reorganised to form the basis for civic corporations. The strengthening of the role of statutory authorities extended eventually to cover both town and country.

The rise of capitalism during this period and the development of the class system reinforced the differences between rich and poor, in terms of possessions, living conditions and access to opportunities for change. The region contains many examples of very grand properties, such as Blenheim, but towns like Oxford had their share of slum tenements eg St Ebbe's parish, and the conditions of the rural poor were described by Flora Thompson in 'Lark Rise to Candleford' (Thompson 1954).

At the beginning of the post-medieval period the monarchy held vast areas of land in the Thames Valley and surrounding area. It was traditional for the monarch to spend much of the year travelling around the kingdom, either staying at their own properties or at the

houses of the courtiers, with Chenies and Quarrendon west of Aylesbury both build to accommodate such visits. Elizabeth I spent time at Rycote Park, of which only the chapel and part of one tower survive. These progresses served several functions: they allowed the populace to see the monarch, ensured that royal justice was enforced, and spread the burden of feeding the royal entourage. Until the improvements to road and river transport it was impossible for the huge numbers of the royal household to obtain sufficient food if they remained in one place for long.

The Thames Valley was particularly popular with royalty because of its suitability for hunting. It was also within fairly easy reach of London, allowing contact to be maintained with the capital and providing a safe haven from outbreaks of disease. Throughout the 16th and 17th century the monarchy began to spend an increasing proportion of their time at the properties near to the capital. Windsor Castle is the only one still remaining, its parkland forming the setting for various lodges built for various family members in the 18th and 19th centuries (Roberts 1997).

The proximity to London and influence of royalty encouraged the nobility and, in later periods, the wealthy, to build their own grand houses within the region. The Tudor mansions of Chenies and Quarrendon have already been mentioned, but the practice has continued. In the 19th century Disraeli purchased Hughenden Manor north of High Wycombe, and both Chequers south of Aylesbury and Dorney Wood west of Slough provide country retreats for serving politicians.

During the later medieval and for much of the post-medieval periods social provision relied on a mixture of private initiatives and organisation at the level of individual parishes. At the beginning of the period the redistribution of monastic property and resources caused difficulties for some of the schools, hospitals and almshouses they had formerly supported. However, in the Solent-Thames region large areas were held by the Bishop of Winchester, the Dean and Chapter of Windsor, Eton College and the Oxbridge colleges who were able to provide continued support. It was not until the 19th century that more even provision began to be established through legislation such as the 'Poor Law Amendment Act' of 1834 and the 'Local Government Act' of 1872.

Municipal buildings and institutions provide the clearest evidence for these changes in responsibility. Oxfordshire has a number of 17th-century examples, including the town hall at Watlington and the former Berkshire county hall at Abingdon (1672-82) and 18th-century buildings at Wallingford and Woodstock, among others. Town halls and corn exchanges from the 19th century can be found at Banbury, Oxfordshire, Reading, Berkshire and Winchester, Hampshire for example. Until the end of the 19th century it remained common for the ground floor of these buildings to be left open to serve as a market, although many have since been enclosed. Witney, Oxfordshire had a separate market structure, the Butter Cross, constructed in the early 17th century. From a later period the Oxford Covered Market has been studied in detail (Graham 1979).

In Oxford the traditional association of the shire authority with the castle continued. The Old County Hall was built in 1840 within the former bailey and in 1914, the 1960s and 1970s additional buildings were added to the complex. Courts were held there until recently. Winchester Castle similarly has housed civic buildings and courtrooms.

Oxford Castle also has a long tradition of use as a prison, finally closing its doors in the 1990s (OA 2006a); others closed earlier including Abingdon, built in the early 19th century but in use as a grain store by the 1870s. There are a number of prisons still in use across the region, including Reading, Berkshire, made famous by Oscar Wilde and the high security establishment at Parkhurst on the Isle of Wight. New prisons opened at Grendon Underwood and Bullingdon, Buckinghamshire in the late 20th century. Some smaller, earlier local lock-ups and prisons have survived, including an unusual pyramidal structure at Wheatley, Oxfordshire and Buckingham Gaol, now a museum. Former police stations also survive, where, even if they are no longer in use, there is evidence of their function, for example at Whitchurch, Hampshire and Wokingham, Berkshire. The magistrates' court in Thame, Oxfordshire (see Fig. 15.1) has recently been converted into a town museum.

The range of provision for the sick and poor is huge. Foundation of almshouses was a popular way in which rich individuals could mark their gratitude for good fortune and this tradition extended into the 20th century. At Newbury, Berkshire there are many sets of almshouses from the 16th century onwards (Plate 17.5), including one block built in 1937 to house retired nurses (Higgott 2001). Newbury Museum occupies what remains of Kendrick's Workhouse. This wealthier clothier established premises in the town and in Reading in 1625 to provide work for the poor. The Reading building has been demolished completely (OA forthcoming).

In the 19th century the workhouse system was established where the poor were housed and put to work. Some of these were later converted into hospitals, often for mental patients. The Thame, Oxfordshire workhouse became an agricultural college and is currently being converted into flats. The Isle of Wight acquired its workhouse in the 1770s (Jones and Jones 1987). Of the purpose-built hospitals the Radcliffe Infirmary in Oxford of 1757 onwards is a particularly fine example. This has recently closed and has been taken over by Oxford University. Newbury's hospital met a less kind fate and was demolished to make way for sheltered housing. The County Lunatic Asylum, Whitecroft, Isle of Wight was built in 1894-6 and is about to undergo partial redevelopment, as is the former Berkshire County Asylum at Fairmile, Cholsey near Wallingford. Also on the Isle of Wight, the Royal National Hospital for Diseases of the chest opened in Undercliff in 1868, but was demolished in 1968 (Laidlaw 1990).

Universal education was not introduced until the 19th century, after which there was a huge expansion in the number and type of school buildings. Most of the earlier foundations have survived, although many have changed from private foundations to become part of the state system, for example St Bartholomew's School, Newbury, Berkshire, which originated as a medieval hospital. The schools established were not all under local authority control. Wellington College, Berkshire, for example, was founded in 1853 as a memorial to the Duke of Wellington (Pevsner 1966).

Further and higher education establishments were also provided along with provision for learning through museums, libraries and institutes. As discussed below the major example in the region is the University of Oxford, but there are large numbers elsewhere, Reading and Southampton being the other two oldest universities in the region, with several more created in the last two decades of the 20th century.

Provision of water was not operated on a large scale in most areas before the 19th century. Many wells and

Plate 17.5 St Bartholomew's Hospital, Newbury, Berkshire, *copyright Jill Hind*

pumps do survive, although few are still operational. At Stoke Row, Oxfordshire is the Maharajah's Well, unusual in being a gift to the poor of England from an Indian ruler, although there is in fact another gift from India at Ipsden, the next village.

There were urban waterworks in towns in the medieval and post-medieval periods, but few survive. The conduit in Abingdon was in place before the end of the medieval period (Baker 1963, 101). In 1610 Otto Nicolson provided Oxford with a conduit, situated at Carfax in the centre of the town and subsequently relocated as a purely ornamental feature to the park at Nuneham Courtenay in 1787, where it remains. A conduit house at North Hinksey, still *in situ*, supplied the original conduit with spring water.

There are various 19th- and early 20th-century waterworks and reservoirs across the region, some still used, for example the Headington Hill reservoir, Oxford. Remains of early sewage and gas works or electricity generation plants are less common, although the Oxford University engineering department now occupies the Oxford power station. This lies on the river, from which supplies of coal were delivered.

Very many public buildings have been replaced, as they do not meet modern needs and it is not thought either economic or possible to update them. As a result demolition or conversion is being carried out on a vast scale, seldom preceded by an adequate period of recording. The former waterworks in Banbury, Oxfordshire, for example, was demolished in 2000 without any record at all being made.

Local government reorganisation in 1974 and 1998 is referred to above. There is as yet little physical evidence of these changes, apart from signage along the new boundaries. Some buildings have become redundant for municipal use; the Berkshire County Hall at Shinfield just south of Reading, for example, was sold in 1998 to the engineering company Foster Wheeler.

Settlement

Patterns of settlement across the region demonstrate considerable variation, linked to the differences in geology and topography. The region is divided between the Central and South Eastern Provinces as defined by Roberts and Wrathmell (2000). Most of Hampshire, the Isle of Wight and parts of Berkshire fall into the East Wessex sub-province, an area of nucleated settlements. In the Thames sub-province the level of dispersed settlement increases, particularly in the Kennet Valley. Most of the rest of the region falls into the Inner Midlands where arable agriculture and nucleated settlement are the norm. Towards the west, in the Cotswold scarp and Vale, are areas of very dispersed settlement.

At the beginning of this period Hampshire was mainly a dairy area, with pigs in the New Forest. Elsewhere farming was mixed between corn and livestock, primarily sheep. In the later period, away from the downs and woods farming was typical of the so-

called 'champion country', with its emphasis on arable cultivation and well-developed nucleated villages.

The greatest influence on rural settlement during this period was enclosure, which was discussed earlier. The impact of this on rural settlement included a shift of farmsteads away from the villages themselves to new locations. The surviving farm buildings in the village were then re-used. The trend for population to transfer to the town increased from this period onwards. Some settlements were abandoned altogether, either because there was no work available, as at Quarrendon, Buckinghamshire, or because their location did not suit the plans of the landowner. Emparking was popular into the 19th century and resulted in the demolition of villages at Stowe, Hartwell and Waddesdon, Buckinghamshire and at Nuneham Courtney, Oxfordshire. Sometimes, as at Nuneham Courtenay, an entirely new village was built, designed to complement the park (Batey 1970; Airs 2002).

The growing influence of larger landowners led to the development of a bipartite division of many parishes into 'open' and 'closed' (Emery 1974). The closed parishes tended to have a single landowner who controlled the availability of housing, partly to protect them from the burden of poor relief. The houses tended to be of better quality, but facilities such as inns were not always provided. The open villages were larger, but of poorer layout and quality. The inhabitants would include craftsmen who travelled to work in local towns and a supply of agricultural workers to supplement the needs of the large estates. Open villages were associated with non-conformism and seen by polite society as disreputable,

Other villages developed around a particular industry, such as textiles or quarrying. Stonesfield (see Fig. 15.1) and Headington east of Oxford were both Oxfordshire open parishes linked to stone extraction.

As well as the model villages built by the great estates there were occasional attempts by social activists during the 19th century to create a more rural alternative to urban life. The Chartist Land Company founded Charterville in 1847-8 close to Minster Lovell, west of Witney, Oxfordshire. Each of the 90 homes was surrounded by its own farm plot. This initiative was not successful (Hadfield 1970, Tiller 1985).

Almost all of the present towns across the region were in existence by the end of the medieval period. Despite the impact of enclosure on the rural population only very limited growth took place before the end of the 18th century. Some towns experienced a downturn in prosperity in the post-medieval period, perhaps associated with difficulties in the wool and textile industries, and not all were able to survive as towns. Some, such as Burford, Oxfordshire, became fossilised.

Urban expansion in the 18th and 19th centuries was fuelled by the success of industries and improvements in communication systems. Better roads, canals and railways all contributed to the establishment of supply centres to meet the needs of the bigger urban areas and the various wars in which Britain was engaged. The relative proximity of the region to London and the presence of important military and naval facilities were important. Initially urban growth was concentrated around the historic core, with open spaces infilled and older properties redeveloped. The characterisation of towns and the morphology of these changes are beginning to form a routine part of urban studies (eg OA 2006b). In Hampshire, Southampton changed from a spa town to a major port in the mid-19th century.

At the very end of the 19th century and throughout the 20th century suburban growth has taken place around most of the historic towns. In some places this has resulted in the absorption into the town of previously distinct villages. Shaw, Speen, Donnington and Greenham have become parts of Newbury, Berkshire and Iffley, Cowley and others parts of Oxford. Although not yet part of the city, Kidlington is another village on the edge of Oxford that has experienced a vast increase in size and is essentially now a town. Didcot is another Oxfordshire village that has evolved into a town, this time as a result of the railway in the 19th century. The railway also had a strong influence on Wolverton, where there was a big engineering works, and on towns such as Amersham and Beaconsfield within Metroland. The growth of Newbury was fuelled by new estates to house workers from the atomic research establishments at Harwell west of Didcot and Burghfield. In the later part of the 20th century the fashion for trading and industrial estates and out-of-town shopping and recreation facilities pushed the urban boundaries further.

Planned new towns are less common across the region. Both Carterton west of Witney and Berinsfield north of Dorchester in South Oxfordshire were built in the mid 20th century to house Oxford overspill. The region contains two much larger designated 'new' towns, Milton Keynes and Bracknell, both of which have engulfed a number of small, historic villages.

The Isle of Wight shows a different pattern of urban development. There were no towns on the island until the mid 17th century, although recent evidence has suggested that Cowes may have begun its development earlier than its present 19th century built form might suggest (Edwards 1999g). The growth of Cowes was linked to its shipbuilding and mineral industries, but most of the other towns owe their status more to the growth in popularity of the seaside for leisure and health. Bournemouth, now part of Dorset, was another village that owes its considerable growth to the popularity of the seaside in the late Victorian period.

The eastern parts of Buckinghamshire and Berkshire became part of the London commuter belt in the early 20th century, places such as Amersham and Little Chalfont, Buckinghamshire forming part of 'Metroland' (Hepple & Doggett 1994). Slough, now in Berkshire, evolved not as a commuter suburb, but as a large trading estate. The light industrial belt of west London now extends further into the region along the so-called Silicon Valley.

The built environment

During the 20th century the systematic study of buildings, vernacular as well as polite, became a popular field of study for professionals and volunteers. The Oxfordshire Architectural and Historical Society (OAHS) founded an Old Houses Committee in 1914, now the Oxfordshire Buildings Record, which is currently involved in VCH initiatives in Burford and Henley. RCHME Inventory volumes were produced for both Oxford itself and Buckinghamshire, which discuss all the significant pre-1715 buildings. The Buildings Record on the Isle of Wight HER contains records for all pre-1840 buildings on the island. Pre-1700 buildings in parts of Buckinghamshire were assessed through the Whittlewood Project (Jones & Page 2006).

Although there have been many detailed surveys of particular buildings or groups of buildings, as described below, there have been fewer attempts to identify patterns in architectural styles on a county-wide scale, much less across the wider region. The use of local building materials and the relationship to the surrounding geology has received attention, in the Chiltern region (Whitehand 1967; CgMs 2006b) and across Oxfordshire (Arkell 1947) for example. Although stone is still used for building in areas where it is naturally abundant brick became the predominant material by the late 19th century. Some flint and rubble persisted, in the Chilterns and Isle of Wight in particular. In Buckinghamshire witchert, a mixture of chalk marl and straw, was less popular after the 17th century, but continued in regular use in the centre of the county until the 1930s.

Urban buildings have been the subject of a number of studies linked to large-scale redevelopment, for example from Oxford during the demolition and site clearance for construction of the New Bodleian Library in 1937 (Pantin 1937, Bruce Mitford 1939) and the Clarendon Hotel in the 1950s (Jope and Pantin 1958). The building stock of the historic core formed part of the surveys of historic towns carried out in the 1970s (Astill 1978, Rodwell 1974, Hughes 1976), and are also featured in the ongoing programme of Extensive Urban Survey funded by EH (Edwards 1999) and a survey of Newbury for West Berkshire Council (OA 2006b). Building recording has also taken place across the Chilterns where there is a plethora of design and materials employed, which might suggest an outward looking, experimental society (Moir 2001).

It is not really possible to make many general statements about housing stock and architecture across the region. Yellow brick features strongly in Victorian north Oxford, where St John's college released land for building in the later part of the 19th century (Hinchcliffe, 1992). In parts of Berkshire rubbed brick is often used for decorative detail. In the Isle of Wight styles are strongly influenced by the development of the island as a holiday resort, with marine villas and *cottage orné* surviving (Boynton 1996). East Cowes also has examples of the earliest concrete housing from 1852 (www.iwias.org.uk/).

Some surviving post-World War II (WWII) prefabricated houses can be found, in Barton, Oxford for example.

There have also been a number of studies of housing in rural areas, for example at Ducklington and Little Milton (Portman 1960), both in Oxfordshire. The latter study investigated the rebuilding which took place during the earlier part of the period. During the development of the new town the Milton Keynes Archaeological Unit carried out a number of detailed studies on the villages which were to form its framework (Croft & Mynard 1993, Mynard & Zeepvat 1992).

Across the region there are many surviving country houses, representing the whole period. By no means all of them survive as private houses and of those that do many, such as Blenheim Palace, Oxfordshire or Beaulieu, Hampshire, rely on the income generated from public opening and event income. Many others have become schools (Stowe, Buckinghamshire), conference centres (Great Missenden Abbey, Buckinghamshire), offices (Hursley, Hampshire) or hotels (Cliveden, Buckinghamshire). Some survive only as monuments, often in the care of English Heritage (Appuldurcombe House, Isle of Wight) or the National Trust (Basildon Park, Berkshire). In some cases, such as the Tudor site at Quarrendon (Everson) and Ascott, near Wing (Rains 1982), only features such as garden earthworks survive. Both of these have been subject to surveys.

The era of the large country house really ended with WW I, during which many families lost heirs. After the second war the added pressures of taxation and poor agricultural returns led to the demolition of many mansions, but the situation in much of the Solent-Thames region was made easier by good communication with London. Rich business men and show business personalities funded restoration work (eg. George Harrison at Friars Park, Henley, Oxfordshire) and even had new mansions built, mostly recently in 1995 when Tusmore House, Oxfordshire was built for Wafic Said (Airs 2002).

A number of former monastic properties formed the basis for secular houses immediately after the Dissolution in the mid-16th century, such as Thame Park, Oxfordshire, Great Missenden Abbey, Buckinghamshire, and Titchfield Abbey, Hampshire. There were also new houses built at that period, for example Shaw House, Berkshire and Wolverton Manor, Isle of Wight. A number of other notable houses were originally built in the 17th century, including Chastleton House, Oxfordshire, Radclive, just west of Buckingham, Bramshill, Hampshire and Stratfield Saye, Hampshire. This last is of particular interest for its later connection to the Duke of Wellington, who was given the estate by the nation. Although he had originally planned to have a new house built, he settled for a remodelling of the original. Similarly, another Prime Minister, Disraeli, altered an existing house at Hughendon Manor for his home. This contrasts with the extravagant Vanburgh and Hawksmoor creation of Blenheim Palace, the Duke of Marlborough's reward from a grateful nation in the 18th century.

Many other fine houses were constructed in the 18th century: in Oxfordshire Nuneham Courtenay for Lord Harcourt; Claydon House for the Verneys, West Wycombe for Sir Francis Dashwood, Stowe, Buckinghamshire; Norris Castle and Appuldurcombe House, Isle of Wight; Broadlands at Romsey, Hampshire; Basildon Park, Berkshire. Building continued throughout the 19th century also and the selection includes examples from both major and less distinguished architects of the Victorian period (Mordaunt Crook, 1999). Major examples of Victorian building include Cliveden, Waddesdon (north-west of Aylesbury) and Mentmore (south-east of Wing), Buckinghamshire. Bearwood (west of Wokingham), Berkshire, Highclere Castle (south of Newbury), Hampshire and Osborne, Isle of Wight, this last built for Queen Victoria and Prince Albert.

The scale of 20th-century country house building is not nearly as great, but includes examples of most of the significant architectural trends. Inter-war examples include Overshot, Hinksey Hill, west of Oxford and High and Over, Amersham, Buckinghamshire. New House, Luccombe, Isle of Wight is a rare war-time construction. In 1964 Stratton Park, Hampshire was completely rebuilt with only the portico of Dance's 1801 house maintained as a linked feature. Charters House, Berkshire was built in 1938. It has recently been divided into seven apartments, with adjoining new blocks providing space for over 20 more.

A wide variety of agricultural buildings were employed across the region and some work has been carried out on these. A RCHM(E) survey of English Farmsteads in the 1990s included parts of West Berkshire (RCHME 1997). A characterisation study of farmsteads in Hampshire has been published (Edwards 2005) and there have been reports on individual buildings or complexes as part of the planning process. Farm buildings on the Isle of Wight were assessed in the 1980s (Brinton 1987). In Buckinghamshire and Oxfordshire the record is patchier, although agricultural buildings are surveyed by groups like the Oxfordshire Buildings Record and the Chilterns Society.

From the evidence available few regional trends or variations specific to the region can yet be identified. On the Isle of Wight lobby-entry farmhouses survive from the 16th and 17th centuries, and other relatively early examples occur elsewhere, including Allbrook near Eastleigh, Hampshire and Mapledurham in Oxfordshire, dated 1659 and 1691 respectively (Roberts 2003; Platt 1994). The barns of south and east Oxfordshire have different patterns of roofing purlins from those in the Cotswold stone areas of the north and west (EH 2006).

Although there are a number of universities within the Solent-Thames region, these are with one exception of late 19th- or 20th-century foundation and their buildings are therefore typical of public architecture from those periods. The exception, the University of Oxford, has a wide range of buildings from all periods. The medieval residential halls and colleges have expanded, through rebuilding and addition of new structures. New colleges have been founded and a large number of institutional buildings constructed, of which the Sheldonian Theatre, designed in 1663 by Sir Christopher Wren, is among the best known.

The buildings of the university and colleges have been celebrated in description and illustration over a long period from Bereblock onwards (Durning 2006; Loggan 1676; etc. etc.). They are well described in summary in the Royal Commission Inventory of 1939 (RCHM 1939) and in the University volume of the VCH (VCH Oxfordshire III 1954). They have also been included in the architectural sections of the History of the University (Catto et al. ed. 1984-2000), although the results of more recent research remain to be integrated in the published literature.

A more art/architectural historical approach is evident in the approach of many writers on Oxford's architecture, one of the best and most accessible accounts being that provided by Tyack (1998).

Some of the city's buildings have also benefited from more detailed archaeological analysis of their fabric, with investigation of the roof of Duke Humphrey's Library (OA 2001), the Radcliffe Camera (Gillam 1995) and the Old Ashmolean (Bennett et al. 2000) among them. Such investigations have raised the question of the plundering for re-use of historic fabric (such as happened with the recycling of the roof of the monastic college of St Mary for the chapel of Brasenose), and it is likely that much more remains to be identified of the practice.

Much new building in Oxford (as well as the extensive repairs to the old over the last 30 years, which have not always been used as an opportunity to record or preserve ancient fabric) has been carried out by local building firms, heirs or successors to those which built Oxford in the past. Some of these firms have been studied and histories published (Sturdy 1997; Law 1998).

Public buildings and structures and those associated with the church, warfare, transport and industry are mainly dealt with under the appropriate sections.

Ceremony, ritual and religion

At the beginning of this period, the Protestant Reformation in England under Henry VIII was in process. A major component of this was the dissolution of the monasteries when their estates and buildings were confiscated and redistributed by the king. As already discussed the effect on rural land organisation was dramatic. The fate of the religious complexes themselves was more varied, as illustrated by large numbers of sites across the Solent-Thames region. In some instances these and their immediate environs became the nucleus of a private estate. The houses at Great Missenden, Buckinghamshire, Thame Park, Oxfordshire and Beaulieu Abbey in Hampshire all incorporate some of the original buildings, while Netley, Mottisfont and Titchfield in Hampshire are spectacular examples of the conversion of the former monastic church itself to

domestic use, a practice that was more common than sometimes thought (Doggett, 2002; Howard 2007).

Elsewhere, many of the buildings were demolished to supply building stone, often over a prolonged period. The church and cloister of Abingdon Abbey were demolished rapidly (Cox 1989), but the nave of Reading Abbey survived until 1643 when the stone was used in the town's civil war defences. Overton church was extended in the 16th century using material from Titchfield Abbey. Elsewhere the former monastic churches survived, becoming either the parish church, as at Dorchester, Romsey and Southwick, while Osney Abbey in Oxford was briefly Oxford Cathedral until this role passed to Christ Church. The latter demonstrates the benefits of associations between religious organisations and the secular authorities. Oxford Cathedral is the former St Frideswide's Priory, which also serves as the college chapel. The royal links with Windsor and Eton College enabled many of their possessions to survive.

Evidence for the monastic past exists in surviving ruins, including those of Reading, Titchfield and Netley Abbeys. However, the region does not have the spectacular, isolated sites seen in other parts of the country. All that remains of Bradwell Priory, near Milton Keynes, for instance, are tithe barn, chapel, and bakehouse.

It was not only the monastic foundations that suffered during the reformation, but also guilds and charitable foundations. Again some of their property was swept away, but in many instances transfer to a secular institution or support from a private individual enabled their charitable activities to continue. In Buckingham the Guild of the Holy Trinity was abolished, but its Chantry Chapel survived as the home of the Royal Latin School. St Bartholomew's Hospital in Newbury (Plate 17.5) survived as a workhouse, although without its burial ground, which disappeared under a new road layout.

The site of Quarr Abbey in the Isle of Wight (see Fig. 15.1) is unique in the region. In the early 20th century a Benedictine house was established on the site of the medieval Cistercian monastery and continues in use today.

Within churches the reformation left its mark. Painted ceilings, statues and stained glass began to disappear, while royal coats of arms and protestant texts took their place. Many of the medieval wall paintings have been lost although careful removal of more recent plaster and whitewashing has uncovered some, eg in Oxfordshire at Dorchester Abbey and St Oswald's Church, Widford. This destruction was accelerated by the actions of Cromwell's armies. Many churches retain the plaques bearing the Royal Arms. Changes in the liturgy, which eliminated the mass and changed the emphasis to communion and preaching, were reflected in the construction of communion tables (though few now survive), box pews and elaborate pulpits and galleries. Few churches still maintain this layout in its entirety, but some box pews can be seen in many buildings including Southwick and at Rycote Chapel in Oxfordshire. This private chapel also has rare remains of the original painted ceiling.

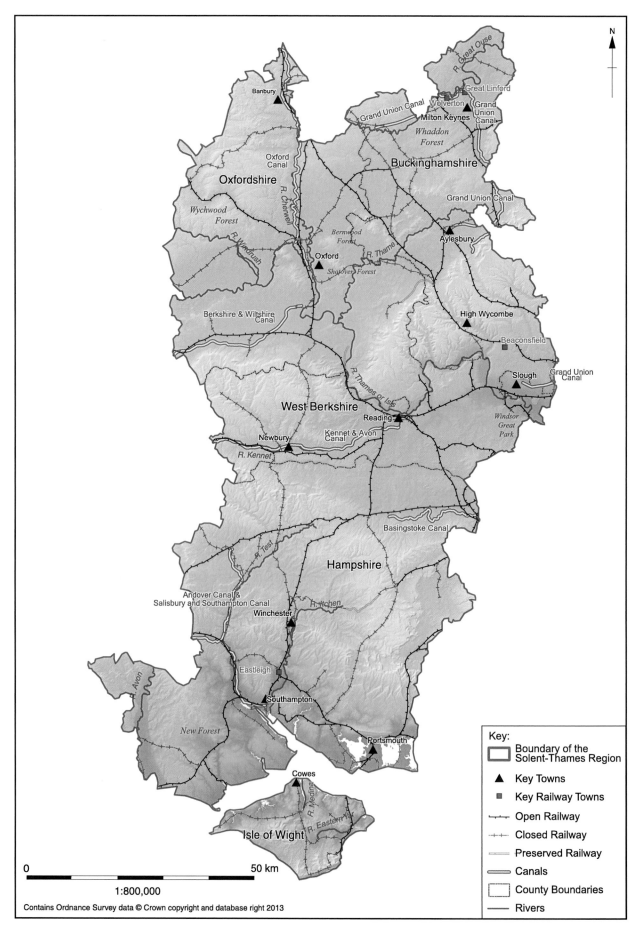

Figure 17.2 Canals, railways, railway towns and forests mentioned in the text

Religious disputes in the 16th and 17th century were not just between protestant and catholic, but involved deep schisms over how the protestant church itself should develop. For many the links between Christianity and social justice were fundamental and a number of groups of non-conformists emerged, who did not accept the tenets of the established church. At Burford in Oxfordshire, where their mutiny was put down, there is a memorial to one short-lived group, the Levellers, a section of the New Model Army. Originally non-conformists were outlawed and their places of worship were created within larger houses, or by converting outbuildings such as stables, such as the Congregational church in Finchdean, Hampshire. The first Oxford Methodist Church, visited by John Wesley in 1783, was in a 16th-century house in New Inn Hall Street. In Niton, Isle of Wight, the village hall began life as a malthouse in *c*. 1760, became a Baptist Church in 1823 and a school in 1848 (Dunning 1951). There are some surviving examples across the region. Probably the best known non-conformist site is the Quaker Meeting House at Jordans near Beaconsfield (see Fig. 17.2 for location), which was built in 1688, but was badly damaged by fire in 2005. Most of the non-conformist churches and chapels date from the late 18th and 19th centuries, utilising mostly Gothic and Classical architecture. The Baptist Chapel at Waddesdon, Bucks, is a rare example of a vernacular style, from 1792.

The Church of England did not undertake much church building in the 16th to 18th century, although some rebuilding took place, some of it on different sites. This rebuilding programme included St Luke's at Stoke Hammond, Bucks in the 17th century, St Peter le Bailey, Oxford in 1726, Banbury in 1790 and Buckingham church. Several new churches were associated with large estates, St Lawrence at West Wycombe and Hartwell church for example. When Lord Harcourt created Nuneham Park a new church was constructed, resembling a classical temple. Most new churches from this period were in towns, including Holy Trinity church (Gosport) in 1696, the church dedicated to St George (Portsmouth) in 1754 in an American-Colonial style and the church of St Peter (Wallingford) in 1760-9.

The 19th century witnessed a resurgence of interest in religion with the growth of the Evangelical and Oxford Movements. This period also saw large numbers of new churches, mainly as the result of population growth in towns generating new parishes. These churches demonstrate a variety of styles, with classical Romanesque and Italianate structures in addition to those in the highly popular 'Middle Pointed' Gothic style. This last was used to correct the 'mistakes' of the past and was the favourite approach used in the many church restoration programmes.

Many of the leading church architects of the period are represented across the region. Gilbert Scott was responsible for Bradfield, Highclere and Ryde amongst others. Street also carried out restoration work and designed new churches, including All Saints, Maidenhead and St Mary in Wheatley. Woodyer designed St

Paul's, Wokingham, Burges the church at Fleet and Butterfield Dropmore and Horton-cum-Studey. Humbert designed Whippingham church, Isle of Wight, apparently with some help from Prince Albert. Blomfield produced the Italianate St Barnabas in Jericho, Oxford, but unfortunately the internal mosaic murals were only completed on one side of the church.

Some major artists of the periods were involved in designing monuments and decorating churches. Oxford Cathedral contains a stained glass window by Morris and Burne Jones, whose Pre-Raphaelite influence can also be seen in the chapel of Exeter College. Extensive restoration work was carried out at the cathedral in 1871 by Sir Gilbert Scott, and more was undertaken in 1887-9. Winchester Cathedral was in danger of collapse until Jackson carried out a major programme of work in 1905-12. Examples of churches by Street (eg Maidenhead, Wheatley) should also be mentioned, as should Victorian restoration work at Oxford and Winchester Cathedrals.

Pugin is only known to be responsible for one church in the region, the new Roman Catholic church in Marlow, Buckinghamshire. Easing of the restrictions on Catholics permitted the restoration of chapels at Stonor (near Henley) and at Milton House in the 18th century, and the construction of a new chapel at Mapledurham in 1794. In the 19th century Roman Catholic parish churches began to be built, and a cathedral was constructed in Winchester in 1926.

The Burial Act of 1854 halted burials in the overcrowded urban churchyards and led to the creation of municipal cemeteries, several of which are now also full. Often these cemeteries contained a number of chapels to serve different denominations, as at Henley-on-Thames. In Oxford, Osney cemetery is located at least in part on the site of the former Osney Abbey. Non-conformists churches often had their own burial ground. Haddenham, north-east of Thame in Buckinghamshire, has the remains of a Quaker burial ground and another has been identified at St Giles Hill, Winchester. Plague pits have been found in Winchester and some Civil War burials in Newbury. One cemetery in Abingdon, a Parliamentary town, contained 250 Commonwealth graves (Allen 1989; 1990b), and another smaller group elsewhere in the town has tentatively also been ascribed to this period (T Allen 1997). There has been little opportunity since to excavate a significant assemblage of burials from this period, but work on the former hospital cemetery at Haslar, Hampshire is being carried out by Oxford Archaeology and Cranfield University. An investigation of a C17 burial vault at Thame Church was carried out in the late 1990s by Julian Lytton from the V &A and David Miles of OAU, but was unfortunately never written up. The vault contained members of the Herbert family, who had built nearby Tythrop House.

The Solent-Thames region has, like almost all of England, a multicultural population. The earliest significant immigrant groups were probably associated with the ports of Hampshire as there is a long tradition of

Chinese and lascar seamen. Southampton experienced two waves of Protestant refugees from France, one in the1560s and then Huguenots in the 17th century. Medieval St Julian's became the French Church.

Little other sign of any religious activity has been identified in connection with these groups and the earliest non-Christian religious institutions recorded are synagogues. Jews settled in Portsmouth in the 1730s and acquired land for a burial ground in 1749, which remained in use until the 1990s. A purpose-built synagogue opened in 1780, but in 1936 the congregation moved to a converted house in Southsea, taking many of the original fittings with them. In Southampton Old Cemetery one of the 1850s mortuary chapels was for the Jews. Another synagogue was built in Reading in 1901 and a school and centre for Jewish studies was founded at Mongewell Park, South Oxfordshire in 1953, although it closed in 1997. The synagogue there, now Listed Grade II, was built in 1963 by Thomas Hancock. During the later 20th century immigration, particularly from the Indian subcontinent, has further diversified the range of religious groups in the region. Of the numerous mosques that have opened, some are in converted buildings, but more recently purpose-built structures have begun to appear, eg in Oxford and Reading.

The recording of churches and their fittings is not as comprehensive as might be expected. A detailed study has been carried out of Buckinghamshire stained glass with a catalogue and photographs available on the web (www.buckinghamshire stainedglass.org.uk) and some survey of Oxfordshire wall paintings was done. NADFAS groups across the counties have been preparing inventories, but these records are not accessible locally.

There is a rich legacy of monuments in the churches, churchyards and cemeteries of the region, particularly those to the royal family in St George's Chapel, Windsor. Elaborate royal mausoleums have been constructed in Windsor Great Park at Frogmore, one for Queen Victoria and Prince Albert and the other for her mother, the Duchess of Kent. Another mausoleum was built by the Empress Eugenie of France at Farnborough, Hampshire together with a small abbey for its support. The numerous parks and estates across the region are full of memorials, for example the Column of Victory in Blenheim Park and an equestrian statue of George I at Hackwood Park and of George III in Windsor Great Park. Petersfield market-place features an equestrian statue of William of Orange. Equestrian statues are generally rare in England. Memorials are common in the region's towns and villages also, one of the most impressive being the Martyrs' Memorial in St Giles, Oxford. Often memorials incorporate a source of water, many for the Diamond Jubilee of Queen Victoria, but others form tributes to individuals or groups, such as the emigrants from Ascott-under-Wychwood, whose ship sank en route to New Zealand.

Of course the largest group of memorials is war memorials, mostly commemorating the fallen of the First and Second World Wars but some, such as that on Coombe Hill near Wendover, Buckinghamshire and in Bonn Square, Oxford, commemorate earlier conflicts. The 1919 Cenotaph in Southampton by Lutyens is thought to have served as a model for the Whitehall example. A particularly unusual monument is the Boer War memorial on the village green at Latimer, Buckinghamshire, with a separate memorial to a horse wounded at the Battle of Boshof and subsequently brought back to England.

Pagan superstition is not completely absent from the archaeological record for this period. Witch bottles, shoes and dead cats among other objects have been found hidden in building and traces of apotropaic marks have also been identified. It is likely that such things are often either not recognised as significant or felt to be too embarrassing to discuss. Alterations to the ruins of Medmenham Abbey and caves at West Wycombe Park (5 kilometres from High Wycombe) have been associated with pagan rituals through the activities of the Hellfire Club.

Warfare, defences and military installations

The Portsmouth Naval Base was first established at the end of the 15th century, but enjoyed a period of growth during the reign of Henry VIII. From the 17th century onwards the facilities were gradually extended, with the establishment of the Haslar Naval Hospital and the Gosport victualling centre for example. Several components of the complex are now Scheduled Monuments. Many of the sites are no longer in use and recent defence cuts mean that the Ministry of Defence is reviewing its holdings. Archaeological work is being carried out in the gunboat yard and hospital cemetery at Haslar (Shortland *et al.* 2008). It was from Portsmouth that the Mary Rose sailed in 1545 only to sink in the Solent where she remained until 1982. The archaeology of the Mary Rose has been extensively recorded, and published, while the ship itself is preserved for public view (see Plate 15.12).

The threat of invasion also influenced the construction of land fortifications. Henry VIII commissioned a series of forts along the Hampshire coast and on the Isle of Wight, including Yarmouth, Cowes, Hurst Castle (see Fig. 15.1) and Southsea (south of Portsmouth). Medieval Carisbrooke castle on the Isle of Wight was surrounded between 1597 and 1602 by a series of artillery defences designed by Federigo Giabnibelli (Young 2000).

The Civil War of the mid 17th century led to many alterations and refurbishments to existing fortifications, some evidence for which has survived, at Donnington (just north of Newbury) and at Old Basing for example. More significant were defences around the more important towns. Some possible traces have been seen at Silver Street, Reading (Foundation Archaeology 2001) and at Abingdon (Devaney 2007). The extensive royalist defences of Oxford have been excavated in several areas, for example Parks Road (Bradley *et al.* 2006). Work in Oxford demonstrates the benefits of a research strategy

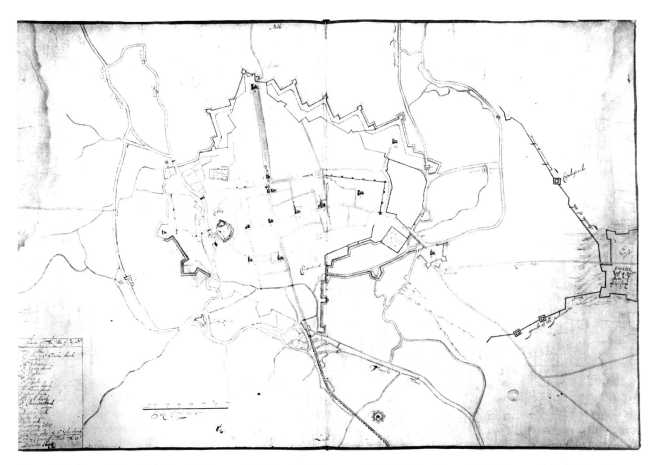

Plate 17.6 Map of the Civil War Defences of Oxford (De Gomme 1644, MS Top. Oxon. B 1678), *copyright Bodleian Library*

as trenches are located after reference to the map created by the engineer of the defences, De Gomme (Plate 17.6). Various battles and skirmishes took place across the region, the locations of the First Battle of Newbury (1643), Chalgrove (1643) and Cropredy Bridge (1644) appearing in the EH Register of Historic Battlefields. Following the Parliamentary victory Cromwell ordered the slighting of many of the defences. Very little archaeological work has been done on this and the evidence from the conflicts themselves is minimal.

Of the fresh round of improvements to coastal defences that took place during the Napoleonic Wars little evidence remains, although some Admiralty Telegraph stations have survived. Semaphore signalling to link Portsmouth and London was established, first using a shutter system in 1796 and then one using fixed arms from 1822. An extension to Plymouth was never completed.

A perceived threat of invasion by the French remained and in the 1860s Palmerston authorised a vast network of coastal defences, one section of which was centred on the Solent. In addition to land forts a road was built along the south coast of the Isle of Wight and a series of seaforts constructed at Spithead. The land fortifications guarded against attack from the sea and from inland, with a number of forts lining Portsdown Ridge above the town of Portsmouth. Many of these defences survive, often adapted for later purposes. A survey was carried out by EH (Saunders 1998), unfortunately not published in its entirety. The Palmerston Forts Society (www.palmer-

stonforts.org.uk) has published several papers on specific sections of the complex.

Elsewhere Britain's standing army and local yeomanry grew in size, accompanied by more demand for barracks and training grounds. Although volunteer rifle ranges and small barracks were to be found in many towns it was on the heathland areas of the south of England, including parts of Berkshire and Hampshire, that the army had the greatest impact. The various barracks, hospitals and training grounds have evolved as military needs and improved attitudes to soldiers' welfare have changed. Many of these establishments have been closed or reduced in capacity and the level of recording of facilities has been disappointing, as they have until very recently not been seen as significant either as individual buildings or monuments. One building was moved to a museum when the Queen Elizabeth Barracks at Fleet west of Farnborough, home to the Gurkhas, was sold for housing (OA 2004d).

Twentieth-century conflicts have had a marked impact on the Solent-Thames region. World War I (WWI) practice trenches have been identified in a number of locations and some of the early military airfields were situated here, including an early seaplane base for the Fleet Air Arm at HMS Daedalus near Gosport, Hampshire. Some continued in use into the World War II (WWII) and beyond. Today several have become industrial parks, Witney, Oxfordshire for example. A grass airstrip constructed for the Royal Flying Corps still exists at Halton. During WWII the US forces established a base in Southampton, the main embarkation port for D-Day.

More airfields were established from the 1930s, with Harwell thought to be the first and RAF Bicester a particularly good example (Hance 2006; various incl CgMs 2003). These housed bombers, fighters, gliders and other specialist planes. Recording of surviving features and airfield history have become popular areas for research and it is not possible to provide a detailed discussion here. During WWII large estates were requisitioned as research establishments (Ditton Park), training centres (Thame Park, Beaulieu), command centres (Langley House) and even prisoner of war camps (Water Stratford). A POW camp survey has been carried out (Thomas 2003) and a museum commemorating the SOE has recently opened at Beaulieu. The most well known example is Bletchley Park, home of the code-breakers, where again a museum has been established. Significant recording of the 'stop lines', systems of pillboxes and other hardened field defences along the Thames, Kennet and other rivers, has been carried out by the Defence of Britain project. One underresearched area is the reason for the development of a network of signal and intelligence facilities in Buckinghamshire. Features associated with the civilian population, such as air raid shelters and home guard stations, are also under-recorded.

During the Cold War a number of bases continued in use. Upper Heyford and Greenham Common are both associated with the US and their nuclear capability (Plate 17.7). The history and archaeology of the latter has been investigated recently (CgMs 2006a) for the proposed Conservation Plan. High Wycombe is still the headquarters of NATO, complete with underground bunkers. Rockets development was carried out on the Isle of Wight by Saunders-Roe, who tested the Black Knight and Black Arrows rockets near The Needles, Isle of Wight (Plate 17.8). Rocket research and development was also carried out at Westcott Royal Ordnance

Plate 17.7 View of GAMA shelters at Greenham Common airbase, Berkshire, *copyright Jon Gill with kind permission of David Arnold*

Factory, Buckinghamshire, where some of the surviving structures are under consideration for Listing.

Art associated with conflict is also found across the region, not just in the form of war memorials of which there are very many examples. US servicemen have left a lasting record at Upper Heyford, and at Greenham Common there are also features left from the antinuclear protest camps. Memorials to victims of WWI can be found at Sandham, Burghclere, south of Newbury, where the purpose-built chapel is decorated with Stanley Spencer murals. The village of Enham Alamein, Hants was originally constructed to house disabled servicemen and its name records a donation by the Egyptian government in recognition of the British success at that battle (some additional development is planned here, which may provide the opportunity for recording work).

What has not been addressed specifically is the reuse of defensive features over time. Bembridge Fort in the Isle of Wight, for example, was constructed as part of the Palmerston defences and later equipped with pillboxes and other more recent structures. The effects on the

Plate 17.8 High Down Rocket Site from the Needles, Isle of Wight, *copyright Isle of Wight Museum*

landscape and society of military establishments should not be underestimated. Airfields require clearance of hedgerows and trees, not just within the perimeter of the site itself. Trees along the Ridgeway were removed to aid take off from Harwell (near Didcot) and the horizon remains empty. The influx of people, including families, associated with military establishments could transform small rural communities.

Material culture

Post-medieval and modern artefacts have been recovered from excavation sites and form an increasing proportion of the entries on HERs, nearly one third for the Isle of Wight. The growth in popularity of metal detecting as a hobby, and the work of the Portable Antiquities scheme, have made a significant contribution to this increase. However, systematic analysis of the collected material has not been carried out to a significant extent. There have been a number of articles published for Oxford in Oxoniensia focusing on particular aspects of material culture, based on the large assemblages obtained during major development work in the city, in the St Ebbe's area and at the site of the Bodleian Library for example. Oxford College bottle seals, ceramics and clay pipes have all received some attention. The surviving wall paintings from Oxford, including the Golden Cross Inn and 3 Cornmarket, and from the rest of the county, such as Upper High Street in Thame, have also been studied. Winchester and Southampton have been the subject of extensive archaeological investigations, which again have produced large assemblages from urban contexts. In Buckinghamshire the work at Bierton near Aylesbury in 1975-9 produced material (Allen 1986) but in common with very many multi-period sites, the later periods were not given a great deal of attention.

Evidence for everyday material culture can also be found in many of the museums and major country houses across the region, where themed exhibitions and preserved room layouts form part of the visitor attractions. Standing buildings often retain features such as fireplaces, ovens and pumps or smaller fixtures and fittings such as bell-pulls, which can add to the understanding of everyday life. It is important that these should feature in building-recording programmes and that householders are made more aware of their significance.

Documentary studies have also played a part in investigation of material culture through detailed inventories and probate records, which list furnishings and other goods on a room by room basis. Much work of this kind has been carried out through local societies.

The evidence for material culture from this period has a bias towards urban areas, where the majority of archaeological investigation has taken place, and towards the upper end of the social scale. Grand houses tend to undergo less radical modernisation. The record has also suffered from the lack of interest in the more recent past, which has still to be overcome in many instances. Historical archaeology emerged as a major field of study in the mid-20th century in the USA, where colonisation by Europeans provided a fairly clear division.

Crafts, trade and industries

As discussed above, across the Solent-Thames region in general agriculture was the principal form of land-use at the start of the post-medieval period, and continues to be so outside the urban areas. Certain trades related to agricultural production have been practised across the whole of the region. Large numbers of water mills and windmills survive across the region and the locations of many more have been identified. In addition a number of tide mills are known from the coastal areas of Hampshire and the Isle of Wight. Mill surveys have been carried out for all the counties, although the Berkshire work dates back to the 1960s and a new book on Buckinghamshire mills has just been compiled (Farley 2007). Durngate Mill, Winchester, was recorded before its demolition in 1966 (Reynolds *et al.* 1967) Working water mills can be found at Mapledurham, Oxfordshire, and Ford End, Ivinghoe, Buckinghamshire (see Fig. 9.1). Buckinghamshire also has two restored post-mills, Brill (Plate 17.9) and Pitstone (see Fig. 13.1), the latter the oldest surviving example in the country. The tower mill at Wheatley has recently undergone restoration (Wheatley Windmill Society) and the sails have been

Plate 17.9 Windmill at Brill, Buckinghamshire, *copyright Jill Hind*

replaced. Another, unrestored example is located nearby at Great Haseley. The windmill at Bembridge, Isle of Wight is now maintained by the National Trust.

Some mills have survived from the medieval period, but sites did change frequently. Survival for mills often depended on diversification from grain to fulling, saw or grist mills. At Bisham, Buckinghamshire, Temple Mills moved to brassworking. Gunpowder was manufactures at Osney Mill, Oxford, during the Civil War. The Schultze factory at Fritham, Hampshire also produced gunpowder from 1865 to 1923 for the military. The Whitchurch 'Silk' Mill, Hampshire is described below.

Although recent years have seen the closure of many breweries, brewing and malting were common across the region. Unfortunately the amount of recording carried out has been very limited, although a survey of the Oxfordshire Industries was published in 1985 (Bond & Rhodes). Major sites developed close to the easy transport route of the River Thames, at Wallingford and at Henley (see Fig. 15.1) where the modern plant from Brakspears was removed in 2002 and the buildings converted to a hotel in 2004-5 (CgMs 2004). In Reading the Courage Brewery remains a major manufacturing site. Many small local breweries have been taken over by larger organisations; for example Halls took over four Oxford brewers in 1897. Morrells was founded in the city in 1597, but in the late 1990s this also was taken over and production ceased. Their St Thomas Street plan has been recorded and excavated (H Moore 2006; Norton 2006). Similar closures have taken place in the other counties, including Strong's of Romsey, Hampshire.

Wool and textiles

Sheep and wool production had developed during the medieval period into a major source of wealth for many landowners and the prosperity of towns across Oxfordshire, Berkshire and Hampshire in particular. Following a peak in the 16th century, the trade began to decay in the 17th century. For some towns this led to a loss of status, for example Burford, or a concentration on other industries, as happened in Reading and Newbury. Other towns managed to maintain their wool industry through specialist production. The most successful example was Witney where the blanket trade only ceased production in the late 1990s. Chipping Norton and Banbury moved to the production of tweed while plush was manufactured in the latter town and its environs. Most of the cloth industry was carried out in relatively small workshops or in weavers' homes, although the specialist towns, particularly Witney, had larger mills operating in the 19th century after mechanisation had taken place.

Bliss Tweed Mill and the mill in Witney retain many original features, but are now residential buildings. Other workshops have experienced similar conversions, but many have been demolished. Little recording has been carried out, although English Heritage has carried out survey work for the Textile Mills of the South-West project, for which the detailed records are not readily accessible. It is important that opportunities to explore buildings, even when the frontage appears to be of recent date, for the survival of workshops, or parts of them, at the rear should be exploited, and that surviving evidence for the cloth industry is recorded. The extensive tenter grounds for drying cloth are generally now only known from historic maps.

Hemp and twine were used by a factory in Abingdon to make sacking. By the later 19th century coconut and rush matting were being produced and soon after 1900 the factory became Abingdon Carpets, now no longer based in the town. Behind Twitty's Almshouses in Abingdon a factory producing hemp sacks and linen was partly destroyed in 1838. It was taken over by a clothier, John Hyde, whose family established a clothing factory, specialising in cotton goods. Trading continued until 1931. In 1977-8 the site of the demolished factory was excavated and its various phases revealed (Wilson 1989).

James I was determined to establish a native silk industry and in 1607 began planting of mulberry trees at Broadlands, Romsey (see Fig. 15.1). Although the king was not successful in his ambitions, silk processing continued in Hampshire and Berkshire with the last operating plant, Whitchurch silk mill, closing in 1985. Huguenot refugees opened a silk factory in Southampton in the 17th century. The mill has been restored by the Hampshire Preservation Trust as a working museum (http://whitchurchsilkmill.org.uk/mill/index. php/history-of-the-mill). Andover had a tradition of home-working and there were also mills in Wokingham (http://www.wokinghamsociety.org.uk/history.html). However, this industry has not been studied in detail

In the south-west of Hampshire another textile crop, flax, was grown. This raw material was woven into canvas, in particular to supply the local shipbuilders with sails. Around 500 looms have been noted in the Fordingbridge area. Sailmaking was also carried out in Reading, originally at the Oracle site and later at a factory in Katesgrove (Childs 1910).

A much smaller-scale production was that of lace. This was carried out in the Aylesbury and High Wycombe area as well as at Olney in the north of Buckinghamshire. In these areas, archaeological evidence is confined to occasional finds of pins or bobbins. A separate industry existed in the Isle of Wight, where a factory operated at Newport in the 19th century (Jones & Jones, 1987, 116).

Geological resources

The Solent-Thames region is crossed by bands of different geological date, the characteristics of which support a range of industries. The major river terraces of the Avon, Coln, Kennet and Thames have experienced large-scale gravel extraction programmes for which archaeological investigations have concentrated on the evidence from earlier periods contained within or overlaid by the gravel. Small-scale local gravel pits are also widespread.

The chalk bands of the Chilterns have also been exploited. A number of chalk pits and mines have been identified in Buckinghamshire (Farley 1979b, 138-9) and the Caversham area of Reading and cement working took place at Pitstone, Buckinghamshire and Chinnor, Oxfordshire. Concrete from the West Medina Mills in the Isle of Wight provided raw materials for some very early concrete houses (www.iwias.org.uk). Surprisingly few lime kilns have been identified in north Buckinghamshire within the limestone belt.

Good building stone occurs in various parts of the region. Probably the quarries at Taynton and Headington in Oxfordshire were the most important of these, and the industries, together with production of slate from Stonesfield, were examined in some detail by Arkell in 1947. Hampshire supplied some malmstone and Berkshire sarsen.

The abundance of clay across the region supported a brick and tile industry. Works were established in Hampshire, Berkshire and on the outskirts of Ryde and Cowes, Isle of Wight. Brick making was particularly common in Buckinghamshire, at Slough, Hedgerley, Great Linford and Calvert/Newton Longville. The plant at Great Linford was adjacent to the canal from which it supplied the building of Wolverton and New Bradwell in the 1880s. The Calvert plant continued to be operated by the London Brick Company into the 1980s and 90s. A brickworks operated at Chawley just west of Oxford in the 18th and 19th centuries, serving the expanding town (Dodsworth 1976). Pottery was also produced, in Tilehurst, Cove, Inkpen and Brill. Evidence for tile production in the post-medieval period is less common, but a 16th-century kiln has recently been excavated at Penn, east of High Wycombe (Broadbent 1983) and there were also tile kilns at Little Brickhill in the 16th century.

Important local brick making centres were found across the Chilterns in the 18th century, several of them surviving into the 20th century and beyond. A well-preserved bottle kiln survives at Nettlebed, Oxfordshire and there are several abandoned clay pits in the vicinity. Chalfont St Giles and Chesham were important brick producing centres in Buckinghamshire: Matthews and Duntons are still producing hand-made bricks today.

Pottery production took place at a number of locations in Buckinghamshire and Oxfordshire, but the major manufacturing site was at Brill, Buckinghamshire (see Fig. 15.1), where it continued until the 1860s. Excavations in the 1970s and 1980s identified the remains of kilns from the 16th century onwards (Farley 1979a, Yeoman 1988, Cocroft 1985).

Glass was produced at a few locations, including Buckholt, Hampshire and at Alum Bay, Cowes. The Ravenscroft Glassworks in Henley finally closed in the 1960s. Its success had been the result of discovery of a recipe for lead crystal, which relied on a particular type of sand from Nettlebed.

Small-scale industry

Several types of small-scale industrial production were taking place across the region. The elm woods of the Chilterns supported the furniture industry around High Wycombe, where there is a museum to the crafts. Paper was produced at a number of locations close to rivers, such as Thatcham, Berkshire, High Wycombe, Buckinghamshire and Wolvercote, near Oxford. A Conservation Area has been designated by South Buckinghamshire Council to protect the remains of the Riverside works in Taplow. The latter site supplied paper to the Oxford University Press. Parchment was produced at a works in Havant, Hampshire, which originated in the early 19th century and continued to the 1920s (CgMs 2006b), and in Andover, the former having closed only recently.

A by-product of this industry was the relatively short-lived production of tarred paper roofs for buildings in the early 19th century, with examples recorded near Abingdon and at Eynsham and Sandford-on-Thames (Airs 1998).

Needles were made in Long Crendon, east of Thame in Buckinghamshire, but the cottage industry never developed and disappeared after its competitors in Redditch (Warwickshire) went over to mechanised mass production. Straw plaiting for hats was another occupation mainly for Buckinghamshire women. Clockmaking was pursued in Oxford, North Oxfordshire (Beeson 1967) and Newbury (Higgott 2001).

Leather production is another industry that uses much water. In Newbury on the Kennet, tanneries were common, possibly supplying manufacture of saddlery for the coach trade. Gloves were made in Witney, Woodstock and Charlbury, Oxfordshire (Leyland and Troughton 1974).

Fishing was obviously important in the coastal areas of the region, but the extent to which it formed a major part of the economy is uncertain. Some remains of a fishing hamlet survive at Steephill Cove, Isle of Wight. Oysters from the Solent were harvested at Emsworth and Langstone Bay and shipped to urban markets. Salt production survived as an important industry from the medieval period into the 19th century along the New Forest coast and at various sites on the Isle of Wight. At Lymington some remains of the salterns and coal-powered boiling houses can still be found. The cost of transporting coal and high salt taxes resulted in the end of manufacture (http://www.lymington.org/history/the saltindustry.html)

Transport

Production of means of transport was a significant element in the industry of the Solent-Thames region. The largest component was shipbuilding, mostly in South Hampshire and on the Isle of Wight, for example at Hamble and at Bucklers Hard at Beaulieu (Plate 17.10). Most were timber craft, made from wood from the New Forest and the Forest of Bere, but some iron ships were produced from metal from Funtley and Sowley. Powerboats were later produced at Hythe, Isle of Wight and Vospers also had a marine engineering works in the area, as well at Southampton. The island was also home to Saunders-Roe, the company which became the British Hovercraft Corporation in the 1960s. The Isle of

Plate 17.10 Model of Bucklers Hard, Hampshire, *copyright Bucklers Hard Museum*

Plate 17.11 Hammerhead Ship Crane at Cowes on the Isle of Wight, *copyright Isle of Wight Museum*

Wight's shipyards are still dominated by the Cowes Hammerhead Crane erected in 1912 (Plate 17.11), and thought to be the earliest extant crane in the UK (http://www.coweshammerheadcrane.org.uk/)

Smaller craft for river use were manufactured elsewhere. Salter's Boatyard in Oxford was one site and there was extensive work carried out on the site before it was redeveloped for housing (OA 2000b). Tooley's Boatyard in Banbury is now a museum.

Aircraft were also manufactured in the region, in Reading, Woodley, Southampton and the Hamble. Saunders-Roe produced sea planes in Cowes and a company in Newbury was switched over to making gliders (Oxford Archaeology 2006b).

Wokingham was for a time a centre for coach building. The most important source of road vehicles is the car plant at Cowley, which grew from William Morris' garage in Longwall Street, Oxford. The plant has changed hands many times since its foundation and the current site, producing Minis for BMW, is much smaller than the extent occupied at the height of production. When the rest was demolished little recording took place. Another car manufacturing plant existed in Abingdon, where MG was established by Cecil Kimber, who had been making sports cars from Morris' vehicles. The plant was sited in a former leather working warehouse. Production finally ceased in Abingdon in 1980 (Moylan 2007). Some of the plant was demolished, again without recording, and some is used by Oxford Engineering. Wantage too has some links with the motor industry, providing bases for the Williams Formula 1 motor racing teams.

Small foundries and engineering works existed across the region. In Wallingford was Wilder's, a company responsible for wells, manhole covers and iron kerbing (examples of which still survive in the town) as well as agricultural machinery. Other companies were known in Reading, Newbury, Andover, Eastleigh, Buckingham, and Lucy's Eagle Ironworks in Oxford. Wolverton (west of Milton Keynes) was established by the London and Birmingham railway company for manufacture of railway engines and carriages. Further south was the Eastleigh carriage and locomotive works.

New industries

New industries were established in the 20th century. Film studios were constructed at Denham, Buckinghamshire, where Alexander Korda made some of his films, but the Hi-tech industries have been particularly important. The Atomic Energy Research Establishment was based at Harwell (west of Didcot) where prototype nuclear reactors were built (Hance 2006). The site and its surrounding area have continued to attract similar initiatives such as the Diamond Light Source and JET at Culham. Radiation was also important to Amersham International and the Atomic Weapons Research Establishments at Aldermaston and Burghfield. From Slough to Reading the computer industry has established bases while Vodafone have made Newbury its headquarters.

Leisure

Entertainment and sport have become more significant 'industries' in recent years. The Solent-Thames region is home to Windsor, Ascot and Newbury racecourses, which have their particular development histories. Horse racing also took place on Port Meadow, Oxford and at Tweseldown, Fleet, Hampshire. The horse racing industry has been influential in the development of the Lambourn Downs area of Berkshire, where many studs and gallops are located. Newbury has its own railway station and now a course range occupies the centre of the racetrack (OA 2006b). Polo is played at Windsor.

The region contains a number of professional football clubs, traditionally a strong feature in the social life of the working classes, although with major new stadia in recent years at Reading, Southampton and Oxford, most have moved away from their original locations, with the old sites redeveloped for housing. Only Portsmouth (at Fratton Park) now remain at their traditional home. Fratton Park contains one of the few remaining stands by the engineer Archibald Leitch, the leading pre-WWII architect for such facilities.

A small well-preserved (former professional) football stadium survives at The Recreation Ground, Aldershot and Buckinghamshire now also has its own professional team, the MK Dons, which relocated from Wimbledon in 2003 and since November 2007 has played at stadium:mk.

The Thames itself has a significant role in water sports, particularly the Henley Regatta (the original 1913 grandstand at Phyllis Court having been rebuilt in the 1990s) and, more recently, international events on the Eton Rowing Course at Dorney Lake. The Solent is of course also a centre for water sport. Yachting takes place in the Hamble area and Cowes Royal Regatta has been taking place for nearly 200 years.

Shopping has developed from a necessity to a leisure activity, although the activity will always have also served a social function, particularly where markets brought people together from dispersed settlements. Recording of markets and shops is uncommon beyond photographic collections. Material from the former Capes store in Oxford is held by the Oxfordshire Museums Service following a survey on its 1970s closure (Foster 1973).

Cinemas and theatres have yet to receive the attention they deserve. Some have existed for a long time such as Theatre Royal in Winchester, which dates from 1850. The Theatre Royal in Windsor opened in 1903 and the Empire Variety Theatre in Southampton in 1928, although this became a cinema in 1933. The Holywell Music Room, Oxford, was the first purpose built concert hall, opening in 1742. The region does have a number of cinema buildings from the early 20th century including the Rivoli, Sandown, Isle of Wight from the 1930s, the Plaza, Southsea, Hampshire from 1928 and in Oxford the Electra of 1910-11 and one in Magdalen Street which was built in 1922-4. This is still operating as a multi-screen cinema.

Recording of industrial premises has been limited. Work was carried out at Spencer Corsets, Banbury (Stradling 1996) and the Lucy's Foundry in Oxford was the subject of an MA dissertation, but this did not include recording of buildings (Warburton 2003).

Transport and communications

Southampton has been an important trading port from the early medieval period, but it was in the mid-19th century that the dock area began to expand. During the post-medieval and modern periods the growth of passenger traffic also increased, – liners, ferries to Europe and the rest of the world (P&O, Cunard etc) and the Isle of Wight. Portsmouth has remained primarily a naval port, although it is now possible to catch ferries to the Isle of Wight and the continent. Several small ports serve the Isle of Wight. Cowes is the largest, but Ryde is the base for the hovercraft service in addition to a passenger ferry to the mainland. Regular ferries from Ryde began in 1796.

To help ensure safe passage for shipping various lighthouses have been erected around the coast. On the Isle of Wight the first lighthouse on the Needles was built in 1785. This and St Catherine's Lighthouse of 1840 have experienced problems with sea mists and have had various improvements made over the years (Insole & Parker 1979). The island also boasts a 6.1 m high triangular pillar, erected in 1735 at Ashey Down, erected as a Sea Mark. Rivers, particularly the Thames, have served as carriage routes for people and goods since the prehistoric period. Use of the Thames was in decline at the end of the medieval period, but from the 17th century onwards efforts were made to improve the navigation through dredging and construction of weirs and locks. These are mainly recorded in drawings and photographs (Siberechts of Henley, Taunt 1872, Banks and Stanley 1990), although some archaeological recording has been carried out at Iffley near Oxford and at Abingdon Swift Ditch lock (WA 2000, OA 2000a). Henley was a major gathering point for goods such as grain and timber (Plot 1677). These and coal were transferred to Oxford as well as London and stone from Headington was taken out (Prior 1981, 1982; Peberdy 1996). There were several wharf areas in Oxford, the best known along Fishers Row and from the 19th century in Jericho, where the boatyard has only recently closed. When Salter's Boatyard in Oxford was redeveloped an extensive programme of recording was carried out (OA 2000b).

Although goods are no longer moved by river the Thames is an important route for recreational cruising and the venue for numerous sporting events. Little work has been carried out on the craft employed although the River and Rowing Museum in Henley does house various sporting craft.

Construction of canals (Fig. 17.2) and the canalisation of stretches of river permitted easier freight movement by water. Construction of canals in the region

actually began in 1611 when the Earl of Southampton dammed the River Meol and built the Titchfield Canal, the second canal in England. Of the major river improvement schemes, the River Wey was improved in 1653, the Itchen Navigation dates from 1710 and the Kennet Navigation section of the Kennet and Avon Canal opened between 1795 and 1810 (Hadfield 1970; see Plate 1.2). This last enabled a significant wharf to be developed at Newbury (WA 1996c, 1998).

A network of other canals was constructed to link the various waterways, including the Basingstoke and Andover Canals (1794) and the Berkshire and Wiltshire Canal in 1810. Further north the major canal linking London with Braunston, Northamptonshire passed through Buckinghamshire. This opened at the end of the 18th century and linked into the Grand Union Canal in the Midlands. A branch to Aylesbury has been closed and largely dismantled although traces remain. The most important site within Buckinghamshire was at Wolverton where an aqueduct, now a Scheduled Ancient Monument, opened in 1811 carrying the canal over the River Ouse (Faulkner 1972). The Oxford Canal from Coventry had opened in 1790 (Bloxham and Bond 1981), finally closing as a coal wharf in the 1950s. The route passed through Banbury where a dock has been excavated. Tooley's Boatyard had closed in 1995, but the historic workshops have been preserved as a museum (Birmingham University Field Archaeology Unit 1999, 2000; OA 2003).

Many of the locks on these navigations were originally constructed with turf-sides, but these have generally been replaced. Garston Lock near Reading has survived as a working lock and that at Monkey Marsh, Thatcham has been excavated and recorded. (Harding and Newman 1990). Canal restoration groups are helping to restore many stretches of waterway and ensure the preservation of features.

One factor in the commercial demise of the canal and river network was the coming of the railways (Fig. 17.2). Railway companies were formed sometimes to build very short branch lines and these were amalgamated in 1921 into the major companies that existed until nationalisation of the railways in 1948. The Solent-Thames region falls mainly within the area operated by the Great Western Railway (GWR), but lines from the north were operated by the London Midland and Scottish Railway (LMS). The various lines are too numerous to discuss in detail here, but their histories are well documented in the vast published literature. Only parts of the network still survive, partly as a result of the cuts in the 1960s under Dr Beeching, although in the late 20th century reopening of lines began, such as the Chiltern Line from Birmingham to London.

There are large number of surviving structures and features of historical interest, usually on smaller or disused lines. Their preservation and recording owes much to volunteer organisations that run museums and operate trains over limited distances. There are six of these within the region: the Isle of Wight Steam Railway; Mid-Hants Watercress Railway; the Didcot Railway

Plate 17.12 LMS railway station, Oxford, *copyright OA*

Centre, Cholsey and Wallingford Railway, Oxfordshire; Chinnor & Princes Risborough Railway (Oxfordshire/ Buckinghamshire) and the Buckinghamshire Railway Centre at Quainton. Didcot owes its present size and significance in the county to the GWR works. The London and Birmingham Railway, later part of LMS, opened a major works at Wolverton in 1838 for manufacture of engines and carriages, which similarly established the town. Among the significant structures associated with the railway is the Wolverton Viaduct over the River Ouse (Cockman 1974).

The LMS station in Oxford was an unusual building utilising the same technology as that employed in the building of the Crystal Palace. It opened in 1851 and then in 1999 it was dismantled and moved to the Railway Centre at Quainton, Buckinghamshire (OA 1999; Plate 17.12). North-west of the present Oxford Station are the remains of a turntable bridge over the Sheepwash Channel (OAU 1996).

The railway network never connected everywhere and in the 1870s the Duke of Buckingham attempted to plug one gap with the horse drawn Wotton Tramway. This operated for 64 years, and some associated earthworks survive (Jones 1974). The Metropolitan Railway expanded into Buckinghamshire in the 1890s, allowing houses to be built on their land holdings route, helping to create the suburbs of Metroland (Hepple & Doggett, 1994).

At one time there was an extensive network of railway lines on Isle of Wight, linking the seaside resorts to the ports of Cowes, Ryde and Yarmouth. Primarily serving the tourist industry, these railways were a response to their development.

Until the post-medieval period responsibility for the maintenance of roads lay with individual parishes, which made little effort to keep the highways in good condition. During the 18th century a series of Turnpike Acts were passed, imposing a toll for travel along a particular section of road which was used to pay for maintenance (Albert 1972). In the Isle of Wight, however, the Turnpike Trust was not established until 1813. Toll collectors were provided with houses, many of which survive and are often now Listed Buildings. In Oxford, for example, there is one on the Botley Road and another at Folly Bridge.

A number of major routes from London, such as A4, A5, A40 and A31, pass through the region. The turnpike system encouraged coach travel along these, bringing with it associated prosperity for a number of towns. Coaching inns survive, including the Kings Head, Aylesbury, Griffin, Amersham and George and Dragon, West Wycombe, Buckinghamshire; Chequers, Newbury, White Hart, Colnbrook and George, Reading, Berkshire; Three Cups, Stocksbridge, White Hart, Andover and Red Lion, Fareham, Hampshire; Old Black Horse, Oxford, Old Crown, Faringdon and George, Dorchester-on-Thames, Oxfordshire. In the 20th century the M3, M4, M40 and M1 motorways have had a similar beneficial impact, most notably for the development of Milton Keynes.

As yet neglected subjects of study are motorway service stations, roadside transport cafés, such as Mac's Cafe on the A4 at Padworth, Berkshire which are currently rapidly disappearing from 'A' roads across the region to be demolished or converted to other uses. Even the distinctive chain of 1960s and 1970s 'Little Chef' restaurants is losing sites.

Milestones are commonly found, sometimes statutorily listed, and on the A4 in Berkshire several pumps set up to reduce the level of dust are still in position (Babtie n.d.). Roadside archaeology includes signposts as well as more recent features such as police boxes and those set up by the AA and RAC. There are only a few examples of early garages that still survive. These often started life as blacksmiths' forges or bicycle repair shops. One early purpose-built garage is the Electric Filling Station, built on the south side of Newbury in 1934 (OA 2006b). The history of road vehicles themselves is recorded at Beaulieu Motor Museum, Hants.

Various forms of public transport have been tried in towns. Tramways were constructed in Oxford, Reading and Southampton, although the only surviving evidence comes from maps. In Oxford the trams were only ever horse-drawn and not electrified as happened elsewhere (Hart 1972). Horse buses were the precursors to motor buses. At Long Hanborough, Oxfordshire there is a Bus Museum documenting their history.

Bridges are important features of the road network and many were originally built before the post-medieval period. Magdalen Bridge in Oxford was rebuilt in the 1770s and widened in 1835 and 1872 (VCH Oxfordshire IV 1979). Some bridges have been the subject of detailed studies, for example Wallingford Bridge, Oxon (Steane 1982). In Buckingham the bridge has some fine Coadstone decoration. Rather more unusual is the Floating Bridge in the Isle of Wight, which is in fact a chain ferry across the River Medina, linking East and West Cowes. This has operated in various forms since 1859 (http://www.simplonpc.co.uk/Cowes.html# anchor71591).

Despite its legacy of former military airfields, the region has not played a major role in the growth in commercial air travel. The only major airport is Southampton and there is a much smaller facility at Kidlington serving the Oxford area. However, the majority of sites which are still open for flying operate at club level, Booker near High Wycombe and Popham near Basingstoke for example.

An aspect of transport that has not been well researched is the place within society of the gangs of construction workers needed to build the canals, railways and major roads. Huge numbers of these would have moved into areas for the lifetime of the project, requiring housing and some supporting infrastructure. For example, little is known about the lives of some 3,000 men employed on the Grand Junction Canal (which includes the Grand Union Canal) in 1793 (Faulkner 1972). In more recent times the camps of environmental protestors have become a feature of major projects, affecting construction of the Winchester by-pass at Twyford Down and the Newbury by-pass.

Legacy

The post-medieval and modern period witnessed the growth of Great Britain as a world power, building a trade network for the products of the industrial revolution. Although the British Empire no longer exists, the Solent remains an important part of the international network through its container port as well as the passenger facilities for cross-channel ferries and cruises.

For Britain, a sea-going nation that led the industrial revolution, the wider world has always been of importance. One sign of globalisation has been the growth of multi-cultural societies, but the presence of immigrant communities did not come as new to Hampshire with its major ports. These are now more common across the region, but particularly so in the east, in Slough, Reading and High Wycombe and some smaller centres like Chesham.

It is still possible to some extent to tell which county is which from the building materials and styles. However, new buildings are not always sensitive to this, employing instead a generic shopping mall or supermarket brand style. This erosion of regional/local character is a marked legacy, although by no means only within the Solent-Thames region.

Until the later 20th century Britain was a manufacturing nation, but most of this capacity has now been exported to the Far East and Eastern Europe where production costs are less. As the Solent-Thames region was never dependent on an industrial base, its prosperity has not suffered as much as that of other parts of Britain. Consumerism has had an impact on the infrastructure of the region through the proliferation of out-of-town shopping facilities, reconstruction of town centres for malls as well as altering the pattern of freight movement from its ports.

Chapter 18

The Post-Medieval and Modern Period (AD 1540 onwards): Research Agenda

by Jill Hind

18.1 Nature of the evidence

The wealth of evidence for this period is immense, much of it from documentary records, contemporary illustrations and eye-witness accounts. The archaeological record is expanding, although excavations are still much rarer than survey work. All types of evidence only provide a partial record, and the documentary sources have a bias away from ordinary people and their lives. Ways in which the various data sources are used in combination need to be improved, as follows:

18.1.1   Areas where the physical and documentary evidence is contradictory need to be identified for further investigation.

18.1.2   The strengths and weaknesses of the various types of evidence across the region should be assessed.

18.2 Chronology

The documentary records for this period mean that chronology and dating should be better understood than for earlier ones. However, this does not mean that there is no uncertainty over the timing of events, particularly those affecting changes to the rural environment and land use. Opportunities to obtain reliable dates for structures or landscapes elements should therefore be taken whenever possible. Specific aims should include the following:

18.2.1   The reliability of chronological markers, particularly for the 16th to 18th century, needs to be tested.

18.2.2   Architectural typologies and dendrochronology should be compared to check consistency.

18.2.3   The precision of ceramic sequences should be tested.

18.3 Landscape and land use

One of the major influences on the rural landscape during this period was enclosure, either by agreement or parlia-mentary act. Enclosure began during the medieval period and still continues at a very low level with loss of commons for example, although the majority had happened by the late 19th century. The changes in the landscape and increasing urbanisation were also influenced by major developments in the transport infrastructure. Listed below are some issues of particular importance for research:

18.3.1   The possible social and economic forces responsible for the distribution of 'champion' and 'ancient' landscapes within the region need to be explored.

18.3.2   Environmental evidence needs to be collected routinely to gather information on the origins of fields and changes in agricultural practice, which may have occurred at different times in different areas.

18.3.3   The impact of large towns (and of London) on their hinterlands would merit further investigation.

18.3.4   Studies of significant gardens and parks, particularly those which are not on the Register of Parks and Gardens, should consider social issues, such as their roles as status symbols and in competition between members of the elite, as well as their design components.

18.3.5   The development of agriculture in the Isle of Wight may inform debate on the perceived insularity of the Island.

18.3.6   Evidence for the impact of the Little Ice Age on the coastal and marine environments should be sought.

18.3.7   The impact of the Little Ice Age on daily life and the wider economy may also be found in the environmental record.

18.3.8   Survival of woods and commons is good across the region, particularly in south Buckinghamshire, but the reasons for this are not well understood.

18.3.9   The date and impact of industry on the landscape needs to be established.

18.3.10   The impact of the agricultural revolution on the landscape needs to be explored.

18.4 Social and administrative organisation

The archaeology of social organisation and administration for this period lies mainly in associated buildings and structures. These can range from a village pump to a large hospital complex. Smaller features are often removed for road schemes or redevelopment, while the larger buildings are frequently seen as unsuitable for modern requirements. This results in major alteration, change of use or even demolition. The following areas of research merit particular attention:

18.4.1   The balance between insularity and population movement should be studied, particularly in the context of the Isle of Wight.

18.4.2   Social hierarchy in settlements should be investigated, through built infrastructure, decoration, symbology and material culture manifestations of social, economic and cultural/racial variation within urban and rural settlement.

18.4.3   More work is needed on changes in standards of living for the lower classes. For example, to what extent was such change uniform or was defined by local circumstance (such as the priorities of major landlords).

18.4.4   The relationships between urban morphology, prosperity and backyard enterprise merit investigation.

18.4.5   The provision of public utilities across the region and its relationship to social hierarchies would merit further investigation.

18.4.6   Evidence should be gathered to illustrate how the proceeds of capitalism were divided and used, both across the region and over time.

18.4.7   Indirect and direct influences on the environment of the region by the monarchy, parliament, the growth of London and the growth of empire, especially with respect to the region's location in the hinterland of London and Southampton, need to be explored.

18.5 Settlement

In rural areas settlement and landscape cannot be

regarded separately. HLC can lead on to more detailed consideration of the development and character of settlements, as it has in Buckinghamshire. Study of towns is a better established discipline, with a number of county based projects in the 1970s and 1980s which are being updated at present through an EH initiative. Key among the areas needing research are the following:

18.5.1   The factors leading to the mix of settlement types across the region should be investigated.

18.5.2   Environmental evidence for the quality of the urban environment should be collected, and used to investigate possible zoning and evidence for social improvement in the later part of the period.

18.5.3   The reasons why some towns failed during the post-medieval period, and the rationale for new ones to be established, are not fully understood.

18.5.4   More parish surveys are needed which explore the development of settlements in more detail, including relationships with outlying farms and hamlets, morphology etc.

18.5.5   Evidence for differences between the rural and urban economies should be collected and analysed.

18.6 Built environment

The types of building materials and building styles used across the region vary considerably, although modern developments seldom maintain this diversity, especially outside Conservation Areas. The work of many leading architects is represented across the Solent-Thames region, in individual houses as well as churches and larger corporate buildings. The efficient communications network and proximity to London led to the creation of commuter belt suburbs in Berkshire and Buckinghamshire, while other major suburban developments have followed industries such as the Harwell and Aldermaston research establishments. Avenues for further study are listed below:

18.6.1   Investigation should be carried out to test whether the nature of the built environment reflects differences in settlement patterns.

18.6.2   Whether anciently enclosed landscapes display greater diversity and innovation than surviving open field areas need to be explored.

18.6.3   Further study of public buildings (local government and justice; schools, hospitals etc) would illuminate their origin, development, aspects of their operation and their social context.

18.6.4   A better understanding of when building materials and techniques change across the region is needed.

18.6.5   The role of built infrastructure, decoration, symbology and material culture as manifestations of social, economic and cultural/racial variation within urban and rural settlement would benefit from systematic study.

18.6.6   The impact of London and other major connurbations on regional building styles, particularly through suburban developments, could be tested.

18.7 Ceremony, ritual and religion

The nature of religious beliefs and practices across the Solent-Thames region has undergone massive changes during the post-medieval and modern periods. The beginning of the period saw the conversion of the established Church from Roman Catholicism to Anglican Protestantism. The new religion itself underwent a series of changes in rite and acceptable church decoration, fittings and furnishing over the next few centuries. Catholicism was never completely eradicated and it was re-established in the 19th century. The number and variety of non-conformist denominations also varied across this period. At all periods, but particularly from the 2nd half of the 20th century onwards, immigrants from abroad have brought a variety of different religions or sects, producing, even within this limited geographical area, a multi-cultural society. The following aspects of evidence of ritual and religion merit further study:

18.7.1   The churches, churchyards and memorials of the region should be studied to provide information about their connections with major architectural and artistic figures, and the roles played by the inhabitants of the region in the wider environment.

18.7.2   The region, in particular Berkshire, was home to a significant Catholic recusant community, and evidence for this movement should be collated.

18.7.3   Systematic study of non-conformism could determine whether its spread reflected socio-economic factors.

18.7.4   Early evidence for places of worships linked to non-Christian groups should be sought, particularly around the major ports.

18.8 Warfare, defences and military installations

The Solent-Thames region has played a major role in Britain's defences throughout this period. The naval bases along the south coast have been in continuous use since Henry VIII began to establish a permanent navy, and the heathlands of Berkshire, Hampshire and neighbouring Surrey saw the development of the country's standing army. Airfields were a 20th century addition to the landscape, and in our region many survived the end of World War II and came to prominence during the Cold War, including Greenham Common, Upper Heyford and the NATO HQ at High Wycombe. Secret establishments such as Bletchley Park also existed within the region. Areas of particular potential include the following:

18.8.1   The many sites connected with the Civil War, including garrisons, skirmishes sieges and defences, should be identified and their archaeological potential assessed.

18.8.2   More work remains to be done on 17th to 19th century military sites and World War I defences, including upon the issues of continuity and re-use.

18.8.3   The scope of information about the region's wide range of World War II defensive arrangements should be extended to include more on civilian defence, particularly air-raid shelters, and should include both identification and recording of sites and accompanying oral testimony.

18.8.4   Further studies of cold war operations and defences should be pursued, partly in order to identify features for future protection.

18.9 Material culture

Material culture generally is not receiving the attention it deserves, but this is particularly true for the post-medieval and modern periods. The close study of ceramic assemblages, grave furniture or the inventory of goods surviving in a building is seldom carried out and finds are often regarded as obscuring the more interesting earlier layers below. Historical archaeology in the USA has demonstrated the value of studying more recent material culture, but adoption of these ideas in the UK is slow. The following measures urgently need implementation or reinforcement.

18.9.1   Post-medieval below-ground archaeology tends to be investigated only as a by-product of sites identified for their medieval interest, in urban situations where later levels may have been extensively disturbed. There is a case for more emphasis in planning conditions upon the proper investigation of sites likely to be productive for their post-medieval interest, both to provide the data for detailed studies of contexts and associations and help to build up a better picture of ceramic and other artefact sequences. This will be particularly productive for urban sites in Oxford, Aylesbury, Reading, Winchester or Cowes.

18.9.2   In particular, more detailed work should be concentrated on ceramics as a dating base, particularly for the 15th/16th century, and on helping to establish patterns of sources and manufacture for the market towns of each county.

18.9.3   Studies are also needed on further developing detailed understanding of non-ceramic artefact types found in excavation, especially bottle glass and tobacco pipes.

18.9.4   It would be helpful to establish a methodology for the analysis of probate records, hearth tax returns etc., in order to improve the integration of documentary and archaeological evidence, including that from building recording.

18.9.5   Patterns in material culture can contribute to the understanding of patterns of trade across the region, the influence of the major south coast ports and the influence of London and royalty on society.

18.10   Crafts, trade and industries

The Solent-Thames region is not usually associated with industry, a term which tends to suggest the heavy manufacturing and extraction processes of the Midlands and North. There has in fact been a wide variety of industries including ship and aircraft manufacture, cloth working and brick and tile production, as well as the furniture production of Buckinghamshire, needle making, straw plaiting and other cottage industries, most of which did not survive when mechanisation was introduced. Ways to enhance our understanding of these practices include:

18.10.1   Collection of environmental evidence for particular industries eg. salt-making.

18.10.2   Exploration of the distribution of industry, the reasons for its existence and, where appropriate, its demise.

18.10.3   Recording of surviving industrial complexes and small-scale rural enterprises before closure.

18.10.4   Further investigaton of the leisure and recreation industries, including those associated with the coast, which are changing rapidly.

18.10.5   Searching for environmental evidence for the use of exotic imports such as spices.

Transport and communications

The Solent and its various harbours established the region as an important part of the maritime transport network. The River Thames continued to be a major link in the transport network into the 20th century, while the importance of the River Kennet was increased when it was incorporated into the Kennet and Avon Canal. The A34 continues to act as one of the major north-south routes in southern England, linking the Solent to Oxford and from there to the M40 and the Midlands. At Newbury this road intersects with the principal route from London to Wales, the A4 and now the M4. These and other long established major routes have been a big influence on the development of the region. Better understanding of the development of the region's transport networks requires the following:

18.11.1   More information about the pre-turnpike road network.

18.11.2   Exploration of the effects of the development of the communications network and related technology upon settlement patterns, land use and local economies.

18.11.3   Evidence for the development of the maritime network, including environmental evidence.

Conclusion

The range of resources available for studying the post-medieval periods is vast, and wherever possible archaeological investigations should be tied to the documentary sources. For the very recent past oral history can also contribute. Post-medieval and modern studies need therefore to operate as collaborations between archaeologists, local and social historians, historical geographers and other interested parties. There are numerous groups and individuals involved in this work, many of them amateurs, and this interest and enthusiasm must be harnessed to provide the best data, and to ensure the continuation of this interest for the future.

Chapter 19

Conclusions

by Gill Hey and Jill Hind

Introduction

The creation of a Resource Assessment and Research Agenda has demonstrated the keen level of interest in the Solent-Thames historic environment and the range of groups and individuals who are actively involved in research in the area. Many of these people have contributed to this volume. There was considerable support for the idea of a Research Framework, and the online version of the county contributions has attracted attention from researchers across the UK and from Europe. People from all sectors of interest have been involved in its preparation, including non-professionals.

Whereas a research-led approach to the examination of the historic environment is well established in archaeology, including in a planning context, this concept is less usual for the built environment and, with some exceptions, the project was unable to generate much enthusiasm to participate from this sector. This area of study is less-well represented in this volume than we would have liked.

The preparation of this document has demonstrated the richness and variety of the historic environment of the Solent-Thames sub-region. Despite the quantity of research that has been carried out to date, a number of areas have been identified where there is insufficient evidence to inform understanding. The reasons for this include:

- advances in research techniques, not available when previous work was carried out;
- lack of knowledge of areas that have seen low levels of development and of archaeological investigation;
- lack of focus on specific research questions in planning work.

Common themes

Although research issues that are specific to each chronological period have been identified, a surprising number of themes have emerged that are common to more than one. Some of these are related to the application of particular approaches to data and investigation, others to a specific geographical area, and some to particular topics.

The need for existing collections to be revisited and re-appraised arose in most of the period agendas. In particular, it is thought that flint artefacts may have been wrongly identified in the past, leading to incorrect assessments about the levels and locations of past activity for different chronological periods (see, for example, the Upper Palaeolithic and Mesolithic chapter).

More accurate dating was seen as desirable for all periods. The use of scientific techniques, such as radiocarbon and OSL (optically-stimulate luminescence) dating, as well as refinements to artefact typologies, are seen as being able to contribute to this objective. These can be applied to both existing collections and as a more regular feature of current and future investigations.

Environmental sampling was another area where more work is observed to be generally necessary. More samples are required, for landscape reconstruction and for targeting specific issues. Greater consistency and co-ordination in sampling strategies over wider areas and in different contexts would also enable a better comparison of results and more rapid acquisition of useful research data (see, for example, the Late Bronze Age and Iron Age chapter). In addition to informing understanding of a particular chronological period, the results will contribute to the developing picture of how the wider landscape of the region has evolved. As has been pointed out in a number of the period assessments and agendas, the full value of much environmental work that has already been undertaken has not been realised, and a synthesis of existing datasets would, in itself, shed much light on the past landscapes of the region.

As has been stressed by a number of the contributors, our current understanding of the historic environment of the region has been biased by our focus on development-led work, which has been concentrated in particular areas (see the late Bronze Age and Iron Age chapter). Other parts of our region are much less well understood. An example is the gaps in our understanding of the Roman settlement pattern (see the Roman chapter).

The importance of understanding the landscape setting and environmental context in order to appreciate human settlement has been stressed by several authors, especially for early periods when finds may be scarce. As the environmental introduction and the Palaeolithic chapters make clear, for some periods reconstructing the contemporary physical geography of the region is a fundamental starting point for assessing where sites of the greatest potential might lie and where different kinds of activity can be expected. Francis Wenban-Smith has described this as understanding the 'lived landscape' (Lower and Middle Palaeolithic chapter). Investigating how people moved through these landscapes and how this changed through time is another cross-period theme. Understanding shifting *vs* permanent settlement, and the changing range and balance of settlement types, are research topics that occur repeatedly throughout this volume.

For our region, extremes of environmental change are clearest in the long period covered by the Lower and Middle Palaeolithic. Even in later periods, however, the significance and effects of natural climatic changes and human modifications to the environment are important. In archaeological terms, some extremely high-quality data has come from remains sealed beneath alluvium and colluvium (see, for example, the Neolithic and Early Bronze Age and the Early Medieval chapters). The relationship between field systems and settlement, boundaries, land rights and the changing balance between clearance, pasture and arable is a persistent theme from the Neolithic to the medieval periods, as is the importance of a better understanding of human impact on the 'wild' environment of plants and animals. The introduction and use of domesticated plants and animals in the Neolithic is still poorly understood, but the availability of new foods and changing diets are research topics raised for all periods (see, for example, the Roman and the Medieval chapters). The relationship between towns and their hinterlands, it is felt, are still little understood, despite the prominence of national research projects like that for Wroxeter (Gaffney and White 2007), and could be much improved by the better use of environmental data.

The importance of understanding taphonomic factors is raised in several chapters, for example the fortuitous relationship between deposition of Palaeolithic implements and their rapid burial by land slips or silt deposits. Ploughing has had an impact on the preservation of fragile deposits of many different periods and understanding the resulting palimpsest of surface finds is a common theme, especially for occupation which pre-dates our present settlement pattern (see, for example, the Upper Palaeolithic and Mesolithic and the Early Medieval chapters). In towns there is the problem of the differential survival of the less substantial remains of early settlement or housing related to lower income groups (see the Medieval and the Post-medieval and Modern chapters). How far this last issue can be addressed in future remains to be seen.

The Solent-Thames region has had a particularly strong association with royalty since the early medieval period, only in part related to its proximity to London. The importance of this region in the emergence and changing composition of elites is a cross-period theme (from the Neolithic to the Post-medieval and Modern period) which would merit more study. The link between the rise of kingship and the re-introduction of Christianity and its developing structure is an issue with great potential for further work in this area, with early bishoprics present at Winchester and at Dorchester-on-Thames. The changing face of Christianity and, latterly, other religions can be charted up to the modern era.

New industries were influenced by the geography and geology of the region, for example potting in the Roman period and the early use of bricks in medieval vernacular architecture (see the Roman and the Later Medieval chapters). Proximity to long-distance contacts and trade routes also played an important role and a main research area to be addressed is the maritime heritage of the region. Work in this area will need to consider the *Maritime Archaeological Research Agenda for England* (Ransley *et al.* 2013). The gradual change of the Solent river into a marine channel, the particular character of the Isle of Wight, Britain as a maritime power and defence against invasion are all relevant here. The interesting relationship between the mainland and the Isle of Wight, and the importance of the Island have been flagged up as meriting greater scrutiny, especially for the Roman, early medieval and later medieval periods. The present Solent hides drowned landscapes of the Mesolithic and earlier periods.

Long-distance links extending beyond the region are relevant for all periods. These can be investigated in terms of migration routes or trading links for example. The Solent-Thames region is not an obviously homogeneous area and its relationships to adjoining regions are important. The role of immigration on its society and the changing cultural affiliations of its population are important research themes and the use of stable isotope analysis and DNA sampling of human and animal remains to shed light on this issue has been highlighted by several authors (see, for example, Late Bronze Age and Iron Age and Early Medieval chapters).

Serendipity will always play a part in archaeological endeavour, and remains of international significance can emerge unexpectedly. It is vital that these are recognised and treated appropriately, whether they are identified in a Research Framework or not. We must not allow what are intended to be helpful commentaries on the known resource and the obvious gaps in knowledge to lead to formulaic responses. We hope they will promote new insights and innovation and the recognition of the genuinely new and unexpected.

Research strategy proposals

A Research Strategy for the region is the next stage in this Research Framework Project. It will examine potential mechanisms for addressing the issues raised in the Research Agendas and will formulate a policy for further research within a national, regional and local framework.

The strategy will look at the many ways that archaeological research can be integrated into strategic and development opportunities to ensure that research funding, whether from developers, public bodies or grant-giving trusts and others, is used in a cost-effective manner. It will also seek to mesh with the Research Frameworks of adjacent areas and those which are period or theme specific, as also with national policy statements that set out the need for research to underpin the public value of the historic environment. It is of vital importance to provide a strategic vision of fundamental values for the historic environment which is related to the public interest.

The Strategy needs to encourage the participation of everyone active in the study of the historic environment for the benefit of the public, part of which is to inform and facilitate curatorial decision making, providing a recognised framework within which judgements can be made and justified.

The Research Framework presents the state of the historic environment at a particular point in time. Levels of knowledge and understanding will change over time and the Research Framework will need to evolve alongside these changes. Part of the Strategy will be to put in place a review process to allow this to happen.

Bibliography

Aberg, F A, 1978 *Medieval moated sites*, CBA Res Rep **17**, London

Abrams, J, 2003 Rose Cottage, Elm Road, Tylers Green, Buckinghamshire, unpublished report

Addyman, P V and Leigh, D, 1973 The Anglo-Saxon village at Chalton, Hampshire: second interim report, *Medieval Archaeology* **17**, 1-25

Addyman, P V, Leigh, D and Hughes, M J 1972, Anglo-Saxon houses at Chalton, Hampshire, *Medieval Archaeology* **16**, 13-32

Adkins, R A and Petchey, M R, 1984 The Secklow hundred mound and other meeting place mounds in England, *Archaeol J* **141**, 243-251

Aiello, L and Wheeler, P, 1995 The Expensive-tissue Hypothesis the Brain and the Digestive System in Human and Primate Evolution, *Current Anthropology* **36**, 199–221

Airs, M, 1998 The strange history of paper roofs, *Trans Ancient Monuments Soc* **42**, 35-62

Airs. M (ed.), 2002 *The 20th Century Great House*, OUDCE, Oxford

Albert, W, 1972 *The turnpike road system of England 1663-1840*, Cambridge

Alcock, N W, 1981 *Cruck Construction. An Introduction and Catalogue*, CBA Res Rep **42**, London

Alexander, J, Ozanne, P C and Ozanne, A, 1960 The excavation of a round barrow on Arreton Down, Isle of Wight, *Proc Prehist Soc* **26**, 263-296

Allen, D, 1982 Salvage excavations at 13-19 Buckingham Street and the Bull's Head redevelopment site, Aylesbury, in 1979 and 1980, *Rec Buckinghamshire* **24**, 81-106

Allen, D, 1983 Iron Age occupation, a Middle Saxon cemetery and twelfth to nineteenth century urban occupation. Excavations at George Street, Aylesbury 1981, *Rec Buckinghamshire* **25**, 1-60

Allen, D, 1986 Excavations in Bierton, 1979 A late Iron Age 'Belgic' settlement and evidence for a Roman villa and a twelfth to eighteenth century manorial complex, *Rec Buckinghamshire* **28**, 1-120

Allen, D and Dalwood, C H, 1983 Iron Age occupation, a Middle Saxon cemetery, and twelfth to nineteenth century urban occupation: excavations in George Street, Aylesbury, 1981, *Rec Buckinghamshire* **25**, 1-59

Allen, J R L, 2012 Iron-smelting at Silchester (Calleva Atrebatum): a re-assessment over time, in Fulford 2012a, 77-103

Allen, J R L, and Allen, S A, 1997 A stratified prehistoric site from the Kennet floodplain at Ufton Nervet, Berkshire, *Berkshire Archaeol J* **75**, 1-8

Allen, J R L and Fulford, M G, 1996 The distribution of south-east Dorset black burnished category 1 pottery in south west Britain, *Britannia* **27**, 223-81

Allen, J R L and Fulford, M G, 2004 Early Roman mosaic materials in southern Britain, with particular reference to Silchester (Calleva Atrebatum): a regional geological perspective, *Britannia* **35**, 9-38

Allen, J R L, Fulford, M G and Todd, J A, 2007 Burnt Kimmeridgian shale at early Roman Silchester, South-East England, and the Roman Poole-Purbeck complex-agglomerated geomaterials industry, *Oxford J Archaeol* **26**, 167-91

Allen, J R L and Todd, J A, 2010 A Kimmeridgian (Upper Jurassic) source for early Roman yellow tesserae and opus sectile in southern Britain, *Britannia* **41**, 317-21

Allen, M J, 1988 Archaeological and environmental aspects of colluviation in south-east England, in *Man-Made Soils*, (eds W. Groenman-van Waateringe & M. Robinson), BAR **S410**, 67-92

Allen, M J, 1991a The environmental (molluscan) evidence, in Bellamy, P S, The investigation of the prehistoric landscape along the route of the A303 improvement between Andover, Hampshire, and Amesbury, Wiltshire, *Proc Hampshire Fld Club Archaeol Soc* **47**, 5-81

Allen, M J, 1991b Analysing the landscape; a geographical approach to archaeological problems, in *Interpreting artefact scatters: contributions to plough-zone archaeology*, (ed. A J Schofield), Oxbow Books, Oxford, 37-54

Allen, M J, 1992 Products of Erosion and the Prehistoric Land Use of the Wessex Chalk, in *Past and Present Soil Erosion*, (eds M G Bell and J Boardman), Oxbow Monograph, 37-92

Allen, M J 1996 Landscape and landuse: priorities in Hampshire 500,000 BC to AD 1500, in *Archaeology in Hampshire: a framework for the future*, (D Hinton and M Hughes eds), Hampshire County Council, 55-70

Allen, M J, 1997a Landscape, land-use and farming, in *Excavations along the route of the Dorchester by-pass, Dorset, 1986-8*, (eds R J C Smith, F Healy, M J Allen, E L Morris, I Barnes, and P J Woodward), Wessex Archaeology Report **11**, 277-283

Allen, M J, 1997b Environment and land-use: the economic development of the communities who built Stonehenge; an economy to support the stones, in *Science and Stonehenge*, (eds B Cunliffe and C Renfrew), Proc British Academy, Oxford, 115-144

Allen, M J, 2000a Wood, farm and field: landuse history of Twyford Down; land snail evidence, in *Twyford Down, Hampshire: archaeological investigations* on the M3 Motorway from Bar End to Compton, 1990-93*, (eds K E Walker and D E Farewell), Hampshire Field Club Monograph **9**, 138-142

Allen, M J, 2000b Landscape and economy: a discussion of the environmental evidence, in *Twyford Down, Hampshire: archaeological investigations on the M3 Motorway from Bar End to Compton, 1990-93*, (eds K E Walker and D E Farewell), Hampshire Field Club Monograph **9** 158-9

Allen, M J, 2001 Land snail evidence for landscape and land-use change, in Ellis, C J, and Rawlings, M, Excavations at Balksbury Camp, Andover 1995-97, *Hampshire Studies* **56**, 54-67

Allen, M J, 2005 Beaker settlement and environment on the chalk downs of southern England, *Proc Prehist Soc* **71**, 219-45

Allen, M J (ed.), 2005 Scientific studies: crew, conditions and environment, in *Before the mast; life and death aboard the* Mary Rose, (eds J Gardiner with M J Allen), The Archaeology of the Mary Rose vol 4, Portsmouth: Mary Rose Trust Ltd, 501-650

Allen, M J, 2008a Some thoughts on fields and field systems in the wider landscape, in Cunliffe, B W, New Danebury Landscape Volume Series **1**, 50-53

Allen, M J, 2008b Land and freshwater Mollusca; the landscape evidence, in Masefield, R, *Prehistoric and Later Settlement and landscape from the Chiltern Scarp to Aylesbury Vale; the archaeology of the Aston Clinton bypass, Buckinghamshire*, BAR **473**, 156-163

Allen, M J, 2011 An environmental archaeology and geoarchaeological revolution?, in *The New Antiquarians: 50 years of archaeological innovation in Wessex*, (ed. R Whimster), CBA Res Rep **166**, York, 179-192

Allen, M J and Gardiner, J, 2000 *Our changing coast. A survey of the intertidal archaeology of Langstone Harbour, Hampshire*, CBA Res Rep **124**, York

Allen, M J, and Gardiner, J, 2009 If you go down to the woods today. A re-evaluation of the chalkland postglacial woodland: implications for prehistoric communities, in *Land and people: papers in memory of John G Evans* (eds M J Allen, N Sharples and T O'Connor), Prehistoric Society Research Paper **2**, 49-66

Allen, M J and Scaife, R, 2007 A new downland prehistory: long-term environmental change on the southern English chalklands, in *Prehistoric and Roman landscapes; landscape history after Hoskins*, (eds A Fleming and R Hingley), Windgather Press, Macclesfield, 16-32

Allen, M J, Morris, M and Clarke, R H, 1995 Food for the living: a reassessment of a Bronze Age barrow at Buckskin, Basingstoke, Hampshire, *Proc Prehist Soc* **61**, 157–90

Allen, M J, Carter, R and Maxted, A, 2008a Rapid field investigation methods and a new Mesolithic site approach for the Weald, UK, *PAST* **59** (July), 5-8

Allen, M J, Maxted, A and Carter, R, 2008b A new Mesolithic for the Weald? Rapid geoarchaeological survey at Chiddinglye Wood Rocks, West Hoathly,

Sussex Past and Present **115** (August), 4-5

Allen, S, 2005 Mesolithic hunter-gatherer exploitation of the Marlborough Downs, in *The Avebury landscape: aspects of the field archaeology of the Marlborough Downs* (eds G Brown, D Field D and McOmish) Oxbow Books, Oxford, 95-102

Allen, T G, 1990 *An Iron Age and Romano-British enclosed settlement at Watkins Farm, Northmoor, Oxon.*, Thames Valley Landscapes Monograph: the Windrush Valley Vol **1**, OAU Oxford

Allen, T G, 1991 An 'oppidum' at Abingdon, Oxfordshire, *CBA South Midlands Archaeol* **21**, 97-9

Allen, T G, 1993 Abingdon, Abingdon Vineyard 1992: Areas 2 and 3, the early defences, *SMA* **23**, 64-6

Allen, T, 1994 A Medieval Grange of Abingdon Abbey at Dean Court Farm, Cumnor, Oxon', *Oxoniensia* **59**, 219–447

Allen, T, 1997 Abingdon: West Central Redevelopment Area, *South Midlands Archaeology* **27**, 47-54

Allen, T, 1998 Locating, evaluating and Interpreting Lithic Scatters: the Eton Rowing Lake experience, *Lithics* **19**, 33-46

Allen, T G, 2000 The Iron Age background, in Henig, M and Booth, P, 1-33

Allen, T, 2002 *The Excavation of a Medieval Manor House of the Bishops of Winchester at Mount House, Witney, Oxfordshire*, Oxford Archaeology Thames Valley Landscapes Monograph **13**

Allen, T G, 2007 Oxfordshire Later Bronze Age and Iron Age Historic Environment Resource Assessment (Draft) http://www.buckscc.gov.uk/ bcc/get/assets/docs/archaeology/Later%20Prehistory %20Oxfordshire%20nature%20of%20evidence.pdf

Allen, T G and Kamash, Z, 2008 *Saved from the grave: Neolithic to Saxon discoveries at Spring Road Municipal Cemetery, Abingdon, Oxfordshire, 1990-2000*, Oxford Archaeology Thames Valley Landscapes Monograph **28**, Oxford

Allen, T (ed.), 2011 *The Lost Abbey of Abingdon*, Oxford Archaeology

Allen, T G and Lamdin-Whymark H, 2000 The Rediscovery of Taplow Hillfort, *CBA South Midlands Archaeol* **30**, 22-8

Allen, T G and Mitchell, N, 2001 Dorney, Eton Rowing Lake, *CBA South Midlands Archaeol* **31**, 26-30

Allen, T and Robinson, M, 1979 Hardwick with Yelford, Mingies Ditch, *Counc Brit Archaeol Group 9 Newsletter* **9**, 115-17

Allen, T G and Robinson, M A, 1993 *The prehistoric landscape and Iron Age enclosed settlement at Mingies Ditch, Hardwick-with-Yelford, Oxon*, Thames Valley Landscapes Monograph: the Windrush Valley **2**, Oxford, OAU

Allen, T and Welsh, K, 1997 Eton Rowing Lake, Dorney, Buckinghamshire. Second interim report, *South Midlands Archaeology* **27**, 25-34

Allen, T G, Miles, D and Palmer, S, 1984 Iron Age buildings in the Upper Thames region, in Cunliffe and Miles (eds) 1984, 89-101

Allen, T G, with Barton, N and Brown, A, 1995 *Lithics and landscape: archaeological discoveries on the Thames Water pipeline at Gatehampton Farm, Goring, Oxfordshire 1985-92*, Thames Valley Landscapes 7, Oxford

Allen, T G, with Hacking, P and Boyle, A, 2000 Eton Rowing Course at Dorney Lake. The Burial Traditions, *Tarmac Papers* **4**, 65-106

Allen, T G, Barclay, A, and Lamdin-Whymark, H, 2004 Opening the wood, making the land: landscape in the Dorney area of the Middle Thames Valley, in Cotton and Field 2004, 82-98

Allen, T G, Hayden, C and Lamdin-Whymark, H, 2009 *Excavations at Taplow Court, Buckinghamshire: a late Bronze Age and Iron Age hillfort*, Oxford Archaeology Thames Valley Landscapes Monograph **30**, Oxford

Allen, T G, Lamdin-Whymark, H and Maricevic, D, 2006 Taplow, Taplow Court (Phase 2), Clivedon Road, (SU907 824), *CBA South Midlands Archaeology* **36**, 19-21

Allen, T, Cramp, K, Lamdin-Whymark, H and Webley, L, 2010 *Castle Hill and its landscape; Archaeological Investigations at the Wittenhams, Oxfordshire*, Oxford Archaeology Monograph **9**, Oxford

Allen, T G, Barclay, A, Cromarty, A M, Anderson-Whymark, H, Parker, A and Robinson, M, 2013 *Opening the wood, making the land: The archaeology of a Middle Thames landscape. The Eton rowing course at Dorney and the Maidenhead, Eton and Windsor flood alleviation channel, Volume 1: Mesolithic to Early Bronze Age*, Oxford Archaeology Thames Valley Landscapes Monograph **38**, Oxford

Allen, T G, Bradley, P and Cromarty, A M, forthcoming *Bridging the River, Dividing the Land: The Archaeology of a Middle Thames landscape. The Eton rowing course at Dorney and the Maidenhead, Eton and Windsor flood alleviation channel, Volume 2: Middle Bronze Age to Roman*, Oxford Archaeology Thames Valley Landscapes Monograph, Oxford

Allison, K J, Beresford, M W and Hurst, D G, 1965 *The Deserted Villages of Oxfordshire*

Ames, R E, 1993 A Mesolithic assemblage from Moor Farm, Holyport, near Maidenhead, *Berkshire Archaeol J* **74**, 1-8

Anderson, E, Goudie, A and Parker A, 2007 *Global Environments through the Quaternary: Exploring Environmental Change*, OUP

Andrews, P (ed.), 1988 *The coins and pottery from Hamwic*, Southampton Finds Volume One, Southampton

Andrews, P (ed.), 1997 *Excavations at Hamwic volume 2: excavations at Six Dials*, CBA Res Rep **109**, York

Andrews, P and Crockett, A, 1996 *Three excavations along the Thames and its Tributaries, 1994; Neolithic to Saxon settlement and burial in the Thames, Colne and Kennet Valleys*, Salisbury, Wessex Archaeology Report **10**

Anthony, S, Hull, G, Pine, J and Taylor, K, 2006 *Excavations in medieval Abingdon and Drayton, Oxfordshire*, Thames Valley Archaeological Services Monograph 8

Antoine, P, Limondin Lozouet, N, Chaussé, C, Lautridou, J-P, Pastre, J-F, Auguste, P, Bahain, J-J, Falguères, C and Galehb, B, 2007 Pleistocene fluvial terraces from northern France (Seine, Yonne, Somme): synthesis, and new results from interglacial deposits, *Quaternary Science Reviews* **26**, 2701-2723

Archaeological Services and Consultancy Ltd, 2003 Watching brief and salvage recording: Claydon Road, Hogshaw, unpublished report

Archaeological Solutions Ltd, 2004 Business/Science Park, Aston Clinton Major Development Area, Aylesbury Buckinghamshire, Archaeological desk-based assessment and earthwork survey, unpublished report

Arkell, W J, 1947 *Oxford stone*, London

Armour-Chelu, R, 2001 128 High Street, Chesham, Buckinghamshire. Archaeological excavation on the site of supermarket development and associated parking, unpublished report

Arnold, C J, 1975 A medieval site at Bouldnor, *Proc Isle Wight Nat Hist Archaeol Soc* **VI**, 664-667

Arnold, C J, 1982 *The Anglo-Saxon Cemeteries of the Isle of Wight*, British Museum Publications Ltd, London

Arthur, B V and Jope, E M, 1962 Early Saxon pottery kilns at Purwell Farm, Cassington, Oxfordshire, *Medieval Archaeol* **6-7**, 1-14

Ashbee, P, 1957 The Great Barrow at Bishop's Waltham, Hampshire, *Proc Prehist Soc* **23**, 137–66

Ashton, N M and Lewis, S G, 2002 Deserted Britain: declining populations in the British late Middle Pleistocene, *Antiquity* **76**, 388-396

Astill, G G, 1978 *Historic Towns in Berkshire*, Berkshire Archaeological Committee 2, Reading

Astill, G G and Lobb, S J, 1989 Excavation of Prehistoric, Roman, and Saxon Deposits at Wraysbury, Berkshire, *Archaeol J* **146**, 68-134

Aston, M, 2000 *Monasteries in the Landscape*, Stroud

Atkinson, R J C, Piggott, C M, and Sandars, N K, 1951 *Excavations at Dorchester, Oxon*, Oxford

Avery, M, 1982 The Neolithic causewayed enclosure, Abingdon, in Case and Whittle (eds) 1982, 10-50

Avery, M, 1993 *Hillforts in Southern England*, BAR Brit Ser **231**, Oxford

Avery, M, Sutton, J E G, and Banks, J W, 1967 Rainsborough, Northants, England: Excavations 1961-5, *Proc Prehist Soc* **33**, 207-306

Balaam, N D and Scaife, R G, 1987 Archaeological pollen analysis, in *Research Priorities in archaeological Science*, (ed. P Mellars), CBA Occasional Papers **17**, London, 7-10

Babb, L, 1997 A thirteenth-century brooch hoard from Hambleden, Buckinghamshire, *Medieval Archaeology* **41**, 233-6

Babtie, n d Industrial Berkshire

Bailey, K A, 1995 Buckinghamshire slavery in 1086, *Rec Buckinghamshire* **37**, 67-78

Bailey, K A, 1997 Mills in Domesday Buckinghamshire, *Rec Buckinghamshire* **39**, 67-72

Bailey, K A, 2002 The population of Buckinghamshire in 1086, *Rec Buckinghamshire* **42**, 1-14

Bailey, K A, 2003 The Church in Anglo-Saxon Buckinghamshire, *Rec Buckinghamshire* **43**, 61-76

Bailey, K A, 2005 Early medieval Stewkley: settlements and fields, *Rec Buckinghamshire* **45**, 93-114

Baines, A H J, 1984 The Danish wars and the establishment of the Borough and County of Buckinghamshire, *Rec Buckinghamshire* **26**, 11-27

Baines, A H J, 1985 The development of the Borough of Buckingham, *Rec Buckinghamshire* **27**, 53-64

Baines, A H J, 1986 The origins of the Borough of Newport Pagnell, *Rec Buckinghamshire* **28**, 128-137

Baker, A R H, 1966 The Evidence in the Nonarum Inquisitiones of Contracting Arable Lands in England during the Early Fourteenth Century, *Economic History Review* 2nd ser **19**, 518-32

Baker, J and Brookes, S, 2013 *Beyond the Burghal Hidage: Anglo-Saxon civil defence in the Viking Age*, Leiden and Boston

Baker, S, 2002 Prehistoric and Romano-British landscapes at Little Wittenham and Long Wittenham, Oxfordshire, *Oxoniensia* **67**, 1-28

Baldwin, R, 1985 Intrusive burial groups in the late Roman cemetery at Lankhills, Winchester – a reassessment of the evidence, *Oxford J Archaeol* **4** (1), 93-104

Banerjea, R, 2011 Microscopic perspectives on the use of Period 3 MRTB 1/ERTB 1, in Fulford and Clarke 2011, 63-95

Bannister, N, 2003 Bembridge and Culver Downs, unpublished report for the National Trust

Banks, L and Stanley, C, 1990 *The Thames, a history from the air*, Oxford

Barber, A, 2011 Denham, The Lea, *CBA South Midlands Archaeol* **41**, 21-22

Barber, M, Field, D, and Topping, P, 1999 *Neolithic Flint Mines in England*, English Heritage/RCHME

Barclay, A J, 1995 The ceremonial complex in its local and national context, in Barclay *et al.* 1995, 106-15

Barclay, A J, 1999 Grooved Ware from the Upper Thames, in *Grooved Ware in Britain and Ireland*, (eds R Cleal and A MacSween), Oxbow Monograph, 9-22

Barclay, A J, 2000 Spatial histories of the Neolithic: a study of the monuments and material culture of central southern England, unpubl. PhD thesis, Univ. Reading

Barclay, A, 2007 Connections and networks: a wider world and other places, in Benson and Whittle 2007, 331-44

Barclay, A J and Bayliss, A, 1999 Cursus monuments and the radiocarbon problem, in Barclay and Harding 1999, 11-29

Barclay, A J and Halpin, C, 1999 *Excavations at Barrow Hills, Radley, Oxfordshire 1: the Neolithic and Bronze Age monument complex*, Thames Valley Landscapes **11**, Oxford

Barclay, A J and Harding, J (eds), 1999 *Pathways and ceremonies: the cursus monuments of Britain and Ireland*, Neolithic Studies Group Seminar Papers **4**, Oxford

Barclay, A, Gray, M and Lambrick, G, 1995 *Excavations at the Devil's Quoits, Stanton Harcourt, Oxfordshire 1972-3 and 1988*, Thames Valley Landscapes Monograph: The Windrush Valley Vol **3**, OAU Oxford

Barclay, A J, Bradley, R, Hey, G and Lambrick, G, 1996 The earlier prehistory of the Oxford region in the light of recent research, *Oxoniensia* **61**, 1-20

Barclay, A J, Lambrick, G, Moore, J and Robinson, M, 2003 *Lines in the landscape: cursus monuments in the Upper Thames Valley*, Oxford Archaeology Thames Valley Landscapes Monograph **15**, Oxford

Barfield, L H, 1977 The excavation of a Mesolithic site at Gerrards Cross, Bucks, *Rec Buckinghamshire* **20** (3), 308-36

Barnes, I and Cleal, R M J, 1995 Neolithic and Bronze Age settlement at Weir Bank Stud Farm, Bray, in Barnes *et al.* 1995, 1-51

Barnes, I, Boismier, W A, Cleal, R M J, Fitzpatrick, A P and Roberts, M R, 1995 *Early settlement in Berkshire: Mesolithic-Roman occupation in the Thames and Kennet valleys*, Wessex Archaeology Report **6**, Salisbury

Barrett, J C, 1973 Four Bronze Age cremation cemeteries from Middlesex, *Trans London Middlesex Archaeol Soc* **24**, 111-34

Barrett, J C, 1980 The pottery of the later Bronze Age in lowland England, *Proc Prehist Soc* **46**, 297–320

Barrett, J C, 1994 *Fragments from Antiquity; an archaeology of social life 2900–1200 BC*, London; Blackwell, Oxford

Barrett, J C and Bradley, R (eds), 1980a *Settlement and society in the British Later Bronze Age*, BAR Brit Ser **83**

Barrett, J C and Bradley, R, 1980b The Later Bronze Age in the Thames Valley, in Barrett and Bradley 1980a, 247-70

Barrett, J C, Bradley, R, and Green, M, 1991 *Landscape, monuments and society: the prehistory of Cranborne Chase*, Cambridge

Barrett J H, Locker, A M and Roberts, C M, 2004 'Dark Age economics' revisited: the English fish bone evidence AD 600–1600, *Antiquity* **78**, 618–636

Barton, R N E, 1986 Experiments with long blades from Sproughton, near Ipswich, Suffolk, *Studies in the Upper Palaeolithic and Britain and Northwest Europe* (ed. D A Roe), BAR Int Ser **296**, Oxford, 129-41

Barton, R N E, 1989 Long Blade Technology in Southern Britain, in *The Mesolithic in Europe* (ed. C Bonsall), John Donald, Edinburgh, 264-71

Barton, R N E, 1992 *Hengistbury Head, Dorset, Volume 2: the Late Upper Palaeolithic and early Mesolithic sites*, Oxford University Committee for Archaeology Monograph **34**, Oxford

Barton, R N E, 1993 Late Upper Palaeolithic Flints, in Allen and Robinson, 16-17

Barton, N, 1995 The long blade assemblage, in Allen, T G, with Barton, N, and Brown, A, 1995, 54-64

Barton, N, 1997 *Stone Age Britain*, Batsford/English Heritage, London

Barton, R N E and Froom, F R, 1986 The Long Blade assemblage from Avington VI, Berkshire, in *The Palaeolithic of Britain and its nearest neighbours: recent advances* (ed. S N Colcutt), Department of Archaeology and Prehistory, University of Sheffield, Sheffield, 80-4

Barton, R N E and Roberts, A J, 1996 Reviewing the British Late Upper Palaeolithic: new evidence for chronological patterning in the Lateglacial record, *Oxford J Archaeol* **15:3**, 245-265

Barton, N and Roberts, A, 2004 The Mesolithic period in England: current perspectives and new research, in *Mesolithic Scotland and its neighbours* (ed. A Saville), Society of Antiquaries of Scotland, Edinburgh, 339-58

Barton, N, Roberts, A J and Roe, D A, 1991 *The Late Glacial in North-West Europe: human adaptation and environmental change at the end of the Pleistocene*, CBA Res Rep 77, York

Barton, R N E, Berridge, P J, Bevins, R E and Walker, M J, 1995 Persistent places in the Mesolithic landscape: an example from the Black Mountain uplands of South Wales, *Proc Prehist Soc* **61**, 81-116

Barton, R N E, Antoine, P, Dumont, S, Hall, S and Munaut, A V, 1998 New optically stimulated luminescence (OSL) dates from a Late-glacial site in the Kennet Valley at Avington VI, Berkshire, UK, *Quaternary Newsletter* **85**, 21-31

Barton, R N E, Jacobi, R M, Stapert, D and Street, M J, 2003 The Creswellian and the lateglacial reoccupation of the British Isles, *Journal of Quaternary Science* **18**, 631-643

Barton, R N E, Jacobi, R M, Stapert, D and Street, M J, 2003 The Late-glacial reoccupation of the British Isles and the Creswellian, *Journal of Quaternary Science* **18**, 631-643

Barton, R N E, Ford, S, Collcutt, S N, Crowther, J, Macphail, R I, Rhodes, E and Van Gijn, A, 2009 A Final Upper Palaeolithic site at Nea Farm, Somerley, Hampshire and some reflections on the occupation of Britain in the Late Glacial Interstadial, *Quärtar* **56**, 7-35

Basford, H V, 1980 *The Vectis Report: A Survey of Isle of Wight Archaeology*, Isle of Wight County Council, Newport

Basford, V, 1989 *Historic Parks and Gardens of the Isle of Wight*, Isle of Wight County Council

Basford, V 2008 Isle of Wight Historic Landscape Characterisation, report for English Heritage and Isle of Wight Council, http://www.iwight.com/az services/documents/1324-HLC%20Final%20Report %202008%20Vol%201.pdf

Basford, V, 2013 Medieval and post-medieval rural settlement and land use on the Isle of Wight: An application of regional models of historic landscape character in an island Context, PhD thesis, Bournemouth University, http://eprints.bournemouth. ac.uk/20803/1/Vol_1_(amended).pdf

Basford, V and Smout, R, 2000 The landscape and history of Wydcombe, Isle of Wight, *Proc Isle Wight Nat Hist Archaeol Soc* **16**, 7-20

Bates, M R, Wenban-Smith, F F, Briant, R and Marshall, G, 2004 Palaeolithic Archaeology of the Sussex/Hampshire Coastal Corridor, Unpublished report submitted to English Heritage, March 2004

Batey, M, 1970 *Nuneham Courtenay*, Oxford

Batey, M, 1982 *Oxford gardens: the university's influence on garden history*, Amersham

Bayley, J, 1998 *Science in Archaeology; an agenda for the future*, London, English Heritage

Bayliss, A and Whittle, A, 2007 Histories of the dead: building chronologies for five southern British long barrows, *Cambridge Archaeological Journal* 17.1 (Supplement)

Bayliss, A and Woodman, P, 2009 A new Bayesian chronology for Mesolithic occupation at Mount Sandel, Northern Ireland, *Proc Prehist Soc* **75**, 101–123

Bayliss, A, Benson, D, Bronk Ramsey, C, Galer, D, McFadyen, L, van der Plicht, J and Whittle, A, 2007 Interpreting chronology: the radiocarbon dating programme, in Benson and Whittle 2007, 221-32

Bayliss, A, Hines, J, Høilund Nielsen, K, McCormac, G and Scull, C, 2013, *Anglo-Saxon graves and grave goods of the sixth and seventh centuries AD: a chronological framework*, Society for Medieval Archaeology, Leeds

BCAS, 1996 Interim report on an archaeological excavation at the Brewery Site, High Street, Marlow, Buckinghamshire, unpubl. report No. 384

Beamish, H F, 1989 A medieval pottery production site at Jack Ironcap's Lane, Great Brickhill, *Rec Buckinghamshire* **31**, 88-92

Beamish H and Parkhouse J, 1993 New archaeological evidence for Anglo-Saxon activity at Newport Pagnell, *Rec Buckinghamshire* **33**, 145-7

Beamish, M and Ripper, S, 2000 Burnt mounds in the East Midlands, *Antiquity* **74**, 37-38

Bean, S C, 2000 *The coinage of the Atrebates and Regni*, Oxford University School of Archaeology Monograph **50**

Bell, M G, 1983 Valley sediments as evidence of prehistoric land-use on the South Downs, *Proc Prehist Soc* **49**, 119-150

Bell, M, 2007 *Prehistoric Coastal Communities: the Mesolithic in western Britain*, CBA Res Rep **149**, York

Bell, M, Chisham, C, Dark, P and Allen, S, 2006 Mesolithic sites in coastal and riverine contexts in southern Britain: current research and the management of the archaeological resource, in *Preserving the early past: investigation, selection and preservation of Palaeolithic and Mesolithic sites and landscapes*, (eds E Rensink and H Peeters), NAR Nederlandse Archeologische Rapporten **31**, Amersfoort, 25-40

Bellamy, P S, 1991 The Investigation of the Prehistoric Landscape along the Route of the A303 Road

Improvement between Andover, Hampshire and Amesbury, Wiltshire, 1984-1987, *Proc Hampshire Fld Club Archaeol Soc* **47**, 5-81

Bendrey, R, 2007 New methods for the identification of evidence for bitting on horse remains from archaeological sites, *J Archaeol Sci* **34**, 1036-1050

Bennet, F J, 1966 A late Mesolithic and secondary Neolithic flint industry at Shorwell, I.W., *Hampshire Field Club Archaeol Soc Newsl* **4**, 44-5

Bennett, J A, Johnston, S A and Simcock, A V, 2000 *Solomon's House in Oxford, new finds from the first museum*, Museum of the history of science, Oxford

Benson, D and Miles, D, 1974 *The Upper Thames Valley, an archaeological survey of the river gravels*, Oxford Archaeological Unit Survey **2**

Benson, D and Whittle, A, 2007 *Building memories: the Neolithic Cotswold long barrow at Ascott-under-Wychwood, Oxfordshire*, Oxford

Beresford, G, 1970 The Old Manor, Askett, *Rec Buckinghamshire* **18**, 343-66

Beresford, M W, 1953-4 A Summary List of Deserted Villages in the County, *Rec Buckinghamshire* **16**, 26-8

Beresford, M W and Hurst, J G, 1971 *Deserted Medieval Villages*, Lutterworth Press

Beresford, M W and St Joseph, J K S, 1958 *Medieval England – An Aerial Survey*, Cambridge

Betts, I M and Foot, R, 1994 A newly-identified late Roman tile group from Southern England, *Britannia* **25**, 21-34

Betts, I, Black, E W and Gower, J, 1997 *A corpus of relief-patterned tiles in Roman Britain*, J Roman Pottery Stud **7** (for 1994)

Biddle, M, 1961/2 The deserted medieval village of Seacourt, Berkshire *Oxoniensia* **26/27**, 70-201

Biddle, M, 1970 Excavations at Winchester, 1969: eighth interim report, *Antiq J* **50 (II)**, 277-326

Biddle, M, 1972 Excavations at Winchester, 1970: ninth interim report, *Antiq J* **52 (I)**, 93-131

Biddle, M, 1975a, *Felix urbs Winthonia*. Winchester in the age of monastic Reform, in Parsons ed. 1975, 123-39

Biddle, M, 1975b Excavations at Winchester, 1971; tenth and final interim report: Part II, *Antiq J* **55 (II)**, 295-337

Biddle M, 1986 *Wolvesey, The Old Bishops Palace, Winchester*, London

Biddle, M (ed.), 1990 *Object and Economy in Medieval Winchester*, Winchester Studies **7 (ii)**, Oxford

Biddle, M (ed.), 2012 *The Winchester mint : and coins and related finds from the excavations of 1961-71*, Winchester Studies **8**, Oxford

Biddle, M, and Hill, D, 1971 Late Saxon planned towns, *Antiq J* **51**, 70-85

Biddle, M and Kjølbye-Biddle, B, 2007 Winchester: from *Venta* to *Witancæstir*, in *Pagans and Christians – from antiquity to the middle ages; Papers in Honour of Martin Henig, presented on the occasion of his 65th birthday*, (L Gilmour ed.), BAR Int Ser **1610**, 189-214

Bingeman, J M, 2010 *The First HMS Invincible (1747-58); her excavations (1980-1991)*, Oxbow Books

Birbeck, V, 2000 *Archaeological investigations on the A34 Newbury Bypass, Berkshire/ Hampshire 1991-7*, Wessex Archaeology report for the Highways Agency, Salisbury

Birbeck, V, 2001 Excavations at Watchfield, Shrivenham, Oxfordshire, 1998, *Oxoniensia* **66**, 221-88

Birbeck, V, 2005 *The Origins of Mid-Saxon Southampton; excavations at the Friends Provident St Mary's Stadium 1998-2000*, Salisbury, Wessex Archaeology

Birmingham University Field Archaeology Unit, 1999 Archaeological field evaluation at Tooley's Boatyard, Banbury, Unpublished client report

Birmingham University Field Archaeology Unit, 2000 Archaeological recording at Tooley's Boatyard, Banbury, Unpublished client report

Blair, J, 1976 A Monastic Fragment at Wadham College, *Oxoniensia* **41**, 161–8

Blair, J, 1978 Frewin Hall, Oxford: A Norman Mansion and a Monastic College, *Oxoniensia* **43**, 48–99

Blair, J, 1994 *Anglo-Saxon Oxfordshire*, Stroud

Blair, J 1995 Anglo-Saxon pagan shrines and their prototypes, *Anglo-Saxon Studies in Archaeology and History*, 8, 1-28

Blair, J, 1996 The Minsters of the Thames, in *The Cloister and the World: Essays in Medieval History in Honour of Barbara Harvey*, (eds J Blair and B J Golding), Oxford, 5-28

Blair, J, 1998a The Anglo-Saxon minsters of Berkshire, *c*. 670-1086, in J Dils (ed.) 1998, 16-17

Blair, J, 1998b Archaeological discoveries at Woodeaton Church, *Oxoniensia* **63**, 221-37

Blair, J, 2002 Anglo-Saxon Bicester: the Minster and the Town, *Oxoniensia* **67**, 133-40

Blair, J, 2005 *The Church in Anglo-Saxon Society*, Oxford University Press, Oxford

Blair, J, 2007a Transport and Canal-Building on the Upper Thames 1000-1300, in J Blair (ed.) 2007, 254-94

Blair, J, 2007b *Waterways and Canal Building in Medieval England*, Oxford

Blair, J, 2010a The Anglo-Saxon Minsters, in K Tiller and G Darkes (eds) 2010, 26-7

Blair, J, 2010b Communications and Urban Origins before 1066, in K Tiller and G Darkes (eds), *An Historical Atlas of Oxfordshire*, Oxfordshire Record Society Vol **67**, 28-9

Blair, J, 2013 *The British Culture of Anglo-Saxon Settlement: The Chadwick Lecture 2013* (Department of Anglo-Saxon, Norse and Celtic, Cambridge, 2013)

Blair, J and Hamerow, H, 2003 Anglo-Saxon plaster-infilled timber wall, in Hardy *et al.* 2003, 207-9

Bloxham, C and Bond, C J, 1981 *The Oxford Canal*, Oxfordshire Museums, Woodstock

Boismier, W A, 2003 A Middle Palaeolithic Site at Lynford Quarry, Mundford, Norfolk: Interim Statement, *Proc Prehist Soc* **69**, 315–324

Boismier, W A and Mepham, L N, 1995 Excavation of a Mesolithic site at Windmill Hill, Nettlebed, Oxon, *Oxoniensia* **60**, 1-19

Bokelmann, K, 1991 Some new thoughts on old data on humans and reindeer in the Ahrensburgian Tunnel Valley in Schleswig-Holstein, Germany, in *The Late Glacial in North-West Europe,* (eds N Barton, A J Roberts and D J Roe), CBA Res Rep 77, chapter 9

Bond, J, 1979 The reconstruction of the medieval landscape: the estates of Abingdon Abbey, *Landscape History* **1**, 59-75

Bond, J, 1986 The Oxford Region in the Middle Ages, in Briggs, Cook and Rowley 1986, 135–59, maps 14–15

Bond, J and Rhodes, J, 1985 *The Oxfordshire Brewer,* Oxfordshire Museums, Woodstock

Bond, J and Tiller, K (eds), 1997 *Blenheim, landscape for a palace,* Stroud

Bonner, D, 1996 Investigations at the County Museum, Aylesbury, *Rec Buckinghamshire* **38**, 1-89

Bonner, D, Parkhouse, J and Smith, N, 1995 Archaeological investigations of the medieval earthworks at Castlethorpe, Buckinghamshire, *Rec Buckinghamshire* **37**, 79-99

Boon, G C, 1974 *Silchester; the Roman Town of Calleva,* Newton Abbot/London

Booth, P, 1997 *Asthall, Oxfordshire, excavations in a Roman 'small town', 1992,* Thames Valley Landscapes Monograph 9, OAU, Oxford

Booth, P (ed.), 2009 Roman Britain in 2008: The midlands-Southern counties, *Britannia* **40**, 240-279

Booth, P (ed.), 2010 Roman Britain in 2009: Southern Counties, *Britannia* **41**, 399-408

Booth, P M and Simmonds, A, 2009 *Appleford's Earliest Farmers: Archaeological Work at Appleford Sidings, Oxfordshire, 1993-2000,* Oxford Archaeology Occasional Paper 17, Oxford

Booth, P and Simmonds, A, 2011 Gill Mill, Ducklington & South Leigh, Oxfordshire: Post-excavation assessment and project design, unpublished client report prepared for Smith & Sons (Bletchington) Ltd and English Heritage

Booth, P, Evans, J and Hiller, J, 2001 *Excavations in the extramural settlement of Roman Alchester, Oxfordshire, 1991,* Oxford Archaeology Monograph 1, Oxford

Booth, P, Dodd, A, Robinson, M and Smith, A, 2007 *The Thames through time; the archaeology of the gravel terraces of the Upper and Middle Thames. The early historical period: Britons, Romans and the Anglo-Saxons in the Thames Valley AD 1-1000,* Oxford Archaeology Thames Valley Landscapes Monograph 27

Booth, P, Gosden, C, Hamerow, H, Hey, G, Metcalfe, J, Morrison, W, Richards, J and Wilkinson, D R P, 2012 *The Discovering Dorchester-on-Thames Project: a report on the excavations 2007-2011,* Dorchester Abbey

Bootle, R and Bootle, V, 1990 *The Story of Cookham,* Cookham

Bourdillon, J, 1988 Countryside and town: the animal resources of Saxon Southampton, *Anglo-Saxon settlements* (ed. D Hooke), Oxford, Blackwell, 177-195

Bourdillon, J, 1993 Animal bones, in Garner, M F, Middle Saxon evidence at Cook Street, Southampton (SOU254), *Proc Hampshire Fld Club Archaeol Soc* **49**, 116-120

Bourdillon, J, 1994 The animal provisioning of Southampton, in *Environment and Economy in Anglo-Saxon England* (ed. J Rackham), CBA Res Rep **89**, 120-125

Bourdillon, J, 1997 The animal bone, in Andrews, P, *Excavations at Hamwic: volume 2; excavations at Six Dials,* CBA Res Rep **109**, 242-245

Bourn, R, 2000 Archaeological desk based assessment – The Courtyard, Frogmoor, High Wycombe, unpubl. report

Bourn, R, 2002 Archaeological desk-based assessment: Land at Market Lane, Slough, CgMs

Bowden, M, Ford, S and Gaffney, V, 1991-3 The Excavation of a late Bronze Age artifact scatter on Weathercock Hill, *Berkshire Archaeol J* **74**, 69-83

Bowden, M, Ford, S and Mees, G, 1993 The Date of the Ancient Fields on the Berkshire Downs, *Berkshire Archaeol J* **74**, 109-133

Bowen, H C, 1961 *Ancient Fields,* London, HMSO

Bowen, H C and Fowler, P J, 1978 *Early Land Allotment,* BAR Brit Ser **48**, Oxford

Bowijk, G and Groves, C, 1997 *Dendrochronological analysis of Timbers from Meadow Lake Excavations, Testwood Lake, Netley Marsh, Hampshire,* ARCUS Report 281

Boyle, A, Dodd, A, Miles, D and Mudd, A, 1995 *Two Oxfordshire Anglo-Saxon cemeteries: Berinsfield and Didcot,* Thames Valley Landscapes Monograph **8**, Oxford. OAU

Boyle, A, Jennings, D, Miles, D and Palmer, S, 1998 *The Anglo-Saxon cemetery at Butler's Field, Lechlade, Gloucestershire Volume 1: Prehistoric and Roman activity and Anglo-Saxon grave catalogue,* Thames Valley Landscapes Monograph **10**, Oxford, OAU

Boyle, A, Jennings, D, Miles, D and Palmer, S, 2011 *The Anglo-Saxon Cemetery at Butler's Field, Lechlade, Gloucestershire, Volume 2: the Anglo-Saxon grave goods, specialist reports, phasing and discussion,* Oxford Archaeology Thames Valley Landscapes Monograph **33**

Boynton, L, 1996 The Marine Villa, in *The Georgian Villa* (ed. D Arnolf), 118-129

Bracknell Forest Borough Council, 2000 The Great Forest

Bradford, C and Steane, J, 1982 Oxford Folly Bridge, *CBA Group 9 Newsletter* **12**, 108–9

Bradley, P and Hey, G, 1993 A Mesolithic Site at New Plantation, Fyfield and Tubney, Oxfordshire, *Oxoniensia* **58**, 1-26

Bradley, P, Charles, B, Hardy, A and Poore, D, 2006 Prehistoric and Roman activity and a Civil War Ditch: Excavations at the Chemistry Research Laboratory, 2-4 South Parks Road, Oxford, *Oxoniensia* **70**, 141-203

Bradley, R J, 1978 *The Prehistoric Settlement of Britain*, Routledge & Kegan Paul

Bradley, R, 1984 *The social foundations of prehistoric Britain*, London and New York

Bradley, R, 1986 A reinterpretation of the Abingdon causewayed enclosure, *Oxoniensia* **51**, 183-87

Bradley, R, 1990 *The passage of arms: an archaeological analysis of prehistoric hoards and votive deposits*, Cambridge

Bradley, R, 1992 The excavation of an oval barrow beside the Abingdon causewayed enclosure, Oxfordshire, *Proc Prehist Soc* **58**, 127-42

Bradley, R, 2005 *Ritual and Domestic Life in Prehistoric Europe*, Routledge, London

Bradley, R, 2006 *The prehistory of Britain and Ireland*, Cambridge University Press, Cambridge

Bradley, R and Chambers, R, 1988 A new study of the cursus complex at Dorchester-on-Thames, *Oxford J Archaeol* **7**, 271-9

Bradley, R and Edmonds, M, 1993 *Interpreting the axe trade: production and exchange in Neolithic Britain*, Cambridge

Bradley, R and Ellison, A, 1975 *Rams Hill: a Bronze Age defended enclosure and its landscape*, BAR Brit Ser **19**, Oxford

Bradley, R and Gordon, K, 1988 Human skulls from the River Thames, their dating and significance, *Antiquity*, 62, 503-509

Bradley, R J and Hooper, B, 1975 Recent discoveries from Portsmouth and Langstone Harbours: Mesolithic to Iron Age, *Proc Hampshire Fld Club Archaeol Soc* **30**, 17–27

Bradley, R and Keith-Lucas, M, 1975 Excavation and pollen analysis on a bell barrow at Ascot, Berkshire, *J Archaeol Sci* **2**, 95-108

Bradley, R J and Lewis, E, 1974 A Mesolithic site at Wakeford's Copse, Havant, *Rescue Archaeology in Hampshire* **2**, 5–18

Bradley, R J and Richards, J C, 1979 The excavation of two ring ditches at Herons House, Burghfield, *Berkshire Archaeol J* **70**, 1–8

Bradley, R, Lobb, S, Richards, J and Robinson, M, 1980 Two late Bronze Age settlements on the Kennet Gravels: excavations at Aldermaston Wharf and Knight's Farm, Burghfield, Berkshire, *Proc Prehist Soc* **46**, 217-95

Bradley, R, Entwistle, R and Raymond, F, 1994 *Prehistoric land divisions on Salisbury Plain: the work of the Wessex Linear ditches Project*, English Heritage

Brady, K, Smith, A and Laws, G, 2007 Excavations at Abingdon West Central Development: Iron Age, Roman, Medieval and Post-Medieval activity in Abingdon, *Oxoniensia* **72**, 107-202

Branch, N P and Green, C P, 2004 Environmental history of Surrey, in *Aspects of Archaeology and History in Surrey: towards a research framework for the county* (eds J Cotton, G Crocker, and A Graham), Guildford, 1-18

Branigan, K, 1971 *Latimer: A Belgic, Roman, Dark Age and early modern farm*, Chess Valley Archaeol & Hist Soc, privately published

Briant, R M, Bates, M R, Hosfield, R T and Wenban-Smith, F F, 2009 *The Quaternary of the Solent Basin and the West Sussex raised beaches: Field Guide*, Quaternary Research Association

Bridgland, D R, 1994 *Quaternary of the Thames*, Chapman & Hall, London

Briggs, G, Cook, J and Rowley, T, (eds) 1986 *The Archaeology of the Oxford Region*, Oxford University Department of External Studies

Brinton, M, 1987 Farmhouses and Cottages of the Isle of Wight, IoWCC

Britnell, R H, 1981 The proliferation of markets in England 1200-1349, *Economic History Review* **34**, 209-21

Broad J, 2004 *Transforming English Rural Society: The Verneys and the Claydons, 1600 -1820*, Cambridge University Press, Cambridge

Broad, J and Hoyle, R (eds), 1997 *Bernwood: the Life and Afterlife of a Forest*

Brodribb, A C C, Hands, A R and Walker, D R, 1968 *Excavations at Shakenoak Farm, near Wilcote, Oxfordshire, Part I: sites A & D*, Oxford

Brodribb, A C C, Hands, A R and Walker, D R, 1971 *Excavations at Shakenoak Farm, near Wilcote, Oxfordshire, Part II: Sites B and H*, Oxford

Brodribb, A C C, Hands, A R and Walker, D R, 1972 *Excavations at Shakenoak Farm, near Wilcote, Oxfordshire, Part III: Site F*, Oxford

Brodribb, A C C, Hands, A R and Walker, D R, 1973 *Excavations at Shakenoak Farm, near Wilcote, Oxfordshire, Part IV: Site C*, Oxford

Brodribb, A C C, Hands, A R and Walker, D R, 1978 *Excavations at Shakenoak Farm, near Wilcote, Oxfordshire, Part V: Sites K and E*, Oxford

Brossler A, Early, R and Allen, C, 2004 *Green Park (Reading Business Park): Phase 2 Excavations 1995: Neolithic and Bronze Age sites*, Thames Valley Landscapes Monograph **19**, OUCA and OA, Oxford

Brossler, A, Brown, F, Guttman, E, Morris, E and Webley, L, 2013 *Prehistoric Settlement in the lower Kennet Valley: Excavations at Green Park (Reading Buisness Park) Phase 3 and Moores Farm, Berkshire*, Oxford Archaeology Thames Valley Landscapes Monograph **37**, Oxford

Brown, A, 1995 The Mesolithic and later flint artefacts, in Allen *et al.* 1995, 65-84

Brown, A and Everson, P, 2005 Earthworks at Lavendon, *Rec Buckinghamshire* **45**, 45-64

Brown, D H, 1994 Pottery and late Saxon Southampton, *Proc Hampshire Fld Club Archaeol Soc* **50**, 127-52

Brown, L, 2009 An Unusual Iron Age Enclosure at Fir Hill, Bossington & a Romano-British Cemetery near Brook, Hampshire: the Broughton to Timsbury Pipeline, Part 2 *Proc Hampshire Fld Club Archaeol Soc* **64**

Brown, M, 2001 *Ivinghoe Beacon, Ivinghoe, Buckinghamshire: Landscape Investigation Report*, English Heritage

Brown, R and Hardy, A, 2011 *Trade and prosperity, war and poverty: an archaeological and historical investigation into Southampton's French Quarter*, Oxford Archaeology Monograph 15, Oxford

Brown, T, 1997 Clearances and clearings: deforestation in Mesolithic/Neolithic Britain, *Oxford J Archaeol* 16, 133-46

Bruce-Mitford, R L S, 1939 The archaeology of the site of the Bodleian extension in Broad Street, *Oxoniensia* 4, 89-146

Brück, J, 1999 Houses, Lifecycles and Deposition on Middle Bronze Age Settlements in Southern England, *Proc Prehist Soc* 65, 145-66

Brück, J, 2000 Settlement, landscape and social identity: the early middle Bronze Age transition in Wessex, Sussex and the Thames Valley, *Oxford J Archaeol* 19(3), 273-300

Brück, J (ed.), 2001 *Bronze Age landscapes: tradition and transformation*, Oxbow, Oxford

Bryant, S R and Burleigh, G, 1995 The later prehistoric dykes of the eastern Chilterns, in Holgate, R, (ed.) *Chiltern Archaeology, Recent Work: A Handbook for the Next Decade*, Dunstable

Buckinghamshire County Museum, 1984 Missenden Abbey, *CBA South Midlands Archaeol* 14, 10-11

Buckinghamshire County Museum, 1985 Missenden Abbey, *CBA South Midlands Archaeol* 15, 26-8

Buckinghamshire County Museum Archaeological Group, 1978 Buckinghamshire windmills, *Rec Buckinghamshire* 20, 516-524

Buckinghamshire County Museum Archaeological Group, 1982 Buckinghamshire watermills, *Rec Buckinghamshire* 24, 34-45

Buckinghamshire County Museum, 1984 Missenden Abbey, *CBA South Midlands Archaeol* 14, 10-11

Buckinghamshire County Museum, 1985 Middenden Abbey, *CBA South Midlands Archaeol* 15, 26-8

Buckley, V (ed.), 1990 *Burnt offerings: International contributions to burnt mound archaeology*, Dublin

Bull, E J, 1978 A medieval settlement area adjacent to Pitstone church, *Rec Buckinghamshire* 20, 646-655

Bull, E J, 1993 The Bi-Axial Landscape of Prehistoric Buckinghamshire, *Rec Buckinghamshire* 35, 11-18

Bull, L, 1975 The ancient saltway from Droitwich to Princes Risborough, *Rec Buckinghamshire* 20, 87-92

Burnett, A M, 1990 Celtic coinage in Britain III: the Waltham St Lawrence treasure trove, *British Numismatic Journal* 60, 13-28

Burnham, B C and Wacher, J S, 1990 *The 'small towns' of Roman Britain*, London

Burnham, B C, Collis, J, Dobinson, C, Haselgrove, C and Jones, M, 2001 Themes for urban research, *c.* 100BC to AD 200, in *Britons and Romans: advancing an archaeological agenda* (eds S James and M Millett), CBA Res Rep 125, York, 67-76

Burrin, P J and Scaife, R G, 1984 Aspects of Holocene sedimentation and floodplain development in southern England, *Proceedings of the Geologists' Association* 85, 81-96

Burrin, P J and Scaife, R G, 1988 Environmental thresholds, catastrophe theory and landscape sensitivity: their relevance to the impact of man on valley alluviation, in *Conceptual Issues in Environmental Archaeology*, (eds J L Bintliffe, D A Donaldson & E G Grant), Edinburgh, Edinburgh University Press, 212-232

Butterworth, C A and Lobb, S J, 1992 *Excavations in the Burghfield Area, Berkshire; development in the Bronze Age and Saxon landscapes*, Wessex Archaeology Report 1, Salisbury

Cahill, N, 1984 Isle of Wight Downlands, unpublished report for Isle of Wight County Council

Campbell, B M S, Galloway, J A, Keene, D and Murphy, M, 1993 *A Medieval Capital and its Grain Supply: Agrarian Production and Distribution in the London Region c. 1300*, London

Campbell, G, 1992 Bronze Age Plant Remains, in Moore and Jennings 1992, 103-12

Campbell, G, 2000 'Plant Utilisation: the Evidence from Charred Plant Remains, in Cunliffe, B *The Danebury Environs Programme The prehistory of a Wessex Landscape Volume 1; Introduction* Oxford University Committee for Archaeology Monograph 48 Oxford Institute of Archaeology, 45-49

Campbell, G, 2008 Plant utilisation in the countryside around Danebury: a Roman perspective, in Cunliffe 2008, 53-74

Campbell, G E, 1992 Excavations at Lower Bolney, Harpsden, South Oxfordshire, 1991, *Oxoniensia* 57, 29-42

Campbell, J B, 1977 *The Upper Palaeolithic of Britain. A study of man and nature in the late ice age. Volumes I & II*, Clarendon Press, Oxford

Cann, R, 1988 DNA and human origins, *Current Anthropology* 17, 127-143

Cantor, L M and Hatherly, J, 1977 The Medieval Parks of Buckinghamshire, *Rec Buckinghamshire* 20, 430-50

Carew, T, Bishop, B, Meddens, F and Ridgeway, V, 2006 *Unlocking the landscape: archaeological investigations at Ashford Prison, Middlesex*, Pre-Construct Archaeol Monograph 5, Great Dunham

Carruthers, W, 2005 Mineralised plant remains, in Birbeck 2005, 157-163

Carruthers, W, 2008 Charred, Mineralied and Waterlogged Plant Remains, in Framework Archaeology, *From Hunter-Gatherers to Huntsmen: A History of the Stansted Landscape*, Wessex Archaeology, Chapter 34

Carter, H H, 1976 Fauna of an area of Mesolithic occupation in the Kennet Valley, considered in relation to contemporary eating habits, *Berkshire Archaeol J* 68, 1-3

Carter, R J, 2001 New evidence for seasonal human presence at the early Mesolithic site of Thatcham, Berkshire, England, *J Archaeol Sci* 28, 1055-60

Cartwright, C R, 1982 Field survey of Chichester Harbour 1982, *Sussex Archaeol Collect* 122, 23-7

Case, H J, 1952-3 Mesolithic finds in the Oxford area, *Oxoniensia* 17-18, 1-13

Case, H J, 1956 The Neolithic causewayed camp at Abingdon, Berks, *Antiq J*, **36**, 11-30

Case, H J, 1956a The Lambourn Seven barrows, *Berkshire Archaeol J* **55**, 15-31

Case, H J, 1963 Notes on the finds and on ring-ditches in the Oxford region, *Oxoniensia* **28**, 19-52

Case, H J, 1982a The linear ditches and southern enclosure, North Stoke, in Case and Whittle 1982, 60-75

Case, H J, 1982b Cassington, 1950-2: late Neolithic pits and the big enclosure, in Case and Whittle 1982, 118-51

Case, H J, 1986 The Mesolithic and Neolithic in the Oxford Region, in Briggs *et al.* 1986, 18-37

Case, H J and Whittle, A W R (eds), 1982 *Settlement patterns in the Oxford Region: excavations at the Abingdon causewayed enclosure and other sites*, Counc Brit Archaeol Res Rep **44**, London

Catt, J A, 1977 Loess and coversands, in F W Shotton (ed.), *British Quaternary Studies, Recent Advances*, Clarendon Press, Oxford, 221–229

Catto 1984-2000 *The History of the University of Oxford*, Oxford

Cauvain, S and Cauvain, P, 1997 Investigations at Pann Mill, High Wycombe, *Rec Buckinghamshire* **39**, 18-44

CgMs, 2003 RAF Bicester, Oxfordshire—Urban Capacity Study, Unpublished client report

CgMs, 2004 Former Brakspears Brewery, Henley-on-Thames – Preparation of Statement of Significance and Impact Assessment through to grant of planning permission, Unpublished client report

CgMs, 2006a Historic Buildings record in respect of Former RAF/USAF Greenham Common Base, New Greenham Park, Near Newbury, Berkshire, Unpublished client report

CgMs, 2006b Havant Parchment Works, Unpublished client report

Chadwick, P, 1985 Berkshire Archaeological Notes 1983-85, *Berkshire Archaeol J* **72**, 75-87

Challinor, D, Petts, D, Poore, D and Score, D, 2003 Excavations at Manor Farm, Drayton, Oxfordshire, *Oxoniensia* **68**, 280-311

Chamberlin, R, 1985 *Carisbrooke Castle*, English Heritage

Chambers, R A, 1987 The late- and sub-Roman cemetery at Queenford Farm, Dorchester-on-Thames, Oxon., *Oxoniensia* **52**, 35-69

Chambers, R and Boyle, A, 2007 The Romano-British cemetery, in R Chambers and E McAdam, *Excavations at Barrow Hills, Radley, Oxfordshire. Volume II: the Romano-British cemetery and Anglo-Saxon settlement*, Oxford Archaeology Thames Valley Landscapes Monograph **25**, Oxford, 13-64

Chambers, R and McAdam, E, 2007 *Excavations at Barrow Hills, Radley, Oxfordshire. Volume II: the Romano-British cemetery and Anglo-Saxon settlement*, Oxford Archaeology Thames Valley Landscapes Monograph **25**, Oxford

Champion, T C, 1977 Chalton, *Current Archaeology* **59**, 364-71

Champion, T C and Collis, J C, 1996 *The Iron Age in Britain and Ireland: Recent Trends*, J R Collis Publications Dept Arch and Prehistory, University of Sheffield

Chapman, A, 2007 A Bronze Age barrow cemetery and later boundaries, pit alignments and enclosures at Gayhurst Quarry, Newport Pagnell, Buckinghamshire, *Rec Buckinghamshire* **47(2)**, 81-211

Chartres, C J, 1975 Soil development on the terraces of the River Kennet, unpublished PhD Thesis, University of Reading

Chatters, C, 1984 The Downs and Heaths of the Isle of Wight, unpublished report for Isle of Wight County Council

Chatters, C, 1991 A brief ecological history of Parkhurst Forest, *Proc Isle Wight Nat Hist Archaeol Soc* **11**, 43-60

Chatterton, R, 2006 Ritual, in *Mesolithic Britain and Ireland: new approaches*, (eds C Conneller, and G M Warren), Stroud, 101-20

Cheetham, G H, 1975 Late Quaternary palaeohy-drology with reference to the Kennet Valley, unpublished PhD Thesis, University of Reading

Chenevix-Trench, J, and Fenley, P, 1979 A base-cruck hall in Denham, *Rec Buckinghamshire* **21**, 3-10

Chenevix Trench, J, and Fenley, P, 1991 The County Museum buildings, Church Street, Aylesbury, *Rec Buckinghamshire* **33**, 1-43

Cherry, J, 1991 Pottery and Tile in *English Medieval Industries*, (eds J Blair and N Ramsay), 189-209, London

Cherryson, A, 2010 'Such a resting place as is necessary for us in God's sight and fitting in the eye of the world': Saxon Southampton and the development of churchyard burial, in *Burial in later Anglo-Saxon England c 650-1100 AD*, (eds J Buckberry and A Cherryson), Oxford, Oxbow Books, 54-72

Chibnall, A C, 1965 *Sherington: Fiefs and Fields of a Buckinghamshire Village*, Cambridge

Childe, V G, 1931 The forest cultures of northern Europe: a study in evolution and diffusion, *Journal of the Royal Anthropological Institute* **61**, 325-48

Chisham, C, 2004 Mesolithic human activity and environmental change: A case study of the Kennet Valley, unpublished PhD Thesis, Department of Archaeology, University of Reading

Churchill, D M, 1962 The stratigraphy of the Mesolithic Sites III and V at Thatcham, Berkshire, England, *Proc Prehist Soc* **28**, 362-370

Christie, N, Creighton, O, Edgeworth, M and Fradley, M, 2010 'Have you found anything intersting?'; exploring late Saxon and medieval urbanism at Wallingford: sources, results and questions, *Oxoniensia* **75**, 35-47

Christie, N and Creighton, O, with Edgeworth, M, and Hamerow, H, 2013 *Transforming Townscapes. From Burh to Borough: The Archaeology of Wallingford AD 800-1400*, Soc Med Archaeol Monograph **35**, London

Clapham, A J, 2000 Plant remains, in K E Walker & D E Farwell, *Twyford Down, Hampshire; archaeological investigations on the M3 motorway from bar End to Compton, 1990-93*, Hampshire Field Club Monograph **9**, 148-150, Winchester

Clapham, A J, 2005 Waterlogged plant remains, in Birbeck 2005, 173-181

Clark, J G D, 1932 *The Mesolithic Age in Britain*, Cambridge

Clark, S, 2007 Early Medieval Berkshire (AD410 – 1066), at http://thehumanjourney.net/pdf_store/ sthames/phase3/County/Early%20Medieval/Early%2 0Medieval%20Berkshire.pdf

Clarke, D L, 1970 *Beaker pottery of Great Britain and Ireland*, Cambridge

Clarke, G, 1979 *Pre-Roman and Roman Winchester: Part 2: The Roman Cemetery at Lankhills*, Oxford

Cleal, R M J, Walker, K E and Montague, R, 1995 *Stonehenge in its landscape: 20th-century excavations*, Engl Heritage Archaeol Rep **10**, London

Clifford, M H, 1936 A Mesolithic flora in the Isle of Wight, *Proc Isle Wight Natur Hist Archaeol Soc* **2**, 582-94

Clinch, G, 1905 Bronze celt found at Crickhowell, *Archaeologia Cambrensis*, **5**, 259-60

Clough, T H McK and Cummins, W A, 1979 *Stone axe studies*, CBA Res Rep **23**, London

Cockman, F G, 1974 The Railway Era in Buckinghamshire, *Rec Buckinghamshire* **19**, 1971-1974

Cocks, A H 1921 A Roman-British homestead in the Hambleden valley, Bucks, *Archaeologia* **71**, 141-98

Cocroft, W D, 1985 Two Post-Medieval Pottery Kilns and Associated Products from Prosser's Yard, Brill, Buckinghamshire, *Rec Buckinghamshire* **27**, 72-93

Cocroft, W, 2000 *Dangerous Energy*, English Heritage

Cocroft, W and Thomas, R J C, 2003 *Cold War*, English Heritage

Cohen, N, 2010 *Thames Archaeological Survey* http:// www.thamesdiscovery.org/riverpedia/the-thames-archaeological-survey

Cole, A, 2010 Place-Name Patterns, in Tiller and Darkes 2010, 22-5

Coles, J M and Coles, B, 1986 *Sweet Track to Glastonbury: the Somerset Levels in prehistory*, London

Coleman, L and Collard, M, 2005 Taplow to Dorney Pipeline, Taplow, Buckinghamshire, Unpublished post-excavation assessment and updated project design, Cotswold Archaeology

Coleman, L, Havard, T, Collard, M, Cox, S, and McSloy, E, 2004 Denham, The Lea, Interim Report, *CBA South Midlands Archaeol* **34**, 14-17

Collard M, Darvill, T and Watts, M, 2006 Ironworking in the Bronze Age? Evidence from a 10th Century BC Settlement at Hartshill Copse, Upper Bucklebury, West Berkshire *Proc Prehist Soc* **72**, 367-421

Collins, A E P, 1952-3 Excavations on Blewburton Hill, 1948-9, *Berkshire Archaeol J* **53**, 21-64

Collins, P E F, 1994 *Floodplain environmental change since the Last Glacial Maximum in the Lower Kennet Valley, South-central England*, unpublished PhD thesis, University of Reading

Collins, P E F, Fenwick, I M, Keith-Lucas, M D and Worsley, P, 1996 Late Devensian river and floodplain dynamics and related environmental change in Northwest Europe, with particular reference to a site at Woolhampton, Berkshire, England, *Journal of Quaternary Science* **11**(5), 357-375

Collis, J R, 1994 An Iron Age and Roman Cemetery at Owlesbury Hampshire, in Fitzpatrick and Morris 1994, 106-8

Collis, J R, 1996 Hillfortts, enclosures and boundaries, in Champion and Collis 1996, 87-94

Colquhoun, I, 1979 The Late Bronze Age Hoard from Blackmoor, Hampshire, in Burgess, C and Coombs, D (eds) *Bronze Age Hoards: some Finds Old and New* BAR (Brit Ser) **67**, Oxford 99-116

Conneller, C and Ellis, C, 2007 A Late Upper Palaeolithic site at La Sagesse Convent, Romsey, Hants, *Proc Prehist Soc* **73**, 191-228

Cook, A M and Dacre, M W, 1985 *Excavations at Portway, Andover 1973-75*, Oxford University Committee for Archaeology Monograph **4**, Oxford

Cook, J and Rowley, T 1985 *Dorchester Through the Ages*, Oxford University Department for External Studies

Cook, S, 1999 Archaeological excavations at 64-66 St. Thomas's Street, Oxford, *Oxoniensia* **64**, 285-296

Cook, S, 2011 The Geochemistry of 'House 1' in Periods 3 and 4, in Fulford and Clarke 2011, 53-62

Cooke, N, Brown, F and Phillpotts, C, 2008 *From hunter gatherers to huntsmen. A history of the Stansted landscape*, Framework Archaeology Monograph **2**, Oxford and Salisbury

Copeland, T, 1988 The North Oxfordshire Grim's Ditch: a fieldwork survey, *Oxoniensia* **53**, 277-292

Cotswold Archaeology, 2003 *Great Western Alternative, Didcot, Oxfordshire: Archaeological Evaluation for Wimpey PLC and Bryant Homes Ltd*, unpub client report CA 02101

Cotswold Archaeology, 2004 Abingdon Pipeline, Oxfordshire. Archaeological Evaluation and Programme of Archaeological Recording, unpublished client report 04010 produced for RSK ENSR Environment on behalf of Transco

Cotton, J and Field, D, 2004 *Towards a new stone age: aspects of the Neolithic in south-east England*, CBA Res Rep **137**, York

Cotton, M and Frere, S, 1968 Ivinghoe Beacon excavations 1963-65, *Rec Buckinghamshire* **18**, 187-260

Cotton, M A and Gathercole, P W, 1958 *Excavations at Clausentum, Southampton, 1951-4*, Ministry of Works Archaeological Reports **2** , London

Countryside Commission, 1994 *The Isle of Wight Landscape: An Assessment of the Area of Outstanding Natural Beauty*

County Museum Archaeological Group, 1973 Moated

sites in Buckinghamshire – a list, *Rec Buckingham-shire* **19**, 336-339

Cox, P W, 1997 Billings Field, Bicester Road (Quarrendon) Aylesbury, Bucks: An archaeological evaluation report, unpublished report

Coy, J, 1989 Animal bones, 111-114, in Astill, G G & Lobb, S J, Excavation of Prehistoric, Roman, and Saxon deposits at Wraysbury, Berkshire, *Archaeol J* 146, 68-134

Cramp, K, 2007 The Flint, in Benson and Whittle 2007, 289-314

Crawford, O G S, 1951 Some Notes on Avington, *Proc Hampshire Fld Club Archaeol Soc* 17, 107-11

Crawford, O G S, 1960 *Archaeology in the Field*, London

Crawford, O G S and Keiller, A, 1928 *Wessex from the Air*, Oxford

Creighton, J, 2000 *Coins and Power in Late Iron Age Britain*, Cambridge University Press

Critchley, D J, 2004 *Addington Church. An Architectural and Historical Study*, Buckinghamshire Papers 4

Crockett, A, 1996 Iron Age to Saxon Settlement at Wickhams Field, near Reading, Berkshire; Excavations on the Site of the M4 Granada Reading Motorway Service Area, in Andrews and Crockett 1996, 112-170

Croft, R A and Mynard, D C, 1993 *The Changing Landscape of Milton Keynes*, Buckinghamshire Archaeological Society Monograph Series 5, Aylesbury

Croft, R A and Pike, A R, 1988 Buckinghamshire fishponds and river fisheries, in *Medieval Fish, Fisheries and Fishponds in England* (ed. M Aston), BAR Brit Ser **182**(ii), Oxford, 229-266

Cromarty, A M, Foreman, S and Murray, P, 1999 The excavation of a late Iron Age enclosed settlement at Bicester Fields Farm, Bicester, Oxon., *Oxoniensia* **64**, 153–233

Cromarty, A M, Barclay, A, Lambrick, G and Robinson, M, 2006 *Late Bronze Age ritual and habitation on a Thames eyot at Whitecross Farm, Wallingford: The archaeology of the Wallingford Bypass, 1986-92*, Oxford Archaeology Thames Valley Landscapes Monograph 22, Oxford

Crook, J 1991 The Pilgrims' Hall, Winchester. Hammerbeams, Base Crucks and Aisle-Derivative Roof Structures, *Archaeologia* 119, 129-59

Crummy, N and Eckardt, H, 2003 Regional identities and technologies of self: nail-cleaners in Roman Britain, *Archaeol J* **160**, 44-69

Cruse, R J, 1987 Further investigation of the Acheulian site at Cuxton, *Archaeologia Cantiana* **104**, 39–81

Cunliffe, B W, 1974 *Iron Age Communities in Britain* (1st edn), London

Cunliffe, B W, 1975 *Excavations at Portchester Castle. Vol. 1: Roman*, Res Rep Comm Soc Antiq London **32**, London

Cunliffe, B, 1976 *Excavations at Portchester Castle Volume II: Saxon*, Res Rep Comm Soc Antiq London **XXXIII**, London

Cunliffe, B, 1984a Iron Age Wessex: Continuity and Change, in *Aspects of the Iron Age in Central Southern Britain* (eds B Cunliffe and D Miles), 12-45

Cunliffe, B W 1984b *Danebury: an Iron Age hillfort in Hampshire* 2 vols, CBA Res Rep **52**, London

Cunliffe, B W, 1987 *Hengistbury Head, Dorset. Vol I: The Prehistoric and Roman Settlement 3500BC – AD 500*, Oxford, Oxford Univ Comm Archaeol Monograph **26**

Cunliffe, B W, 1991 *Iron Age Communities in Britain* (3rd ed.), London, Longman

Cunliffe, B W, 1993 *Wessex to AD 1000: A Regional History of England*, London, Longman, 205-219

Cunliffe B 1995 *Danebury: An Iron Age Hillfort in Hampshire: Vol 6 A Hillfort Community in Perspective*, CBA Res Rep **102**, York

Cunliffe, B W (ed.), 2000 *The Danebury environs programme: the prehistory of a* Wessex landscape, 1 and 2, Oxford University School of Archaeology Monographs **48** and **49**

Cunliffe, B W, 2001 *The Danebury Environs Project 5: Fullerton Villa Excavation, 2001*, Interim Report, Oxford, Danebury Trust/Institute of Archaeology

Cunliffe, B W, 2005 *Iron Age Communities in Britain*, (4th ed.), Routledge, London

Cunliffe, B, 2008 *The Danebury Environs Roman Programme. A Wessex Landscape during the Roman Era, Volume 1, Overview*, English Heritage & Oxford University School of Archaeology Monograph 70, Oxford

Cunliffe, B, 2012 Calleva in context, in Fulford 2012a, 14-21

Cunliffe, B W and de Jersey, P (eds), 1997 *Armorica and Britain: cross Channel relationships in the late first millennium BC*, Oxford, OUCA Monograph **45**

Cunliffe, B W and Miles, D (eds), 1984 *Aspects of the Iron Age in central southern Britain*, OUCA Monograph **2**, Oxford

Cunliffe, B W and Poole, C, 1991a *Danebury: an Iron Age Hillfort in Hampshire* 4, *the Excavations, 1979-1988: the site*, CBA Res Rep **73**, London

Cunliffe, B W and Poole, C, 1991b *Danebury: an Iron Age Hillfort in Hampshire* 5, *the Excavations, 1979-1988: the finds*, CBA Res Rep **73**, London

Cunliffe, B W and Poole, C, 1994 *Houghton Down, Stockbridge, Hants, 1994. The Danebury Environs Programme. The prehistory of a Wessex Landscape*, English Heritage and OUCA Monograph, Institute of Archaeology, Oxford

Cunliffe, B W and Poole, C, 2000a *Suddern Farm, Middle Wallop, Hants, 1991 and 1996. The Danebury Environs Programme. The Prehistory of a Wessex Landscape*, English Heritage and OUCA Monograph **49**, Institute of Archaeology, Oxford

Cunliffe, B W and Poole, C, 2000b *The Danebury Environs Programme – The Prehistory of a Wessex Landscape, Volume 2, Part 2 – Bury Hill, Upper Clatford, Hants*, English Heritage and OUCA Monograph 49 (Part 2), Institute of Archaeology, Oxford

Cunliffe, B W and Poole, C, 2000b *Houghton Down, Stockbridge, Hants, 1994. Danebury Environs Programme. Vol. 2 Part 6,* English Heritage/Oxford Univ Comm Archaeol Monograph **49**, Oxford, 78-102

Cunliffe, B W and Poole, C, 2000c *Nettlebank Copse, Wherwell, Hants, 1993.* The Danebury Environs Programme. Vol. 2. Part 5. English Heritage/Oxford Univ Comm Archaeol Oxford, 53-83

Cunliffe, B W and Poole, C, 2000d *Bury Hill, Upper Clatford, Hants, 1990. Danebury Environs Programme. Vol. 2 Part 2,* English Heritage/Oxford Univ Comm Archaeol Monograph **49**

Cunliffe, B and Poole, C, 2008a *The Danebury Environs Roman Programme. A Wessex Landscape during the Roman Era, Volume 2, Part 1, Houghton Down, Longstock, Hants, 1997,* English Heritage and Oxford Univ School of Archaeology Monograph **71**, Oxford

Cunliffe, B and Poole, C, 2008b *The Danebury Environs Roman Programme. A Wessex Landscape during the Roman Era, Volume 2, Part 2, Grateley South, Grateley, Hants, 1998 and 1999,* English Heritage and Oxford University School of Archaeology Monograph **71**, Oxford

Cunliffe, B and Poole, C, 2008c *The Danebury Environs Roman Programme. A Wessex Landscape during the Roman Era, Volume 2, Part 3, Fullerton, Hants, 2000 and 2001,* English Heritage and Oxford University School of Archaeology Monograph **71**, Oxford

Cunliffe, B and Poole, C, 2008d *The Danebury Environs Roman Programme. A Wessex Landscape during the Roman Era, Volume 2, Part 4, Thruxton, Hants, 2002,* English Heritage and Oxford University School of Archaeology Monograph **71**, Oxford

Cunliffe, B and Poole, C, 2008e *The Danebury Environs Roman Programme. A Wessex Landscape during the Roman Era, Volume 2, Part 5, Rowbury Farm, Wherwell, Hants, 2003,* English Heritage and Oxford University School of Archaeology Monograph **71**, Oxford

Cunliffe, B and Poole, C, 2008f *The Danebury Environs Roman Programme. A Wessex Landscape during the Roman Era, Volume 2, Part 6, Flint Farm, Goodworth Clatford, Hants, 2004,* English Heritage and Oxford University School of Archaeology Monograph **71**, Oxford

Cunliffe, B and Poole, C, 2008g *The Danebury Environs Roman Programme. A Wessex Landscape during the Roman Era, Volume 2, Part 7, Dunkirt Barn, Abbotts Ann, Hants, 2005 and 2006,* English Heritage and Oxford University School of Archaeology, Monograph **71**, Oxford

Cunliffe, B and Poole, C, 2008 *The Danebury Environs Roman Programme. A Wessex Landscape During the Roman Era. Vol. 2 The Sites (Part 1: Houghton Down, Longstock, Hants, 1997; Part 2: Grateley South, Grateley, Hants, 1998 and 1999; Part 3: Fullerton, Hants, 2000 and 2001; Part 4: Thruxton, Hants, 2002; Part 5: Rowbury Farm, Wherwell, Hants, 2003; Part 6: Flint Farm, Goodworth Clatford, Hants, 2004. Part 7: Dunkirt Barn, Abbotts Ann, Hants, 2005 and 2006).* English Heritage and OUCA Monograph, Institute of Archaeology, Oxford

Currie, C K, 1999 An archaeological and historical landscape survey of the Mottistone Manor Estate, Mottistone, Isle of Wight, report to the National Trust (Southern Region)

Currie, C, K, 2000 An archaeological and historical survey of the Newtown Estate, Newtown, Isle of Wight, report to the National Trust (Southern Region)

Currie, C K, 2001 An archaeological and historical survey of the Knowles Farm and St Catherine's Hill & Down Estates, Isle of Wight, report to the National Trust (Southern Region)

Currie, C K, 2002 An archaeological and historical survey of the Ventnor Downs and Luccombe Farm Estate, Isle of Wight, Volume 1: historical text and archaeological inventory report to the National Trust (Southern Region)

Currie, C K, 2003 An archaeological survey of earthworks on Castle hill, Mottistone, Isle of Wight, *Proc Hampshire Fld Club Archaeol Soc* **58**, 24-32

Currie, C K, 2007 Early water management on the lower River Itchen in Hampshire, in J Blair (ed.) 2007, 244-53

Currie, C R J, 1992 Larger Medieval Houses in the Vale of White Horse, *Oxoniensia* **57**, 81–245

Dacre, M and Ellison, A, 1981 A Bronze Age cemetary at Kimpton, Hampshire, *Proc Prehist Soc* **47**, 147-199

Dalwood, H, Dillon, J, Evans, J and Hawkins, A, 1989 Excavations in Walton, Aylesbury, 1985-1986, *Rec Buckinghamshire* **31**, 137-221

Darby, H C, 1977 *Domesday England,* Cambridge

Darby, H C, 1986 *Domesday England* – concluding volume of the *Domesday Geography of England*

Darby, H C and Campbell, E M J, 1962 *The Domesday Geography of South-East England,* Cambridge

Dark, P, 2000a Revised 'absolute' dating of the early Mesolithic site of Star Carr, North Yorkshire, in the light of changes in the early Holocene tree-ring chronology, *Antiquity* **74**, 304-7

Dark, P, 2000b *The Environment of Britain in the First Millennium AD,* Duckworth, London

Dark, P, 2011 The Pollen and Trichurid Ova from Pit 5251, in Fulford and Clarke 2011, 294-300

Darvill, T, C, 1992 Monument evaluation manual part iv, urban areas, English Heritage and author, London

Darvill, T, 2004 *Long barrows of the Cotswolds and surrounding areas,* Stroud

Davies, J S, 1883 *A history of Southampton, partly from the MS. of dr. Speed,* Southampton

Davies, S M, 1981 Excavations at Old Down Farm, Andover: Part II: Prehistoric and Roman, *Proc Hampshire Fld Club Archaeol Soc* **37**, 81-163

Davies, S M, Bellamy, P S, Heaton, M J and

Woodward, A, 2002 *Excavations at Allington Avenue, Fordington, Dorchester, Dorset, 1984-87* Dorset Natural History and Archaeological Society Monograph Series **15**

Dawson, M, 2002 Archaeology desk based assessment and trial trench evaluation at the Grand Junction Hotel, Buckingham, unpubl. report

Day, S P, 1991 Post-glacial vegetational history of the Oxford region, *New Phytologist* **119**, 445-70

Day, S P, 1993 Woodland origin and 'ancient woodland indicators': a case-study from Sidlings Copse, Oxfordshire, UK, *The Holocene* **3(1)**, 45-53

De Roche, C D, 1977 An analysis of selected groups of early Iron Age pottery from the Oxford region, BLitt thesis, Univ Oxford

De Roche, C D, 1978 The Iron Age pottery, in Parrington, M 1978, *The Excavation of an Iron Age Settlement, Bronze Age Ring-Ditches and Roman Features at Ashville Trading Estate, Abingdon (Oxfordshire) 1974-76*, Oxford Archaeological Unit Report 1, CBA Res Rep **28**, London, 40-74

Dennel, R W, 1983 *European economic prehistory: a new approach*, Academic Press, London

Dennell, R, 2003 Dispersal and colonisation, long and short chronologies: how continuous is the Early Pleistocene record for hominids outside East Africa? *Journal of Human Evolution* **45**, 421–440

Department for Culture Media and Sport, 2001 *The Historic Environment: A Force for Our Future*

Department for Culture Media and Sport, 2001 *The Government's Statement on the Historic Environment for England 2010*

Devoy, R J N, 1979 Flandrian sea-level changes and vegetational history of the lower Thames estuary, *Phil Trans Royal Soc London* Series B **285**, 355-410

Dewar, H S L, 1929 The field archaeology of Doles, *Proc Hampshire Fld Club Archaeol Soc* **10** (1926-30), 118-126

Dewey, H, 1924 Implements from the Clay-with-flints of north Kent, *Antiq J* **4**, 147-149

Dewey, J and Dewey, S, 1977 *The Book of Wallingford*

Dickinson, T M, 1976 The Anglo-Saxon burial sites of the Upper Thames Region and their bearing on the history of Wessex, circa AD 400-700, 3 volumes, Oxford D. Phil. thesis (unpublished)

Dils, J (ed), 1998 *An Historical Atlas of Berkshire* Berkshire Record Society, Reading

Dinwiddy, K E, 2011 An Anglo-Saxon Cemetery at Twyford, near Winchester, *Hampshire Studies* **66**, 75-126

Dixon, P, 1994 *The Hillfort Defences. Crickley Hill Vol.* **1**, University of Nottingham, Nottingham

Dobney, K and Ervynck, A, 2007 To fish or not to fish? Evidence for the possible avoidance of fish consumption during the Iron Age around the North Sea, in Haselgrove and Moore 2007, 403-18

Dobney, K, Jacques, S and Irving, B, 1995 *Of Butchers and Breeds: Report on vertebrae remains from various sites in the city of London*, Lincoln, City of Lincoln Archaeological Unit Studies **5**

Dodd, A (ed.), 2003 *Oxford before the University: the late Saxon and Norman archaeology of the Thames Crossing, the defences and the town*, Oxford Archaeology Thames Valley Landscapes Monograph **17**, Oxford

Dodd, A, 2010 Early Anglo-Saxon settlement, in Tiller and Darkes, 2010, 18-19

Dodds, D, 2002 Berryfields, Aylesbury, Buckinghamshire: An Archaeological Evaluation, Oxford Archaeology, unpublished client report

Doggett, N, 2002 *Patterns of Re-use: The Transformation of Former Monastic Buildings in Post-dissolution Hertfordshire, 1540-1600*, BAR Brit Ser **331**

Doubleday, H A (ed.), 1900 *A History of Hampshire and the Isle of Wight, Volume One*, The Victoria History of the Counties of England, Westminster

Downey, R, King, A and Soffe, G, 1979 The Hayling Island Temple, London, Downey

Draper, C, 1951 Stone industries from Rainbow Bar, Hants, *Archaeological Newsletter* **3.9**, 147–9

Draper, C, 1953 Further Mesolithic sites in south Hampshire, *Archaeological Newsletter* **4.12**, 193

Draper, C, 1968 Mesolithic distribution in south-east Hampshire, *Proc Hampshire Fld Club Archaeol Soc* **23**, 110–19

Drewett, P L, 1970 The excavation of two round barrows and associated fieldwork on Ashey Down, Isle of Wight, 1969, *Proc Hampshire Fld Club Archaeol Soc* **27**, 33-56

Duncan, C, 2000 The comparative palaeopathology of males and females in English medieval skeletal samples in its social context, Leicester, University of Leicester, Unpublished PhD Thesis

Dunning, G, 1939 A thirteenth century midden near Niton, *Proc Isle Wight Nat Hist Archaeol Soc* **3**, Part II, 128-137

Dunning, G, 1951 The history of Niton, Isle of Wight, *Proc Isle Wight Nat Hist Archaeol Soc* **4** Part VI, 191-204

Dunning, G C, 1976 Salmonsbury, Bourton-on-the-Water, Gloucestershire, in Harding (ed.) 1976, 75-118

Durham, B, 1977 Archaeological Investigations in St. Aldate's Oxford, *Oxoniensia* **42**, 83–203

Durham B, 1978 Traces of a Late Saxon church at St Mary's, Aylesbury, *Rec Buckinghamshire* **20**, 621-6

Durham, B, 1984 The Thames Crossing at Oxford. Archaeological Studies, 1979–82, *Oxoniensia* **49**, 87-

Durham, B, 1991 The Infirmary and Hall of the Medieval Hospital of St. John the Baptist at Oxford, *Oxoniensia* **56**, 17–75

Durham, B and Bell, C, 1993 All Souls' College: medieval cloister, *CBA South Midlands Archaeol* **23**, 74

Durham, B, Halpin, C and Palmer, N, 1983 Oxford's Northern Defences. Archaeological Studies 1971–1982, *Oxoniensia* **48**, 13-40

Durning, L (ed.), 2006 *Queen Elizabeth's Book of Oxford*, Oxford

Dyer, A, 1991 *Decline and Growth in English Towns 1400-1640*, Basingstoke

Dyer, C, 2002 *Making a Living in the Middle Ages. The People of Britain 850-1520*, London

Dyer, C, 2005 *An Age of Transition? Economy and Society in the Later Middle Ages*, Oxford

Dyer, J F, 1961 Barrows of the Chilterns, *Archaeol J* **116**, 1-24

Dyer, J, 1991 The Five Knolls and associated barrows at Dunstable, *Bedfordshire Archaeol J* **19**, 25-9

Eckardt, H, 2002 *Illuminating Roman Britain*, Monographies Instrumentum **23**, Éditions Monique Mergoil, Montagnac

Eckardt, H, 2006 The character, chronology and use of the late Roman pits: the Silchester finds assemblage, in Fulford *et al.* 2006, 221-45

Eckardt, H (ed), 2010 *Roman Diasporas. Archaeological Approaches to Mobility and Diversity in the Roman Empire*, Journal of Roman Archaeology Supplementary Series **78**, Portsmouth, Rhode Island

Eckardt, H, 2011 The mid-Roman pits in context, in Fulford and Clarke 2011, 301-18

Eckardt, H, Chenery, C, Booth, P, Evans, J A, Lamb, A and Müldner, G, 2009 Oxygen and Strontium Isotope evidence for mobility in Roman Winchester, *J Archaeol Sci* **36**(12), 2816-2825

Edmonds, N, Sly, T and Strutt, K, 2002 Quarr Abbey Geophysical Survey Report, November 2002, University of Southampton

Edwards, B, 1999a Historic Newport: Archaeological assessment document, *An Extensive Urban Survey of the Isle of Wight's Historic Towns*, Hampshire County Council

Edwards, B, 1999b Historic Yarmouth : Archaeological assessment document, *An Extensive Urban Survey of the Isle of Wight's Historic Towns*, Hampshire County Council

Edwards, B, 1999c Historic Newtown: Archaeological assessment document, *An Extensive Urban Survey of the Isle of Wight's Historic Towns*, Hampshire County Council

Edwards, B, 1999d Historic Brading: Archaeological assessment document, *An Extensive Urban Survey of the Isle of Wight's Historic Towns*, Hampshire County Council

Edwards, B, 1999e Historic Carisbrooke: Archaeological assessment document, *An Extensive Urban Survey of the Isle of Wight's Historic Towns*, Hampshire County Council

Edwards, B, 1999f Historic St Helens: Archaeological assessment document, *An Extensive Urban Survey of the Isle of Wight's Historic Town*, Hampshire County Council

Edwards, B, 1999g Historic Cowes: Archaeological assessment document, *An Extensive Urban Survey of the Isle of Wight's Historic Towns*, Hampshire County Council

Edwards, R, 1999 An Extensive Urban Survey of Hampshire's Historic Towns

Edwards, R, 2005 Historic Farmsteads and Landscape Character in Hampshire

Ehrenberg, M R, 1977 *Bronze Age Spearheads from Berkshire, Buckinghamshire and Oxfordshire*, BAR Brit Ser **34**, Oxford

Elliott, D J, 1975 *Buckingham. The Loyal and Ancient Borough*, Chichester

Ellis, C J, Allen, M J, Gardiner, J, Harding, P, Ingrem, C, Powell, A, and Scaife, R G, 2003 An early Mesolithic seasonal hunting site in the Kennet Valley, Southern England, *Proc Prehist Soc* **69**, 107-36

Ellis, P, Hughes, G and Jones, L, 2000 An Iron Age boundary and settlement features at Slade Farm, Bicester, Oxfordshire: a report on excavations, 1996, *Oxoniensia* **65**, 211–265

Ellison, A B, 1980 Deverel Rimbury urn cemeteries: the evidence for social organisation, in Barrett and Bradley 1980, 115-26

Ellison, A B, 1981 Towards a socio-economic model for the Middle Bronze Age in southern England, in *Pattern of the Past: Studies in Honour of David Clarke*, (eds I Hodder, G Isaac & N Hammond), Cambridge, 413–38

Ellison, A and Rahtz, P, 1987 Excavations at Whitsbury Castle Ditches, *Proc Hampshire Fld Club Archaeol Soc* **43**, 63-81

Elvey, E M, 1965 Aylesbury in the fifteenth century – a bailiff's notebook, *Rec Buckinghamshire* **17**, 321-335

Elvey, E M, 1977 The history of nos. 1 & 2 Market Hill, Buckingham, *Rec Buckinghamshire* **20**, 301-7

Emery, F, 1974 *The Oxfordshire landscape*, London

English Heritage, 1991 *Exploring our past: strategies for the archaeology of England*, English Heritage

English Heritage, 1993 Monuments Protection Programme: single monument class descriptions for 'Medieval Villages' and 'Medieval Dispersed Settlements'

English Heritage, 1996 *Frameworks for our past*

English Heritage, 1998 *Identifying and Protecting Palaeolithic Remains: Archaeological Guidance for Planning Authorities and Developers*, English Heritage, London

English Heritage, 2000 *Power of place*

English Heritage/Prehistoric Society, 1999 *Research Frameworks for the Palaeolithic and Mesolithic of Britain and Ireland*, English Heritage, London

English Heritage/Prehistoric Society, 2008 *Research and Conservation Framework for the British Palaeolithic*, English Heritage, London

Enright, D and Parkhouse, J, 1996 Archaeological Investigation at Weston Underwood in 1994, *Rec Buckinghamshire* **38**, 175-98

Entwistle, R, 2001 A Bronze Age round barrow and Deverel-Rimbury cremation cemetery at Zionshill Copse, Chandler's Ford, Hampshire, *Proc Hampshire Fld Club Archaeol Soc*, **56**, 1–20

Entwistle, R, Raymond, F and Stedman M, 2005 A surface collection project and finds from metal detecting at Shavards farm, Meonstoke, Hampshire, *Proc Hampshire Fld Club Archaeol Soc* **60**, 13-53

Evans, C, Pollard, P, and Knight, M, 1999 Life in woods: tree-throws, 'settlement' and forest cognition *Oxford J Archaeol* **18(3)**, 241-54

Evans, J, Stoodley, N and Chenery, C, 2006 A Strontium and Oxygen Isotope Assessment of a possible Fourth Century Immigrant Population in a Hampshire Cemetery, Southern England, *J Archaeol Sci* **33**, 265-72

Evans, J G 1972 *Land snails in archaeology*, Seminar Press, London and New York

Evans, J G, 1975 *The environment of early man in the British Isles*, Paul Elek, London

Evans, J G, 1992a River valley bottoms and archaeology in the Holocene, in *The wetland revolution in prehistory*, (ed. B Coles), Warp, The Prehistoric Society, 47-53

Evans, J G, 1992b Mollusca, In C A Butterworth & S J Lobb, *Excavations in the Burghfield Area, Berkshire; developments in the Bronze Age and Saxon landscapes*, Wessex Archaeological Report **1**, Salisbury, 130–43

Evans, J G and Valentine, K W G, 1974 Ecological changes induced by prehistoric man at Pitstone, Buckinghamshire, *J Archaeol Sci* **1**, 343-351

Evans, J G, Limbrey, S, Maté, I and Mount, R, 1993 An environmental history of the Upper Kennet Valley, Wiltshire, for the last 10,000 years, *Proc Prehist Soc* **59**, 139-95

Everard, C E, 1954 Submerged gravel and peat in Southampton Water, *Proc Hampshire Fld Club Archaeol Soc* **18**, 263–285

Everitt, A, 1974 The Banburys of England, *Urban History Yearbook* 1974, repr. in *Landscape & Community In England* (London, 1985)

Everson, P, 2001 Peasants, Peers and Graziers: the Landscape of Quarrendon, Buckinghamshire, interpreted in *Rec Buckinghamshire* **41**, 1-45

Evison, V I, 1969 A Viking grave at Sonning, Berks, *Antiq J* **49**, 330-45

Evison, V I, 1988 *An Anglo-Saxon Cemetery at Alton, Hampshire*, Hampshire Fld Club Archaeol Soc Monograph **4**

Eyers, J E, 2011 *Romans in the Hambleden Valley. Yewden Roman Villa*, High Wycombe

Fairbrother, J R, 1990 *Faccombe Netherton. Excavations of a Saxon and medieval manorial complex*, British Museum Occasional Paper **74**, London

Farley, M E, 1972 A Bronze Spearhead from Princes Risborough, *Rec Buckinghamshire* **19**, 215-217

Farley, M E, 1973 Note in *Rec Buckinghamshire* **29**, 344

Farley, M, 1974 Aylesbury – a defended town?, *Rec Buckinghamshire* **19**, 429-48

Farley, M, 1976 Saxon and medieval Walton, Aylesbury, Buckinghamshire 1973-4, *Rec Buckinghamshire* **20**, 153-292

Farley, M E, 1978 Excavations at Low Farm, Fulmer, Bucks, 1: the Mesolithic occupation, *Rec Buckinghamshire* **20**, 601-16

Farley, M, 1979 Burials in Aylesbury and the early history of the town, *Rec Buckinghamshire* **21**, 116-21

Farley, M 1979a Pottery and pottery kilns of the post-medieval period at Brill, Buckinghamshire *Post-Medieval Archaeology* **13**, 127-152

Farley, M, 1979b A Bell-Pit or Chalk Well at Lane End, *Rec Buckinghamhire* **21**, 135-140

Farley, M, 1980 Middle Saxon Occupation at Chicheley, Bucks, *Rec Buckinghamshire* **22**, 92-104

Farley, M, 1982a Excavations at Low Farm, Fulmer, Bucks: II, the medieval manor, *Rec Buckinghamshire* **24**, 46-72

Farley, M, 1982b A medieval pottery industry at Boarstall, Buckinghamshire, *Rec Buckinghamshire* **24**, 107-117

Farley, M, 1983a A mirror burial at Dorton, Buckinghamshire, *Proc Prehist Soc* **49**, 269-302

Farley, M E, 1983b Archive notes and finds, CASS 5276, BCM 417.1983

Farley, M, 1991a A late Bronze Age sickle from Great Kimble, Buckinghamshire, *Rec Buckinghamshire* **33**, 142-4

Farley, M, 1991b Ravenstone Priory: the church located, *Rec Buckinghamshire* **33**, 114-127

Farley, M, 2001 Medmenham Abbey, Medmenham, Bucks; results from some archaeological watching briefs, unpublished report

Farley, M, 2006 Buckinghamshire Early Medieval Solent-Thames Research Framework

Farley, M, 2007 *The Watermills of Buckinghamshire: A 1930s account by Stanley Freese with original photographs*, Buckinghamshire Archaeological Society, Aylesbury

Farley, M, 2008 Early Medieval Buckinghamshire, at http://thehumanjourney.net/pdf_store/sthames/phase3/County/Early%20Medieval/Early%20Medieval%20Buckinghamshire.pdf

Farley, M, 2009 The Mesolithic period, in *An archaeological research framework for Buckinghamshire: collected papers from the Solent-Thames Research Framework*, (ed. D Thorpe), Buckinghamshire Papers **15**, Aylesbury, 13-9

Farley, M and Jones, G, 2012 *Iron Age ritual, a hillfort and evidence for a minster at Aylesbury, Buckinghamshire*, Oxbow, Oxford

Farley, M and Lawson, J, 1990 A fifteenth-century pottery and tile kiln at Leyhill, Latimer, Buckinghamshire, *Rec Buckinghamshire* **32**, 35-62

Farley, M and Leach, H, 1988 Medieval pottery production areas near Rush Green, Denham, Buckinghamshire, *Rec Buckinghamshire* **30**, 53-102

Farley, M and Manchester, K, 1989 The Cemetery of the Leper Hospital of St Margaret, High Wycombe, Buckinghamshire, *Medieval Archaeology* **33**, 82-89

Fasham, P J, 1983 Fieldwork in and around Micheldever Wood, Hampshire, 1973-1980, *Proc Hampshire Fld Club Archaeol Soc* **39**, 5-45

Fasham, P J, 1985 *The Prehistoric Settlement at Winnall Down, Winchester*, Hampshire Field Club Monograph **2**

Fasham, P J and Keevill, G, 1995 *Brighton Hill South*

(Hatch Warren); an Iron Age farmstead and deserted medieval village in Hampshire, Wessex Archaeology Report 7, Salisbury

Fasham, P J and Whinney, R J B, 1991 *Archaeology and the M3*, Hampshire Field Club Monograph 7, Wessex Trust for Archaeology/Hants Field Club, Winchester

Fasham, P J, Farwell, D E and Whinney, R J B, 1989 *The archaeological site at Easton Lane, Winchester*, Hampshire Field Club Monograph 6, Winchester

Faulkner, A H, 1972 *The Grand Junction Canal*, David and Charles, Newton Abbot

Faulkner, P A, 1975 The surviving medieval buildings, in Platt, C, and Coleman Smith, R, *Excavations in Medieval Southampton 1953-1969*, 56-124

Favis-Mortlock, D, Boardman, J and Bell, M G, 1997 Modelling long-term anthropogenic erosion of a loess cover, South Downs, UK, *The Holocene* 7, 79–90

Featherstone, R and Bewley, R, 2000 Recent aerial reconnaissance in north Oxfordshire, *Oxoniensia* 65, 13-26

Fell, D, 2001 An archaeological evaluation of Rose Cottage, Tylers Green, Buckinghamshire, unpublished report

Fennelly, L R, 1969 A late medieval kiln at Knighton, I.O.W., *Proc Hampshire Fld Club Archaeol Soc* 26, 97-110

Field, D, 2004 Use of land in central southern England during the Neolithic and early Bronze Age, unpublished PhD dissertation, University of Reading

Field, D, 2006 *Earthen long barrows: the earliest monuments in the British Isles*, Stroud

Field, D, 2008 *Use of land in Central Southern England during the Neolithic and Early Bronze Age*, BAR Brit Ser 459, Archaeopress, Oxford

Finlayson, C, Pacheco, F G, Rodríguez-Vidal, J, Fa1, D A, Gutierrez López, J M, Pérez, A S, Finlayson, G, Allue, E, Preysler, J B, Cáceres, I, Carrión, J S, Jalvo, Y F, Gleed-Owen, C P, Jimenez Espejo, F J, López, P, López Sáez1, J A, Cantal J A R, Marco, A S, Guzman, F G, Brown, K, Fuentes, N, Valarino, C A, Villalpando, A, Stringer, C B, Martinez Ruiz, F and Sakamoto, T, 2006 Late survival of Neanderthals at the southernmost extreme of Europe, *Nature* 443, 850-853

Fischer, A, 1991 Pioneers in deglaciated landscapes: the expansion and adaptation of the late Palaeolithic societies in Southern Scandinavia, in Barton *et al.* 1991, 100-21

Fitzpatrick, A P, 1984 The deposition of La Tène Iron Age metalwork in watery contexts in southern England, in Cunliffe and Miles 1984,178-88

Fitzpatrick, A P, 2001 Cross-Channel Exchange, Hengistbury Head and the End of Hillforts, in *Society and Settlement in Iron Age Europe Actes du XVIIIe Colloque de l'AFEAF,* (ed. J Collis) *Winchester, April, 1994*, Sheffield, 83-97

Fitzpatrick, A P, 1998-2003 A Late la Tene Dagger from the Thames at Windsor Berks, *Berkshire*

Archaeol J 76, 14-6

Fitzpatrick, A P, Barnes, I and Cleal, R M J, 1995 An Early Iron Age settlement at Dunston Park, Thatcham, in Barnes *et al.* 1995, 65-92

Fitzpatrick, A P and Morris, E L, (eds) 1994 *The Iron Age in Wessex: Recent Work*, Association Française D'Etude de L'Age du Fer, Trust for Wessex Archaeology, Salisbury

Fitzpatrick, A P and Timby, J, 2002 Roman Pottery in Iron Age Britain, in *Prehistoric Britain; The Ceramic Basis*, (ed. A Woodward and J D Hill), PCRG Occ Publ 3, Oxbow, Oxford, 161-172

Fitzpatrick, A P, Ellis, C and Allen, M J, 1996 Bronze Age 'jetties' or causeways at Testwood Lakes, Hampshire, Great Britain, *PAST* 24, 9-10

Fitzpatrick, A P and Ellis, C, 2000 A Middle Bronze Age bridge at Testwood Lakes, Hampshire, Great Britain, *News Warp* Issue 27

Ford, B M and Teague, S, with Biddulph, E, Hardy, A and Brown, L, 2011 *Winchester – a City in the Making. Archaeological excavations between 2002 and 2007 on the sites of Northgate House, Staple Gardens and the former Winchester library, Jewry St*, Oxford Archaeology Monograph 12, Oxford

Ford, B M, Poore, D, Shaffrey, R and Wilkinson, D R P, 2013 *Under the Oracle: excavations at the Oracle Shopping Centre site 1996-8. The medieval and post-medieval urban development of the Kennet floodplain in Reading*, Oxford Archaeology Thames Valley Landscapes Monograph 36

Ford, S, 1982 Fieldwork and excavation on the Berkshire Grims Ditch, *Oxoniensia* 47 13-36

Ford, S, 1982-3 Linear Earthworks on the Berkshire Downs, *Berkshire Arch J* 71, 1-20

Ford, S, 1987a *East Berkshire archaeological survey*, Berkshire County Council Department of Highways and Planning Occas Pap 1, Reading

Ford, S, 1987b Flint scatters and prehistoric settlement patterns in south Oxfordshire and east Berkshire, in *Lithic analysis in later British prehistory* (eds A Brown and M Edmonds), BAR Brit Ser 162, 101-35, Oxford

Ford, S, 1991-3 Excavations at Eton Wick, *Berkshire Archeol J* 74, 27-36

Ford, S D, 1992 The nature and development of prehistoric settlement and land-use in the Middle Thames Region (8000–500 BC), with special reference to the evidence from lithic artefacts, unpublished PhD thesis, University of Reading

Ford, S D, 1997a Loddon Valley (Berkshire) fieldwalking survey, *Berkshire Archaeol J* 75, 11-33

Ford, S, 1997b The Excavation of Late Saxon and Medieval Features at Kintbury Square, Kintbury, Berkshire, 1995, *Berkshire Archaeol J* 75, 75-92

Ford, S, 2002 *Charnham Lane, Hungerford, Berkshire, archaeological investigations 1988–97*, TVAS monograph 1, Reading

Ford, S and Howell, I, 2004 Saxon and Bronze Age settlement at the Orchard site, Walton Road, Walton, Aylesbury, 1994, in Ford, S, Taylor, K and Howell, I,

2004, *The archaeology of the Aylesbury-Chalgrove pipeline and a Saxon site at The Orchard, Walton*, TVAS monograph **5**, 60–88

Ford, S and Pine, J, 2003 Neolithic ring ditches and Roman landscape features at Horton (1989-1996), in *Prehistoric, Roman and Saxon sites in eastern Berkshire: excavations, 1989-1997* (ed, S Preston), Reading, 12-85

Ford, S and Preston, S, 2002 Medieval occupation at The Orchard, Brighthampton, *Oxoniensia* **67**, 287-312

Ford S and Taylor K, 2001 Iron Age and Roman settlements with prehistoric and Saxon features, at Fenny Lock, Milton Keynes, Buckinghamshire, *Rec Buckinghamshire* **41**, 79-123

Ford, S, Bowden, M, Mees, G and Gaffney, V, 1988 The date of the 'Celtic' Field-Systems on the Berkshire Downs, *Britannia* **19**, 401-404

Ford, S, Entwistle, R and Taylor, K, 2003 *Excavations at Cippenham, Slough, Berkshire, 1995-7*, TVAS Monograph **3**, Reading

Foreman, S, Hiller, J and Petts, D, 2002 *Gathering the People, Settling the Land: The Archaeology of a Middle Thames Landscape, Anglo-Saxon to Post Medieval*, Oxford Archaeology Thames Valley Landscapes Monograph **14**, Oxford

Foster, R, 1973 *F. Cape & Co. of St Ebbe's Street, Oxford*, Woodstock

Foundation Archaeology 1999 The Red Lion Hotel, Oxford St, Lambourn, West Berkshire, an archaeological evaluation, unpublished client report

Foundations Archaeology, 2001 Silver Street, Reading, Unpublished client report

Fowler, M J, 1986 Over Wallop – Martin's Clump, *Archaeology in Hampshire* **4**

Fowler, P J, 1960 Excavations at Madmarston Camp, Swalcliffe, 1957-8, *Oxoniensia* **25**, 3-48

Fox, G E and St John Hope, W H, 1891-1906 *Excavations on the Site of the Roman City of Silchester, Hants, 1890-1905*, London, Society of Antiquaries (Fifteen volumes)

Framework Archaeology 2006 *Landscape Evolution in the Middle Thames Valley: Heathrow Terminal 5 Excavations Volume 1, Perry Oaks*, Framework Archaeology Monograph **1**

French, C, 2007 Deer Park Farm; micromorphological analysis of the soil profile, in French *et al.* (eds) 2007, 398-9

French, C, Lewis, H, Allen, M J, Green, M, Scaife, R G, and Gardiner, J, 2007 *Prehistoric landscape development and human impact in the upper Allen valley, Cranborne Chase, Dorset*, McDonald Institute Monograph, Cambridge

Frere, S S, 1962 Excavations at Dorchester on Thames, 1962, *Archaeol J* **119**, 114-149

Frere, S S, 1984 Excavations at Dorchester on Thames, 1963, *Archaeol J* **141**, 91-174

Frere, S, 1987 *Britannia a history of Roman Britain*, London (3rd ed.)

Froom, F R, 1963 An axe of Dorset chert from a Meso-

lithic site at Kintbury, *Berkshire Archaeol J* **61**, 1-3

Froom, F R, 1970 The Mesolithic around Hungerford Part VI: further results of the surface survey, *Trans Newbury Dist Fld Club* **12**, 58-67

Froom, F R, 1972 A Mesolithic site at Wawcott, Kintbury, *Berkshire Archaeol J* **66**, 23-44

Froom, F R, 1976 *Wawcott III: a stratified Mesolithic succession*, BAR Brit Ser **27**, Oxford

Froom, R, 2005 *Late Glacial Long Blade sites in the Kennet Valley. Excavations and fieldwork at Avington VI, Wawcott XII and Crown Acres* (ed. J Cook), British Museum Research Publications **153**, Bloomsbury Press, London

Froom, R, Cook, J, Debenham, N and Ambers, J, 1993 Wawcott XXX: an interim report on a Mesolithic site in Berkshire, in *Stories in Stone* (eds N Ashton and A David), Lithic Studies Society Occasional Paper **4**, Oxford, 206-12

Fulford, M G, 1975 *New Forest Roman Pottery: manufacture and distribution, with a corpus of pottery types*, BAR Brit Ser **17**, Oxford

Fulford, M G, 1984 *Silchester Defences, 1974-80*, Britannia Monograph **5**, Gloucester

Fulford, M, 1989 *The Silchester Amphitheatre. Excavations of 1979-85*, Soc for Promotion of Roman Studies Britannia Monograph **10**, London

Fulford, M, 1992 Iron Age to Roman: a Period of Radical Change on the Gravels, in Fulford and Nichols (eds) 1992, 23-38

Fulford, M, 1993 Silchester: the early development of a civitas capital, in *Roman Towns: the Wheeler Inheritance* (ed. S J Greep), CBA Res Rep, **93**, York, 16-33

Fulford, M, 2000 Human remains from the North Gate, Silchester: an 'early' and a 'late' radiocarbon date from the city, *Britannia* **31**, 356-8

Fulford, M, 2007 Coasting Britannia: Roman trade and traffic around the shores of Britain, in *Communities and Connections: essays in Honour of Barry Cunliffe* (eds C Gosden, H Hamerow, P de Jersey and G Lock), OUP, Oxford, 54-74

Fulford, M, 2001 Links with the past: pervasive 'ritual' behaviour in Roman Britain, *Britannia* **32**, 199-218

Fulford, M (ed.), 2012a *Silchester and the Study of Romano-British Urbanism*, Journal of Roman Archaeology Supplementary Series **90**, Portsmouth, Rhode Island

Fulford, M, 2012b Calleva Atrebatum (Silchester, Hampshire, UK): An Early Medieval Extinction, in *Urbes Extinctae. Archaeologies of Abandoned Classical Towns* (eds N Christie and A Augenti), Ashgate, Farnham, 331-51

Fulford, M and Clarke, A, 2011 *Silchester: City in Transition. The Mid-Roman Occupation of Insula IX c. AD 125-250/300*, Soc for Promotion of Roman Studies Britannia Monograph **25**, London

Fulford, M and Creighton, J, 1998 A Late Iron Age Mirror Burial from Latchmere Green, near Silchester, Hampshire, *Proc Prehist Soc* **64**, 331-342

Fulford, M G and Hodder, I, 1974 A regression

analysis of some later Romano-British pottery: a case study, *Oxoniensia* **39**, 26-33

Fulford, M and Nichols, E (eds), 1992 *Developing Landscapes of Lowland Britain. The Archaeology of the British Gravels: a Review*, Soc of Antiqs Occ Paper **14**, London

Fulford, M G and Rippon, S J, 1994 Lowbury Hill, Oxon: A Re-assessment of the Probable Romano-Celtic Temple and the Anglo-Saxon Barrow, *Archaeol J* **151**, 158-211

Fulford, M and Timby, J, 2000 *Late Iron Age and Roman Silchester. Excavations on the site of the forum-basilica 1977, 1980-86*, Soc for Promotion of Roman Studies Britannia Monograph **15**, London

Fulford, M G, Powell, A B, Entwistle, R and Raymond, F, 2006 *Iron Age and Romano-British Settlements and Landscapes of Salisbury Plain*, Wessex Archaeology Report **20**, Salisbury

Fulford, M G, Rippon, S, Ford, S, Timby, J and Williams, B, 1997 Silchester: excavations of the North Gate, on the north walls, and in the northern suburbs 1988 and 1991-3, *Britannia* **28**, 87-168

Fulford, M G, Clarke, A and Eckardt, H, 2006 *Life and Labour in Late Roman Silchester: Excavations in Insula IX since 1997*, Britannia Monograph **22**, London

Gaffney, V and Tingle, M, 1989 *The Maddle Farm project: an integrated survey of Prehistoric and Roman landscapes on the Berkshire Downs*, BAR Brit Ser **200**, Oxford

Gaffney, V L and White, R H with Goodchild, H, 2007 *Wroxeter, the Cornovii and the urban process Final report on the Wroxeter Hinterland Project 1994-1997, Volume 1: Researching the hinterland*, J Roman Archaeol Suppl Ser **68**, Portsmouth RI

Gale, A, 2000 *The Story Beneath the Solent*, Hampshire and Isle of Wight Trust for Maritime Archaeology, 2nd edition

Galloway, J A, Keene, D A and Murphy, M, 1996 Fuelling the city: production and distribution of firewood and fuel in London's region, 1290-1400, *Economic History Review* **49**, 447-72

Gamble, C S and Steele, J, 1999 Hominid ranging patterns and dietary strategies, in *Hominid Evolution: Lifestyles and Survival Strategies*, (ed. H Ullrich), Archea, Schwelm, 396–409

Gardener, W, 1793-1810 manuscript drawings of the Isle of Wight, British Library Map Library, Ordnance Survey Drawings 67-74

Gardiner, J P, 1984 Lithic distributions and Neolithic settlement patterns in central southern England, in *Neolithic studies I: a review of some current research*, (eds R J Bradley and J P Gardiner), Oxford, BAR Brit Ser **133**, 15-40

Gardiner, J, 1987 The Neolithic and Bronze Age, in Cunliffe, B W, *Hengistbury Head Dorset, Vol 1: the prehistoric and Roman settlement 3500 BC–AD 500*, Oxford University Committee for Archaeology Monograph **13**, Oxford, 329–36

Gardiner, J, 1988 The composition and distribution of Neolithic surface flint scatters in central southern England, unpublished PhD thesis, University of Reading

Gardiner, J, 2002 The Palaeolithic and Mesolithic, in *The Millennium Publication: a review of archaeology in Hampshire 1980–2000* (ed. N Stoodley), Winchester, 1–3

Gardiner, J with Allen, M J (eds), 2005 *Before the mast; life and death aboard the Mary Rose*, The Archaeology of the Mary Rose vol 4, Mary Rose Trust Ltd, Portsmouth

Gardner, A, 2007 *An Archaeology of Identity. Soldiers and Society in Late Roman Britain*, Left Coast Press, Walnut Creek CA

Garmonsway, G N (translated and ed.), *The Anglo-Saxon Chronicle*, Dent, London

Garton, D, 1980 An early Mesolithic site at Rackham, east Sussex, *Sussex Archaeol Collect* **118**, 145–52

Garwood, P, 1999 Discussion, in Barclay and Halpin 1999, 275-309

Garwood, P, 2007 Before the hills in order stood: chronology, time and history in the interpretation of early Bronze Age round barrows, in *Covering old ground: barrows as enclosures* (ed. J Last), Oxford

Gelling, M, 1974 *Place-names of Berkshire*

Gelling, M, 1976 *The Place-Names of Berkshire: Part III*, English Place-Name Society, **51**, London

Gem, R, 2005 The Church of All Saints, Wing, Buckinghamshire, in Holmes, M, Excavation of a Late Saxon – Medieval Cemetery at the site of the former Victorian School, Wing, Buckinghamshire May–June 1999, unpublished report

Gibbard, P L, 1995 The formation of the Strait of Dover, in *Island Britain: a Quaternary Perspective*, (ed. R C Preece), The Geological Society, London, 15–26

Gibson, A M, 1992 Possible timber circles at Dorchester on Thames, *Oxford J Archaeol* **11.1**, 85-91

Giggins, B L, 1983 A brief history of the site of Valentin, Ord and Nagle's factory in Fenny Stratford, unpubl. Report

Gilbert, D, 2008 Excavations west of St Mary's Church, Black Bourton, Oxfordshire: early, middle and late Anglo-Saxon activity, *Oxoniensia* **73**, 147-60

Gillam, S, 1995 The Radcliffe Camera (1992), *CBA South Midlands Archaeol* **25**, 67

Glasscock, R E, 1980 England circa 1334, in *A New Historical Geography of England before 1600*, (ed. H C Darby), 141

Godwin, H and Godwin, M E, 1940 Submerged peat at Southampton, data for the study of post glacial history V, *New Phytologist* **39**, 303–307

Gooder, J, 2007 Excavation of a Mesolithic house at East Barns, East Lothian, Scotland: an interim report, in *Mesolithic studies in the North Sea basin and beyond*, (eds K L Pedersen and C Waddington), Oxbow Books, Oxford, 49-59

Gosden, C and Lock, G, 2001 The Hillforts of the

Ridgeway Project Excavations at Alfred's Castle 2000, CBA *South Midlands Archaeol* **31**, 80-9

Gosden, C, Lock, G, and Daly, P, 2005 University of Oxford The Ridgeway and Vale project: excavations at Marcham/Frilford 2004, *CBA South Midlands Archaeol* **35**, 94-105

Gover, J, 2000 A geophysical investigation of Ivinghoe Beacon, Chiltern Hills, Unpublished report adapted from an MSc dissertation submitted to Reading University

Grace, R, 1992 Use wear analysis, in Healy *et al.* 1992, 53-63

Graham, M, 1979 The building of Oxford Covered Market, *Oxoniensia* **44**, 81-91

Grant, A, 1984 Survival or sacrifice? A critical appraisal of animal burials in Britain in the Iron Age, in *Animals and archaeology. Vol. 4. Husbandry in Europe*, (ed. C Grigson and J Clutton-Brock), BAR Int Ser **227**, 221-227

Grant, A, 1975 The Animal Bones, in Cunliffe 1975, 375-408

Grant, A, 2000 Diet, Economy and Ritual Evidence from the Faunal Remains, in Fulford and Timby 2000, 425-82

Gray, H L, 1915 *English Field Systems*, Cambridge, Mass.

Green, C, and Rollo-Smith, S, 1984 The excavation of eighteen round barrows near Shrewton, Wiltshire, *Proc Prehist Soc* **50**, 255-318

Green, D and Kidd, A, 2006 Buckinghamshire and Milton Keynes Historic Landscape Characterisation, Buckinghamshire County Council

Green, F, 1991 Mesolithic structures in the Test Valley: Bowman's Farm, *PAST* **11**, 1–2

Green, F J, 1979 Medieval plant remains: methods and results in archaeobotanical analysis from excavations in southern England with special reference to Winchester and urban settlement of the 10th-15th centuries, Unpubl. M.Phil thesis, University of Southampton

Green, F J, 1981 Iron Age, Roman and Saxon crops from Wessex, in *The Environment of Man; the Iron Age to the Anglo-Saxon period*, (ed. M Jones & G Dimbleby), Oxford, BAR Brit Ser **97**, 129-153

Green, F J, 1994 Cereals and plant foods: a re-assessment of the Saxon economic, in *Environment and Economy in Anglo-Saxon England*, (ed. J Rackham), CBA Res Rep **89**, York, 83-8

Green, F J, 1996 Mesolithic or later houses at Bowmans Farm, Romsey Extra, Hampshire, England?, in *Neolithic houses in Northwest Europe and beyond* (eds T Darvill and J Thomas), Neolithic Studies Group Monograph **1**, Oxbow Books, Oxford, 113-22

Green, H S, 1974 Early Bronze Age territory and population in Milton Keynes, Buckinghamshire, and the Great Ouse Valley, *Archaeol J* **131**, 75-139

Green, H S, 1981 The Dating of Ivinghoe Beacon, *Rec Buckinghamshire* **23**,1-3

Green, M, 1969 *Churches of the Isle of Wight*, Winton Publications Ltd, Winchester

Green, M, 2000 *A Landscape Revealed – 10,000 years on a chalkland farm*, Tempus, Stroud

Green, M, 2005 Medieval tile industry at Penn, *Rec Buckinghamshire* **45**, 115-160

Green, M, Barton, R N E, Debenham, R E and French, C A I, 1998 A new late-glacial open-air site at Deer Park Farm, Wimborne St Giles, *Proc Dorset Natur Hist Archaeol Soc* **120**, 85-8

Green, M J (ed.), 1995 *The Celtic World*, Routledge, London

Griffiths, R, 1979 Rescue excavations of a medieval house at Whaddon, Buckinghamshire, *Rec Buckinghamshire* **21**, 40-76

Grigson, C, 1989 The animal remains, in Stainton 1989, 49-74

Grimes, W F, 1960 *Excavation on defence sites, 1939-1945, 1: mainly Neolithic – Bronze Age*, Ministry of Works Archaeological Report **3**, HMSO, London

Grinsell, L, 1938–40 Hampshire barrows parts 1–3, *Proc Hampshire Fld Club Archaeol Soc* **14(1–3)**, 9–40, 195–230, 346–66

Grinsell, L V and Sherwin, G A, 1940 Isle of Wight barrows, *Proc Isle Wight Natur Hist Antiq Soc* **3**, 1

Gulland, D, 2003 Aston Clinton Manor House: from moated site to classical mansion, *Rec Buckinghamshire* **43**, 195-207

Guttman, E B, 2005 Midden cultivation in prehistoric Britain: arable crops in gardens, *World Archaeol* **37** (2), 224-39

Gwilt, A and Haselgrove, C (eds),1997 *Reconstructing Iron Age societies : new approaches to the British Iron Age*, Oxbow, Oxford

Hadfield, A M, 1970 *The Chartist Land Company*

Hadfield, C, 1970 *The Canals of the East Midlands, including Part of London*, Newton Abbot

Hadley, D, 2001 *Death in Medieval England: an archaeology*, Stroud

Hadley, D, 2006 *The Vikings in England: Settlement, Society and Culture*

Hall, D, 2001 *Turning the Plough. Midland open fields: landscape character and proposals for management*, Northampton

Hall, R A, 1975 An excavation at Hunter Street, Buckingham 1974, *Rec Buckinghamshire* **20**, 100-133

Hallam, H E (ed.), 1988 *The Agrarian History of England and Wales Volume 2. 1042–1350*

Hall-Torrance, M and Weaver, S D G, 2003 The excavation of a Saxon settlement at Riverdene, Basingstoke, Hants, 1995, *Hampshire Studies* **58**, 63-105

Halliwell, G and Parfitt, K, 1993 Non-river gravel Lower and Middle Palaeolithic discoveries in East Kent, *Kent Archaeol Rev* **114**, 80–89

Hambleton, E, 1999 *Animal husbandry regimes in Iron Age Britain: a comparative study of faunal assemblages from Iron Age sites.* BAR (Brit Ser) **282**, Oxford

Hambleton, E, 2008 *Review of Middle Bronze Age-Late Iron Age Faunal Assemblages from Southern Britain*, English Heritage Research Dept. Report **71**, http://

services.english-heritage.org.uk/ResearchReports Pdfs/071_2008WEB.pdf

Hamerow, H, 2012 *Rural settlements and society in Anglo-Saxon England*, Oxford

Hamerow, H, Hayden, C and Hey, G, 2007 Anglo-Saxon and earlier settlement near Drayton Road, Sutton Courtenay, Berkshire, *Archaeol J* **164**, 109-196

Hamilton-Dyer, S, 2000 The Fish Remains, in Fulford and Timby 2000, 482-4

Hamilton-Dyer, S, 2005 Animal bones, in Birbeck 2005, 140-154

Hamlin, A, 1963 Excavations of ring ditches and other sites at Stanton Harcourt, *Oxonienia* **28**, 1-19

Hammon, A, 2008 Animal husbandry: an overview of the evidence from the animal bones, in Cunliffe 2008, 74-100

Hammond, N, 1974 *Rural life in the Vale of White Horse*

Hammond, S, 2011 An Iron Age Iron Smelting Site at Baird Road, Arborfield Garrison, Berkshire, 2002, in *Archaeological Investigations in the Silchester Hinterland, Exploring Landscape use around the Roman Town* (ed. S Preston), TVAS monograph **9**, Reading, 33-42

Hampshire and Wight Trust for Maritime Archaeology, 2005 Archaeological and palaeo-environmental investigations of a Mesolithic site 11.5m below sea level, unpublished report for SCOPAC

Hance, N, 2006 *Harwell: the Enigma Revealed*

Hancock, A, 2010 Excavation of a mid Saxon settlement at Water Eaton, Bletchley, Milton Keynes, *Rec Buckinghamshire* **50**, 5-24

Hands, A R, 1993 *The Romano-British roadside settlement at Wilcote, Oxfordshire I. Excavations 1990-92*, BAR Brit Ser **232**, Oxford

Hands, A R, 1998 *The Romano-British roadside settlement at Wilcote, Oxfordshire II. Excavations 1993-96*, BAR Brit Ser **265**, Oxford

Hands, A R and Cotswold Archaeology, 2004 *The Romano-British roadside settlement at Wilcote, Oxfordshire III. Excavations 1997-2000*, BAR Brit Ser **370**, Oxford

Hanley, H, 1976 The Friarage, Rickfords Hill, Aylesbury, *Aylesbury Society Newsletter* **7**, 5-6

Harden, D B, and Treweeks, R C, 1945 Excavations at Stanton Harcourt, Oxon, 1940, II, *Oxoniensia* **10**, 16-41

Harding, D W (ed), 1976a *Hillforts: Later Prehistoric Earthworks in Britain and Ireland*, Academic Press, London

Harding, D W, 1976b Blewburton Hill, Berkshire: Re-excavation and Reappraisal, in Harding, D, (ed.) 1976, 133-46

Harding, D W, 1987 *Excavations in Oxfordshire, 1964-66*, University of Edinburgh Department of Archaeology Occasional Papers **15**, Edinburgh

Harding, J, 2003 *Henge monuments of the British Isles*, Stroud

Harding, P A, 1998 An interim report of an archaeological watching brief on Palaeolithic deposits at Dunbridge, Hants, in *Stone Age Archaeology: Essays in Honour of John Wymer*, (eds N Ashton, F Healy and P Pettitt), Oxford, Oxbow Books, 72-76

Harding, P A and Andrews, P, 2002 Anglo-Saxon and medieval settlement at Chapel Street, Bicester: excavations 1999-2000, *Oxoniensia* **67**, 141-79

Harding, P and Newman, R, 1990 The excavation of a turf-sided lock at Monkey Marsh, Unpublished client report

Harding, P A and Richards, J C, 1982 Sample excavation of a Mesolithic flint scatter at Whistley Court Farm, Unpubl Wessex Archaeology client report

Hardy, A, 1996 Archaeological excavations at 54-55 St. Thomas's Street, Oxford, *Oxoniensia* **61**, 225-273

Hardy, A, Dodd, A and Keevill, G D, 2003 *Aelfric's abbey: excavations at Eynsham Abbey, Oxfordshire, 1989-1992*, Oxford Archaeology Thames Valley Landscapes Monograph **16**, Oxford

Hare, J, 1988 Bishop's Waltham Palace, *Archaeol J* **145**, 222-54

Hare, J, 1999 *The Dissolution of the Monasteries in Hampshire*, Hampshire Papers **16**

Harrison, D, 2004 *The Bridges of Medieval England. Transport and Society 400-1800*, Oxford

Harrison, S, 2003 The Icknield Way: some queries, *Archaeol J* **160**, 1-22

Harvey, I M W, 1997 Bernwood in the middle ages, in *Bernwood. The Life and Afterlife of a Forest* (eds J Broad and R Hoyle), 1-18, Preston

Harvey, P D A, 1985 Mapping the Village : the Historical Evidence, in *Medieval Villages* (ed. D Hooke), Oxford, 33-45

Hase, P H, 1988 The Mother Churches of Hampshire, in *Minsters and Parish Churches: The Local Church in Transition, 950-1200* (ed. J Blair), Oxford University Committee for Archaeology, Monograph **17**, 45-46

Hase, P H, 1994 The Church in the Wessex Heartlands, in *The Medieval Landscape of Wessex* (eds M Aston and C Lewis), Oxbow Monograph **46**, Oxford, 47-81

Haselgrove, C, 1989 The Later Iron Age in southern Britain and beyond, in Todd, M, *Research on Roman Britain, 1960-89*, Society for the Promotion of Roman Studies, 1-19

Haselgrove, C (ed), 2000, *Understanding the British Iron Age: An agenda for action* http://www.personal.rdg.ac.uk/~lascretn/IAAgenda.htm

Haselgrove, C and Moore, T (eds), 2007 *The Later Iron Age in Britain and Beyond*, Oxbow, Oxford

Haselgrove, C and Pope, R (eds), 2007 *The Earlier Iron Age in Britain and the Near Continent*, Oxbow, Oxford

Hassall, T G, 1986 Archaeology of Oxford City, in Briggs *et al.* 1986, 115–34

Hassall, T G, Halpin, C E and Mellor, M, 1989 Excavations in St. Ebbes, Oxford, 1967–76, *Oxoniensia* **54**, 71–279

Hawkes, C F C, 1925 Old roads in Central Hants, *Proc Hampshire Fld Club Archaeol Soc*, **9**, 324-333

Hawkes, C F C, 1927 Excavations at Alchester 1926, *Antiq J* **7**, 155-184

Hawkes, J W and Heaton, M J, 1993 *Jennings Yard, Windsor: a closed-shaft garderobe and associated medieval structures*, Wessex Archaeology Report **3**

Hawkes, S C, 1986 The early Saxon period, in Briggs *et al.* (eds) 1986, 64-108

Hawkes, S C and Dunning, G C, 1961 Soldiers and settlers in Britain, fourth to fifth century, *Medieval Archaeol* **5**, 1-70

Hawkes, S C with Grainger, G, 2003 *The Anglo-Saxon Cemetery at Worthy Park, Kingsworthy, near Winchester, Hampshire*, Oxford, Oxford University School of Archaeology

Hayward, K M J, 2009 *Roman Quarrying and Stone Supply on the Periphery – Southern England*, BAR Brit Ser **500**, Oxford

Hayward, K M, 2011 The Worked Stone, in Fulford and Clarke 2011, 204-19

Healy, F, Heaton, M and Lobb, S J, 1992 Excavations at a Mesolithic site at Thatcham, Berkshire, *Proc Prehist Soc* **58**, 41-76

Hearne, C M, 2000 Archaeological evaluation in the Vale of the White Horse, near Abingdon, 1992–99, *Oxoniensia* **65**, 7–12

Henig, M, 1993 *Roman sculpture from the Cotswold Region with Devon and Cornwall*, Corpus Signorum Imperii Romani, Great Britain, Vol **1**, Fascicule 7, Oxford

Henig, M and Booth, P, 2000 *Roman Oxfordshire*, Sutton, Stroud

Hepple, L W and Doggett, A M, 1992 *The Chilterns*, Phillimore, Chichester

Hepple, L W and Doggett, A M, 1994 *The Chilterns*, Phillimore, Chichester (2nd edn)

Hesse, R, 2011 Reconsidering animal husbandry and diet in the northwest provinces, *J Roman Archaeol* **24**, 215-48

Hewitson, C, Nichol, K, Litherland, S and Rátkai, S, forthcoming *Excavations in Banbury Castle and Town*, (BAR Brit Ser)

Hey, G, 1995 Iron Age and Roman settlement at Old Shifford Farm, *Oxoniensia* **60**, 93-176

Hey, G, 2004 *Yarnton: Saxon and medieval settlement and landscape Results of excavations 1990-96* Oxford Archaeology Thames Valley Landscapes Monograph **20**, Oxford

Hey, G, and Barclay, A, 2007 The Thames Valley in the late 5th and early 4th millennium cal BC: the appearance of domestication and the evidence for change, in *Going over: the Mesolithic-Neolithic transition in North-West Europe* (eds A Whittle and V Cummings), Proc British Academy **144**, London, 399-422

Hey, G and Lacey, M, 2001 *Evaluation of archaeological decision-making processes and sampling strategies*, Oxford Archaeological Unit monograph

Hey, G, with Robinson, M, 2011 Mesolithic communities in the Thames Valley: living in the natural landscape, in G Hey, P Garwood, M Robinson, A Barclay, and P Bradley (eds) 2011, 193-220

Hey, G, Bayliss, A, and Boyle, A, 1999 Iron Age

inhumation burials at Yarnton, Oxfordshire, *Antiquity* **73**, 551-62

Hey, G, Dennis, C, and Mayes, A, 2007 Archaeological investigations on Whiteleaf Hill, Princes Risborough, Buckinghamshire, 2002-5, *Rec Buckinghamshire* **47** (2), 1-80

Hey, G, Booth, P and Timby, J, 2011a *Yarnton: Iron Age and Romano-British settlement and landscape: results of excavations 1990-98*, Oxford Archaeology Thames Valley Landscapes Monograph **35**, Oxford

Hey, G, Garwood, P, Robinson, M, Barclay, A and Bradley, P, 2011b Part 2 Mesolithic to early Bronze Age, in A Morigi, D Schreve, M White, G Hey, P Garwood, M Robinson, A Barclay and P Bradley, *Thames through Time. The archaeology of the gravel terraces of the Upper and Middle Thames: Early Prehistory to 1500 BC*, Oxford Archaeology Thames Valley Landscapes Monograph **32**, 151-463

Hey, G, Dennis, C and Bell, C, in prep. *Yarnton: Neolithic and Bronze Age settlement and landscape*, Thames Valley Landscapes Monograph, OA Oxford

Higgott, T, 2001 *The Story of Newbury*

Highfield, J R L, 1986 The Early Colleges, in *History of the University of Oxford, 1: The Early Oxford Schools*, (ed. J L Catto), 236

Hill, J D, 1995 *Ritual and Rubbish in the Iron Age of Wessex: a study on the formation of a specific archaeological record*, BAR Brit Ser **242**, Oxford

Hill, J D, 1996 Hillforts and the Iron Age of Wessex, in Champion and Collis 1996, 95-116

Hill, J D, 2007 The dynamics of social change in later Iron Age eastern and south-eastern England *c*. 300 BC-AD 43, in Haselgrove and Moore 2007, 16-40

Hiller, J, 2000 Oxford, The Kitchen Project, Lincoln College, *CBA South Midlands Archaeol* **30**, 64–7

Hills, C M and O'Connell, T C, 2009 New light on the Anglo-Saxon succession: two cemeteries and their dates, *Antiquity* **83**, 1-13

Hindle, P, 2002 *Medieval Roads and Tracks*, Princes Risborough

Hindmarch, E, 2002 Church Hill, Buckingham, Buckinghamshire. An archaeological evaluation for Buckingham Town Council, unpubl. report

Hines, J (ed.), forthcoming *Anglo-Saxon England c. 570-720: The Chronological Basis*, London, Society for Medieval Archaeology Monograph Series

Hinchcliffe, T, 1992 *North Oxford*, Newhaven and London

Hingley, R, 1984a The Archaeology of settlement and the social significance of space, *Scottish Archaeological Review* **3**, 22-7

Hingley, R, 1984b Towards Social Analysis in Archaeology: Celtic Society in the Iron Age of the Upper Thames Valley (400-0BC), in *Aspects of the Iron Age in Central Southern Britain* (eds B Cunliffe and D Miles), Oxford University: Committee for Archaeology Monograph **2**, 72-88

Hingley, R, 1999 The creation of later prehistoric landscapes and the context of the reuse of Neolithic and earlier Bronze Age monuments in Britain and Ireland, in *Northern Exposure: Interpretative Devolution and the Iron Age in Britain,* (ed. B Bevan), Leicester Archaeology Monograph **4**, Leicester, 233–51

Hingley, R, 2006 Defining Community: iron, boundaries and transformation in later prehistoric Britain, in Harding, A, Sievers, S & Venclova, N, *Enclosing the Past*, Sheffield Academic Monograph **15**, 116-25

Hinton, D A, 1968 Bicester Priory, *Oxoniensia* **33**, 22-52

Hinton, D A, 1969 Excavations at Bicester Priory, *Oxoniensia* **34**, 21-28

Hinton, D A, 1983, The Anglo-Saxon church at Yateley, *ProcHampshire Fld Club Archaeol Soc* **39**, 111-20

Hinton, D A, 1996 *The Gold, Silver and other non-Ferrous alloy objects from Hamwic*, Southampton Finds Vol **2**, Stroud

Hinton, D A, 1997 Reviews, *Medieval Archaeology* **41**, 332-4

Hinton, D A, 2005 *Gold and Gilt, Pots and Pins. Possessions and People in medieval Britain*, Oxford, Oxford University Press

Hinton, D, 2008 Anglo-Saxon Hampshire, at http://thehumanjourney.net/pdf_store/sthames/phase3/County/Early%20Medieval/Early%20Medieval%20Hampshire.pdf

Hinton, D A and Hughes, M (eds), 1996 *Archaeology in Hampshire: A framework for the Future*, Hampshire County Council

Hirst, S and Rahtz, P, 1996 Liddington Castle and the battle of Badon: excavations and research 1976, *Arch J* **153**, 1-59

Hockey, S F, 1970 *Quarr Abbey and its Lands*, Leicester University Press

Hockey, S F (ed.) 1981 *The Cartulary of Carisbrooke Priory*, Isle of Wight Record Office, Newport

Hockey, S F, 1982 *Insula Vecta: The Isle of Wight in the Middle Ages,* London, Phillimore & Co. Ltd

Hockey, S F, 1991 *The Charters of Quarr Abbey,* Isle of Wight County Record Office, Newport

Hogg, A H A, 1979 *British Hill-Forts. An Index*, BAR Brit Ser **62**

Hogg, A H A and Stevens, C E, 1937 The defences of Roman Dorchester, *Oxoniensia* **2**, 41-73

Hohler, C, 1941 Medieval paving tiles in Buckinghamshire, *Rec Buckinghamshire* **14**, 1-49

Holden, B, 1985 The Deserted Medieval Village of Thomley, Oxfordshire, *Oxoniensia* **50**, 215–37

Holgate, R, 1988a *Neolithic settlement of the Thames Basin*, BAR Brit Ser **194**, Oxford

Holgate, R, 1988b The flints, in Lambrick, G, *The Rollright Stones: megaliths, monuments and settlement in the prehistoric landscape*, English Heritage, London, 85-90

Holgate, R, 2004 Flintwork, in Lambrick and Allen 2004, 93-9

Holmes, J, and Rielly, K, 1994 Animal Bone from the 'Mausoleum' Site, in Williams and Zeepvat 1994, 515-536

Holmes M, 2000 Wing, *CBA South Midlands Archaeol* **30**, 21

Holmes, M, 2005 Excavation of a Late Saxon – Medieval Cemetery at the site of the former Victorian School, Wing, Buckinghamshire May – June 1999, unpublished report

Holmes, M and Chapman, A (eds), 2008 A middle-late Saxon and medieval cemetery at Wing Church, Bucks, *Rec Buckinghamshire* **48**, 61-123

Holyoak, D T, 1980 Late Pleistocene sediments and biostratigraphy of the Kennet Valley, England, unpublished PhD thesis, University of Reading

Holyoak, D T, 1983 A late Pleistocene interglacial flora and molluscan fauna from Thatcham, Berkshire, with notes on mollusca from the interglacial deposits at Aveley, Essex, *Geological Magazine* **120** (6), 623-9

Hood, S and Walton, H, 1948 A Romano-British Cremating Place and Burial Ground on Roden Downs, Compton, Berkshire, *Trans Newbury Dist Fld Club* **9**(1), 1-62

Hooke, D, 1987 Anglo-Saxon estates in the Vale of the White Horse, *Oxoniensia* **52**, 129-43

Hooke, D, 1988 Regional Variation in Southern and Central England in the Anglo-Saxon Period and its Relationship to Land Units and Settlement, in *Anglo-Saxon Settlements*, (ed. D Hooke), Oxford, 123-151

Hosfield, R T, 1999 *The Palaeolithic of the Hampshire Basin: a regional model of hominid behaviour during the Middle Pleistocene*, BAR Brit Ser **286**, Oxford

Hosfield, R T and Chambers, J C, 2002 Processes and Experiences – Experimental Archaeology on a River Floodplain, in *River Systems and Environmental Change in Wales*: *Field Guide*, (eds M G Macklin, P A Brewer and T J Coulthard), British Geomorphological Research Group, Aberystwyth, 32–39

Hoskins, W G, 1955 *The Making of the English Landscape*, Hodder and Stoughton, London

Hughes, M, 1976 *The Small Towns of Hampshire*, Southampton

Hughes, M W (ed.), 1942 *A Calendar of the Feet of Fines for Buckinghamshire, 7 Richard I to 44 Henry III*, Bedford

Hull, B, 2008 Social differentiation and diet in early Anglo-Saxon England: stable isotope analysis of archaeological human and animal remains, Unpublished D.Phil thesis, University of Oxford

Humphrey, R, 2004 The Oxford Road Watermill, Aylesbury, *Rec Buckinghamshire* **44**, 67-103

Hunn A, Lawson J and Farley M, 1994 The Anglo-Saxon cemetery at Dinton, Buckinghamshire, *Anglo-Saxon Studies in Archaeology and History* **7**, 85-148

Hunn, A, Lawson, J, and Parkhouse, J, 1997 Investigations at Magiovinium 1990-91: the Little Brickhill and Fenny Stratford by-passes, *Rec Buckinghamshire* **37**, 3-66

Hunter, J R and Heyworth, M P, 1998 *The Hamwic Glass*, CBA Res Rep **116**, York

Hunter, K L, 2005 Charred plant remains, in Birbeck 2005, 163-173

Hutchinson, G E and Hutchinson, A L, 1969 The "idol" or sheela-na-gig at Binstead, *Proc Isle Wight Nat Hist Archaeol Soc* **6**, Part IV, 237-251

Iliffe, J H, 1929 Excavations at Alchester 1927 *Antiq J* **9**, 105-36

Iliffe, J H, 1932 Excavations at Alchester 1928 *Antiq J* **12**, 35-67

Ingrem, C, 2006 The Animal Bone, in Fulford *et al.* 2006, 167-88

Ingrem, C, 2011 The Animal Bone, in Fulford and Clarke 2011, 244-70

Ingrem, C, 2012 Animals in the economy and culture of Roman Britain: a case study from southern England, in Fulford 2012a, 184-212

Insole, A and Parker, A G (eds) 1979 Industrial Archaeology in the Isle of Wight, IoWCC Isle of Wight Medieval Landscape Project http://www.arch.soton.ac.uk/Research

Ivens, R J, 1981 Medieval pottery kilns at Brill, Buckinghamshire: preliminary report on excavations in 1978, *Rec Buckinghamshire* **23**, 102-106

Ivens, R J, 1982 Medieval Pottery from the 1978 excavations at Temple Farm, Brill, *Rec Buckinghamshire* **24**, 144-169

Ivens, R, 1984 Deddington Castle Oxfordshire and the English Honour of Bayeux, *Oxoniensia* **49**, 101-19

Ivens, R, 2004 Bradwell, Bradwell Abbey, *CBA South Midlands Archaeol* **34**, 28-30

Ivens R, Busby P and Shepherd N, 1995 *Tattenhoe and Westbury: two deserted Medieval settlements in Milton Keynes*, Buckinghamshire Archaeol Soc Monograph **8**

IWCAHES, 2000 Isle of Wight coastal audit: report prepared for English Heritage by the Isle of Wight County Archaeology and Historic Environment Service, second draft

Jacobi, R, 1978 The Mesolithic of Sussex, in *The archaeology of Sussex to AD 1500* (ed. P Drewett), CBA Res Rep **29**, London, 15–22

Jacobi, R, 1981 The last hunters in Hampshire, in *The archaeology of Hampshire* (eds S J Shennan and R T Schadla Hall), Hampshire Fld Club Archaeol Soc Monograph **1**, Winchester, 10–25

Jacobi, R M, 1999 Some observations on the British Upper Palaeolithic, in *Dorothy Garrod and the progress of the Palaeolithic*, (eds W Davies and R Charles), Oxbow Books, Oxford, 35–40

James, T B, 1997 *Winchester*, English Heritage/Batsford

Jarvis, K S, 1983 *Excavations in Christchurch 1969-1980*, Dorset Nat Hist and Archaeol Soc Monograph **5**

Jenkins, J G, 1934 An early coroner's roll for Buckinghamshire, *Rec Buckinghamshire* **13**, 163-185

John Moore Heritage Services, 2002 An archaeological investigation at Town Farm Barns, Market Square, Princes Risborough, Buckinghamshire, unpubl. report

Johnson, A E, 1975 Excavations at Bourton Grounds, Thornborough 1972-3, *Rec Buckinghamshire* **20**, 3-56

Johnson, S, 1979 *The Roman Forts of the Saxon Shore* (2nd ed.) London, Paul Elek

Johnston, D E 1998 A Roman and Anglo-Saxon site at Northbrook, Micheldever, Hampshire, *Proc Hampshire Fld Club Archaeol Soc* **53**, 79-108

Jones, G E M, 1989 The charred plant remains, 124-8 and mf M1 83-96, in Astill, G G & Lobb, S J, Excavation of Prehistoric, Roman, and Saxon deposits at Wraysbury, Berkshire, *Archaeol J* **146**, 68-134

Jones, G, 2000 Evaluating the importance of cultivation and collecting in Neolithic Britain, in *Plants in Neolithic Britain and beyond*, (ed. A S Fairbairn), Neolithic Studies Group Seminar Papers **5**, Oxford, Oxbow Books, 79-84

Jones, J D, 1978 The Isle of Wight 1558-1642, unpublished PhD thesis, Southampton University

Jones J, and Jones J, 1987 *The Isle of Wight: An illustrated History*, Wimborne, The Dovecote Press

Jones, K, 1974 The Wotton Tramway (Brill Branch), *Locomotion Papers* **75** (Oakwood)

Jones, M J, 1989 Thirteenth century gardens in Carisbrooke Castle, *Proc Isle Wight Nat Hist Archaeol Soc* **9**, 135-136

Jones, M J, 1991 A survey of the manors of Swainston and Brighstone, 1630, Part 1 *Proc Isle Wight Nat Hist Archaeol Soc* **11**, 61-84

Jones, M J, 2003 The 1630 survey of Swainston – farm Buildings and farm lands, Part 2 *Proc Isle Wight Nat Hist Archaeol Soc* **19**, 69-100

Jones, M K, 1984 Regional Patterns in Crop Production, in *Aspects of the Iron Age in Central Southern Britain*, (eds B Cunliffe and D Miles), Oxford University Committee for Archaeology Monograph **22**, 120-125

Jones, M K, 1985 Archaeobotany beyond subsistence reconstruction, in *Beyond Domestication in Prehistoric Europe: Investigations on Subsistence Archaeology and Social Complexity*, (eds G Barker and C Gamble), London, 107-28

Jones, R, 2004 Signals in the Soil: the Use of Pottery in Manure Scatters in the Identification of Medieval Arable Farming Regimes, *Archaeol J* **161**, 159-88

Jones, R and Page, M, 2006 *Medieval Villages in an English Landscape: Beginnings and Ends*, Macclesfield

Jones, R L C, 2003 Whittlewood Project: Fieldwalking 2002 – The Pottery Part 1, unpublished report

Jope, E M, 1954 Medieval pottery kilns at Brill, Buckinghamshire: preliminary report on excavations in 1953, *Rec Buckinghamshire* **16**, 39-42

Jope, E M, 1956 Saxon Oxford and its region, in *Dark Age Britain: studies presented to E T Leeds*, (ed. D B Harden), London, 234-58

Jope, E M, 1958 The Clarendon Hotel, Oxford, Part I: the site, *Oxoniensia* **23**, 1-83

Jope, E M, and Ivens, R J, 1981 Some early products of the Brill pottery, Buckinghamshire, *Rec Buckinghamshire* **23**, 32-38

Jope, E M and Threlfall, R I, 1959 The twelfth-century castle at Ascott Doilly, Oxfordshire, *Antiq J* **39**, 219-73

Kamash, Z, Gosden, C and Lock, G, 2010 Continuity and Religious Practice in Roman Britain: The Case of the Rural Religious Complex at Marcham/ Frilford, Oxfordshire, *Britannia* **41**, 95-125

Keen, L, 1989 Coastal salt production in Norman England, *Anglo-Norman Studies*, **11**, 133-79

Keen, L, 2002 Windsor Castle and the Penn Tile Industry, in *Windsor. Medieval Archaeology, Art and Architecture of the Thames Valley* (eds L Keen and E Scarff), Brit Archaeol Assoc Conf Trans **XXV**, 219-37

Keene, D, 1995 Small towns and the Metropolis: the experience of medieval England, in *Peasants and Townsmen in Medieval Europe* (eds J-M Duvosquel and E Thoen), Ghent

Keene, D J, 1985 *Survey of Medieval Winchester*, Winchester Studies 2, Oxford

Keene, D J, (forthcoming) Old Windsor, in The British Historic Towns Atlas, volume **V**, Windsor and Eton

Keevill, G D, 1992 An Anglo-Saxon site at Audlett Drive, Abingdon, Oxfordshire, *Oxoniensia* **52**, 55-79

Keevill, G D and Campbell, G E, 1991 Investigations at Danesfield Camp, Medmenham, Buckinghamshire, *Rec Buckinghamshire* **33**, 87-99

Keith-Lucas, M, 2000 Pollen analysis of sediments from Moor Farm, Staines Moor, Surrey, *Surrey Archaeol Collect* **87**, 85-93

Keith-Lucas, D M, 2002 Pollen Analysis, in Ford, S, *Charnham Lane, Hungerford. Archaeological investigations 1988-1997*, TVAS Monograph **1**, Reading

Kelly, S, 2000 *Charters of Abingdon Abbey: Part 1*, Anglo-Saxon Charters, VII, Oxford

Kemp, B R, 1968 The Mother Church of Thatcham, *Berkshire Archaeol J* **63**, 15-22

Kenward, R, 1982 A Neolithic burial enclosure at New Wintles Farm, Eynsham, in Case and Whittle 1982, 51-4

Kidd, A M, 2004 Hillforts and Churches: a coincidence of locations?, *Rec Buckinghamshire* **44**, 105-9

Kidd, A, 2005 Buckinghamshire Historic Towns, Draft Project Design V2, unpubl. report

Kidd, A, 2006 The Cistercian grange at Grange Farm, Shipton Lee, Quainton, *Rec Buckinghamshire* **46**, 149-56

Kidd, A M, 2007 Buckinghamshire Later Bronze Age and Iron Age Historic Environment Resource Assessment (2nd draft) Solent-Thames Archaeological Research Framework, http://www.buckscc.gov.uk/bcc/get/assets/docs/Bucks_Iron_Age.pdf

Kimble G D, 1933 Cholesbury Camp, *J Brit Arch Assn* **39(1)**, 187-212

King, A C and Soffe, G, 1994 The Iron Age and Roman temple on Hayling Island, in *The Iron Age in Wessex: recent work*, (eds A P Fitzpatrick and E L Morris), Salisbury: Trust for Wessex Archaeology, 114-16

King, A C and Soffe, G, 1998 Internal Organisation and Deposition at the Iron Age Temple on Hayling Island, *Proc Hampshire Fld Club Archaeol Soc* **53**, 35-48

King, C, 2000 Bourne House Stables, Oxford Road, Lambourn, Foundation Archaeology Report 112

King, C C, 1887 *A History of Berkshire*, Elliot Stock, London

King, D C, 1983 *Castellarium Anglicanum*

King, J E, 1962 Report on animal bones, in Wymer 1962, 355-60

Kjølbe-Biddle, B, 1992 Dispersal or Concentration: the disposal of the Winchester dead over 2000 years, in *Death in Towns: urban responses to the dying and the dead 100-1600* (ed. S Bassett), Leicester, 210-47

Knight, D, 1984 *Late Bronze Age and Iron Age settlement in the Nene and Great Ouse basins*, BAR Brit Ser **130**, Oxford

Knight, D, 2002 A Regional Ceramic Sequence: Pottery of the First Millennium BC between the Humber and the Nene in *Prehistoric Britain: the Ceramic Basis,* (eds J D Hill and A E Woodward), Oxbow Monograph, Oxford

Knocker, G M, 1956 Early burials and an Anglo-Saxon cemetery at Snell's Corner near Horndean, Hampshire, *Proc Hampshire Fld Club Archaeol Soc* **19ii**, 117-70

Knocker, G, 1963 Excavation of a Round Barrow, in Rag Copse, near Hurstbourne Tarrant, Hampshire, *Proc Hampshire Fld Club Archaeol Soc* **22(3)**, 125-50

Knowles, D and Hadcock, R N, 1953 *Medieval religious houses England and Wales*, 2 edn, London

Kökeritz, H, 1940 *The Place-Names of the Isle of Wight*, Uppsala

Kukla, G J, 1975 Loess stratigraphy of Central Europe, in *After the Australopithecines: Stratigraphy, Ecology and Culture Change in the Middle Pleistocene*, (eds K W Butzer and G L Isaac), Mouton, The Hague, 99–188

Lacaille, A D, 1963 Mesolithic industries beside Colne Waters in Iver and Denham, Buckinghamshire, *Rec Buckinghamshire* **17** (3), 143-181

Lack, W, Stuchfield, H M and Whittemore, P, 1994 *The Monumental Brasses of Buckinghamshire*, London

Laidlaw, E F, 1990 *The Story of the Royal Naval Hospital Ventnor*, Crossprint, Newport

Lakin, D, 2006 The former Sanderson site, Oxford Road, Denham, Buckinghamshire: an archaeological post-excavation assessment and updated project design, Site Code BM-SSU02, Museum of London Archaeology Service, London

Lamb, H H, 1981, *Climate from 1000 BC to 1000 AD* in *The Environment of Man: the Iron Age to the Anglo-Saxon Period*, (eds M Jones and G Dimbleby), BAR Brit Ser **87**, Oxford, 53-65

Lambrick, G H, 1978 Iron Age Settlements in the Upper Thames Valley, in Cunliffe and Rowley 1978, 103-19

Lambrick, G H, 1984 Pitfalls and possibilities in Iron Age pottery studies: experiences in the Upper Thames Valley, in Cunliffe and Miles 1984, 162-77

Lambrick, G H (ed.), 1985a *Archaeology and Nature Conservation*, Oxford University Department for External Studies, Oxford

Lambrick, G, 1985b Further Excavations on the Second Site of the Dominican Priory, Oxford, *Oxoniensia* **50**, 131–209

Lambrick, G H, 1988 *The Rollright Stones: megaliths, monuments and settlement in the prehistoric landscape*, English Heritage Archaeological Report **6**, London

Lambrick, G H, 1992a The development of late prehistoric and Roman farming on the Thames gravels, in Fulford and Nichols 1992, 78-105

Lambrick, G H, 1992b Alluvial archaeology of the Holocene in the Upper Thames Basin 1971-1991: a review, in *Alluvial Archaeology in Britain* (eds S Needham and M G Macklin), Oxbow Monograph **27**, Oxford, 209-226

Lambrick, G, 2010 *Neolithic to Saxon social and environmental change at Mount Farm, Berinsfield, Dorchester on Thames*, Oxford Archaeology Occasional Paper **19**, Oxford

Lambrick, G H, 2013 Prehistoric Oxford, *Oxoniensia* **78**, 1-48

Lambrick, G H and Allen, T G, 2004 *Gravelly Guy, Stanton Harcourt, Oxfordshire: the Development of a Prehistoric and Romano-British Community*, Oxford Archaeology Thames Valley Landscapes Monograph **21**, Oxford

Lambrick, G H and Bramhill, P, 1999 *Hampshire historic landscape assessment, final report*, Hampshire County Council and English Heritage, Winchester

Lambrick, G H and McDonald, A, 1985 The archaeology and ecology of Port Meadow and Wolvercote Common, Oxford, in Lambrick 1985, 95-109

Lambrick, G H and Robinson, M A, 1979 *Iron Age and Roman riverside settlements at Farmoor, Oxfordshire*, CBA Res Rep **32**, Oxford Archaeological Unit Report **2**, London

Lambrick, G, (with Robinson, M and contributions by Allen, T), 2009 *The Thames through time; the archaeology of the gravel terraces of the Upper and Middle Thames. Volume 2: The Thames Valley in late prehistory: 1500 BC-AD 50*, Oxford Archaeology Thames Valley Landscapes Monograph **29**, Oxford

Lamdin-Whymark, H, 2008 *The residue of ritualised action: Neolithic depositional practices in the Middle Thames Valley*, BAR Brit Ser **466**, Oxford

Lane-Fox, A, 1870 On the threatened destruction of the British earthworks near Dorchester, *Jn Ethnological Soc London* **2**

Lang, A T O, 2009 *The Iron Age Archaeology of the Upper Thames and North Oxfordshire Region, with Especial Reference to the Eastern Cotswolds* DPhil thesis, University of Oxford http://ora.ox.ac.uk/objects/uuid%3A6e97faa5-a3de-4ea0-a5e4-c59b c2d7a650

Larsson, L, 1991 The late Palaeolithic in Southern Sweden: investigations in a marginal area, in *The Late Glacial in North-West Europe*, (eds N Barton, A J Roberrts and D J Roe), CBA Res Rep 77, York, chapter 12

Law, B R, 1998 *Building Oxford's heritage*, Oxford

Laws, G, 2002 Stratford House, Buckingham, Buckinghamshire. Archaeological evaluation, unpubl. Report

Lawson, A J, 1999 The Bronze Age hoards of Hampshire, in *Experiment and Design; archaeological studies in honour of John Coles*, (ed. AF Harding), Oxford, Oxbow books, 94-107

Lawson, A J, 2000 *Potterne 1982-5: animal husbandry in later prehistoric Wiltshire*, Wessex Archaeology Report **17**, Salisbury

Le Patourel, H E J, and Roberts, B K, 1978 The significance of moated sites, in *Medieval moated sites* (ed. F A Aberg), CBA Res Rep **17**, 46-55, London

Leeds, E T, 1923 A Saxon village near Sutton Courtenay, Berkshire, *Archaeologia* **73**, 147-92

Leeds, E T, 1927a A Neolithic site at Abingdon, Berks., *Antiq J* **7**, 438-64

Leeds, E T, 1927b A Saxon village at Sutton Courtenay, Berkshire, second report, *Archaeologia* **76**, 59-80

Leeds, E T, 1928 A Neolithic site at Abingdon, Berks. (second report), *Antiq J* **8**, 461-77

Leeds, E T, 1936 Round barrows and ring-ditches in Berkshire and Oxfordshire, *Oxoniensia* **1**, 7-23

Leeds, E T, 1947 A Saxon village at Sutton Courtenay, Berkshire, third report, *Archaeologia* **92**, 79-93

Leeds, E T and Harden, D B, 1936 *The Anglo-Saxon cemetery at Abingdon, Berkshire*, Oxford

Lobb, S J and Rose, P G, 1996 *Archaeological Survey of the Lower Kennet Valley, Berkshire*, Wessex Archaeology Report **9**, Salisbury

Leland, J (ed. Toulmin Smith, L), 1964 *The Itinerary 1535-1543 1*

Letters, S, *et al.*, 2003 *Gazetteer of Markets and Fairs in England and Wales to 1516* (List & Index Soc. Vol. 32 & 33). Available: http://www.history.ac.uk/cmh/gaz/gazweb2.html Accessed: 20 July 2006

Lewis, C, Mitchell-Fox, P and Dyer, C, 1997 *Village, Hamlet and Field. Changing Medieval Settlements in Central England*, 2 edn, Macclesfield

Lewis, J, 1991 A Late Glacial and early post-glacial site at Three Ways Wharf, Uxbridge, England: interim report, in Barton *et al.* 1991, 246-255

Lewis, J S C, Wiltshire, P, and Macphail, R I, 1992 A late Devensian/ early Flandrian site at Three Ways Wharf, Uxbridge: environmental implications, in *Alluvial archaeology in Britain*, (eds S Needham and M G Macklin) Oxbow Monograph **27**, Oxford, 235-247

Lewis, J, Leivers, M, Brown, L, Smith, A, Cramp, K, Mepham, L and Phillpotts, C, 2010 *Landscape Evolution in the Middle Thames Valley. Heathrow*

Terminal 5 Excavations Volume 2, Framework Archaeology Monograph **3**, Oxford and Salisbury

Lewis, J S C with Rackham, J, 2011 *Three Ways Wharf, Uxbridge: a Lateglacial and Early Holocene hunter-gatherer site in the Colne Valley*, Museum of London Archaeology Monograph Series **51**

Leyland, N and Troughton, J E, 1974 *Glovemaking in West Oxfordshire*, Woodstock

Lilley, K D, 1999 *Norman Towns in Southern England: Urban Morphogenesis in Hampshire and the Isle of Wight 1066-1215*; Urban Morphology Research Monograph **5** (University of Birmingham, School of Geography and Environmental Sciences),

Limbrey, S and Robinson, S, 1988 Dry Land to Wet Land: Soil Resources in the Upper Thames Valley, in *The Exploitation of Wetlands,* (eds P Murphy, P and C French), BAR (Brit Ser) **186**, Oxford, 129-44

Lingham, B F, 2005 *The long years of obscurity : a history of Didcot. Vol.1, to 1841*

Lipscomb, G, 1847 *The History and Antiquities of Buckinghamshire Vols 1-4*, London

Litherland, S and Nichol, K, 1999 Banbury Town Centre, *CBA South Midlands Archaeol* **29**, 40–42

Little, A G, 1942 The Grey Friars of Aylesbury, *Rec Buckinghamshire* **14**, 77-98

Lloyd, D W and Pevsner, N 2006 *The Buildings of England: The Isle of Wight*, Yale University Press, New Haven and London

Loader, R, 2006 *Isle of Wight: Upper Palaeolithic and Mesolithic resource assessment*, www:thehuman-journey.net/pdf_store/sthames/phase3/County

Loader, R Westmore, I, and Tomalin, D, 1997 *Time and Tide: An Archaeological Survey of the Wootton-Quarr Coast*, Isle of Wight Council

Lobb, S J, 1992 Excavation at Shortheath lane, Abbotts Farm Sulhamstead, in Butterworth and Lobb 1992, 73-8

Lobb, S J and Morris, E L, 1991-3 Investigation of Bronze Age and Iron Age features at Riseley Farm Swallowfield, *Berkshire Archaeol J* **74**, 37-68

Lobb, S J and Rose, P G, 1996 *Archaeological survey of the Lower Kennet Valley, Berkshire*, Wessex Archaeology Report **9**, Trust for Wessex Archaeology, Salisbury

Lock, G and Gosden, C, 2004 The Ridgeway and Vale project: excavations at Marcham/Frilford 2003 – interim report, *CBA South Midlands Archaeol* **34**, 84-94

Lock, G, Gosden, C, Griffiths, D and Daly, P, 2003 Hillforts of the Ridgeway project: excavations at Marcham/Frilford 2002, *CBA South Midlands Archaeol* **33**, 84-91

Lock, G, Gosden, C and Daly, P, 2005 *Segsbury Camp: Excavations in 1996 and 1997 at an Iron Age Hillfort on the Oxfordshire Ridgeway*, OUCA Monograph **61**, Oxford

Loggan, D, 1676 *Oxonia Illustrata*, Oxford

Long, A J and Tooley, M J, 1995 Holocene sea-level and crustal movements in Hampshire and Southeast England, United Kingdom, *Journal of Coastal Research*, Special Issue **17**, 299-310

Long, A J, Scaife, R G and Edwards, R G, 2000 Stratigraphic architecture, relative sea level and models of estuarine development in southern England; new data from Southampton Water, in *Coastal and estuarine environments: sedimentology, geomorphology and geoarchaeology,* (eds K Pye and J R L Allen), Geological Society Special Publications Vol **175**, London, 253-279

Longley, D, 1976 *The archaeological implications of gravel extraction in north-west Surrey*, Res Vol Surrey Archaeol Soc **3**, 1-35

Longley, D, 1980 *Runnymede Bridge 1976: Excavations on the Site of a Late Bronze Age Settlement*, Res Vol Surrey Archaeol Soc **6**

Loveday, R, 1999 Dorchester-on-Thames: ritual complex or ritual landscape?, in Barclay and Harding 1999, 49-66

Loveday, R, 2006 *Inscribed across the landscape: the cursus enigma*, Tempus Publishing Ltd, Stroud

Luff, R and Rowley-Conwy, P, 1994 The (dis)integration of environmental archaeology, in *Whither Environmental Archaeology*, (eds R Luff & P Rowly-Conwy), Oxford, Oxbow Monograph **34**, 1-3

Lyne, M A B, 1994 Late Roman Handmade Wares in South-East Britain, Unpubl PhD thesis University of Reading

Lyne, M A B, 2012a The Iron Age and Roman pottery, in Tomalin *et al.* 2012, 311-45

Lyne, M A B, 2012b The Iron Age and Roman coins from Wootton Haven, in Tomalin *et al.* 2012, 417-24

Lyne, M A B, 2012c The Combley Farm Hoard, in Tomalin *et al.* 2012, 424-8

Lyne, M A B, 2012d The Iron Age and Roman coins from Fishbourne Beach, in Tomalin *et al.* 2012,

Lyne, M A B and Jefferies, R S, 1979 *The Alice Holt/Farnham Roman Pottery Industry*, London, CBA Res Rep **30**

Macdonald, A and Gowing, C, 1989 Excavations at The Hamlet in Bedgrove, Aylesbury, 1964-5, *Rec Buckinghamshire* **31**, 120-36

McGregor, R, 1962 A Late Bronze Age Barrow at Berry Wood, Burley, New Forest, *Proc Hampshire Fld Club Archaeol Soc* **22**, 45-50

McInnes, R G, and Jakeways, J, 2001 *Coastal change, climate and instability: final technical report. Volume 2: palaeoenvironmental study areas, Study Area P1*, LIFE Project no **97 ENV/UK/000510**, Isle of Wight Centre for the Coastal Environment, Ventnor

McOmish, D, 1996 East Chisenbury: ritual and rubbish at the late Bronze Age-Iron Age transition, *Antiquity* **70**, 68-76

McOmish, D, Field, D and Brown, G, 2002 *The Field Archaeology of the Salisbury Plain Training Area*, English Heritage, Swindon

Maddicott, J R, 2005 London and Droitwich, *c.* 650-750: trade, industry and the rise of Mercia, *Anglo-Saxon England* **34**, 7-58

Maitland, F W, 1897 *Domesday Book and beyond*, Cambridge

Mallet Morgan, F de, 1959 The excavation of a long barrow at Nutbane, Hants, *Proc Prehist Soc* **25**, 15–51

Maltby M, 1985 Assessing variations in Iron Age and Roman butchery practices: the need for quantification, in *Palaeobiological Investigations: Research Design, Methods and Data Analysis*, (eds N R J Fieller, D D Gilbertson and N G A Ralph), BAR Int Ser **S266**, Oxford, 19-30

Maltby, M, 1989 Urban-rural variations in the butchering of cattle in the Romano-British Hampshire, in *Diet and Crafts in Towns: the evidence of animal remains from the Roman to Post-medieval Periods,* (eds D Serjeantson and T Waldron), Oxford, BAR Brit Ser **199**, 75-106

Maltby M, 2002 Animal bones in archaeology: how archaeozoologists can make a greater contribution to British Iron Age and Romano-British archaeology, in *Bones and the Man: studies in honour of Don Brothwell,* (eds K Dobney & T O'Connor), Oxford, Oxbow Books, 88-94

Maltby, M, 1994 The animal bones from a Romano-British well at Oakridge II, Basingstoke, *Proc Hampshire Fld Club Archaeol Soc* **49**, 47-76

Maltby, M, 2010 *Feeding a Roman Town. Environmental evidence from excavations in Winchester, 1972-1985,* Winchester Museums Service and English Heritage, Winchester

Manning, W H, 1974 Excavations on late Iron Age, Roman, and Saxon Sites at Ufton Nervet, Berkshire, in 1961-63, *Berkshire Archaeol J* **67**, 1-61

Margham, J, 1982 Isle of Wight village morphology Part 1, *Proc Isle Wight Nat Hist Archaeol Soc* **7**, 475-487

Margham, J, 1983 Isle of Wight village morphology Part 2, *Proc Isle Wight Nat Hist Archaeol Soc* **7**, 601-608

Margham, J, 1988 Domesday population of the Isle of Wight, *Proc Isle Wight Nat Hist Archaeol Soc* **8**, 56-60

Margham, J, 1990 Thorley – a parish survey, *Proc Isle Wight Nat Hist Archaeol Soc* **10**, 113-126

Margham, J, 1992a Freshwater – man and the landscape, *Proc Isle Wight Nat Hist Archaeol Soc* **12**, 95-124

Margham, J, 1992b Carisbrooke: a study in settlement morphology, *Southern Hist* **14**, *1-28*

Margham, J, 1997 Saints in an Island landscape: a study in church dedications, *Proc Isle Wight Nat Hist Archaeol Soc* **13**, 91-106

Margham, J, 2000 St Mary's Brading: Wilfred's church, *Proc Isle Wight Nat Hist Archaeol Soc* **16**, 117-136

Margham, J, 2003 Charters, landscapes and hides on the Isle of Wight, *Landscape History* **25**, 17-43

Margham, J, 2005 The Anglo-Saxon charter bounds of the Isle of Wight. Part 1: The West Medine, *Proc Isle Wight Nat Hist Archaeol Soc* **21**, 77-106

Margham, J, forthcoming a The Anglo-Saxon charter bounds of the Isle of Wight. Part 2: The East Medine, *Proc Isle Wight Nat Hist Archaeol Soc* **23**

Margham, J, 2012 The place-names and settlement history of Binstead and Wootton parishes in Tomalin, D J, Loader, R D, and Scaife R G, 2012 *Coastal archaeology in a dynamic environment: a Solent case study,* BAR Brit Ser **568**

Martin, R, n d The Reclamation of Brading Haven, Available: http://www.iwhistory.org.uk

Masefield, R, 2008 *Prehistoric and Later Settlement and landscape from the Chiltern Scarp to Aylesbury Vale; the archaeology of the Aston Clinton bypass, Buckinghamshire,* BAR Brit Ser **473**, Oxford

Massey, R, 2006 Solent-Thames Historic Environment Research Framework Hampshire: The Roman Period 50 BC–AD 410, Second Draft

Mayes, A, Hardy, A and Blair, J 2000 The excavation of early Iron Age and medieval remains on land to the west of Church View, Bampton Oxon., *Oxoniensia* **65**, 267-90

Meaney, A, 1964 *A Gazetteer of Early Anglo-Saxon Burial Sites,* London

Meaney, A and Hawkes, S C, 1970 *Two Anglo-Saxon Cemeteries at Winnall, Winchester, Hampshire,* Soc Med Archaeol Monograph **4**

Mellars, P, 1975 Ungulate populations, economic patterns and the Mesolithic landscape, in *The effects of man on the landscape: the Highland zone,* (eds J G Evans, S Limbrey and H Cleere), CBA Res Rep **11**, London, 49-56

Mellars, P, 1976 Settlement Patterns and Industrial Variability in the British Mesolithic, in *Problems in Economic and Social Archaeology*(eds G Sieveking, I H Longworth, and K Wilson), 375-99, London

Mellars, P A, 2004 Neanderthals and the modern human colonisation of Europe, *Nature* **432**, 461–465

Mellars, P and Dark, P, 1998 *Star Carr in context: new archaeological and palaeoecological investigations at the early Mesolithic site of Star Carr, North Yorkshire,* McDonald Institute Monograph, Cambridge

Mellor, M, 1994 A synthesis of Middle and Late saxon, medieval and early post-medieval pottery in the Oxford region, *Oxoniensia* **59**, 17-217

Mellor, M, 1997 *Pots and People,* Oxford

Mepham, L and Brown L, 2007 The Broughton to Timsbury pipline, Part 1: A Late Saxon pottery kiln and the production centre at Michelmersh, Hampshire, *Proc Hampshire Fld Club and Archaeol Soc* **62**, 25-68

Miles, D (ed.), 1986 *Archaeology at Barton Court Farm, Abingdon, Oxon: an investigation into the late Neolithic, Iron Age, Romano-British and Saxon settlements,* Oxford Archaeolical Unit Rep **3**, CBA Res Rep **50**, Oxford and London

Miles, D and Rowley, T, 1976 Tusmore Deserted Village, *Oxoniensia* **41**, 309–15

Miles, D, Palmer, S, Lock, G, Gosden, C and Cromarty, A M, 2003 *Uffington White Horse and its landscape: investigations at White Horse Hill, Uffington, 1989-95 and Tower Hill Ashbury, 1993-4,* Oxford Archaeology Thames Valley Landscapes Monograph **18**, Oxford

Millard, L, 1965 A Mesolithic industry from Bolter End, *Rec Buckinghamshire* **17**, 343-9

Miller, E (ed.), 1991 *The Agrarian History of England and Wales Volume 3. 1348-1500*

Millett, M, 1986 An early Roman cemetery at Alton, Hampshire, *Proc Hampshire Fld Club Archaeol Soc* **42,** 43-87

Millett, M, 1987 An early Roman burial tradition in Central Southern England, *Oxford J Archaeol* **6,** 63-8

Millett, M and Graham, D, 1986 *Excavations on the Romano-British Small Town of Neatham, Hants. 1969-1979*, Hants Field Club and Farnham District Museum Society

Millett, M with James, S, 1983 Excavations at Cowdery's Down, Basingstoke, Hampshire, 1978-81, *Archaeol J* **140**, 151-279

Moffett, L, 2006 The archaeology of medieval plant foods, in *Food in Medieval England. Diet and nutrition*, (eds C M Woolgar, D Serjeantson and T Waldron), Oxford Oxford University Press, 41-55

Moffett, L, Robinson, M A and Straker, V, 1989 Cereals, fruit and nuts: Charred plant remains from Neolithic sites in England and Wales and the Neolithic Economy, in *The Beginnings of Agriculture*, (eds A Milles, D Williams & N Gardner), BAR Int Ser **496**, Oxford, 243-61

Moir, J, 2001 The Canadian Red Cross Memorial Hospital, Cliveden, Unpublished Report

Momber, G, 2000 Drowned and deserted: a submerged prehistoric landscape in the Solent, England, *International Journal of Nautical Archaeology* **29**, 86-99

Momber, G, 2001 Recent investigation of deeply submerged human occupation site on the floor of the Western Solent, in McInnes and Jakeways 2001, 36-41

Momber, G, 2004 The inundated landscapes of the Western Solent, in *Submarine prehistoric archaeology of the North Sea* (ed. N C Fleming), CBA Res Rep **141**, York, 37-42

Montgomery, J, Budd, P and Evans, J, 2000 Reconstructing the lifetime movements of ancient people: a Neolithic case study from Southern England, *European Journal of Archaeology* **3(3),** 370-385

Moore, J, 2001a Excavations at Oxford Science Park, Littlemore, Oxford, *Oxoniensia* **66**, 163-219

Moore, J, 2001b An archaeological evaluation at The Courtyard, Frogmoor, High Wycombe, unpubl. report

Moore, J, 2002 Hedgerley, Knights Rest, Moat farm Barns, Hedgerley Llane, Gerrards Cross, *CBA South Midlands Archaeol* **32**, 16

Moore, J and Jennings, D, 1992 *Reading Business Park: a Bronze Age Landscape*, Thames Valley Landscapes: the Kennet Valley **1**, OAU, Oxford

Moore, H, 2006 Medieval Buildings and Land Reclamation at the former Lion Brewery, St Thomas' Street, Oxford, *Oxoniensia* **71**, 393-412

Moore, T, 2006 *Iron Age Societies in the Severn-Cotswolds: Developing Narratives of Social and Landscape Change*, BAR Brit Ser **421**, Oxford

Moorey, P R S, 1982 A Neolithic ring-ditch and Iron Age enclosure at Newnham Murren, near Wallingford, in Case and Whittle 1982, 55-9

Mordaunt Crook, J, 1999 *The Rise of the Nouveaux Riches, Style and Status in Victorian and Edwardian Architecture*

Morris, E L, 1981 Ceramic exchange in western Britain: a preliminary view, in *Production and distribution: a ceramic viewpoint*, (eds H Howard and E L Morris), BAR Int Ser **120**, Oxford, 67-81

Morris, E L, 1985 Prehistoric salt distributions: two case studies from western Britain, *Bull Board Celtic Studies* **32**, 336-79

Morris, E L, 1994a The organisation of salt production and distribution in Iron Age Wessex, in Fitzpatrick and Morris 1994, 14-16

Morris, E L, 1994b The organisation of pottery production and distribution in Iron Age Wessex, in Fitzpatrick and Morris 1994, 26-9

Morris, E 1997 Where is the Danebury ware? in *Reconstructing Iron Age Societies*, (eds A Gwilt and C Haselgrove), 36-9

Morris, E L, 2013 The Middle to Late Bronze Age ceramic transition in the Lower Kennet Valley and beyond, in Brossler *et al.* 2013, 103-114

Morris, J (ed.), 1978 *Domesday Book: Buckinghamshire*, Chichester

Morris, J, 2011 *Investigating Animal Burials. Ritual, mundane and beyond*, BAR Brit Ser **535**, Oxford

Morris, R, 1989 *Churches in the Landscape*, London

Morton, A D, 1992 *Excavations at Hamwic Volume 1: excavations 1946-83, excluding Six Dials and Melbourne Street*, CBA Res Rep **84**, London

Moylan, B, 2007 *Those Were The Days... MG's Abingdon factory*

Mudd, A, 1995 The excavation of a late Bronze Age / early Iron Age site at Eight Acre Field, Radley, *Oxoniensia* **60**, 21-65

Muir, J and Roberts, M R, 1999 *Excavations at Wyndyke Furlong, Abingdon, Oxfordshire, 1994*, Thames Valley Landscapes Monograph **12**, OAU, Oxford

Mulville, J and Levitan, B, 2004 The animal bone, in Lambrick and Allen 2004, 463-78

Munby, J, 1975 126 High Street: the Archaeology and History of an Oxford House, *Oxoniensia* **40**, 254-308

Munby, J, 1978 Tackley's Inn and Three Medieval Houses in Oxford, *Oxoniensia* **43**, 123-69

Munby, J (ed.), 1982 *Domesday Book: Hampshire*, Phillimore, Chichester

Munby, J, 1992 Zacharias's: a 14th-century Oxford New Inn and the Origins of the Medieval Urban Inn, *Oxoniensia* **57**, 245-311

Munby, J and Steane, J, 1995 Swalcliffe: A New College Barn in the Fifteenth Century, *Oxoniensia* **60**, 333-378

Museum of London Archaeological Service, 2000 *The Archaeology of Greater London: an Assessment of*

Archaeological Evidence for Human Presence in the Area now Covered by Greater London, London

Musson, C, 1970 House plans and prehistory, *Current Archaeology* **21**, 267-75

Mynard, D C, 1979 Stone weights from the Rivers Great Ouse, Ouzel, Nene and Tove, *Rec Buckinghamshire* **21**, 11-28

Mynard, D C, 1984 A medieval pottery industry at Olney Hyde, *Rec Buckinghamshire* **26**, 56-85

Mynard, D C (ed.), 1987 *Roman Milton Keynes*, Buckinghamshire Archaeol Soc Monograph Ser **1**, Aylesbury

Mynard, D C, 1991 *Excavations at Great Linford, 1974-80*, Buckinghamshire Archaeol Soc, Aylesbury

Mynard, D C, 1994 *Excavations on Medieval Sites in Milton Keynes*, Buckinghamshire Archaeol Soc Monograph Ser **6**, Aylesbury

Mynard, D C and Ivens, R J, 2002 The excavation of Gorefields: a medieval nunnery and grange at Stoke Goldington, Buckinghamshire, *Rec Buckinghamshire* **42**, 19-101

Mynard, D C, Woodfield, P and Zeepvat, R J, 1994 Bradwell Abbey, Buckinghamshire research and excavation, 1968 to 1987, *Rec Buckinghamshire* **36**, 1-61

Mynard, D C and Zeepvat, R J, 1992 *Great Linford*, Buckinghamshire Archaeol Soc Monograph Ser **3**, Aylesbury

Mytum, H, 1986 An early Iron Age site at Wytham Hill, near Cumnor, Oxford, *Oxoniensia* **51**, 15-24

Mytum, H and Taylor, J W 1981 Stanton Harcourt: Linch Hill Corner, *CBA Group 9 Newsletter* **11**, 139-41

National Trust, 1993 The King's Head, Aylesbury. An historic building survey 1992/3, unpubl. report

Myres, J N L, 1937 A prehistoric and Roman site on Mount Farm, Dorchester, *Oxoniensia* **2**, 12-40

Nayling, N and McGrail, S, 2004 *Barlands Farm Romano-Celtic boat*, CBA Res Rep **138**, York

Neal, D S, 1987 Excavations at Magiovinium, Buckinghamshire, 1978-80, *Rec Buckinghamshire* **29**, 1-124

Needham, S P, 1991 *Excavation and salvage at Runnymede Bridge 1978, The Late Bronze Age Waterfront Site*, British Museum Press and English Heritage, London

Needham, S P, 1992 Holocene alluviation and interstratified archaeological evidence in the Thames valley at Runnymede Bridge, in Needham and Macklin (eds) 1992, 249-60

Needham, S P, 2002 Contribution in *Treasure Annual Report 2000*, London, Department of Culture, Media and Sport, 12-15

Needham, S, 2006 The beginnings of the Channel Bronze Age, in *The Ringlemere Cup: Precious Cups and the Beginning of the Channel Bronze Age*, (eds S Needham, K Parfitt and G Varndell), British Museum Press, London

Needham, S P, 2007 800 BC, the Great Divide, in Haselgrove and Pope 2007, 39-63

Needham, S P and Ambers, J, 1994 Redating Rams Hill and reconsidering Bronze Age enclosure, *Proc Prehist Soc* **60**, 225-243

Needham, S P and Burgess, C B, 1980 The later Bronze Age in the lower Thames valley: the metalwork evidence, in Barrett and Bradley 1980a, 437-469

Needham, S P and Macklin, M G (eds), 1992 *Alluvial Archaeology in Britain*, Oxbow Monograph **27**, Oxford

Needham, S P, Ramsey, C B, Coombs, D, Cartwright, C and Pettitt, P, 1997 An independent chronology for British Bronze Age metalwork: the results of the Oxford radiocarbon accelerator programme, *Archaeol J*, **154**, 55-107

Needham, S P, and Spence, T, 1996 *Refuse and Disposal at Area 16 East Runnymede*, Runnymede Bridge Research Excavations 2, British Museum Press, London

Nelson, S, 1984 A French Saintonge jug from Newport, Isle of Wight, *Proc Hampshire Fld Club Archaeol Soc* **40**, 133-14

Network Archaeology Ltd, 2003 Land to the rear of 10 High Street, Winslow, Buckinghamshire, unpubl. report

Network Archaeology, 2005 Somerton Farm to Knight's Cross reinforcement 300mm gas pipeline Archaeological Watching Brief, 2000, Network Archaeology Transco Report 162

Newton, P A, 1979 *The County of Oxford. A Catalogue of Medieval Stained Glass (Corpus Vitrearum Medii Aevi), Great Britain*, i

North Buckinghamshire Archaeological Society, 2000 Excavation report for Tickford Abbey dig of 21st-22nd October 2000, http://www.nbas.org.uk/tickford.html Accessed 10 June 2006

Northamptonshire Archaeology, 2001 Excavation of an Iron Age Enclosure at Kennel Farm, Basingstoke, Hampshire, Northamptonshire Archaeology Report

Northamptonshire Archaeology, 2002 Excavation of an Iron Age and Romano-British Enclosure at Kennel Farm, Basingstoke, Hampshire, 1998, Northamptonshire Archaeology Report

Northover, J P, 1984 Iron Age bronze metallurgy in central southern England, in Cunliffe and Miles 1984, 126-45

Northover, J P, 1995 The technology of metalwork, in Green 1995, 285-309

Norton, A, 2006 Excavations at 67-69 St Thomas' Street, Oxford, *Oxoniensia* **71**, 347-392

O'Drisceoil, D 1988 Burnt mounds: cooking or bathing?, *Antiquity* **62**, 671-80

O'Malley, M and Jacobi, R, 1978 The excavation of a Mesolithic occupation site at Broom Hill, Braishfield, Hampshire 1971–1973, *Rescue Archaeology in Hampshire* **4**, 16–38

Oliver, M, 1992 Excavation of an Iron Age and

Romano-British Settlement Site at Oakridge, Basingstoke, Hampshire, 1965-6, *Proc Hampshire Fld Club Archaeol Soc* **48**, 55-93

Oliver, M, 1993 The Iron Age and Romano-British settlement at Oakridge, *Proc Hampshire Fld Club and Archaeol Soc* **48**, 55-94

Oliver, M and Applin, B, 1979 Excavation of an Iron Age and Romano-British Settlement at Rucstalls Hill, Basingstoke, Hampshire, 1972-5, *Proc Hampshire Fld Club Archaeol Soc* **35**, 41-92

Oram, R, 2006 A Middle Bronze Age burnt mound at Greywell Road, Hatch, Basingstoke, *Hampshire Stud* **61**, 1-15

Oswald, A, 1997 A doorway on the past: practical and mystic concerns in the orientation of roundhouse doorways, in Gwilt and Haselgrove 1997, 87-95

Oswald, A, Dyer, C, and Barber, M, 2001 *The creation of monuments: Neolithic causewayed enclosures in the British Isles*, London

Oxford Archaeological Unit, 1996 Railway turntable, Sheepwash Channel, Oxford, Unpublished client report

Oxford Archaeological Unit, 1999 Oxford LMS Station, Unpublished client report

Oxford Archaeological Unit, 2000a Abingdon Swift Ditch Lock, Unpublished client report

Oxford Archaeological Unit, 2000b Salters' Boatyard, Unpublished client report

Oxford Archaeology, 2000 Hampshire Water Meadows Survey, Unpublished client report

Oxford Archaeology, 2001 The Bodleian Library, Oxford: The Roof Carpentry of Duke Humfrey's Library: A Report on the Archaeological and Dendrochronological Studies of the BOLD Project, Unpublished client report

Oxford Archaeology, 2003 Banbury, Cherwell Wharf, *CBA South Midlands Archaeol* **33**, 74

Oxford Archaeology, 2004a Church of the Holy Cross and St Mary, Quainton, Buckinghamshire, unpublished archaeological watching brief report

Oxford Archaeology, 2004b St Leonards Church, Grendon Underwood, Buckinghamshire, unpublished archaeological watching brief report

Oxford Archaeology, 2004c Notley Abbey, Long Crendon, Buckinghamshire, Historic Buildings Assessment, unpublished report

Oxford Archaeology, 2004d Queen Elizabeth II Barracks, Fleet: Archaeological Assessment, Unpublished client report

Oxford Archaeology, 2006a Client Report: Oxford Castle Development, Post Excavation Assessment and Research Design, Unpublished client report

Oxford Archaeology, 2006b Newbury Historic Character Study: Assessment Report, Unpublished client report

Oxford Wessex Archaeology, 2005 Solent-Thames Archaeological Research Framework Project Design, client report for ALGAO South East and English Heritage, October 2005

Oxley, J (ed.), 1988 *Excavations at Southampton Castle*, Southampton Archaeology Monograph **3**, Southampton

Page, M, 2005 Destroyed by the Temples: the Deserted Medieval Village of Stowe, *Rec Buckinghamshire* **45**, 189-204

Page, P, Atherton, K and Hardy A, 2005 *Barentin's Manor: Excavations of the moated manor at Hardings Field, Chalgrove, Oxfordshire 1976-9*, Oxford Archaeology Thames Valley Landscapes Monograph **24**, Oxford

Page, W (ed.), 1905 *A History of the County of Buckingham*, The Victoria History of the Counties of England, London

Page, W (ed.), 1912 *A History of Hampshire and the Isle of Wight Vol.* **5**, The Victoria History of the Counties of England, London

Palmer, R, 1984 *Danebury an Iron Age hillfort: an aerial photographic interpretation of its environs*, RCHME Supplementary Series **6**, London

Palmer, S, 1872-5 On the antiquities found in the peat of Newbury, *Trans Newbury Dist Fld Club* **2**, 123-34

Palmer, S, 1977 *Mesolithic cultures of Britain*, Dolphin Press, Poole

Pantin, W A, 1937 The recently demolished houses in Broad Street, Oxford, *Oxoniensia* **2**, 171-200

Pantin, W A, 1941 Notley Abbey, *Oxoniensia* **6**, 22-43

Pantin, W A, 1958 Monuments or Muniments? The Interrelation of Material remains and Documentary Sources, *Med Archaeol* **2**, 158-68

Palmer, N, 1980 A Beaker Burial and Medieval Tenements in the Hamel, Oxford', *Oxoniensia* **45**, 124–225

Parfitt, S A, Barendregt, R W, Breda, M, Candy, I, Collins, M J, Coope, G R, Durbidge, P, Field, M H, Lee, J R, Lister, A M, Mutch, R, Penkman, K E H, Preece, R C, Rose, J, Stringer, C B, Symmons, R, Whittaker, J E, Wymer, J J & Stuart, A J, 2005 The earliest record of human activity in northern Europe, *Nature* **438**, 1008–1012

Parker, A G, 1975 *Isle of Wight Local History: A Guide to Sources*, Newport, Isle of Wight Teachers' Centre

Parker, A G, 1977 *The Story of Victorian Shanklin*

Parker, A G and Robinson, M A, 2003 Palaeoenvironmental investigations on the Middle Thames at Dorney, UK, in *Alluvial archaeology in Europe* (eds A J Howard, M Macklin and D G Passmore), 43-60, Rotterdam

Parker, R F, and Boarder, A W F, 1991 A medieval settlement site at Fillington Wood, West Wycombe, *Rec Buckinghamshire* **33**, 128-39

Parker Pearson, M, 1993 *Bronze Age Britain*, London

Parkhouse, J and Bonner, D, 1997 Investigations at the Prehistoric Site at Coldharbour Farm Aylesbury in 1996, *Rec Buckinghamshire* **39**, 73-139

Parkhouse, J and Smith, N, 1994 An Anglo-Saxon cemetery at Bottledump Corner, Tattenhoe, Milton Keynes, Buckinghamshire, *Rec Buckinghamshire* **36**, 103-19

Parkhouse, J, Roseff, R and Short, J, 1996 A late

Saxon cemetery at Milton Keynes village, *Rec Buckinghamshire* **38**, 199-221

Parrington, M, 1978 *The Excavation of an Iron Age Settlement, Bronze Age Ring-Ditches and Roman Features at Ashville Trading Estate, Abingdon (Oxfordshire) 1974-76*, Oxford Archaeolical Unit Report **1**, CBA Res Rep **28**, London

Parsons, D (ed), 1975 *Tenth-Century Studies*, Chichester

Pasmore, A H, 2000 Millersford Bottom boiling mound, New Forest Section site 73/4 – excavation 1998, *Hampshire Field Club Newsletter 33*, New Forest Annual Report **37** iii-vii

Pasmore, A H and Pallister, J, 1967 Boiling mounds in the New Forest, *Proc Hampshire Fld Club Archaeol Soc* **24**, 14-19

Pavry, F H and Knocker, G M, 1957 The Mount, Princes Risborough, Buckinghamshire, *Rec Buckinghamshire* **16**, 131-178

Payne, A, Corney, M and Cunliffe, B, 2006 *The Wessex Hillforts Project: extensive survey of hillfort interiors in central southern England*, English Heritage

Peacock, D PS, 1987 Iron Age and Roman Quern Production at Lodsworth, West Sussex, *Antiq J* **67**(i), 61-85

Peake, A E, 1913 An account of a flint factory with some new types of flints excavated at Peppard Common, Oxon, *Archaeol J* **70**, 33-68

Peake, A E, 1917 A prehistoric site at Kimble S. Bucks, *Proc Prehist Soc of East Anglia* **II** (3), 437-58

Peake, H J E, 1931 *The Archaeology of Berkshire*, London

Pearson, E and Robinson, M, 1994 Environmental evidence from the villa, in Williams and Zeepvat 1994, 565-583

Peberdy, R, 1996 Navigation on the River Thames between London and Oxford in the late Middle Ages. A Reconsideration, *Oxoniensia* **61**, 311–40

Peers, C R, 1902 The Benedictine Nunnery of Little Marlow, *Rec Buckinghamshire* **8**, 419-34

Peers, Sir C, 1975 *Carisbrooke Castle*, London, HMSO, fifteenth impression

Pelling, R, 2012 *Dowd's Farm, Hedge End, Hampshire Supplement to Publication Charred Plant Remains* http://www.wessexarch.co.uk/system/files/Dowds_Farm_CharredPlant.pdf

Petchey, M R, 1978 A Roman field system at Broughton, Buckinghamshire, *Rec Buckinghamshire* **20.4**, 637-45

Peters, J E C, 1964 The tithe barn at Arreton, I.W., *Trans Ancient Monuments Soc* **12**, 61-79

Pevsner, N, 1966 *The Buildings of England: Berkshire*, Harmondsworth

Pevsner, N and Lloyd, D, 1967 *The Buildings of England: Hampshire and the Isle of Wight*, Yale University Press

Pevsner, N, and Williamson, E, 1960 *The Buildings of England – Buckinghamshire*, London

Pevsner, N and Williamson, E 1994 *The Buildings of England; Buckinghamshire*, Penguin, London, 2nd edn

Phillips M, 2005 Excavation of an early Saxon settlement at Pitstone, *Rec Buckinghamshire* **45**, 1- 32

Phythian-Adams, C, 1993 *Societies, Cultures and Kinship, 1580-1850*, Leicester, 1993

Piggott, S, 1937 The excavation of a long barrow in Holdenhurst Parish, near Christchurch, Hants, *Proc Prehist Soc* **3**, 1-14

Piggott, S, 1938 The Early Bronze Age in Wessex, *Proc Prehist Soc* **4**, 52-106

Piggott, S, 1947 The Arreton Down Bronze Age Hoard, *Antiq J* **27**, 177-8

Pike, A, 1995 Earthwork enclosures in the Buckinghamshire Chilterns, in *Chiltern Archaeology – recent work. A Handbook for the Next Decade* (ed. R Holgate), Dunstable, 118-9

Pine, J, 2003a Late Bronze Age occupation, Roman enclosure and Early Saxon occupation at Waylands Nursery, Welley Road, Wraysbury, Berkshire, 1997, in *Prehistoric, Roman and Saxon Sites in eastern Berkshire* (ed. S Preston), TVAS Monograph **2**, 118-137

Pine, J, 2003b Excavation of a medieval settlement, Late Saxon features and a Bronze Age cremation cemetery at Loughton, Milton Keynes, *Rec Buckinghamshire* **43**, 77-126

Pine, J, 2010 Roman occupation at the Former Turnpike School, Gaywood Drive, Newbury, West Berkshire, in Pine, J, *Archaeological Investigations along the line of Ermin Street in West Berkshire, 1992-2008*, TVAS Monograph **12**, Reading,

Pine, J and Ford, S, 2003 Excavation of Neolithic, late Bronze Age, early Iron Age and early Saxon features at St Helen's Avenue, Benson, *Oxoniensia* **68**, 131-78

Pine, J and Taylor, K 2006 Chapter Two: late Saxon, medieval and post-medieval occupation, with a post-medieval tannery, at Morlands Brewery, Abingdon, in Anthony *et al.* 2006, 41-84

Pitts, M and Roberts, M B, 1997 *Fairweather Eden: Life in Britain Half a Million Years Ago as Revealed by the Excavations at Boxgrove*, Century, London

Platt, C, 1994 *The great rebuildings of Tudor and Stuart England : revolutions in architectural taste*, UCL Press, London

Plot, R, 1677 *The Natural History of Oxfordshire*, Oxford

Pollard, A M, 2012 Science, archaeology and the Romans, or 'What has scientific archaeology ever done for the Romans?', in *More than Just Numbers? The Role of Science in Roman Archaeology* (ed. I Schrüfer-Kolb), Journal of Roman Archaeology Supplementary Series **91**, Portsmouth, Rhode island, 177-88

Pollard, A M, Ditchfield, P, Piva, E, Wallis, S, Falys, C and Ford, S, 2012 'Sprouting like cockle amongst the wheat': the St Brice's Day massacre and the isotopic analysis of human bones from St John's College, Oxford, *Oxford J Archaeol* **31**(1), 83-102

Pollard, J, 1999 'These places have their moments': thoughts on settlement practices in the British Neolithic, in *Making places in the prehistoric world:*

themes in settlement archaeology (eds J Brück and M Goodman), London, 76-93

Poole, H F, 1929 Roman British Midden at Ventnor, *Proc Isle of Wight Nat Hist & Archaeol Soc* for 1928, **1** part 9, 610-11

Poole, H F, 1936 An outline of the Mesolithic flint cultures of the Isle of Wight, *Proc Isle Wight Natur Hist Archaeol Soc* **2**, 551-581

Poore, D, 2000 Oxford Sackler Library, *CBA South Midlands Archaeol* **30**, 68-9

Poore, D and Wilkinson, D, 2001 *Beaumont Palace and the White Friars. Excavations at the Sackler Library, Beaumont St., Oxford*, Oxford Archaeological Unit Occasional Paper **9**

Pope, M I and Roberts, M B, 2009 The archaeological and sedimentary records from Boxgrove and Slindon, in Briant *et al.* 2009, 95-116

Pope, R, 2007 Ritual and the Roundhouse: a critique of recent ideas on the use of domestic space in later British Prehistory, in Haselgrove and Pope 2007, 204-228

Portable Antiquities Scheme http://www.finds.org.uk.

Portman, D, 1960 Little Milton, the rebuilding of an Oxfordshire village, *Oxoniensia* **25**, 55-111

Potter, J F, 2006 A geological review of some Hampshire Anglo-Saxon churches, *Proc Hampshire Fld Club Archaeol Soc* **61**, 134-52

Poulton, R and Scott, E, 1993 The hoarding, deposition and use of pewter in Roman Britain, in *Theoretical Roman Archaeology: First Conference Proceedings*, (ed. E Scott), Aldershot, 115-132

Powell, K, Laws, G and Brown, L, 2009 A late Neolithic or early Bronze Age enclosure and Iron Age and Romano-British settlement at Latton Lands, Wiltshire, *Wiltshire Archaeol Nat Hist Mag* **102**, 22-113

Powell, K, Smith, A, and Laws, G, 2010 *Evolution of a Farming Community in the Upper Thames Valley. Excavation of a Prehistoric, Roman and Post-Roman landscape at Cotswold Community, Gloucestershire and Wiltshire. Volume 1: Site Narrative and Overview*, Oxford Archaeology Thames Valley Landscapes Monograph **31**

Preece, R C, 1986 Faunal remains from radio-carbon dated soils within landslip debris from the Undercliff, Isle of Wight, Southern England, *J Arch Sci* **13** 189-200

Preston, S, 2003 *Prehistoric, Roman and Saxon Sites in Eastern Berkshire. Excavations 1989-1997*, TVAS Monograph **2**, Reading

Preston, S, 2007 Bronze Age occupation and Saxon features at the Wolverton Turn Enclosure, near Stony Stratford, Milton Keynes, *Rec Buckinghamshire* **47 (1)**, 81-117

Preston, S (ed), 2011 *Archaeological Investigations in the Silchester Hinterland*, TVAS Monograph **9**, Reading

Preston, S (ed), 2012 *Settlement and Landscape Archaeology in the Middle Thames Valley: Slough and Environs, Reading*, TVAS Monograph **14**

Prior, M, 1981 The accounts of Thomas West of Wallingford, a sixteenth century trader on the Thames, *Oxoniensia* **46**, 73-93

Prior, M, 1982 *Fisher Row*, Oxford

Pryor, F, 1996 Sheep, stocklands and farm systems; Bronze Age livestock populations in the Fenlands of eastern England, *Antiquity* **370**, 313-24

Phythian-Adams, C, 1992 An Agenda for English Local History, in *Societies, cultures and kinship, 1580–1850* (Leicester, 1993), 1-23

Qualmann, K, 1978 St Paul's Church, in Collis, J, 1978 *Winchester Excavations Volume: 1949-1960. Excavations in the suburbs and western part of the town*, Winchester, 265-70

Qualmann, K E, Rees, H, Scobie, G D and Whinney, R, 2004 *Oram's Arbour: The Iron Age Enclosure at Winchester: Vol. 1: Investigations 1950-1999*, Winchester Museums Service, Winchester

Rackham, O, 1986 *The History of the Countryside*, Dent, London

Rahtz, S and Rowley, T, 1984 *Middleton Stoney: excavation and survey in a north Oxfordshire parish*

Ralston, I, 2006 *Celtic Fortifications*, Tempus, Stroud

Rankine, W F, 1949 *A Mesolithic survey of the west Surrey Greensand*, Res Vol Surrey Archaeol Soc **2**, Guildford

Rankine, W F, 1951 A Mesolithic site on the foreshore at Cams, Fareham, Hants, *Proc Hampshire Fld Club Archaeol Soc* **17**, 141–2

Rankine, W F, 1952 A Mesolithic chipping floor at the Warren Oakhanger, Selborne, Hants, *Proc Prehist Soc* **18**, 21–35

Rankine, W F, 1953 Mesolithic research in east Hampshire: the Hampshire Greensand, *Proc Hampshire Fld Club Archaeol Soc* **18**, 157–72

Rankine, W F, 1956 *The Mesolithic of Southern England*, Res Vol Surrey Archaeol Soc **4**, Guildford

Ransley, J, Sturt, F, Dix, J, Adams, J, and Blue, L (eds) 2013 *People and the Sea: A Maritime Archaeological Research Agenda for England*, CBA Res Rep **171**

Raymond, F, 1987 *Monument Protection Programme Single Monument Class Description: Burnt Mounds*, London

RCHME, 1979 *Long barrows in Hampshire and the Isle of Wight*, HMSO, London

Reed, M, 1978 Markets and fairs in medieval Buckinghamshire, *Rec Buckinghamshire* **20**, 563-585

Reed, M, 1979 *The Buckinghamshire Landscape*, London

Reed, M, 1986 Decline and Recovery in a provincial urban network: Buckinghamshire towns, 1350-1800, in *English Towns in Decline 1350-1800* (ed. M Reed), Leicester

Reed, M, 1993 *A History of Buckinghamshire*, Chichester

Rees, H, Crummy, N, Ottaway, P J and Dunn, G, 2008 *Artefacts and Society in Roman and Medieval Winchester. Small finds from the suburbs and defences, 1971-1986*, Winchester Museums Service and English Heritage, Winchester

Renn, D F, 1954 The enceinte wall of Quarr Abbey, *Proc Isle Wight Nat Hist Archaeol Soc* **5** Part IX, 350-1

Reynier, M J, 1998 Early Mesolithic settlement in England and Wales: some preliminary observations, in *Stone Age archaeology: essays in honour of John Wymer*, (eds N Ashton, F Healy, and P Pettit), Oxford, 174–84

Reynier, M, 2000 Thatcham revisited: spatial and stratigraphic analysis of two sub-assemblages from Site III and its implications for Early Mesolithic typo-chronology in Britain, in *Mesolithic lifeways: current research from Britain and Ireland* (ed. R Young), Leicester University Archaeological Monograph 7, Leicester, 33–46

Reynolds, A, 2003 Boundaries and settlements in later sixth- to eleventh-century England, *Anglo-Saxon Studies in Archaeology and History* **12**, 98-136

Reynolds, S, 1977 *An Introduction to the History of English Medieval Towns*, Oxford

Rhodes, P P, 1948 A prehistoric and Roman site at Wittenham Clumps, Berkshire, *Oxoniensia* **13**, 18-31

Richards, J, 1978 *The archaeology of the Berkshire Downs: an introductory survey*, Berkshire Archaeol Comm Publ **3**, Reading

Richards, J, 1986-90 Death and the past environment: the results of work on barrows on the Berkshire Downs, *Berkshire Archaeol J* **73**, 1-42

Richmond, A, Rackham, J and Scaife, R, 2006 Excavations of a prehistoric stream-side site at Little Marlow, Buckinghamshire, *Rec Buckinghamshire* **46**, 65-102

Rigold, S E, 1969 Recent investigations into the earliest defences of Carisbrooke Castle, Isle of Wight, *Chateau Gaillard* **3**, 128-138

Riley, H, 2001 Stowe Park, Stowe, Buckinghamshire. Survey report, English Heritage Archaeological Investigation Report series AI/21/2001, unpubl.

Rivers-Moore, C N, 1939 Excavations ar St. Mary's Priory, Hurley: Second Report, *Berkshire Archaeol J* **43 [1]**, 23-29

Roberts, A J, Barton, R N E, and Evans, J, 1998 Early Mesolithic mastic radiocarbon dating and analysis of organic residues from Thatcham III, Star Carr and Lackford Heath, in *Stone Age archaeology: essays in honour of John Wymer* (eds N M Ashton, F Healy and P B Pettit), Oxbow Monograph **102**/Lithic Studies Occas Pap **6**, Oxford, 185-92

Roberts, B K and Wrathmell, S, 2000 *An Atlas of Rural Settlement in England*, English Heritage, London

Roberts, B K and Wrathmell, S 2002 *Region and Place: a study of English Rural Settlement*, English Heritage, London

Roberts, E, 1998 The rediscovery of two major monastic buildings at Wherwell, *Proc Hampshire Fld Club Archaeol Soc* **53**, 137-53

Roberts, E, 2003 *Hampshire Houses 1250-1700 their Dating and Development*, Hants County Council

Roberts, J, 1997 *Royal landscape : the gardens and parks of Windsor*, Yale University Press, London

Roberts, K, 2003 *First Newbury: The turning point*, Osprey Press

Roberts, M B, 1986 Excavation of a Lower Palaeolithic site at Amey's Eartham Pit, Boxgrove, West Sussex: A preliminary report, *Proc Prehist Soc* **52**, 215-245

Roberts, M B and Parfitt, S A (eds), 1999 *Boxgrove: a Middle Pleistocene Hominid Site*, English Heritage, London

Roberts, M R, 1993 Lady Lamb Farm, Fairford, Oxford Archaeological Unit unpublished client report

Roberts, M R, 1995 Excavations at Park Farm, Binfield, Berkshire 1990: an Iron Age and Romano-British settlement and two Mesolithic flint scatters, in Barnes *et al.* 1995, 93-139

Roberts, M R, 1996 A tenement of Roger of Cumnor and other archaeological investigations in medieval North Oseney, Oxford, *Oxoniensia* **61**, 181-224

Robinson, M A, 1992a Environmental archaeology of the river gravels : past achievements and future directions, in Fulford and Nichols (eds) 1992, 47-62

Robinson, M A, 1992b Environment, archaeology and alluvium on the river gravels of the South Midlands, in Needham and Macklin 1992, 197-208

Robinson, M A, 1993 The pre-Iron Age environment and finds, in Allen and Robinson 1993, 7-19

Robinson, M A, 2000a Further considerations of Neolithic charred cereals, fruits and nuts, in *Plants in Neolithic Britain and beyond*, (ed. A S Fairbairn), Neolithic Studies Group Seminar Papers 5, Oxbow Books, 85-90

Robinson, M A, 2000b Middle Mesolithic to Late Bronze Age insect assemblages and an Early Neolithic assemblage of waterlogged macroscopic plant remains, in *The passage of the Thames: Holocene environment and settlement at Runnymede* (ed. S Needham), London, 146-67

Robinson, M, 2005 Insect remains, in Birbeck 2005, 181-183

Robinson, M, 2006 The macroscopic plant remains, in Fulford *et al.* 2006, 206-18 and 374-79

Robinson, M 2011 The macroscopic plant and invertebrate remains, in Fulford and Clarke 2011, 281-93 and 485-96

Robinson, M A, 2011 The Thames and its changing environment in our era, in Hey *et al.* 2011, 173-191

Robinson, M A, in prep. The palaeohydrology, in Hey *et al.* in prep.

Robinson, M A and Lambrick, G H, 1984 Holocene alluviation and hydrology in the Upper Thames Basin, *Nature* **308**, 809-814

Roden, D, 1966 Field systems in Ibstone, a township of the south-west Chilterns during the later middle ages, *Rec Buckinghamshire* **18**, 43-57

Roden, D, 1969 Demesne Farming in the Chiltern Hills, *Agricultural History Review* **17**, 9-23

Roden, D, 1973 Field Systems of the Chiltern Hills and their Environs, in *Studies in the Field Systems in the British Isles* (eds A R H Baker and R A Butlin), Cambridge, 325-76

Rodwell, K, 1974 *Historic towns in Oxfordshire: a survey of the new county*, OAU, Oxford

Rodwell, W, 2009 *Dorchester Abbey Oxfordshire: the archaeology and architecture of a cathedral, monastery and parish church*, Oxford

Roe, D A, 1981 *The Lower and Middle Palaeolithic Periods in Britain*, London, Routledge & Kegan Paul

Roe, D A, 2001 Some earlier Palaeolithic find-spots of interest in the Solent region, in *Palaeolithic Archaeology of the Solent River, (eds* F F Wenban-Smith and R T Hosfield), Lithic Studies Society Occasional Paper 7, London, 47–56

Roe, F, 1979 Typology of stone implements with shaftholes, in Clough and Cummins 1979, 23-48

Roebroeks, W and van Kolfschoten, T, 1994 The earliest occupation of Europe: a short chronology, *Antiquity* **68**, 489–503

Roebroeks, W van Kolfschoten, T (eds), 1995 *The Earliest Occupation of Europe*, University of Leiden, Institute of Prehistory, Leiden

Rohl, B, and Needham, S, 1998 *The Circulation of Metal in the British Bronze Age*, British Museum Occasional Paper **102**, British Museum Press, London

Rouse, E C, 1977 The wall paintings at nos. 1 & 2 Market Hill, Buckingham, *Rec Buckinghamshire* **20**, 293-300

Rowley, T and Brown, L, 1981 Excavations at Beech House Hotel, Dorchester-on-Thames 1972, *Oxoniensia* **46**, 1-55

Royal Commission on Historical Monuments (England), 1912 *An Inventory of the Historical Monuments in Buckinghamshire I (South)*, London

Royal Commission on Historical Monuments (England), 1913 *An Inventory of the Historical Monuments in Buckinghamshire II (North)*, London

Royal Commission on the Historical Monuments of England (RCHM(E)), 1939 *An Inventory of the historical monuments in the City of Oxford*

Royal Commission on the Historical Monuments of England (RCHM(E)), 1986 *Nonconformist Chapels and Meeting Houses; Buckinghamshire*

Royal Commission on the Historical Monuments of England (RCHM(E)), 1997 *English Farmsteads 1750-1914*

Royal Commission on the Historical Monuments of England (RCHM(E)), 1998 *English Hospitals, 1660-1948: A survey of their architecture and design*, London

RPS Consultants, 2001 SeaClean Wight Pipelines: Archaeological Assessment Report (3 vols)

RPS, 2005 Archaeological Investigations for the A41 Aston Clinton Bypass, Buckinghamshire, unpublished report

Ruben, I and Ford, S, 1992 Archaeological Excavations at Wallingford Road, Didcot, South Oxfordshire, 1991, *Oxoniensia* **57**, 1-28

Russel, A, 1990 Two Beaker burials from Chilbolton, Hampshire, *Proc Prehist Soc* **56**, 133–72

Russel, A, 2002 Anglo-Saxon, in Stoodley (ed) 2002, 202-5

Russell, P D D (ed.), 1981 *Hearth Tax Returns for the Isle of Wight 1664 to 1674*, Isle of Wight County Record Office

Salter, C, 2004 Ferrous metalworking debris, in Hey 2004, 307-11

Salter, C and Ehrenreich, R, 1984 Iron Age iron metallurgy in central southern Britain, in Cunliffe and Miles 1984, 146-61

Sauer, E W, 1999 Aves Ditch: an Iron Age tribal boundary? *Current Archaeol* **163**, 268-9

Sauer, E, 2000 Alchester, a Claudian 'Vexillation Fortress' near the western boundary of the Catuvellauni: new light on the Roman invasion of Britain, *Archaeol J* **157**, 1-78

Sauer, E W, 2005a *Linear Earthwork, Tribal Boundary and Ritual Beheading: Aves Ditch from the Iron Age to the Early Middle Ages*, BAR Brit Ser **402**, Oxford

Sauer, E W, 2005b Inscriptions from Alchester: Vespasian's base of the Second Augustan Legion(?), *Britannia* **36**, 101-133

Saunders, A, 1998 *Fortifications of Portsmouth and the Solent: a Review of Pre-20th Century Coastal Defence Sites and Associated Remains*, English Heritage, London

Saunders, C, 1971 The Pre-Belgic Iron Age in the Central and Western Chilterns, *Archaeol J* **78**, 1-30

Saville, A, 1983 Excavations at Condicote Henge monument, Gloucestershire 1977, *Trans Bristol Gloucestershire Archaeol Soc* **101**, 21-47

Saville, A, 1990 *Hazleton North: the excavation of a Neolithic long cairn of the Cotswold-Severn group*, English Heritage Report **13**, London

Scaife, R G, 1987 The Late-Devensian and Flandrian vegetation of the Isle of Wight, in *Wessex and the Isle of Wight: Field Guide*, (ed. K E Barber), Quaternary Research Association, Cambridge, 156-80

Scaife, R, 1992 Plant macrofossils and pollen analysis, in Healy *et al*. 1992, 64-70

Scaife, R G, 1996 Charred and waterlogged plant remains, in Crockett, A, 1996, 157-163

Scaife, R, 2000 Pollen analysis from Farlington Marshes: a vegetational history of Langstone Harbour, in Allen and Gardiner 2000, 171–5

Scaife, R G and Burrin, P J, 1992 Archaeological inferences from alluvial sediments: some findings from southern England, in *Alluvial Archaeology in Britain*, (eds S Needham and M G Macklin), Oxford: Oxbow Books, 75-91

Schofield, A J, 1995 The changing face of 'landscape' in field archaeology: an example from the upper Meon valley, in *The evolution of the Hampshire landscape: the Meon valley landscape project* (ed. M Hughes), Hampshire County Council Archaeological Report **1**, Winchester, 1–14

Schulting, R J, 2000 New AMS dates from the Lambourn long barrow and the question of the earliest Neolithic in southern England: repacking the Neolithic package, *Oxford J Archaeol* **19**, 25-35

Schulting, R J and Richards, M P, 2000 The use of

stable isotopes in studies of subsistence and seasonality in the British Mesolithic, in *Mesolithic lifeways: current research from Britain and Ireland*, (ed. R Young), Leicester Archaeology Monographs **7**, Leicester, 55-65

Schumer, B, 1975 An Elizabethan survey of North Leigh, Oxfordshire, *Oxoniensia* **40**, 309-24

Schumer, B, 1984 *The evolution of Wychwood to 1400: pioneers, frontiers and forests*, Leicester

Scobie, G D, Zant, J M and Whinney, R, 1991 *The Brooks, Winchester. A preliminary report on the excavations, 1987-88*, Winchester: Winchester Museums Service Archaeology Report **1**

Scott, I R, 1996 *Romsey Abbey. Report on the excavations 1973-1991*, Hampshire Fld Club Archaeol Soc Monograph **8**

Scott, I R, 2001 Romsey Abbey: Benedictine Nunnery and parish church, in *Monastic Archaeology: papers on the study of medieval monasteries*, (eds G Keevill, M Aston and T Hall), Oxford, 150-60

Scott-Jackson, J E, 2000 *Lower and Middle Palaeolithic Artefacts from Deposits mapped as Clay-with-Flints*, Oxbow Books Ltd, Oxford

Scull, C, 1992 Excavation and survey at Watchfield, Oxfordshire, 1983-92, *Archaeol J* **149**, 124-281

Seaby, W A, 1932 Some pre-Roman remains from south Reading, *Berkshire Archaeol J* **36**, 121-5

Secker, D, 2005 A survey of earthworks and structural remains at Bray's Wood, The Lee, *Rec Buckinghamshire* **45**, 65-73

Seebohm Rowntree, B, 1913a *The Land*

Seebohm Rowntree, B, 1913b *How the Labourer Lives*

Seeley, F, and Drummond-Murray, J, 2005 *Roman pottery production in the Walbrook Valley. Excavations at 20-28 Moorgate, City of London, 1998-2000*, MoLAS Monograph **25**, London

Sellwood, B, 1984 The rock types represented in the town walls of Silchester, in Fulford 1984, 224-30

Sellwood, L, 1984 Tribal boundaries viewed from the perspective of numismatic evidence, in Cunliffe and Miles 1984, 191-204

Semple, S, 2013 *Perceptions of the Prehistoric in Anglo-Saxon England: Religion, Ritual, and Rulership in the Landscape*, Oxford

Serjeantson, D, 2006 Food or feast at Neolithic Runnymede, in *Animals in the Neolithic of Britain and Europe* (eds D Serjeantson and D Field), Neolithic Studies Groups Seminar Papers **7**, Oxford, 113-34

Serjeantson, D and Rees, H (eds), 2009 *Food, craft and status in medieval Winchester: the plant and animal remains from the suburbs and the city defences*, Winchester Museums

Sewell, J, 2000 An investigation into the origin and continuity of the parish boundary of Carisbrooke, Isle of Wight, *Proc Hampshire Fld Club Archaeol Soc* **55**, 31-45

Shaffrey, R, 2006a The Worked Stone, in Fulford *et al.* 2006, 133-4

Shaffrey, R, 2006 *Grinding and milling A study of Romano-British rotary querns and millstones made from Old Red Sandstone*, BAR Brit Ser **409**, Oxford

Shapland, M G, 2012 Buildings of Secular and Religious Lordship: Anglo-Saxon Tower-nave Churches, unpubl. PhD thesis, University College London

Sharp, J, 1985 Oseney Abbey, Oxford, Archaeological Investigations, 1975–83, *Oxoniensia*, **50**, 95–131

Sheahan, J, 1861 *History and Topography of Buckinghamshire*, Longman

Shennan, S, 1985 *Experiments in the collection and analysis of archaeological field data: the East Hampshire Field Survey*, Sheffield

Shennan, S, 1999 The Excavation of a Burnt Mound at Harbridge, Hampshire, *Hampshire Studies* **54** 172-9

Sheridan, R, Sheridan, D, and Hassell, P, 1967 Rescue excavation of a Mesolithic site at Greenham Dairy Farm, Newbury, 1963, *Trans Newbury Dist Fld Club* **11.4**, 66-73

Sheridon, R K, 1974 *Lords, Captains and Governors of the Isle of Wight*, London, HMSO

Sherratt, A, 1981 Plough and Pastoralism: aspects of the secondary products revolution, in *Pattern of the Past: studies in honour of David Clark*, (eds I Hodder, G Isaac and N Hammond), Cambridge, Cambridge University Press, 261-305. Reprinted in Sherratt, A 1997, *Economy and Society in Prehistoric Europe: changing perspectives*, Edinburgh, Edinburgh University Press

Sherwin, G A, 1936 Arreton Down Bronze Hoard, *Proc Isle Wight Nat Hist Archaeol Soc* **2**, 612-3

Sherwin, G A, 1936-42 Archaeological Survey of the Isle of Wight, unpubl. Manuscript

Sherwood, J and Pevsner, N, 1974 *The buildings of England: Oxfordshire*, Harmondsworth

Shortland, A J, Masters, P, Harrison, K, Williams, A and Boston, C, 2008 Burials of eighteenth-century Naval personnel: preliminary results from excavations at the Royal Hospital Haslar, Gosport (Hants), *Antiquity* **82** Issue 317

Sidell, J, and Wilkinson, K, 2004 The central London Thames: Neolithic river development and floodplain archaeology, in Cotton and Field 2004, 38-49

Simmonds, A, Anderson-Whymark, H and Norton, A, 2011 Excations at Tubney Wood Quarry, Oxfordshire, 2001-9, *Oxoniensia* **76**, 105-72

Simmons, I, Dimbleby, G W and Grigson, C, 1981 The Mesolithic, in *The environment in British Prehistory*, (eds I Simmons and M Tooley), London, 82–124

Sister Jane Mary SPB, Miller, D D and Miller, D M, 1985 The Manor and Abbey of Burnham, *Rec Buckinghamshire* **27**, 94-106

Slatcher, D and Samuels, J, 2004 Multi-period activity at Main Street, Ashendon: excavations in 1999, *Rec Buckinghamshire* **44**, 1-20

Sly, T J T, 1988 A Survey of Deserted Medieval Villages on the Isle of Wight, unpublished undergraduate dissertation, University of Southampton

Sly, T J T and Clark, K M, 1997 Survey at Quarr

Abbey, IOW: The West & South-West Precinct Wall, unpublished report, Southampton University

Smith, P S H, 1985 Hardmead and its Deserted Village, *Rec Buckinghamshire* **27**, 38-52

Smith, R A, 1905 Anglo-Saxon Remains, in *VCH Buckinghamshire* **1**, 195-205

Smith, R A, 1906 The Anglo-Saxon Remains, in *VCH Berkshire* (ed. W Page and P H Ditchfield) **1**, London

Somerville, E, 1994 The Oysters, in Fulford and Rippon 1994, 188 and M1, 25-35

Southampton City Council (accessed 13.8.13): http://www.southampton.gov.uk/s-leisure/artsheritage/history/archaeology/archaeology-unit/sitesbyarea/bargate-ward/westquay.aspx

Southern Archaeological Services, 2005 Summary report on an archaeological investigation at Hursts, Lugley Street/Chain Lane, Newport, Isle of Wight, January 2001-March 2002

Spickernell, W, 1859 *The Roman Villa, Carisbrooke, Isle of Wight; with Ground Plan*, Kentfield, Newport

Stainton, B, 1989 Excavation of an early prehistoric site at Stratford's Yard, Chesham, *Rec Buckinghamshire* **31**, 49-74

Stanford, C B and Bunn, H T (eds), 2001 *Meat Eating and Human Evolution*, Oxford University Press, New York

Stead, I M and Renfrew, C, 2000 *The Salisbury Hoard*, Stroud

Steane, J M, 1982 Wallingford Bridge, *CBA South Midlands Archaeol* **12**, 110-3

Steane, J, 1994 Stonor, a Lost Park and a Garden Found, *Oxoniensia* **59**, 449–71

Steane, J, 1996 *Oxfordshire*

Steane, J, 1998 The Grounds of Magdalen College 1480–1880, *Oxoniensia* **63**, 91–105

Steane J, 2001 Medieval Oxfordshire 1100-1540, *Oxoniensia* **66**, 1-12

Steane, J and Gosling, E, 1980 Oseney Mill, surviving part of Oseney Abbey, *CBA Group 9 Newsletter* **10**, 96–7

Stenton, F M, 1936 The road system of medieval England, in *Preparatory to Anglo-Saxon England* (ed. D M Stenton), 234-52

Stevens, C, 2004 Iron Age and Saxon settlement at Jugglers Close, Banbury, Oxfordshire, *Oxoniensia* **69**, 385-416

Stevens, C J, 2003 An investigation of consumption and production models for prehistoric and Roman Britain, *Environmental Archaeology* **8**, 61-67

Stevens, C J, 2008 Environment and Agricultural Economy, in Booth, P, Crockett, A D, and Fitzpatrick, A P, *The Archaeology of the M6 Toll 2000-2003* Oxford, Salisbury, Oxford-Wessex Archaeology Monograph **2**, 457-460

Stevens, C J, 2009 The Iron Age Agricultural Economy, in Wright *et al.* 2009, 78-83

Stevens, J C, 1888 *A Parochial History of St. Mary Bourne*

Stevens, J, 1894 The Discovery of a Saxon Burial Place, near Reading, *Journal of the British Archaeological Association* **50**, 150-157

Stevens, S, 2004 An Archaeological Evaluation of Land at East Anton Manor Farm, East Anton, Andover, Hampshire, Archaeology South East Report: Project 1760

Stewart, I J, 1990 Cold Harbour Farm, Aylesbury : an Archaeological Investigation, *Rec Buckinghamshire* **32**, 91-104

Stocker, D and Went, D, 1995 Evidence for a pre-Viking church adjacent to the Anglo-Saxon barrow at Taplow, Buckinghamshire, *Archaeol J* **152**, 441-454

Stone, P, 2011 Saxon and medieval activity at Walton Street, Aylesbury, *Rec Buckinghamshire* **51**, 99-129

Stone, P G, 1891 *The Architectural Antiquities of the Isle of Wight*, 2 volumes, London

Stoodley, N (ed.), 2002 *The Millennium Publication. A review of archaeology in Hampshire 1980-2000*, Hampshire Field Club and Archaeological Society

Stoodley, N, 2006 Changing burial practice in seventh-century Hampshire; the Anglo-Saxon cemetery at Portway West, Andover, *Proc Hampshire Fld Club Archaeol Soc* **61**, 63-80

Stoodley, N and Stedman, M, 2001 Excavations at Shavards Farm, Meonstoke: the Anglo-Saxon cemetery, *Proc Hampshire Fld Club Archaeol Soc* **56**, 129-69

Stout, A, 1994 *Where two rivers meet: the story of Kennet Mouth*, Two Rivers Press, Reading

Straker, V, 2000 The Charcoal, in Fulford and Timby 2000, 512-23

Sturdy, D, 1997 *A history of Knowles and Son, Oxford builders for 200 years*, BAR Brit Ser **254**, Oxford

Sweet, R, 2004 *Antiquaries: The Discovery of the Past in Eighteenth Century Britain*, Hambledon and London, London

Sykes, N, Whites, J, Hayes, T and Palmer, M, 2006 Tracking animals using strontium isotopes in teeth: the role of fallow deer (*Dama dama*) in Roman Britain, *Antiquity* **80**, 948-959

Tate, W E, 1947 Field systems and enclosures in Hampshire, *Proc Hampshire Fld Club Archaeol Soc* **16**, 257-79

Taunt, H W, 1872 *A new map of the river Thames from Oxford to London*, Oxford

Taylor, H M and Taylor, J, 1980-84 *Anglo-Saxon Architecture*, Cambridge University Press

Taylor-Moore, K, 2006 The comparative development of Aylesbury and Buckingham up to c. 1550, unpubl. MA dissertation, University of Leicester

Teague, S, 2005 Manor Farm, Monk Sherborne, Hampshire: archaeological investigations in 1996, *Hampshire Studies* **60**, 64-135

Thames Valley Archaeological Services,1989 Southam Common, Blackmoor, East Hampshire: archaeological evaluation, unpublished report BM89/5

Thomas, G, 2012 The prehistory of medieval farms and villages: from Saxons to Scandinavians, in N

Christie and P Stamper (eds), *Medieval Rural Settlement: Britain and Ireland, AD 800-1600*, Oxford

Thomas, J, 1999 *Understanding the Neolithic*, Routledge, London

Thomas, R, 1999 Rise and fall: the deposition of Bronze Age weapons in the Thames Valley and the Fenland, in *Experiment and Design: Archaeological Studies in Honour of John Coles*, (ed. A F Harding), Oxbow Books, Oxford, 116-22

Thomas, R, 2010 Monastic Town Planning at Abingdon, *Oxoniensia* **75**, 49-60

Thomas, R J C, 2003 *Twentieth Century Military Recording Project: Prisoner of War Camps (1939-1948)*, English Heritage

Thorne A, 2005 Wolverton Mill, *CBA South Midlands Archaeology* **35**, 19

Thorne, A T, and Walker, C, 2003 Excavations at the former Cowper Tannery, Olney, unpublished report

Thornes, R and Fradgley, N, 1988 Upton Court, Slough: an Early Fourteenth-Century Open Hall, *Archaeol J* **145**, 211-221

Tiller, K, 1985 Charterville and the Chartist Land Company, *Oxoniensia* **50**, 251-66

Tiller, K, and Darkes, G (eds), 2010 *An historical atlas of Oxfordshire*, Oxfordshire Record Society Vol **67**, Chipping Norton

Timby, J, 2003 The Pottery, in Preston 2003, 125-128

Timby, J, 2011 The Pottery, in Fulford and Clarke 2011, 143-203

Timby, J, 2012 The language of pots: an overview of pottery supply to Silchester and its hinterland, in Fulford 2012a, 127-50

Tingle, M, 1991 *The Vale of the White Horse survey*, BAR Brit Ser **218**, Oxford

Tipper, J, 2004 *The Grubenhaus in Anglo-Saxon England*, Yedingham: Landscape Research Centre

Tipping, R, 2004 Interpretative issues concerning the driving forces of vegetation change in the Early Holocene of the British Isles, in *Mesolithic Scotland and its neighbours* (ed. A Saville), Society of Antiquaries of Scotland, Edinburgh, 45-53

Tomalin, D J, 1980 The Neolithic in *The Vectis Report*, (ed. H V Basford), Newport, 15-17

Tomalin, D, 1987 *Roman Wight. A Guide Catalogue to "The Island of Vectis, very near to Britannia"*, Newport

Tomalin, D, 1996 Towards a new strategy for curating the Bronze Age landscape of the Hampshire and Solent region, in *Archaeology in Hampshire; a framework for the future* (ed. D Hinton and M Hughes), 13–25, Winchester

Tomalin, D J, 2002 'Wihtgarasbyrig' explored: a review article considering 'Excavations at Carisbrooke Castle, Isle of Wight, 1991-1996', *Proc Isle Wight Nat Hist Archaeol Soc* **18**, 55-80

Tomalin, D J, 2003 From Gat Cliff to Carisbrooke Castle: a medieval quarry re-located, *Proc Isle Wight Nat Hist Archaeol Soc* **19**, 101-108

Tomalin, D J, n d The villa estate in Rock Roman Villa, Draft Excavation Report (unpublished)

Tomalin, D, 2012a Maritime activity in the Iron Age, in Tomalin *et al.* 2012, 250-3

Tomalin, D, 2012b The significance of the east Solent coast in Roman times, in Tomalin *et al.* 2012, 253-63

Tomalin, D and Scaife, R, 1987 The excavation of the first piped-water system at Newport, I.W. and its associated urban palynolgy, *Proc Isle Wight Nat Hist Archaeol Soc* **8**, Part II, 68-81

Tomalin, D J, Loader, R D, Scaife, R G, (eds) 2012 *Coastal Archaeology in a Dynamic Environment. A Solent case study*, Oxford, BAR Brit Ser **568**

Tomlin, R S O, 1996 A five-acre wood in Roman Kent, in *Interpreting Roman London: papers in memory of Hugh Chapman*, (eds J Bird, M Hassall and H Sheldon), Oxbow Monograph **58**, 209-215

Torrance, L and Ford, S, 2003 A late Bronze Age burnt mound at Barkham Square, Wokingham, 1992, in Preston 2003, 87–97

Torrance, M and Weaver, S D G, 2003 The Excavation of a Saxon Settlement at Riverdene, Basingstoke, *Hampshire Studies* **58**, 63-105

Toulmin Smith, L (ed.), 1964 *The Itinerary of John Leland in or about the years 1535-1543. Parts IV and V*, Fontwell

Trott, K, 1999 A Rescue Excavation at the Brading Roman Villa Coach Park, Isle of Wight, *Proc Hampshire Fld Club Archaeol Soc* **54**, 189-215

Trott, K, 2000a Mersley Farm fieldwalking assessment, *Proc Isle Wight Nat Hist Archaeol Soc* **16**, 113-116

Trott, K, 2000b The evaluation excavation at Mersley Farm, Newchurch, Isle of Wight, *Proc Isle Wight Nat Hist Archaeol Soc* **16**, 95-112

Trott, K, 2003 Pyle Farm, Chale, Isle of Wight Archaeological Field-walking Project, *Proc Isle Wight Nat Hist Archaeol Soc* **19**, 59-68

Trott, K, 2006 An archaeological watching brief at the Willows, Shalfleet, Isle of Wight, unpublished report deposited in Isle of Wight HER

Trott, K and Tomalin, D, 2003 The maritime role of the island of Vectis in the British pre-Roman Iron Age, *International Journal of Nautical Archaeology* Vol **32** Issue 2, 158-181

Tubbs, C R, 2001 *New Forest History Ecology and Conservation*, New Forest Ninth Centenary Trust second edition revised

Turner, M E, 1973a Some Social and Economic Consequences of Parliamentary Enclosure in Buckinghamshire 1738-1866 2 Volumes Unpublished PhD (University of Sheffield)

Turner, M E, 1973b The Cost of Parliamentary Enclosure in Buckinghamshire, *Agricultural History Review* **21**, 33-46

Turner, M E, 1977 Enclosure Commissioners and Buckinghamshire Parliamentary Enclosure, *Agricultural History Review* **25**,

TVAS, 1989 Southam Common, Blackmoor, East Hampshire: archaeological evaluation, Unpublished report **BM89/5**

TVAS, 1997 Excavation of Iron Age and early Roman Features at Viking Way, Andover, Hampshire, 1996,

Thames Valley Archaeol Services Archaeol Rep, unpublished, Reading

Tyack, G, 1998 *Oxford, an architectural guide*, Oxford

Tyldesley, J A, 1987 *The Bout Coupé Handaxe: a Typological Problem*, BAR Brit Ser **170**, Oxford

Tyler, R, 2001 Archaeological investigations during refurbishment of St Aldate's Church, *Oxoniensia* **66**, 369-409

Ulmschneider, K, 1999 Archaeology, history and the Isle of Wight in the Middle Saxon period, *Medieval Archaeol* **43**, 19-44

Ulmschneider, K, 2000 *Markets, Minsters and Metal-detectors. The archaeology of middle Saxon Lincolnshire and Hampshire*, BAR Brit Ser **307**, Oxford

Ulmschneider, K, 2003 Markets around the Solent: unravelling a 'productive' site on the Isle of Wight, in *Markets in Early Medieval Europe* (eds T Pestell and K Ulmschneider), Windgather Press, 73-83

Van de Noort, R, Middleton, R, Foxon, A and Bayliss, A, 1999 The Kilnsea boat and some implications from the discovery of England's oldest plank boat, *Antiquity* **73** No **279**, 131-135

Van de Noort, R, 2006 Argonauts of the North Sea – a Social Maritime Archaeology for the 2nd Millennium BC, *Proc Prehist Soc* **72**, 267-287

van der Veen, M, 1987 The plant remains, in Heslop, D H, *The Excavation of an Iron Age Settlement at Thorpe Thewles, Cleveland, 1980–1982*, CBA Res Rep **65**, London, 93-61

van der Veen, M, 1992 *Crop Husbandry Regimes. An Archaeobotanical Study of Farming in Northern England: 1000BC–AD5000*, Sheffield, J.R. Collis Publications, Sheffield Archaeological Monograph **3**

van der Veen, M, 1999, The economic value of chaff and straw in arid and temperate zones, *Vegetation History and Archaeobotany* **8**, 211-24

van der Veen, M and O'Connor, T P, 1998 The expansion of agricultural production in late Iron Age and Roman Britain, in *Science in Archaeology, an agenda for the future*, (ed. J Bayley), London, English Heritage, 127-144

Van der Veen, M and Jones, G, 2007 The production and consumption of cereals: a question of scale, in *The Later Iron Age of Britain and Beyond*, (eds C Haselgrove and T Moore) Oxford, Oxbow Books, 419-429

Varndell, G L, 1979 The Andover Hoard, a Late Bronze Age Hoard of the Wilburton Tradition from Hampshire, in *Bronze Age Hoards: some Finds Old and New*, (eds C Burgess C and D Coombs), BAR Brit Ser **67**, Oxford, 93-9

Varndell, G, Coe, D and Hey, G, 2007 The Crow Down hoard, Lambourn, West Berkshire, *Oxford J Archaeol* **26(3)**, 275–301

Veal, R, 2012 Examining continuity in landscape exploitation: Late Roman fuel consumption in Silchester's Insula IX, in Fulford 2012a, 227-45

Victoria History of the County of Berkshire, 1906-24 (VCH Berkshire)

Victoria History of the County of Buckingham, 1905-53 (VCH Buckinghamshire)

Victoria History of the County of Hampshire and the Isle of Wight, 1900-12 (VCH Hampshire)

Victoria History of the County of Oxfordshire, 1907-2000 (VCH Oxfordshire)

Waddington, K E and Sharples, N 2010 *The Whitchurch excavations 2006-9: an interim report*, Cardiff University, Cardiff Studies in Archaeology Specialist Report **29**

Wainwright, A, 1989 Ashridge Park Survey, draft report for National Trust

Wainwright, A P, Marshall, G, and Salkeld, G, 2010 Archaeological Survey of the Ashridge Estate, Vol. 1, Land Use History, National Trust

Wait, G A, 1985 *Ritual and Religion in Iron Age Britain*, BAR Brit Ser **149**, Oxford

Wakeham, G and Bradley, P, 2013 A Romano-British malthouse and other remains at Weedon Hill, *Rec Buckinghamshire* **53**, 1-44

Wakely, J, 1993 Bilateral congenital dislocation of the hip, spina bifida and spondylolysis in a female skeleton from the medieval cemetery at Abingdon, England, *Journal of Palaeopathology* **5**, 37-45

Walker, K E and Farwell, D E, 2000 *Twyford Down, Hampshire. Archaeological Investigations on the M3 Motorway from Bar End to Compton, 1990-93*, Hampshire Fld Club Monograph **9**

Waller, R, 2006 Archaeological Resource Assessment of the Isle of Wight: Early Medieval period, at http://thehumanjourney.net/pdf_store/sthames/phase 3/County/Early%20Medieval/Early%20Medieval%20Isle%20of%20Wight.pdf

Wallis, S, 2005 The Rear of 12 Church Gate, Thatcham: an archaeological evaluation for Westbuild Homes (Reading) Ltd

Walton, P J, 2012 Rethinking Roman Britain: Coinage and Archaeology, *Collection Moneta* **137**, Wetteren

Warren, G M, 2006 Technology, in *Mesolithic Britain and Ireland: new approaches*, (eds C Conneller, and G M Warren), Stroud, 13-34

Warry, P, 2012 The Silchester tile industry, in Fulford 2012a, 49-75

Waton, P V, 1982 Man's impact on the Chalklands: some new pollen evidence, in *Archaeological aspects of woodland ecology*, (eds M Bell and S Limbrey), BAR Int Ser **146**, Oxford, 75-91

Waton, P V, 1983a The pollen evidence 159-62, in Millett with James 1983, 159-62

Waton, P V, 1983b A palynological study of the impact of man on the landscape of Central Southern England with special reference to the Chalklands, unpublished PhD thesis, University of Southampton

Waton, P V, 1986 Palynological evidence for early and permanent woodland on the Chalk of Central Hampshire, in *The scientific study of flint and chert*, (eds G de G Sieveking and M B Hart), Cambridge University Press, Cambridge, 169-74

Watts, M and Langdon, J, 2004 An early tower windmill? The Turweston 'post-mill' reconsidered, *History of Technology* 25, 1-6

Webster, C n d The Gentry's Role in the Development of the Isle of Wight, unpublished notes for WEA Lectures

Webster, L and Cherry, J, 1976 Medieval Britain in 1975, *Medieval Archaeol* 26, 158-201

Wenban-Smith, F F, 2001a Review of *Lower and Middle Palaeolithic Artefacts from Deposits mapped as Clay-with-flints* by J Scott-Jackson, *Antiquity* 75, 893–894

Wenban-Smith, F F, 2001b As represented by the Solent River: handaxes from Highfield, Southampton, in *Palaeolithic Archaeology of the Solent River*, (eds F F Wenban-Smith and R T Hosfield), Lithic Studies Society Occasional Paper 7, London, 57–69

Wenban-Smith, F F, 2004a Handaxe typology and Lower Palaeolithic cultural development: ficrons, cleavers and two giant handaxes from Cuxton, in *Lithics 25 (Papers in Honour of R J MacRae)*, (eds M Pope and K Cramp), 11–21

Wenban-Smith, F F, 2004b Bringing behaviour into focus: Archaic landscapes and lithic technology, in *Lithics in Action: Proceedings of the Lithic Studies Society Conference held in Cardiff, September 2000*, (eds E A Walker, F F Wenban-Smith and F Healy), Lithic Studies Society Occasional Paper 8, Oxbow Books, Oxford, 48–56

Wenban-Smith, F F and Bridgland, D R, 2001 Palaeolithic archaeology at the Swan Valley Community School, Swanscombe, Kent, *Proc Prehist Soc* 67, 219–259

Wenban-Smith, F F, Gamble C S and ApSimon, A M, 2000 The Lower Palaeolithic site at Red Barns, Portchester, Hampshire: bifacial technology, raw material quality and the organisation of Archaic behaviour, *Proc Prehist Soc* 66, 209–255c

Wenban-Smith, F F, Schwenninger, J-L and Scaife, R, 2005 New OSL dates and pollen records from the Bembridge Raised Beach sequence, Isle of Wight (UK), *Quaternary Newsletter* 107, 1–19

Wessex Archaeology, 1990 Area W, Brighton Hill South, Basingstoke, Hampshire, Trust for Wessex Archaeology Rep

Wessex Archaeology, 1993a *The Southern Rivers Palaeolithic Project, Report No. 1 – The Upper Thames Valley, the Kennet Valley and the Solent Drainage System*, Wessex Archaeology, Salisbury

Wessex Archaeology, 1993b *The Southern Rivers Palaeolithic Project, Report No. 2 – The South West and South of the Thames*, Wessex Archaeology, Salisbury

Wessex Archaeology, 1994 *The Southern Rivers Palaeolithic Project, Report No. 3 – The Sussex Raised Beaches and the Bristol Avon*, Wessex Archaeology, Salisbury

–Wessex Archaeology, 1996a *English Rivers Palaeolithic Project, Report No. 1 – The Thames Valley and the Warwickshire Avon*, Wessex Archaeology, Salisbury

Wessex Archaeology, 1996b *English Rivers Palaeolithic Project, Report No. 2 – The Great Ouse Drainage and the Yorkshire and Lincolnshire Wolds*, Wessex Archaeology, Salisbury

Wessex Archaeology, 1996c Newbury Wharf – Assessment Report on the Excavation, Unpublished client report

Wessex Archaeology, 1996d Land Adjoining the Former Rooksdown Hospital, Basingstoke, Hampshire: Excavations Undertaken in 1989 and 1995, Wessex Archaeology Project 33077, Salisbury

Wessex Archaeology, 1997 *English Rivers Palaeolithic Project, Report No. 3 – East Anglian Rivers and the Trent Drainage*, Wessex Archaeology, Salisbury

Wessex Archaeology, 1998 Newbury Wharf, Newbury: assessment report on the excavation, Unpublished client report

Wessex Archaeology, 2000 Iffley Lock Oxford, *CBA South Midlands Archaeol* 30, 69

Wessex Archaeology, 2004a *Artefacts from the sea. Catalogue of the Michael White Collection* (2 volumes), Salisbury

Wessex Archaeology, 2004b Round Hill, Wittenham Clumps, Oxfordshire: evaluation Time Team/Wessex Archaeology report 52568.09, Salisbury

Wessex Archaeology, 2005a Chamberhouse Farm, Thatcham Berkshire, unpublished draft client report 1998 (issued 2005) report ref 43211, Salisbury

Wessex Archaeology, 2005b Preferred Area 4, Denham, Buckinghamshire: archaeological evaluation report, unpublished client report 50692.08, Salisbury

Wessex Archaeology, 2006 Kingsmead Quarry, Horton, Berkshire, parts of extraction phases 4-7, post-excavation assessment report, Wessex Archaeology report 54635.03

Wessex Archaeology/Time Team, 2010 Sutton Courtenay, Oxfordshire: Archaeological Excavation and Assessment of Results, at http://www.scribd.com/doc/56051394/Time-Team-

Whimster, R, 1981 *Burial practices in Iron Age Britain*, BAR Brit Ser 90, Oxford

Whinney, R, 1994 Oram's Arbour: the Middle Iron Age Enclosure at Winchester, in Fitzpatrick and Morris 1994, 86-91

White, M J and Jacobi, R M, 2002 Two sides to every story: *bout coupé* handaxes revisited, *Oxford J Archaeol* 21, 109–133

Whitehand, J W R, 1967 Traditional Building Materials in the Chilterns: A Survey based on Random Sampling, *Oxoniensia* 32, 1-9

Whitehead, B and Higgins, P, 1995 Summary Report on an Archaeological Evaluation at Priory Farm Orchard, Carisbrooke, Southern Archaeological Services, Southampton

Whitehead, J L, 1911 *The Undercliff of the Isle of Wight*, Ventnor

Whittaker, K, Beasley, M, Bates, M R and Wenban-Smith, F F, 2004 The lost valley, *Brit Archaeol* 74, 22–27

Whittle, A, 1990 A model for the Mesolithic-Neolithic

transition in the Upper Kennet Valley, North Wiltshire, *Proc Prehist Soc* **56**, 101-10

Whittle, A, 1991 Wayland's Smithy, Oxfordshire: excavations at the Neolithic tomb in 1962-63 by R J C Atkinson and S Piggott, *Proc Prehist Soc* **57**(2), 61-101

Whittle, A, 2007 The temporality of transformation: dating the early development of the southern British Neolithic, in Whittle and Cummings 2007, 377-98

Whittle, A and Bayliss, A, 2007 The times of their lives: from chronological precision of kinds of history and change, *Cambridge Archaeological Journal* **17:1**, 21-8

Whittle, A and Cummings, V (eds), 2007 *Going over: the Mesolithic-Neolithic transition in North-West Europe*, Proc British Academy **144**, London

Whittle, A, Atkinson, R J C, Chambers, R and Thomas, N, 1992 Excavations in the Neolithic and Bronze Age complex at Dorchester-on-Thames, Oxfordshire, 1947-1952 and 1981, *Proc Prehist Soc* **58**, 143-201

Whittle, A, Bayliss, A, and Wysocki, M, 2007 Once in a lifetime: the date of the Wayland's Smithy long barrow, *Cambridge Archaeol J* **17**(1) (**suppl.**), 103-21

Whittle, A, Barclay, A, Bayliss, A, McFayden, L, Schulting, R, and Wysocki, M, 2007 Building for the dead: events, processes and changing worldviews from the 38th to the 34th centuries cal BC in southern Britain, *Cambridge Archaeol J* **17**(1) (**suppl.**), 123-47

Wilkinson, I P, Williams, M, Young, J R, Cook, S R, Fulford, M G and Lott, G K, 2008 The application of microfossils in assessing the provenance of chalk used in the manufacture of Roman mosaics at Silchester, *J Archaeol Sci* **35**, 2415-2422

Wilkinson, K, and Straker, V, 2008 Neolithic and Early Bonze Age environmental background, in *The archaeology of South West England: South West archaeological research framework, resource assessment and research agenda*, (ed. C J Webster), Somerset County Council, Taunton, 63-74

Williams, A, 1946-7 Excavations at Langford Downs, Oxon (near Lechlade) in 1943, *Oxoniensia* **11-12**, 44-64

Williams R J, 1993 *Pennyland and Hartigans: two Iron Age and Saxon sites in Milton Keynes*, Buckinghamshire Archaeol Soc Monograph **4**

Williams, R J, and Zeepvat, R J, 1994 *Bancroft: a late Bronze Age/Early Iron Age settlement, Roman villa and temple-mausoleum. Vol 1: Excavations and building materials, Vol 2: Finds and environmental evidence*, Buckinghamshire Archaeol Soc Monograph **7**, Aylesbury

Williams, R J, Hart, P J, and Williams, A T L, 1996 *Wavendon Gate, a Late Iron Age and Roman Settlement in Milton Keynes*, Buckinghamshire Archaeol Soc Monograph **10**, Aylesbury

Williams-Freeman, J, 1915 *An Introduction to Field Archaeology – As Illustrated By Hampshire*, London

Williamson, T, 2002 *Shaping Medieval Landscapes: Settlement, society, environment*, Macclesfield

Willis, G W, 1947 Hampshire Palaeoliths and the Clay-with-flints, *Proc Hampshire Fld Club Archaeol Soc* **16**, 253-256

Wilson, C E, 1981 Burials within settlements in southern Britain during the pre-Roman Iron Age, *Bull Inst Archaeol Univ London* **18**, 127-70

Wilson, D M, and Hurst, J G, 1958 Medieval Britain in 1957, *Medieval Archaeology*, **2**, 183-185

Wilson, K and Edmunds, R, 2006 Brading Haven Sea Wall, *Bulletin of the Isle of Wight Natural History and Archaeological Society*, 46

Wilson, K, and Edmunds, R, 2006 Newport Bus Station, *Bulletin of the Isle of Wight Natural History and Archaeological Society*, 6-7

Wilson, R, Hamilton, J, Bramwell, D and Armitage, P, 1978 The animal bones, in Parrington 1978, 110-139

Wilson, T, 2008 *A Narrow View across the Upper Thames Valley in Late Prehistoric and Roman Times: Archaeological Excavationsalong the Chalgrove to East Ilsley Gas Pipeline*, BAR (Brit Ser) **467**, Oxford

Winchester Museums Service 1993 *Nunnaminster. A Saxon and medieval community of nuns*, Winchester, Winchester Museums Service

Wintle, W, Hawes, J and Boyer, K, 2009 Geophysical Survey at and near Cherbury Camp, Oxfordshire, *CBA South Midlands Archaeol* **39**, 67-71

Winton, H, 2001 A possible Roman small town at Sansom's Platt, Tackley, Oxon., *Britannia* **32**, 304-9

Wise, J, 1991 A survey of prehistoric and later earthworks on Whiteleaf Hill, *Rec Buckinghamshire* **33**, 108-13

Wood, A, 1674 *Historia et Antiquitates Univ. Oxon*, Oxford

Wood, A, ed. Clark, A, 1891-5 *Wood's Life and Times*, 3 vols., Oxford

Woodfield, C, 1977 A Roman military site at Magiovinium?, *Rec Buckinghamshire* **20.3**, 384-99

Woodward, A, 2000 *British barrows: a matter of life and death*, Stroud

Woodward, A, and Woodward, P, 1996 The topography of some barrow cemeteries in Bronze Age Wessex, *Proc Prehist Soc* **62**, 275-91

Wordie, J R, 1984 The south: Oxfordshire, Buckinghamshire, Berkshire, Wiltshire and Hampshire, in *The agrarian history of England and Wales Vol.1 1640-1750*, (ed J Thirsk), Cambridge

Worsley, Sir R, 1781 *The History of the Isle of Wight*, London

Wright, J, 2004 Excavation of early Saxon settlement and Mesolithic activity at Goch Way, near Charlton, Andover, *Proc Hampshire Fld Club Archaeol Soc* **59**, 116-38

Wright, J, Leivers, M, Seager-Smith, R and Stevens, C J, 2009 *Cambourne New Settlement, Iron Age and Romano-British settlement on the clay uplands of west Cambridgeshire*, Salisbury, Wessex Archaeology Report **23**

Wymer, J J, 1958 Excavations at the Mesolithic site at

Thatcham, Berkshire, 1958, *Trans Newbury Dist Fld Club* **10**, 31-48

Wymer, J J, 1959 Excavation on the Mesolithic site at Thatcham, Berkshire, 1958: interim report with a report on the pollen analysis by Dr G W Dimbleby, *Berkshire Archaeol J* **57**, 1-33

Wymer, J J, 1960 Excavations at the Maglemosian sites at Thatcham, Berkshire: second interim report, *Trans Newbury Dist Fld Club* **11**, 12-9

Wymer, J J, 1962 Excavations at the Maglemosian sites at Thatcham, Berkshire, England, *Proc Prehist Soc* **28**, 329-61

Wymer, J J, 1963 Excavations at Thatcham: final report, *Trans Newbury Dist Fld Club* **11**, 41-52

Wymer, J J, 1968 *Lower Palaeolithic archaeology in Britain as represented by the Thames Valley*, John Baker, London

Wymer, J J, 1977 *A gazetteer of Mesolithic sites in England and Wales*, CBA Res Rep **20**, London

Wymer, J, 1991 *Mesolithic Britain*, Shire Publications, Princes Risborough

Wymer, J J, 1995 The contexts of palaeoliths, in *Lithics in Context* (ed. A J Schofield), Lithic Studies Society Occasional Paper 5, London, 45–51

Wymer, J J, 1996 The Palaeolithic and Mesolithic periods in Hampshire, in *Archaeology in Hampshire: a framework for the future* (eds D A Hinton and M Hughes), Winchester, 1–6

Wymer, J J, 1999 *The Lower Palaeolithic Occupation of Britain*, Salisbury, Wessex Archaeology

Yates, D, 1999 Bronze Age field systems in the Thames Valley, *Oxford J Archaeol* **18**, 157-170

Yates, D, 2001 Bronze Age agricultural intensification in the Thames Valley and estuary, in Brück 2001, 65-82

Yates, D T, 2007 *Land, Power and Prestige: Bronze Age Field Systems in Southern England*, Oxford, Oxbow

Yates, M H, 2007 *Town and Countryside in Western Berkshire, c. 1327 to c. 1600. Social and Economic Change*, Boydell Press, Woodbridge

Yeoman, P A St. J, 1986 Excavations at the motte, Weston Turville Manor, 1985, *Rec Buckinghamshire* **28**, 169-178

Yeoman, P, 1988 Excavation of an early Post-medieval kiln at Temple Street, Brill, 1983, *Rec Buckinghamshire* **30**, 123-155

Yeoman, P A, and Stewart, I J, 1992 A Romano-British villa estate at Mantles Green, Amersham, Buckinghamshire, *Rec Buckinghamshire* **34**, 107-182

York, J, 2002 The life cycle of Bronze Age metalwork from the Thames, *Oxford J Archaeol* **21** (1), 77-92

Young, C J, 1975 The defences of Roman Alchester, *Oxoniensia* **60**, 136-170

Young, C J, 1977 *The Roman pottery industry of the Oxford region*, BAR (Brit Ser) **43**, Oxford

Young, C J, 2000 *Excavations at Carisbrooke Castle Isle of Wight 1921-1996*, Wessex Archaeology, Salisbury

Zant, J M, 1993 *The Brooks, Winchester, 1987-88. The Roman Structural Remains*, Winchester Museums Service Archaeology Report 2, Winchester

Zeepvat, R J, 1988 Another Roman building at Wymbush?, *Rec Buckinghamshire* **30**, 111-16

Zeepvat, R J, Roberts, J S and King, N A, 1994 *Caldecotte. Excavations and Fieldwork, 1966-91*, Buckinghamshire Archaeol Soc Monograph Ser **9**, Aylesbury

Other internet sites of reference

http://www.dendrochronology.net/oxfordshire.asp
www.iwias.org.uk/
www.palmerstonforts.org.uk

Abbreviations:

IWCAHES: Isle of Wight County Archaeology and Historic Environment Service

Index

This index is not intended to be comprehensive. With such a wide-ranging volume, both in terms of time and subject matter, the aim has been to provide indexing to places, and to subjects, that span more than one period. Readers should first refer to the headings within each chapter in the contents, and the lists of figures and plates.